The Modern Bogo 1.d4 e6

Dejan Antic & Branimir Maksimovic

The Modern Bogo 1.d4 e6

A Complete Guide for Black

New In Chess 2014

© 2014 New In Chess
Published by New In Chess, Alkmaar, The Netherlands
www.newinchess.com

Cover design: Steven Boland
Translation: Vladimir Krpan and Aleksandar Davidovic
Supervisor: Peter Boel
Proofreading: René Olthof
Production: Anton Schermer

Have you found any errors in this book?
Please send your remarks to editors@newinchess.com. We will collect all relevant corrections on the Errata page of our website www.newinchess.com and implement them in a possible next edition.

ISBN: 978-90-5691-495-0

Contents

Part II: 3.♘d2 355

Part III: 3.♘c3 397

Foreword

Two years ago the undersigned authors completed their work on *The Modern French*. This book was warmly received by chess fans and experts alike. As a logical continuation we now present the book *The Modern Bogo*, with which we complete a fully-fledged opening repertoire for black players.

One of the questions that readers as well as the New In Chess editors asked during the course of writing this book, was what our recommendation is if after 1.d4 e6 White continues with 2.e4. With our answer that we recommend 2...d5, entering the French Defence, the next dilemma was whether this book is only for people who play the French with black. Of course, our reply is: no, it is not. More than 90 percent of the material is comprised of the popular theoretical lines in the Bogo- and Nimzo-Indian, which are regularly reached via the move order 1.d4 ♘f6 2.c4 e6. With this in mind, the book is aimed at a wide reading auditorium. However, because we recommend the move order 1.d4 e6, the book has a particular significance to fans of the French Defence.

As mentioned, more than 90 percent of the lines are also reached through the standard transposition with 1.d4 ♘f6 2.c4 e6. Less than 10 percent of the material covers lines without 2...♘f6. As you will find in the book, with this course of action Black deprives White of many Nimzo-Indian lines, and also retains the possibility of striking at the centre while the knight is still on g8. The resulting positions are very original already early in the opening.

The book structure is offering the following chapters: the Bogo-Indian after 2...♗b4+, with transpositions to the standard positions, as well as the regular move order 1.d4 ♘f6 2.c4 e6 3.♘f3 ♗b4+ 4.♗d2, and now the options 4...♗xd2+, 4...a5 and 4...c5, in all cases with excellent play for Black. In the line with 4...a5 we have also covered the Catalan Opening, with the currently most popular set-up for Black.

In the line 1.d4 ♘f6 2.c4 e6 3.♘f3 ♗b4+ 4.♘bd2 we suggest 4...0-0, and then possibly 5.a3 ♗e7 6.e4 d5. The play is very dynamic and bears lots of similarities to the Tarrasch French, where the extra tempo with the white pawn on a3 doesn't make a difference since his pawn on c4 and knight on d2 are not compatible. Tournament practice suggests that these lines are the most popular continuations for Black and we believe that our contribution and our new ideas will cement their solid reputation.

In order to increase the legibility of this book we have used a special feature in the Index of Variations (in the back of the book). Although we advocate (and use) the move order 1.d4 e6 2.c4 ♗b4+ throughout this book we appreciate that the great majority of the material in this monograph can be classified under the regular Bogo-Indian Defence: 1.d4 ♘f6 2.c4 e6 3.♘f3 ♗b4+.

So we strictly follow the order in which each line is presented but have made a distinction between lines with or without the insertion of ♘f3 and ♘f6. Hence the page numbers in the Index of Variations may at times seem slightly chaotic, but we feel it's the best way to enable the reader to find where any given line or position is examined in our book.

We are grateful to the people who actively participated in the work on this book: the translators Mr Vladimir Krpan and IM Aleksandar Davidovic, as well the editors of New In Chess. Our gratitude also goes out to Mr Goran Urosevic, the founder of Chessdom.com, who helped with corrections in the final stages.

Dejan Antic and Branimir Maksimovic, June 2014

Explanation of Symbols

**The chessboard
with its coordinates:**

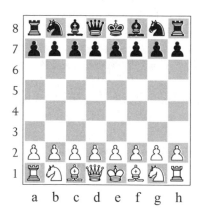

±	White stands slightly better
∓	Black stands slightly better
±	White stands better
∓	Black stands better
+−	White has a decisive advantage
−+	Black has a decisive advantage
=	balanced position
∞	unclear position
⯎	compensation for the material
!	good move
!!	excellent move
?	bad move
??	blunder
!?	interesting move
?!	dubious move
↑	initiative
⇄	counterplay
#	mate
corr.	correspondence

❏	White to move
■	Black to move
♔	King
♕	Queen
♖	Rook
♗	Bishop
♘	Knight

Part I: 3.♗d2

Section I

The Exchange 3...♗xd2+

3...♗xd2+ is the favourite line of Swedish Grandmaster Ulf Andersson, its basic idea being quick development and simplification. Similar set-ups usually emerge from the Queen's Gambit, the Catalan or the Queen's Indian, but here the dark-squared bishops are quickly exchanged and the resulting positions bear specific features.

Chapter 1

The Sideline 4.♘xd2

The reply 4.♘xd2 is nothing unusual. White captures Black's bishop on the d2-square, developing his piece. However, strategically speaking, this position of the knight on d2 has two drawbacks: 1. the knight is more passive than on the more natural c3-square, and 2. it weakens the protection of the central d4-pawn, because it disrupts the queen's influence on the d-file. These strategic details, especially the weakened pawn on d4, send a clear message to Black: he must choose a plan that involves attacking White's centre, with...d7-d6 and ...e6-e5.

We will analyse the main line 4...d6, the solid 4...♘c6, and the inferior 4...d5. We will add that using 4...♘f6 Black can transpose to the regular Bogo-Indian.

4...d6!

The most flexible and best continuation applied on grandmaster level. It is especially favoured by grandmaster Dragan Kosic, who uses this move order exclusively. With this move order, Black has a bigger choice of continuations to support his main plan of ...e6-e5. Instead:

A) With **4...♘c6** Black immediately attacks the unprotected d4-pawn: **5.♘gf3** Not dangerous for Black would be 5.d5 ♘ce7 6.e4 d6 7.♘gf3 (or 7.♗d3 ♘f6 8.♘e2 0-0 9.0-0 c6⇄) 7...♘f6 8.♗d3 0-0 9.0-0 ♘g6∞. Black has nice squares for his minor pieces.

5...d6

Black continues preparing the attack on White's centre with ...e6-e5. White now has a choice between two types of positions, depending on the diagonal he wants to place his light-squared bishop on:

A1) After **6.e4 ♘f6**

A11) **7.♗e2 0-0 8.0-0 e5 9.d5** If he wishes to continue the fight, White must close down the centre. Now it is a matter of preference, as is the case in the variation with 7.♗d3, whether the black knight will be moved to the kingside (9...♘e7) or continue participating in the fight on the queenside with 9... ♘b8:

A111) **9...♘b8** A common retreat. The knight keeps fighting for the critical queenside squares. **10.c5 ♗g4** Black finishes development, planning maximum simplification. **11.cxd6 cxd6 12.♖c1 ♘bd7 13.♘e1 ♗xe2 14.♕xe2 ♖c8=**. After a likely trade of all rooks on the c-file the players are very close to a draw;

A112) **9...♘e7** The black knight clearly aims for the f4-square, from where it can put pressure on the opponent's king or potentially simplify the position by being traded for the white bishop. **10.♘e1 10.c5 ♘g6=. 10...c5!? 11.♕c2 ♘g6∞**

Black has a lack of space, but active pieces and better dark-square play, Dridi-Zysk, Sharjah 1985.

A12) **7.♗d3 0-0 8.0-0 e5**

Black's idea, with the white knight on the d2-square, comes to fruition. He opens up his light-squared bishop and attacks his opponent's most vulnerable spot in the centre. **9.d5** A practically forced shutdown of the centre. White gains some space, but his pawn centre loses mobility, thereby enabling Black to play more freely on the flanks. This type of centre, which most commonly appears in the King's Indian Defence, is not so beneficial for White in this instance, because the dark-squared bishops have been traded and White has sensitive squares on c5, f4, d4, and b4, which the opponent can make use of for his counterplay.

Black can now keep his queenside knight with 9... ♘b4 or switch it to the kingside with 9...♘e7.

A121) **9...♘e7** Black again wants to move the knight to the kingside for an attack on the opponent's king. **10.b4 ♘g6 11.♖e1 h6!?** With the idea ...♘f6-h7. **12.♗f1 ♘h7 13.c5 f5 14.♖c1** with good play on both sides, but on different flanks. However, Black's kingside initiative is clearly more dangerous than the opponent's initiative on the queenside. The game Kasimdzhanov-Andersson, Germany 2000, ended in a draw here;

A122) **9...♘b4** Black attacks the opponent's bishop, gaining some time, but his main goal is the fight for the critical c5- and b4-squares. **10.♗e2 a5 11.a3 ♘a6 12.b4 ♗g4** Black has a little less space, but he can play effectively on both flanks due to the pawn structure, which is compatible with his light-squared bishop:

A1221) **13.♕b1 c5!?**

With this thematic thrust, without opening up the a-file with ...axb4, Black wants to provoke his opponent into shutting down the queenside with b4-b5 or win the b4-, c5- or d4-square for his knight. **14.b5** After 14.dc6 bc6 15.c5 dc5 16.♗a6 ♖a6 17.bc5 the position is on the verge of a draw. **14...♘c7 15.h3 ♗f3 16.♗f3 g6** Play transfers to the kingside. Black wants to place his knight on the g7-square, from where it can support the thematic ...f7-f5 thrust. **17.♕d3 ♘ce8 18.g3 ♘g7 19.♗g2 ♘fh5 20.f4** 20.♖ae1∞. **20...ef4 21.gf4 ♕h4∓**

A typical middlegame position. After f2-f4 and gxf4. White seems to have formidable power in the centre, but the support by his pieces is insufficient. Any advance of the e-pawn or the f-pawn will leave behind a vulnerable square. That is why White's centre is more of a target for Black rather than a powerful weapon with which White can make progress, Krasenkow-Miton, Warsaw 2003;

A1222) After **13.♕b3** Black can apply a nice and simple plan with **13...♗f3 14.♗f3 ab4 15.ab4 c5!** and the black knight gains a stronghold on b4, e6 or c5, depending on White's reaction: **16.bc5?!** 16.b5 ♘b4=; 16.dc6 bc6= with the idea ...♘c7-e6. **16...♘c5** This gives Black a solid position, since White has no bishop to challenge the knight on c5.

Back to the position after 5...d6.
A2) **6.g3 ♘f6 7.e4** 7.♗g2 0-0 8.0-0 e5 9.d5 ♘b8 10.e4 transposes. **7...e5**

Analysis diagram

White does not respond to Black's plan in the centre. Will he fianchetto the bishop, or will he place it on the f1-a6 diagonal? He sets up his planned pawn centre in a way that is compatible with his light-squared bishop. **8.d5 ♘b8 9.♗g2 0-0 10.0-0 a5 11.♘e1 ♘a6**

The position looks like a King's Indian, where the absence of the dark-squared bishops clearly favours Black. **12.♘d3** and now:

A21) **12...♗g4!?N 13.f3** On 13.♕c2 ♗e2 14.♖fe1 ♗d3 15.♕d3 ♘c5 Black will be more solid, because his knight stands better than the opponent's bishop. **13...♗d7 14.a3 c6⇄**

This thematic move combines excellently with the queen on the d8-square. Black has a good game, especially on the dark squares after the possible ...♕b6;

A22) An interesting move would be **12...♘d7**, with the idea of trading the active d3-knight via c5. **13.f4?!** It seems that White is still not ready for this standard assault. Better would be 13.a3 ♘ac5 14.♘c5 ♘c5 15.b4↑. Now instead of 13...f6∞ (Mikhalevski-Krush, Edmonton 2012), a better move would be **13...ef4!**

... and Black would gain the initiative. For example: **14.♖f4** (14.gf4 ♘b4↑) **14...♘b4∓**;

A23) Black can use **12...♕e7** to move on to a well-known theoretical position, which can come about via several different move orders, but most commonly after 1. d4 ♘f6 2. c4 e6 3. ♘f3 ♗b4 4. ♗d2 ♕e7 etc. The fight usually continues as follows: **13.a3 ♗g4 14.f3 ♗d7 15.b4 ab4** 15...c6 16.bxa5 (after 16.♕b3 Black achieves excellent play with 16...cxd5 17.cxd5 axb4 18.axb4 ♘c7 19.♕b2 ♗b5, Skembris-Beliavsky, Igalo 1994) 16...cxd5 17.cxd5 ♗b5 18.♕b3 ♗xd3 19.♕xd3 ♘c5 20.♕c3 ♘fd7 21.♗h3± Jussupow-Winants, Brussels (rapid) 1992. **16.axb4 c6 17.♖e1** Or 17.dxc6 bxc6 18.♕c2 with the idea of c4-c5, with good prospects for both sides, Seirawan-Jussupow, Belgrade 1991. **17...♖fc8 18.dxc6 bxc6 19.♘f1** with mutual chances, Rogozenco-Parligras, Hamburg 2008.

B) A bad response to the knight recapture would be **4...d5** because it leaves Black in an inferior position due to the passive light-squared bishop. For example: **5.♘gf3 ♘f6 6.g3 0-0 7.♗g2 ♕e7** Or 7...♘bd7 8.0-0 c6 9.♕c2 b6 10.e4 dxe4 11.♘xe4 ♘xe4 12.♕xe4 ♗b7 13.♖ac1 with the idea c4-c5: 13...♘f6 14.♕e3 ♕c7 15.c5

15

± Agzamov-Gonzalez, Tunja 1984. **8.0-0 ♘bd7 9.♕c2 c5 10.dxc5 ♕xc5 11.♖fc1 ♘b6 12.♘e5 dxc4 13.♘dxc4 ♘xc4 14.♘xc4 ♖b8 15.♘e3 ♕xc2 16.♖xc2 ♗d7 17.♖ac1 ♖fc8 18.♘c4±** White increased his advantage later on: **18...♔f8 19.e4 ♔e7 20.f4 ♘e8 21.e5 b6 22.♔f2 ♖c7 23.♘e3 ♖bc8 24.♗e4 h5 25.b3 g6 26.a4 ♖c5 27.h3 ♖5c7 28.a5±** Postny-Kosic, Dresden 2008;

C) **4...♘f6 5.♘gf3 ♘gf3** switches to the regular Bogo-Indian, i.e. 1.d4 ♘f6 2.c4 e6 3.♘f3 ♗b4 4.♗d2 ♗xd2 5.♘xd2.

5.♘gf3

Here Black usually either chooses 5...♘f6 or supports his thematic attack on White's centre with 5...♕e7 or 5...♘c6.

5...♘f6

Black switches to the regular Bogo-Indian that usually comes about after 1.d4

♘f6 2.c4 e6 3.♘f3 ♗b4 4.♗d2 ♗xd2 5.♘xd2 d6. We chose this continuation, because in this move order Black has a sound opportunity to support his thematic assault ...e6-e5 with a rook on e8, after castling. As usual, White can either fianchetto his bishop with 6.g3 or develop it to d3 or e2 after the active 6.e4, or the more cautious 6.e3.

5...♕e7 (5...♘c6 is dealt with in the move order under 4...♘c6) Black does not want to expose his queenside knight on c6 to an attack with d4-d5, but rather uses the queen to support the central push ...e6-e5. The queen is comfortable on the e7-square, because with the white knight on d2, Black doesn't need to worry about its sortie to d5 after the thematic...e6-e5. Besides, the knight on b8 has the choice between three destinations: c6, d7 or a6.

As usual, White has two diagonals to choose from for his bishop:

A) **6.e4 e5**

7.♕c2 7.♗e2 ♘f6 8.0-0 0-0 (8...exd4 9.♘xd4 0-0=) **9.♖e1 c5 10.d5 ♘a6 11.a3 ♗d7 12.♖b1 ♘c7 13.b4 b6 14.g3 ♖fb8 15.♕c2 a5 16.bxc5 bxc5 17.♕c3 a4** with mutual chances, Postny-Golod, Biel 2012. **7...♘f6 8.♗e2 0-0 9.0-0 ♗g4 10.♖fe1 a5 11.♗f1 c5 12.d5 ♘bd7**

∞, Degerman-Ulibin, Stockholm 1999;
B) **6.g3 ♘f6 7.♗g2 0-0 8.0-0 e5**

9.e4 Alternatives are 9.♕c2 c6 10.e4 ♗g4 11.h3 ♗xf3 12.♘xf3 c5 13.d5 ♘bd7= Rogers-Nikolic, Manila 1992; Black also gets an easy game after 9.e3 ♘c6 10.h3 a5= Bogosavljevic-Kosic, Jahorina 2012.

B1) **9...a5 10.♕c2 ♘c6!? 11.d5 ♘b8 12.b3 ♘a6 13.a3 ♗d7 14.♘e1 c6⇄** Indjic-Arsovic, Cetinje 2013;

B2) **9...c5!?** is an understandable idea. Black doesn't worry about his lack of space and creates a pawn structure in the centre which is compatible with his light-squared bishop, forcing the opponent to shut down the centre with d4-d5. He will seek counterplay on the queenside with ...a7-a6 and ...b7-b5 or on the kingside with ...f7-f5. **10.d5 ♗g4 11.♕c2 ♗xf3 12.♘xf3 ♘bd7 13.♘e1 a6** A logical plan. Black makes use of the absence of the white bishop

on the f1-a6 diagonal, and organizes play on the queenside. In the game Velikov-Inkiov, Sunny Beach 2013, Black probably wanted to attack the white king and played 13...g6. However, after 14.♘d3 ♘h5 15.♖ae1 ♖ae8 16.f4 f5 17.fxe5 dxe5 18.♗h3± he was in a critical position. **14.a4 ♖ab8** Black can make use of his opponent's unconnected rooks by playing the liberating strike 14...b5! 15.axb5 axb5 16.♖xa8 ♖xa8 17.cxb5 ♘b6⩲. Black will easily retrieve the pawn with ...♕e8 or gain a strong initiative on the a-file by playing ...♕a7. **15.a5 g6 16.♘d3 ♘h5 17.♖ae1 ♕d8 18.♕d2 f5 19.exf5 gxf5 20.f4 e4 21.♘f2±** with the idea of ♘d1-e3, with pressure on the f5-pawn, Manea-Benidze, Rijeka 2010.

6.g3

A) **6.e4 0-0 7.♗d3 e5** For 7...♘c6 8.0-0 e5 see under 4...♘c6. **8.0-0** (8.dxe5 dxe5 9.♘xe5 ♖e8⩱) Interestingly, here Black has four continuations that promise him equality, which only proves the flaws of the white knight being on d2. Both **8...♘c6**, **8...♗g4**, **8...♖e8** and **8...♕e7** are equal.

B) **6.e3** This humble move grants Black more options and better play. **6...0-0 7.♗d3 ♘c6** With 7...b6!? 8.0-0 ♗b7 9.♕c2 ♘bd7= Black gets a flexible position and can prepare various assaults on the opponent's centre without any worries. The chances are equal. **8.a3 e5 9.dxe5 ♘xe5 10.♘xe5 dxe5 11.♕c2 h6 12.h3 ♕e7 13.0-0-0 ♗d7 14.♘e4 ♗c6** with a good position for Black, Mosnegutu-Jobava, Brasov 2011.

6...0-0 7.♗g2

And Black can now choose between three solid continuations that support his typical assault on the opponent's centre: 7...♖e8, 7...♕e7 and 7...♘c6.

7...♖e8

A) For **7...♕e7**, see under 5...♕e7;

B) For **7...♘c6 8.0-0 e5** see under 4...♘c6.

8.0-0 e5 9.e4 a5

A move in the spirit of the King's Indian Defence. Black prepares for the standard plan with ...exd4 and moving the queen's knight to c5. The lack of dark-squared bishops and the passive white knight on d2 give Black good play on the dark squares, in spite of the small space advantage his opponent has in the centre.

10.♕c2 ♘a6

Or immediately 10...exd4 11.♘xd4 ♘a6 12.♖fe1 ♘c5=, Vorobiov-Maiorov, Kazan 2013.

11.♕c3 exd4 12.♘xd4 ♘c5 13.♖fe1 c6 14.b3 ♗d7 15.h3 h6 16.♖e3 ♕c7 17.♖ae1 ♖e7 18.f4 ♖ae8⇄

In this dynamic position both sides have good prospects, Nakamura-Giri, Zug 2013.

Conclusion

As we have seen, in the positions where White has captured with his knight on d2, Black should focus on building a central pawn structure with ...d7-d6 and ...e6-e5. The interesting thing is that Black can support his thematic assault in three ways:

1. with the rook on e8,
2. with the queen on e7 or
3. with the knight on c6,

... maintaining good play in all cases.

In the game Nakamura-Giri, Zug 2013, where Black supported his thematic attack on the centre with ...♖e8, we see the next stage of the game developing in the spirit of the King's Indian Defence, with ...exd4, ...a7-a5 and moving the queen's knight to the standard c5-square. Black easily achieves good play, due to the absence of dark-squared bishops and the passive position of the white knight on d2.

In the positions where White closes the centre with d4-d5, to relieve the pressure on his d4-pawn, (most commonly in the lines with ...♘c6), White gains space, but the central pawn structure is not compatible with his remaining bishop. In addition, White's centre also loses its flexibility, which eases Black's play on both flanks. It follows that with the knight on the d2-square White can't count on an advantage.

Exercises

1 (1) Find the plan.
(solution on page 437)

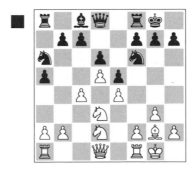

1 (2) Find the plan.
(solution on page 437)

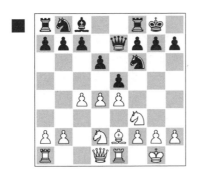

1 (3) Find the plan.
(solution on page 437)

Chapter 2

Black Fianchetto: 4.♕xd2 ♘f6 5.♘f3 b6

Chapter 2.1

Central Strategy: 6.♘c3

1.d4 e6 2.c4 ♗b4+ 3.♗d2 ♗xd2+ 4.♕xd2 ♘f6 5.♘f3 b6 6.♘c3

4.♕xd2 is a logical continuation. White doesn't capture with his knight, because he wants to put the latter on the natural c3-square. After 4...♘f6 White can choose between two strategies: either the fianchetto 5.♘f3 followed by g2-g3, or first 5.g3 and then ♘f3; or the central strategy 5.♘c3 with the idea e2-e4, when the light-squared bishop is developed on the f1-a6 diagonal. We will concentrate on the latter option in this chapter.

1.d4 e6 2.c4 ♗b4+ 3.♗d2 ♗xd2+ 4.♕xd2 ♘f6 5.♘f3

A) **5.♘c3 d5 6.♘f3 0-0 7.g3**. This continuation with an early ♘c3 is not the most fortunate of solutions. For 7.e3 see Chapter 5. **7...dxc4** For 7...♘c6 see Chapter 3.2. **8.♗g2 ♘c6 9.0-0 ♖b8∓** White will have a hard time proving compensation for the missing pawn, Ernst-Nikolic, Netherlands 2011;

B) **5.g3!?** This order is clearly aimed against the Queen's Indian bishop development with ...b7-b6. **5...d5 6.♗g2 ♘bd7** Or 6...c6 7.♘f3 ♘bd7. **7.♘f3 c6** – see 5.♘f3.

Black is now at a great and important crossroads. 5...d5 is the standard high-level continuation, with a clearly defined centre, to which we will devote most of our attention; it is covered in the final chapters of this Section. 5...0-0 (Chapter 3) leaves Black the choice between various approaches in the centre, e.g. 6...d6, 6...b6 or the standard 6...d5.

Let us start the introduction to the following chapters with Black's attempt to quickly establish control of e4 with 5...b6.

5...b6 6.♘c3

A logical move. White develops a piece and threatens e2-e4.

A) **6.e3**

A calm and not overly ambitious continuation, which gives Black a wider choice of plans and easier play. **6...♗b7 7.♗e2 0-0 8.♘c3 d6 9.0-0 ♘bd7=** and Black will set up his preferred position, either using ...e6-e5 or ...c7-c5, made possible by his flexible position and White's unambitious play. For example: **10.♖fd1** 10.b4 c5 (10...♘e4 11.♘xe4 ♗xe4=) 11.a3 ♘e4 12.♘xe4 ♗xe4 13.♖fd1 ♘f6 14.♕b2 ♕c7 15.♘d2 ♗b7 16.♗f3 ♗xf3 and the players agreed to a draw because after 17.♘xf3, an obviously equal position emerges, Spassky-Bronstein, Tallinn 1975. **10...♕e7 11.♖ac1 ♖ad8** 11...♘e4 12.♘xe4 ♗xe4=. **12.♕c2 c5 13.dxc5 bxc5!?**

Black has already achieved a dynamic position with good control of the centre, which is not all that common for the hyper-modern systems that are covered in our book. **14.♘b5 ♘b8 15.♘d2 ♘c6 16.♗f3 a6 17.♘c3 ♘d7 18.g3 ♘de5** and the odds favour Black, as in the game Stamos-Kotronias, Vrachati 2013;

B) For the move **6.g3** please consult Chapter 2.2.

6...♗b7

We shall take a look at three different plans which White can use to fight for the upper hand: the restricting 7.d5, the developing 7.g3, and 7.♕f4 with the idea of e2-e4.

7.d5
White uses the central d5-pawn to limit the influence of the opponent's bishop. However, without the dark-squared bishop, this strategic plan is not very promising.
First the alternatives:

A) **7.g3** The fianchetto of the light-squared bishop generally gives White the best chances of an advantage in positions with the Queen's Indian bishop on b7, however in this order it gives his opponent the additional option of **7...♗xf3!?**. Black can surrender his strong bishop, since he is ruining his opponents pawn structure. For 7...0-0 8.♗g2 see Chapter 3.1. **8.exf3 0-0 9.f4 d5 10.♗g2 c6!**

Black's plan is typical and clear. He's building a pawn structure in the centre that limits the influence of his opponent's pieces, getting ready to move the queen's knight to the ideal d6-square.

Now **11.♕d3** is a new move, invented by a very strong engine that obviously doesn't think that White needs 11.b3, which is the usual practice, when after 11...♘a6 12.0-0 ♕d7 13.♖ad1 ♘c7 14.♖fe1 ♖fd8 15.♕e2 the players agreed to a draw in a balanced position, Ljubojevic-Speelman, New York 1995. After 11.♕d3 a fight between two highly rated machines went as follows: **11...♘a6 12.a3 ♘c7 13.0-0 ♕d7 14.♖ac1 ♘ce8!** With the idea ...♘d6. **15.c5 bxc5 16.dxc5 ♘c7 17.♘e2 ♖fb8 18.♖c2 ♘b5 19.♔h1 a5 20.♘g1 ♕e7 21.♘f3 a4 22.♖e1 ♘d7 23.♕e3 ♕f6 24.♗f1 ♖b7 25.♗d3 ♖ab8**

With mutual chances, Komodo 5-Houdini 3, Internet 2012;

B) After **7.♕f4** White obviously wants to play e2-e4 and get a full centre, using his most powerful piece to control the e4-square, which is somewhat unorthodox. Black can either foil his opponent's plans with 7...d5 or allow them and continue developing with 7...0-0:

B1) **7...0-0 8.e4**

White places all three of his pawns in the centre, but is late with his development. Let us look at the dynamic reply 8...♘c6 and the calmer 8...d6.

B11) **8...♘c6!?N** Now a hyper-modern position emerges. Black is not interested in the centre, but exclusively in the development and activity of his own pieces. The essential question is: can the activity of Black's minor pieces compensate for the opponent's strong centre?

Also, this continuation is perfect for aficionados of hypermodern chess, where the opponent's centre is attacked by pieces. In this particular position, Black has an additional motif in the exposed white queen on f4, so he wants to transfer his knight to g6.

9.♗e2 It is too early to proceed with 9.e5 ♘h5 10.♕e3 (weaker would be 10.♕g4 g6 11.0-0-0 f6∓) 10...f6 11.0-0-0 fxe5 12.dxe5 ♕e7 with a good, active position for Black. **9...♘e7 10.0-0 ♘g6 11.♕e3 ♘g4** 11...d6 leads after 12.h3 ♕e7 to the same position. **12.♕d2 d6 13.h3 ♘f6 14.♕e3 ♕e7 15.♖ad1 h6 16.♗d3 ♘d7∞.**

Black has active pieces and a flexible pawn structure, but less space. However, there are plenty of players who love this type of position, which is somewhat passive but with a healthy and flexible pawn structure in the centre. And now you will probably be surprised to hear that this hyper-modern game was played by two machines!! – Houdini 2.0 Pro-Houdini 2.0 Pro, Internet 2011. Of course, we called for their aid, since there are no practical human games with this line;

B12) **8...d6** Flexible, but more passive. **9.0-0-0** A safer move would be 9.♗e2±. **9...♘bd7 10.♗e2 c5** A questionable move was 10...♘h5?! 11.♕e3 ♘hf6 12.h3 ♕e7 13.g4± when White had a spatial advantage and the initiative in Piket-Danielsen, Leeuwarden 1993. **11.e5** Weaker would be 11.dxc5 e5 12.♕d2 ♘xc5 13.♕xd6 ♕c8⇆. **11...cxd4 12.exf6** 12.♕xd4 dxe5 13.♘xe5 ♘xe5 14.♕xe5 ♕e7=. **12...dxc3 13.fxg7 cxb2+ 14.♔xb2 ♔xg7 15.♖xd6 ♕f6+ 16.♕xf6+ ♘xf6** with a clear draw.

B2) **7...d5!?** Black is playing a weaker version of the Queen's Gambit, since there are no dark-squared bishops on the board, but instead relies on the time White has spent with his queen:

B21) **8.e3 0-0 9.♖c1** 9.♗e2 dxc4 10.♗xc4 ♕d6=. **9...♘c6** More passive would be the development with 9...♘bd7 10.cxd5 ♘xd5 11.♘xd5 ♗xd5 12.♕xc7±.

10.♗e2 10.cxd5 ♘xd5 11.♘xd5 ♕xd5 12.♗c4 ♕d6 13.♕xd6 cd6=.

10...dxc4 11.♗xc4 ♕d6 12.♕xd6 Or 12.♘e5 ♕e7 13.♘xc6 ♗xc6 14.0-0 ♗b7 15.♖fd1 ♖fd8= and it is unclear how White is going to fare against the liberating and equalizing ...c7-c5. **12...cxd6 13.0-0 a6** with equality, as in the game Deep Rybka 4-Deep Rybka 4, Internet (blitz) 2010;

B22) **8.cxd5 ♘xd5 9.♘xd5 ♕xd5!** Of course, Black is ready to sacrifice his c-pawn because his opponent will fall behind in development. **10.♕xc7 ♘d7 11.♕c3** 11.e3? ♖c8 12.♕f4 ♕a5+∓. **11...0-0⇆**

With an advantage in development and sufficient compensation for the pawn in the game Kiselev-Kazantsev, Moscow 1996;

B23) Nothing is achieved by **8.♘b5 ♘a6 9.e3 0-0 10.a3 ♕e7 11.♖c1 ♖fd8** with good play for Black.

7...0-0 8.g3

8.e4 is a logical continuation of White's plan. However, Black has multiple options to neutralize White's centre and simplify the position: **8...exd5 9.exd5** 9.cxd5?! ♖e8∓. **9...♘a6!?N** On 9...c5 10.♗e2 d6 11.0-0 White has better chances due to his space advantage, Sherbakov-Kholmov, Smolensk 1986. **10.♗e2 ♘c5 11.0-0 c6 12.♖fe1 ♖e8 13.♗f1 ♘ce4 14.♘xe4 ♘xe4 15.♕d4 cxd5 16.cxd5 ♘f6** with obviously equal chances.

To the text Black can respond: a) with counterplay against White's centre by ...c7-c6; b) with 8...exd5 or c) with the blockade 8...d7-d6 and ...e6-e5.

8...c6

This is a logical response to the early d4-d5. Black is eager to activate his light-squared bishop before his opponent finishes his development and fortifies the centre.

A) **8...exd5** Black opens up the e-file, but loses control over f5, which is an important square in this type of position, as White frequently attacks with ♘h4-f5 or ♘d4-f5. **9.cxd5 b5!?**

Black trades his b-pawn for the opponent's central pawn, but now his c- and d-pawns become exposed to threats by White's rooks. Safer would be 9...c6=. **10.♘xb5 ♗xd5 11.♗g2 a6** 11...c6 12.♘c3 ♘e4 (another option is 12...♗xf3N 13.♗xf3 d5 14.0-0 ♘bd7 15.♗g2 ♖b8 16.♖fd1 ♕b6 with chances of equality) 13.♘xe4 ♗xe4 14.0-0 ♖e8 15.♖ac1 ♘a6 16.♖fd1± Arbakov-Vospernik, Bled 1995. **12.♘c3 ♗b7 13.0-0 d6 14.♖ac1 ♘bd7 15.♘d4 ♗xg2 16.♔xg2±** White has a better pawn structure and has pressure on his opponent's weakened queenside, Kaidanov-Cherniaev, New York 1993;

B) For **8...d6 9.♗g2 e5** see Chapter 3.1. **9.d6 c5 10.♗g2 ♘e4 11.♕d3!?** 11.♘xe4 ♗xe4 12.0-0 ♘c6 13.♕f4 f5=. **11...♘xc3**

Also possible is 11...f5!?=.

12.♘g5 ♕xg5 13.♗xb7 ♘xe2! 14.♕xe2 ♘c6 15.♗xa8 ♖xa8♔

With a fortified knight in the centre, Black has obvious compensation for his slight lack of material, Christiansen-Seirawan, Estes Park 1986.

Conclusion

In the critical position after 5.♘f3 b6 6.♘c3 ♗b7 Black uses the early fianchetto to control the important e4-square. Here White has tried various methods to gain an advantage:

a) On 7.g3 Black achieves equality by ruining his opponent's structure with 7...♗xf3.

b) In reply to the attempt to box in the bishop with 7.d5 Black easily copes with White's centre by playing 7...c6.

c) If White plays for a full centre with 7.♕f4, Black has the choice between a hypermodern position with 7...0-0 8.e4 ♘c6!? and a position in the spirit of the Queen's Gambit with 7...d5.

In this chapter we have covered the material where White plays the logical developing move 6.♘c3. We can conclude that this gives White less chances of an advantage than 6.g3, which we will cover in Chapter 2.2.

Exercises

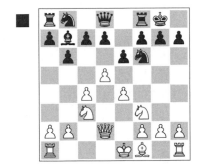

2.1 (1) Find the plan.
(solution on page 437)

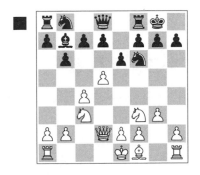

2.1 (2) Find the plan.
(solution on page 438)

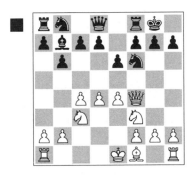

2.1 (3) Find the plan.
(solution on page 438)

Chapter 2.2

Fianchetto 6.g3

1.d4 e6 2.c4 ♗b4+ 3.♗d2 ♗xd2+ 4.♕xd2 ♘f6 5.♘f3 b6 6.g3

This is the most frequent continuation, although Black now has the opportunity to develop his bishop on the f1-a6 diagonal as well. However, White does not wish to reckon with Black's strategic threat of ...♗b7xf3, with the destruction of his pawn structure, as was the case in Chapter 2.1 where we covered 6.♘c3 ♗b7, and instead timely fianchettoes his bishop.

Now Black has the choice between two diagonals for his light-squared bishop.

6...♗a6

Black obviously wants a more active role for his bishop on this diagonal, instead of neutralizing the activities of the Catalan bishop by developing on b7. This idea is backed up by Black's option to reduce the white light-squared bishop's activity on g2 with his c- and d-pawns.

Also, this variation has increased in popularity and it frequently emerges in the move order of the Queen's Indian: 1.d4 ♘f6 2.c4 e6 3.♘f3 b6 4.g3 ♗b4+ 5.♗d2 ♗xd2+ 6.♕xd2 ♗a6.

White can defend the c4-pawn with the logical 7.b3, or else overload his pieces with 7.♕c2 or 7.♘a3.

For 6...♗b7 7.♗g2 0-0 8.♘c3 see Chapter 3.1.

7.b3

The most efficient move. Using his b-pawn to defend c4, White doesn't put too much strain on his pieces, and also frees the b2-square, from which White's queen can perform useful tasks in the absence of the dark-squared bishop. In this position, Black can play our favourite system of 7...c6 with the idea of ...d7-d5, or else 7...0-0, preparing for a total confrontation in the centre with ...d7-d5 and ...c7-c5. We shall also take a look at the less frequently played continuations 7...d5 and 7...c5, though they often transpose into the positions with hanging pawns covered under 7...0-0.

To summarize, Black can realistically play one of two systems:

1. with the central pawns on d5 and c6;
2. with the pawns on d5 and c5, which can be achieved via different move orders in combination with castling kingside.

A) **7.♕c2** By thus defending the pawn White relinquishes control of the d-file, so Black has the opportunity to destroy the opponent's centre with A1) 7...♗b7 with the idea of ... c7-c5 or, immediately, A2) 7...c5.

A1) **7...♗b7**

With no dark-squared bishops on the board, ...♗xf3!? is often a strategic

threat, since White can't compensate for the ruined pawn structure with the bishop pair.

A11) **8.♘c3 c5** Or immediately 8...♗xf3 9.exf3 ♘c6⇄. **9.dxc5 ♗xf3 10.exf3 bxc5 11.♗g2 ♘c6⇄** Black has given up his powerful bishop, but in return has gained the excellent d4-square for his knight;

A12) **8.♗g2 c5!** The standard method of simplifying and achieving equal play, but only under the condition that White does not have the option of d4-d5. **9.dxc5** 9.0-0 cxd4 10.♘xd4 ♗xg2 11.♔xg2 0-0= Evdokimov-Sethuraman, Philadelphia 2012. **9...bxc5 10.0-0 0-0 11.♖d1** and now:

A121) **11...♕e7** The best place for the queen. Now Black intends to develop his pieces naturally with ...♘b8-c6, ...d7-d6, ...♖fd8 etc. **12.♘c3 ♘c6 13.♖d2 ♖fd8 14.♖ad1 d6 15.♘e4 ♘xe4 16.♕xe4 ♘e5 17.♕c2 ♘xf3+ 18.♗xf3 ♗xf3 19.exf3 ♖d7 20.♕e4 ♖ad8 21.♔g2 g6 22.h4 h5 23.f4 ♕f6=** Ramirez Alvarez-Onischuk, Saint Louis 2013;

A122) A weaker move would be **11...♕b6** because of **12.♘c3 d6** (12...♘c6 13.e4±) **13.♖d2 ♖d8 14.♖ad1** and because of the weakness of the d6-pawn, Black can't develop his knight on the natural square c6.

14...♘a6 15.e4 with better play for White, due to the d6 weakness and the useless knight on a6, Indjic-Perunovic, Vrnjacka Banja 2013.

A2) It's possible to immediately play **7...c5**, though here White has the aggressive **8.e4!?** at his disposal (8.♗g2 ♘c6 9.dxc5 bxc5 10.0-0 ♖b8 11.♖d1 0-0 12.b3 ♕e7 13.♘c3 ♖fd8 with chances for both sides, Brkljaca-Bojkovic, Banja Koviljaca 2013), for example: **8...cxd4 9.♘xd4 0-0 10.♘c3 ♗b7 11.0-0-0 a6 12.♖g1!? ♕c7 13.f4 ♘c6 14.♘xc6 ♗xc6 15.e5 ♘g4 16.♗d3,** Beliavsky-Razuvaev, Ashkhabad 1978.

B) **7.♘a3**

White seems to imitate his opponent by placing his piece on the edge of the board to defend his c4-pawn. However, the bishop is a long-range piece and can swiftly readjust its position if need be. **7...0-0 8.♗g2 ♗b7** and now:

B1) **9.0-0 d6 10.♖ad1 ♘bd7 11.♖fe1** 11.♘b5 a6 12.♘c3 b5⇄ Torre-Miles, Wijk aan Zee 1984. **11...♕e7 12.♘h4 ♗xg2 13.♘xg2 c5 14.♘e3 ♖fd8=** Pelletier-Carlsen, Biel 2006;

B2) **9.♘b5 a6 10.♘c3 ♘e4 11.♕c2 ♘xc3 12.bxc3** Now the famous tactical motif does not work, since Black has a pawn on a6: 12.♘g5? ♕xg5 13.♗xb7 and Black can play 13...♖a7∓; and if

12.♕xc3 d6 13.0-0 ♘d7=. **12...♘c6 13.0-0 ♘a5** with equal chances, Elianov-Efimenko, Kiev 2012.

7...0-0

This flexible developing move is usually chosen by players who strive for dynamic and active play. Black aims at a direct confrontation in the centre with ...d7-d5 and ...c7-c5.

A) **7...c6**

This variation hasn't lost its popularity over the years and is occasionally, or even frequently, on the repertoire of many grandmasters, including Michael Adams, the late Lev Polugaevsky, Ulf Anderson, and Predrag Nikolic. However, the most persistent player who applied it was the UK-born original grandmaster Anthony Miles, so the variation could very well be named after him.

Black prepares ...d7-d5 with the intention of attacking the c4-pawn and increasing the influence of his bishop on a6, at the same time limiting his opponent's strong light-squared bishop on the h1-a8 diagonal. White can generally develop in two directions: either a central strategy with A1) 8.♘c3 or A2) 8.♕f4 and carrying through e2-e4, or a fianchetto strategy in the spirit of the Closed Catalan with A3) 8.♗g2 and queenside play.

A1) **8.♘c3 d5**

A11) 9.♗g2 This continuation usually leads to positions we have covered under 8.♗g2 above. Here we will just have a look at 10.♕b2 since it has independent meaning. **9...♘bd7 10.♕b2!?** We already mentioned in the note to 7.b3 that the white queen is often placed on the comfortable b2-square, possible due to the disappearance of the dark-squared bishop. From there the queen can perform an array of useful tasks, including controlling the dark squares. **10...0-0 11.0-0 dxc4 12.bxc4 ♗xc4 13.♘d2 ♗a6 14.♗xc6 ♖c8 15.♗g2 ♘b8 16.♘b3 ♕e7 17.♖fe1**

17...♖c4 17...♘c6!?N 18.♖ac1 ♘b4 with active play and equal chances. **18.e4 ♖fc8 19.♖ac1 ♕c7 20.♗f1±** Torre-Miles, Thessaloniki 1984;

A12) 9.e4 White threatens e4-e5, practically forcing his opponent to give up the centre and trade the d-pawn, which is the pillar of Black's strategy.

A121) 9...dxe4 10.♘g5 ♘bd7 For 10...c5 11.♘gxe4 ♘xe4 12.♘xe4 see under 11...c5. **11.♘gxe4 0-0 12.♗g2 ♘xe4 13.♘xe4 ♘f6 14.0-0 ♖c8 15.♖fd1 ♘xe4 16.♗xe4 ♕c7 17.♕e3 g6 18.♖d2 ♗b7 19.c5 e5 20.♖ad1 ♖fe8 21.b4±** Vyzhmanavin-Ikonnikov, Cheliabinsk 1990;

A122) 9...0-0 Black ignores White's centre and strives for positions similar to the French Defence. **10.e5 ♘e8** On 10...♘fd7 White continues as planned with 11.cxd5 ♗xf1 12.♔xf1 cxd5 13.♔g2±. **11.cxd5 ♗xf1 12.♔xf1 cxd5 13.♔g2 ♘c6 14.♖ac1 ♖c8 15.h4 h6 16.♘e2 f6 17.♘f4 ♕d7 18.♖he1±** Black has some trouble with the central e5- and e6-squares, as is often the case with this type of centre in the French Defence, Dautov-Nikolic, Moscow 2001;

A123) 9...♘xe4 10.♘xe4 dxe4 11.♘g5

11...c5!?
A good continuation to achieve active and dynamic play.

11...♘d7 would lead to a passive position. After 12.♘xe4 ♘f6 13.♗g2 ♘xe4 14.♗xe4 ♗b7 15.0-0 0-0 16.♖fd1 ♕f6 17.♕e3 has a problematic bishop on b7, for example: 17...♖fd8 (or 17...♖ad8 18.♖d2 ♖d7 19.♖ad1 ♖fd8 20.h4 g6 21.b4± S. Savchenko-Balogh, Baku 2007) 18.♖d2 ♖d7 19.♖ad1 g6 20.h4 h5 21.dxc5± Tkachiev-Bauer, France 2007.

12.♗g2
12.♘xe4 cxd4 (12...0-0? 13.dxc5± Kortchnoi-Greenfeld, Beer-Sheva 1987) 13.♗g2 0-0 14.♘g5 ♘d7 15.♗xa8 ♕xa8 16.0-0 ♘f6 17.♕xd4 h6

31

18.♘h3 ♗b7⩱ M. Marin. Let us extend the analysis of the great Romanian grandmaster: 19.♘f4 ♘e4 (with the idea of ...♘g5) 20.h4 (White can lose his way with 20.♘h5 f6 21.♕d7?! ♖f7⩱ and the e6-pawn is poisoned, so Black is taking matters into his own hands) 20...♖d8 21.♕e3 ♘d2 22.♖fd1 ♘f3+=.

12...♘c6 13.dxc5 ♕xd2+ 14.♔xd2 f5

15.♘xe6 After 15.cxb6, as in the game Saric-Riazantsev, Budva 2009, Black is also able to activate his pieces and gets sufficient compensation: 15...♔e7 16.bxa7 ♖hd8+ 17.♔c1 h6 18.♘h3 ♘d4 19.♖d1 e5 20.♔b2 ♖xa7 21.♖d2 g5⩱ 22.♘g1? ♗xc4−+. **15...♔f7 16.♘f4** 16.♘c7 doesn't change the evaluation: 16...♖ad8+ 17.♔c1 ♘b4 18.cxb6 axb6 19.♘xa6 ♘xa6 20.♖d1 ♘b4 with sufficient compensation for Black, Khismatullin-Shomoev, Khanty-Mansiysk 2012.
16...bxc5 17.f3 ♖ad8+ 18.♔c3 e3 19.♘d3 ♖he8 20.f4 After 20.♘xc5 Black easily drew with 20...e2 21.♘xa6 ♖e3+ 22.♔c2 ♖ed3 23.♖ae1 ♖d2+ 24.♔c1 ♖xa2 25.f4 ♖dd2 and Black had perpetual check in Aronian-Grischuk, Moscow 2012. **20...e2 21.♗d5+ ♖xd5 22.cxd5 ♖e3 23.dxc6 ♖xd3+ 24.♔c2 ♔e6 25.♖ae1 ♖d5 26.♖hf1 ♔d6 27.♖f3 ♔xc6 28.♖e3**

♔d7 Black can maintain his position due to the protected pawn on the second rank, Gueci-Schuster, FICGS email 2010.

A2) **8.♕f4!?**

Also a solid way to enforce the main idea of the central strategy, the e2-e4 advance. In addition, White activates the queen, taking control of the dark squares and freeing the d2-square for his queen's knight. **8...d5 9.♘bd2 ♘bd7 10.e4 dxe4 11.♘xe4**
Here Black can play either A21) 11...♘xe4 or the elastic A22) 11...0-0, which gives him a wider array of choices. However, after this continuation, White also has a solid additional option in 12.♘xf6+!?:

A21) **11...♘xe4 12.♕xe4 ♕c7** 12...0-0 13.♕xc6 (after 13.♗g2 ♗b7 we are in the game Georgiev-Nikolic, Kragujevac 2013) 13...♖c8 14.♕d6 14...♗b7⩱; or 14.♕e4 b5⩰ and White's king will be under attack by the opponent's queen after ...♕a5. **13.♗g2 ♗b7 14.0-0** 14.♘e5 f5 15.♕e3 ♘xe5 16.dxe5 0-0-0=. **14...0-0** and again we are in the game Georgiev-Nikolic, Kragujevac 2013, given under 11...0-0 below. After the immediate 14...c5 there could follow 15.♕e3 0-0 16.♖ad1 ♖fd8 17.♖d2 with the idea of ♖fd1, with an easier game for White, which is otherwise typical of this type of position, due to his pawn majority and a potential passed pawn on the queenside.

A22) **11...0-0** and now:

A221) **12.♗g2 ♞xe4 13.♕xe4**

A2211) **13...b5!?** A logical attempt to activate the bishop on the f1-a6 diagonal and to continue without it returning to b7.

A22111) After **14.0-0 bxc4** White should play **15.♕e2** with equal chances, because after 15.♕xc6?! ♞b6 16.bxc4 ♗xc4 Black is also better off, due to the weakness of the d4-pawn, Morovic Fernandez-Sisniega, New York 1988;

A22112) **14.c5 ♕a5+ 15.♔f1** 15.♞d2 ♜ad8 16.♕c2 e5↑ and Black takes over. **15...♕c3 16.♜e1 b4+ 17.♔g1=** Beliavsky-Miles, Moscow 1990;

A22113) **14.♕xc6!N** Surprisingly this has not been played in practice, though it gives White the best chances. **14...♕a5+ 15.♞d2 ♞b6 16.c5 ♜ac8 17.♕e4 ♞d5 18.♕d3! ♜fd8 19.0-0** and Black finds it difficult to prove compensation for the missing pawn. If a reader ever finds a solution to this problem it will be very fortunate for the fans of this variation!

A2212) **13...♗b7 14.0-0 ♕c7** With the idea ...c6-c5, which would solve the

last strategic problem in this opening. **15.♞e5 ♞xe5 16.dxe5** 16.♕xe5 ♜ac8= with the idea ...c6-c5. **16...♜ad8 17.♜fd1**

White seems to be better off strategically, but the essential question is whether it is enough for something substantial in the endgame. **17...h6** Black plays a useful move and waits for the opponent to play the logical b2-b4, so that after the liberating ...c6-c5 he could open up the b-file for his rooks.

However, more precise seems 17...♗a8!?N 18.♕e3 c5 19.♗xa8 ♜xd1+ 20.♜xd1 ♜xa8 21.♜d6 ♜d8. (Black must not allow the doubling up on the d-file, because it would be a torture to play such an endgame) 22.♕d2 ♜xd6 23.exd6 ♕d7± . White's pawn looks dangerous, but our analyses do not show a win for White. Please have a look at the similar endgame without the b-pawn in the game Georgiev-Nikolic, Kragujevac 2013. **18.b4 ♗a8 19.♕e3** With the idea c4-c5. Better odds are offered by 19.c5!? bxc5 20.bxc5 ♜d5 21.♜ac1 ♜xe5 (21...♕xe5 22.♕xe5 ♜xe5 23.♜d7≋; 21...♜fd8 22.♕a4±) 22.♕f4≋ and in all instances White has strong compensation for the pawn due to the weak bishop on a8.

19...c5 20.♗xa8 ♖xd1+ 21.♖xd1 ♖xa8 22.bxc5 bxc5 23.♖d6 ♖b8 24.♔g2 ♖b6= and thanks to the open b-file, Black can exchange the rooks and with relative ease achieve a draw in the queen ending: **25.♕d3 ♖xd6 26.exd6 ♕d7 27.h4 a6 28.h5 ♔f8 29.♔h2 ♔e8 30.♕d2 ♕d8 31.♕d1 ♕d7 32.a3 ♕c6=** An important game for the evaluation of the topical continuation 8.♕f4, Georgiev-Nikolic, Kragujevac 2013.

A222) **12.♘xf6+**

12...♕xf6 On 12...♘xf6 after 13.♘e5 ♗b7 14.♗g2 ♖c8 15.0-0 ♕e7 16.♖fe1 ♖fd8 17.♖ad1± White achieves an advantage which is typical of this position, due to the passive bishop on b7, Kortchnoi-Kudrin, Titograd 1984. **13.♕xf6 gxf6!?** An interesting idea, ruining his own pawn structure to prevent the unpleasant posting of White's knight on e5. **14.0-0-0 ♖fd8 15.♗g2 ♖ac8 16.♖d2 ♔f8 17.♔b2 f5 18.♖hd1±** White has better chances because his position is clearly more sound strategically. However, the players simplified in the following moves, steering towards a draw: **18...♖c7 19.d5 cxd5 20.cxd5 ♘f6 21.dxe6 ♖xd2+ 22.♖xd2 fxe6 23.♘e5 ♗b5 24.a4 ♗e8 25.♖d4 ♔e7=** A draw was agreed in this equal posi-

tion in Cheparinov-Georgiev, Bol 2013.

A3) **8.♗g2 d5**

Black has placed his main strategic pillars on d5 and c6. What's left is ...♘d7, ...0-0, ...♕e7 and a rook on c8, and he can successfully round off his opening concept.

A31) **9.♘e5 ♘fd7 10.f4** For 10.♘c3 ♘xe5 11.dxe5 ♘d7 12.f4 ♕e7 13.0-0 0-0 see under 7...0-0 8.♘c3 d5 9.♗g2 c6 10.0-0 ♘bd7 11.♘e5 ♘xe5 12.dxe5 ♘d7 13.f4 below; 10.♘xd7 (all this work just to exchange the knight on d7 achieves nothing) 10...♘xd7 11.cxd5 cxd5 12.0-0 ♖c8 13.♘c3 ♘f6 14.♖fc1 0-0 15.♖c2 ♕d6 16.♖ac1 ♖c7 17.♘e4 ♘xe4 18.♗xe4 ♖xc2 19.♗xc2 ♕d7 20.♗d3 ♗xd3 21.♕xd3 ♖c8 with absolutely equal chances, Spiess-Sergeev, Guben 2013; 10.♘d3 0-0 11.0-0 is dealt with under 9...c6. **10...0-0 11.♘c3 ♘xe5 12.fxe5** For 12.dxe5 ♘d7 13.0-0 ♕e7 see under 7...0-0 8.♘c3 d5 9.♗g2 c6 10.0-0 ♘bd7 11.♘e5 ♘xe5 12.dxe5 ♘d7 13.f4 below. **12...♘d7 13.cxd5 cxd5 14.e4 dxe4 15.♘xe4 f6 16.0-0-0 ♗b7 17.exf6 ♘xf6** with a clearly equal position, Shirov-Navara, Germany 2012;

A32) **9.♕c2** White is striving for ♘d2 and e2-e4, a typical plan in the Closed Catalan. **9...0-0 10.♘bd2 ♘bd7** and now:

A321) **11.0-0 c5 12.♖ac1** For 12.e4 see under 11.e4. **12...♖c8 13.♕b2 ♖c7** 13...♗b7 14.♖fd1 ♖c7 (also natural seems to be 14...♕e7!?= and Black can't have any problems) 15.dxc5 bxc5 16.e3 ♕b8 17.♘e5 ♘xe5 18.♕xe5 ♖d8 19.cxd5 exd5 20.♘b1± with the idea of ♘c3, and White will build up some unpleasant pressure against his opponent's hanging pawns. **14.♖fd1 ♕b8** Another option is 14...♕e7!?, which has already proven itself as a solid square for the queen in the absence of dark-squared bishops. **15.e3 ♖fc8** with equal chances, Xu Jun-Arnason, Thessaloniki 1984;

A322) **11.e4 c5** Black is the first to complete his development, so there's no reason for him to shy away from attacking the opponent's centre. **12.0-0 cxd4 13.exd5 exd5** 13...d3! – though this was played in a blitz game Carlsen-Andreikin, Moscow 2013, this insertion, which had not yet appeared in practice, probably surprised Carlsen, since now the position quickly became equal: 14.♕xd3 exd5 15.♖fe1 ♖c8=.
After **14.♘xd4 ♖c8 15.♖fe1 g6 16.♖ac1** (weaker would be 16.b4?! ♗xc4 17.♕a4 ♕c7 18.♗h3 ♖ce8 19.♘xc4 ♖xe1+ 20.♖xe1 ♕xc4∓ D. Gurevich-Christiansen, Estes Park 1987; but 16.a4!?±, preventing the relieving ...b7-b5, maintains the initiative, thanks

to his bishop on g2 and a potentially dangerous knight on d4) **16...b5!=** Black increases the influence of his queenside rook and bishop, gaining equal play, Gelfand-Psakhis, Haifa 2000.
  A33) **9.0-0 ♘bd7**

The basic and the most important position of the 'Miles System', which can also work with castling instead of putting the knight on d7. After a few more moves, the positions usually merge and we have covered them under the line 7...0-0 8.♗g2 d5 9.0-0 c6 below.
However there are several important issues to consider when making this choice. By playing 7...c6 and ...♘bd7 instead of castling, Black diverts his opponent from the natural development of his knight on c3, which would mean giving the pawn on c4, because without the standard invasion of White's knight on e5 he has no compensation for the pawn. In addition, with the knight on d7, Black doesn't have to reckon with his opponent's manoeuvre ♘e5-d3, because he would simply exchange on e5.
Finally, in the order with 7.0-0, Black can't count on playing the Miles System if his opponent plays 8.♘c3. Here we will take a look at Miles's set-up alone, which has independent meaning, and at the original continuation ...♖c8 (9...0-0 – 7...0-0 8.♗g2 d5 9.0-0 c6).

10.cxd5

For 10.♘e5 ♘xe5 11.dxe5 ♘d7 12.f4 ♕e7 13.♘c3 0-0 see under 7...0-0 8.♘c3 d5 9.♗g2 c6 10.0-0 ♘bd7 11.♘e5 ♘xe5 12.dxe5 ♘d7 13.f4 below. For 10.♖c1 0-0 see under 7...0-0 8.♗g2 d5 9.0-0 c6.

In practice the natural 10.♘c3 is never seen...

... because after 10...dxc4∞ it is more difficult for White to prove compensation for the pawn, in a position where Black has the knight on d7 with control of the e5-square, which is one of the advantages of delaying castling for Black (for 10...0-0 instead, see the line 7...0-0 8.♘c3 d5 9.♗g2 c6 10.0-0 below).

10...cxd5 11.♘c3 11.♖c1 ♘e4 (for 11...0-0 12.♘c3 ♕e7 see under 7...0-0 8.♗g2 d5 9.0-0 c6 10.♖c1 ♘bd7 11.cxd5 cxd5 12.♘c3) and after 12.♕b2 in the game Lajthajm-Jeremic, Subotica 2008, Black unexpectedly faced difficulties: 12...♖c8 13.e3 0-0 14.♘bd2 ♘xd2 (14...♕e7!?) 15.♘xd2 ♕e7 16.b4 ♗b7 17.a4 ♕d6 18.♗f1 ♖fe8 19.♘f3 and White has activated and harmonized his pieces, and is better. **11...♖c8!?** The continuation of Anthony Miles, who played the system with 6... ♗a6 for years and contributed to a better understanding of it (for 11...0-0 see under 7...0-0 8.♘c3 d5

9.♗g2 c6 10.0-0 ♘bd7). **12.♖ac1 0-0 13.♖c2 ♖c7 14.♖fc1 ♕b8 15.♘e5 ♖fc8** with equality, Portisch-Miles, Lucerne 1985.

B) **7...d5**

This move is usually played by those who favour positions with ...c7-c5, with a direct and total confrontation in the centre. However, without castling, Black has to take into account the additional possibility for his opponent to exchange queens and force Black into an inferior endgame by 8.cxd5 exd5 and 9.♕e3+.

B1) **8.♗g2 0-0** For 8...c6 see under 7...c6. **9.0-0 ♘bd7** (9...c5 is covered under 8...d5)

Black wants to keep both options of ...c7-c5 and ...c7-c6 open. But now that the knight has declared its intentions on d7, he can exploit the inferior positioning of his opponent's pieces.

B11) **10.♖c1**

Or 10.♖d1 c6 (now 10...c5 is weaker because of 11.♘c3!±) 11.♕c2 ♖c8 12.♘c3 c5 13.dxc5 ♖xc5 14.e4 dxc4 15.b4 ♖c7 16.♖d4 h6 17.♖ad1⩲ Zilka-A. Saric, Meissen 2013; if 10.♘e5 c5 11.♘xd7 ♕xd7 12.dxc5 bxc5 13.♕a5 ♗b7 14.♖d1 ♖fc8 15.e3 h5 16.♘d2 ♕e7 17.♖ac1 h4 with chances for both sides, Ballow-Magallanes, ICCF email 2011.

10...c5 For 10...c6 see under 7...0-0. **11.cxd5** 11.♕b2 dxc4 12.bxc4 ♗b7 13.e3 ♖c8 14.♘bd2 ♖c7 15.a4 a5 16.♘e1 ♗xg2 17.♘xg2 ♕a8 18.♘f4 ♖fc8= Midoux-Saric, Vienna 2009. **11...♘xd5** 11...exd5!? deserves attention, since the white rook will have to regroup: 12.♘c3 ♖e8 13.dxc5 ♘xc5 14.♘d4 ♖c8∞ Markus-Cabrilo, Teslic 2006. Black has fully activated pieces in compensation for the isolated d5-pawn. **12.♘a3 ♖c8 13.♘c4 ♘5f6 14.♕b2 cxd4 15.♘xd4 ♗xc4 16.♖xc4 ♖xc4 17.bxc4 ♘c5 18.♘c6 ♕c7** with equal chances, Girya-Koneru, Tashkent 2013;

B12) **10.cxd5!**
Denying Black the option of transposing to positions with ...c7-c6. Now usually a pawn structure emerges where Black's central pawns are objects rather than any real power, because they are exposed to attack. **10...exd5** For 10...♘e4 11.♕b2 exd5 see under 9...♘e4. **11.♘c3 ♖e8**

With the idea ...♘e4. **12.♕b2!** The queen hides from the assault with ...♘e4 and strengthens the control of the dark squares on the queenside. Black can now put his pawn either on c5 or on c6, but in both instances White has easier play with no risk, due to his clear plan and his pressure on the vulnerable black pawns in the centre.

After 12.♖fd1 ♘e4 13.♘xe4 dxe4 14.♘e1 ♘f6 15.♘c2 ♘d5 16.♘e3 ♗b7 17.♖ac1 ♕e7 18.♖c2 ♘xe3 19.♕xe3 ♗d5 the players drew in this equal position, Gen. Timoschenko-Rodriguez Cespedes, Belgrade 1988.

12...♗b7 For 12...c5 13.♖fd1± see under 10...♘bd7 11.♕b2. **13.♖ac1 a6 14.♖fd1 ♕e7 15.e3 ♕d6 16.b4 c6 17.♘a4 b5 18.♘c5 ♘xc5 19.dxc5 ♕c7 20.a4±** Polak-Cvek, Prague 2007.

B2) **8.cxd5**

B21) **8...♘e4** A weaker move would be 8...♘xd5 9.e4±. **9.♕c2** 9.♕b2 exd5 10.♗g2; 9.♕b4 9...exd5 10.♕a4+?! (better is 10.♘c3 c5 (for 10...♘xc3 11.♕xc3 0-0 12.♖c1 see under 9.♕c2 below) 11.♕a4+ ♔f8∞) 10...c6!N (White will experience difficulties due to his queen being badly placed on a4. 10...♕d7 11.♕xd7+ ♘xd7 12.♘bd2 ♔e7 13.♗h3 c5 14.dxc5 ♘dxc5= Sargissian-Efimenko, Valjevo 2012) 11.e3 ♕f6 12.♘bd2 ♗xf1 13.♔xf1 a5

14.♔g2 (14.♘xe4? ♕xf3—+) 14...♕e7∓ with the idea ...b6-b5. **9...exd5** and now:

B211) **10.♗g2 0-0 11.0-0 ♘d7 12.♘bd2** 12.♖e1 ♘df6 (12...c5!? 13.♘c3 ♗b7 14.♖ac1 ♖c8 15.♕b2 ♕e7⇄) 13.♘bd2 c5 14.dxc5 ♘xc5 15.♕b2 ♖e8 16.♘d4 ♕d7 17.♖ad1 ♗b7∞ Lintchevski-Kovalenko, Kazan 2013. **12...♖e8** 12...♗xe2 13.♘xe4 dxe4 (13...♗xf1 14.♘eg5±) 14.♕xe2 exf3 15.♕xf3 ♖c8 16.♖fd1± and Black has critical weaknesses on the light squares. **13.♘xe4 dxe4 14.♘e5 ♘f6** Weaker would be 14...♘xe5 15.dxe5 ♖xe5 16.♗xe4± with a double attack on a8 and h7. **15.♘c6 ♕d7** 15...♕d6!?N 16.♖ac1 ♗b7= with the idea ...♘d5. **16.♖ac1 ♗b5 17.♖fd1±** Black hasn't solved all his problems, M.M. Hansen-Vervoort, ICCF email 2006.

B212) **10.♘c3 ♘xc3 11.♕xc3 0-0 12.♖c1 ♕e7 13.e3** 13.♕xc7?! ♘d7⩱. **13...♕e4 14.♗e2 c6 15.♕c2 ♗xe2 16.♔xe2 ♕e6 17.♖he1 ♖c8 18.♔f1 f6 19.♘h4±** Ponomariov-Efimenko, Kiev 2013.

B22) **8...exd5 9.♕e3+** For 9.♘c3 0-0 see under 7...0-0. **9...♕e7 10.♕xe7+ ♔xe7 11.♘c3**

This type of central pawn structure, with or without queens, usually gives White comfortable play, for example:

B221) **11...♖e8 12.♖c1 c6 13.♗g2 ♘bd7 14.0-0 ♔f8 15.♖fe1 ♗b7 16.♗h3 ♖ad8 17.e3** It is enough to look at the pawns on c6 and e3 and to compare the bishops to reach the conclusion that Black has an inferior position. **17...h6 18.b4 g5 19.♗f5±** Bogdanovski-Cabrilo, Bijeljina Dvorovi 2002;

B222) **11...c5 12.0-0-0!?** A logical move, though White is castling to the side where Black has the pawn majority (for 12.♗g2± see under 10.♕e3). **12...cxd4?!** Better would be 12...♗b7!? 13.♗g2 ♘bd7∞ and Black has a chance to draw even due to his opponent's not so secure king. **13.♖xd4 ♘c6 14.♘xd5+ ♘xd5 15.♖xd5±** Hracek-Cifka, Karlovy Vary 2005;

B223) **11...♘bd7 12.♗h3 ♘f8** Or 12...c6 13.0-0 ♖he8 14.a4 ♔d6 15.♖fe1 ♖e7 16.a5 and White achieves nothing on the side where Black has the pawn majority, Gazi-Sergeev, corr. 2009; if 12...♖he8 13.0-0 ♔f8 14.♖fc1 c6 15.e3 h6 16.b4± Hjartarson-Agdestein, Gausdal 1987. **13.0-0 ♘e6 14.♖fd1 ♖hd8 15.♘e5 ♗b7 16.♖ac1 c6 17.e3 ♖ac8 18.b4±** with a typical advantage in this type of position, Timman-Short, Montpellier 1985.

C) **7...c5**

This continuation, which stopped being modern long ago, usually leads to positions containing hanging pawns, which we cover under 7...0-0.

8.♗g2 Or 8.dxc5 bxc5 9.♘c3 ♘c6 10.♗g2 0-0 11.0-0 d5 12.cxd5 exd5; with 8.d5?! White personally activates the opponent's passive bishop on a6: 8...exd5 9.cxd5 0-0 10.♘c3 ♖e8↑ and Black comes first, since his bishop has been activated with the reckless 8.d5.

8...d5 Black can hardly do without this move, since he is weaker on the d-file: 8...♗b7? 9.dxc5 bxc5 10.♘c3 0-0 11.0-0 ♕e7 (perhaps more resistant would be 11...d5 12.cxd5 exd5 13.♖fd1 ♘a6 14.♘h4 ♘c7 15.♘f5 ♖e8 16.♖ac1 ♖c8 17.♘e3±

with a nice and instructive position, illustrating the strategy against hanging pawns) 12.♖fd1 ♖d8 13.♕d6± Atalik-Oll, Nova Gorica 1999. **9.cxd5 exd5 10.♘c3** Also good would be 10.♕e3+ ♕e7 11.♕xe7+ ♔xe7 12.♘c3 ♘c6 13.dxc5 bxc5 14.♖c1 (14.♘h4!? ♘d4 15.0-0-0± Ruzele-Balashov, Böblingen 1998) 14...♖he8 15.0-0 ♔f8 16.♖fe1 d4 17.♘a4 ♗xe2 18.♘xc5 (better is 18.♘d2 ♗b5 19.♘xc5±) 18...♖ac8 19.♘d2 (19.♘g5!?) 19...♘b4= Van Wely-A. Sokolov, Ohrid 2001. **10...♘c6** Black strives for dynamic and active play. On 10...♘bd7 White can simplify with 11.♕e3+ ♕e7 12.♕xe7+ ♔xe7 13.♘e5±, or if 10...0-0 then 11.♘e5±.

11.0-0 0-0 12.dxc5 bxc5 A weaker move would be 12...d4?! 13.♘a4±, Solomunovic-Cabrilo, Valjevo 2012.

This critical position with hanging pawns can emerge in several ways.

13.♖fd1 The standard and best positioning of the rook in positions with hanging pawns. White attacks d5 while moving out of the black light-squared bishop's range. 13.♘h4 ♖c8 14.♖ac1 ♖e8 15.♖fe1 d4 16.♘a4 c4 17.bxc4 ♘e5 18.♘b2 ♘xc4 19.♘xc4 ♖xc4 20.♖xc4 ♗xc4= Gyimesi-Pelletier, Turin 2006. **13...d4 14.♘a4±** with strong pressure on Black's hanging pawns, Polugaevsky-Bronstein, Yerevan 1975.

8.♗g2

The major alternative is **8.♘c3**. White develops and aims for e2-e4, not allowing the Miles System with ...c7-c6 and ...d7-d5.

8...d5 (for 8...c6?! 9.e4 d5 10.e5± see under 9...0-0) Now White can choose between A) 9.♗g2 and B) 9.cxd5.

A) **9.♗g2** This natural developing move allows Black to return to the Miles System with 9...c6 (line A2). In this move order, White is denied the opportunity to play solidly with 11.a4, since his eighth move was 8.♘c3.

A1) **9...c5?!** An active move, preferred on different occasions by grandmasters Aleksandar Kovacevic and Goran

Cabrilo. For 9...♘bd7?! 10.♘e5 c5 see under 10...♘bd7. Now:

A11) For **10.0-0 ♘c6** see under 9.0-0 c5 10.♘c3;

A12) For **10.cxd5 exd5 11.♘e5** see under 10.♘c3;

A13) **10.dxc5 bxc5 11.cxd5 exd5** White can easily lose his way in this position, which is riddled with weak hanging pawns. However, one thing to bear in mind is their potential dynamic power, especially if they are well supported by other pieces. **12.♘e5** For 12.0-0 ♘c6 see under 10.♘c3; 12.♘h4 ♘c6 13.0-0 (13.♘xd5? ♘xd5 14.♕xd5 (14.♗xd5 ♕f6 15.♖c1 ♖ad8∓) 14...♕f6 15.0-0 ♘d4∓) can also be found under 10.♘c3. With the text, White immediately attacks d5, but thanks to the open e-file Black's mobile central pawns can easily show their strategic qualities when supported by other active pieces. **12...♖e8! 13.♘d3 ♘bd7 14.0-0 d4 15.♘a4 ♖c8 16.♖fc1 ♘e4 17.♕f4 ♘df6⇄** Blagojevic-A. Kovacevic, Vrnjacka Banja 2006.

A14) **10.♘e5!** seems like the best and simplest way to aim at the hanging pawns in this particular instance. White strengthens the pressure on the d5-square and the h1-a8 diagonal, intending to further simplify the position by exchanging the opponent's queenside knight:

A141) **10...♘bd7**

11.♘xd7 One of the aims of the plan with ♘e5. White simplifies the position, thereby weakening the dynamic power of the opponent's centre. Also an option is 11.♘c6!? ♕e8 12.cxd5 exd5 13.♘xd5 ♘xd5 14.♗xd5 ♘f6 15.♗f3 ♘e4 16.♕e3 f5 17.d5. **11...♕xd7 12.dxc5 bxc5 13.cxd5 ♗b7 14.0-0 exd5 15.♘a4±**;

A142) **10...♗b7 11.0-0 ♘bd7 12.♖fd1 ♖e8 13.♖ac1** Also good is 13.♘xd7 ♕xd7 14.dxc5 bxc5 15.♘a4 ♖ac8 16.♕a5± with strong pressure on the queenside. **13...cxd4 14.♕xd4±** Vaganian-Balashov, Leningrad 1974.

A2) **9...c6** A typical scene we can also see in the Closed Catalan, where the dark-squared bishops haven't been exchanged. Black's main idea is very clear. He raises obstacles before the Catalan bishop, trying to prove that his bishop on the f1-a6 diagonal is better.

Now after 10.♘e5 ♘fd7⇄ it seems that Black's light-squared bishop has become more dangerous than its counterpart on g2, since White suffers unpleasant pressure on the c4-pawn, Khalifman-Nikolic, New York 1994.

After **10.0-0** Black can either continue with his chosen plan, or take the c4-pawn, but in this case he has to be prepared for assaults by White's activated pieces:

A21) **10...dxc4!?** Not exactly orthodox to tear down the wall you have built against the Catalan bishop for a mere pawn. Black will have an extra pawn, but he will have to suffer through the long-term initiative of White's well developed pieces.

11.bxc4 It is difficult to assess what the best course of action could be for White. Leave the pawn on the a-file? Or on the b-file? With the a-pawn, at an opportune moment, White can play the rather unpleasant a2-a4-a5, and with the pawn on the b-file there will be activity on the a-file.

On 11.♘e5 cxb3 12.axb3 ♗b7 13.♖fc1!?, obviously here too White has compensation for his pawn.

11...♗xc4 12.♘e5 ♗a6 and now:

A211) **13.♖fc1 ♗b7** 13...♘d5 14.a4♙. **14.a4 ♕e7 15.♕b2 c5 16.♗xb7 ♕xb7 17.dxc5±** Da Silva-Bonow, Brazil CXEB 2001;

A212) Weaker would be **13.♘xc6 ♘xc6 14.♗xc6 ♖c8∓** and Black's pieces will be more active, Socko-Hou Yifan, Istanbul 2012;

A213) **13.♖fd1 ♗b7 14.♖ac1** White has maximum activity and excellent piece coordination, which provides him with obvious compensation for the pawn, Johansson-Overton, corr. 2009.

A22) **10...♘bd7**

11.♘e5 Giving up the centre with 11.cxd5 is typical for the variations with the white knight on c3, where White is forced to either exchange on d5 or sacrifice his c4-pawn. Though in the Closed Catalan the trade on d5 usually has a purpose if White can make progress on the c-file, in other cases it bodes well for Black, because it opens up the a6-f1 diagonal and strengthens the black bishop on the a6-square: 11...cxd5 12.♖fc1 ♕e7 – see under 7...0-0 8.♗g2 d5 9.0-0 c6 10.♖c1 ♘bd7 11.cxd5 cxd5 12.♘c3.
11...♘xe5 12.dxe5 ♘d7 13.f4 ♕e7 A nice place for the black queen, from which it controls many dark squares. The move also connects the rooks. **14.♖fd1** The rook moves out of the range of the black bishop and indirectly defends the c4-pawn. **14...♖fd8!**

Black wants the rooks on the d- and c-files, and this seems to be the optimal solution.

14...♖ad8 is a logical move, but not optimal. Black removes the rook from the dangerous Catalan diagonal, leaving the other rook on the kingside to support the attack with ...f7-f6. However, this relieves White of the doubled pawns and gives him time to develop more activity: 15.cxd5 (15.♕e3 ♖fe8 16.a4 ♕b4 17.♘a2 ♕c5= Topalov-Kamsky, Sofia 2007) 15...cxd5 (15...exd5 16.e4 dxe4 17.♕d6 ♕xd6 18.♖xd6 f5 19.♖ad1± Lukacs-Wahls, Budapest 1988) 16.♖ac1 f6 17.exf6 ♘xf6 18.♕d4↑ Piantedosi-Nenciulescu, corr. 2011.

15.cxd5 cxd5 16.e4! Without this thrust, White cannot hope for anything, since the activity of Black's pieces grows stronger with each move. Now:

A221) Interesting is **16...d4!?**. Black gives up his pawn since he doesn't wish to activate the opponent's minor pieces. **17.♕xd4 ♖ac8** 17...♘c5 18.♕e3±. **18.♕e3** 18.♖ac1 ♘c5♟. Black now uses the weak c3-square to displace the opponent's queen: 19.♕b4 g5!N (with the idea 20...gxf4 21.gxf4 ♕h4. Weaker would be 19...♕e8 20.♖xd8 (20.♕a3!±) 20...♖xd8 21.♖d1 ♘d3 22.♕a4 ♕e7= Greenfeld-l'Ami, Dieren 2013). The continuation might be 20.♖xd8+ ♕xd8 (20...♖xd8 21.♘a4±) 21.♖d1 ♘d3 22.♕d6 ♕c7 23.♗f1 ♕xc3 24.♗xd3 ♔g7=.
18...♕b4

A critical position for the evaluation of the pawn move 16...d4. Analyses show that Black has certain compensation due to his active pieces, but it is hard to say whether it is enough for a draw. It will require more practical games and more time to find the right answers. The only thing that is certain is that Black is the one who is constantly threatening things, so White needs a solid amount of chess knowledge and patience to make something out of this doubled pawn on the e-file, if it is even possible. **19.♘e2** 19.♖ac1!? ♘c5♟ with certain compensation; 19.♘a4!? (White does not allow Black to play the critical ...♘c5) 19...♕b8♟. **19...♘c5 20.♖xd8+ ♖xd8 21.♕c3 ♕xc3** 21...♕b5!?. **22.♘xc3 ♔f8♟** Tukmakov-Miles, Wijk aan Zee 1984.

A222) **16...♖ac8** also doesn't equalize because of **17.♕e3!** and White will likely get a strong centralized knight on the e4-square. A weaker move would be 17.♖ac1?! because of 17...d4! 18.♕xd4 ♘c5 and Black gets sufficient compensation due to the weak d3-square, Greenfeld-l'Ami, Dieren 2013;

A223) **16...dxe4 17.♕d6 ♕xd6 18.♖xd6 ♘c5 19.♖ad1** 19.♘xe4 ♘xe4 20.♗xe4 ♖xd6 21.exd6 ♖d8 22.♖d1 ♗b5=. **19...♖xd6 20.♖xd6 ♖c8 21.♘xe4 ♘xe4**

And the players agreed to a draw in Sosonko-Ljubojevic, Wijk aan Zee 1988. There might have followed **22.♗xe4 ♗b5 23.a4 ♗e8 24.♔f2 ♔f8=**. White has a strategically tempting position, but with the rooks on the board it is probably not enough for the win.

B) **9.cxd5 exd5** 9...♘xd5 10.♖c1±.
10.♗g2

10...♖e8 With the idea ...♘e4. **11.0-0** For 11.♘e5! see under 7...0-0. **11...♘e4 12.♘xe4 dxe4 13.♘g5 ♘c6** and now:

B1) **14.♖fd1 ♘xd4 15.♘xf7 ♘xe2+ 16.♕xe2 ♗xe2 17.♖xd8 ♖axd8 18.♘xd8 ♖xd8 19.♗xe4 c5 20.♖c1 ♖d4↑** and Black has better odds in the endgame, Eingorn-Gelfand, Moscow 1990;

B2) **14.♕f4 f6 15.♘xe4 ♘xd4 16.♘c3 g5! 17.♕g4 ♘xe2+ 18.♘xe2 ♗xe2∓** and White will not gain sufficient compensation by his opponent's weakened king: **19.♕a4 ♗xf1 20.♗xa8 ♕xa8** 20...♗h3 21.♗g2 ♗xg2 22.♔xg2 ♕a8+ 23.♔g1 ♖e7∓ Beliavsky-Gelfand, Linares 1993. **21.♖xf1 ♖e7∓** Ruban-Nikolenko, Moscow 1991;

B3) Probably the best course for White is **14.♘xe4N ♘xd4 15.♖fe1 ♗b7 16.♖ad1 ♗xe4 17.♕xd4 ♕xd4 18.♖xd4 ♗xg2 19.♔xg2 ♖ad8 20.♖ed1=**.

8...d5

Or 8...c6 if we aim for the Miles System: 9.0-0 d5, see under 8...d5.

9.0-0

A major alternative is **9.cxd5** and now:

A) **9...exd5 10.♘c3** For 10.0-0 ♖e8 11.♘c3 see under 8.♘c3 (for 11.♖e1 ♘bd7 12.e3 ♘e4 13.♕b2 see under 9...♘e4; 11.♘e5 ♘bd7 12.♘c6? ♖xe2∓ CBM 36.-E15. Survey Opening 1993, Dautov). **10...♖e8** Black aims for ...♘e4. **11.♘e5!** For 11.0-0 see under 8.♘c3. **11...c5** 11...♘bd7 12.♘c6 ♕c8 13.e3 ♘b8 14.♘xd5± Vyzhmanavin-Smirin, Leningrad 1990; 11...♗b7 12.0-0 ♘bd7 (for 12...c5 see under 11...c7-c5) 13.f4 ♕e7 14.♖ac1 a6 15.e3± Magerramov-Ikonnikov, Cheliabinsk 1991. **12.0-0 ♗b7** 12...♕d6? 13.♘xd5! ♘xd5 14.♘xf7± Dautov. **13.♖fd1 ♘a6 14.♕f4!** A simple but strong move with which White controls a cluster of important squares, also planning a strategically lucrative exchange with ♘g4. If 14.e3 ♕e7 15.♕e2 ♘c7 16.♖ac1 ♖ad8∞ Magerramov-King, Baku 1986. **14...♘c7** 14...♕c7 15.♘c4 (15.♘b5 ♕e7 16.e3± Van der Wiel) 15...♖ad8 16.♘e3 (16.♕xc7 ♘xc7 17.dxc5 bxc5 18.♘a5 ♗a8 19.♘a4 ♖xe2 20.♘xc5± Van der Wiel) 16...♕xf4 17.gxf4 ♘c7 18.dxc5 bxc5 19.♘a4 ♗a6⇄ Tukmakov-Van der Wiel, Rotterdam

1988; 14...♕e7 15.♘g4! ♘xg4 16.♕xg4±.

15.♘g4! Typical for the hanging pawns strategy. White exchanges his pieces and reduces the dynamic power of the opponent's centre. **15...♘xg4 16.♕xg4 ♕f6 17.e3 ♖ad8 18.♖ac1** Without the knight on f6, Black's pawn pair makes a different picture altogether. Black will have to focus on the defence of these pawns later in the game. **18...♕e7 19.dxc5 bxc5 20.♕a4±** with pressure on the hanging pawns, whose strategic power has been altered due to the exchange of two of Black's pieces, Leko-Carlsen, Morelia/Linares 2007.

B) 9...♘e4!?

10.♕b2 For 10.♕c2 exd5 see under 10.♗g2. **10...exd5 11.0-0 ♘d7** The knight on d7 is the most suitable for the protection of the soon-to-be hanging pawns. For 11...c5 12.♖d1 ♘c6 see

under 10.♖d1; 11...♖e8 12.♖e1 c5 13.dxc5 ♘c6 14.♘fd2 ♘xc5 15.♘c3 ♕f6⇄ Polak-Babula, Kouty nad Desnou 2012. **12.♖e1** 12.b4 c5 13.b5 ♗b7 14.♘c3 ♖e8 15.e3 ♕f6 16.♖fd1 (16.♘e2 h5 17.h4 g6 18.♘f4 ♘f8 19.♗h3 ♗c8 20.♗g2 ♗b7 21.♗h3 ♗c8 and the opponents agreed to a draw in a nearly equal position, Torre-Ljubojevic, Brussels 1986) 16...♘xc3 17.♕xc3 a6 18.a4 c4⇄ with chances on both sides, Antic-A. Kovacevic, Kopaonik 2005; 12.♖d1 ♖e8 13.e3 ♕f6 14.♘bd2 c5 15.♖ac1 ♖ad8⇄ Marszalek-Sygulski, Chotowa 2007. **12...♖e8 13.e3 c5 14.♘c3** and now:

B1) 14...cxd4

15.exd4 15.♘xd4 ♘dc5⇄; 15.♘xd5!± dxe3 (15...d3 16.♘b4±) 16.♖xe3 ♗b7 17.♘d2 ♗xd5 18.♘xe4 ♗xe4 19.♗xe4 ♖c8 20.♖d1±. **15...♘df6 16.♘e5 ♘xc3 17.♕xc3 ♘e4** If 17...♖c8 18.♕b2 ♕d6 White's position is strategically more pleasing but Black has a serious chance to reach equality: 19.b4!? (19.♗h3 ♖c7 20.♖ac1 ♖ee7= Farago-Lau, Wuppertal 1986) 19...♗b7 (19...♗b5 20.a4 ♗d7 21.b5±) 20.b5↑. **18.♕f3** 18.♕b4!?. **18...f6 19.♘g4 ♖c8 20.♘e3 ♗b7=** Pogonina-Dzagnidze, Belgrade 2013.

B2) 14...♗b7 15.♖ac1 a5?! It's still not the time for this standard move.

Better would be 15...♕f6N 16.♖ed1 ♖ad8⇄ with mutual play. For example: 17.dxc5 bxc5 18.♖c2 ♕f5 19.♘xe4 dxe4 20.♘h4 ♕f6 21.♕xf6 ♘xf6 22.♖dc1 ♖e5 23.♗f1 g5 24.♘g2 ♖c8 25.b4 ♘d7= and Black has compensation for the weakness of the c-file due to the weak knight on g2. **16.♖ed1↑** Prusikin-Saric, Rogaska Slatina 2009.

Going back to the main move **9.0-0**: Black can now choose between the Miles System with 9...c6, the direct confrontation in the centre with 9...c5, and the developing move 9... ♘bd7.

9...c6
A) **9...c5!?**

The second-most important position in Chapter 2.2, which can come about via different move orders. Black directly confronts his opponent in the centre, striving for dynamic and active play. The emerging positions are essentially different from the Miles System, and are best suited for players who love complications on the board and who are bored with the calm positional battle of the system with 7...c6.
Most frequently, positions with hanging pawns emerge, where Black aims for the support of his hanging centre using maximum activity of his pieces, thereby granting it mobility and dynamic power.

Of course, White will do the opposite. His two main strategic missions will be:

1. Limiting the mobility of the opponent's hanging pawns and putting pressure on them;

2. Exchanging the opponent's active pieces and simplifying the position, for the purpose of removing the support of the hanging pawns so as to destruct them more easily.

We'll look at the natural moves A1) 10.♘c3, A2) 10.cxd5, which usually transposes, and A3) 10.♖d1.

A1) **10.♘c3 ♘c6 11.♖fd1** Both sides have finished their development, planning the best set-up for the clash in the centre. However, it is Black's turn to move, so he can continue in the spirit of the system, creating complications: **11...dxc4!?** 11...♖c8 12.cxd5 exd5 13.dxc5 bxc5 14.e3 (14.♘xd5 ♘xd5 15.♕xd5 ♗e2 16.♕xd8 ♖fxd8 17.♖xd8+ ♖xd8 18.♖e1 ♖d1 19.♖xd1 ♗xd1 20.♘d2 ♘b4 21.a4 (21.a3!?) 21...c4= Gligoric-Szabo, Moscow 1956) 14...♘e4 15.♘xe4 dxe4 16.♕xd8 ♖fxd8 17.♖xd8+ ♖xd8 18.♘g5 f5 19.g4± Baranowski-Sheretiuk, ICCF email 2008. Now:

A11) **12.bxc4 ♖c8 13.d5** 13.dxc5 bxc5=. **13...♘a5 14.♕c2** 14.♕f4 ♗xc4 15.dxe6 ♕e7 16.exf7+ ♗xf7 17.♘e5 ♗e6∞. **14...♕e8** Safer would be

14...♗xc4!?N 15.dxe6 ♕e7 16.exf7+ ♗xf7 with equal chances. **15.dxe6 ♕xe6 16.♘g5 ♕xc4?** 16...♕e5!∞. **17.♖d6?!⩱** Khasin-Kharitonov, Sverdlovsk 1979 (17.e4!+−);

A12) **12.dxc5 bxc5 13.♕d6 ♕xd6 14.♖xd6 ♖ac8 15.♘d2 ♖fd8 16.♘xc4 ♗xc4 17.♖xc6 ♖xc6 18.♗xc6 ♗a6=** Nikolaev-Shaposhnikov, St Petersburg 1999;

A13) **12.♘e5 ♘xd4 13.e3 ♘f5 14.♗xa8** 14.♕e1!? with mutual chances. **14...♕xa8** with sufficient compensation for Black, for example **15.bxc4?! ♘e4 16.♕b2 f6−+** Ilincic-Cabrilo, Novi Sad 2000.

A2) **10.cxd5 exd5 11.♘c3 ♘c6** 11...♘bd7 12.♘h4±xd5. 11...♖e8 12.♖fd1±. **12.dxc5 bxc5** This is again the critical position with hanging pawns, which was covered under 7...c5 8.♗g2 d5 9.cxd5 exd5 10.♘c3 ♘c6 11. 0-0 0-0.

A3) **10.♖d1** White prepares for a clearance of the centre with cxd5 and dxc5 and an attack on the d5-pawn, avoiding the black bishop's x-ray pressure on the f1-a6 diagonal. This is the standard and best position for the rook, but only in positions with hanging pawns. However, in this particular instance, the centre is still undefined, so Black now gets the opportunity to obtain a good game. **10...♘c6**

Black aims for a maximum activation of his pieces, so he develops his knight on the natural c6-square.

Of course, also possible is 10...♘bd7 because it is well-known that the queen's knight is best suited for the defence of the potential hanging pawns. However, this leads to a completely different type of position where there are no fireworks as seen in the continuation with the knight on c6: 11.♘c3± dxc4?! 12.♘e5!±.

11.cxd5 For 11.♘c3 see under 10.♘c3. **11...♘e4** After 11...exd5 12.dxc5 bxc5 13.♘c3 we are in the game Polugaevsky-Bronstein, Yerevan 1975 (under 10.♘c3 on page 39). **12.♕b2** A weaker move would be 12.♕c2 exd5∓ 13.e3?! (13.dxc5? ♕f6!−+) 13...♘b4∓. **12...exd5** and now:

A31) **13.e3 ♕f6** Weaker would be 13...♖e8 14.♘c3 ♘xc3 15.♕xc3 ♕f6 16.♕b2 ♖ad8 17.♖ac1 h6 18.♖d2± Eingorn-Short, Reykjavik 1990. **14.♘e5** 14.♘bd2 ♖fe8 15.♖ac1 cxd4 16.♘xe4 dxe4 17.♘xd4 ♘b4 18.♕d2 ♘d3 with active play for both sides, Van der Sterren-Van der Wiel, Rotterdam 1990. **14...♖ad8** 14...♖fe8= and the players agreed to a draw in a nearly equal position in Novikov-Ca.Hansen, Debrecen 1990. **15.♘xc6 ♕xc6 16.dxc5 ♕xc5 17.♖c1 ♕b4 18.a3 ♕e7 19.♘d2 ♘c5** with equal chances and a draw in Malakhatko-Pelletier, Cap d'Agde 2006;

A32) **13.dxc5 bxc5 14.e3 ♖c8 15.♘bd2** 15.♘c3?! ♕f6∓; 15.♘fd2!? ♕f6 (also functional is 15...♗e2!? 16.♖c1 ♗d3 17.♘xe4 ♗xe4 18.♖xc5 ♕e7⩱) 16.♕xf6 ♘xf6 17.♘c3 ♖fd8=. Here, noteworthy is the simple **15...♕e7!?N** (with 15...♕f6 Black trades queens, though this facilitates things for his opponent, considering he has hanging pawns: 16.♕xf6 ♘xf6 17.♗h3 ♖c7 18.♖dc1 ♘a5 19.♖c3 ♘b7 20.b4± Vachier-Lagrave-Navara, Haguenau 2013), with which Black strengthens the dynamic power of his central pawns.

16.♘xe4

16.a3 ♖fd8⇄ And White probably already feels the strength of his opponent's central pawns.

16...dxe4 17.♘d2

17.♘e1 ♖fd8 18.♖ac1 ♘b4⇄ with mutual play.

17...f5!?

Black pawn structure in the centre is not impressive but it also limits the influence of white pieces and controls many important squares. So the attack on the weak d3-square by the black knight can prove to be most unpleasant for the opponent.

18.♗f1

18.♘c4 ♗xc4 19.bxc4 ♘e5↑.

18...♗xf1 19.♔xf1 ♘e5⇄

B) For **9...♘bd7** see under 7...d5.

We go back to the position after 9...c6. We will pause at this important and critical crossroads, since we have before us the elementary and most important position of the Miles System. We will also cover the other position of the said

system (regardless of the fact that after a while they merge) with the queenside knight on d7, instead of castling by Black, because it has certain advantages, which we have explained under 7...c6.

The position greatly resembles the Closed Catalan with its typical pawn structure in the centre. The essential question is: which side is better off with the missing dark-squared bishops? Let us start with Black. If we look at Black's pawn structure in the centre, his light-squared chain f7/e6/d5/c6 simply cries out for a dark-squared bishop, a guardian of the dark squares. Let us consider that the ever unpleasant white knight on e5 is not dangerous for Black when the dark-squared bishop is present, because after ...♘xe5 and dxe5, Black faces no difficulties on d6 or any other critical dark squares.

On the other hand, if we picture White's bishop on f4 or b2 and Black's bishop on e7, where they usually stand in the regular Closed Catalan, we will remember that Black always had difficulties to find a safe place for his queen. In our system, the queen has the comfortable e7-square, from where the dark-squared bishop is easily traded for control of the dark squares, and the minor and major pieces are harmonized. In addition, the lack of these two pieces simplifies the position, which is psychologically more in favour of Black.

Of course it is not exactly a bed of roses for Black. One of White's unavoidable and more dangerous plans will be the assault with ♘e5!? when after the practically inevitable exchange White will use the e5-pawn to try and make use of the weakness of the d6-square, by opening up the d-file or preferably with ♘c3-b5(e4)-d6.

White has more options, but here we will cover 10.♖c1, 10.♘e5, and 10.♕b4.

10.♖c1

Or **10.♘e5** 10.cxd5 cxd5 11.♖c1 ♘bd7 under 10.♖c1; nothing is achieved by 10.♕b4 ♗b7 11.♘bd2 (11.♘c3 c5=) 11...c5!? 12.♕a3 (12.dxc5 ♘a6 13.♕a3 ♘xc5=) 12...♘bd7 13.♖fd1 a5= Adianto-Short, Jakarta 1996; 10.♘c3 ♘bd7 is seen under 7...0-0 8.♘c3 d5 9.♗g2 c6 10.0-0 (or 10...dxc4, which is also covered under 7...0-0 8.♘c3 d5 9.♗g2 c6 10.0-0). **10...♘fd7 11.♘d3** 11.♘c3 ♘xe5 12.dxe5 ♘d7 13.f4 ♕e7 is analysed under 7...0-0 8.♘c3 d5 9.♗g2 c6 10.0-0 ♘bd7 11.♘e5 ♘xe5 12.dxe5 ♘d7 13.f4; 11.♘xd7 ♘xd7 12.cxd5 cxd5 13.♘a3 ♕e7 14.♘c2 ♗b7 15.a4 a5= Baramidze-Lupulescu, Germany 2013. **11...dxc4** Black takes the pawn, because it is not easy for White to prove compensation with the knight on d3. Interesting is the calm 11...♘f6 12.♕c3 ♘bd7 13.♘d2 c5∞ S. Savchenko-Ionov, Rostov on Don 1993. **12.♘b4 cxb3** Also possible is 12...♕c8 13.bxc4 ♗xc4 14.♖c1 ♗a6 15.♘xc6 ♘xc6 16.♖xc6 ♕d8 17.♖c3 ♖c8 18.e3 ♕e7= Karpov-P. Nikolic, Thessaloniki 1988. **13.♘xa6 ♘xa6 14.axb3** After 14.♗xc6 ♖c8 15.♗e4 ♘f6 the oppo-

nents quickly agreed to a draw in this position where the chances are nearly equal, Atalik-De Firmian, Reykjavik 1994. **14...♘db8** 14...♘ab8 15.♘a3 a5 16.♘c4 ♖a7 17.b4 a4 18.♖fc1 ♕e7 19.♕b2 b5 20.♘a5♔; White has sufficient compensation for the pawn, Kovacs-Rahde, LSS email 2008. **15.♘a3 ♘c7 16.♘c4 ♘d5 17.♘e5 a5 18.♖fc1** White has compensation for the pawn but not more, Antic-Ostojic, Banja Koviljaca 2002.

10...♘bd7

In this important position, we will take a look at the recently popular 11.a4 and the usual A) 11.♕b2 and B) 11.cxd5.

11.a4

The introduction to a solid plan. White can't move his knight to c3, so he prepares to play ♘a3 and advance his queenside pawns. Black can continue with 11...♕e7 or immediately hit the centre with 11...c5. We will also look at 11...♖c8, though after White has chosen the plan with 11.a4 with the strategic threat of a4-a5, it is more prudent to wait with the development of this rook.

A) **11.♕b2**

The best strategic position for the white queen. Here it controls the important cluster of dark squares, vacating the d2-square for the queenside knight, creating a harmonious and active position for the upcoming battle in the centre, where White usually plans queenside play with b2-b4. Black can continue his attack on the centre with A1) 11...c5 or first comfortably position his queen with A2) 11...♕e7:

A1) **11...c5 12.cxd5** 12.♘bd2 ♗b7 13.b4 cxb4 14.♕xb4 ♖c8 15.a4 dxc4 16.♘xc4± ♗d5 17.♘e3 (on 17.♘d6 Black can root the white knight with 17...♕e7 18.♘e5 ♗xg2 19.♔xg2 ♘e4 20.♘xd7 ♖fd8 21.♘e5 ♕xd6 22.♕xd6 ♘xd6) 17...♗e4 18.♕a3 ♖xc1+ 19.♖xc1= and two legends of Russian chess agreed to a draw in Smyslov-Polugaevsky, Leningrad 1962. The game could continue with 19...♘b8 (with the idea ...♘c6, xd4,e5,a5) 20.♖d1 ♘c6 21.♘c4 ♕a8=. **12...exd5** On 12...♘xd5 after 13.♘c3 White also has some initiative in the endgame after 13...♘xc3 (13...♗b7 14.♘xd5 ♗xd5 15.dxc5 ♘xc5 16.b4 ♘e4 17.♘e5↑) 14.♖xc3 ♖c8 15.♖ac1↑ White has more active play, but Black has a shot at equality. **13.♘c3 ♖e8 14.♖d1 ♖c8** 14...♗b7 15.e3 ♕e7 16.♖ac1 ♘f8 17.♘h4±,

Chernin-Razuvaev, Tilburg (rapid) 1994.

15.dxc5 bxc5 16.e3 The start of a typical plan. White first limits the mobility of the opponent's d-pawn and will then

continue with ♘e1-d3-f4, increasing the pressure on the hanging pawns. 16.♘xd5!? is an alternative. **16...♗b7 17.♘e1 ♘b6 18.♘d3 ♕e7 19.♘f4 ♖ed8 20.♕a3 ♗c6 21.♖ac1±** White has a standard amount of pressure on the opponent's centre, but without his dark-squared bishop; Black fails to create anything substantial out of his hanging pawns, Ruban-Rodriguez Cespedes, Havana 1990.

A2) **11...♕e7**

An interesting and strategically instructive picture. Two queens are settled on positions that are normally occupied by their dark-squared bishops. This shows their desire to pick up some of the bishops' tasks.

12.♘bd2 White has completed his development and is ready to proceed on the queenside with b2-b4. **12...c5** On 12...♗b7 after 13.b4 Black obviously has a more passive position, where his opponent has easier play and better perspectives.

A21) **13.dxc5 bxc5 14.♘e5** 14.cxd5 exd5⇄. **14...♗b7!?N** Black returns the bishop to the central diagonal and intends to continue playing with his hanging pawns in spite of the simplified position. 14...♘xe5 15.♕xe5 ♘d7 (worthy of attention is 15...♖fd8!? 16.cxd5 ♘xd5 with the idea ... ♖ac8

17.♘c4 ♖ac8= and despite his weaker pawn structure, Black has a real chance to obtain full equality, due to his active pieces and the simplified position) 16.♕c3 ♗b7 17.♕a5 ♕d8 Black wishes to exchange as the white queen exerts a lot of pressure on the queenside, but ends up in an inferior endgame. 18.♕xd8 ♖fxd8 19.cxd5 ♗xd5 20.♘e4± Damljanovic-M. Adams, Palma de Mallorca 1989. **15.cxd5 exd5 16.♘xd7 ♘xd7 17.b4!?** The last chance to make some progress, considering the knight's passive position on the d2-square. 17.e3 ♘e5⇄; 17.♖c2 a5⇄. **17...cxb4 18.♖c7 ♗a6 19.♖ac1** On 19.♗xd5 Black easily achieves full equality with 19...♕d6 20.♗xa8 ♕xc7 21.♗f3 ♖b8 22.♖c1 ♕e5=.

White connects his rooks and now has clear compensation for the pawn. In addition, Black is tied on the 7th rank and weak on the long diagonal. Black's situation presents a paradox, as he has to capture on e2 if he wants an equal endgame, walking into a pin on the e-file.

19...♗xe2! 20.♗xd5 If 20.♖e1 ♖ae8 with the idea of ...♕d6. Black is tied on the 7th rank and the e-file, and the position can be assessed as equal. However, there are no practical games, so we have to trust the machines, which ap-

parently have taken over our lives. **20...♖ad8 21.♘c4** 21.♖xa7 ♕f6=; 21.♗g2 a5 22.♘b3 ♕e5 23.♕xe5 ♘xe5 24.♘xa5=. **21...♖xc4 22.♗xc4 ♕d6 23.♖xa7 ♘e5 24.♗e2 g6=**;

A22) Black's situation is more complicated after **13.♘e5**. A logical turn of events. White must seek an advantage on the central h1-a8 diagonal, or attack his opponent's future hanging pawns. **13...♗b7** Weaker is 13...♘xe5 14.dxe5 ♘d7 15.cxd5 exd5 16.♗xd5 ♖ad8 17.♘f3±; or 13...cxd4 14.♘c6 (in case of 14.♕xd4 ♘xe5 15.♕xe5 ♖ad8= Black has no difficulties) 14...♕d6 15.cxd5 exd5 16.♘xd4±.

A221) **14.cxd5 ♗xd5**

Black captures with his bishop, intending to play the variations we have seen under 14.♘xd7 ♘xd7 15.cxd5. **15.e4** For 15.♘xd7 ♘xd7 see under 15.cxd5. **15...♗b7 16.♘ec4** White is trying to build up with e4-e5, creating a stronghold on d6. For 16.♘xd7 ♘xd7 see under 14.♘xd7 ♘xd7 15.cxd5. **16...♖ad8!** Black prepares for combat with the knight on the c6-square, vacating a square for his bishop's retreat. **17.e5 ♘d5 18.♘d6 ♗a8 19.♘2c4 cxd4 20.♕xd4 f6!** Black weakens his e6-pawn, but also White's stronghold on d6. In addition, the f-file is opened and the rook activated. **21.f4** A weaker move would be 21.exf6? ♘7xf6∓. **21...fxe5 22.fxe5 a6!** With the idea ...b7-b5. **23.a4** 23.♖f1 b5 24.♖xf8+ ♖xf8 25.♘d2 ♘b8=. **23...b5 24.axb5 axb5 25.♘d2** 25.♘xb5 ♘c5 26.♖a7 ♕g5 27.♖f1 ♘xb3=. **25...♘xe5=**

A222) **14.♘xd7 ♘xd7** No good comes from 14...♕xd7? 15.dxc5 bxc5 16.cxd5± and White captures the c5-pawn. **15.cxd5** On 15.♖c2 Black can get rid of the hanging pawns with 15...cxd4!? 16.cxd5 ♗xd5 17.♗xd5 exd5 18.♘f3 d3 19.exd3 ♖ac8 with nearly equal play, Pravec-Raessler, ICCF email 2010 (19...♘c5!?).

15...♗xd5!?N After 15...exd5 16.♘f1 ♘f6 17.♖c2 ♖fc8 18.♖ac1 ♖c7 19.♘e3± Black is exposed to constant pressure on his central pawns with not enough counterplay. Among other things, White has the unpleasant manoeuvre ♗f3-♘g2-f4 at his disposal, Chernin-Razuvaev, Tilburg 1994.
16.e4 On 16.♗xd5, after 16...exd5 17.♘f3 a5!? it would seem that the trade of the light-squared bishop changes the character of the position. Now the game turns into a fight against Black's majority on the queenside. **16...♗b7 17.b4!?** This pawn sacrifice might be the best move for White, allowing him to continue the search for an advantage. If 17.♘c4 cxd4 18.♕xd4 ♘c5=. **17...cxb4 18.♖c7 ♖ab8**

And now we will now analyse two logical moves for White:

A2221) **19.♖ac1 ♖fc8 20.e5 ♖xc7 21.♖xc7 ♗xg2 22.♔xg2 ♕d8** 22...a5 23.♕c2 ♕d8 24.♕c6 ♘f8=. **23.♖xa7** 23.♕c2 ♘c5∓. **23...♖a8 24.♖xa8 ♕xa8+ 25.♔g1 b5!?** Vacating b6 for a possible ...♘b6-d5. **26.♕xb4 ♕xa2 27.♕xb5 ♕a1+ 28.♔g2 ♕xd4=;**

A2222) **19.e5 ♗xg2 20.♔xg2 a5 21.♖ac1** 21.♘e4 ♕d8 22.♖c2 (22.♖c6 ♖c8 23.♖d6 ♖c7∓) 22...f5 23.♘d6 ♘f6!∓. **21...♕d8∞** with the idea ...♘c5.

B) 11.cxd5
Also one of the common plans for White. He gets rid of the weak c4-pawn, with the option of developing his queen's knight on its natural square c3 and activating the rooks on the c-file.
11...cxd5

As we see, Black has gained something as well. He no longer has to worry about the c6-pawn and plans a liberating strike with ...e6-e5. The bishop on a6 has its diagonal lengthened, whereby its activity is increased. In addition, the open c-file increases the possibility of rook exchanges, i.e. simplifications of the position. All in all, Black is closer to a draw here than in the continuations with 11.♕b2 and 11.a4.
12.♘c3 12.a4 ♕e7 13.b4 ♖fc8 14.♘a3 ♕f8 15.♘e5 ♖xc1+ 16.♖xc1 ♖c8

17.♖xc8 ♕xc8 18.b5 ♗b7 with an equal endgame. After 19.♘xd7 the players agreed on a draw in Andreikin-Harikrishna, Havana 2013.

12...♕e7 As we can see, the black queen practically always goes to e7 in the Miles System. But... 12...♖c8!? – this is how grandmaster Miles dealt with the battery on the c-file. He delays the queen's development to e7, preparing a battery of his own on the c-file. 13.♖c2 (in response to other moves by White, Black can place his queen on e7 and end all his opening troubles) 13...♖c7 14.♖ac1 ♕b8 15.♘e5 ♖fc8= Portisch-Miles, Lucerne 1985. **13.♖c2** On 13.♘e5 Black has equal play after 13...♘xe5 (or 13...♖ac8!?=) 14.dxe5 ♘d7⇄ Gunina-Kosteniuk, Batumi 2012. Or 13.a4 ♖ac8 14.a5 bxa5 15.♖xa5 ♘b8 16.♖aa1 ♖c7 17.♕b2 and the players agreed to a draw in this equal position. Fridman-Gustafsson, Germany 2006.

Now the important question is: which rook positioning is the better one from the following two games?

B1) **13...♖fc8** 14.♖ac1= draw agreed, Illner-Lutz, Germany 2013;

B2) **13...♖ac8** 14.♖ac1 ♖fd8 15.♕f4 ♕f8 (15...h6!?=) 16.♗f1 ♘h5 17.♕d2 ♘hf6= Olafsson-Short, Istanbul 2000.

11...♕e7!

Let's remind ourselves! This is a strategically important move. The queen takes the whole cluster of dark squares under control and connects the rooks by vacating the 8th rank.

A) **11...c5 12.♘a3** 12.e3 ♖c8 13.♘a3 ♘e4 14.♕b2 ♗b7∞ Khenkin-Sukandar, Cammeray 2013. **12...♗b7 13.b4** There seems to be no other way to improve the position. **13...♖c8 14.cxd5 ♗xd5 15.dxc5!** White's best shot. He intends to create a distant passed pawn. **15...bxc5 16.b5** With initiative on the queenside. **16...a6** 16...♘e4!?N 17.♕e3 ♘d6⇄ White has the initiative on the queenside, but Black has sufficient counterplay thanks to his passed c-pawn. **17.a5↑** Postny-Cvitan, Budva 2009.

B) **11...♖c8 12.♘a3 ♕e7** 12...c5?! 13.cxd5 (13.♘b5!?) 13...exd5 14.♘b5 ♗xb5?! 15.axb5 ♖c7 16.♘e5± Antic-Mladenovic, Kragujevac 2013. **13.♕b2 ♖fd8** 13...c5 14.♘b5 ♘b8 15.♘e5 dxc4 16.bxc4 cxd4 17.♘xd4 (17.♕xd4!? ♖fd8 18.♕e3± Postny) 17...♗b7 18.♗xb7 ♕xb7 19.a5 ♘bd7 20.♘xd7 ♘xd7 21.axb6 axb6 with a drawish position in Bronstein-Polugaevsky, Baku 1961. **14.♖c2** 14.b4!?. **14...♘e4 15.♖ac1 ♕f6 16.b4 c5 17.dxc5 ♕xb2 18.♖xb2 bxc5 19.b5 ♗b7** with mutual chances, Girya-Kosteniuk, Moscow 2011.

12.♘a3

Or first 12.a5, continuing the advance of the a-pawn to keep the black rook on a8. It seems, however, that Black has no difficulties in neutralizing his opponent's initiative both in the centre and on the queenside: 12...♖fd8 (Black activates his kingside rook, keeping the other rook on a8 until further notice, to protect the a-file) 13.♕b2 c5 (also the right moment to attack the centre. The black bishop waits with switching to the central h1-a8 diagonal until his opponent activates his knight) 14.♘bd2 ♗b7 (Black's light-squared bishop has no more purpose on a6, so it moves to b7 to neutralize White's play on the long diagonal) 15.cxd5 ♗xd5 16.♘c4 h6 17.axb6 axb6. Black has equal play. Obviously, in this sensitive middlegame, three simple yet strong moves, ...♕e7, ...♖fd8 and ...♗b7 and their right playing order, played a key part in achieving equality for Black, Gelfand-Grischuk, Astana 2012.

12...♗b7

As a rule, Black's bishop moves to the central diagonal in order to neutralize the opponent's play with ...c6-c5, as soon as the white queen's knight loses the option to develop to c3
12...c5!?N and on 13.♘b5 (if 13.cxd5 ♘xd5= Black can't have any problems, since he has a nice stronghold for the knight on b4) 13...♗b7 (with the idea ...a7-a6) 14.a5 ♗c6!= with the idea ...♗b5 (see under 13... c6-c5).

13.a5

13.b4?! is suspect because of 13...a5! and White loses control of the c5-square: 14.b5 c5↑ and Black takes over, since the move ♘a3 loses all its meaning.

13...c5

13...♖fc8 has also been played: 14.b4 (better is 14.♘e5N ♘xe5 15.dxe5 ♘d7 16.♘c2↑ with the idea a5-a6) 14...bxa5 15.bxa5 c5= with a good position for Black, Gunina-Karavade, Istanbul 2012. 15...♗a6!?= also works, because Black's light-squared bishop seems more active than its esteemed colleague on g2.

14.♘b5 ♗c6!N

With the idea of ...♗xb5, and White won't be able to achieve anything on the queenside. If 14...dxc4 15.bxc4 cxd4 16.♘fxd4 ♗xg2 17.♔xg2↑ and despite Black's stronghold on c6, White has a certain initiative on the queenside, Shen Yang-Kosteniuk, St Petersburg 2012.

15.♘c7

15.♘e5 ♗xb5 16.cxb5 ♘xe5 17.dxe5 ♘d7⇄.

15...♖ac8 16.axb6 axb6 17.cxd5 ♘xd5 18.♘xd5 ♗xd5=

Conclusion

1. The system with black pawns on d5 and c6 usually leads to a calm and positional battle; we have named this line after grandmaster Anthony Miles;
2. The system with pawns on d5 and c5 leads to a tough and complicated battle.

Against the Miles System we could not find more than a symbolic or at most minimal advantage for White, though we have covered many practical games, old and new, and spent plenty of time on the computer analyses. Therefore the system is applicable, and especially suited for positional players aiming for a calm and solid game. Apart from that, the concept is very simple and understandable, which can be seen in the critical position after 7...c6 (please keep in mind that if we castle first with 7...0-0, White can avoid this system with 8.♘c3) 8.♗g2 d5 9.0-0 ♘bd7 10.♖c1 0-0 and now Black always responds to his opponent's strategic attempts 11.a4, 11.♕b2 with ...♕e7!, releasing the rooks and preparing for the liberating thrust ...c6-c5. The same goes for the more drawish continuation 11.cxd5 cxd5 12.♘c3: Black places his queen on e7 and then a rook on the open c-file, which can only speed up the draw outcome.

System 2, with the pawns on d5 and c5, is tougher and more complex, and it usually leads to positions with hanging pawns. There are plenty of riddles and traps for White, but with correct play White can eventually reach the positions where he has more comfortable play. Usually these positions contain hanging pawns for Black, which are more of a target than a dynamic force.

Exercises

2.2 (1) Find the plan.
(solution on page 438)

2.2 (2) Find the plan.
(solution on page 438)

2.2 (3) Find the plan.
(solution on page 439)

Chapter 3

5...0-0

5...0-0 is a flexible developing move with which Black is keeping all options in the centre and on the queenside open. White has two good plans to choose from: the fianchetto with 6.g3 (Chapter 3.1), or central play with 6.♘c3, which we will cover in Chapter 3.2.

Chapter 3.1

Fianchetto 6.g3

1.d4 e6 2.c4 ♗b4+ 3.♗d2 ♗xd2+ 4.♕xd2 ♘f6 5.♘f3 0-0 6.g3 b6

In this move order Black is on time to control the central e4-square, as opposed to the lines starting with 6.♘c3 which we cover in Chapter 3.2. However, it appears that in this type of Queen's Indian Defence, without dark-squared bishops, this is not enough for full equality. We should also note that this position can be reached with a different move order: 1.d4 ♘f6 2.c4 e6 3.♘f3 b6 4.g3 ♗b4+ 5.♗d2 ♗xd2+ 6.♕xd2 0-0.

For 6...d5 – see Chapter 4.1.

For 6...d6 7.♗g2 ♘c6 8.♘c3 e5 – see Chapter 3.2.

7.♘c3 ♗b7

7...♗a6 8.e4±.

8.♗g2

Here Black usually chooses between simplifying with 8...♘e4, the classical 8...d5, or the flexible 8...d6.

8...d6

Introducing the standard plan, with the main idea of attacking the white centre with ...e6-e5 or ...c7-c5.

A) The thematic **8...♘e4** does not promise equality.

A1) **9.♕c2** is inaccurate, however: **9...♘xc3 10.♘g5 ♕xg5 11.♗xb7**

♘xe2! This move would not be possible with the white queen on d3. **12.♕xe2** Now if 12.♗xa8 ♘xd4!. **12...♘c6 13.♗xa8 ♖xa8 14.♕d3 d5 15.0-0 ♖d8** with certain compensation, Komodo CCT-Critter 1.6, Internet (blitz) 2013. **16.f4 ♕f5 17.♕xf5 exf5 18.cxd5 ♘xd4 19.♔f2 ♖xd5 20.♖ac1 c5 21.b4 ♔f8 22.bxc5 bxc5 23.♖fe1**;

A2) **9.♘xe4 ♗xe4** Black is controlling the important e4-square, but this is only temporary. **10.0-0 d6**

Now White has three typical procedures to fight for the key square e4:

A21) **11.♕f4 ♗b7** 11...f5? 12.♘g5±. **12.e4 ♘d7 13.♖fe1 ♕e7 14.♖ad1 e5 15.♕d2±** transposes to the type of position we cover under 8...d6 9.0-0 ♘e4;

A22) **11.♕e3 ♗b7 12.♕d3 f5 13.♕e3** Or 13.♘e1 ♗xg2 14.♘xg2 ♘d7 with approximate equality, Ma Zhonghan-Yu Shaoteng, Tianjin 2013. **13...♖e8 14.c5 ♘d7 15.cxd6 cxd6 16.♖ac1 ♘f6 17.♘h4 ♗xg2 18.♘xg2 ♘d5 19.♕d3 ♕d7=** Vallejo Pons-Safarli, Nakhchivan 2011;

A23) **11.♘e1 ♗xg2 12.♘xg2 ♘d7 13.e4 e5 14.♘e3** White has exchanged the bishops and succeeded in pushing e2-e4. Despite his somewhat passive set-up, Black has a healthy pawn structure and the material is reduced. It shouldn't be difficult to hold a draw:

14...exd4 15.♕xd4 ♕f6 16.♕xf6 ♘xf6 17.f3 with some space advantage for White but the most likely result is a draw, Lengyel-Ivkov, Stip 1977.

A3) **9.♕d3 ♘xc3** No equality even after 9...f5 10.♘e5! (also possible is 10.0-0 ♘xc3 11.♕xc3 ♗e4 12.♖ac1 ♕f6 13.d5 ♕xc3 14.♖xc3 ♘a6 15.dxe6 dxe6 16.♘d4± Eingorn-Grekh, Cappelle la Grande 2013) 10...♘c5 (10...♘d6 11.d5±) 11.dxc5 ♗xg2 12.♖g1 ♗c6 13.0-0-0 ♕f6 14.f4 bxc5 15.♘xc6 dxc6 16.e4 ♘a6 17.e5 ♕e7 18.♕f3± Polugaevsky-Dokhoian, Belgrade 1988. **10.♘g5**

Here 10...♕xg5 simply fails to 11.♗xb7 ♘xe2 12.♗xa8!, so **10...♘e4**, and now:

A31) **11.♗xe4 ♗xe4 12.♕xe4 ♕xg5 13.♕xa8 ♘c6 14.♕b7 ♘xd4**

This is the critical position for the evaluation of the exchange. Black has given up the rook for the pawn and for an active knight on d4. His pawn structure is healthy and intact and his king is safer. White is still having trouble with the king in the centre.

The position is very dynamic and interesting to explore further, so it is no wonder that it was seen in a game between two World Champions.

15.♖d1 c5 15...♕e5?! is weaker: 16.e3 ♘c2+ 17.♔e2 d5 18.♖d2± and there is no good escape route for the knight, Euwe-Capablanca, 8th match game, Amsterdam 1931; 15...♕a5+ is also okay: 16.♔f1 ♕e5 17.♔g2 d5 with fine play for Black, Cordova-Cori Tello, Montcada 2012. **16.e3 ♘c2+ 17.♔d2 ♕f5 18.♕g2 ♘b4↑**

And Black is at least equal, Euwe-Capablanca, 10th match game, Amsterdam 1931.

A32) 11.♘xe4 ♘c6 12.0-0 ♖b8 Or 12...f5 13.♘c3 ♕f6 14.e3 ♘b4 15.♕d2 ♗xg2 16.♔xg2 ♘c6 17.b3 ♘d8 18.f4 ♘f7 19.e4± with a massive centre and active play for White, Indjic-Radovanovic, Vrnjacka Banja 2012. **13.♘c3 ♘b4 14.♕d2 ♗xg2 15.♔xg2 c6 16.a3 ♘a6 17.e4 d5 18.cxd5 cxd5 19.e5** Black has succeeded in trading the bishop but he is left with a passive knight. **19...♘c7 20.♖ac1 ♕d7 21.♖c2 ♖bc8 22.♖fc1 ♘b5 23.♘xb5 ♖xc2 24.♖xc2 ♕xb5 25.♖c7±**

White has seized the c-file and the 7th rank, Sargissian-Yu Yangyi, Ningbo 2011.

B) Black can also try **8...d5**, after which White can apply different methods in the fight for the initiative: **9.cxd5** Or 9.♘e5 ♘bd7 10.0-0 ♕e7 11.♕f4 (11.♖fd1 ♖fd8 12.♕f4±, Z. Polgar-A. Schneider, Stara Zagora 1990) 11...c6 12.♖fd1 ♖fd8 (12...♘xe5 13.dxe5 ♘d7=) 13.♖ac1 ♘f8 14.e4± Antic-Lajthajm, Vrnjacka Banja 2008. **9...exd5** In case of 9...♘xd5 White would have an advantage in the centre: 10.0-0 ♘d7 11.♖ac1±, Gligoric-Tartakower, Saltsjöbaden 1948. **10.0-0 ♕e7** Or 10...♘bd7 11.♖ac1 ♖e8 12.♖fd1 a6 13.♕c2 ♘f8 14.b4 ♕e7 15.♕b3 ♘e6 16.e3 ♖ab8 17.♘e5±, Beliavsky-Kasimdzhanov, Pune 2004. **11.♖ac1 ♘bd7 12.♖fe1 c6 13.♕f4 ♖fe8 14.♘h4±**

White has better chances, with the black bishop passively placed on b7,

Miljkovic-Karpov, Nis (rapid match) 2010.

9.0-0

It is also possible to play the thematic 9.d5 e5 (or 9...a5 10.♘d4 e5 11.♘db5 ♘a6 12.0-0 ♗c8 13.b3 ♗d7 14.a3 with a small space advantage for White, Sargissian-Parligras, Legnica 2013) 10.0-0 ♘bd7 11.♘e1 a5 12.♘d3 ♘c5 13.f4 exf4 14.gxf4 ♖e8 15.♘xc5 bxc5 16.e4 ♗a6 17.b3 a4 18.♖ae1 ♘d7 with mutual chances, Ivanchuk- Kharitonov, Tashkent 1987.

9...♘bd7

On **9...♘e4**, after **10.♘xe4 ♗xe4 11.♕f4** (11.♖fd1 ♘d7 12.♖ac1 ♕e7 13.♕e3 ♘f6 14.d5 ♗xf3 15.exf3 c5= Gavrilov-Milosevic, Basle 2013) **11...♗b7 12.e4 ♘d7 13.♖fe1 ♕e7 14.♖ad1 e5 15.♕d2 a5...**

White can now immediately take on e5. In case of 15...♖fe8, after 16.dxe5!? (with 16.♕c2 we can transpose to Kasparov-Akopian below) 16...♘xe5 17.♘d4 f6 18.b3 ♖ad8 19.f4 ♘f7 20.♘f5 ♕f8 21.♕c3± White has lots of space and very active play, Dautov-Larsen, Bad Homburg 1998. **16.dxe5!** Earlier 16.♕c2± was played, and although the white bishop is not very attractive, White's surplus in space and good central control grant him some advantage, Feller-Dorfman, Internet (blitz) 2006. **16...♘xe5 17.♘d4±** with a slight space advantage that is typical for this structure.

10.♕c2 ♕e7 11.e4 e5 12.♖fe1 ♖fe8 13.♖ad1±

White is more active thanks to his space advantage in the centre, Kasparov-Akopian, Internet (blitz) 1998.

Conclusion

In the opening stage, Black manages to control the e4-square, however this doesn't provide equality. The problem is that Black doesn't have any direct influence on the centre, and quite often White can align three pawns on the 4th rank. In truth, Black's position is flexible and without weaknesses, although somewhat passive. His play is based on undermining White's centre with ...d7-d6 and ...e6-e5, or ...d7-d6 and ...c7-c5. In case Black implements ...d7-d5, White will also have an easier and more active game due to the absence of dark-squared bishops.

Exercises

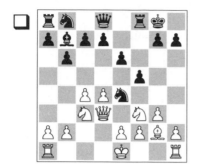

3.1 (1) Find the plan.
(*solution on page 439*)

3.1 (2) Find the plan.
(*solution on page 439*)

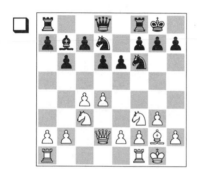

3.1 (3) Find the plan.
(*solution on page 439*)

Chapter 3.2

Central Strategy: 6.♘c3

1.d4 e6 2.c4 ♗b4+ 3.♗d2 ♗xd2+ 4.♕xd2 ♘f6 5.♘f3 0-0 6.♘c3

This natural developing move is also often seen in practice. Here White focuses on the development of the centre without declaring the placement of his light-squared bishop, as we have seen in Chapter 3.1. Apart from the main and principled response 6...d5, which we will analyse in Chapter 5, Black can play the flexible 6...d6, the cunning 6...♘c6 or the fianchetto with 6...b6.

6...d6

The logical set-up after the exchange of the dark-squared bishops. Black is preparing ...e6-e5 or ...c7-c5, trying to seize control over the dark-square complex. However, the problem is that White should fianchetto his light-squared bishop, which will then not be obstructed on the long and open a8-h1 diagonal, thanks to Black's pawn structure with d6/e5 or d6/c5.

A) **6...♘c6!?** A cunning alternative, directed against the move 7.g3. Black continues his development, not committing himself with the d-pawn and with the pawn structure in the centre.

A1) **7.g3 d5!=**

This is the point. Black has waited until White decided on the fianchetto and now he immediately gets good play. The combined development of the knight on c3 and the pawn on g3 is not the best solution.

8.cxd5 Weaker is 8.♘e5?!; without the light-squared bishop on g2, this knight jump is not good: 8...♘xe5 (a better move would be 8...dxc4!N 9.♘xc6 bxc6 10.♗g2 ♖b8 11.♖d1 (it doesn't look good for White after 11.♗xc6 ♕d6 12.♗f3 ♖d8 13.♖d1 ♕b6∓) 11...♕d6∓ with the idea ...c7-c5) 9.dxe5 ♘d7 10.cxd5 ♘xe5 11.♗g2 exd5 12.♕xd5 ♕e7 (better is 12...♕xd5 13.♘xd5 c6=) 13.♕e4↑ Chernikov-Kolbak, Rogaska Slatina 2012. **8...exd5 9.♗g2 ♘e4!?=**;

A2) After **7.d5 ♘e7 8.e4 d6 9.♗e2 ♘g6⇄** Black has counterplay on the weakened dark squares;

A3) Or **7.e4 d6**, which is covered below under 6...d6;

A4) **7.e3** is the best reaction to 6...♘c6. White continues his development, building a strong and stable centre. **7...d6 8.♗e2**

Now Black can finish his development by activating his light-squared bishop on the h3-c8 diagonal with 8...e5, or on the central diagonal with 8...b6. In both cases, Black has a healthy and flexible position, but White keeps a slight lead, due to his small spatial advantage in the centre. **8...e5** In case of 8...b6 9.0-0 ♗b7 10.♖fd1 ♘e7 Black has a

flexible pawn structure and active minor pieces, especially the b7-bishop, but he also suffers from a lack of space. 11.♘e1 (better is 11.♕c2± with a slight space advantage) 11...a6 12.♗f3 ♕b8 13.♕c2 ♖d8 14.b4 b5 with mutual chances, Arounopoulos-Eingorn, Bad Wiessee 2012. **9.0-0 exd4 10.exd4** It seems logical to liberate the f3-square for the bishop with 10.♘xd4!? ♗d7 11.♖ac1 ♖e8 12.♖fd1± with more active play for White. **10...♖e8 11.♖fe1 a6** 11...♗g4!?. **12.h3 ♗f5 13.♗d3 ♕d7 14.b3 ♖xe1+ 15.♖xe1 ♗xd3 16.♕xd3 ♖e8 17.♖xe8+ ♕xe8** and the opponents agreed to a draw in a near equal position, Dumitrache-Nevednichy, Creon 2002.

B) **6...b6**

Black wants to operate on the long diagonal, but in this move order he is late with taking control of the e4-square. White has a pleasant choice between two types of position:

7.g3, in the spirit of the Queen's Indian Defence, which was covered in Chapter 3.1; or 7.e4, like in the English Defence (1.d4 e6 2.c4 b6), where Black hasn't done anything to challenge the strong white centre.

7.e4 For 7.g3 ♗b7 8.♗g2 see Chapter 3.1. **7...♗b7 8.♗d3** For 8.♕f4 see Chapter 2.1. **8...d6 9.0-0 ♘bd7**

10.♖fe1 e5 11.♖ad1±. We have already seen similar positions with the white bishop on g2. This small detail doesn't change the evaluation as White still has the better chances due to his space advantage and more active major pieces.

7.g3!

White is more than happy to fianchetto the bishop, because there are no obstacles on the central diagonal.

A different plan is **7.e4**. With no dark-squared bishops this active move in the centre provides Black with easier counterplay: **7...♘c6** and now:

A) **8.0-0-0 ♕e7** Black wants to play ...e6-e5. **9.h3** 9.e5 dxe5 10.♘xe5 ♖d8⇄ with good play for Black. **9...e5 10.d5 ♘b4!? 11.a3 ♘a6 12.♗d3** Weaker is 12.b4 ♘b8 with the idea ...a7-a5. Black gets the a-file or the strong outpost on c5. **12...♘c5 13.♗c2 a5∞** and White's position is not trustworthy, Krasenkow-Meier, Germany 2005;

B) **8.♗e2 e5 9.d5 ♘e7 10.0-0 ♘g6** Black is obviously happy that the dark-squared bishops have been traded. **11.g3** 11.♘e1 c6 12.♘d3 cxd5 13.cxd5 ♕b6 14.♖ac1 ♗d7 15.g3 ♖ac8 16.♗f3 ♖c7 17.♗g2 ♖fc8 18.♖c2 ♘e8↑ with the idea ...f7-f5, with excellent play for Black, Rybka 4.1-Stockfish 2.2.2, Internet 2012. **11...♗h3 12.♖fd1 h6 13.♘e1 ♘h7∞**

with active play for Black, Ovetchkin-Meier, Internet (blitz) 2006.

7...♘c6 8.♗g2 e5 9.0-0 ♗g4
Black is completing his development and indirectly presses on d4. However, White has multiple continuations which he can use to fight for the upper hand.

10.d5

White decides on a position which gives him a small but stable edge due to his space advantage. Instead:

A) **10.e3** is a reasonable idea. White maintains the centre while not closing off the diagonal for his strong light-squared bishop. **10...♕d7** 10...h6 11.h3 ♗d7 is not satisfactory because now White could have continued 12.dxe5N ♘xe5 (12...dxe5 13.♖fd1±) 13.♘xe5 dxe5 14.♖fd1± with greater piece activity, in Sakaev-Zviagintsev, Novi Sad 2000. **11.dxe5** White combines pressure on the d-file and the central diagonal. If 11.♘d5!? ♘e4 12.♕d3 f5 (on 12...♗xf3 13.♗xf3 ♘g5 14.♗g2

White stands better with his centralized knight and strong bishop, Van Wely-Ulibin, Leeuwarden 1997) 13.♘h4 ♘g5 14.f3 (on 14.f4 in the game Van Wely-Porte, Vlissingen 2001, Black could have played 14...♘h3+ to even the chances, for example 15.♗xh3 (15.♔h1 e4∞) 15...♗xh3 16.♖fe1

e4!?=) 14...♗h3 15.♗xh3 ♘xh3+ 16.♔g2 ♘g5 17.f4 exf4 18.exf4 ♘e4∞ Troia-Giobbi, ICCF email 2010. **11...dxe5 12.♕xd7 ♘xd7 13.h3 ♗e6 14.♖fd1 f6 15.a3** Better is 15.♘d2N ♖fd8 16.♘b3 with slightly superior play for White due to his better control of the centre, e.g. 16...♗xc4 17.♗xc6 bxc6 18.♘a5. **15...♖ad8 16.♘d5 ♘b6↑** Baumgartner-Schwierzy, ICCF corr 1999.

B) **10.dxe5!?** is also a sound plan, though it simplifies the game and brings it closer to a draw. White combines the pressure on the d-file and the central diagonal. **10...♘xe5 11.♘xe5 dxe5 12.♕g5 ♕d4** 12...c6!?N 13.♕xe5 ♖e8 14.♕f4 ♗xe2 15.♖fe1 ♗h5 16.♖xe8+ ♕xe8 17.♕c7 ♕d7=. **13.h3** 13.♖fd1!? ♕xc4 14.♕xe5 c6 15.♖d4 ♕a6 16.♗f1↑. **13...♗e6 14.♖fd1 h6 15.♕c1 ♕xc4 16.♗xb7 ♖ad8** with equal chances, Rombaldoni-Dimitrov, Veliko Tarnovo 2013.

10...♘e7 11.♘e1 ♕d7 12.e4 ♗h3 13.♘d3

Also possible is 13.♗xh3 ♕xh3 14.♘d3 ♘g6 15.f3 ♕d7 16.♕e3 c6 17.dxc6 ♕xc6? (Black relinquishes the control of the very important d5-square for no reason, thereby also destroying the mobility of his d-pawn − better is 17...bxc6 18.♖fd1↑) 18.b3 with a clear advantage for White, due to his opponent's permanent weaknesses on the d-file, Markus-Danner, Hungary 2011.

13.f4?! is an aggressive move White isn't quite prepared for: 13...exf4 14.gxf4 ♘g6∓ and White's centre is more of a liability than a formidable force, Ernst-Van den Doel, Netherlands 2010.

13...♗xg2 14.♔xg2 c6 15.f3 cxd5 16.cxd5 ♖fc8 17.♖ac1

White has a slight space advantage, Halkias-Mikkelsen, Reykjavik 2013.

> ### Conclusion
> In this chapter, we considered the alternatives 6...d6, 6...♘c6 and 6...b6 as the responses to the popular continuation 6.♘c3.
>
> After the first alternative, 6...d6, the best plan for White is to fianchetto his bishop with 7.g3, thereby developing maximum activity along the unobstructed central diagonal. The critical position comes after 7...♘c6 8.♗g2 e5 9.0-0 ♗g4 and now White has several different ways to continue the fight for a win and come out on top after the opening.
>
> With the cunning 6...♘c6, Black will easily achieve good play in the case of 7.g3 with 7...d5! or, after the aggressive 7.e4, with 7...d6 followed by the central break 8...e5. However, White can choose the calm 7.e3, building a strong and stable centre, which gives him a solid shot at the upper hand.
>
> With 6...b6, Black doesn't get enough counterplay, for the concessions he has made to the opponent in the centre.

Exercises

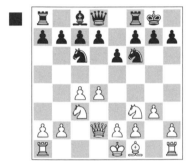

3.2 (1) Find the plan.
(solution on page 439)

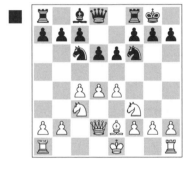

3.2 (2) Find the plan.
(solution on page 439)

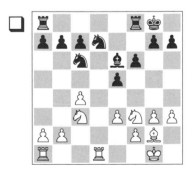

3.2 (3) Find the plan. *(solution on page 440)*

Chapter 4

The Classical Centre –
4.♕xd2 ♘f6 5.♘f3 d5: The Fianchetto 6.g3

1.d4 e6 2.c4 ♗b4+ 3.♗d2 ♗xd2+ 4.♕xd2 ♘f6

The first major and important crossroads for White in this variation with 4.♕xd2. White can choose between two strategies: the fianchetto with 5.♘f3 followed by g3 (or vice versa), and the central strategy with 5.♘c3 with the idea of playing e2-e4, where the light-squared bishop usually develops on the f1-a6 diagonal.
5.♘f3 d5

The classic reaction in the centre from which many stable opening systems spring. Black often castles first, but the chess elite applies this order. White still has the choice between the fianchetto and central positioning (which will be dealt with in Chapter 5), depending on the diagonal he chooses for his bishop. In this chapter we will concentrate on:
6.g3
White uses his light-squared bishop to influence the central diagonal.

Chapter 4.1

Black Plays in the Centre with ...♕e7

6...0-0 7.♗g2

7...♘bd7

A flexible developing move in accordance with the idea of the system. The black knight doesn't take up its natural position on c6, saving this square for his c-pawn and building a fortress to face the white bishop on g2. In addition, as was previously mentioned, the black knight on c6, which is usually combined with the ...dxc4 capture, isn't a good solution here without the dark-squared bishop, since White can win back his pawn with ♘a3xc4, which means that Black has opened up the diagonal for the white bishop for nothing.

For 7...c6 8.0-0 ♘bd7 see under 7...♘bd7.

7...♕e7 8.0-0 ♖d8

This ideal placement for Black's major pieces is very popular in the system where White develops his bishop on the f1-a6 diagonal. However, delaying the development on the queenside might not be the best solution with the Catalan bishop on g2.

For 8...♘bd7 see under 7...♘bd7.

9.♖c1

A) **9...♘c6** Black strives for more active influence in the centre and pressure on the d4-pawn.

White also needs to be wary of the potential threat of ...dxc4 with ...e6-e5. On the other hand, blocking his own c-pawn and keeping the light-squared bishop passive on c8 do not give cause to great optimism.

A1) **10.♘e5!?**

This continuation, as it was noted in Boris Avrukh's *Grandmaster Repertoire 2*, promised White the most substantial advantage, until the machines came up with an unusual plan to complicate the game:

10...♘xe5!? A weaker move is 10...♗d7 11.♕e3 (11.♕f4 is not as good but it also works: 11...♗e8 12.♘d2 a5 13.♘df3 a4 14.♘xc6 ♗xc6 15.♘e5± Z. Polgar-Dzindzichashvili, New York 1992) 11...♗e8 12.♘d2 a5 13.♘b3 a4 14.♘c5 ♘a5 15.cxd5 exd5 16.b4 and White has a clear advantage, Maksimovic-Benkovic, Vrnjacka Banja 2010. **11.dxe5 ♘g4** After 11...♘d7 12.♕e3 c6 13.♘d2 Black still hasn't obtained equality. **12.♕f4 h5∞**

Unusual play by Black, but he already threatens 13...g5 to endanger White's e5-pawn. White will probably have to sacrifice the pawn, to try and exploit Black's weakened kingside;

A2) **10.♕c3!? ♘e4 11.♕e3 ♘d6 12.cxd5 ♘f5 13.♕f4 exd5 14.♘c3±** Notkin-Jankovskis, Passau 1994;

A3) **10.♘a3** White develops his piece and wants to recapture with his knight in case of ...dxc4. However, Black doesn't need to fulfill his opponent's wishes, and with his knight at the edge of the board, White is unlikely to get an advantage. **10...♗d7 11.♖ab1 ♗e8=** D. Gurevich-Kavalek, Estes Park 1986;

A4) **10.e3** is a subtle move, by which White neutralizes the influence of the black knight on c6, and opens up e2 for the queen. **10...dxc4** 10...♗d7 11.♕e2 ♖ac8 12.♘bd2± and Black is weaker in the centre with his c-pawn in the starting position. **11.♖xc4±** 11.♘a3?! e5 and Black carries through his idea, with an excellent position. **11...e5? 12.♖xc6 bxc6 13.♘xe5±** with superior compensation.

B) **9...c6**

White now has a comfortable choice between two good moves.

10.♕e3 With 10.b4 White immediately springs into action on the queenside, vacating the b2-square for his queen: 10...dxc4 11.♖xc4 ♘bd7 12.♕b2 a5 13.bxa5 ♖xa5 14.♘bd2 ♕a3 15.♗c2 ♕xb2 16.♖xb2 ♖a4 17.♖c1 ♘e8 18.♘c4 f6 19.♘fd2 ♔f8 20.♘b3 ♖a7 21.e4± I. Sokolov-Short, Malmö 2013. **10...♗d7**

Black intends a completely new role for his light-squared bishop. Instead of the usual position on the queenside, the idea for it is to be activated on the h5-e8 diagonal, on the kingside. Besides, in the event of potential lucrative exchanges in the centre, this bishop will have the option of operating on the a4-e8 diagonal. A noteworthy idea, but hard to achieve, so Black will be stuck in a passive position for a while. **11.♘bd2 ♗e8** In practice, White usually plays in one of two ways: moving the knight to e5, or advancing his queenside pawns.

B1) **12.a3 a5**

B11) **13.♕f4 ♘a6 14.g4** A safer move would be 14.c5± with better prospects for White. **14...c5 15.g5 ♘e4 16.cxd5 exd5 17.e3 ♖ac8** Better would be 17...♘xd2 18.♘xd2 ♖ac8= (Timman). **18.♘xe4 dxe4 19.♘h4±** Timman-Nikolic, Tilburg 1988;

B12) **13.c5 a4 14.♘e5 ♘fd7** Of course, the only substantial plan for Black is to activate his light-squared bishop with ...f7-f6. **15.♘d3 f6**

16.♗h3 ♗f7 17.f4 ♖e8 18.♘f3 b6 19.cxb6 ♘xb6 20.♘d2 ♖a5 Black had an interesting option in 20...♘c8!? 21.♖c3 ♘d6⇄ and in spite of the backward c6-pawn, Black has active play due to the excellent position of his knight on d6 and the option of activating his light-squared bishop on g6. **21.♖c3 ♕a7** 21...♘c8!? with the idea ...♘d6. **22.♖ac1±** and the c6-pawn remains the main factor in the evaluation of the position, Timman-Nikolic, Reykjavik 1988.

B2) **12.♘b3**

Black has two options of activating his knight on b8 and thus finish his development:

B21) **12...♘a6** Black does not want a cramped position with the knight on d7, but there is also no bright future for it at the edge of the board. **13.a3 ♖ac8 14.♘e5** A questionable plan. White moves the knight to d3 but that also gives Black some time to activate his bishop on e8. 14.cxd5 cxd5 15.♘e5 ♘c7= with the idea ...♘b5-♘d6; 14.c5!?± Kholmov. **14...dxc4 15.♖xc4 ♘d5 16.♕c1 f6 17.♘d3 ♘b6 18.♖c3 ♘a4 19.♖c2 ♗f7 20.♖c4** White could have played 20.♘a5!? to continue fighting in a more active position, for example 20...♖xd4? 21.♗xc6! bxc6 22.♘xc6 ♖xc6 23.♖xc6±. **20...♘b6**

21.♖c3 ♘a4 22.♖c4 and the opponents reached a truce in Razuvaev-Kholmov, Moscow 1991;

B22) **12...♘bd7 13.♘a5 ♖ab8 14.♖ab1 ♖dc8 15.cxd5 ♘xd5 16.♛d2 c5 17.e4 ♘5b6 18.e5 h6 19.a3 ♘d5 20.♘c4±** and in this tense position Black has problems with the weak d6-square, Kasparov-Timman, Belgrade 1989.

8.0-0

We shall take a look at the main continuation 8...c6 and the not so highly regarded 8...♛e7 or 8...dxc4.
For 8.♛c2 c6 9.♘bd2 b6 see Chapter 4.2.

8...c6

With this unavoidable move Black builds the foundation of his position. The next phase will be aimed at developing the light-squared bishop.

A) **8...♛e7?!**

The queen is not meant to be here in this move order. This move is usually combined with putting the rook on d8, so with the knight on d7 Black is combining two different systems, with which he risks allowing his opponent to find a plan to make one of these two pieces dysfunctional. **9.♛c2!** In case of the stereotypical 9.♖c1, after 9...c6 Black will not be punished for his inaccuracy. This line is covered under 8...c6.

Now Black's previous move loses its meaning. White returns to the standard plan with ♘d2 and e2-e4, knowing that the queen is not supposed to be on e7 in this position.

9...c6 There is no full equality even after 9...c5 10.cxd5 ♘xd5 11.♘c3± and Black is late with his development. **10.♘bd2 b6 11.e4 dxe4 12.♘xe4 ♗b7 13.♖fe1 ♘xe4 14.♛xe4** And now it is obvious that the black queen is not comfortable on e7. **14...♘f6 15.♛c2 ♖ad8 16.♖ad1 c5 17.d5±** Pharaon 3.3-RedQueen 1.1.3, Internet (blitz) 2013.

B) **8...dxc4?!** Giving in in the centre and opening the diagonal to the now powerful Catalan bishop, which is not in the spirit of Black's general strategy and now leads to a comfortable game for his opponent. **9.♖c1** 9.a4± (Avrukh, *Grandmaster Repertoire*). A weaker move would be 9.♘a3 because of the small tactical detail 9...e5!

10.dxe5 ♘xe5 11.♕xd8 ♘xf3+ 12.♗xf3 ♖xd8 13.♘xc4 ♗e6 14.♖fc1 (or 14.♖ac1 c6= Tomashevsky-Nisipeanu, Moscow 2012) 14...♗d5 15.♗xd5 ♖xd5 16.b4 ♖e8= Horvath-Erdös, Bratto 2013. **9...♕e7 10.♖xc4 c6 11.b3** With the idea ♕b2 and ♘bd2. **11...♖e8 12.♘e5 ♘d5 13.♕b2 f6 14.♘xd7 ♗xd7 15.♘d2 e5 16.dxe5 ♕xe5 17.♕xe5 ♖xe5 18.♘e4 ♘b6 19.♖d4 ♗e6 20.♖ad1±** and White controls the d-file and has better prospects, Meier-Naiditsch, Baden-Baden 2013.

9.♖c1

Logical and, likely, the strongest move in the fight with the very popular fianchetto system against Black's slightly passive but solid position. However, Black can boast two very different but solid plans to get full equality: a) the active 9...♕e7 with the idea of ...dxc4 and ...e6-e5, and b) the calm 9...b6 followed by the development of the bishop to b7 or a6, which we will discuss in Chapter 4.2.

For 9.♕c2 b6 10.♘bd2 ♗b7 see Chapter 4.2; for 9.♘e5 see Chapter 4.2.

9...♕e7

An active and excellent choice. Black makes use of the opponent's current eagerness to play on the queenside by organizing his own play in the centre, usually with ...e6-e5. This plan is legiti-

mate, because the trade at c4 exposes the white rook to his knights and enforcing ...e6-e5 will activate Black's light-squared bishop. In most cases, White will try 10.♕f4, 10.♕e3 or 10.♘a3, to foil this idea.

For 9...b6 see Chapter 4.2.

10.♕e3

A) **10.♘a3** White develops and defends the c4-pawn, but with the knight on the edge of the board. Black has not weakened himself on the c-file with ...b7-b6, so it is unclear how, without sufficient control of the centre, White could improve his position. **10...♖e8** Weaker would be 10...e5 11.cxd5 ♘xd5 12.dxe5 ♘xe5 13.♘xe5 ♕xe5 14.♘c4±. **11.e3** 11.♘xe5 ♘xe5 12.dxe5 ♘d7⇄. **11...♖d8** Again risky is 11...e5 12.dxe5 ♘xe5 13.♘xe5 ♕xe5 14.cxd5 ♘xd5 15.♗xd5 cxd5 16.♘b5± and White has the strategically desired position. **12.♕c3 a5 13.♘e5** This continuation leads directly to an equal position. **13...♘xe5 14.dxe5 ♘d7 15.e4 dxe4 16.♗xe4 ♕c5 17.♖e1 ♘xe5 18.♗xh7+ ♔xh7 19.♖xe5 ♕d4=** Borovikov-Cifuentes Parada, Dos Hermanas 2004.

B) **10.♕f4** White strengthens his control of the e5-square, at the same time vacating the usual square for his queenside knight. Now:

B1) **10...b6 11.cxd5** 11.♘bd2 ♗a6 (it is better for Black to play 11...♗b7!?N to prepare for the thematic 12.e4 dxe4 13.♘xe4 c5 14.♕d6 ♕e8! 15.♘xf6+ ♘xf6 16.♕c7 ♕b8 17.♕xb8 ♖axb8=) 12.e4 dxe4 13.♘xe4 ♘xe4 14.♕xe4± Lalic-Radlovacki, Budapest 2012, and Black still hasn't caught up. **11...cxd5 12.♘e5** 12.♘c3 ♗a6=. **12...♘xe5 13.dxe5 ♘d7 14.♘c3 ♗a6 15.♕a4 ♗b7** Better is 15...♘c5!?N

16.♕a3 (16.♕d4 ♖ac8= with a good position for Black: 17.b4?! ♘d7 18.b5 ♗b7∓ and White has significantly weakened his own queenside) 16...♗b7= 17.♘b5 a5= (with the idea ... ♗a6) 18.♘d6 ♗a6 19.♕e3. **16.♕d4 ♗c6 17.♖c2 f6 18.exf6 ♘xf6 19.♖ac1 ♖ad8 20.f4±** Cheparinov-Gagunashvili, Legnica 2013;

B2) **10...dxc4 11.♖xc4 ♘d5 12.♕d2** 12.♕g5 f6 (on 12...♕xg5 13.♘xg5 ♖d8 14.♘d2 ♘e7 15.♘df3 b6 16.♘e4± White has a more pleasant game, Caruana-Bruzon Batista, Khanty-Mansiysk 2009) 13.♕d2 ♖d8 14.♖c1 e5=. **12...♘5b6** Black would unnecessarily complicate things with 12...♖d8 13.e4 ♘5b6 14.♖c1 e5 15.♖d1 exd4 16.♕xd4 ♖e8 17.♘c3 and now in the game Cheparinov-Zviagintsev, Khanty-Mansiysk (blitz)

2013, Black could have obtained a satisfactory game with 17...♘c5!?. **13.♖c2 e5** Black has played the last few moves according to his plan, which we explained after 9...♕e7.

14.♘c3 e4↑ and Black takes the initiative, Stockfish 2.2.2-Houdini 3.0, Internet (blitz) 2012.

10...dxc4 11.♖xc4 ♘d5 12.♕a3 ♖e8 13.♕xe7 ♖xe7 14.e4 ♘5b6 15.♖c2 e5

With or without the queens, Black enforces this liberating thrust, attacking White's centre and at the same time freeing the h3-c8 diagonal for the development of his light-squared bishop.

16.♘bd2 a5 17.a3 g6 18.♖ac1 exd4 19.♘xd4 ♘e5

with equal prospects, Kramnik-Andreikin, Moscow 2013.

Conclusion

In this chapter we covered a solid system for Black where he manipulates the game via the centre. In the critical position after 9...♕e7, Black plans ...dxc4 with the liberating strike ...e6-e5. White usually responds with 10.♕e3 or 10.♕f4 – however, after both continuations, Black achieves satisfactory play relatively easily, carrying through his plan. In case of 10.♘a3, White has even less of a chance to do something meaningful with his queenside knight.

Exercises

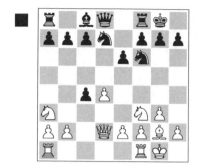

4.1 (1) Find the plan.
(solution on page 440)

4.1 (2) Find the plan.
(solution on page 440)

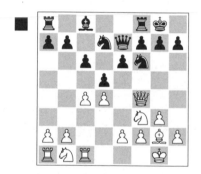

4.1 (3) Find the plan.
(solution on page 440)

Chapter 4.2

The Black Queenside Fianchetto

1.d4 e6 2.c4 ♗b4+ 3.♗d2 ♗xd2+ 4.♕xd2 ♘f6 5.♘f3 d5 6.g3 ♘bd7

Black wants to achieve the standard set-up for this type of position which involves the rapid development of his queenside with ...c7-c6, ...b7-b6, ...♗c8-b7 or ...♗c8-a6. In this type of Catalan, with the dark-squared bishops exchanged, the plan with the knight on c6, which is usually combined with ...dxc4, is not recommended since, due to the absence of the bishop on e7, White can conveniently play ♘a3-♘c4.

Also possible is first 6...c6 7.♗g2 ♘bd7.

7.♗g2 c6

Of course, here Black can first castle and then proceed to develop his queenside.

However, we will follow the preferred order of the chess elite, who regularly delay kingside castling. In his book *A Rock-Solid Chess Opening Repertoire*, grandmaster Viacheslav Eingorn gives the following line as one of the reasons for delaying castling: 8.♕c2 b6 9.♘bd2 ♗b7 10.e4 dxe4 11.♘xe4 ♘xe4 12.♕xe4 ♕c7 13.♘e5 ♘xe5 14.dxe5 and now Black has the option of castling queenside: 14...0-0-0!. The idea is ...c6-c5 after which chances are equal.

7...b6?! 8.cxd5 exd5 Not many players prefer this pawn structure, and besides

White can now exchange the queens. 8...♘xd5?! makes Black's life even more difficult for it makes the opponent's pawn centre extra mobile. For example: 9.0-0 ♗b7 10.♖e1 0-0 11.e4 ♘5f6 12.♘c3±. **9.♕e3+ ♕e7 10.♕xe7+ ♔xe7 11.♘c3±**

8.0-0

In the following we will see how two good moves (8...b6 and 8...0-0) and two suspicious moves (8...dxc4?! and 8...♘e4?!) work in this situation. White can also play **8.♕c2,**

introducing the typical plan with ♘d2 and e2-e4, known from the Closed Catalan. However, it should be noted that here White has one tempo less, lost by the white queen during the exchange of the dark-squared bishops on d2. **8...b6 9.♘bd2 ♗b7**

A) **10.e4 dxe4** Or 10...♘xe4 11.♘xe4 dxe4 12.♕xe4 ♕c7 13.♘e5 ♘xe5 14.dxe5= and the opponents agreed on a draw, Zhukova-Chiburdanidze, Plovdiv 2010. We have already mentioned grandmaster Eingorn's opinion that Black can now castle queenside with the idea ...c5 and an equal position. **11.♘xe4 ♘xe4 12.♕xe4 ♕c7 13.0-0 c5 14.♕e2 0-0 15.♖fd1 ♖ad8 16.♘e1 ♗xg2 17.♔xg2 ♘f6** and both sides can make easy-to-find moves and have equal chances,

Blagojevic-Shengelia, Porto Carras 2011;

B) **10.0-0 0-0 11.e4**

In the regular Closed Catalan with the bishops on c1 and e7, it would be White's turn now. In the present case, Black's chances are equal thanks to his one extra tempo to play in the centre. Black has three replies, which can result in three different types of position: the thematic but passive B1) 11...dxe4, the prophylactic B2) 11...h6, and the active and principled B3) 11 ...c5.

B1) **11...dxe4 12.♘xe4 ♘xe4** 12...c5 13.♘d6! ♗c6 14.♖fd1 ♕c7 15.dxc5 ♘xc5 16.♘b5 ♕b7 17.♕e2 a5 18.♘d6 ♕c7 19.♘e5± Van Wely-Andersson, Villarrobledo 1998. **13.♕xe4 ♕c7 14.♘e5 ♘xe5 15.dxe5** Or 15.♕xe5 ♖ac8 16.♖ad1 ♖fd8 17.b4 ♖d7 18.c5 ♖cd8=. Despite being a blitz game, this game has certain theoretical importance, P.H. Nielsen-Short, Internet (blitz) 2004. **15...♖ad8 16.♖fd1** Attention! Please compare an important analysis of practically the same position, only White has a pawn on b3 instead of b2, as it occurred in the game Georgiev-Nikolic, Kragujevac 2013. That game was dealt with under Miles' system in Chapter 2.2. **16...♗a8 17.♕e3 c5 18.♗xa8 ♖xa8** It is safer to immediately exchange one rook, as in the above-mentioned game between K. Georgiev and P. Nikolic: **18...Ξxd1+ 19.Ξxd1 Ξxa8 20.Ξd6 Ξd8. 19.Ξd6** With an initiative for White along the d-file. The game will probably have a dramatic ending with a passed d-pawn, which is very uncomfortable for Black, but objectively close to a draw. For example, Moranda-Stupak, Krakow 2011. **19...Ξad8 20.Ξad1 Ξxd6 21.Ξxd6** 21.exd6!?. **21...Ξd8 22.Ψd2 Ξxd6 23.exd6 Ψd7=** In the above-mentioned game, Nikolic relatively easily kept a similar queen endgame in which b-pawns were exchanged;

B2) **11...h6** is an interesting and useful move: **12.Ξac1 Ξc8 13.e5 ♘h7 14.cxd5 cxd5 15.Ψa4 a6 16.Ψb4 Ξe8 17.♘b3 ♘hf8∞** with a slightly more passive but solid position, Cernousek-Stocek, Slovakia 2012;

B3) **11...c5!**

12.cxd5

12.exd5 exd5 13.Ξfe1 Ψc7=. In this position, which is typical for the Closed Catalan, without dark-squared bishops, Black can breathe more easily and has no problems balancing the game: **12...exd5 13.e5 ♘e4 14.♘xe4 dxe4 15.♘h4 cxd4 16.♗xe4 ♗xe4 17.Ψxe4 ♘c5** with equal chances, Ju Wenjun-Ding Yixin, Olongapo City 2010.

8...b6

This is a good moment to remember Anthony Miles' system in which we have the same position, but with the insertion of ...♗c8-a6 and b2-b3, which we dealt with in Chapter 2.2.

A) **8...dxc4?!** Since Black cannot keep the pawn and has opened a diagonal for the Catalan bishop, thus doing a strategic favour to his opponent, a good solution is **9.Ψc2** (9.a4!?±) **9...b5 10.b3N** 10.♘c3 ♗b7 11.e4 0-0 12.e5?! ♘d5 13.♘e4 c5!∓ White does not have sufficient compensation for the pawn, Gelashvili-Benidze, Rijeka 2010. **10...♗a6 11.♘bd2±** with obvious compensation for the pawn;

B) **8...♘e4?! 9.Ψc2 0-0 10.♘bd2 f5** It is illogical to build a Stonewall position without the dark-squared bishop, which is usually the strategic pillar for Black in this type of position. **11.Ξac1 Ψf6 12.e3 g5?! 13.♘e1** A thematic move. One of White's knights goes to d3, and the other to e5, taking absolute control, whereas the mobile pawn on f2 can control the delicate central square e4 with f2–f3. **13...Ψh6?! 14.♘d3 ♘df6 15.♘f3 ♗d7 16.♘fe5 Ξad8 17.b4 ♗c8 18.a4 a6 19.Ψb2±** Black cannot attack, while White has a clear advantage in the centre and on the queenside, Erdös-Jäschke, Deizisau 2012;

C) **8...0-0 9.♘e5** For 9.♕c2 b6 10.♘bd2 ♗b7 11.e4 see under 8.♕c2. On 9.♖c1 Black can choose between two completely different but both solid plans: the active and good 9...♕c7 (dealt with under 8...c6) and the calm and equalizing 9...b6 (dealt with under 8...b6). **9...♘xe5 10.dxe5 ♘d7 11.f4 f6!** A tried and tested method of playing in the opponent's centre in the manner of the French Defence. Weaker is 11...♘b6 12.♘a3 ♕e7 13.♖ac1 a5 14.♖fd1, Moranda-Jobava, Warsaw (rapid) 2011. **12.exf6 ♘xf6 13.♘c3 dxc4!**

This strategically bad move is sometimes good! Black breaks up the pawn structure in the centre but captures a pawn and simplifies the position, since White is practically forced to exchange queens. Besides, White will need more time to regain the pawn on c4 because his knight is now on c3 – time which Black will use to complete his development and correct his structural defects. **14.♕xd8 ♖xd8 15.♖ad1 ♖e8 16.♘e4 ♘xe4 17.♗xe4 a5** Better is 17...g6!?N with the idea ...e6-e5.**18.♖c1 e5 19.f5 ♗xf5 20.♗xf5 gxf5 21.♖xf5=** Black has an extra pawn, but White's active rooks secure him a draw. **18.♖c1 a4 19.a3 ♖a5 20.♖xc4 ♖d8 21.♗d3±** Black has not solved all his problems yet

and has to keep on fighting to equalize, Vitiugov-Zviagintsev, St Petersburg (rapid) 2012.

9.♖c1

The key move in White's general plan, in which the c-file is the battle arena. We can already sense White's further intentions, such as opening the c-file with cxd5 and the rush of the white knights to e5 and b5 for the purpose of supporting the rook.

A) **9.♘e5**

A logical alternative, always unpleasant for Black. White increases the pressure from this central square and often moves the knight to the flexible square d3. Consequently, an exchange on e5 usually occurs at some point, which changes the position completely. By the way, after some time, practical games have brought up two questions for both sides. For White: When is the best moment to move the knight to e5? For Black: When is the best moment to exchange the knight on e5? The quality of the game depends on the right answers to these important strategic questions.

For 9.♕c2 ♗b7 10.♘bd2 see under 10.0-0.

9...♗b7 Right on time! Black develops the bishop and defends the pawn on c6. This would not have been possible if Black had castled instead of playing 8...b6. Now is not the time to exchange the knight since after 9...♘xe5 10.dxe5 ♘d7 11.cxd5 cxd5 White has two simple moves that yield him a better position: 12.f4± or 12.e4±. **10.♘c3 0-0** Again weak was 10...♘xe5? 11.dxe5 ♘d7 12.cxd5 cxd5 13.♘b5±.

11.♖fd1 11.♖ac1 ♕e7 12.e4 dxe4 13.♘xe4 ♘xe4 14.♗xe4 ♘xe5 15.dxe5 c5 16.♗xb7 ♖ad8 17.♕e2 ♕xb7 18.♖fd1 and in this absolutely equal position the opponents agreed on a draw, Khalifman-Dominguez Perez, St Petersburg (rapid) 2012. **11...♕e7 12.♖ac1 ♖ac8 13.f4 ♖fd8 14.e3** This is slightly more complicated than the exchange 14.cxd5 cxd5 15.♘b5 a6 16.♘a7 ♖xc1 17.♖xc1 ♕d6 18.♘ac6 ♖c8 19.♘xd7 ♘xd7 20.♘e5 ♖xc1+ 21.♕xc1 ♘xe5 22.fxe5 ♕c6 23.♕xc6 ♗xc6 24.♔f2 a5 25.♔e3 ♔f8= and the game will obviously end in a draw,

Miton-Fedorchuk, Lublin 2012. **14...dxc4!?N** 14...h6 15.♗f3 ♗a8 16.♕g2 with slightly better chances for White, Elianov-Vitiugov, Eilat 2012.

Attention should be paid to the position of the white queen on the d-file. **15.♘xc4 ♗a6 16.♗f1** 16.b3 c5⇄; 16.♘e5? ♘xe5 17.fxe5 ♘g4∓. **16...♗xc4 17.♗xc4 e5∞** with mutual chances;

B) **9.♘a3** usually transposes into the familiar position dealt with under our main line 9.♖c1: **9...0-0 10.♖fc1 ♗b7** Also possible is 10...♗a6 11.♘e5 ♖c8 12.cxd5 ♘xe5 13.dxe5 ♘xd5 14.♘c4 ♗xc4 15.♖xc4 c5∞ with mutual chances. **11.cxd5 ♘e4!?** 11...cxd5 is dealt with under 11...♗b7. **12.♕f4 exd5** 12...cxd5 13.♘b5±. **13.♘c4 ♘df6 14.♘fd2 ♘xd2 15.♘xd2 ♖e8 16.e3 ♕e7** with approximately equal chances, Ivanchuk-Quesada Perez, Havana 2012.

9...0-0

9...♗a6?! Is this the original position from the system of Anthony Miles described in Chapter 2.2? The answer has to be yes if White responds with 10.b3. However, in this position White does not have to waste time on this prophylactic move since there is a better move, which leads to a superior position: **10.♘e5!** and White gets into the familiar position with an extra tempo (for 10.b3 see Chapter 2.2; for 10.cxd5 cxd5 11.♘c3 0-0 see under 11...♗a6) **10...♘xe5** 10...♖c8?! Black has not yet connected his rooks, so an exchange on the c-file will suit the opponent better. 11.cxd5 cxd5 12.♘a3 ♘xe5 (12...0-0? 13.♘c6±) 13.dxe5 ♘d7 14.♖xc8 ♕xc8 15.♖c1 ♕b8 16.f4± 0-0? 17.e4±. **11.dxe5 ♘d7 12.cxd5 cxd5 13.f4 0-0 14.♘c3±** (for 14.♘a3 see under 12.♘e5).

After 9...0-0 we have the second most important key position in the fianchetto system.

In Chapter 4.1 we had this position, only with the queen on e7 instead of the b-pawn on b6, which clearly indicates two essentially different concepts. In the former situation Black played in the centre, preparing ...dxc4 and ...e6-e5, while here Black plays on the queenside, planning to develop the light-squared bishop on the central diagonal with ...♗b7 or more actively, on the diagonal f1-a6. We will analyse the following moves for White: 10.cxd5, A) 10.b4, B) 10.a4 and C) 10.♘e5.

10.cxd5

White continues according to the plan started with 9.♖c1, opening the c-file for the forthcoming moves on the queenside.

A) **10.b4** is the introduction to a logical plan, although it is more attractive in positions where the white knight defends the pawn on c4. White intends to improve his pieces with ♕b2 and ♘bd2, and his queenside pawns should advance further. On the other hand, this gives Black more time to organize his counterplay. **10...♗b7 11.♕b2 dxc4** It is clear: Black captures on c4 before the opponent has managed to play ♘d2. Also a good move is 11...♖b8 12.♘bd2 ♕e7 13.e3 ♖fc8 14.♖c2 c5 15.bxc5 bxc5 16.♕a3 ♖c6 17.♖ac1 ♗a6 18.♕d3 h6∞ with mutual chances, Topalov-Carlsen, Nanjing 2010. On 11...♕b8, after 12.♘bd2 ♖c8 13.♘e5 ♘xe5 14.dxe5 ♘d7 15.f4± White has won the theoretical duel, Bacrot-Fedorchuk, Fujairah City 2012. **12.♖xc4 a5 13.bxa5 ♖xa5∞** with mutual chances;

B) **10.a4**

With the obvious intention of pushing a4-a5. **10...a5** It is risky to ignore White's plan with 10...♗b7 11.a5 ♘e4 12.♕f4 c5 13.a6 (better is 13.cxd5 ♗xd5 (after 13...exd5 14.♘c3± all white pieces are operative) 14.♘c3 ♘xc3 15.bxc3± when White has the more active position) 13...♗c6 14.♘bd2 f5∞, Damljanovic-Antic, Valjevo 2011. **11.cxd5** White relies on the fact that the new pawn structure on the queenside is a strategic advantage and enables the knight to move to the conquered square b5. **11...cxd5 12.♘a3 ♗a6 13.♘b5 ♖c8!** A more passive move is 13...♕b8 14.♘e1 ♖c8 15.♖xc8+ ♕xc8 16.♖c1 ♕d8 17.♘c7 ♖a7 18.♘xa6 ♖xa6 19.♖c6 ♖a8 20.♕c3 ♕b8 21.♘d3 and with his control over the c-file White has better chances, Avrukh-Grachev, Sibenik 2012. **14.♘e1 ♖xc1 15.♖xc1 ♕b8=** Next will be 16...♖c8 with an obvious draw, Hammer-Mchedlishvili, Khanty-Mansiysk 2010.

C) **10.♘e5**

10...♘xe5 A risky trade. Black is now in danger of losing control of the dark squares. Squares d4 and d6, usually targeted by the white knight, are especially critical.

For 10...♗b7 11.cxd5 cxd5 see under 11...♗b7.

11.dxe5 ♘d7 12.f4 ♗b7 For 12...♗a6 13.cxd5 cxd5 14.♘c3± see under 11.♘e5. **13.♘c3!?** White finishes his development, without hurrying to complete the exchanges in the centre. For 13.cxd5 cxd5 see under 12...♘d7. **13...a6** A slow move for this type of position, but there is no better plan: after 13...b5 14.cxd5 ♕b6+ 15.e3 cxd5 16.b4± White is better thanks to his more active men and his domination over the dark squares. If 13...dxc4

14.♘e4♕ White has more than sufficient compensation for the pawn. And if 13...f6?! 14.cxd5 cxd5 15.♘b5± with the idea ♘c7. **14.♖d1** 14.b4!?N ♕e7 15.cxd5 cxd5 16.e4!±. **14...b5** A weaker solution is 14...f6?! 15.cxd5 cxd5 16.e4 fxe5 17.exd5±. **15.cxd5 cxd5 16.e4 b4 17.♘e2** Better is 17.♘a4 ♕a5 18.b3 ♘c5 19.♘xc5 ♕xc5+ 20.♕d4±. However, the analysis shows that Black ends up in a difficult position with a pawn less, but with sufficient compensation for a draw thanks to the position of the opponent's king, for example 20...♕a5 21.exd5 ♗xd5 22.♗xd5 ♖ad8 23.a3 ♖xd5 24.♕xb4 ♕d8 25.♖xd5 ♕xd5♕. **17...♕b6+ 18.♔h1 ♖ad8** 18...f6! 19.exf6 (if 19.exd5 fxe5 20.dxe6 ♘f6♕ Black also has sufficient compensation thanks to White's weakened king) 19...♘xf6 20.♕d4 ♕xd4 21.♘xd4 dxe4 22.♘xe6 ♖fc8 with equal chances. **19.exd5 exd5** Logical but weaker is 19...♗xd5 20.♗xd5 ♘b8 (20...♘c5 21.♕e3±) 21.♕c2 ♖xd5 22.♖xd5 exd5 23.♖d1±. White will place the knight on d4, thus gaining a considerable strategic advantage. **20.♖ac1±** Black does not have any appropriate counter-moves to compensate for his strategic weaknesses, Ganguly-Markidis, Kavala 2012.

10...cxd5

An important crossroads for White. Now he has a choice between 11.♘a3, A) 11.♘c3, B) 11.♘e5 and C) 11.♕b4.

11.♘a3

White finishes his development by moving the knight to the rim, with the manoeuvre ♘c2-d4 in mind, after the usual exchange of the knights on e5. Besides, White does not lose the possibility to threaten ♘a3-b5.

Black can finish his development with either 11...♗a6 or 11...♗b7.

A) **11.♘c3**

White completes his development by placing the knight on c3. Black can again choose between two positions for his bishop:

A1) **11...♗a6**

The position which we had in Miles' system (Chapter 2.2), only in this instance White has a tempo more, since he has not played b2-b3. However, practical games and analyses do not show a clear path to a better position for White. In practice we have seen 12.a4 and 12.♖c2 here:

A11) **12.♖c2!?** This simple plan seems to be underestimated in practice. After doubling the rooks on the c-file, White intends to play e2-e3 and exchange the light-squared bishops with ♗f1, in order to weaken the opponent's light squares and move the play to the

queenside. **12...♖c8** 12...♕e7 has become a standard move in the system with 3...♗xd2, and it is even more effective in positions where White has played b2-b3. However, in this particular position, the queen move is not the best solution if we bear in mind White's above-mentioned plan. After 13.♖ac1 ♖ac8 14.e3± the players agreed on a draw in Braga-Andersson, Calvi 2004, although White had a slightly better position.

The game could continue as follows: 14...h6 15.♗f1 ♗b7 (a weaker solution is 15...♗xf1 16.♔xf1 with the idea ♘xd5, with a strong white initiative on the queenside) 16.♘b5 ♖xc2 17.♖xc2 a6 18.♘a7!↑. It is unusual, but White has the initiative on the queenside, with his knight on a7. Of course, controlling the c-file and the crucial points e5 and c6 is of the essence.

13.♖ac1 White's chances are slightly better in this unique ending thanks to the more natural positioning of his pieces and more attacking motifs. White's advantages are not great, but they are sufficient to make the opponent feel inferior. We may remind you that we dealt with the same ending in Miles' system (Chapter 2.2), only there White had played b2-b3. Let's expand the analysis a little:

13...h6!? A useful move when the queen is on e7, because of the insufficiently protected rook on c8. Black's backup plan is Miles' plan (Chapter 2–2) with ...♖c7,...♕b8 and ...♖fc8. **14.e3 ♖c7 15.a4** Now 15.♗f1 leads to a certain draw after 15...♗xf1 16.♔xf1 ♕b8= with the idea ...♖fc8. **15...♕b8** A more passive square for the queen than e7. **16.♘e5 ♖fc8 17.♘d3±** with slightly more active play for White;

A12) **12.a4 ♖c8** It is a waste of time to play 12...♗c4 13.♘b5 ♕e7 14.♘a3 (better is 14.♘e5 ♗xb5 15.axb5 ♘xe5 16.dxe5 ♘g4 17.♕f4 ♘h6 18.♖c6± and Black has to continue tackling serious problems) 14...♘e4 15.♕d1 ♗a6 16.♘b5 ♗xb5 17.axb5 ♕b4 18.♕a4 ♕xa4 19.♖xa4 ♘d6 20.♖c7 ♖fd8 21.♖axa7 ♖xa7 22.♖xa7 ♘xb5 23.♖a1 ♔f8= Portisch-Spassky, Reykjavik 1988. Or 12...♕e7 13.♘b5 ♘e4 14.♕e3 (better is 14.♕e1 ♗xb5 15.axb5 ♘d6 16.♕b4 ♖fc8 17.♘e5±) 14...♗xb5 15.axb5 ♕b4= Sargissian-Georgiev, Khanty-Mansiysk (rapid) 2013. **13.♘b5 ♖xc1+** 13...♘e4 14.♕f4 ♕e7 15.♖c7 ♗xb5 16.axb5 ♘d6 17.♕c1 ♖xc7 18.♕xc7 ♖c8 19.♕xa7 ♕d8 20.♕a4 h6 21.♕b4 ♕f8 22.b3 (better is 22.e3±) 22...♘e4 23.♕xf8+ ♔xf8= Wang Yue-Carlsen, Nanjing 2010. **14.♖xc1**

14...♕b8 Black does not have to hurry with capturing on b5, but he gets ready to exchange the rooks on the c-file. If 14...♗xb5 15.axb5 ♘e4 16.♕f4 (a logical move, but it seems that the white queen's place is on the queenside. Better is 16.♕c2 ♘d6 17.♕a4 ♕b8 18.e3 ♖c8 19.♖c6± and White maintains the pressure) 16...♘df6 17.♘e5 ♘d6 18.♘c6 ♕d7 19.♘xa7 ♘xb5 20.♘xb5 ♕xb5= Chadaev-Grigoriants, Moscow 2011. **15.♕f4** 15.♗f1 ♖c8 16.♖xc8+ ♗xc8 17.♕f4 a6 18.♕xb8 ♘xb8 19.♘d6 ♗d7 20.♘e5 ♗e8=. White will have the initiative for some time, but after the arrival of the black king on e7 a draw cannot be avoided, Sanner-Kruijer, corr. 2012.

After the double exchange with **15...♗xb5 16.axb5 ♕xf4** (or 16...h6 17.♕xb8 ♖xb8 18.♖c7 ♖a8 19.♘e5 ♘xe5 20.dxe5 ♘g4 21.f4 ♘e3 with an equal position, Ganguly-Grachev, Biel 2013) **17.gxf4 ♖a8 18.♖c7 ♘f8 19.e3 ♘e8 20.♖c3 ♘d6 21.♗f1 ♖c8 22.♖a3 ♖c7 23.♘e5 ♘g6=** a draw was agreed, since Black has neutralized all of the opponent's threats, Borroni-Meißen, corr. 2012.

A2) **11...♗b7** Black finishes the development of his minor pieces and defends the critical square c6. Now he only has to play ...♕e7 and ...♖fc8 and all his opening wishes will come true. **12.♖c2** With 12.♘b5 we enter the game Kramnik-Carlsen, Wijk aan Zee 2011, which we tackled under 11.♘a3. For 12.♘e5 see under 11.♘e5. **12...♕e7** The standard square for the queen in the system without dark-squared bishops. **13.♖ac1 ♖fc8** Black has realized his plan. In the forthcoming battle, there is a tendency to exchange the major pieces along the open c-file, which usually leads to a draw. **14.♘e5** 14.♘e1 ♕d8 (14...♘e8!? 15.♘d3 ♘d6∞) 15.♘d3 h6 (15...♘e4!? 16.♕f4 ♘xc3 17.♖xc3 ♖xc3 18.♖xc3 ♖c8=) 16.f3 ♘b8 17.♘e5 ♘c6 18.♘b5↑ De Blois Figueredo-Zarnescu, ICCF email 2011.

A21) 14...♘xe5?!

This exchange should be always considered very carefully, for it changes the type of position – usually to White's benefit. The pawn on e5 brings White significant strategic advantages:

– It expels the black king's knight from f6;

– The new pawn structure in the centre offers White a new possibility in the form of a tremendous attack on the opponent's centre with e2-e4;

– It enables the white pieces, especially the knight, to take up a centralized position on the vacated square d4;

– In Black's structure a weak square appears on d6.

15.dxe5 ♘d7 16.f4± 16...♘c5 17.b4± (or 17.♘b5±); 16...f6? 17.♘xd5!+−; 16...a6 17.e4!±. The tremendous attack by the pawn in the new structure, which often indicates the superiority of White's strategy in this type of position.

A22) 14...h6 Black continues building his position while trying to read the intentions of the opponent, who is having trouble strengthening his position because of the potential exchange of the major pieces along the c-file and the resulting possible draw. **15.f4** A tempting move. White increases his control of the board, but at the same time loses control of the central square e4, so Black's immediate reaction is a typical manoeuvre. **15...♘e8!** With the obvious idea ...♘d6, after which the black knight has a variety of squares to choose from. **16.♘b5 ♖xc2 17.♖xc2 a6 18.♘c3 ♖c8=** with ...♘d6 next. White has active pieces, but Black has good control over the position and chances are equal, Grachev-Fedorchuk, Sibenik 2012.

B) 11.♘e5

A thematic move which can be used at different moments during the game, and without which White can hardly make any progress. Black can now either continue developing with 11...♗b7 or change the type of position by changing the central pawn structure with 11...♘xe5.

B1) 11...♘xe5 We have already pointed to the risks of this plan tending to simplification and giving White control over the dark squares d4 and d6, as well as allowing a strong strategic attack in the centre with e2-e4. **12.dxe5 ♘d7**

Black has problems even after 12...♘e4 13.♗xe4 dxe4 14.♕f4 ♗b7 15.♘c3 ♕d4 16.♖d1 ♕b4 17.♖d2 ♖ad8 18.♖ad1 ♖xd2 19.♖xd2±. **13.f4**

Black can finish his development with the defensive move 13...♗b7 or the active move 13...♗a6:

B11) 13...♗a6 The bishop is more active here and it also prevents an excellent manoeuvre by the white knight: ♘c3(♘a3)-b5-d4(d6). Although it is strategically more appropriate to place the light-squared bishop on b7 to defend against the even more dangerous strategic threat e2-e4, especially if White can play ♘c3. We will see later that Black can play ...♗a6 if the white knight is on a3 (under 11.♘a3), thanks to the important theoretic novelty 15...♘a4!N. **14.♘c3±** (for 14.♘a3 see under 11.♘a3) White finishes his development and poses the tremendous threat of e2-e4. In the new situation, Black hardly has any smart moves. The bishop on a6 prevents the manoeuvre ♘b5-d4(d6), but how to fight against the even more dangerous strategic threat e2-e4 ? **14...b5** 14...♕e7 15.e4±; 14...f6? 15.♘xd5±; 14...♘c5? (this continuation is possible if the white knight is on a3) 15.b4±. **15.e3 b4 16.♘a4** 16.♘e2 ♗xe2 17.♕xe2 ♕b6=. **16...♕e7 17.♕d4±;**

B12) 13...♗b7

More passive, but safer! The black bishop is in its favourite shelter, from where it can defend all the vulnerable light squares and participate in the battle against e2-e4. Black can easily deal with the problem of White's knight move to b5 by playing ...a7–a6. **14.♘c3** With 14.♘a3 we would enter the game Georgiev-Antic, Plovdiv 2012. **14...a6** An important prophylactic move. From the b5, the white knight would have two excellent squares at its disposal: d4 and d6. **15.e4** The thematic and most dangerous attack. See the critical game Ganguly-Markidis, Kavala 2012, under 10.♘e5. For 15.♖d1 b5 16.e4, see also under 10.♘e5. **15...dxe4 16.♖d1** On 16.♘xe4 Black immediately evens the score with 16...♗xe4 17.♗xe4 ♘c5=. Probably the best move for White is 16.♗xe4! ♘c5 17.♕xd8 ♖fxd8 18.♗xb7 ♘xb7 19.b4±

with a slightly better ending because of the passive knight on b7, but it probably leads to a draw.

16...♘c5 17.♕e3 ♕c7 It is better to avoid the c-file with 17...♕e7!?N 18.b4 ♘d3 19.♘xe4 ♘xb4 20.♕xb6 ♗d5!?=. **18.b4 ♘d3 19.♘xe4 ♘xb4 20.♖ac1±**

Li Chao-Xiu Deshun, Xinghua Jiangsu 2011.

B2) **11...♗b7**

Now White usually continues his development with 12.♘c3 but he can also make other knight moves – 12.♘c6, 12.♘d3 or 12.♘a3.

B21) The exchange **12.♘c6** rarely brings profits to White. The knight on e5 is the piece with the greatest energy, so its pointless exchange usually leads to a quick draw, for example: **12...♗xc6 13.♖xc6 ♖c8 14.♖xc8 ♕xc8 15.♘c3 ♕b8 16.e3 ♖c8 17.♖c1 ♘e8 18.b3**

♘d6= Atalik-Stojanovic, Sarajevo 2007;

B22) **12.♘d3** This manoeuvre is not suitable in positions where the c-pawns have been exchanged. Now Black has more time to remove all of the remaining potential threats along the c-file and on b5. **12...♕e7 13.♖c7 ♖fb8 14.♘a3 ♘e8 15.♖c2 ♖c8 16.♖ac1 ♕d8=** and Black emerges out of the opening with equal chances. Cornette-Chernuschevich, Belfort 2010;

B23) For **12.♘a3** see under 12.♘e5;

B24) **12.♘c3** Here, Black is not forced to obey the opponent's will and exchange the knights on e5, for as the queen's knight closes off the c-file there is no threat of ♘e5-c6. Black can choose between several solid options: 12...♕e7, 12...a6 or 12...♘e8:

B241) **12...a6** The standard prophylactic move in this type of position. For 12...♘xe5 13.dxe5 ♘d7 14.f4 see under 10.♘e5.

13.♘a4 Principled and good. White's main plans take place on the queenside, so he focuses on Black's only, newly-created weakness. 13.♘xd7 ♕xd7 14.e3 was seen in Dominguez Perez-Bruzon Batista, Havana 2011. **13...♖c8** It is possible to play 13...♘xe5, though after 14.dxe5 ♘d7 15.♕d4 b5 16.♘c5 ♘xc5 17.♖xc5 ♖c8 18.♖ac1 ♖xc5

19.♕xc5 ♕a8± Black has an inferior position, remaining weak on the dark squares. However, after the likely exchange of the rooks, Black ends up with a queen and bishop against queen and bishop, and has chances to achieve a draw. **14.♕b4** In case of 14.♖xc8 the game could continue in the following way: 14...♕xc8 15.♖c1 ♕b8 16.♘xd7 ♘xd7 17.♕b4 a5! (Black drives the white queen away from b4, controls the critical diagonal a3-f8 and attacks the pawn on b6) 18.♕e7 (18.♕b5 ♕d6=) 18...♖c8 19.♖c3 ♖xc3 20.♘xc3 ♘f6 21.e3 ♗c6 22.♗f1 ♕c8 23.♕a7 ♕d8 24.♗d3 ♘e8= and in spite of the fact that all three of White's pieces are more active, Black can hold this position. **14...a5** The white queen has to be chased away from b4. Was this the right moment to exchange with 14...♘xe5 ? Let's see: 15.dxe5 ♘d7 16.♖xc8 ♗xc8 17.♕d6 b5 18.♘c5 ♘xc5 19.♕xc5 ♗b7 20.♖c1 ♕a8 21.♕b6 ♖c8 22.♖c7 ♖xc7 23.♕xc7± and White has a comfortable position. Black has weak dark squares but still has chances to hold the draw, Li Chao-Moradiabadi, Jakarta 2011. **15.♕b5 ♖c7!**

It is not easy to find this multi-purpose move which is in perfect accordance with the position. Black vacates the c8-square for the queen thanks to his control on the c-file, and now the ex-

change on e5 becomes more powerful. If this exchange is made at the wrong moment, Black faces problems along the c-file or on the dark squares. The further course of the game testifies to the validity of Black's strategy. **16.♘c6** If 16.♘d3 ♘e8= and Black keeps control; or 16.e3?! ♘xe5 17.dxe5 ♘d7 18.f4 ♕c8 and Black takes the initiative. **16...♗xc6 17.♖xc6 ♕b8 18.♖ac1 ♖fc8 19.e3 ♕b7 20.♖xc7 ♖xc7 21.♖c3 g6 22.♕d3 ♔g7 23.♕c2 ♖xc3 24.♘xc3** 24.♕xc3 ♘e8=. **24...♕c7=**

And obviously this game can end in peace. Black has not lost the battle for the c-file and only needs to move the knight from f6 to d6 to take care of his only weakness on b5, Cheparinov-Dominguez Perez, Loo 2013;

B242) **12...♘e8!?**

Also a common move in Black's defensive arsenal. Black covers the critical square c7 and intends to move the knight to the ideal square d6 at the right time. However, being more active, White manages to keep the initiative: **13.♕f4 ♘df6 14.a4 ♖c8 15.♘b5 a6 16.♘a7!** An interesting move. As if the white knight wanted to leave the chessboard! But joking aside – it has a safe exit on c6. **16...♖xc1+ 17.♖xc1 ♘d6 18.♘ac6 ♗xc6 19.♖xc6 ♘f5 20.♕d2 ♘e7 21.♖c1 ♕d6** Better is 21...♖b8!? with the idea ...♖c8 with good chances to equalize. **22.♕c3 ♖b8 23.♕c7** White begins to rampage along the c-file and the seventh rank. **23...♘e8 24.♕a7 f6 25.♘d3?** White had a better option in 25.♘d7! ♖c8 26.♖xc8 ♘xc8 27.♕b7 but probably Sjugirov did not see that on 27...♕c7 there was a tactical shot:

28.♗xd5!±. **25...♘c8!∓** led to a draw but White was worse here, Sjugirov-Fedorchuk, Cappelle la Grande 2013;
  B243) **12...♕e7**

13.♘b5 A typical motif. White plans to make progress by activating and coordinating his rook and knights. **13...a6 14.♖c7 ♖fb8!=** 14...♖ab8?! 15.♖xb7 ♖xb7 16.♘c6 ♕e8 17.♘d6 ♕a8

18.♘e7+! (weaker is 18.♖c1 ♘b8 19.♘xb7 ♕xb7 20.♕c3 ♘xc6 21.♕xc6 ♕xc6 22.♖xc6 ♖b8 23.e3 a5 24.♗f1 ♔f8 25.♗d3 h6 26.♔f1 ♘e8= and Black holds, Sedlak-Antic, Eretria 2011) 18...♔h8 19.♖c1 ♖bb8 (19...♘b8? 20.♘xf7+− with checkmate in three) 20.♕f4 (with the idea ♖c7) 20...b5 (20...♖be8 21.♘xe8 ♖xe8 22.♕d6± ♖d8 23.e3 g6 24.a4± with the idea ♗f1) 21.♖c7± and White has superb compensation.

15.♕g5! In the style of former World Champion Mikhail Tal. Without imagination and good intuition, this queen move is not easy to find. The alternatives lead to exchanges or to the retreat of the white army, which would bring the game closer to a draw. If 15.♘a3 ♛d6=; or 15.♘xd7 ♘xd7 16.♘a3 ♛d6 17.♖ac1 ♘f6= with the idea ...♘e8. **15...h6 16.♛h4 ♛b4!** White threatened to capture the knight with ♖xd7. **17.♘xd7** In case of 17.♘d3 ♛f8 White has to retreat (17...♛xb5? 18.a4 ♛b3 19.♖c3±). **17...♘xd7 18.♖xd7 ♛xb2 19.♘d6** 19.♖f1 ♗c6 20.♖xf7 ♔xf7 21.♘d6+ ♔g8 22.♗h3 ♗d7 23.♛e7≌. **19...♛xa1+ 20.♗f1 ♗c6 21.♖c7 ♗b5** If 21...♗e8 22.♛f4 ♔h8 23.e3≌ White has sufficient compensation for a draw. **22.♛h5 ♛xd4 23.♛xf7+ ♔h8 24.♛xe6≌** with compensation, but just for a draw, Li Chao-Gagunashvili, Jakarta 2012.

C) 11.♛b4 White wants to prevent the black queen from coming to e7 and controlling the dark squares, but it is a delusion to think that the white queen can retain a stable position here, among so many enemy pieces. **11...a5 12.♛b3** 12.♛d6 ♗a6=. **12...b5 13.♘c3 ♗a6 14.♘xb5 ♗xb5 15.♛xb5 ♖b8 16.♛a6 ♖xb2** with equal chances, Melkumyan-Giri, Schwetzingen 2013.

11...♗a6

The more passive but more stable development of the light-squared bishop, which does not obstruct the a-pawn, is **11...♗b7** and now:

A) 12.♘b5 A continuation of White's logical plan to use the c-file and activate his knights to obtain a concrete advantage. **12...a6 13.♘d6 ♛b8 14.♛b4 a5 15.♛a3 ♗a6 16.♘e5** White's initiative is growing and it seems very dangerous. However, Black's next move demonstrates that the knight on d6 is unstable. After 16.♖c6 ♗xe2 17.♖ac1 White has compensation for the pawn but it leads only to a draw. **16...b5!** With the idea ...b5-b4. **17.♛xa5?!** Better is 17.♘dxf7 ♖xf7 18.♘xf7 ♔xf7 19.♛xa5=; if 17.♘c6? b4 18.♘xb8 bxa3 19.♘xd7 axb2∓. **17...♛xd6 18.♖c6 ♛b8 19.♖xa6 ♖xa6 20.♛xa6 ♘xe5 21.dxe5 ♛xe5 22.♛xb5 ♖b8 23.♛d3 ♖xb2∓** White's hopes are tied to the a-pawn, but the excellent coordination of Black's pieces give him the better chances, Kramnik-Carlsen, Wijk aan Zee 2011;

B) 12.♛b4 As said, the white queen cannot do anything in this unstable position. **12...a5 13.♛a4 ♗a6** 13...♖c8!?=. **14.♗f1 ♖c8 15.e3 ♗xf1 16.♔xf1 ♛e7=** Likavsky-Vesselovsky, Orlova 2012;

C) 12.♘e5 and now;

C1) In case of **12...♘e4** White has the good reaction **13.♛f4** (13.♗xe4 dxe4 14.♘ec4 ♘f6∞ with mutual chances; 13.♛b4 a5 14.♛b3 ♘xe5 15.dxe5 ♗a6 (15...♘c5!? 16.♖xc5 a4 17.♛b4 bxc5 18.♛xb7 ♖b8 19.♛a7 ♖xb2 20.♛xc5 ♛b8 21.e4 ♖c8≌) 16.♛e3 (better is 16.♗xe4 dxe4 17.♘c4 ♗xc4 18.♖xc4 ♛d5 19.♛c3 with a minimal advantage for White player thanks to the fact that he can play e2-e3 and ♖d4 at a suitable moment) 16...♘c5 17.♘c2 ♛d7 18.♘d4 ♖fc8= with mutual chances, Pashikian-Markowski, Legnica 2013) **13...♘xe5 14.dxe5** with slightly better chances, since the black knight does not have a solid basis. A weaker solution is 14.♕xe5 as after 14...♘d6 the white queen will not feel comfortable among the enemy pieces;

C2) **12...♘xe5 13.dxe5 ♘d7 14.f4 a6 15.♘c2**

15...♖c8 15...♕e7!? 16.♘d4 ♖fc8∞ deserves attention. **16.♘d4 ♕e7 17.a3 ♖fd8 18.e3 ♘c5 19.♕b4 ♕c7 20.♗f1 a5 21.♕e1 a4** with unclear play, Georgiev-Antic, Plovdiv 2012.

Back to the main line.

Black wants his light-squared bishop to play an active role instead of the defensive role on b7. Along the diagonal f1-a6 it seems more significant than its colleague on g2. However, the text also has some disadvantages because the bishop blocks the a-pawn and does not control the important c6–square, which White wants to use to force a change of pawn structure in the centre with ♘e5.

12.♘e5

This thematic move is probably the best way for White to make progress. In the case of an exchange, White can rely on square d4 for his knight that is momentarily inactive on the edge of the board. The alternative is 12.♘c2. Since square b5 is now out of bounds, White wants to activate the knight via b4. Two games have been played so far, in which Black reached a clearly equal position relatively easily: 12...♘e4 13.♕e1 ♗b7 14.♘b4 ♕b8=

Kursova-Ghader Pour, Istanbul 2012; and 12...♖c8 13.♘b4 ♗b7 14.♘d3 ♖xc1+ 15.♖xc1 ♕b8 16.♘fe5 ♘xe5 17.♘xe5 ♖c8 18.♕f4 ♖xc1+ 19.♕xc1 ♘e8 20.e3 ♕c7 with an equal ending, Farago-Lobzhanidze, Siebenlehn 2011.

12...♘xe5

Black is practically forced to exchange because of the strategic threat ♘e5-c6, which is in fact one of the reasons why White developed the knight on a3.
If 12...♕e7 13.♘c6 ♕d6 14.e3 ♖fc8 15.♘b4 ♗b7 16.♘b5±; 12...♖c8? 13.♘c6±.

13.dxe5 ♘d7 14.f4 ♘c5

There is no better plan. Black plans to jump with this knight to the central square e4 at the right moment.
If 14...♖c8 15.♖xc8 ♕xc8 16.♖c1 ♕d8 Black has simplified the position by exchanging one rook, but the differ-

ence in the activity of the remaining pieces is obviously advantageous to White (better is 16...♛b7!? with the idea ...♜c8, with chances to equalize) 17.♘c2 ♘b8 18.♘d4± with a clear advantage for White, Nogueiras Santiago-Andersson, Sarajevo 1985.

Or 14...♛e7 15.♘c2 ♜ac8 16.♘d4 ♘c5 17.♜c2 ♝b7 18.♜ac1 a5 19.b4 axb4 20.♛xb4± Sethuraman-Rakhmanov, Voronezh 2013.

Or 14...f6 15.♜c6!±.

15.b4

15.♘c2 ♜c8!? (the immediate 15...♘e4 gives White a slight advantage after 16.♛e3 ♜c8 17.♘d4±, Wen Yang-Golizadeh, Zaozhuang 2012) 16.♘d4 ♛d7 17.♜c2 ♘e4 18.♝xe4 dxe4 19.♜ac1 ♜xc2 20.♜xc2 ♜d8 21.e3 f6 with equal chances.

15...♘a4!N

An unusual position of the two opposing knights on the a-file. The white knight probably dreams of d4, while the best place for the black knight is right next to it, on c4.

A weaker solution was 15...♘e4 16.♛e3±, when Black is in danger of ending up with a bishop against the excellent knight on d4.

16.♜c6!?

16.♘c2 (with the idea ♘d4); 16...♘b2= (with the idea ...♘c4).

16...♜c8 17.♜ac1 ♜xc6 18.♜xc6 ♝b7 19.♜c1

19.♜d6 ♛c8 20.♘b5 (in case of 20.♘c2 ♘c3∞ White has problems with the rook on d6) 20...a5 21.a3 axb4 22.axb4 ♛c4=.

19...a6 20.♘c2 b5

20...♛b8!? 21.♘d4 ♜c8=.

21.♘d4 ♘b6=

Judging by the activity of the pieces and the colour of the squares on which the pawns are standing, the position should suit the white player. However, the situation is quite peculiar since the white pawns on dark squares can easily become targets for the queen and the knight. For example:

22.f5?! ♘c4 23.♛f4 exf5 24.♘xf5 ♝c8⇄

Conclusion

In this chapter we have dealt with the fianchetto system in which Black builds the following standard set-up: ...d7-d5, ...c7-c6, ...♘bd7, ...b7-b6, ...♝c8-b7 or ...♝c8–a6, ...♛e7 and ...♜fc8 or ...♜ac8, which can often be seen in the regular Closed Catalan. The pawn triangle e6/d5/c6 neutralizes the Catalan bishop and secures a stable position in the centre for Black.

White usually fianchettoes the bishop after having played ♘f3, but many players choose the opposite move order, i.e. firstly g2-g3 and then ♘g1–f3, in order to avoid a situation similar to the Queen's Indian or the solid system devised by Anthony Miles, which was tackled in Chapter 2.2.

The critical position occurs after 8.0-0 b6 9.♖c1 0-0 10.cxd5 cxd5 and now White mostly chooses to finish his development by playing A) 11.♘a3 or B) ♘c3.

A) By moving to the edge of the board with 11.♘a3, White usually intends to play the thematic ♘e5, and then, after the virtually forced exchange on e5, the instructive strategic manoeuvre ♘a3-c2-d4 follows, centralizing the knight.

Our main proposal here is the active 11...♗a6, although it is a solid solution to place the bishop on b7 as in the game Kramnik-Carlsen, Wijk aan Zee 2011. In this middlegame, White has no better plan than 12.♘e5, when due to the threat ♘e5-c6 Black is virtually forced to an exchange 12...♘xe5, and after 13.dxe5 ♘d7 14.f4 White achieves his desired position, by moving the queen's knight to the edge of the board and the king's knight to e5.

This position is strategically dangerous for the black player, since the opponent plans to centralize the knight on d4 and thus gain an advantage. However, it turns out that after 14...♘c5 15.b4 Black has the unusual possibility 15...♘a4!N, which secures equal chances.

B) In the case that White plays the usual 11.♘c3, we recommend the more passive but safer option 11...♗b7. Then, after the aggressive 12.♘e5, Black is not forced to exchange on e5 (since White does not threaten to play ♘c6 because of the closed c-file), and we can suggest up to three solid responses for the black player: 12...♕e7, 12...a6 or 12...♘e8, all three of which yield Black an advantage or at least equal chances.

As a reaction to White's plan with 12.♖c2 (instead of 12.♘e5), with the intention to double the rooks, Black should opt for the standard set-up with 12...♕e7 and ...♖fc8.

We can notice the following important characteristics of both players' plans, if we limit ourselves to the best set-up for Black:

White often makes use of aggressive and unpleasant attacks by the knight on e5 at various moments during the game. The question of when White carries out the invasion on e5, or when Black should make the exchange, may depend on the slightest details in the position, and this is one of the most important strategic questions in this opening.

Nevertheless, White's most dangerous plan involves the rook on the open c-file and the white knight jump to b5. The situation becomes even more dangerous when the knight on e5 joins the battle, or when White's queen enters via the dark squares. Of course, this is all hypothetical, but we have seen numerous games in which this was possible.

The second player possesses sufficient resources to fend off the opponent's attack or initiative, which usually occurs on the queenside. Please take note of the prophylactic move ...a7-a6, which can prevent aggressive intentions by the white player via square b5. Besides, Black can often move the bishop to a6, where it is more active. Numerous games can be found with such positions in which the bishop on a6 is more valuable than the Catalan bishop, which is only a powerless observer.

Exercises

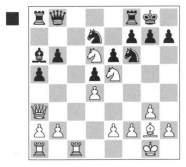

4.2 (1) Find the plan.
(solution on page 440)

4.2 (2) Find the plan.
(solution on page 440)

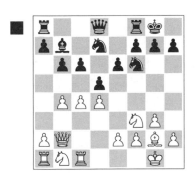

4.2 (3) Find the plan.
(solution on page 441)

Chapter 5

White Builds the Centre

4.♕xd2 ♘f6 5.♘f3 d5 6.e3 0-0 7.♘c3

Or first 6.♘c3 and then 6...0-0 7.e3.

The first critical crossroads for Black. It is clear that Black should continue development and fight for the centre. However, without the knowledge of chess theory and practical experience, it is difficult to find the best solution, especially here where the active ...c7-c5 can be backup by the pawn, the knight or the queen, and the best solution for the development of the minor pieces on the queen's side is not yet clear. In this position, Black has a relatively wide choice of moves that can lead to various types of positions.

Chapter 5.1

The Flexible 7...♞bd7

1.d4 e6 2.c4 ♝b4+ 3.♝d2 ♝xd2+ 4.♛xd2 ♞f6 5.♞f3 d5 6.e3 0-0 7.♞c3 ♞bd7!?

The favourite move of grandmaster Keith Arkell. Black combines the development of the knight with covering e5 and supporting the potential attack with ... c7-c5. Besides, Black does not choose any particular option, keeping the pawn structure in the centre and the queenside intact and preserving the choice between various types of positions. A negative point is the fact that Black renounces the development of the knight to the more active square c6.

White can react with: 1. the standard exchange in the centre with cxd5, or 2. with moves that delay the clarification in the centre, like 8.♝d3 and 8.♖c1.

A) **7...b6?!**

This move enables the development of the bishop on b7 and prepares ...c7-c5, after which usually positions with hanging pawns ensue. However, in our opening, in which the dark-squared bishops have been exchanged early, the ensuing positions are not very comfortable to play. This is logical if we keep in mind that each exchange directly affects the hanging pawns in a negative way, as it reduces their mobility and the game becomes more and more focussed on their defence. A good example where the move ...b7-b6 does work is the famous Tartakower Variation in the Queen's Gambit: 1.d4 d5 2.c4 e6

3.♘c3 ♘f6 4.♘f3 ♗e7 5.♗g5 h6 6.♗h4 0-0 7.e3 b6.

8.cxd5 Standard, and the best response to 7...b6. Black can recapture in two ways, but both of them lead to an inferior position: **8...exd5**

White can now focus on positions in which the early exchange of the dark-squared bishops is to his advantage.

With 8...♘xd5 Black aims to preserve the opened central diagonal h1-a8 for the bishop, but loses time playing with the same piece twice, and loses Black's usual control over e4: 9.♗d3 ♗b7 10.♖c1 ♘d7 (10...♘xc3 11.♕xc3±; 10...♘f6 11.♕e2 ♘bd7 12.0-0 c5 13.♗a6 ♕c8 14.♗xb7 ♕xb7 15.♖fd1 ♖fd8 16.e4±) and now White could play 11.♘xd5! (11.♘e4 ♖c8 12.0-0 ♕e7 13.a3 ♖fd8= with the idea ...e6-e5 or ...c7-c5, Nikolic-Vratonjic, Nis 1997) 11...♗xd5 12.♕c2 ♗xf3 13.gxf3 c5 14.♗xh7+ ♔h8 15.♗e4 ♖c8 16.d5 exd5 17.♗xd5± and have an extra pawn.

A1) **9.♗d3** has the disadvantage that, in positions with hanging pawns on c5 and d5 and the bishop on b7, Black may threaten ...d5-d4 with the aim to capture ...♗f3, destroying White's pawn structure on the kingside. **9...♘bd7** is the best order to develop Black's pieces, since it neutralizes White's most active

plan with ♘e5. Now **10.0-0±** will tackled in the main line with 7...♘d7;

A2) **9.♘e5!?** is the most active plan, but it is also double-edged. White uses the fact that the black knight does not yet control e5 to create a stronghold for his knight with the help of the f-pawn. **9...♗b7** A weaker solution is 9...♘bd7 because of 10.♗b5±. **10.♗d3 c5 11.0-0 ♘c6** Another possible solution is 11...♘bd7 12.f4 cxd4 13.exd4 ♘e4 14.♕e3 ♘df6∞ with mutual chances. **12.f4 ♕e7! 13.♖ad1 ♖ad8!∞**

One of Black's main recipes in this type of position. The white position seems powerful because of the maximal activity of all his pieces, especially the aggressive knight on e5, but it has one important flaw: the potentially weak e4-point. Therefore, Black's main strategy should be directed at this point. Black has the idea to jump to e4 at the right moment, which would give him satisfactory counterplay;

A3) **9.♗e2** White finishes his development, planning to place the rooks on d1 and c1 after castling and to wait for what will happen next. Most probably we will have the scenario with hanging pawns for Black. **9...♗b7** Or first 9...♘bd7 and then 10...♗b7. A weaker solution is 9...c5, as after 10.dxc5 bxc5 11.♖d1 Black loses a pawn. **10.0-0**

♘d7 11.♖ac1 Or 11.♕c2 c5 12.♖fd1± and, at the right moment, with dxc5, White will either enforce hanging pawns on d5 and c5 or an isolani on d5 in case Black recaptures on c5 with a piece. Both cases will be favourable for the first player. **11...c5 12.♖fd1±**

B) **7...dxc4?!**

This continuation is not good at this point, since White will gain an advantage in develop. Therefore, we will adopt one rule: Black should not give in with ...dxc4 if White's light-squared bishop is still undeveloped on f1. Of course, as all chess rules this one should be observed with some reserve just as all rules in chess. We will see later that the gain or loss of a tempo on c4 will be an important strategic motif in selecting various plans on both sides. In the similar situation in the Queen's Gambit Accepted (1.d4 d5 2.c4 dxc4 3.e3 ♘f6

4.♗c4 e6 5.♗xc4 c5), the centre can be handed over without any consequences, since, with the bishop on e7, Black can quickly catch up with ...c7-c5. **8.♗xc4 ♘bd7** The immediate 8...c5? is not good because of 9.dxc5 ♘bd7 10.♖d1± and White has an extra pawn without having makde any compromises, Barlov-Govedarica, Sibenik 1986. **9.0-0 c5** 9...b6 10.e4 ♗b7 11.♖fe1!?± with an advantage in the centre. **10.♖fd1 ♕e7 11.♖ac1±**

With an obvious advantage in development for White;

C) **7...c5?** simply does not work, since after **8.dxc5±** White has an extra pawn and also threatens to leave the black pawn on d5 isolated and weak. In the QGA position after 1.d4 d5 2.c4 e6 3.♘c3 ♘f6 4.♘f3 ♗e7 5.♗f4 0-0 6.e3 c5 we see that Black can make this important move immediately after 6.e3, since it is backed by the bishop on e7.

8.♗d3!

White continues his development, without being afraid to enter a position similar to the QGA, since the loss of a tempo after ...dxc4 is less important than the passive position of the black queen's knight and the absence of dark-squared bishops.

Besides 8...c6 we will also have a look at 8...♕e7, 8...dxc4 and 8...b6.

But first let's examine White's major alternatives to the main move.

A) **8.cxd5 exd5 9.♗d3**

Black can now choose between three different pawn structures on the queenside: A1) ...b7-b6 with ...c7-c5, which usually leads to a position with hanging pawns; A2)...c7-c6 leads to a Carlsbad structure; and A3) ...c7-c5 usually leads to a position with an isolated black pawn on d5. Of course, Black can make other moves such as 9...♖e8 or 9...♕e8, but they do not have separate significance since they usually transpose to positions with ...c7-c6.

A1) **9...b6**

Black does not want to lose control over the important central square d4 and prepares the pawn push to c5. In addition, Black vacates square b7 for his bishop. **10.0-0 ♗b7** A better move order is 10...c5 to avoid White's additional possibility given in line A13).

A11) White achieves nothing with **11.♘e5**, since after the exchange **11...♘xe5 12.dxe5** the simple **12...♘e4** evens out the chances;

A12) With **11.♖ac1** White prepares to fight against the hanging pawns: **11...c5 12.♖fd1** and White has a comfortable position (it is too early for 12.dxc5 bxc5 13.♘a4 ♘e4!

... with equality, Ikonnikov-Ugoluk, Frankfurt 2004) **12...c4 13.♗b1 ♕e7 14.b3 cxb3** A weaker solution is 14...♖ac8 15.bxc4 ♘e4 16.♘xe4 dxe4 17.♕c2 f5 18.♘d2± Vidmar-Réti, Mannheim 1914. **15.axb3** and with more active pieces, especially the light-squared bishop, White has better chances;

A13) **11.b4!?±**

With the thematic idea of b4-b5, reducing the mobility of Black's queenside pawns. Now Black has a choice between two uncomfortable positions.

11...c5 11...♕e7 12.b5! a6 13.a4 axb5 14.axb5±; Black's majority on the queenside loses its value and there are no plans in sight. White has a better position, Doch 09.980-Ktulu 9.0, Internet 2009. **12.bxc5 bxc5 13.♖ab1 ♖b8 14.dxc5 ♘xc5 15.♖fc1±** This type of position with the isolated pawn on d5 we have seen in the line 9...c5, only with the b-pawns still on the board. However, that does not change the essence of the situation. White is better.

A2) **9...c6**

A careful move which does not allow any isolated or hanging pawns, that is, it does not expose his central pawns to pressure by the opponent. Of course, we will have a completely different story with the Carlsbad scenario. The current position has the same central pawn structure as the positions which occur in the Exchange Variation of the Queen's Gambit (1.d4 d5 2.c4 e6 3.♘c3 ♘f6 4.cxd5 exd5 5.♗g5 ♗e7 6.e3 0-0 7.♗d3 ♘bd7), and the most important ideas and plans are the same. With the typical b2-b4-b5 push, White will try to create conditions for a minority attack on the queenside, while Black will focus on control of the important central square e4. He will try to move his knight there in order to further simplify the position, or to create counterchances on the kingside.

In general, the absence of dark-squared bishops has simplified the position and reduced Black's problems in obtaining a draw. However, this conclusion should be taken with some reserve, since from a strategic point of view, Black's central pawn structure seems to be suffering from the lack of his dark-squared bishop.

10.0-0 ♕e7 11.♕c2 ♖e8 Black takes control over e4. This is one of the most important positions with the Carlsbad structure in the centre, which can be reached in several ways. Chess players who do not like complications like this type of position, since both sides have a clear and simple plan. White will play ♖ab1 and b4-b5 with the idea to weaken the opponent's pawn structure on the queenside, while Black will play ...♘e4, followed by either more simplifications or counterchances on the kingside. **12.♖ab1**

The critical position in the Carlsbad structure without dark-squared bishops, and an important crossroads for Black. We will look at three different plans: A21) 12...♘e4, A22) 12...a5 and A23) 12...g6.

It is hard to determine which plan of the two – the prophylactic 12...g6 or the standard 12...♘e4, is more acceptable. This probably was also a dilemma for the brilliant grandmaster Leinier Dominguez, who recently used both options in important games.

A21) **12...♘e4 13.b4 ♘df6 14.♘e5** 14.b5 c5! Obviously the best choice among the three types of pawn structure on the queenside. Allowing White to put his knight on c6 or to capture on b5 leaves Black in an inferior position. 15.dxc5 ♘xc5= Gunawan-Trifunovic,

Vrnjacka Banja 1988. **14...♘xc3 15.♕xc3 ♘e4 16.♕c2 g6** 16...f6!? – compare this with the similar position in the game Kasimdzhanov-Dominguez Perez, Macedonia Palace 2013, in which the white rook was on d1 and the pawn on a3, while the black pawn was on a6. This line is tackled under 8.♖d1 a6. **17.♖fc1** 17.♗xe4 dxe4 gives equal chances, although Black has many pawns on the squares of his own bishop's colour. **17...♗f5 18.♖b3 a6 19.a4 ♘d6 20.♗xf5 ♘xf5 21.h3** and the opponents agreed on a draw in this equal position, Onischuk-Dominguez Perez, Tromso 2013;

A22) With **12...a5!?** Black wants to exchange a-pawns and open the a-file, though grandmaster Eingorn believes that the queenside should not be weakened and assesses this move as suspicious in his book. **13.a3 g6** We have already commented on this useful move, which liberates the black knight from the obligation to defend the h7-pawn. 13...♘e4 14.b4 axb4 15.axb4 ♘df6 16.b5 (16.♘e5 ♘xc3 17.♕xc3 ♘e4 18.♕c2 f6 19.♗xe4 dxe4 20.♘c4 ♗e6=) 16...c5!?N (16...♖a3 Ushenina-Stefanova, Khanty-Mansiysk 2012)

17.dxc5 ♘xc5 with an equal position. In the position after 13...g6, White has used two active plans: **14.b4** 14.♘a4

♘e4 yields White fewer benefits from the thematic 15.b4 (15.♗xe4 ♕xe4 16.♕xe4 ♖xe4 17.♖bc1 ♖e8= and Black has nothing to fear), for example:15...axb4 16.axb4 b5

17.♘c5 (17.♘c3 ♘d6=) 17...♘dxc5 18.dxc5 ♕f6=. **14...axb4 15.axb4 b5!?**

One of the important plans, but it only works if Black can realize the manoeuvre ...♘b6-♘c4. If not, this structure would make no sense.

The thematic 15...♘e4 does not yield enough possibilities for counterplay because of 16.♖fc1 ♘df6 17.b5± with the initiative.

16.♖fe1 White wants to play e2-e4, focusing on the centre in order to emphasize the weaknesses in Black's pawn structure, especially after 15...b5. Now:

A221) **16...♗b7 17.e4** 17.♘d2 ♘b6 18.♘b3 ♘c4= Gabriel-Arkell, Fügen 2006. **17...dxe4 18.♗xe4±** 18.♘xe4

♘xe4 19.♗xe4 ♕d6=. **18...♘xe4?!
19.♘xe4** and the white knight is much
more active than the black bishop;

A222) A more logical option is
16...♘e4, when after the temporarily
defensive **17.♘d2?!** (17.♘e2! ♗b7 and
after the exchange of the black knight
with 18.♗xe4 dxe4 19.♘d2± White
keeps an advantage because of the problematic black bishop) **17...♘xd2
18.♕xd2 ♘b6∞** Black has a good position because of the weak pawn on d4,
while he will be able to cover the flaws
in his own pawn structure with the active ...♘c4, Krush-Arkell, York 1999;

A223) Black should continue with his
idea and play **16...♘b6!N 17.e4 ♗e6**
with play on both sides, for example:
18.♘e5 A weaker option, though seemingly logical, is 18.exd5 ♘bxd5∓ when
the pawn on b4 is more vulnerable than
the one on c6. For example, 19.♘xd5
♘xd5 and now 20.♕xc6?! ♖ac8
21.♕a6 (21.♕xb5 ♘c3∓) 21...♘c3!∓.
An unbelievable knight. Not only does
it threaten the rook and the pawn on
b4, it also puts the white queen in a
cage. **18...♖ec8=;**

A23) **12...g6**

A useful prophylactic move directed
against White's play along the diagonal
b1-h7. **13.b4 b6** A solid plan. Black
wants to develop the bishop on b7, and
at the same time he is ready to respond

to the thematic b4-b5 with ...c6-c5.
14.a4 14.♕e2 a5 15.b5?! (a better solution is 15.a3 or 15.bxa5 with equal
chances) 15...c5 16.♖bc1 ♗b7
17.♖fd1 ♖ac8 with a good position for
Black, Braun-Bischoff, Bad Zwesten
2005; if 14.b5 c5 with mutual chances.
14...a5 15.bxa5 15.b5?! c5 and Black
takes the initiative thanks to his majority on the queenside. **15...♖xa5
16.♖fd1 ♗b7 17.h3 ♖ea8 18.♘d2 ♗a6**
Maybe more tenacious is 18...c5!?
19.♗b5 ♘f8 20.♘b3 ♖5a7 21.dxc5
bxc5 22.a5 ♖d8 23.♘a4 ♘e6⇄ and
Black has good counterchances thanks
to his strong support for the mobile
hanging pawns. **19.♘b3 ♗xd3
20.♖xd3 ♖5a6**

... with equal chances since both sides
have weaknesses on the queenside,
Bacrot-Dominguez Perez, Makedonia
Palace 2013.

A3) **9...c5 10.dxc5**

A logical and good move. White does not want to worry whether Black's pawn majority after the advance ...c5-c4 is dangerous or not. He is satisfied with the situation around the isolated pawn on d5, which can be characterized as weak since the critical d4-square is under White's control.

Although the activity of Black's pieces has increased thanks to the exchange in the centre, not many players like such positions, or are capable of playing it well. We will see further on that things are not that simple and that one single detail (for example the white pawn being on a3 instead of a2) can affect the situation. We will only mention that this type of position is one of the critical weapons for the black player in the battle for an equal position.

10...♘xc5 11.0-0 b6 12.♗e2 ♗b7 13.♖fd1 ♖c8 14.♖ac1 ♕e7 15.♘d4±

White has comfortable play against the isolated pawn, while Black tries to compensate this with active moves. Chadaev-Stupak, Mumbai 2012.

Another nice example of play in this type of position is the game Nikolic-Kosic, Plovdiv 2008.

B) 8.♖c1 White places the rook on the usual square in this type of position, waiting for the opponent to show his intentions on the queenside. On the other hand, this rook move seems premature since the rook will be needed on b1 in case White switches to the Carlsbad structure.

Black can maintain the mystery by playing 8...♕e7, or else move any of his queenside pawns: 8...dxc4, 8...c6, 8...b6 or 8...a6, although this way he will determine the pawn structure and reveal his future plans to the opponent:

B1) 8...c6 A more passive approach. 8...dxc4 would be contrary to the rule we defined under 7...dxc4, and justifies the opponent's move 8.♖c1. For example: 9.♗xc4 c5 10.0-0 cxd4 11.♘xd4 ♕e7 12.♖fd1 ♘b6 13.♗b3 ♗d7 14.e4

... with an edge for White, Portisch-Andersson, Tilburg 1982.

8...a6 does not have any significance on its own; for 8...b6 9.cxd5 exd5 10.♗d3 ♗b7 11.0-0 see under 9...b6.

9.♗d3 ♕e7 and now:

B11) 10.cxd5 Switching to the Carlsbad structure with the rook on c1 does not bring White anything. **10...exd5 11.0-0** If 11.♕c2 ♖e8 12.0-0 ♘f8 (for 12...♘e4 see the main line) 13.♕b1 the white rook is not on the right square, so White has to lose time with his queen in order to start his typical attack: 13...♘g6 14.b4 a6 15.a4 ♗g4⇄ (Black obviously has enough counterplay on the kingside) 16.♘d2

♘h4 17.♖fe1 ♕d7 (White certainly
does not feel comfortable in the face of
the opponent's attacks on the kingside)
18.♘e2 ♗xe2 19.♗xe2 ♘e4 20.♘xe4
♖xe4= 21.b5? axb5 22.axb5 and now,
in the game A. David-Zysk, Paris 2011,
Black could easily have obtained a clear
advantage with 22...♘xg2!∓ 23.bxc6
(23.♔xg2? ♖h4−+) 23...bxc6 24.♗f3
♘xe1∓. **11...♘e4 12.♕c2 ♖e8 13.♖ce1**
13.♗xe4 dxe4 14.♘d2 ♘f6=
Quinteros-Andersson, Rio de Janeiro
1985. **13...♘df6 14.♘e5 ♗f5
15.♘xe4?! ♗xe4 16.♗xe4 ♘xe4=**
Wirig-Eingorn, Metz 2008;

B12) **10.0-0 dxc4 11.♗xc4 e5
12.♘xe5** Better is 12.e4!? exd4
13.♕xd4±. **12...♘xe5 13.dxe5 ♕xe5
14.h3 ♗f5 15.♖fd1 ♕e7 16.♕d6
♕xd6 17.♖xd6 ♖fd8 18.♖cd1 ♖xd6
19.♖xd6 ♔f8=** Tregubov-Zviagintsev,
Moscow 2010.

B2) **8...♕e7 9.♕c2**
9.♗e2 dxc4 10.♗xc4 c5 11.0-0 ♘b6
12.♗e2 ♖d8 13.♖fd1 (13.♘e5 cxd4
14.exd4 ♗d7 15.♗f3 ♗e8∞)
13...cxd4 14.♘xd4 (14.exd4 ♗d7
15.♘e5 ♗c6=) 14...♗d7 and Black
emerges from the opening with equal
chances, Kunte-Zviagintsev, Khanty-
Mansiysk 2007.

It is disputable whether White can play
9.cxd5 since after 9...exd5 10.♗d3 c6
11.♕c2 ♖e8

the black rook is on the right square for
this type of position, while we cannot
say the same for the white rook. We
tackled this position under 8...c6.
In case of 11...b6, after 12.0-0 ♗b7
13.♗f5 (13.e4!?±) 13...g6 14.♗xd7
♘xd7 15.♖fd1 White obviously has a
more comfortable position, although
Black could obtain equality in a few
moves, see 15...♖fd8 16.a3 ♘f6 17.h3
♘e8 18.b4 ♘d6 19.a4 a5 20.bxa5
♖xa5=, Bacrot-Arkell, France 2002.
9...♖d8 Still both opponents do not determine their pawn structure. If 9...c6
10.♗e2 (for 10.cxd5 exd5 11.♗d3
♖e8 see under 8...c6) 10...b6
(10...dxc4!?) 11.0-0 ♗b7 12.♖fd1
♖fd8 13.a3 a6 14.cxd5 cxd5 15.b4
♖dc8 16.♕b2 ♖c7 17.b5 a5 18.♘a4
♖ac8= Speelman-Arkell, England 2013.
10.a3 10.cxd5!? exd5 11.♗d3 ♘f8
12.0-0 − this switch to the Carlsbad position has sense since the black rook is
on the d-file. **10...a6**

Black is ready to capture on c4 and next
play ...b7-b5. We should mention that
we have dealt with some variations
which start from this position also in
Chapter 5.2, but there Black first plays
9...a6 and then 10...♘bd7, as in the
game Aronian-Carlsen, London 2013.
White can react in the following ways:
1. The virtually unavoidable exchange

on d5 enables him to keep the initiative to a certain extent; or 2. With moves that ignore Black's plan, giving White an equal position after 11.♗e2 or an inferior position after 11.h3.

For 10...dxc4 see Chapter 5.2.

11.cxd5 11.♗e2 dxc4!

Though with a slightly different move order, we have arrived at the game Aronian-Carlsen, London 2013, Chapter 5.2.

11.h3 dxc4! 12.♗xc4 c5 13.0-0 b5 14.♗a2 ♗b7∓ was seen in Mukhaev-Kholmov, Moscow 1997.

11...exd5 12.♗d3 Despite the fact that it has not been played in practice, we should check the knight jump 12.♘a4!? c6 13.♗d3 ♖e8 14.0-0 ♘e4. White's position is slightly more comfortable, considering that Black has not yet solved the problem of his queenside development. **12...c6** In this Carlsbad structure, the inserted moves a2-a3 and ...a7-a6 do not affect the assessment of the position, which is almost equal. True, the white pawn on a3 has both a strategic advantage and a disadvantage, since it does not only defend its friend on b4, but it can mean the loss of a tempo for White in case he chooses to follow the main plan with b2-b4-b5. Black having the pawn on a6 also has a disad-

vantage since it weakens b6, and also an advantage since it slows down White's b2-b4-b5 push.

12...c5 13.dxc5 ♘xc5 14.0-0 b5 15.h3 ♗b7∞ with active pieces for Black and equal chances.

13.0-0 ♖e8 with the idea ...♘f6-e4, with equality.

Now back to the main line after **8.♗d3!**.

8...c6

Among other things, Black proposes to play the Carlsbad structure, which would occur after 9.cxd5 exd5. However, not even this careful move will yield Black an equal position, since White is not obliged to simplify. Besides, one look at the central pawn structure after 8...c6 is enough to reject this move. The gap on d6 is so noticeable that one may think that Black's dark-squared bishop has fallen off the board.

This central pawn structure limits the scope of White's bishop, but only in positions where it is fianchettoed, as we described in Chapter 4.

A) **8...dxc4** The right reaction at the right time. Black adheres to the rule defined above, under 7...dxc4, and captures on c4 since White has already 'lost' a move with his bishop.

However, the passive knight on d7 reduces the activity of Black's pieces, so White retains more activity and better chances. **9.♗xc4 c5 10.♖d1!?** With the idea dxc5. On the natural 10.0-0, after 10...b6 11.♖fd1 ♗b7 12.♕e2 ♕c7 (on 12...♕e7 13.♗a6↑ Black has problems with the light squares on the queenside) 13.♗a6 ♖ac8= Black is close to equal. **10...b6** 10...cxd4 11.♕xd4±; 10...♕e7 11.0-0 under 8...♕e7; 10...♘b6? 11.dxc5 ♕c7 12.cxb6 ♕xc4 13.bxa7±, Poulsen-Jensen, Vejgaard 1992. **11.d5 exd5 12.♗xd5!** That is the point. Black has problems developing his queenside (12.♘xd5 ♗b7=). **12...♘xd5 13.♕xd5 ♖b8 14.0-0 ♕e7 15.♕d6↑** White has the initiative since he controls the d-file;

B) **8...♕e7**

A useful developing move that gives Black the choice to switch to various types of positions.

9.0-0 For 9.cxd5 exd5 10.0-0 c6 see under 9...c6. **9...dxc4** Black gains a tempo on the white bishop, but the passive knight on d7 prevents him from reaching full equality. **10.♗xc4** and now:

B1) **10...a6** is a familiar topic from the Queen's Gambit Accepted with the idea to get better control over the queenside squares. However, thanks to his strong centre, White keeps the better position: **11.a4 b6 12.e4 ♗b7 13.♖fe1 ♖fd8 14.♖ad1 ♕b4 15.b3±** Black manages to gain control over the squares b4 and b5, but leaves the opponent more space, Houdini 3-Bouquet 1.5, Internet 2012;

B2) **10...e5 11.♕c2!** White increases his control over the important e4-square, which reduces Black's chances of becoming active. **11...c6** 11...e4 12.♘g5 ♘b6 13.♗b3 ♗f5 14.f3±. **12.♗b3!±** Prophylaxis against the move ...♘d7-b6. When he loses his two key ideas of ...e5-e4 and... ♘d7-b6, Black will end up in an inferior position since White has more active pieces and better control of the centre. Black can open the centre with ... exd4, but in that case White's rooks will become important. **10...c5 11.♖ad1!** ♘b6 Black wants to finish his development and move the knight to an unusual square. However, if we compare this position with the game Kunte-Zviagintsev, given under 8.♖c1, we will see that there Black managed to realize this plan and got a good position because White had spent a move on ♖a1-c1.

If Black tries to place the bishop on the standard diagonal with 11...b6 12.d5 exd5 13.♘xd5 ♘xd5 14.♕xd5 ♖b8 15.♕d6±, White will be in charge of the d-file. **12.♗b3 ♗d7** The move

12...♖d8 does not achieve much because of 13.e4±. The queen is not bound to the d-file since the white rook is on it, Batsiashvili-Melia, Anaklia 2011. **13.e4 cxd4** And now White should capture with **14.♘xd4±**, not only to control c6, on which the black bishop can be activated, but also to make way for the f-pawn. If we add the strategic threat e4-e5, against which there are no good solutions, we can see that Black is going to have some serious problems.

On 14.♕xd4, after 14...♖fd8 15.e5 Black can move his pieces to the centre and get equal chances: 15...♘fd5 16.♘xd5 and the players agreed to a draw in Smyslov-Andersson, Bugojno 1984. After 16...♘xd5= a suspicious move is 17.♗xd5?! because of 17...♗c6∓, when Black would take over the initiative thanks to the strong bishop. **14...♖fd8** Neither does 14...e5 help in view of 15.♘f5 ♗xf5 16.exf5 ♖ad8 17.♕e3±. **15.e5 ♘e8** More tenacious is 15...♘fd5 16.♘e4±. **16.f4 ♘c7 17.♕f2 ♗c6 18.f5**

With a clear advantage for White, Sherbakov-Kholmov, Voronezh 1988.

C) **8...b6** As we know, this move usually leads to a position with hanging pawns.

9.cxd5 exd5 10.0-0 ♗b7 11.♖ac1 (11.b4±) **11...c5 12.♖fd1±** was seen under 9...b6 in the game Vidmar-Réti.

Back to the main line after 8...c6.
    9.0-0
Here Black usually chooses 9...dxc4 or A) 9...♕e7, but we will also look at B) 9...b6.
For 9.cxd5 exd5 see under 9...c6.
    9...dxc4

A) **9...♕e7**

A1) White's pieces are better developed, so with the typical **10.e4!?** (for 10.cxd5 exd5 see under 9...c6) he can open the centre, which is known from similar situations with dark-squared bishops on the board. In this situation, Black can breathe more easily without them since there are comfortable squares for the queen, but still he will have more problems on the dark squares. Now:

A11) **10...dxe4 11.♘xe4** 11.♗xe4!? ♘xe4 12.♘xe4 ♘f6 13.♘xf6+ ♕xf6 14.♖fe1±. **11...♘xe4 12.♗xe4 e5 13.♖fe1 f5 14.♗c2 e4 15.♕c3 ♘f6 16.♘d2±** with the idea f2-f3;

A12) **10...dxc4 11.♗xc4 b5** For 11...e5 12.♗b3 see under 11.♗b3. **12.♗b3 b4 13.e5 bxc3 14.exf6 ♘xf6 15.♕xc3±**.

A2) **10.♖fd1 dxc4 11.♗xc4 e5**

With the idea ...e5-e4. White is leading in development, but the position is very delicate and he has to find the right plan, since the initiative can easily transfer into the opponent's hands.

A21) **12.♗b3?!** is often a useful prophylactic move, but in this situation it does not work since Black can realize his plan and take the initiative with **12...e4 13.♘g5 ♘b6** Black threatens 14...h6. **14.f3 exf3 15.♘xf3 ♗e6 16.♗xe6 ♕xe6∞** with a better position for Black, since White has landed in a French defense but with one vulnerable pawn on the e-file;

A22) **12.e4!?N** White increases control in the centre, not allowing the opponent to organize counterplay with ...e5-e4. **12...exd4 13.♕xd4±** White retains better control in the centre and better development. For example: **13...♖e8** 13...♘b6 14.e5±. **14.♖e1 ♘e5 15.♕xe5 ♕xe5 16.♘xe5 ♖xe5 17.♖ad1±**;

A23) **12.dxe5 ♘xe5 13.♘xe5 ♕xe5=** Arkell-Galego, London 2011. The opponents agreed to a draw in a position where White has a minimal advantage for he temporarily controls the d-file. There could have followed: **14.♕d6 ♕xd6 15.♖xd6 ♖e8 16.♖ad1 ♗e6 17.♗xe6 ♖xe6 18.♖xe6 fxe6=.** From a strategic point of view, White is better since he controls the d-file and has a

better pawn structure. However, Black does not have great problems to draw since the isolated pawn on e6 only appears to be weak. For example, on e2-e4 Black plays ...e6-e5!, controlling the centre and keeping the opponent's pawn majority in check. The issue of White's control of the d-file is solved by moving the king to e7 followed by ...♖d8.

B) On **9...b6** after **10.cxd5** Black has a tough choice between two types of positions: **10...cxd5** Or 10...exd5 **11.♖fe1±** with a not very enviable pawn structure in the centre. **11.♖fc1±** with an inferior position for Black, with his passive bishop and knight on d7.

10.♗xc4 e5

Black makes use of the position of the white queen on d2 to conduct a typical attack on the centre and open up his light-squared bishop. Nevertheless, in positions without dark-squared bishops this suits the white player better, as was shown by Alekhine almost 100 years ago.

11.♗b3!

The white bishop maintains control over the important diagonal a2-g8, dodging a potential attack with ...♘b6, which is an important strategic motif for Black.

11.♗xf7+ leads to a draw after 11...♖xf7 12.dxe5 ♘g4 13.e6 ♖xf3!

14.exd7 (14.gxf3 ♘xh2!=) 14...♗xd7 15.gxf3 ♘xh2 16.♔xh2 ♕h4+ with perpetual check.

After 11.dxe5?! ♘xe5 Black can destroy White's pawn structure with no compensation.

11...♕e7

Opening the centre with 11...exd4 leads to a quicker activation of the white rooks: 12.exd4 ♘b6 13.♖fe1±. White retains a more active position, and the situation suits White more because of the absence of dark-squared bishops in this typical position with a semi-open centre.

If 11...e4?! 12.♘g5±.

12.e4!

White has more active pieces and good control of the centre, and his general plan is to be the first to activate his pawn majority on the kingside.

12...exd4 13.♘xd4 ♘c5 14.♗c2 ♖d8 15.♖ad1 ♗g4 16.f3 ♘e6 17.♕f2 ♘xd4 18.♖xd4 ♗e6 19.♖fd1 b6 20.h3±

White is ready to proceed with f2-f4.

20...c5 21.♖4d2 ♖xd2 22.♕xd2 c4?! 23.f4±

White's control of the d-file and strong mobile centre are sufficient to win, Alekhine-Bogoljubow, Budapest 1921.

Conclusion

In this chapter on the Central System we have discussed positions in which Black immediately moves his queen's knight, which is flexible but passive: 7...♘bd7. Practical games and analyses have shown that the development of the black knight on d7 does not make the same strong impression as in the regular positions of the Queen's Gambit with dark-squared bishops on the board. This is understandable, if we keep in mind that there Black's plans in the centre, regardless whether they include ...c7-c5 or ...dxc4 and then ...e6-e5, involve the presence of dark-squared bishops.

However, White has to be careful since the opponent can easily create counterplay with ...♕e7, followed by ...dxc4 and ...c7-c5, as a reaction to the logical 8.♖c1. Of course, at many points White can switch to a position with the Carlsbad structure with cxd5 (keeping in mind that in that case the switch with the rook to c1 is not effective, since the rook has to be on b1 in order to carry out the main plan with b2-b4-b5), though this should not worry Black much, since he will usually like such positions.

The best thing to do for White is continue with 8.♗d3! and castle, without being afraid of losing a tempo after ...dxc4 as this is less important than Black's passive knight on d7 and the absence of dark-squared bishops.

Black can choose between various set-ups, either with hanging pawns or with an isolated pawn on d5, but black players more frequently opt for the set-up with the queen on e7 and the capture on c4, and after that ...e6-e5 or ...c7-c5. It seems that the knight on d7 is passive in all of these cases, and therefore White is better.

Exercises

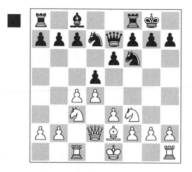

5.1 (1) Find the plan.
(solution on page 441)

5.1 (2) Find the plan.
(solution on page 441)

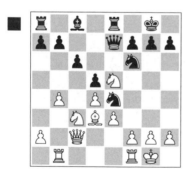

5.1 (3) Find the plan.
(solution on page 441)

Chapter 5.2

7...♛e7: Main Line 8.♖c1

1.d4 e6 2.c4 ♝b4+ 3.♝d2 ♝xd2+ 4.♛xd2 ♞f6 5.♞f3 d5 6.e3 0-0 7.♞c3 ♛e7!

This position can also be reached if White plays first 6.♞c3 and then 6...0-0 7.e3.It is not easy to find the multipurpose move 7...♛e7, which postpones the development of the minor pieces. Black actively prepares ...c7-c5 with the intention of creating a balance in the centre, where, for the time being, his opponent has an extra pawn. Before the main strike with ...c7-c5, Black plans to play ...dxc4, in order to open the central diagonal h1-a8 for his light-squared bishop and avoid the creation of an isolated pawn at d5.

Otherwise, this queen move with the queen perfectly meets the requirements of the position and gives Black the best chances to achieve complete equality. The best proof of its strength is that the chess elite applies it, among whom the current stars Carlsen and Ponomariov.

Knowing the basic rule of opening theory, which states that the development of the minor pieces has priority, the question arises: is it not better to prepare this important strike in the centre with .... ♞bd7 or ...b7-b6, linking it to the development of the queenside? The answer is very easy: d7 is not the only square to which the knight can move. By developing it to this less active position, we deprive our knight of a possibly more successful career, which it might have had with the development to its natural square c6. In the case of ..b7-b6, Black usually ends up with loose, unprotected pawns, especially when there are no dark-squared bishops on the board.

White can react in two essentially different ways 1. immediately yielding in the centre with 8.cxd5, or else 2. getting on with development (♖c1, ♖d1, ♝d3) or prophylactic moves (a2-a3, ♛c2).

8.♖c1

The most frequent follow-up among grandmasters. This practical, patient rook developing move is the most logical one with this type of pawn structure in the centre.

White has a number of alternatives: 8.♖d1, 8.♗d3, 8.a3 and 8.♕c2. We will look at each of them.

A) 8.♖d1!?

This move seems a bit unusual, because the natural square for the rook in this pawn structure is c1. However, not everything is as it seems to be. This move has been seen in high-rated games and has the reasonable idea that the rook will be more useful on the d-file with the future developments in the centre. We will look at the following moves for Black: A1) 8...a6 and A2) 8...♖d8, which may transpose but also have individual significance, and the risky A3) 8...dxc4.

A1) 8...♖d8 9.♕c2

9.cxd5 is weaker because after 9...exd5 White can't prevent the opponent's development with ...♗g4 or ...♗f5, which will both lead to absolutely equal positions.

White synchronizes his pieces, taking control of the central square e4. Black should adjust his plan to the current position and postpone ...dxc4 and ...c7-c5 until a more appropriate opportunity. For the time being it is best to keep the pawn structure with a pawn on d5. This is not bad and will almost inevitably result in a Carlsbad structure in case White plays cxd5. But how should Black proceed? With ...♘bd7 or with ...a7-a6?

A11) 9...c6 10.♗d3± has no independent significance, as it transposes to positions already presented;

A12) 9...dxc4?! Obviously White's pieces will now be ideally placed, without losing a tempo with the recapture on c4: **10.♗xc4 c5 11.0-0 cxd4 12.exd4 ♘c6 13.♖fe1±** Black's development is hindered and he faces the dangerous threat of d4-d5, Matlakov-Dominguez Perez, St Petersburg 2012;

A11) 9...a6!? is a well-known idea from the Queen's Gambit. Black plans ...dxc4 followed by quick development with ...b7-b5 and ...♗b7 and ...♘bd7, followed by the weakening of the opponent's centre with ...c7-c5. In addition, Black can also harbour hopes of moving his knight to a more active position on c6. **10.cxd5** 10.a3 is given in line C) 8.a3, below; 10.♗d3 dxc4 11.♗xc4 b5 12.♗e2 ♗b7

with equality; not effective is 10.e4 dxe4 11.♘xe4 ♘c6 (also 11...♘bd7=

is possible) 12.♘xf6+ ♕xf6= Hecht-Zoler, Schwarzach 1997.

10...exd5 11.h3 ♘c6 12.a3 ♘e4 13.♘xe4 dxe4 14.♘d2±

With a more pleasant game for White, I. Sokolov-Krush, Reykjavik 2013;

A12) **9...♘bd7** Black is developing, waiting for the best moment to implement the basic plan with ...dxc4 and ...c7-c5. White can now either resolve the centre with 10.cxd5 or delay this for another move with 10.♗e2 or 10.a3. **10.cxd5** On 10.♗e2 Black easily equalizes by gaining a tempo on the white bishop: 10...dxc4! 11.♗xc4 c5 12.0-0 ♘b6 13.♗e2 ♗d7 14.e4 cxd4 15.♖xd4 (or 15.♘xd4 ♖ac8= with a great position for Black) 15...e5 16.♖d2 ♗c6 17.♖fd1= and the opponents agreed a draw in this absolutely equal position, Kasparov-Andersson, Lucerne 1982; for 10.a3 see under 8.a3. **10...exd5 11.♗d3**

Black can now either become active with 11...c5 or aim for restrained and more passive positions with 11...c6 or 11...♘f8.

A121) With **11...♘f8** Black does not fully equalize: **12.h3 ♘g6 13.0-0 c6 14.♖fe1±**

Nikolic-Andersson, Tilburg 1987;

A122) **11...c6** leads to a typical Carlsbad structure with the rooks unusually positioned on the d-file. White's rook is normally on b1 to support his main plan of b4-b5; the black rook will normally be on e8, also to support his main plan of ...♘e4. The key question is whether one of the opponents can take profit from his rook position on d1 or d8. It turns out that White can, thanks to his backup plan of ♖e1 and e3-e4, which we will see in the following examples. **12.0-0 ♖e8** Black returns the rook to its usual place. If 12...♘f8, after 13.h3 (on 13.♘e5 follows the typical 13...♘g4) 13...♘g6 14.♖fe1±, by transposition we reach the above-mentioned game Nikolic-Andersson, Tilburg 1987, where White has the slightly better chances. **13.♖fe1!?** With 13.♖b1 we would reach the typical position already covered in Chapter 5.1. **13...♘e4∞** The standard attack with the knight, in order to keep drawing chances. In case of 13...♘f8 White would justify the position of his rook on d1 with 14.♘e5 ♗e6 15.h3 ♖ac8 16.f4

... with better central control, Kortchnoi-Nei, Riga 1955.

A123) 11...c5!? Black strives for active play, instead of manoeuvring in a solid but passive 'Carlsbad position' with an untypical position of the rook on d8. White has his bishop on d3 but the time he has spent on ♖d1 and ♕c2 is an extra motive for Black to enter into this position. He is not afraid of having a weak pawn on d5, because he relies on his active pieces.

12.dxc5 In case of 12.0-0 Black creates a majority on the queenside with 12...c4 13.♗e2 (it's helpful to compare this position with Bommhardt-Langheld, corr. 2005, given under 9...a6) 13...a6∞ with excellent play on the queenside. **12...♘xc5 13.♗e2** 13.h3 ♗e6 14.0-0 ♖ac8=; 13.♘d4 would lead to a position that is almost identical to the one in the exemplary game P. Nikolic-D. Kosic, Plovdiv 2008 – only the white pawn is on a3 instead of a2. In that game, Black played ...♗e6 and it also led to a draw (he game is given under 10...♖d8). Here, with 13...♗d7!? Black actively avoids the possibly annoying move ♕e5: 14.0-0 ♖ac8=. **13...♗e6 14.0-0 ♘ce4=**

This type of position is usually acceptable for White but in these specific circumstances, Black can easily achieve a draw, because he is already threatening 15...♖ac8 with the idea of ...♘xc3, breaking up the white pawn structure on the queenside, Goldin-Balashov, Klaipeda 1988.

A2) 8...a6

The start of a typical plan. Black prepares a quick development of his queenside starting with ...dxc4, and he is ready to play in a Carlsbad structure after cxd5. **9.a3** Both sides keep postponing clarifications in the centre, anticipating the opponent's plans.

On 9.♕c2 Black can realize his favourite idea with 9...dxc4 (for 9...♖d8 see under 9...a6) 10.♗xc4 c5 11.dxc5 ♕xc5 12.♘e4 ♘xe4 13.♕xe4 ♘d7 14.0-0 ♘f6 15.♕d4 ♕xd4 16.♘xd4 ♗d7 with an apparently equal position, Giri-Vitiugov, Olginka 2011.

9...♘bd7 Black is now ready to take on c4 (there's no need to rush with 9...dxc4 because after 10.♗xc4 White can defend along the d-file in case of ...c7-c5). **10.cxd5** Practically the last chance for White to prevent the quick development of Black's queenside. For example: 10.♕c2 dxc4 11.♗xc4 b5= and Black easily develops his own queenside. **10...exd5 11.♗d3**

The crucial moment for Black. He has to choose between two moves that lead to essentially different types of position – the solid but passive 11...c6 and the active 11...c5, which we prefer:

A21) **11...c6** This development is more appealing for players who prefer a solid pawn structure with clear plans. Here, grandmaster L. Dominguez probably opted for the Carlsbad structure because of the untypical position of the rook on d1. **12.♕c2 ♖e8 13.0-0 ♘e4!**

Black gains control of the central square e4 after White plays cxd5, and generally he will use this square for a further transformation of the position. **14.♖fe1** In case of 14.♗xe4 dxe4 15.♘d2 ♘f6 16.♘c4 Black could proceed with 16...♗g4 17.♖c1 ♖ad8 18.♘e5 ♗h5∞ with chances for both sides. **14...♘df6 15.♘e5 ♘xc3 16.♕xc3 ♘e4 17.♕c2 f6** Look up for this position in the game Onischuk-Dominguez Perez, Tromsø

2013 in Chapter 5.1, where Black continues with ...g7-g6 and ...♘e4-d6 with the idea of trading off the light-squared bishops with ...♗f5. **18.♗xe4 dxe4 19.♘c4 ♗g4 20.♖c1 ♖ad8∞**

In compensation for his weakened queenside Black has an adequate counterattack via the central square d5. However, one can't shake off the impression that Black has many pawns on the squares of his own bishop, which is strategically not favourable, Kasimdzhanov-Dominguez Perez, Greece 2013;

A22) **11...c5!?N**

Black threatens ...c5-c4, creating a mobile queenside pawn majority. Besides, the inclusion of the moves a2-a3 and ...a7-a6, which rather favours Black in this type of position, and the untypical position of White's bishop on d3 are

117

two additional reasons for Black to opt for this active plan. The game could develop as follows:

12.dxc5 White creates an isolated pawn for the opponent, but he also increases the mobility of his pieces. The following developments show that Black easily compensates for the blockaded pawn with the mobility of its pieces.

On 12.0-0, after 12...c4 13.♗c2 b5 14.♖fe1 ♗b7∞ Black has good perspectives thanks to the progress of his queenside pawn majority. **12...♘xc5** Black activates his knight, anticipating a jump to e4. A similar position results after 8.a3 ♖fd8 9.♖ad1 a6 10.♕c2 ♘bd7, but in that case White has made the additional move ♕d2-c2 and Black ...♖f8-d8.

Let's have a look at several choices for White:

A221) In reply to the prophylactic **13.h3**, after **13...♗e6 14.0-0 ♘ce4 15.♕e1 ♖ac8⇄** Black has active development and equal chances;

A222) In case of **13.♗b1 ♗g4 14.b4 ♘ce4 15.♘xd5 ♘xd5 16.♕xd5 ♘c3 17.♕d3 ♘xb1 18.♕xb1 ♕f6⩱** Black gains back his pawns and equalizes, keeping an active position;

A223) **13.♘d4 ♗d7 14.0-0 ♖ac8⇄**;

A224) **13.0-0 ♗g4 14.♗e2 ♖fd8⇄** with active play for Black. He can continue with the simple moves ...♖ac8 and ...♘ce4. In this typical position, White gains control over the critical blockade square d4, but that is not enough to make progress, especially since his opponent has maximum activity and counterplay via the e4-square.

A3) **8...dxc4?!** A justification of White's previous move. Besides, the white bishop develops to c4 in one move. **9.♗xc4 c5 10.0-0±** White obvi-

ously has the advantage. He will develop his rook to d1 and is ready to play with an isolated pawn or battle along the d-file.

B) **8.♗d3**

This common developing move seems like an inadequate reaction to Black's plan of developing with gain of tempo. In actual games, things are not that simple. Black has to play extra cautiously in order not to end up in an inferior position.

8...dxc4 Of course this would also follow if White played 8.♗e2. **9.♗xc4**

B1) **9...♖d8**

B11) **10.♕e2 a6!?**

A typical move in QGA positions. Before striking at the centre with ...c7-c5, Black will gain a tempo with ...b7-b5 and develop his bishop to b7. If 10...c5 11.dxc5 (for 11.0-0 ♘c6 12.♖ad1 see under 9...c5) 11...♕xc5 12.0-0 ♘c6

13.♖fd1 (13.♖ac1 ♝d7 14.♝b3 ♛h5 15.♖fd1 and a draw was agreed in this almost equal position in Krivoshey-Kholmov, Rovno 2000) 13...♝d7 14.a3 ♘e5 15.♘xe5 ♛xe5 16.♝b5 with a draw in an equal position, Vladimirov-Spassky, Salamanca 1991. **11.0-0** 11.a4 is weaker: 11...c5 (11...♘c6 12.0-0 e5=) 12.0-0 ♘c6 and in both cases White has damaged his position by weakening square b4. **11...b5 12.♝d3 ♝b7 13.e4 ♘bd7 14.e5 ♘d5 15.♘xd5 ♝xd5 16.♝e4 ♝xe4 17.♛xe4 c5=** Houdini 2.0c Pro-Houdini 2.0c Pro, Internet (blitz) 2012;

B12) **10.0-0 c5**

B121) **11.♛c2 cxd4 12.exd4** After 12.♘xd4 ♝d7 13.♖fd1 ♘c6 Black has emerged from the opening without problems, Drenchev-Jobava, Plovdiv 2012. **12...♘c6 13.♖ad1 a6!?N** Following the plan of grandmaster Nikita Vitiugov in his game against Evgeny Tomashevsky, Sochi 2012, though White had a queen on e2 in that game (if 13...b6 14.♖fe1 ♝b7 15.d5! – the last moment for this typical breakthrough, otherwise Black gains control of d5 and achieves a good game. 15...♘a5 16.♝d3. But now Black usually takes: 16...♘xd5 17.♝xh7+ ♚h8 18.♘xd5 ♝xd5 19.♝e4 ♖ac8 20.♛b1 ♝xe4 21.♛xe4 ♚g8 with almost equal chances. **14.a3 b5 15.♝a2 ♝b7∞** with play on both sides, e.g **16.d5** (16.♖fe1 b4⇄) **16...exd5 17.♖fe1 ♛c5 18.b4 ♛f8∞** and it is not easy for White to prove compensation for his pawn.

B122) **11.♛e2** Removing the queen from the d-file and putting it on the best square. **11...cxd4** For 11...♘c6!?= see under 10.♛e2. **12.exd4 ♘c6 13.♖ad1**

B1221) **13...b6 14.♖fe1!±** Black can't prevent the d4-d5 break. White has no time for the prophylactic 14.a3 since Black then creates a strong blockade in the centre with 14...♝b7 15.♖fe1 ♘a5 16.♝a2 ♘d5∞, Melkumyan-Vitiugov, Plovdiv 2012. **14...♘a5 15.d5! ♘xc4 16.♛xc4 ♛f8 17.♘g5 exd5** 17...h6 18.♘xf7 ♛xf7 19.dxe6 ♝xe6 20.♛xe6± and White has an extra pawn. **18.♘xd5±** White has more active pieces and better chances;

B1222) **13...♝d7** This back-up plan works better with the e-file closed, reducing the peril from the typical breakthrough d4-d5. **14.a3 ♖ac8 15.♖fe1 ♝e8 16.♝a2** And White is ready for the breakthrough with the central pawn. 16.♛f1 ♛c7 17.d5 exd5 18.♘xd5 ♘xd5 19.♖xd5 ♛f4 20.♛d3 ♖xd5 21.♝xd5 h6 22.g3 ♛f6 23.♛b3 b6 24.♖e4 ♖d8 25.♛e3 was seen in Neverov-Kholmov, Voskresensk 1990. **16...♛c7 17.d5 exd5 18.♘xd5 ♘xd5 19.♝xd5±** as White's light-squared bishop is more mobile, Indjic-Sedlak, Vrnjacka Banja 2013;

B1223) **13...a6!** The move that probably saves Black in this line. Grandmaster Vitiugov improved on his own game against Hrant Melkumyan, played only a month earlier, where he played the risky 13...b6. **14.♖fe1** On 14.a4 after

14...♗d7 Black gets an improved version of line B1222 above, because he has control of the critical square b4: 15.♖fe1 ♖ac8 with equal chances. Now the logical follow-up from the game Indjic-Sedlak would be inappropriate: 16.♗a2?! ♘b4∓. **14...b5 15.d5** 15.♗b3 ♘a5 16.♗c2 ♗b7=; 15.♗d3 ♘b4=. **15...exd5 16.♘xd5 ♘xd5 17.♖xd5 ♕xe2 18.♖xd8+ ♘xd8 19.♖xe2 ♔f8 20.♗b3 ♗e6**

The position is equal, Tomashevsky-Vitiugov, Sochi 2012.

B2) 9...c5 10.0-0 ♘c6 11.♖ad1 ♖d8 12.♕e2 12.♕c2 cxd4 13.♘xd4 (for 13.exd4 see under 11.♕c2) 13...♗d7=, S. Schmidt-Tereick, Germany 2009. **12...♗d7** Black refrains from the exchange on d4, to avoid opening the e-file, which White will often exploit with ♖e1, to strengthen the typical break d4-d5. However, 12...cxd4 13.exd4 a6! equalizes, as we described under the line with 8.♗d3 dxc4 9.♗c4 ♖d8 10.0-0 c5 11.♕e2 cxd4 12.exd4 ♘c6 13.♖ad1 a6.

13.a3 ♗e8 The immediate 13...♖ac8!?N deserves attention, and if 14.♖fe1 a6, creating activity on the queenside, with equal play, for example 15.♗a2 ♗e8∞ with equal chances after 16.d5 exd5 17.♘xd5 ♘xd5 18.♗xd5 ♘d4!. **14.h3 ♖ac8 15.♗a2 h6** and Black

has a solid, yet passive position, Almeida Quintana-Fedorchuk, Madrid 2010.

C) 8.a3

A prophylactic move, taking control of the dark squares on the queenside, also providing a safe haven on a2 for the light-squared bishop in case of Black's typical queenside moves ...a7-a6 with ...b7-b5 or ...♘a5. Although White takes precautionary measures against this, it will be very dangerous for Black to abandon this plan and carrying on passively, with the standard ...dxc4 and ...c7-c5.

White usually follows up with 8.♖d1 and ♕c2, when the same positions appear with a different move order. Where original positions appear, we will discuss them.

We will analyse the risky A) 8...dxc4 and the regular B) 8...♖d8.

C1) 8...dxc4?! This doesn't work in the given position, because the move 8.a3 is less of a tempo loss than 8.♗d3. **9.♗xc4 c5 10.0-0 ♖d8 11.♖ad1 ♘c6 12.♕e2 cxd4** Black continues according to the standard plan. The light-squared bishop still has to be developed, after which he will finally have successfully finished the opening stage. **13.exd4**

A typical position, from the game Tomashevsky-Vitiugov, Sochi 2012, only here White has a pawn on a3. Thanks to this tiny detail, Black's standard plans will not work here, as we will demonstrate. We will consider the currently very risky 13...a6 and 13...b6, and then the strongest move, 13...♘d5.

C11) At this moment it is not good to proceed with **13...a6** in view of **14.♖fe1 b5 15.♗a2** (the main point of 8.a3) **15...b4 16.d5 exd5 17.♕f1!±♕c5?! 18.♘xd5 ♘xd5 19.♖xd5 ♕f8 20.♘g5+−;**

C12) **13...b6? 14.♖fe1 ♗b7 15.d5!** and now after **15...♘a5** White can simply move his bishop to the free square: **16.♗a2+−;**

C13) **13...♘d5 14.♕e4** 14.♗xd5!? exd5 15.♕xe7 ♘xe7 16.♖fe1 ♔f8 with equal chances. **14...♘xc3 15.bxc3 ♗d7 16.♖fe1 ♖ac8** And now White plays **17.♗d3!?**

On 17.h4 comes 17...h6 18.d5 exd5 19.♕xe7 ♘xe7 20.♖xe7 ♔f8 21.♖xd7 ♖xd7 22.♗xd5 ♖xc3 with equal chances, Beliavsky-Jobava, Porto Carras 2011. **17...g6 18.d5 ♘a5 19.♕f4±** and White has the initiative because his pieces are more active and better coordinated, which compensates for his weak queenside pawn structure.

C2) **8...♖d8** This development has become standard in QGD structures. **9.♖d1** See also line 8.♖d1. Yielding in the centre with 8...dxc4 is still risky, as on the previous move after 8.a3. Now the usual follow-ups are 8...a6, 8...b6 and 8...♘bd7, after which Black wilol achieve a desirable outcome in the centre: he will either manage to take on c4 at a convenient moment or will have a solid pawn centre in case the opponent is the first to yield with cxd5.

C21) **9...a6 10.♕c2 ♘bd7** The last preparation before opening the centre with ...dxc4. It seems that 10...dxc4!? is already possible at this point: 11.♗xc4 c5 and the time White has lost on prophylactic moves with his rook, queen and pawn seems to enable Black, to break up the white centre and gradually develop the queenside (unclear is 11...b5 12.♗e2 ♗b7 13.0-0 ♘bd7 because of 14.b4) 12.dxc5 ♖xd1+ 13.♕xd1 ♕xc5 14.♕d8+ ♕f8 15.♕c7 ♘bd7 with an equal position.

A game between two elite players continued in an unusual way. After the rarely played but apparently anticipated 10...h6 11.cxd5 exd5 and now White's unusual set-up 12.h3 ♘bd7 13.g4 c5 14.♗g2 c4∞ an unusual position was reached with about equal chances, Le Quang Liem-Jobava, Khanty-Mansiysk 2010.

After 10...♘bd7 we reach a critical moment. There is no way back.

11.cxd5 11.c5 e5∞ with a great game for Black; on 11.♗d3 dxc4 12.♗xc4 b5 13.♗e2 c5 14.dxc5 ♛xc5 15.0-0 ♗b7↑ Black takes over initiative with his strong bishop and harmonious development. **11...exd5 12.♗d3 c5!?N**

A solid choice. Black doesn't have to play the Carlsbad position and instead chooses an active plan, motivated by the interjected a2-a3 and ...a7-a6 and White's time loss with the moves ♖d1 and ♛c2. **13.dxc5** In case of 13.0-0 c4 14.♗e2 b5 15.♖fe1 ♗b7 Black has an advantageous position because he has a small spatial advantage and a mobile majority on the queenside, Bommhardt-Langheld, corr. 2005. **13...♘xc5 14.♘d4 ♗d7 15.0-0 ♖ac8** The activity of Black's pieces obviously gives him a good game and compensates for the blockaded pawn on d5.

C22) 9...b6

Black is not afraid of isolated pawns because of the successive positions of the major pieces on the d-file. Moreover, usually having the pawn on a3 is useless in that pawn configuration. **10.cxd5** Now 10.♛c2 is weaker because after 10...dxc4 11.♗xc4 ♗b7 12.♛e2 c5 Black overtakes White in development and strikes at the centre, White having spent his time on prophylactic moves with the queen and the rook and on a2-a3. **10...exd5 11.♗e2** Or 11.♗d3 ♗b7 12.0-0 c5 with equal chances, Wilder-Kavalek, Estes Park 1986. **11...c5 12.0-0 ♘c6**

13.♗b5 The transition into a position with isolated pawns with 13.dxc5?! does not gain anything for White, because the pawn on a3 and the positions of white pieces don't agree with this pawn formation: 13...bxc5 14.♛c2

♖b8 15.h3 ♗e6∓ and Black takes over the initiative. **13...♗b7 14.♕d3 ♘a5 15.♕f5 ♖ac8 16.♘e5 ♕e6 17.♕xe6 fxe6 18.h3 cxd4 19.exd4 a6 20.♗d3 ♘c4 21.♗xc4 dxc4=**, Critter 1.6a-Stockfish 2.2.2, Internet 2012;

C23) **9...♘bd7 10.♕c2 dxc4**

Despite the fact that White now doesn't lose a tempo with his bishop, Black is completely equipped for carrying out his main plan in the centre. For 10...a6 see under 9...a6.

11.♗xc4 c5 12.0-0 ♘b6 This back-up manoeuvre on the queenside usually works well if White has played a2-a3 and his queen stands on the c-file. **13.♗e2 ♗d7 14.♖d2 cxd4 15.♘xd4 ♖ac8 16.♖fd1 ♘a4 17.♘db5 ♘xc3 18.♘xc3 ♗c6** and the players agreed a draw in this apparently equal position, Jussupow-Andersson, Belfort 1988.

D) **8.♕c2** This move rarely has independent significance. **8...♖d8 9.cxd5** It seems as if the transition to the Carlsbad structure benefits White, since Black has put his rook on d8. For 9.♖c1 see under 8.♖c1; for 9.♖d1 see under 8.♖d1. **9...exd5 10.♗d3** 10.a3 c5! 11.dxc5?!∓ d4; for 10.♖c1 see under 8.♖c1. **10...♘c6** and White cannot prevent both ...♘c6-b4 and ...♗c8-g4 at once.

Back to the position after **8.♖c1**.

8...♖d8!

Eyeing the white queen, strengthening the strategic threat of ...dxc4 and ...c7-c5. It is a bit unusual that Black's queen and rook play first, while the development of the minor pieces is delayed. Have chess rules changed? This might be the new era of super-modern chess!

Jokes aside, the development of the knight on b8 and bishop on c8 is not Black's main worry at this moment, so it is useful to await developments and then determine which squares are appropriate for them. The value of this plan is approved by the chess elite, who employ it. Among them are such current stars as Carlsen and Ponomariov.

Alternatively, **8...dxc4** is also possible, although Black is playing on the edge, against the rules we defined above: **9.♗xc4** This position resembles those in the Queen's Gambit Accepted, where Black is behind in development. **9...c5** Black has to neutralize White's advantage in the centre and on the c-file as soon as possible. Weaker is 9...b6 10.0-0 ♗b7 11.♕e2 c5 (with 11...♘bd7 Black allows the typical 12.♗a6± by which White advantageously exchanges the light-squared bishops, weakening the opponents' queenside and setting up a squeeze there) 12.dxc5 ♕xc5 13.♖fd1± with an advance in development, RobboLito 0.21Q-Bouquet 1.6, Internet 2013.

A) **10.dxc5 ♕xc5 11.♗b3 ♕a5**
11...♕e7?! 12.e4 ♖d8 is more passive.
White should play 13.♕e3!?N

... with the idea e4-e5, with better
chances. 13.♕f4 was played in the
game, when after the passive
13...♘bd7?! (13...♕b4!?N is a better
option, for example 14.0-0 ♘c6
15.♖fd1 ♗d7 with chances to reach a
draw) 14.e5 ♘e8 15.♗c2± Black's position is critical, Azmaiparashvili-Saric,
Nova Gorica 2006. **12.0-0 ♘c6
13.♖fd1 ♖d8 14.♕e2 ♗d7 15.h3 ♗e8**
with near-equality, Ovetchkin-
Zviagintsev, St Petersburg 2012.

B) **10.0-0** White is obviously ahead
in development. The key question is
whether this is only temporary.
**10...♖d8 11.♕e2 cxd4 12.exd4 ♘c6
13.♖fd1** 13.♖cd1 a6!= – check under
8.♗d3 dxc4 9.♗c4 ♖d8 10.0-0 c5
11.♕e2 cxd4 12.exd4 ♘c6 13.♖ad1
a6. **13...♗d7 14.a3 ♗e8 15.h3 ♖ac8∞**
Black has managed to finish his development with his bishop standing passively on e8. White has an isolated
pawn in the centre but there is still the
danger that it breaks through with
d4-d5, Matveeva-Saric, Solin 2005.
After the text, White may either delay
the decision in the centre with 9.♕c2,
9.a3 or 9.♗d3, or release the tension
with 9.cxd5.

9.♕c2
The queen leaves the d-file, taking control of the e4-square.
A) **9.a3**
A useful move for White, which can be
played in different move orders.
**9...dxc4 10.♗xc4 c5 11.0-0 ♘c6
12.♖fd1 b6 13.♕e2 cxd4** Now d4-d5
is not dangerous, so Black can open the
e-file. **14.exd4 ♗b7**

It is very useful to compare this
position with the game Haik-Spassky,
given below.
15.♗a2 ♖ac8= In this typical, dynamic
position, both sides have their chances.
For instance: **16.h3!? h6** 16...♕f8!
(with the idea ...♘c6-e7) 17.d5 exd5
18.♘xd5 ♘xd5 19.♗xd5 ♘d4!
20.♘xd4 ♖xd5= N. Sedlak. **17.♕e3
♕d6** Black controls the diagonal h2-b8
and intends the strategic manoeuvre
♘c6-e7-d5. Also possible is 17...♗a8
18.♘e5 ♖e8 19.♘xc6 ♗xc6 20.d5
exd5 and in this position the opponents
agreed to a draw, Rantanen-Nokso
Koivisto, Finland 1992.
18.d5 The last opportunity for this typical blow. **18...exd5 19.♘xd5 ♘xd5
20.♗xd5 ♕f6** with equal play, Sedlak-
Maksimovic, Vrnjacka Banja 2014.
B) **9.♗d3** After this move, the essence
of Black's plan can very nicely and
clearly be discerned. **9...dxc4!**

Since the black knight can still be developed to the active c6-square, capturing on c4 with tempo is an ideal solution. Here it gives Black easy equality in a comfortable position. It is useful to study the following sequence of moves: **10.♗xc4 c5 11.0-0 ♘c6 12.♖fd1 b6 13.♕e2 cxd4 14.exd4 ♗b7 15.a3 ♖ac8** with an equal game, Haik-Spassky, Cannes 1987.

C) **9.cxd5 exd5**

C1) **10.♕c2 c5!** 10...c6 is more passive: 11.♗d3 ♘bd7 12.0-0 ♘f8 13.h3 (13.a3 ♘g6 14.h3 ♖d6 15.♖fe1 ♗d7 16.♘d2 ♖e8 17.♘f1 ♘e4∞ Van der Sterren-Andersson, Wijk aan Zee 1988) 13...♘e8 14.♖fe1 ♘d6 15.b4 a6 16.a4 ♕f6 17.♘e5 ♘g6 18.♗xg6 hxg6 19.b5. White has managed to reach his goals in this line. Black now has to choose between two evils. Either he will have a weak pawn on c6, or, after capturing on b5, two disconnected and

weak pawns on b7 and d5, for example 19...axb5 20.axb5 ♘xb5 21.♘xb5 cxb5 22.♕b3≅ Hracek-Kosic, Sibenik 2010. **11.♗e2** White shouldn't play 11.dxc5? because of 11...d4∓. **11...♘c6 12.dxc5 ♕xc5 13.0-0 d4 14.exd4 ♘xd4 15.♘xd4 ♖xd4 16.♘d5 ♕xd5 17.♕xc8+ ♖xc8 18.♖xc8+ ♕d8 19.♖xd8+ ♖xd8=** Stockfish 2.3.1-Critter 1.6a, Internet 2013.

C2) **10.♗d3** Black has two possible approaches to this position – active play with 10...♘c6 or the more passive 10...♘bd7.

C21) **10...♘bd7 11.0-0 c6** leads to a typical position with a Carlsbad structure: **12.♕c2 ♖e8 13.♖b1** The rooks occupy positions that are in accordance with White's general plan. We have reached the critical position as given above, in Chapter 5.1.

C22) **10...♘c6** Black develops his knight to the most active square, taking control of the critical square e5 and aiming to finish his development with ...♗g4. White may respond with either of the prophylactic moves 11.h3 or 11.a3, or the aggressive 11.♗b5:

C221) On **11.a3 ♗g4 12.0-0** as in the game Andreikin-Quesada Perez, Havana 2013, Black should capture **12...♗xf3!** when after **13.gxf3 ♕d7 14.♔h1 ♘e7 15.♖g1 ♘g6∞** he achieves an equal position. It is highly recommended to compare this position with the one in the game Beliavsky-Makarov, Novosibirsk 1995;

C222) Sacrificing the bishop for the c6-knight did not change anything in the following game between two grandmasters: **11.♗b5 ♖d6 12.♗xc6 ♖xc6 13.♘e5 ♖e6 14.f3 b6 15.0-0 ♗b7 16.♖fe1 h6 17.♘e2 c5 18.♘f4 ♖d6 19.dxc5 bxc5 20.♘ed3 c4 21.♘b4**

♖ad8 22.♘c2 ♘d7 23.♘d4 ♘e5∞ Bacrot-Carlsen, Biel 2012.

C223) 11.h3 ♘e4 12.♕e2 ♗f5 12...♘b4 is not as efficient as in the positions already discussed with the white rook on a1: 13.♗b1 ♗f5 14.0-0± when White has ideally positioned pieces and has the better chances, Sedlak-Kosic, Novi Sad 2012. **13.a3** White deprives the black knight from the b4-square. **13...a6!**

A useful prophylactic move for many different reasons. Not only because it controls the b5-square or because Black can now simplify and open the a-file after b4-b5, but it also opens a new path for a strategic transfer of the knight to the square d6. **14.♘d2** 14.0-0 ♘xc3 15.♖xc3 ♗xd3 16.♕xd3 ♘a7!=, with the idea ...♘b5/c8-♘d6. **14...♘xc3 15.♖xc3 ♗xd3 16.♕xd3 ♘a7 17.0-0 ♘b5 18.♖c5 c6 19.a4 ♘d6=** An ideal place for Black's knight in this type of position, as here it control the critical squares e4, c4, b5, f5, and b7, Vachier-Lagrave-Mchedlishvili, Melilla 2011.

After the text, Black can choose between the simple and safe 9...dxc4 and a more complex strategy with 9...a6.

9...a6

As already said, this prophylactic and at the same time preparatory move for action on the queenside, has become the main line in this system.

As mentioned, **9...dxc4** should be avoided if White hasn't already made a move with his bishop. On the other hand, White's two prophylactic moves ♖c1 and ♕c2 help Black gain time in order to fulfill his main plan in the centre starting with ...♕e7 and ..♖d8. The possibility to move the black knight to the active square c6 should also be considered. **10.♗xc4 c5 11.0-0** After 11.dxc5 ♕xc5 12.♗e2 ♘c6 13.0-0 a draw was agreed in Markus-Nikolic, Sarajevo 2013. The game could have continued as follows: 13...♗d7 14.♖fd1 ♗e8=. This position, with a modest light-squared bishop on e8, usually results in a draw after the exchange of the major pieces and the black king arriving on on square e7. **11...cxd4 12.♘xd4** A draw also results after 12.exd4 ♘c6 13.♖fd1 ♗d7 14.♕e2 ♖ac8 and Black has equalized, even though his bishop is not on the standard diagonal h1-a8, Naum 2.1-Rybka 2.3.1, Diksmuide 2007. **12...♗d7 13.♗b5** 13.♖fd1 ♘c6=. **13...a6 14.♗xd7 ♘bxd7=** Leko-Ponomariov, Zug 2013.

10.a3

10.cxd5 exd5 11.♗d3 ♘c6 Posing two strategic threats: ...♘b4 and ...♗g4. **12.♗e2 ♗g4 13.0-0 ♘e4 14.h3 ♗h5** Better is 14...♗f5N with equal chances. **15.♘e5 ♘b4 16.♕d1 ♗xe2 17.♕xe2**

Black is usually OK after the exchange of the light-squared bishops, but due to the bad position of the knight on b4 he has to weaken his structure, which further complicates matters: **17...f6 18.♘f3 ♖d7 19.a3 ♘c6 20.b4?!** After this promising-looking but haphazard move, Black manages to transfer his knight to the ideal square d6. Better was 20.♘xe4 ♕xe4 21.♘d2 ♕f5 22.♘b3 ♖e7 23.a4 ♘d8 24.♘c5 c6 25.b4 ♘f7 26.b5 axb5 27.axb5 ♘d6 28.bxc6 bxc6±. Black has a weak piece on c6 but also a vulnerable king due to the move 17...f6. **20...♘xc3 21.♖xc3 ♘a7 22.♖c5 ♘c8 23.♖fc1 c6 24.a4 ♘d6=** White's crucial plan is undermined, Akobian-Krush, Philadelphia 2012.

10...♘bd7

It can easily be noticed that Black's last four moves – ...♕e7, ...♖d8, ...a6 and ...♘d7, have been often seen in various positions and that they are obviously the backbone of his main strategic plan in this central system. At this point, Black is ready to a maximum degree to execute his main plan in the centre with ...dxc4. White can either allow the opponent to resolve the centre by developing with 11.♗e2, or release the tension himself by playing 11.cxd5.

11.♗e2

Now Black can easily execute his ideal plan.
For 11.cxd5 exd5 and 11.h3, see Chapter 5.1.
11...dxc4 12.♗xc4 c5 13.♗e2 b5 14.dxc5 ♕xc5 15.b4 ♕e7 16.0-0 ♗b7=

And Black has no problems.
17.a4!
Otherwise White risks ending up in an inferior position.
17...♕xb4 18.axb5 axb5 19.♕b1 ♕xb1 20.♖xb1 ♗xf3 21.♗xf3 ♖ab8 22.♘xb5 ♘e5 23.♘d4 ♘xf3+ 24.♘xf3 ♖xb1 25.♖xb1 h6
The opponents agreed the draw in this absolutely equal position, Aronian-Carlsen, London 2013.

Conclusion
Let's start with the critical position after 7.♘c3. Black has many possibilities here, just like in positions in the Queen's Gambit where the dark-squared bishops have not been traded. In spite of this, the great move 7...♕e7! increases Black's chances to reach a draw.
Above all, Black plans to neutralize the opponent's centre with ...dxc4 and ...c7-c5, which will bring him closer to a draw. Accordingly, White can react in two radically different manners:
A) Yielding in the centre by trading pawns on d5, and:
B) Playing useful or prophylactic moves without yielding in the centre, for as long as the position allows.

In Variation A, 8.cxd5 usually leads to positions with a Carlsbad structure, which is mainly covered in Chapter 5.3. In Variation B, high-ranked players mostly use the common follow-up 8.♖c1 or the very popular 8.♖d1. The other alternatives, such as 8.a3 or 8.♕c2, usually transpose to the system with the rook on d1, so they rarely have any independent significance. The inadequate though solid 8.♗d3 should also be mentioned because it enables Black to execute his plan with gain of tempo by capturing ...dxc4. Finally, it should be pointed out that the four successive moves ...♕e7, ...♖d8, ...♘bd7 and ...a7-a6 are frequently found in different orders and positions, and that they are obviously the backbone of Black's main strategic plan in this Central system. After these moves, Black is completely ready to execute his main plan in the centre with ... dxc4. The best example to illustrate this is the game Aronian-Carlsen, London 2013.

Exercises

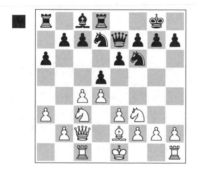

5.2 (1) Find the plan.
(solution on page 441)

5.2 (2) Find the right idea.
(solution on page 442)

5.2 (3) Find the plan.
(solution on page 442)

Chapter 5.3

7...♕e7: Releasing the Tension – 8.cxd5

1.d4 e6 2.c4 ♗b4+ 3.♗d2 ♗xd2+ 4.♕xd2 ♘f6 5.♘f3 d5 6.e3 0-0 7.♘c3 ♕e7 8.cxd5

This is the standard follow-up mostly seen in similar positions in the Queen's Gambit. It is especially favoured by those who prefer solid and simple play, because the removal of the tension in the centre means there is a problem less to worry about. By this exchange, White wants above all to thwart the opponent's plans involving ....dxc4. By giving up the centre White does Black one great service: the second player gains an open diagonal for his bishop and an open e-file for his major pieces, which enables him to gain control of the important e4-square. In addition, the trade of pawns in the centre brings about a considerable change in the position. The plans are simpler, and the opponent's ideas are easier to predict. In this specific line the game develops along the lines of Carlsbad structures.

8...exd5

It is not advisable to yield the centre to White with 8...♘xd5?!. After **9.♖c1±** (or 9.♗d3±) the first player has an obvious advantage, since it is harder for Black to play ...c7-c5.

The evaluation of this position would be much easier compared to the Tartakower Variation in the Queen's Gambit: 1.d4 d5 2.c4 e6 3.♘c3 ♘f6 4.♗g5 ♗e7 5.e3 0-0 6.♘f3 h6 7.♗h4 b6 8.cxd5 ♘xd5 9.♗xe7 ♕xe7. Evidently, there Black is practically two tempi ahead since he has made the useful moves ...b7-b6 and ...h7-h6, while the white queen is on the less favourable initial square d1. With a timely ...c7-c5 Black can neutralize the white centre.

In our position, Black's main plan is delayed, for example: (9.♖c1) **9...b6 10.♘xd5 exd5 11.♗d3** White already

129

threatens 12.♕c2 with a double strike at h7 and c7. **11...c5?!** More advisable is 11...♘a6. **12.dxc5 bxc5 13.♗b1!±** With the idea ♕d5 and ♕c2. After 13.♕c2 ♘a6 14.♗xh7+ ♔h8 15.♗f5 ♘b4 16.♕b1 ♗xf5 17.♕xf5 g6 18.♕b1± White has an extra pawn but Black has certain compensation.

9.♗d3

Without the bishop on the b1-h7 diagonal, White cannot make any progress.

A) **9.♗e2** quickly leads to a draw in many ways, because it allows Black easy development and good control over the centre. For example: **9...c6** (also fine is 9...♗g4 10.0-0 ♘bd7=; or 9...♗f5 10.0-0 ♘bd7=) **10.0-0 ♘bd7 11.♕c2 ♖e8 12.♖ab1 ♘b6!? 13.b4 ♗g4** with an excellent position for Black;

B) **9.♕c2 ♘c6** For 9...c6 10.♗d3 ♘bd7 11.0-0 ♖e8 12.♖ab1 see Chapter 5.1. **10.h3 ♘b4 11.♕d1** Weaker is 11.♕b3 ♗f5 12.♖c1 c5∞ when White has difficulties with the d3-square. **11...♗f5 12.♖c1 ♖ad8 13.a3 ♘c6 14.♗d3 ♗xd3 15.♕xd3 ♘b8 16.0-0 c6 17.b4 ♘bd7** and Black is close to equality.

To shed light on this important position, we will analyse the active 9...♘c6, the solid but more passive 9...c6, the risky 9...♖d8 as well as less strong continuations such as 9...♗g4 and 9...c5.

9...♘c6

Since 8.cxd5 has activated Black's light-squared bishop, by developing the knight to c6 Black achieves rich and active play. Players who prefer the harmonious pawn structure in the centre with ...c7-c6, still retain this possibility after the more active text. At an appropriate moment, the knight can come into action and make way for the c-pawn.

A) **9...c6 10.♕c2** For 10.0-0 ♘bd7 11.♕c2 ♖e8 12.♖ab1 see Chapter 5.1. **10...♖e8** 10...♗g4 11.♘e5± Kozul-Tratar, Rijeka 2011; for 10...♘bd7 11.0-0 ♖e8 12.♖ab1 see Chapter 5.1. **11.♘e5** This move leads to further simplifications and a drawish ending. For 11.0-0 ♘bd7 12.♖ab1 see Chapter 5.1. **11...♘bd7 12.♘xd7** Weaker is 12.f4 because of 12...♘xe5 13.fxe5 ♘g4↑ when Black takes over the initiative thanks to his pressure on the opponent's kingside. **12...♗xd7=** Beliavsky-Nikolic, Belgrade 1987;

B) **9...♖d8!?** is a move often used by GM Dragan Kosic. Usually the rook is on e8 but here, besides defending d5 and preparing ...♘e4, Black has an exceptional possibility to activate the rook along the 6th rank via d6. Although not very common, this plan is not at all pleasant for White as Black's initiative on the kingside can be very dangerous. **10.0-0 ♘c6 11.h3!** Please check David-Kosic, Milan 2011, under 11.0-0;

C) **9...♗g4?!** Without any control of the e5-square, this move is just a waste of time. **10.♘e5 c6 11.0-0 ♘bd7** (Teixeira-Rego, Rio de Janeiro 2012) **12.f4!?±** and the black bishop obviously doesn't belong on g4;

D) **9...c5?!** A risky move. With the previous exchange on d5 this strike has become less effective, and offers White a comfortable position with a weak black pawn on d5: **10.dxc5 ♘c6 11.0-0 ♕xc5 12.♖ac1±** Movsziszian-Kholmov, Budapest 1991.

10.h3!

White hampers Black's ideal development with 10...♗g4, although later the h-pawn may fall prey to an attack by the opponent, especially if the latter has his rook on d8, with the possibility to transfer it to the kingside via d6. Please check the analysis of David-Kosic, Milan 2011, below.

However, without this prophylactic move White has no chance to fight for an advantage. With **10.0-0** White finishes his development but also allows the opponent to develop freely. The following variations lead to equality:

A) **10...♖d8 11.a3 ♗g4 12.♘e1** The knight has to retreat in order to find a more secure position. **12...♗h5** Naturally, trading the light-squared bishops is to Black's advantage, especially if afterwards White opts for the plan with b2-b4. **13.b4 a6 14.f3 ♘a7!** Black intends to transfer his knight to the ideal d6-square via c8. **15.♘c2 ♗g6 16.a4 ♘c8 17.♖ae1 ♘d6 18.♗xg6 hxg6** After this important strategic trade of light-squared bishops, White should be satisfied with a draw. **19.♕d3 ♖e8 20.♖e2 c6=** Giri-Jobava, Melilla 2011;

B) **10...♗g4 11.♕d1** Weaker is 11.a3 because after 11...♗xf3 White's pawn structure is destroyed without any compensation: 12.gxf3 ♘d8 13.b4 ♘e6 14.♔h1 a5 15.♖ab1 axb4 16.axb4 c6 17.f4 ♖fe8 18.f3 ♖a3 19.♕b2 ♖ea8 20.♖be1 ♘h5 21.♖g1 ♕h4 22.♖c1 ♘hxf4 23.exf4 ♕xf4 24.♗e2 ♕xd4 25.b5 ♘f4∓ Beliavsky-Makarov, Novosibirsk 1995. **11...♖fd8 12.♗e2 ♖d6 13.♘b5 ♖d7 14.♖c1 ♘e4 15.♘d2 ♗xe2 16.♕xe2 ♘xd2 17.♕xd2 ♘d8 18.♖c2 ♘e6 19.♖fc1 c6 20.♘c3 ♘g5 21.♘e2 ♘e4 22.♕d3 ♖e8 23.♘g3 ♘xg3 24.hxg3 a6=** Seirawan-Andersson, Biel 1985.

After 10.h3, Black has two main ways to continue:

10...♘b4!

This knight immediately moves into action, as if it wants to prove that the right developing square for it was c6. Black now has a clear strategic plan to develop his light-squared bishop with ...♘e4 and ...♗f5, as the d5-pawn is now defended. Besides, he makes way for his c-pawn to move, making use of the time gained by the attack on the strong white bishop.

10...♖d8 is the other way for Black to continue his development with ...♘e4 and ...♗f5. On d8 the rook seems more passive than on the e- file, yet, again, it can be activated via d6. Active players who prefer attacks and tactics are here probably already considering placing the rook on g6 and attacking the white king, especially after White has pushed his pawn to h3.

A) **11.0-0 ♘e4 12.♕d1** Now Black can either continue with the aggressive ...♖d6 or first finish his development with 12...♗f5:

A1) **12...♖d6**

13.♕b3 ♗e6 14.a3 14.♕xb7? ♖b8 15.♕a6 ♘xd4–+. **14...♖e8** Weaker is 14...♖ad8 15.♖ac1 a6 (if 15...♗f5 16.♘e2± – an important defensive manoeuvre that should be remembered. With ♘f4 White will neutralize Black's attack and gain the better chances) 16.♖fe1 ♕d7 17.♘e2 ♗xh3 18.gxh3 ♖g6+ (18...♕xh3? 19.♗xe4 dxe4 demonstrates why the black rook is better on e8 than on d8. With the rook on e8, Black could capture with the rook on e4 and gain stronger compensation. Now 20.♕xf7+ gives White a winning advantage) 19.♔h2±. **15.♖fe1 ♖a8 16.♖f1 ♖e8!** Black plans an attack with ..♕d7 and ....♗h3, so his rook will be more effective on the e-file. **17.♖fe1** Both players probably want to check the opponent's intentions. The main plan is 17.♖ac1 a6 18.♘e2!.

The same important manoeuvre.
17...a6 The immediate 17...♕d7?! is impossible because of 18.♘b5 and the road of the rook towards the white king is blocked! **18.♖ad1?!** After this seemingly logical move, which plans ♘e5 and opening the d-file, the problems start for White. 18.♖ac1 would also give Black the chance to attack on the kingside with 18...♕d7! 19.♗f1 (19.♘e2 ♗xh3 20.gxh3 ♕xh3 21.♗xe4 ♖xe4 22.♘g3 ♖g6∓) 19...♗xh3∓. White should immediately defend his kingside with the manoeuvre we know well by now: 18.♘e2! ♕d7 19.♘f4±.
18...♕d7!

An unusual position with the black rook on d6. It is not easy to find a good solution against the threatened attack with 19...♗xh3, even though White has great control in the centre and his pieces are so harmoniously positioned!

A11) **19.♕xb7? ♗xh3–+;**

A12) **19.♘e2? ♗xh3 20.gxh3 ♕xh3 21.♗xe4 ♖xe4 22.♘g3 ♖g6**

−+; this diagram nicely illustrates the activity of and coordination between Black's major pieces in this line;

A13) **19.♘e5?! ♘xe5 20.dxe5** and now Black should first play **20...♖b6!N**. In the game 20...♘xc3 was played, and after 21.bxc3 ♖b6 22.♕c2 g6 23.c4 ♖c6 24.♕b1 ♖b6 25.♕c2 ♖c6 26.♕b1 ♖b6 the players agreed on a draw, A. David-Kosic, Milan 2011.

21.♕c2 ♘xc3 22.♕xc3 ♗xh3!∓;

A14) Chances are equal after **19.♗f1** but after **19...♗xh3!?** White has to find **20.♘e5!** (weak is 20.gxh3? because of 20...♖g6+ 21.♔h2 ♕d6+−+ and Black wins quickly) **20...♕f5 21.♘xe4 dxe4= 22.gxh3? ♘xe5−+**.

A2) **12...♗f5**

Black finishes development but has problems with the defence of d5.
13.♕b3 13.♖c1 a6!? (13...♘b4 14.♗b1 c6 is almost equal, Critter

1.6a-Stockfish 2.3.1, Internet 2013) 14.a3 ♘xc3 15.♖xc3 ♗xd3 16.♕xd3 ♘a7

and the knight will reach the ideal d6-square.
13...♘b4 For 13...♘a5 14.♕c2 ♘c6 15.a3± see under 13.0-0; if 13...♘c5?! 14.dxc5 ♗xd3 15.♖fd1±. **14.♗b1 c6 15.a3 ♘a6 16.♗xe4**

16...♗xe4?! Better is 16...dxe4!?N 17.♘e5 ♗e6 18.♕a4 ♗d5=. **17.♘e5** Better is 17.♘xe4 dxe4 18.♘e5± when the black knight needs time to improve its position. **17...♗f5 18.♕d1 f6 19.♘d3 ♗xd3 20.♕xd3 ♘c7 21.b4 a6 22.a4 ♕d7 23.♖ab1 ♘e8 24.♘e2 ♘d6=** Monteban-Etmans, corr. 2005.

B) **11.♗b5** gives nothing: **11...♖d6 12.♗xc6 bxc6** 12...♖xc6 13.♘e5 ♖d6=. **13.♕c2 ♗a6 14.♘e5 c5=** Rybka 2.3.2a-Toga II 1.3.1, Internet 2007;

C) **11.a3**

After ...♘e4 White considers placing his queen on the more natural c2-square. **11...♘e4 12.♕c2 ♗f5 13.0-0** The multiple exchange on e4 with 13.♗xe4 ♗xe4 (13...dxe4 14.♘d2±) 14.♘xe4 ♕xe4 15.♕xe4 dxe4 16.♘d2 ♖d5 17.♖c1 (17.♔e2 ♖e8 18.♖ac1 ♖e7 19.♖c4 g6 20.♖hc1 ♖dd7 21.b4± deserves attention. In both cases White has a comfortable position, Schwenck-Bucur, corr. 2010) 17...f5 18.♔e2 ♔f7 19.♖c2 g6 20.♖hc1± Equinox 1.65-Rybka 2.3.2a, Internet 2013; or 13.♘e2 ♖d6 14.♘d2 ♖e8 15.♗xe4 ♗xe4 16.♘xe4 ♕xe4 17.♕xe4 ♖xe4 18.♖c1 ♖e7 19.b4 a5 20.b5 ♘a7 21.♘c3 f5 22.♔d2 ♘c8 23.♔c2 ♘b6= Granda Zuniga-Fedorchuk, Pamplona 2010.

13...♖d6 Black gives preference to the active plan, probably hoping that after ...♖ad8 he can play ...♖g6 with an attack on White's kingside. However,

White could undermine this aggressive plan relatively easily. The cautious but passive 13...♗g6 also leads to a more comfortable position for White after 14.b4 ♖d6 15.b5 (15.♖fc1 ♖e8 16.♘b5 ♖f6 17.♘c3 ♖d6 18.♘b5 ♖f6 19.♘c3 Ilincic-Kosic, Budapest 2007) 15...♘d8 16.♘e5 ♘xc3 17.♗xg6 hxg6 18.♕xc3± Graf-Tereick, playchess.com INT 2012.

C1) With **14.♖fe1!?** the strategic threat of ♘d2 becomes more dangerous because on ...♘xd2 could interject ♗xf5 as there is no rook under attack on f1. The following variants lead to more comfortable positions for White: **14...♖e8** 14...♗g6 15.♖ac1 ♘xc3 16.♕xc3 ♗xd3 17.♕xd3 ♖e8 18.b4 a6 19.♖e2 ♘a7 20.♖ec2 c6 21.a4 ♖dd8 22.♕b3±; 14...♘xc3 15.♗xf5± ♘e4 16.♖ac1±; 14...♖ad8 15.♘d2±. **15.♖ac1 ♕f6** 15...♗g6 16.♘e2 ♗h5 17.♘h2 ♗xe2 18.♖xe2 a6±; 15...a6 16.♘d2±. **16.♘h2** With 16.♘d2± White could now have gained an advantage. **16...h5 17.♘f1∞** Siegel-Zoler, Biel 1997;

C2) **14.♖ae1 ♖ad8 15.♘d2 ♘xd2 16.♕xd2 ♗xd3 17.♕xd3 ♘b8 18.b4 a6 19.♘a4 c6 20.♘c5 ♕c7 21.a4 ♘d7 22.♖b1±** Riazantsev-Kulicov, Dubai 2005;

C3) **14.♘d2 ♘xd2 15.♕xd2 ♗xd3 16.♕xd3 ♕d7** The multi-purpose move 16...a6!? has already been discussed: 17.♖fe1 ♖e8 18.♖ad1 ♕d8 19.♖e2 h6 20.♘a4 since the e3-e4 strike is prevented, White now tries to build up pressure on the queenside. The game could continue as follows: 20...♕c8 21.♘c5 ♘e7 22.♖de1 ♘g6 23.♔h2 ♘f8 24.♕c3 ♘e6 25.♘d3 ♘g5∞ with play for both sides. **17.b4 ♘e7 18.♖fc1 a6 19.a4 ♖g6** 19...♖c6!?.

20.♘e2∞ ♖c6 21.♖c5 ♖d6 22.♖ac1 c6 23.b5 axb5 24.axb5± with characteristic pressure on c6, Lysyj-Arutinian, Cappelle la Grande 2012;

C4) **14.♖ac1 ♖ad8** (or 14...♖e8 15.♘e2±) Black strengthens the poorly defended central pawn, waiting for the appropriate moment to trade minor pieces on c3 and d3 without discarding the possibility of attacking the white king. We have to admit that this is courageous, but basically this artificial construction is not the best solution for Black. White has already prepared the strong defensive move ♘e2 and the possibility of an initiative on the queenside gives him better perspectives. **15.♘e2** The crucial defensive move again, taking control of the important square f4 and neutralizing Black's attack. **15...h6 16.♕b3 ♘a5 17.♕a4 ♘c6 18.♕c2 ♖e8 19.♘f4 g5 20.♘e2 g4 21.hxg4 ♗xg4 22.♗xe4 dxe4 23.♘h2 ♗xe2 24.♕xe2±** Rybka 3-Rybka 3, Internet (blitz) 2010.

11.♗b1

On 11.♗e2, 11...♘c4 with the idea ...♗f5 is an even more convincing way to achieve equality.

11...♘e4

The thematic knight jump, which serves to help developing the light-squared bishop to f5.

The instant **11...c6** provides a swift transition to the 'Carlsbad-type position', with an unusual positioning of the knight on b4 instead of the usual d7-square. Let's consider the differences: From b4 the black knight will first move to c7, which also had its positive sides:

1. it controls the important squares d5 and b5 in case White breaks through with e3-e4 or b2-b4;

2. It doesn't disturb the activity of the light-squared bishop on the h3-c8 diagonal, so that Black can play actively with ...♘e4 and ...♗f5;

3. The ideal d6-square is only two jumps away, e.g. ...♘e8/d6. Black can now, after ...♘e4, activate his light-squared bishop with ...♗f5, because the queen's knight is not blocking his diagonal anymore.

It must be mentioned that the queen's knight spends more time, but this is usually not a problem in positions with a fixed pawn structure in the centre, where manoeuvring and searching for the best piece positions are the most important elements. We can conclude that this original variation with the active queen's knight is completely playable, and just as good as the standard line with the knight on d7.

12.0-0 ♘e4

The thematic knight jump, enabling ...♗f5. We will consider several white replies:

So far, we have only two correspondence chess games with **13.♕e2**. If 13.♘xe4 dxe4 14.♘e5 (on 14.♗xe4 after 14...♕xe4 15.♕xb4 Black has the tactical strike 15...♗xh3!=) 14...f6 with equal chances; 13.♕d1 ♗f5 14.♕b3 ♘a6=; 13.♕c1 ♗f5= and the position tends to simplification, whereas the black knight on b4 is secured a retreat on a6.

13...♗f5 13...♘a6 14.♖c1 ♘c7 15.♗d3 ♗f5 16.♕c2 ♘e8 17.♘d2 and now 17...♘8d6, with equal chances, was more appropriate than 17...♘8f6, after which the opponents agreed on a draw in Makarov-Szczepanski, corr. 2006. **14.♘d2 ♘xd2 15.♕xd2 ♕g5 16.♗xf5 ♕xf5 17.♘e2 ♘a6 18.♖ac1** with equal chances, Ziegler-Balosetti, corr. 2009.

12.♕d1

If 12.♕c1 c6 13.0-0 and now Black should play the simple 13...♗f5!? obviously with further simplifications and an equal position. Instead, 13...♘g5?! is extravagant but risky: 14.♘xg5 ♕xg5 15.f4 ♕e7 16.f5 f6 17.♕d2 ♗d7 18.a3 ♘a6 19.e4 dxe4 20.♗a2+ ♔h8 21.♖ae1± with a difficult position for Black, Matlakov-Vitiugov, St Petersburg (rapid) 2012.

White could capture a pawn with 12.♘xe4 dxe4 13.♗xe4 ♕xe4 14.♕xb4 but after 14...b6! White is faced with threats by the black bishop along three diagonals: 15.♖c1 (15.0-0?! ♗xh3∓) 15...c5 16.♕c4 ♕g6∞ and Black has adequate compensation thanks to his play on the light squares.

Or 12.♕e2 b6= with the idea ...♗a6.

After the text, again, Black has the choice between the active 12...c5 and the passive 12...c6.

12...c5

For the more solid 12...c6 13.0-0 ♗f5= see under 11...c6.

It is too early for 12...♗f5? because of 13.a3 ♘xc3 14.bxc3 ♗xb1 15.♕xb1 ♘c6 16.♕xb7±.

13.0-0 ♗e6

The critical position, important for the evaluation of the line with 12...c5.

Here 13...♗f5 is not possible because of 14.a3 ♘xc3 15.bxc3 ♗xb1 16.axb4 ♗e4 17.dxc5± and White would be left with an extra pawn.

Worthy of attention is 13...♖d8 14.a3 ♘xc3 15.bxc3 ♘c6 16.♖e1 ♕d6 17.e4 dxe4 18.♗xe4 cxd4 19.♕d3 h6 20.cxd4↑. White has a certain advantage thanks to the strong, unblocked pawn on d4 and the good coordination of its pieces, however Black has a healthy pawn structure and chances to hold the draw.

White has a choice here:

14.a3

With **14.dxc5** White gives Black some problems with d5 but the same goes for him at square c3: **14...♘xc3 15.bxc3 ♘c6 16.♗d3 ♕xc5** Everything is crystal-clear in this typical pawn structure, which also occurs in many other openings. Chances are equal, but White shouldn't forget that the pawn on c3 presents a serious weakness, and if possible he should prepare trading it off as soon as possible with c3-c4, for example **17.♖b1 b6 18.♕a4 ♖ac8 19.♖fc1 ♕e7 20.c4 ♘a5 21.cxd5 ♗xd5=** Houdini 3 Pro-Houdini 3 Pro, Internet (blitz) 2013.

14.♗xe4 dxe4 15.♘xe4 cxd4 Also possible is 15...♗c4 16.♘xc5 ♗xf1 17.♕xf1 b6 18.♘a4 ♘d5 19.♘c3 ♘xc3 20.bxc3 ♖ac8 21.c4 ♕a3∞. **16.♘xd4 ♗c4 17.♕g4 ♗xf1 18.♘f5 ♕e5= 19.f4? ♗e2–+**.

14.♘xe4?! dxe4 15.♗xe4 ♗c4∓

14...♘xc3 15.bxc3

Black rejoices, since the white pawn moves to c3 and so White's strategic threat of dxc5 is eliminated.

15...♘c6=

White has strengthened his centre with 15.bxc3, and he will try to continue with ♖e1 and e3-e4, but he has also weakened his pawn structure on the queenside. Therefore, chances are approximately equal.

Conclusion

In the variations where White trades pawns with 8.cxd5, usually a Carlsbad structure ensues, which, due to the lack of dark-squared bishops, evidently eases Black's game and offers him equal chances. An interesting possibility to play original positions in this structure is 8...♘c6, when the black knight travels via b4 and a6 to c7.

Exercises

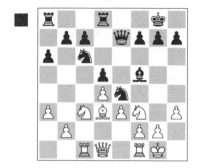

5.3 (1) Find the plan.
(solution on page 442)

5.3 (2) Find the plan.
(solution on page 442)

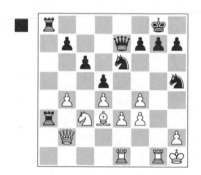

5.3 (3) Find the plan.
(solution on page 442)

Section II

The 3...c5 System: 3...c5 4.♗xb4 cxb4 5.♘f3 ♘f6

In this unusual system, Black voluntarily allows his important c-pawn to be moved away from the centre, doubling the pawns on the b-file, thus leaving his opponent with a pawn majority in the centre.

At first glance, Black's strategy appears to be utterly wrong, because of the doubling of the pawns and because it is made easier for White to build a strong centre. First impressions can be deceiving, though: the pawn on b4 makes it impossible for the white knight to land on its natural c3-square, allowing Black to play ...d7-d6 and ...e6-e5 and undermine his opponent's central formation without any fear for an incursion with ♘c3-d5. In fact, restricting the mobility and flexibility of his opponent's centre and obtaining control of the critical e5-square are the key points of Black's strategy.

To counter Black's plans, White most often removes the b4-pawn by playing a2-a3, which boils down to exchanging his a-pawn for the opponent's c-pawn. From a theoretical standpoint, this exchange is firmly in White's favour: there are practically no openings whereby the c-pawn does not participate in the battle for the central squares. However, this exchange works well for Black too, as the b4-square is cleared for his knight.

The 3...c7-c5 system is therefore hyper-modern, and builds on the foundations postulated by Réti and Nimzowitsch. White indeed builds a powerful centre, but for Black's actively-placed pieces, this will be a target.

Chapter 6

The Early 6.♘bd2

1.d4 e6 2.c4 ♗b4+ 3.♗d2 c5 4.♗xb4 cxb4 5.♘f3 ♘f6 6.♘bd2

This is a logical developing move, often also seen in the main variations with 6.e3, 6.a3 and 6.g3, which are covered in the next chapters. This continuation, however, is not the optimal solution despite the fact that it aids the central e2-e4 advance, because White declares his intentions for his ♘b1 too early, giving up on the natural c3-square.

In this chapter, we will first examine a few minor alternatives for White.

A) **6.♕d3**

Grandmasters Vladimir Epishin and Ivan Farago are quite fond of this early queen excursion, which aims to strengthen the control over the central squares. The one thing that White does not want in particular, is to lose control of the d4-square after placing the knight on d2. A serious drawback is the fact that from d3 the queen seriously hampers the coordination of the white forces, making it easier for Black to plan and execute the thematic ...e6-e5 push.

6...0-0 7.♘bd2 d6 8.e4 ♕c7 9.♗e2 e5 10.0-0 ♗g4 11.♘e1?! There is no need to part with the pawn. Better is 11.♖fe1, even though after 11...♘c6∞ Black has every reason to be satisfied with the position thanks to the awkward position of the white queen. **11...♗xe2 12.♕xe2 exd4 13.♘c2 ♘c6**

14.♕d3 ♕b6∓ Farago-Balogh, Eppingen 2013;

B) **6.♕c2** also brings the queen into the game too early. The idea is to build a full centre with e2-e4, but with the queen on c2 Black's standard plan with ...d7-d6 and ...e6-e5 becomes even stronger because of the weakened pawn on d4. **6...d6 7.e4 e5!** Black exploits the early queen move and the fact that White has not castled yet, to block the e-pawn. **8.♘bd2** 8.dxe5 dxe5 9.♘xe5 ♕e7 10.f4 ♘bd7♟. **8...0-0N** Weaker is 8...♘fd7 because of 9.c5±, Kaabi-Fauland, Novi Sad 1990. **9.♗d3** Or 9.dxe5 dxe5 10.♘xe5 ♖e8♟. **9...exd4**

Black's plan is simple and sound: to organize counterplay by utilizing his control of the weakened dark squares. **10.♘xd4 ♕b6 11.♘2f3 ♘c6** Another good plan is 11...♗g4 12.0-0 ♖e8 13.♖fe1 ♘bd7=. **12.♘xc6 bxc6=** with a good position for Black. This analysis points out the drawbacks of the plan involving the early ♕c2 and e2-e4.

6...0-0

This a natural and a flexible move, allowing Black to adjust his approach on the queenside and in the centre, depending on White's next move. **6...d5?!** is not consistent with the key ideas in this system because it favours White's central pawn formation. However, in

the variations with a2-a3, Black sometimes ends up with a pawn majority on the queenside, in which case hitting the centre with ...d7-d5 makes sense. **7.e3 0-0 8.♗d3 ♘c6 9.0-0±**

Black is a pawn down in the centre and doesn't have much to show for the doubled b-pawns. White is better, Ascic-Juranic, Sibenik 2012.

After 6...0-0 White has the choice between three obvious continuations, leading to three different types of position: 7.e4, 7.e3 and 7.g3.

7.e4

White's threat is to play e4-e5, with a significant advantage. It is worth noting that building a powerful centre is always an appealing option, favoured particularly by young and inexperienced players. One needs to keep in mind that a central pawn formation can be sensitive. In the blink of an eye its strength can turn into a weakness and vice versa, depending on minute factors in the position. Here, without the dark-squared bishop, a good plan for Black is to block White's e-pawn with ...d7-d6 and ...e6-e5, and utilize the dark squares as the launching pad for his forces.

A) 7.e3 Similar to lines after 7.g3, here too Black has the choice between A1) 7...d6, in preparation of the ...e6-e5 thrust, and A2) 7...b6 followed by the fianchetto. These two continuations often transpose, ultimately leading to the same set of positions.

A1) 7...d6 Black is busy building his standard pawn formation and preparing ...e6-e5.

A11) 8.♗e2 ♘c6 9.0-0 e5 and now:

A111) 10.d5 ♘b8 11.a3 ♘a6 12.♕b3 ♕b6 13.axb4 ♘xb4 14.♖a4 14.c5!? dxc5 15.e4 ♗g4=. **14...a5∞** and Black has the very type of position he was aiming for, Seres-Ilincic, Törökbalint 2005;

A112) 10.a3 bxa3 11.♖xa3

White has an extra pawn in the centre and well-positioned pieces, but with the bishop placed on e2 instead of d3, and the knight on d2 instead of c3, it is hard to see how he can make progress. In a similar position, but with the knight on c3, covered under 6.a3, White obtains an advantage thanks to

the d-file in combination with the potential ♘c3-d5. **11...♖e8 12.♘b3** Even though it means wasting two moves, 12.♘b1!? followed by ♘c3 deserves attention, because the pawn structures with d6 and e5 tend to be sensitive to ♘d5. **12...♗g4 13.h3 ♗h5 14.♖e1 ♕b6 15.d5 ♘b4=** Kaufman-Macieja, Freemont 2012;

A12) 8.♗d3 Here Black's most common replies are: 8...b6, 8...♘c6 and 8...♖e8.

A121) For **8...b6** see under 7...b6;

A122) 8...♘c6 is a natural developing move, which has the added benefit of making the thematic ...e6-e5 easier. However, the more precise plan is to postpone the development of the knight and go for the fianchetto, as seen in the 7...b7-b6! variation. **9.0-0** Also good is 9.♕c2 e5 10.dxe5 dxe5 11.♘e4 h6 12.0-0 ♗g4 13.♖ad1 (13.♘xf6+!? ♕xf6 14.♗h7+ ♔h8 15.♗e4 ♕e7 16.h3±) 13...♗xf3 14.gxf3 ♘xe4 15.♗xe4 ♕g5+ 16.♔h1 ♖ad8 17.♖g1 ♕h5 18.♗d5 ♔h8 19.♖g3 f5 20.♖dg1 ♖d7 21.♕a4↑ and White has a strong initiative, Antal-Ilincic, Kecskemet 2013. **9...e5**

Black has executed his plan, obtaining a reasonable position in the centre, and opening the diagonal for the ♗c8. However, White still has the upper hand in the centre, and he has more than one continuation to choose from. The three most common continuations are 10.h3, 10.d5 and 10.♕c2

A1221) The prophylactic **10.h3** prevents the black bishop from utilizing the only active square on the h3-c8 diagonal. **10...♖e8 11.d5** 11.♕c2? fails because of the nice tactical blow 11...b3!∓, when Black has a clear advantage thanks to the combined threats on the b4- and e4-squares, Eingorn-Kortchnoi, Odessa 2006. **11...♘b8 12.♘g5 ♘a6** 12...h6!?N deserves attention: 13.♘ge4 ♘xe4 14.♘xe4 ♗f5 15.♘g3 ♗xd3 16.♕xd3 ♘d7 and thanks to the strong outpost on c5, full equality is not far away for Black. **13.a3 ♘c5?!** This move surrenders the control over the important b4-square. 13...bxa3!? 14.♖xa3 ♘b4 with the idea of playing ...a7-a5 and maintaining the control over the b4 outpost. **14.♕b1 ♘xd3 15.♕xd3 bxa3 16.♖xa3 ♗d7 17.b4 ♕e7 18.♘ge4 ♘xe4 19.♕xe4 a6 20.♖c1 ♖ac8 21.♖ac3±** Lautenbach-Grasis, corr. 2010;

A1222) **10.d5 ♘b8 11.♕b3 a5 12.c5 dxc5 13.♘xe5 ♕xd5 14.♕xd5 ♘xd5 15.♖ac1⩲** White has compensation for the material, but cannot obtain more than a draw, Morchiashvili-Badev, Plovdiv 2008;

A1223) **10.♕c2**

Having a powerful and stable centre and well-positioned pieces, White wants to mount an attack on the black king. **10...♗g4** Black completes his development, successfully completing the opening phase of the game. However, White can keep the initiative going for a while longer, because of his good position in the centre and active pieces. **11.dxe5!?** White realizes that his chances lie in maintaining activity, and goes for the d-file, utilizing his better control over the d4- and d5-squares. The next phase is to exchange the ♘f6, and take the e4-square under control. **11...dxe5 12.♘g5 h6 13.♘h7** 13.♘ge4!?. **13...♘xh7 14.♗xh7+ ♔h8 15.♗e4 ♖c8 16.h3 ♗e6 17.♘f3** Weaker is 17.♘b3 b6∞ Andonovski-Bogdanovski, Struga 2013 (17...♘e7=). **17...♕a5** A better move is 17...♕c7!?N 18.♖fd1 ♘e7⇄. Black controls important central squares, and counts on the centre and the queenside for counterplay. **18.b3 ♕c5 19.♖fd1 ♖fd8 20.♖xd8+ ♖xd8 21.♖d1±** White's plan has come to fruition, and his actively placed pieces exert pressure on the opponent's forces. Black is experiencing serious problems with the d-file and the e5-pawn, Riazantsev-Berescu, Dresden 2007.

A123) **8...♖e8 9.0-0 e5 10.♕c2 ♗g4 11.dxe5 dxe5 12.♘g5 h6 13.♘ge4** Now is a good time to compare the 8...♘c6 and 8...♖e8 variations. It turns out that having the knight on c6 is more important for Black than having the rook on e8. The following two games confirm this assessment, as Black has problems maintaining control over the dark squares, with the d6-square particularly vulnerable. **13...♘bd7** and now:

A1231) **14.a3! ♕e7** If 14...bxa3 15.♖xa3 ♕c7 16.♖fa1 a6 17.c5±.

15.axb4 ♕xb4 16.c5± with the idea of playing ♖a4. White has the upper hand thanks to his space advantage and better piece coordination, Davidov-Olcayoz, ICCF email 2008;

A1232) Also possible is **14.h3**, even though after **14...♗e6 15.c5** (15.♘d6!?) **15...♕c7 16.♖ac1 ♗d5∞** Black has better chances of equalizing, Khenkin-Fauland, Vienna 2011.

A2) **7...b6**

It is hard to imagine a better option for the ♗c8 than to turn it into a Queen's Indian bishop, patrolling the central h1-a8 diagonal, especially in the positions in which White refrains from the fianchetto. **8.♗d3** For 8.♗e2 see Chapter 7. **8...♗b7**

A21) **9.♕c2 d6** 9...a5 10.e4!±.

A211) **10.g4!?** This recently discovered aggressive move deserves our full attention: **10...♘xg4 11.♗xh7+ ♔h8 12.♖g1 f5 13.d5 exd5?** 13...♘d7!

14.dxe6 ♘de5 15.♘xe5 ♘xe5 16.♗xf5 ♕f6 17.e4 ♗xe4 18.♕xe4 ♕xf5 19.0-0-0 ♖ae8= and Black gets his pawn back. **14.♗xf5 ♘h6 15.♗e6+−** Bacrot-Farago, Deizisau 2013;

A212) **10.0-0** is covered under 9.0-0;

A213) **10.♘e4**

The idea is a well-known one: to use the e4-square to trade off Black's active pieces. The exchanges simplify the position, though, leading the game closer to a peaceful outcome.

10...♘xe4 11.♗xe4 ♗xe4 12.♕xe4 ♘d7 13.0-0 Harmless is 13.♕c6 ♘f6 14.♕b5 a5 15.0-0 ♕d7 16.♕xd7 ♘xd7 17.a3 ♖fc8 18.♖fc1 bxa3 19.bxa3 ♔f8= Goldin-Verat, Clichy 1989. **13...♖c8 14.♕d3** 14.b3 a5 15.a3 bxa3 16.♖xa3 ♕e7 and the opponents agreed to a draw in this equal position, Orel-Jakovljevic, Bled 2003. **14...♕c7 15.♘d2 a5 16.a3 bxa3 17.bxa3 e5 18.♖ab1 ♖fe8=** Black has enough activity to force a draw because of the weaknesses in White's pawn structure, Fressinet-Akopian, Porto Carras 2011.

A22) **9.0-0 d6** This move is the cornerstone of Black's strategy, because without it the much-needed ...e6-e5 push is next to impossible. **10.♕c2** White's development is simple and harmonious.

In the forthcoming middlegame, White can choose between two good plans: a) ♘g5, f2-f4, ♖ae1 with the idea of utilizing the centre to obtain the advantage on the kingside, or b) ♘g5-e4, whereby the idea is to exchange the knight and the strong light-squared bishop via e4. On his end, Black continues by preparing the ...e6-e5 advance, usually in combination with ...♛c7 or ...♛e7, and by reinforcing the b4-square with ...a7-a5, while waiting for the opportunity to place the knight on one of three possible squares, a6, c6, or d7, depending on White's set-up.

A221) **10...♛e7 11.♘g5 h6** Also possible is 11...g6 12.♘ge4 ♘fd7∞ with the idea of playing ...f7-f5, Berczes-Romanov, Cappelle la Grande 2012. **12.♘ge4 ♘fd7**

A strategic retreat. 12...♘bd7 is also possible. Black prefers to keep the knight in reserve in case of the typical

a2-a3 push, and opens up the interesting possibility of playing actively with ...f7-f5 (12...♘bd7 13.a3 bxa3 14.♖xa3 a5 15.♘c3± with slightly easier play for White because of the extra space in the centre). **13.f4** 13.a3 bxa3 14.♖xa3 ♘c6= with a good position for Black. **13...f5** Simpler is 13...♘c6!?N

with the idea of playing ...♖ac8 and ...d6-d5. Here is a possible continuation: 14.♘f3 d5 15.♘ed2 ♖ac8 16.♕d1 dxc4 17.♘xc4 ♖c7 18.♖c1 ♖fc8∞.

Black has a sound position despite the doubled b-pawns. His pieces are active, and the nicely-positioned Queen's Indian ♗b7 guarantees good counterplay against any aggression by White, who has weakened his pawn structure and the central h1-a8 diagonal by grabbing the extra space with f2-f4. **14.♘g3 g6 15.e4 ♘c6 16.♘f3 ♕g7 17.♘e2 ♘e7**

18.♖ae1 fxe4 19.♗xe4 d5 20.cxd5 ♘xd5 21.♕d2± Gonda-Andreev, Budapest 2013;

A222) 10...♕c7 11.a3 This is a natural way to strengthen the position: White wants to open the file in order to activate his rooks. **11...bxa3 12.♖xa3 ♘c6!** Clearly, in this position the optimal destination for the knight is the b4-square. **13.♕c3 a5=** The resulting position is strategically balanced. White enjoys the extra space and the sound control over the central squares, whereas Black has the strong outpost on b4, and well-positioned and active pieces, Livshits-Dizdar, Moscow 1994;

A223) 10...♘bd7 A flexible developing move. As previously noted in the comments after the move 10.♕c2, Black has better chances to reach equality by delaying the development of his knight. **11.a3 bxa3 12.♖xa3 ♕c7 13.b4 a6 14.♖c1 ♖ac8 15.♖c3±** with some spatial advantage for White, but a solid position for Black, who maintains the flexible pawn formation, Zysk-Balogh, Achaia 2013.

B) 7.g3 Now Black can opt for his standard plan with ...d7-d6 and ...e6-e5, whereby the future of the light-squared bishop usually resides on the h3-c8 diagonal, or on b7 after the preparatory ...b7-b6. **7...b6** For 7...d6 8.♗g2 ♘c6 9.0-0 see Chapter 9.2.

8.♗g2 ♗b7

B1) To **9.♘f1**, with the idea of transferring the knight to the active e3-square, Black can respond with **9...b5!? 10.cxb5** 10.♘e3 bxc4 11.♘xc4 ♗d5 12.♖c1 ♘c6 13.0-0 ♗xf3 14.♗xf3 d5 15.e3 ♖c8 16.♘d2 ♕a5= Cvitan-Fries Nielsen, Forli 1990; 10.c5 d6 11.cxd6 ♕xd6 12.♘1d2 ♘bd7 13.0-0 ♖ac8=; Black's activity compensates for the deficiencies in his pawn structure, Tukmakov-Nikolic, Elenite 1993. **10...♕a5 11.♘e3 ♗xf3** Safer is 11...♕xb5=. **12.♗xf3 d5 13.♕d3 ♘bd7 14.0-0 ♖fb8 15.♖fc1 ♖xb5 16.b3?! ♖bb8 17.♖c2 ♖c8=** Khenkin-Baklan, Trieste 2009;

B2) 9.0-0 d6

B21) 10.♕c2 ♕c7 For 10...a5 see Chapter 9.3. **11.e4** 11.♖ac1 ♘bd7 12.♕b1 a5 13.♘e1 e5 with good play for Black, Annageldiev-Kuzubov, Alushta 2004. **11...e5=** Zimmerman-Vincze, Kobanya 1996;

B22) 10.♖e1 ♕c7 11.e4 e5 12.d5 With 12.♕c2 White keeps the tension in the centre while activating the ♖a1. Black, however, can take on d4 at the right moment, and utilize the dark central squares for active counterplay. 12...♖e8 13.♖ad1 ♘bd7 14.♗h3 exd4 15.♘xd4 ♘e5∞ with chances for both sides. **12...♘bd7 13.♘h4 ♘c5∞** Black has reached one of the typical positions he aims for, with good play, Zatonskih-Harika, Rogaska Slatina 2011.

7...d6 8.♗d3 e5

A timely reaction, obtaining the standard pawn structure in the centre. White controls more squares, but has potential weaknesses on d4 and c5. Besides, after ...e6-e5 Black, for the time being, does not risk running into the ♘d5 incursion with White's knight on d2.

9.0-0

No advantage is achieved by **9.dxe5 dxe5 10.♘xe5 ♕d4** and Black gets the pawn back with equal play, Rogule-Berzina, Riga 2012. (Also possible is 10...♖e8!?

11.♘df3 ♕c7 12.♗c2 ♘g4 13.♘xg4 ♗xg4 14.h3 ♖d8 15.♕e2 ♗xf3 16.♕xf3 ♘c6⯑ and Black easily organizes his play via the dark squares, in exchange for being a pawn down.)

In case of **9.d5**, after **9...♘a6 10.0-0 ♗g4 11.♖e1 ♘c5 12.♗c2 a5∓** Black succeeds in reaching an important milestone. He has curbed the flexibility of White's central formation, and secured the important c5 outpost, Haik-Speelman, Lucerne 1985.

9...exd4!?

Black has the option of playing 9...♖e8, but he prefers active play on the dark squares

The natural-looking move **9...♘c6?** is a typical mistake that is worth remembering. Black needs to keep in mind that in the centre he is fighting with two pawns versus White's three, and that White's possible pawn advances need to be re-examined after every move: **10.d5 ♘b8** 10...♘e7 11.c5± as the important c5- and e5-squares are not sufficiently protected and Black is experiencing the strategic collapse of his position; 10...♘a5 11.a3± bxa3? (a mistake one can learn from!) 12.b4+− . It is interesting that in this game White makes full use of the b4-square, which is normally controlled by Black, Garcia Luque-Mompo Ballester, Valencia 1990. **11.c5!** This is one the most dangerous weapons at White's disposal, which instantly changes the nature of the position, destroying the opponent's centre and with it the c5 outpost. **11...dxc5 12.♘xe5 ♖e8 13.f4±** White has a powerful initiative in the centre, Wiecek-Mulet, Chorzow 2008.

10.♘xd4 ♕b6 11.♘2f3 ♘c6 12.♗c2 ♗g4 13.h3 ♗xf3

Also good is 13...♗h5=.

14.♘xf3 ♕c5 15.♖c1 ♖fe8 16.♖e1 ♖e6 17.♖e3 ♖ae8

Black's active and well-coordinated pieces compensate for the pawn structure, Mostowik-Prieditis, corr. 1990.

Conclusion

After placing his bishop on d3 or e2, White attempts to obtain an advantage by playing A) e2-e4 or B) e2-e3.

A) In the e2-e4 variations, Black has no difficulties blocking the white e-pawn with ...e6-e5. As a result, Black has good dark-square play with pressure on d4. With his knight on d2, White has no way of making use of the square that has been weakened with ...e6-e5, namely d5.

B) In the e2-e3 variations, White often looks for chances along the b1-h7 diagonal, by playing ♗d3, ♕c2, ♘g5 etc., but this leads to exchanges on the e4-square, taking the game closer to a peaceful resolution.

Revealing his cards early by placing the knight on d2, thus eliminating the possibility of placing it on the natural c3-square, does not bode well for White, regardless of whether he goes for the fianchetto or places his bishop on d3 or e2. Black goes for the fianchetto himself, and organizes counterplay with ...d7-d6 and ...e6-e5.

Exercises

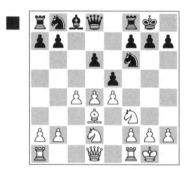

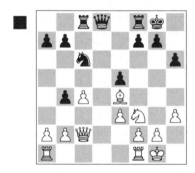

6 (1) Find the plan. *(solution on page 443)*   **6 (2)** Find the plan. *(solution on page 443)*

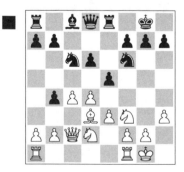

6 (3) Find the plan. *(solution on page 443)*

Chapter 7

The Stable Centre: 6.e3

1.d4 e6 2.c4 ♗b4+ 3.♗d2 c5 4.♗xb4 cxb4 5.♘f3 ♘f6 6.e3

White develops his forces in the spirit of centralized systems, aiming for stability in the centre with harmoniously positioned pieces. In most cases, this entails placing the bishop on d3, the queen's knight on c3 or d2, and the queen on c2 or e2. In the ensuing positions, Black has a range of continuations, which often transpose to the same formations via different move orders.

Our starting point is the flexible and frequently played move...

6...0-0

White can now opt for the active 7.♗d3, or the more peaceful 7.♗e2. The continuations 7.♘bd2 and 7.a3 transpose into the positions covered in Chapters 6 and 8.

7.♗d3

With **7.♗e2** White develops modestly, maintaining a strong and stable centre, and planning to obtain an advantage through strategic manoeuvring. With the bishop on the relatively passive e2-square, Black has a wide choice of continuations, though, and better chances to fully equalize.

In planning and choosing the battleground, Black relies on the following strategic ideas:

1. Counterplay in the centre with ...d7-d6, followed by ...e6-e5 at the right time;

2. Going for the fianchetto with ...b7-b6; and

3. Supporting the b4 outpost with ...a7-a5, and placing the knight on a6 or c6.

We examine the three different continuations, having in mind that they often transpose into the same positions: A) 7...b6, B) 7...a5 and C) 7...d6.

A) **7...b6**

With no opposition on the long h1-a8 diagonal, the bishop fianchetto is a sound solution. The Queen's Indian bishop on b7 is more imposing than its counterpart on e2, which is why White often wants to neutralize its activity with ♘e1 and ♗f3. For this reason, the g2-g3 system with the bishop fianchetto is more popular than the e2-e3 systems. **8.0-0 ♗b7** 8...a5 is covered under B) 7...a7-a5.

A1) **9.a3** White chooses the right moment to play this modest but strategically much-needed move: when Black does not have full control over the important b4-square. **9...bxa3 10.b4!?** One of the most solid plans in the 3...c5 system. Prior to recapturing on a3, White takes control over the critical b4-square, and grabs extra space on the queenside. On the other hand, this gives Black the time to fully activate all of his forces and compensate for the lack of space on the queenside. For 10.♖xa3 and 10.♘xa3 see Chapter 8.

A11) **10...♘c6!?N** Black has active piece play on his mind. **11.b5 ♘a5** The knight is at the edge of the board, but it exerts pressure against the c4-pawn, and Black enjoys plenty of piece activity. For example: **12.♘xa3** Or 12.♖xa3 ♗xf3 13.gxf3 d6∞ when White has

more space and the good control over the central squares. However, this is not enough for an advantage because of his damaged pawn structure and weak pawn on c4. **12...♖c8 13.♕a4 ♘e4** With the idea of playing ...♘c3. **14.♕b4 f5⇄** and all of Black's pieces are highly functional. The position offers chances to both players;

A12) **10...♕e7 11.b5 d5 12.♘xa3 ♘bd7 13.cxd5 ♘xd5** Or 13...♗xd5 14.♕b1 ♖fc8 15.♕b2 ♘e4 16.♖fc1±. **14.♕b3 a5 15.bxa6 ♗xa6 16.♗xa6 ♖xa6 17.♘c4** This is the position White aims for. He has a small but durable advantage, which is reflected in the compact pawn structure. **17...♖aa8 18.g3 h6 19.♘fd2±** With the idea to play e2-e4. White has the upper hand thanks to his better pawn structure and extra space, Tregubov-Meier, Merida 2007.

A2) **9.♘bd2**

A similar position with the bishop on d3 and White's active play on the b1-h7 diagonal is covered in Chapter 6. In this case, White has a new idea in mind. He utilizes the stable centre for the strategic manoeuvre ♘f3-e1-d3, from where it takes aim at the critical b4-square, and also plays ♗e2-f3 to exchange the bishop for its strong counterpart.

A21) **9...d6** The move orders with ...d7-d6 and ...b7-b6 are often interchangeable, and represent the corner-stone of Black's strategic plans.

A211) **10.♘e1** The introduction to a plan often seen in this type of the position. Since the centre is stable, White has the opportunity to transfer the knight to one of the more active squares d3 or c2, and apply pressure to his opponent's important outpost on b4. Furthermore, White wants to exchange Black's now active bishop by playing ♗f3. On the other hand, the stability in the centre gives Black the time to bring to bear his defensive schemes.

We will look at the flexible 10...♕e7 and 10...♕c7 continuations, since it is still unclear what the best destination for the queenside knight might be.

A2111) **10...♕e7** As seen in a number of variations, Black delays the development of the queenside knight until White plays a2-a3. After ...bxa3, Black knows what the best destination for the knight will be, depending on how White recaptures on a3. **11.♘d3 a5 12.a3 bxa3 13.bxa3 ♘bd7** It is now clear that d7 is the right place for the knight. Since White has opened the b-file with his last move, the knight goes to d7 to defend the backward pawn on the b-file. In the game Cvitan-Arlandi, Geneva 1997, Black avoided the exchange of the light-

squared bishops with 13...e5!? and equalized after 14.♖b1 ♘bd7=. **14.♗f3 ♖ab8** 14...♗xf3 15.♕xf3 e5= Kramnik. **15.♗xb7 ♖xb7 16.♖b1 ♖c8 17.e4 e5 18.d5 ♖cb8** with even chances, Kramnik-Kosten, Oviedo (rapid) 1992;

A2112) **10...♕c7 11.♗f3 ♘bd7** 11...a5 12.♘d3 ♘a6 13.a3 bxa3 14.bxa3± is covered under 7...d6. **12.♖c1 ♖ac8 13.♘c2** 13.♘d3!?. **13...a5 14.a3 b3 15.♘e1 a4=** In this position, with the unusual pawn structure on the queenside, the chances are approximately equal, Nickoloff-Petursson, Winnipeg 1994.

A212) To **10.a3** Black responded with **10...bxa3 11.♖xa3** in the game Nikcevic-Drasko, Cetinje 2013, and the opponents quickly agreed to a draw. It is clear that after **11...a5** followed by ...♘a6, Black will have control of the critical b4-square, with equal chances.

A22) Also possible is **9...a5 10.a3** and now:

A221) **10...♘a6 11.♘e1 d5** As mentioned earlier, ...d7-d5 is not often seen when Black has doubled b-pawns, because it leaves White with an extra pawn in the centre. Despite its drawbacks, one should not underestimate the dynamics of the position after the ...d7-d5 strike, especially if Black centralizes his knight on d5. 11...♕e7 12.♘d3 ♖fc8 transposes into the game Chuchelov-Greenfeld, Ohrid 2009, which is covered under B) 7...a5; in the spirit of Black's basic strategies, 11...d6 12.♘d3 bxa3 13.bxa3 leads to one of the standard positions, which is covered under 11...♗b7. **12.cxd5 ♘xd5** On 12...bxa3, to undouble the b-pawns and secure a queenside majority, White has the in-between move 13.dxe6 axb2 followed by 14.exf7+ ♖xf7 15.♖b1 ♘b4 16.♖xb2 with a clear advantage with his extra pawn. **13.a4 ♘ac7 14.♘ef3 ♘e7 15.♘e5 ♖c8 16.♖e1 ♘cd5 17.♗f1** White is slightly better because of his mobile central pawn majority. However, Black's chances should not be underestimated with his active and highly mobile pieces, Ehlvest-Georgiev, Vrsac 1987;

A222) Better is **10...bxa3!N**

Black wants to see his opponent's reaction before deciding what to do with his queenside knight. In case of **11.♖xa3** the black knight travels to its outpost on b4; on 11.bxa3 it is clear that the knight needs to be placed on d7 to protect the backward pawn on the b-file: 11...d6 12.♖b1 ♘bd7. The position is equal, with both sides nursing the deficiencies in their respective pawn structures. **11...♘a6=** This is one of the

key positions that Black is aiming for, with active minor pieces, the outpost on b4, and the mobile e6- and d7-pawns, which have more than one way of striking at the white centre.

A3) **9.♘e1**

This continuation often transposes into the positions that we have already covered. Here we look at two useful games with original ideas. **9...d6 10.♘d3 a5 11.a3 bxa3 12.♘xa3** 12.bxa3 ♕c7 13.♕b3 ♗a6 14.♖c1 ♖c8 15.♘d2 ♘bd7 16.♖ab1 e5 17.h3 ♖e8 18.♕d1 ♖ac8 19.a4 ♕d8= Gabriel-Meier, Germany 2006; 12.♖xa3 ♘bd7 13.♗f3 ♗xf3 14.♕xf3 ♖c8 15.♘d2 e5=. **12...♘a6 13.♘b5 ♖e8 14.♗f3 ♗xf3 15.♕xf3 e5=** Tregubov-Georgiev, France 2006.

B) **7...a5**

A solid plan, reinforcing the important b4 outpost.

B1) 8.0-0 b6 This move order by Black is not to be recommended, for reasons that are evident in the game we examine below. 8...d6! prevents the plan from the game Burmakin-Kasparov, Metz 2007. Please note that the continuation 8...d6 is covered under 7...d6 8.0-0 a5. **9.a3! ♘a6** 9...bxa3?! is weaker because of 10.bxa3! and White obtains control of the critical b4-square, securing the natural c3-square for his knight, and a possible outpost on the weakened b5-square. As a reminder, taking on a3 is good when White's knight is on d2, or when Black has not played ...a7-a5.

10.♘e5! The correct move order. White avoids the ...d7-d6 variation (10.♘bd2 d6=, covered under 7...d6 8.0-0 a5). **10...♗b7 11.♘d2 ♕e7!?** Using the queen to support the b4 outpost is an idea worth investigating. Since White's central e-pawn poses no immediate threats, Black does not opt for the standard ...d7-d6, but activates the queen instead. However, White is in no hurry to take on b4, and this will make it harder for Black to play the usual ...d7-d6. If 11...d6 12.♘d3 bxa3 13.bxa3 Black has to place the knight on d7 to keep an eye on the weak b6-pawn, with good chances of fully equalizing. This is covered under

11...♗b7. **12.♘d3 ♖fc8 13.♗f3!** An unnecessary simplification of the position would be 13.axb4 ♘xb4 14.♕b3 ♘e4 15.♘xe4 ♗xe4 16.♘xb4 ♕xb4 with equality, Chuchelov-Greenfeld, Ohrid 2009. **13...♗xf3** 13...d5 14.cxd5 ♗xd5 15.♗xd5 ♘xd5 16.a4± White enjoys the pawn majority, and the ♘a6 is out of play for the time being. **14.♕xf3 bxa3!?N** To 14...♖ab8 White responded with 15.♖fc1± with better chances in the endgame, Burmakin-Kasparov, Metz 2007. **15.bxa3!** 15.♖xa3 ♘b4=. **15...d5!?**

As said, this classical Queen's Gambit move makes sense when Black has the chance to obtain a pawn majority on the queenside, which is the case in this position after the c-pawn and d-pawn are exchanged. Then Black will have good counterplay. Testing this position with an engine produced the following continuation: **16.♖fc1 ♖c7 17.cxd5 ♖xc1+ 18.♖xc1 exd5 19.♘b1 b5 20.♕d1 b4 21.♕a4 bxa3 22.♘c3 g6 23.♖a1 ♘b4 24.♕xa3 ♖e8 25.♘e5** and White has the upper hand in the endgame, thanks to his better pawn structure;

B2) 8.a3 ♘a6 8...♘c6 fails because of the unpleasant 9.d5±. **9.♘e5** For 9.0-0 d6 10.♘bd2 b6 see under 7...d6 8.0-0 a5. **9...d6 10.♘d3 bxa3** Black is not afraid of exchanging on a3 because he has not played ...b7-b6 and ...♗b7. Furthermore, White has spent lots of time transferring the knight to d3, which allows Black to organize counterplay in the centre with ...e6-e5. **11.♘xa3** 11.bxa3 ♖e8 12.0-0 e5 13.♘c3 exd4 14.exd4 ♘c7 15.♗f3 ♖b8 16.♘f4 ♗d7= with the idea of playing ...b7-b5; 11.♖xa3 ♖e8 12.0-0 e5=. **11...♖e8 12.♘b5 ♘c7 13.♕b3 ♘xb5 14.♕xb5 b6 15.0-0 ♗a6 16.♕a4 ♖c8 17.♖fc1 e5 18.dxe5 dxe5 19.b3 ♕e7 20.b4 ♖xc4 21.♖xc4 ♗xc4 22.bxa5 ♗xd3 23.♗xd3 bxa5 24.♕xa5 ♖c8** and the opponents agreed to a draw in this completely even position, Giri-A. David, France 2011.

C) **7...d6 8.0-0** and now:

C1) **8...a5 9.a3 ♘a6 10.♘bd2 b6 11.♘e1** The idea is to neutralize the activity of the black bishop along the central diagonal with ♗f3, and to transfer the knight to d3, controlling the important b4-square.

C11) **11...e5 12.♘d3** 12.♗f3 doesn't lead to an advantage: 12...♖b8= and the black bishop functions on the h3-c8 diagonal. **12...♗f5** 12...bxa3!? 13.bxa3 ♖e8= Kramnik. **13.dxe5 ♗xd3 14.exf6 ♗xe2 15.♕xe2 ♕xf6 16.♘f3 ♖fd8 17.♖ad1±** and White is slightly better because of Black's weaknesses along the d-file, Kramnik-Mokry, Austria 1993;

C12) **11...♗b7 12.♘d3 bxa3 13.bxa3!?**

This leads to a new type of position and a different pawn structure in our 3...c5 system. White normally takes on a3 with his rook, but in this specific position taking with bxa3 is fully justified, even though it spoils White's own pawn structure, by the fact that the ♘a6 is now out of play and ...a7-a5 has been played, creating a backward b-pawn.

C121) **13...♕c7 14.♗f3** Or 14.♕b3 ♘b8 15.♘b2 ♘bd7 16.♘a4 e5 17.♖fc1 exd4 18.exd4 ♖fe8 19.♘c3± Rogozenco-Jakubowski, Germany 2011. **14...♖ab8 15.♖b1** and White's chances are slightly better because of his extra space and Black's inactive ♘a6, Brynell-Kockum, Sweden 2013 (also possible is 15.♖c1, even though the rook is more active on the b-file, Brynell-Warakomski, Germany 2010);

C122) It is better to play **13...♘b8** with the straightforward idea of continuing with ...♘bd7 and protecting the weakened b6-pawn **14.♗f3 ♗xf3 15.♕xf3 ♘bd7** Black is somewhat worse, but with good chances to fully equalize, thanks to the deficiencies in White's pawn structure. It is worth noting that Black has spent two extra moves by travelling with his knight to d7 via a6, compared to the similar position in the game Kramnik-Kosten, Oviedo (rapid) 1992, which we covered under 10...♕e7.

C2) **8...b6 9.a3** 9.♘bd2 ♗b7= is covered under 7...b6. **9...bxa3 10.b4** We have seen the same idea in a similar position with the bishop on b7 instead of the pawn on d6 – see the comments after the move 7...b6. For 10.♖xa3 and 10.♘xa3 see Chapter 8. **10...♘c6 11.♕b3** Or 11.b5 ♘a5⇄. Black compensates for his lack of activity on the queenside by his actively placed pieces. **11...a5 12.bxa5 ♘xa5 13.♕c2 ♗a6 14.♖xa3 ♕c7⇄** and Black's slightly inferior pawn structure is offset by the pressure on the c4-pawn, Laketic-Ilincic, Sombor 2004;

C3) **8...♘c6** This natural developing move is the precursor to the standard ...e6-e5 thrust. This plan is the most efficient in the positions with e2-e4 and the white knight on the relatively passive d2-square. This way Black attacks the d4-pawn, and does not have to worry about the incursion of the white knight on the weakened d5-square. **9.a3 bxa3 10.♖xa3 e5 11.♘c3±** See Chapter 8.

Back to the main line after 7.♗d3.

Now Black has a dilemma as to which of the following two plans to go for:
a) 7...d6 and getting ready to follow up with ...e6-e5 and the possible activation of the bishop on the h3-c8 diagonal, or:
b) 7...b6 with the idea of playing ...♗b7, with activity along the h1-a8 diagonal.

7...d6

This is the key move, and the cornerstone of Black's strategy in the 3...c5 system.

Black prepares the counterpunch ...e6-e5, which opens the h3-c8 diagonal for the bishop. This does not mean that Black has given up on the fianchetto idea and the possible deployment of the bishop on the h1-a8 diagonal. As previously noted, these two continuations often transpose into the same positions, but the move order directly influences the quality of all further plans.

7...b6 8.e4 For 8.♘bd2 see Chapter 6. **8...♗b7 9.e5** 9.♘bd2 d6 10.0-0 e5= 11.dxe5?! dxe5 12.♘xe5 ♖e8∓. **9...♘e4 10.0-0** 10.♕c2 ♘g5= Kanellos-Galopoulos, Peristeri 2011. **10...f5 11.a3 ♘g5 12.♘bd2 bxa3 13.♖xa3 ♘c6∞** In this dynamic position, both sides have their chances.

8.0-0

For 8.♘bd2 see Chapter 6.
Black now has a number of continuations at his disposal, of which we will examine: 8...♘c6, 8...b6 and 8...♖e8.

8...♘c6

A sound developing move, giving Black a satisfactory position. Black does not wait for White to reveal his cards before developing the knight, but prepares to strike at the centre with ...e6-e5.

With **8...b6** Black goes for the fianchetto, but after the important move ...d7-d6. It's a sound plan against the 7.♗d3 variations.

Now, **9.a3** is a thematic move, with the idea of activating the queenside rook and the knight. This important strategic move can appear in different move orders, and is found in all the chapters dealing with the 3...c7-c5 system 8. For **9.♘bd2** see Chapter 6.

9.e4 allows Black to block the white e-pawn with no preparation by playing directly **9...e5!** because **10.dxe5 dxe5 11.♘xe5** allows the well-known tactical motif **11...♕d4=**.

For **8...♖e8 9.♘bd2** see Chapter 6.
After the text, we will analyse only the continuations 9.e4 and 9.d5. 9.♘bd2 transposes to the positions covered in Chapter 6, and 9.a3 to the ones in Chapter 8.

9.e4

A) **9.d5** For 9.♘bd2 see Chapter 6.
9...exd5 10.cxd5 ♘e7 11.e4 After 11.♕b3 in the game Perez Manas-Narciso Dublan, Barbera del Valles

2012, Black could have obtained better chances with 11...♘exd5∓, for example: 12.♗c4 ♗e6 13.♘d4 ♕e7 14.♘d2 a5∓. **11...♘g6=** Black's forces are more active. Despite the weakened pawn structure, Black has a good position, Petkov-Shavtvaladze, Kavala 2007;

B) **9.a3 e5** For 9...bxa3 10.♖xa3 see Chapter 8. **10.♗e2 bxa3 11.♖xa3 ♗g4** 11...♗f5!? deserves attention, as it leads to the positions covered in Chapter 8 with an extra move for Black. **12.♘xe5?!** Better is 12.♘c3. **12...dxe5 13.♗xg4 exd4 14.exd4 ♕xd4 15.♕xd4 ♘xd4=** Schmidlechner-Dizdar, Austria 2010.

To the text, Black can respond with the standard 9...e5, or with the powerful 9...♕b6!.

9...e5
9...♕b6!N

As you can see, Black does not have to block the e-pawn immediately. Instead, he is utilizing the dark squares to organize his play. **10.d5** Risky is 10.e5 dxe5 11.dxe5 ♘d7 12.♖e1 ♖d8⇄. Black's counterplay is more dangerous than the opponent's initiative on the kingside. **10...♘d4 11.♘bd2 exd5 12.cxd5 ♗g4⇄** with active play and a good position for Black.

10.d5 ♘e7

Only in rare cases is this knight retreat, away from the c5 outpost, better than the usual ...♘b8. However, having in mind the weakened f4-square and the fact that the dark-squared bishops have been swapped off, the knight can be activated on the kingside.

To the standard **10...♘b8** with the intention of reaching c5 as fast as possible, White has an unpleasant response in the form of **11.c5!↑ dxc5 12.♘xe5** and now:

A) **12...♖e8 13.f4 ♘bd7 14.♘d2 ♘xe5 15.fxe5 ♖xe5 16.♕f3!⟳** White has the full compensation for the pawn, thanks to the strategic threat of ♘c4, for instance 16.♘c4?! **♖g5↑. 16...♗f5 17.♕g3 ♗xe4 18.♗xe4 ♖xe4 19.♖xf6 ♕xf6 20.♘xe4 ♕d4+ 21.♘f2 ♕xd5** Black has re-established the material equilibrium, but the endgame is not simple, and White can continue to press for an advantage;

B) Or **12...♕e7 13.♘f3!** 13.f4 ♘bd7⟳. **13...♗g4 14.♘bd2 ♘bd7 15.♕b3** and White has a pleasant game.

11.c5

This is a typical strike, with the intention of destroying the potential c5 outpost, and rendering Black's pawn structure ineffective. From a strategic point of view, the idea is a sound one, but the moment to realize it is wrong because Black has a simple but strong tactical blow at his disposal.

Better is 11.♘bd2 ♘g6 (11...b6 leads to a white initiative on the queenside after 12.a3 bxa3 13.♖xa3 a5 14.b4 ♗g4 15.c5!) 12.a3 bxa3 13.♖xa3 ♗g4 14.♕c2± and White is better. His chances on the queenside are more concrete than Black's counterplay on the kingside.

11...♘exd5!N

This tactical blow solves all of Black's opening problems.

In the only game we could find, Black continued with 11...♘g6 and after 12.cxd6 ♘e8 13.♖e1 ♘xd6 14.♕b3 a5 15.♘bd2± he had good play via dark squares and the strong blockading knight.

However, White still has an advantage because of the pawn majority in the centre, Shkurikhin-Rogovsky, Sochi 2006.

12.exd5 e4 13.♗xe4 ♘xe4 14.c6

After 14.cxd6?! **♕xd6∓** White has problems defending the d5-pawn.

14...bxc6 15.dxc6 ♕b6 16.♘bd2 ♕xc6 17.♘xe4 ♕xe4 18.♕xd6 ♗b7

The position is about equal, even though the black bishop looks more imposing than the white knight.

Conclusion

We have looked at 6.e3 followed by 7.♗d3 or 7.♗e2. The number of original positions is not great because White often plays ♘d2 or a2-a3 at some stage, leading to Chapter 6 or 8.

In the critical position after 8.0-0, Black has two equally effective continuations, 8...♘c6 and 8...b6, either of which gives him good play. In the line with 7.♗d3 d6 8.e4, Black's best option is 8...♕b6! instead of the usual 8...e5, after which White keeps the initiative with 9.d5, denying Black the critical c5-square.

After 7.♗e2 the bishop is not as active as on d3, minimizing White's possibilities of making use of his better centre. The best option for Black is to fianchetto his bishop with 7...b6. In the critical position arising after 9...d6 White usually opts for 10.♘e1, with the idea of exchanging the strong ♗b7. The recipe for equal play for Black is the recommendation by Kramnik.

The three key strategic ideas in organizing Black's counterplay are:

1. Preparation the central strike with ...d7-d6 followed by...e6-e5 at an opportune moment;

2. The bishop fianchetto; and

3. Supporting the b4 outpost with...a7-a5, and utilizing it with the knight via either a6 or c6.

Exercise

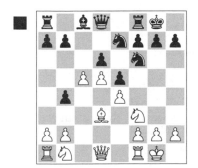

7 (1) Find the plan.
(solution on page 443)

7 (2) Find the plan.
(solution on page 443)

7 (3) Find the plan.
(solution on page 444)

Chapter 8

Play on the Queenside: 6.a3

1.d4 e6 2.c4 ♗b4+ 3.♗d2 c5 4.♗xb4 cxb4 5.♘f3 ♘f6 6.a3

White gives priority to active piece play on the queenside, at the moment when his opponent is unable to support the b4 outpost with ...a7-a5. Because of its strategic importance, the modest but important a2-a3 move features in all of White's plans. It activates the rook and the knight, and White may play it either on move 5 or later, in both the g2-g3 and e2-e3 systems. Of course, the downside of this move is that it frees the opponent of his doubled pawns and vacates b4 for the black knight.

The key question is whether this is the optimal moment to play the unavoidable a2-a3. After it, Black is practically forced to exchange the pawns, since attempting to defend the pawn with 6...♘c6 or 6...♕e7 leads to problematic positions.

6...bxa3

A) **6...♘c6?! 7.d5 exd5 8.cxd5 ♘e7 9.d6 ♘c6 10.axb4**

A1) **10...♘xb4 11.♕d2** White is intrigued by the possibility of giving a check on e3. There is also 11.♘c3! 0-0 12.e4! (White must continue aggressively, otherwise the pawn on d6 might turn into a liability) 12...♖e8 13.♗c4 ♘xe4 14.0-0 and White has an obvious advantage. At the cost of a pawn he has obtained quicker development with more activity and a better coordination of his forces. **11...a5 12.♘c3** Harmless is 12.♕e3+ ♔f8 13.♘a3 b6 14.g3 ♕e8 15.♕xe8+ ♘xe8 with an equal position. **12...0-0 13.e3** 13.g3 gives better chances to fight for an advantage, even though after 13...b6 14.♗g2 ♗b7 15.0-0 ♖e8∞ Black's pieces have plenty of activity, and the chances are approximately equal. **13...b6 14.♗e2 ♗b7 15.0-0 ♖c8 16.♘d4 ♖c5 17.f3 ♘e8 18.♘db5 ♕h4 19.e4 ♖h5 20.h3 ♕g3=** Pert-Bagheri, Paris 2004;

A2) **10...♕b6 11.♘c3 ♕xb4 12.♕d2 0-0 13.e3 ♖b8 14.♖a4±** White is more active and has better chances. Mamedyarov-Fridman, Khanty-Mansiysk 2011.

B) **6...♕e7?! 7.e3 b6 8.♗e2 ♗b7 9.0-0 ♘a6 10.♕a4** With the idea of playing c4-c5. **10...bxa3 11.♘xa3±** Black is in an inferior position, and must divert his attention to defending against the concrete strategic threat of ♘b5, Le Quang Liem-Yu Yangyi, Ho Chi Minh City 2012.

White can now either continue with 7.♖xa3, or opt for the somewhat unprincipled 7.♘xa3. There is no need to analyse 7.bxa3, whereby White needlessly damages his pawn structure.

7.♖xa3

This is a consistent and healthy continuation. White recaptures with his rook, getting ready to develop the knight on the natural c3-square.

With **7.♘xa3** White develops a piece, but this move is not consistent with the idea behind the a2-a3 advance, which is to secure the c3-square as the natural destination for the knight. Black now plans to exploit the inactivity of the knight at the edge of the board and its inability to control the important central squares e4 and d5. **7...0-0** and now:

A) After **8.e3** Black has more than one way to make use of the awkward posi-

tion of the white knight at the edge of the board.

A1) **8...♘c6**

This simple developing move takes aim at the important b4-square, and underscores the deficiencies of White having the knight on a3. Another good point behind this move is that it keeps the pawn formation flexible until White develops his light-squared bishop. If White plays 9.♗d3 on the next move, Black is ready to respond with ...d7-d6 and ...e6-e5, and after 9.♗e2 Black goes for the fianchetto with 9...b6, with pressure along the poorly controlled central diagonal. In both cases it is apparent that without having the knight on c3 White cannot adequately control the central squares e4 and d5.

We will examine the three logical continuations: the calm 9.♗e2, the active 9.♗d3 and the prophylactic 9.♘c2.

A11) **9.♗e2 b6**

This is almost always an excellent choice in the systems with the pawn on e3 and the white bishop on the f1-a6 diagonal. The ♗b7 is even stronger when the white knight is on a3, from where it has no control over the important central squares e4 and d5. **10.0-0 d6 11.♕b1 a5** There is no need to surrender control of the important b4-square, which is a great potential outpost for the black knight. Now:

A111) **12.♖d1 ♗a6** Also sound is 12...♗b7 13.e4 ♘b4⇄ and Black's actively placed pieces exert plenty of pressure on the white centre. The absence of the ♘ on c3 shows up. **13.♘c2 d5 14.b3 ♘e4=** Beliavsky-Salov, Szirak 1987;

A112) **12.♘b5 ♗a6** Also good is 12...♘b4 13.e4 ♗b7 14.♘c3 ♕e7 15.♖d1 ♖ac8∞ with chances for both sides. **13.♘c3 ♖c8 14.♖e1 ♘b4 15.♘d2 d5 16.b3 ♕e7=** and Black has a good position, Tsiganova-Akhmilovskaya, Manila 1992.

A12) **9.♗d3N** The bishop is more active here than on e2, but the absence of the ♘ on c3 makes Black's standard plan with ...d7-d6 and ...e6-e5 more appealing. **9...d6 10.0-0 e5** Black's plan in the centre has come to fruition − he now threatens a double attack with ...e5-e4. For this reason, White's optimal strategy is probably to retreat his bishop to e2, which does not give much hope for an advantage. For example: **11.♗e2** 11.dxe5 leads to good play for Black after 11...dxe5 12.♘g5 ♗b4=. **11...a6!? 12.♘b5 ♗g4 13.♘c3 ♗xf3 14.♗xf3 exd4 15.exd4 ♕b6=** and Black has counterplay along the dark squares;

A13) **9.♘c2** An understandable idea. White wants more space and action on the queenside. **9...d6 10.b4 b6 11.♗e2**

♗b7 12.0-0 a5 13.bxa5 After 13.b5, even though White cements his space advantage, his bishop and the knight on c2 are not well-positioned, allowing Black to organize his counterplay easily: 13...♘b8 14.♗d3 ♘bd7=. The black forces are well-coordinated. White's pawn structure in the centre is less than impressive and Black has the opportunity to further undermine it with ...d6-d5. **13...♘xa5 14.♕b1 ♖c8⇄**

Black's pawn structure is slightly inferior, but this is compensated for by his actively placed pieces, and the possibility of piling up pressure on the c4-pawn, Iotov-Amin, Manama 2009.

A2) **8...d6** This is a good move order, which supports all of Black's plans. **9.♗d3 e5!** Black again exploits the poor placing of the ♘a3, and executes the advance in the centre with no prior preparation, knowing that White cannot capture the offered pawn because of the check on a5. **10.♗e2** 10.dxe5 dxe5 11.♘xe5?? ♕a5+−+. **10...♘c6=**;

A3) **8...b6** The third option in Black's bid to achieve equality. However, it is better to keep the fianchetto in reserve, until White reveals his plans for his light-squared bishop. Now White's best option is to put this bishop on d3, followed by e3-e4, which curbs the activity of the bishop on b7:

A31) **9.♗d3** The most active continuation, and the best way for White to fight for an advantage. **9...d6** The rarely seen plan with ...d7-d5 was employed in a game between two strong chess-playing programs: 9...♘c6 10.0-0 ♘b4 11.e4 d5!? 12.cxd5 exd5 13.e5 ♘e4 14.♘c2 ♘xd3 15.♕xd3 a5 16.♖fc1 ♗a6 17.♕b3 ♗c4 18.♕e3 ♕d7∞ with chances for both sides, Spark 0.5-Stockfish 2.0.1, Internet 2011. **10.0-0 ♗b7** 10...♘c6 11.♖e1 ♗b7 12.e4 e5 13.♕d2 a5 14.♖ad1±. **11.b4!?**

Simply grabbing more space, aiding White in his future activities in the centre and on the queenside. On his part, Black attempts to make use of the weakened control over the central squares e4 and d5, which are under pressure because of the out-of-play ♘a3:

A311) **11...♕e7 12.♖e1 ♘c6 13.♘c2** Better is 13.♕b1

... and White has the upper hand because of his extra space and weakness-free pawn structure. For instance: 13...a5 14.bxa5 bxa5 15.e4 e5 16.d5 ♘b4 17.c5! dxc5 18.♘c4⩲. White gets his pawn back, and has slightly better chances. **13...a5 14.b5 ♘b8 15.e4 ♘bd7 16.e5 dxe5 17.♘xe5** 17.dxe5 is also good for Black: 17...♘g4 18.♗e4 ♗xe4 19.♖xe4 f5 20.exf6 ♘gxf6 21.♖e1 e5∞. **17...♘xe5 18.♖xe5 ♖fd8∞**

Black has obtained a sound position. The knight on c2 is anything but impressive, Beliavsky-Dizdar, Slovenia 2011.

A312) After **11...♘bd7** Black has a flexible pawn structure with harmoniously developed pieces, which are however somewhat passive. For this reason Black's position is reactive rather than 'pro-active'. **12.♘b5 ♕b8 13.♘d2 a6 14.♘c3 ♖c8 15.♕e2** (15.♕b3±) **15...d5 16.♖fc1 dxc4 17.♘xc4 ♘d5 18.♕b2±** Riazantsev-Kuzubov, St Petersburg 2003.

A32) **9.♗e2** is too passive. It is hard to see any advantages in allowing the Queen's Indian bishop on b7 to remain unopposed on the central diagonal. **9...♗b7** Another good option is 9...d6 10.0-0 ♘c6, which is covered under 8...♘c6. **10.0-0 ♘c6 11.♘b5** Or 11.♘e5 d5 12.♘xc6 ♗xc6 13.♗f3 ♕e7

14.♖c1 ♖fc8= Beliavsky-Timman, Tilburg 1993. **11...d5 12.cxd5 ♘xd5 13.♖a3 ♕e7** and in this equal position the opponents agreed to a draw;

B) **8.g3** also does not lead to an advantage: **8...♘c6 9.♗g2 d5** Exchanging the queen leads to an inferior endgame for Black: 9...♕a5+ 10.♕d2 ♕xd2+ 11.♔xd2 d5 12.♖hd1 ♖d8 13.♔e1 b6 14.♘e5± Gostisa-Grosar, Bled 1991. **10.0-0 b6 11.♘e5 ♗b7 12.♘c2 ♕d6=** Gligoric-Hulak, Palma de Mallorca 1989.

In the ensuing position Black has the choice between two fundamentally different plans, leading to two different types of position: the flexible 7...0-0, which allows White to build a full centre but aims to put it under pressure, or the rarely seen 7...b6 with the idea of playing ...♗b7 and ...d7-d5, and challenging the white centre directly.

7...0-0

7...b6 8.♘c3

A) **8...♗b7 9.e3 0-0 10.♗d3** White develops his forces and prepares the advance of the e-pawn, the key factor in the future attack on the black king. 10.♗e2 d6 is covered under 9...b6. **10...d5!?** This type of position rarely appears in the variations with 3...c5, but in this case, without the doubled b-pawns, the...d7-d5 advance becomes a real possibility. An exchange of the d-pawn for the c-pawn would favour both White's majority in the centre and Black's queenside majority. 10...d6 11.0-0 is covered under 8...d6. **11.cxd5 ♘xd5 12.0-0** Or 12.♘xd5 ♕xd5 13.0-0 ♖c8 14.♖c3 ♖xc3 15.bxc3 ♘d7 with an about equal position.

A1) **12...♘b4!?N** By attacking the strong light-squared bishop Black wants to avoid the unpleasant move ♕b1 with a weakening of pawns on the kingside – the side where White enjoys a majority. **13.♗b1** 13.♗e4 ♗xe4 14.♘xe4 ♘8c6=. **13...♘8c6 14.e4 ♘e7∞** The strong pawn pair gives White the upper hand in the centre, but Black is not without chances. His flexible pieces keep White's mobile centre in check, and his intention is to activate his queenside majority at the first opportunity.

A2) **12...♘c6 13.♕b1** 13.♘xd5!? deserves attention, for example 13...♕xd5 14.♕b1 g6 15.♗e4 ♕d7 16.♖c1 ♖fc8 17.♖ac3 ♘b4 18.♘e5 ♕e7 19.♗xb7 ♕xb7 20.h4 a5 21.h5±. **13...♘f6 14.♘e4 h6** An interesting possibility is 14...g6!? 15.♘xf6+ ♕xf6 16.♗e4 ♕e7 17.♖c1 ♖ac8 18.♖ac3 ♘b4 19.♘e5 ♔g7=; the black king is better placed here than in the game. **15.♘xf6+ ♕xf6 16.♗h7+ ♔h8 17.♗e4 ♕e7 18.♖c1 ♖fc8 19.♖ac3 ♘b4 20.♘e5⇄** The white pieces, and the centralized knight in particular, have more potential than the black pieces, Christiansen-Timman, Linares 1985.

B) **8...0-0 9.e4 d6 10.♗d3 ♘c6** and now:

B1) **11.d5 ♘b4 12.dxe6 ♗xe6 13.♘d4 ♕c8 14.♘xe6 fxe6 15.0-0 ♕c5=** Bilobrk-Drazic, Split 2013;

B2) Better is **11.0-0 e5** (11...♘b4 12.♗b1±) **12.dxe5 dxe5 13.h3 ♗b7 14.♘d5±**.

8.♘c3

The critical position has been reached, with two applicable plans for Black. The first one is the Central Plan A, and it involves playing along the dark central squares with 8...d6 and 9...♘c6, or vice versa with 8...♘c6 and 9...d6, followed by the thematic ...e6-e5 push. The light-squared bishop gets activated on the h3-c8 diagonal. The second plan is the Fianchetto Plan B, and it entails occupying the b4 outpost with the knight, and activating the bishop via b7 or a6.

8...d6

As seen in the aforementioned analysis, this move is the cornerstone that lays the foundation for Black's subsequent plans.

With **8...d5** Black builds the structure in the centre similar to that in the Queen's Gambit, but the pawn on d5 is rarely an asset in Bogo-Indian positions without the dark-squared bishop. However, in the variations with a2-a3 and the exchange on b4, the ...d7-d5 advance is fully playable because the exchange of the c- and d-pawns will give Black a queenside majority. **9.e3 b6** 9...♘c6 was played in the game Ponomariov-El Gindy, Khanty-Mansiysk 2009. After 10.c5 a6 11.♗e2 ♖b8 12.0-0 ♕c7 13.♘a4± White had the upper hand because of his more active pieces and better control of the dark squares. **10.cxd5 ♘xd5 11.♗d3 ♗b7** is covered under 7.♖a3 b6 8.♘c3 ♗b7.

8...♘c6

This natural developing move often follows the ...d7-d6 advance. Playing 8...♘c6 first is more flexible, because it gives Black the opportunity to continue with the solid 9...d5. On the negative side, after 9.e3 Black cannot opt for the bishop fianchetto.

A) **9.d5** (9.e3 d6 is covered under 8...d6; 9.e4 d6 is covered under 8...d6) Black has secured a good outpost for his knight on b4, rendering this aggressive d-pawn push harmless. On the contrary, it is White who has to worry about adequately protecting his central pawn. **9...♘b4** Another possibility is to play 9...exd5 first. Black opens the e-file, but the c4-pawn disappears as the potential target for an attack: 10.cxd5 ♘b4 11.d6 b6 12.g3 ♗b7 13.♗g2 a5 14.0-0 ♖c8 15.♘d4 ♗xg2 16.♔xg2 g6 17.e4 ♖c4∞ with chances for both sides, Jasnikowski-Juroszek, Chotowa 2007.

A1) **10.d6 b6 11.e4 ♗b7 12.♗d3 ♕c8 13.0-0 ♕c5∞** Black has plenty of activity, and has the chance to target White's unusual pawn formation in the centre;

A2) Weaker is **10.g3 ♕c7 11.♕b3 a5 12.dxe6 dxe6 13.♗g2** and now:

A21) **13...b6!N 14.♘d4** 14.0-0 ♗a6 15.♘b5 ♕c5 16.♘fd4 ♖ac8∓. **14...♖b8 15.♘db5 ♕c5 16.0-0 ♗a6∓** with the idea to play ...♗b5. Black has the upper hand against the poorly coordinated white forces on the queenside;

A22) **13...e5 14.♘d2? ♖d8∓** Chenaux-Dizdar, Geneva 1999.

B) To **9.g3** Black can respond effectively by attacking the c4-pawn with **9...d5!?=**. As a reminder, this continuation is dubious when Black has the doubled b-pawns, because it favours White's pawn majority in the centre. 9...d6 is covered under 9...♘c6. **10.cxd5 exd5 11.♗g2 ♖e8 12.0-0 a6!?** Black stops the opponent's activity that would otherwise be possible after 12...♗f5 13.♘e5!? ♘xe5 14.dxe5 ♖xe5 15.♕d4♗. **13.e3 ♗f5=** With simple play, Black has equalized. White has the majority in the centre, and the isolated d5-pawn is likely to become the primary object of attack. However, Black enjoys several strategic advantages in having the active pieces and the pawn majority on the queenside.

After 8...d6, White can choose between three logical continuations, 9.e3, 9.e4 and finally 9.g3, which gives the best chances for an advantage.

9.e3

A) **9.e4** White has the full centre, but without the dark-squared bishop the d4-pawn becomes more vulnerable after the usual ...e6-e5 advance. Besides, White's ♗d3 is less than impressive on the b1-h7 diagonal, which has been closed by the e4-pawn. **9...♘c6**

A1) **10.♗d3 e5 11.dxe5** Weaker is 11.d5 ♘b4 12.♗b1 ♗g4= when Black has achieved all the key objectives and has an excellent position, Inkiov-Bagheri, Guingamp 2002. **11...dxe5 12.h3 ♘b4 13.♘d5 ♘fxd5 14.cxd5 ♕d6 15.0-0 ♗d7 16.♕d2 a5 17.♖c1 b6 18.♗f1 f5 19.♖e3 ♖ae8∞** with chances for both sides, Ionchev-Dimitrov, corr. 2009;

A2) **10.♗e2 e5 11.d5** 11.0-0 ♗g4=. **11...♘b4 12.0-0** Or 12.♘d2 a5 13.♘a2 ♘xa2 14.♖xa2 ♕b6=; Black compensates for the lack of space by utilizing the dark squares, Bouaziz-Dizdar, Dubai 2004. **12...b6 13.♘d2 a5=** Black reinforces his control of the critical c5- and b4-squares, with equal chances, Deidun jr-Nickel, corr. 2002.

B) After **9.g3** Black has the choice between two different types of position, depending on the diagonal on which the bishop operates: a) fianchetto with 9...b6, or b) 9...♘c6 with the idea of playing ...e6-e5.

9...b6 9...♘c6 10.♗g2 e5 (for 10...♖e8 11.0-0± see Chapter 9.2) 11.0-0± Chapter 9.1. The text is an introduction to a solid plan, even though the fianchetto is less effective compared to the positions where White's light-squared bishop is on d3 or e2. In this position, Black's dark-squared bishop has a powerful opponent on g2. **10.♗g2 ♗b7 11.0-0 a5!** Weaker is 11...♕e7 12.♘e1 (a better option is the thematic 12.d5!±) 12...♖c8 13.♕d3 ♗xg2 14.♘xg2 ♘c6 15.e4 e5⇄ Thorsteins-Arnason, Grundarfjordur 1986. The best chance for equality is to secure the outpost for the knight on b4. In practice, White usually supports the advance of his e-pawn with either 12.♖e1 or 12.♕b1. The prophylactic 12.b3 as well as the blockading 12.d5 lead to positions that Black desires.

B1) **12.♖e1**

B11) **12...♘a6 13.e4**

13...♖c8 If 13...♘b4 14.e5 dxe5 15.dxe5 ♘d7 (15...♕xd1 16.♖xd1 ♘e4 17.♘d4±) 16.♘b5 ♘c5 17.♘d6⇄. Now:

B111) **14.♘d2 e5⇄** To compensate for his opponent's full centre, Black has strong counterplay along the dark squares, Bensdorp-Royset, Rethymnon 2010. To 14...♘b4 White responds by stopping Black from castling: 15.e5! ♗xg2 16.exf6 ♗b7 17.fxg7, with a strong attack against the black king;

B112) **14.e5 dxe5 15.♘xe5** 15.dxe5 ♕xd1 16.♖xd1 ♘e4=. **15...♗xg2 16.♔xg2 ♘d7 17.b3 ♘xe5 18.♖xe5 ♘b4⇄** White has somewhat better control over the central squares, but Black has sufficient counterplay because of the exposed d4-pawn and the opponent's slightly weaker king.

B12) Also possible is to stop the e-pawn with **12...♘e4 13.♕b1** 13.♘xe4 ♗xe4=; 13.♘b5!?. **13...♘xc3 14.bxc3 ♕c7?!** (14...♖a7!

Next, Black will place his knight on d7 and complete the development of his forces, with equal chances. **15.♘g5 g6 16.♗xb7 ♕xb7 17.♕e4±** Renaze-Verat, Royan 1988.

B2) **12.♕b1 ♘a6 13.e4** and now:

B21) **13...♖c8?!** was played in the game Ushenina-Zdebskaya, Kharkov 2001, where White could have exploited the position of the black rook on c8 to obtain a clear advantage with **14.e5!N dxe5 15.dxe5 ♘g4** 15...♗xf3 16.♗xf3 ♘d7 17.♗b7±. **16.♘g5 ♕xg5 17.♗xb7 ♕h5 18.h4 ♘xe5 19.♕d1!±**;

B22) **13...♘d7?!** **14.♘b5±** Plachetka-Cabrilo, Stara Pazova 1988;

B23) **13...♘b4 14.e5 dxe5!?N** Not as active is 14...♘e8 15.d5 exd5 16.♘xd5⇄ Notkin-Schönthier, Germany 1995. **15.dxe5 ♘d7 16.♖d1 ♕e7⇄** In this dynamic position Black has strong counterplay by targeting the e5- and c4-pawns. Besides, White has yet to reactivate the poorly-functioning ♖a3. Here is one possible continuation: **17.♘b5** Weaker is 17.♘g5?! ♕xg5 18.♗xb7 ♖ad8 19.f4 ♕h5∓. **17...♗c6 18.♖e3 ♖ac8 19.♘d6 ♖cd8 20.♘b5 ♖c8=**

B3) **12.b3** is meek and after **12...♘a6 13.♖a1 ♘b4=** Black has nothing to worry about, Markus-Tratar, Ljubljana 2012;

B4) **12.d5 e5 13.♘e1 ♘a6 14.♘d3 ♘d7 15.♕d2 ♖c8 16.♘b5 ♕e7 17.♖c1 ♘dc5=** Zontakh-Nyzhnyk, Kiev 2008.

9...b6

Black opts for the Fianchetto Plan B, outlaid under the diagram after 8.♘c3. Black allows White to build the full centre by advancing the e-pawn, whereas Black activates all of his forces and looks for counterplay against the weaknesses uncovered by White's aggressive advances.

With **9...♘c6** Black would opt for the Central Plan A. However, we are not convinced because Black chooses to fight in the centre, where he is a pawn down. White can choose between placing his bishop on the safer but more passive e2-square, or playing actively with 10.♗d3. In both cases White has

more space and better control over the central squares.

A) **10.♗d3** Placing the bishop on the diagonal with the maximum punch is usually White's best choice against the Central System. Surprisingly, in practice it is not used as often as the passive 10.♗e2, probably because of seemingly dangerous replies like A1) 10...e5 and ...♗g4 or A2) 10...♘b4. Regardless of its deficiencies, we are of the opinion that this continuation represents White's best chance to fight for an advantage in the 6.a3 systems that we cover in this chapter.

Black is at a crossroads. He has to choose between A1) Central plan with 10...e5 and A2) 10...♘b4.

A1) **10...e5** With the bishop on d3, this standard attack on White's centre in combination with the potential ...♗g4 seems promising. **11.0-0** 11.h3 leads to easy equality for Black after 11...exd4 12.exd4 ♖e8+=. White has to either deactivate a piece or lose the right to castle. Now:

A11) **11...♖e8 12.dxe5 dxe5 13.♘e4** More precise is 13.♘g5± when Black has difficulties because of the weak d6-square. **13...♗e6** Better is 13...♗f5!? with chances to equalize. **14.♘fg5±** Toloza Soto-Nogueiras Santiago, Buenos Aires 2005;

A12) 11...♗g4 12.♗e2 White is playing the variation we have covered under 10.♗e2, but with one move less. Since the extra pawn in the centre is a permanent fixture, an extra move more or less is of secondary importance. Weaker is 12.h3 ♗xf3 13.♕xf3 exd4 14.exd4 ♕b6=; or 12.d5 ♘b4 13.♗b1 ♘d7!? when Black keeps his favourite c5 and b4 outposts under control, and has good play, Oney-Ollier, Avoine 2009.

A121) 12...a6!?N

Black is safeguarding against potential problems with the d6-square after the d-file gets opened or after ♘b5. Still, after **13.h3 ♗h5 14.♕d2 ♖c8 15.♖d1** White will pursue the simple plan of opening the d-file and preparing the knight incursion on the weakened d5-square. The chances are on White's side. **15...h6 16.dxe5 dxe5 17.♘d5 ♖e8 18.♖b3 e4 19.♘d4 ♗xe2 20.♘xe2 ♘e5∞** The position is approximately equal, but with somewhat easier play for White;

A122) 12...♗xf3 does not lead to equality either after **13.♗xf3 exd4 14.exd4** (14.♗xc6 dxc3=) **14...♕b6** because of the pretty in-between move **15.♖b3!±;**

A123) 12...♖e8 13.h3

A1231) 13...♗xf3 14.♗xf3 e4 14...exd4 15.♗xc6 bxc6 16.♕xd4±.

15.♗e2 a5 16.♕b3 b6 17.♖c1 The players agreed to a draw in this position, where White has a slight advantage. Closing the centre with ...e5-e4 is not the best solution from a strategic point of view because it makes things easier for White on the queenside, Kottusch-Tawakol, Schleswig Holstein 1989;

A1232) 13...♗h5

A12321) 14.♘xe5 dxe5 15.♗xh5 exd4 16.♘d5 ♘xd5 17.cxd5 ♕xd5 18.♗f3 ♕d7 19.♗xc6 and the draw was agreed in Orr-Fauland, Haifa 1989;

A12322) Better is **14.♘b5± xd6**, when it is not easy for Black to find an acceptable plan, for instance: **14...a6** 14...♗xf3 15.♗xf3 e4 16.♗e2 a6 17.♘c3 a5. **15.dxe5 dxe5 16.♘d6 ♖e7 17.c5±;**

A2) 10...♘b4

Black commences with the activation of his queenside, implementing the Fianchetto Plan B. The knight occupies the outpost on b4, whereas the light-squared bishop aims for b7 or a6. Black's central pawns stay on e6 and d6, allowing the opponent's central pawns to advance and become a target for counterplay. This kind of plan is typical for Hypermodern chess. As a reminder, Hypermodern chess is the style of controlling the centre by pieces instead of pawns. In other words, the emphasis is on rapid piece development at the expense of pawn moves. **11.♗b1 b6 12.e4** White advances his third pawn to the centre, planning an attack on the black king. Black has to react energetically, by attacking the centre, but the key question is whether to focus on the e4-pawn with 12...♗b7, or on the c4-pawn with 12...a5 followed by ...♗a6:

A21) **12...♗b7 13.0-0 a5!?N** After 13...♖e8 in the game Svensson-Cornu, ICCF corr 1990, White probably could have continued with 14.e5!? dxe5 15.dxe5 ♕xd1 16.♖xd1 ♗xf3 (16...♘g4 17.♖e1± with the idea of playing h2-h3) 17.gxf3 ♘h5 18.♗e4 ♖ac8 19.♖xa7 ♖xc4 20.♖dd7 ♖f8 21.♖a4±.

13...a5!? is a multipurpose move typical for this kind of position. It reinforces the ♘b4, takes the pressure off the a7-pawn and liberates the rook to attack the potentially weak c4-pawn. **14.♕e2** It is too early to play 14.e5 because of 14...dxe5 15.dxe5 ♕xd1 16.♖xd1 ♗xf3 17.gxf3 ♘h5= when Black has a great position. **14...♖c8** with the idea of playing ...♗a6, and now:

A211) **15.♖d1 ♗a6 16.b3 d5⇄** with mutual chances;

A212) **15.e5 dxe5 16.dxe5 ♗xf3 17.♕xf3 ♘d7 18.♕e4** (18.♗xh7+=)

18...g6 19.♘b5 ♕e7 20.♖h3 ♖cd8 21.♕e3 f6 22.exf6 ♕xf6= with the idea of playing ...♘c5;

A213) **15.b3±** A nice prophylactic move, aimed against Black's counterplay with ...♗a6. In the resulting postion, Black is passive and devoid of counterplay;

A22) **12...a5!?N** deserves attention, with the idea of immediately attacking the weakened c4-pawn: **13.0-0 ♗a6 14.e5** White has no choice but to enter into a direct confrontation if he wants to fight for an advantage, since 14.b3 is easily met by 14...d5 15.e5 ♘d7∞ with chances for both sides. **14...dxe5 15.dxe5** Weaker is 15.♘xe5 because of 15...♖c8 16.b3 ♕d6 17.♖a1 ♖cd8 and Black takes over the initiative because the d4-pawn is now a liability. **15...♘d7** 15...♕xd1 16.♖xd1±. **16.♕d4!** White defends the c4-pawn, planning to transfer the king to the kingside and launch an attack on the black king. **16...♘c5** 16...♕e7 17.♕f4!, with the idea of playing ♗xh7+. **17.♕g4**

The critical position. The situation on the kingside is getting more and more dangerous. The white queen has joined the attack and White already threatens 18.♗xh7+ with a win. Black's pieces are active, but far away from the kingside. **17...g6** Weaker is 17...h6?!

18.♘e4! with a strong attack. **18.♘e4** The natural-looking 18.♖d1 improves the position for Black after 18...♕e7 with the idea of continuing with ...♖d8; 18.h4!. **18...♘xe4 19.♗xe4 ♗xc4 20.♗xg6 fxg6** Black allows the splitting of his pawns in order to activate the rook on the f-file. **21.♕xc4 ♕d5!?=** with equal play.

B) **10.♗e2**

To meet Black's obvious intention to play ...e6-e5 and ...♗g4, White develops his bishop on e2, which gives the game a quiet, positional character. Here too Black has the choice between the Central Plan A with 10...e5, the Fianchetto Plan B with 10...♘b4 and possibly C) 10...a5. Our recommendation is to go for the active and dynamic plan with 10...♘b4 followed by the bishop fianchetto, since the standard 10...e5 leads to positions in which Black has to struggle for a draw:

B1) **10...e5** Black continues with the implementation of his plan. To complete his development, all he needs to do is put the light-squared bishop on g4 or f5. However, since the struggle is taking place in the centre, where White has an extra pawn, we are not convinced that this is the best solution here. Our advice for Black is to opt for the more active plan with 10...♘b4. **11.0-0**

White has finished the development of his forces, has the upper hand in the centre, and enjoys good piece coordination. We will examine the three most logical continuations for Black: 11...♗g4, 11...♗f5 and 11...♖e8.

B11) **11...♗g4** Black's development is harmonious, and he exerts indirect pressure on the d4-pawn. However, further analysis shows that Black does not have enough for equality: **12.h3 ♗h5** 12...♗xf3 13.♗xf3± White has a clear advantage thanks to his powerful centre in combination with his active pieces. On 13...exd4 14.exd4 ♕b6, with pressure against d4, White has the strong in-between move 15.♖b3!± Ikonnikov-Hackel, Germany 2002. **13.♕a4!**

An unusual but strong move, after which Black is powerless. White controls the critical b4-square, which is usually in Black's hands, and frees the d1-square for the rook. **13...e4** This type of pawn structure in the centre is not good for Black. By releasing the pressure on the d4-pawn, Black makes it easier for his opponent to attack on the kingside. 13...a5 does not help: 14.dxe5 dxe5 15.♖d1± with the idea of playing ♘d5. **14.♘d2 ♗xe2 15.♘xe2 a5 16.♘c3 ♖e8 17.♕b5 ♘b4 18.♘a2 ♘xa2 19.♖xa2±** Black has numerous weaknesses and no active counterplay, Critter 1.01-Zappa Mexico II, Internet 2011;

B12) **11...♗f5**

Activating the bishop on the b1-h7 diagonal, which is the preferred option of grandmaster Milan Drasko, also fails to give Black satisfactory play.

12.♕d2 More active and better is 12.♕b3N, with pressure on b7 and with the strategic threat of 13.dxe5 dxe5 14.♖d1. Now Black is facing unsurmountable problems, for example: 12...exd4 13.♘xd4 ♘xd4 14.exd4 ♕d7 15.♗f3±. 12.♘h4 ♗d7 13.♘f3 ♗f5 with equality was seen in the game Kozhuharov-Arnaudov, Bankya 2013. **12...b6 13.♖d1 a5?!** Black reinforces his favourite b4-square, but at this stage in the game Postny-Drasko, Novi Sad 2009, White missed the opportunity to create major problems for his opponents with the tactical blow **14.e4!N**

♗g4 14...♘xe4? does not work because of 15.♘xe4 ♗xe4 16.dxe5 dxe5 17.♕e3+− with a double attack and an easily winning position. **15.dxe5 dxe5 16.♕e3±**;

B13) **11...♖e8 12.dxe5** This is the introduction to a plan that is typical for this kind of position. White has better control of the centre, and wants to obtain an advantage by opening the d-file and placing the knight on d5. **12...dxe5 13.♕b1±** Dworakowska-Socko, Krakow 2008 (White is also better after 13.♕b3± with the idea of playing ♖d1).

B2) **10...♘b4**

Before fianchettoing, Black first occupies the stronghold on b4, moving the knight away from possible attacks with d4-d5. **11.0-0 b6** In this position White usually strives to trade off the strong black knight on b4 with 12.♘a2 or 12.♘e1, or plays the aggressive and unclear 12.e4.

B21) **12.♘a2 ♘xa2 13.♖xa2 ♗b7 14.b4** and now:

B211) **14...a6 15.♘d2 ♕c7 16.♘b3 ♘d7** 16...a5= again leads to simplifications and a drawish position. **17.♗d3⇄** White has the upper hand thanks to his extra space, Glek-Kiselev, Moscow 1989;

B212) Safer is **14...a5!?N**

15.♕b3 15.b5?! ♘e4⇄. 15...♕c7 16.♖fa1 axb4 17.♕xb4 ♖xa2 18.♖xa2 ♖a8= with a drawish endgame;

B22) 12.♘e1 The logical plan. White wants to continue fighting for the important b4-square, and starts by exchanging the knight. White is also ready to neutralize the activity of the black light-squared bishop with ♗f3 in case of ...♗b7.

B221) 12...♗b7 13.♘d3 13.♕b3 a5 14.♘d3 ♘xd3 15.♗xd3 ♗a6 16.♖d1 ♖c8 with equal chances, Wagner-Levin, Germany 2012. 13...a5 14.♖b3 ♘xd3 15.♗xd3 ♖b8 16.♖a3 ♕e7 17.♖e1 e5 18.♗f1 ♖fd8= Romanishin-Arlandi, Reggio Emilia 1998, As we can see from the last two games, even though White is successful in trading off the ♘b4, he fails to obtain an advantage;

B222) More dynamic is 12...a5!?N with the idea of playing ...♗a6: 13.♗f3 13.♘d3 ♗a6=; 13.♘c2 ♗a6 14.e4 ♕c7⇄. 13...d5 14.cxd5 ♘fxd5 15.♘xd5 ♘xd5 16.♘d3 ♗a6=;

B23) 12.e4 ♗b7⇄ Purely in the spirit of hypermodern chess. White has established the full pawn centre, but now has to face Black's counterplay against it. 13.♕b1 a5 is covered under 9.e3 b6 10.♗e2 ♗b7 11.0-0 a5 12.♕b1 ♘a6 13.e4 ♘b4.

B3) 10...a5?! This move order is risky because Black is bound to be late with

the development of his bishop. 11.0-0 b6 11...♘b4 12.e4± Without the bishop on b7, the idea of playing e4-e5 gains in strength, Granda Zuniga-Nikolic, Havana 1987:

B31) 12.♕b1 ♗a6!? 13.♖d1 d5!? 14.♘e5 ♘b4 15.♗f3 ♖c8= Vokac-Vujic, Württemberg 1996;

B32) 12.♘e1 e5?! 12...♗a6!. 13.♗f3± (Dlugy-Delaune, Philadelphia 1987) Better is 13.dxe5!?N dxe5 14.♕xd8 ♖xd8 15.♗f3 ♗b7 16.♖b3 ♘d7 17.♘d3 ♖ab8 18.♖d1± with strong pressure on the black position;

B33) 12.e4!?N A show of strength! White places his third central pawn on the fourth rank, but this exposes the centre even more and gives Black new targets there. 12...♗b7 13.♕c1 13.e5 dxe5 14.dxe5 ♘d7⇄, White has weakened his central formation; 13.d5 ♘b4⇄ and White has weakened his dark-square complex; 13.♕b1 ♘b4 is covered under 9.e3 b6 10.♗e2 ♗b7 11.0-0 a5 12.♕b1 ♘a6 13.e4 ♘b4. 13...♘b4!

The right plan, and probably the only way to guarantee active play for Black. Black wants to weaken the white centre by provoking it into advancing. This way, the pawn structure loses its flexibility, while creating vulnerable squares in the process, which Black can exploit to organize his counterplay. It is worth noting that we covered a similar position in Chapter 7 in the variation with 7.♗d3, but with the white queen on d1. **14.♕f4** White maintains the mobility of his centre, postponing any advances until a better opportunity presents itself. **14...♘h5 15.♕d2 ♖c8 16.♖c1 ♘f6 17.♕e3 ♕e7 18.e5** Finally White comes into action. **18...dxe5 19.♘xe5 ♖fd8∞**

White has good control over the central squares, but Black is well-developed and quite active. Particularly impressive are the black rooks on the c-file and the d-file;

B34) **12.d5! ♘b4** 12...exd5 13.cxd5 ♘b4 14.♘d4 ♗d7 15.e4± with a space advantage and a better position for White. **13.♘d4 ♗d7** 13...e5?! 14.♘c6±. **14.dxe6 fxe6 15.♕b3 ♖c8 16.♖d1⇄** Black's central pawns have become targets.

10.♗d3

White places the bishop on the square that promises the maximum activity, but allows Black to transfer his knight to b4 without losing any time. Instead, if **10.♗e2 ♗b7**:

A) The aggressive **11.b4** allows Black to obtain sufficient counterplay after **11...♘c6 12.♕b1** Weaker is 12.b5?! because of 12...♘a5⇄ with the idea to play ...♗xf3. White has difficulties protecting the weakened c4-pawn. **12...a5 13.bxa5 ♘xa5 14.0-0**

A1) **14...♖c8 15.♘d2 ♗a6 16.♕b4** and White's advantage is minimal, Ponomariov-Naiditsch, Moscow (blitz) 2009. **16...d5 17.cxd5 ♖xc3 18.♗xa6 ♘xd5 19.♕b2 ♖xa3 20.♕xa3 ♕a8 21.♗b5 ♖c8 22.♖c1 ♖xc1+ 23.♕xc1 ♕d8 24.♘e4 g6 25.g3 ♕c7;**

A2) **14...♗a6 15.♘b5** Better is 15.♘d2 d5 16.cxd5 ♗xe2 17.♘xe2 ♕d6 18.♖a1 ♘xd5 19.♖c1 and White has a slight plus because of his marginally better pawn structure. **15...♕d7=** Houriez-A. David, Fourmies 2011;

A3) **14...♗xf3!N 15.gxf3 d5 16.cxd5 ♘xd5 17.♘xd5 exd5** with equal chances;

B) **11.0-0 a5** 11...♘c6?! 12.d5 exd5 13.cxd5 ♘b4 14.e4± ♖e8 15.♗b5 ♖e7 16.♖e1 a6 17.♗f1± leads to a better position for White, Akesson-Kosten, West Berlin 1987.

Black prepares to transfer the knight to b4 via a6, because placing it on c6 is fraught with danger due to the unpleasant d4-d5 advance. The best chance for White to make something out of this position is to prepare the advance of the e-pawn with 12.♕b1, or to play 12.♘e1 with the idea of obtaining control of b4 with ♘d3 or ♘c2. An integral part of this plan is using the f3-square to neutralize the activity of Black's strong light-squared bishop. We will also examine the inferior continuations 12.♖a1 and 12.♘d2, which do not impede Black's plans:

B1) An unnecessary waste of time is **12.♖a1 ♘a6 13.♕b3 ♘b4 14.♘a2.** The exchange of knights brings the game one step closer to a peaceful resolution. **14...♘xa2 15.♕xa2 ♕c7 16.b3 ♖fe8 17.♘d2 e5 18.♗f3 exd4 19.exd4 d5=** Black has successfully solved all his opening problems, Nowak-Hracek, Poznan 1987;

B2) **12.♘d2** White plans to exchange the strong ♗b7, similar to the 12.♘e1 variation below. However, on d2 the knight's future is not as bright: **12...♕e7** Better is 12...♘c6 when after 13.♗f3 Black avoids the exchange of the light-squared bishops with 13...d5=. **13.♗f3 ♘c6 14.♕b1 ♖fc8 15.♖b3 ♘b4 16.♗xb7 ♕xb7=** Szymczak-Stempin, Slupsk 1989;

B3) **12.♕b1 ♘a6 13.e4** 13.♘a2 does not give an advantage: 13...♕e7 14.b4 d5= Baquero-Arnason, Thessaloniki 1988.

B31) **13...♘d7** This knight retreat is utterly unnecessary. Black is reacting to the possible e4-e5 advance, which however has the potential to bring problems only to White. **14.♘b5** White sees no useful purpose for the rook on the a-file after ...a7-a5, so he moves the knight away to free the e3-square. From e3 the rook can support the advance of the e-pawn. **14...♕e7 15.♖e3 ♖ad8 16.♖e1 e5 17.♘c3** The white knight reaches its natural square, and aims at the weakened d5-square. This is critical for the assessment of the position. **17...♘b4 18.♘d5±** Johansson-Petursson, Stockholm 1992;

B32) A better option for Black is to keep the knight on f6 and play **13...♘b4!?N**

and in the ensuing position Black compensates for the opponent's full centre by his piece activity, for example: **14.♖d1 ♕e7 15.e5 dxe5 16.♘xe5** Weaker is 16.dxe5 ♘d7 17.♘b5 ♖ad8 with the idea of playing ...♗xf3, dxe5 and White is the only side with potential problems. **16...♖fd8=**

B4) **12.♘e1** White wants to challenge the black light-squared bishop,

175

which is dominating the h1-a8 diagonal, with ♗f3, and to place the knight on d3 or c2, from where it controls the important b4-square. **12...e5 13.♘c2 ♞a6 14.♘b5 ♛c7 15.♖b3 ♖fd8 16.♘c3 ♛c7 17.♘b5 ♛c6 18.f3 d5 19.cxd5 ♞xd5=** Indjic-Huschenbeth, Athens 2012.

10...♗b7

Better is **10...♞c6!?N**. Black hurries to occupy b4 with his knight. **11.0-0** 11.d5 ♞b4 12.♘d4 a5!=. **11...♞b4**

A) **12.e4 a5**

The control of the b4-square and the activation of the light-squared bishop with ...b7-b6 are two crucial elements of Black's strategy. We have a position that is typical for the Hypermodern chess style, seen in the past in the games of old masters such as Réti and Nimzowitsch. White has a full and mobile centre, which Black hopes to undermine with his active pieces. For instance:

A1) **13.♗e2 ♗a6⇄** White needs to be cautious not to advance the central pawns too early, which could leave them exposed. For example: **14.e5 dxe5 15.dxe5** Safer is 15.♘xe5 with an equal position. **15...♞d7⇄** Black has an excellent position. The only effects of the aggressive e4-e5 push are the aggravated problems for White with defending the e5- and c4-pawns;

A2) **13.♖e1 ♗a6⇄** with the pressure against the centre that is typical for this kind of position;

A3) **13.♗b1 ♗a6⇄** is covered under 8...d6 9.e3 ♞c6 10.♗d3 ♞b4 11.♗b1 b6 12.e4 a5;

A4) **13.e5 dxe5 14.♘xe5** 14.dxe5 ♛xd3 15.exf6 ♖d8∓. **14...♗b7** Black completes the development of his light-squared bishop on the central h1-a8 diagonal. 14...♞xd3 is risky, even though there is no denying that eliminating the strong light-squared bishop is an appealing proposition. However, from b4 the knight controls the whole range of important squares, and is in no way less active than the ♗d3. Besides, by keeping the knight Black leaves open the possibility of playing ...♞c6! at the right moment to challenge the strong white knight on e5 square: 15.♛xd3 ♗a6 16.♛e3 ♖c8 17.b3±.

To 14...♗a6 White responds with the unpleasant 15.♘e4!?⇄ with the idea of activating his rook via the third rank, and using it to support the attack on the black king.

15.♖e1 ♖c8⇄

In this dynamic position, both sides have their chances and there is a wealth of possible strategic plans. White has mobile central pawns on d4 and c4, but they require a fair amount of support. If the white bishop retreats to b1 or f1, Black can respond with ...♘c6, with the aim of simplifying the position and exchanging the strong and centralized white knight.

B) **12.♗b1 a5** The advantage of this move order is that it leaves open the possibility of playing ...♗a6 with instant pressure on the c4-pawn. **13.e4 ♗a6⇄** is covered under 8...d6 9.e3 ♘c6 10.♗d3 ♘b4 11.♗b1 b6 12.e4 a5.

11.♕b1

From b1 the queen reinforces the control over the important square e4, and also supports the b2-b4 advance. Its downside is that it allows Black to exchange on f3, damaging the pawn structure around the white king.

For 11.0-0 ♘c6 12.e4 ♘b4 13.♗b1 see under 10...♘b4.

11...a5

11...♗xf3!?N 12.gxf3 ♘c6∞ with chances for both sides.

With 11...a5 Black executes one of the key plans in this position, which entails transferring the knight to b4, activating the bishop on the h1-a8 diagonal, and keeping a flexible pawn structure in the centre, ready for the possible advances ...e6-e5 or ...d7-d5. Also possible is ex-

changing the strong light-squared bishop on f3, in order to spoil the opponent's pawn structure.

12.b4

White obviously does not want to surrender the b4 outpost to his opponent.

12...axb4

12...♗xf3!?N is good in this position too: 13.gxf3 ♘c6 14.bxa5 bxa5 with equal play.

13.♖xa8 ♗xa8 14.♕xb4

14...e5

Kortchnoi, who was Black in this game, passes over the third opportunity to take on f3, which is the move persistently favoured by the chess-playing computers: 14...♗xf3! 15.gxf3 e5! with mutual chances.

15.d5±

Black has obtained an important outpost on c5, but his opponent controls more space while keeping the pawn structure compact. White's chances are somewhat better. We have to admit that Kortchnoi's stubbornness not to exchange the bishop on f3 has influenced our assessment of the position, regardless of what the chess software may suggest, Petursson-Kortchnoi, Reykjavik 1987.

Conclusion

In this chapter we have examined the positions that arise when White engages his opponent in a battle for the queenside with 6.a3. The critical position is reached after the forced 6...bxa3 7.♖xa3 (7.♘xa3 poses no problems for Black, who easily equalizes by exploiting the awkward position of the knight at the edge of the board, and its inability to control the central e4- and d5-squares) 7...0-0 8.♘c3, and in this position the right move order for Black is to first play 8... ♘c6 because now after 9.g3 Black immediately obtains a good position with 8...d5.

9.e3 is the main line. (The positions after the immediate 9.e4 are harmless for Black, who easily equalizes with the standard advance 9...e5.) 9...d6. Now Black is at a crossroads. He has a choice between the active and dynamic 10.♗d3, and the passive but solid 10.♗e2.

Since the set-up with ♗d3, ♘c3 and the recapture ♖a3 can be dangerous for Black, especially in the variations with ...♘b4 followed by placing the bishop on b7 or a6, we suggest that Black goes for the safer plan with 10...e5 followed by...♗g4.

In the positions with the passively placed ♗e2, we suggest to start active counterplay with 10...♘b4 and developing the bishop on b7 or a6, which gives Black good and dynamic play in the Hypermodern style, where the key is that he uses pieces instead of pawns to control the central squares.

Our conclusion is that the set-up with ♗d3, ♘c3, a2-a3 and the recapture ♖a3, which can arise via different move orders, presents the best opportunity for White to fight for an advantage. At this stage there are no effective plans for Black to combat this dangerous combination of a strong centre with active pieces. Because of this, it is a good idea to keep the alternative ...d7-d5 up your sleeve, which is rarely seen in the 3...c7-c5 system because it favours White's pawn majority in the centre. However, after 6.a3 and the subsequent exchange of the doubled pawn on b4, this plan has a point because Black gets a pawn majority on the queenside after the practically inevitable exchange of the c- and d-pawns. The critical position for this plan arises after 6.a3 bxa3 7.♖xa3 b6 8.♘c3 ♗b7 9.e3 0-0 10.♗d3 d5!? 11.cxd5 ♘xd5 12.0-0 ♘b4 !?N.

Exercises

8 (1) Find the plan.
(solution on page 444)

8 (2) Find the plan.
(solution on page 444)

8 (3) Find the plan.
(solution on page 444)

Chapter 9

The Fianchetto: 6.g3 0-0 7.♗g2 d6 8.0-0

6.g3 is the most common continuation. White goes for the fianchetto, leaving a2-a3 and the queenside development for later, and he does not want to free his opponent from the doubled b-pawns. Placing the light-squared bishop on the central h1-a8 diagonal makes a lot of sense because neutralizing its activity is not an easy task for Black. The positions arising after ...d7-d5 are generally not advisable for Black because of White's central pawn majority, and the ...b7-b6 fianchetto transposes into Queen's-Indian positions with doubled b-pawns. Nevertheless, the strong bishop and the doubled pawns should not frighten Black. Having a pawn on b4 has its advantages, and Black has the option of either opposing the 'Catalan' bishop by putting its counterpart on b7, or ignoring it and building a successful career for his own bishop on the f1-a6 diagonal. From a6, the bishop attacks the c4-pawn, the Achilles' heel in the fianchetto systems, which in combination with ...d7-d5 usually guarantees Black satisfactory play.

Chapter 9.1

The Flexible 8...♖e8

1.d4 e6 2.c4 ♗b4+ 3.♗d2 c5 4.♗xb4 cxb4 5.♘f3 ♘f6 6.g3 0-0 7.♗g2 d6 8.0-0 ♖e8

In the past, this flexible move was a formidable weapon for Black. It paves the way for the standard advance of the e-pawn, and Black no longer needs to worry about the d4-d5 push, which is always a threat in the variations with 8...♘c6. Besides, this continuation keeps all Black's options in the air while waiting for White to reveal his intentions on the queenside.

Nevertheless, in a recent game against Bassem Amin in Reykjavik, 2013, grandmaster David Navara recently uncovered an effective plan against Black's clever move order.

9.a3!

This is a standard reaction in this kind of position. White aims to open the a-file and secure the c3-square for his knight.

For **9.♘bd2** see Chapter 9.2.

9...♘c6

9...bxa3 also does not lead to equality: 10.♖xa3 (also good is 10.♘xa3 ♘c6 11.♘b5± with the intention to play c4-c5 and render the move 8...♖e8 a waste of time. Arencibia Rodriguez-Rivera, Santa Clara 1998) 10...♘c6

11.♘c3 e5 12.dxe5 dxe5 13.♘g5±. White has more activity and better control over the central squares. As you can see, in this line 8...♖e8 serves no purpose, Züger-Milosevic, Switzerland 2008.

10.axb4

10.d5 poses no danger for Black: 10...exd5 11.cxd5 ♘e7 12.axb4 ♘exd5 13.b5 ♗d7 14.♘d4 ♕b6=. Black has no difficulty in activating his forces, and the position is about equal, Garcia Padron-Kortchnoi, Las Palmas 1991.

10...♞xb4 11.e4!

This surprising pawn sacrifice, with the clear threat of e4-e5, hits Black's position like a thunderbolt. Black was expecting the obvious ♞b1-c3, and all of a sudden there's an unprotected central pawn on c4! What makes this aggressive advance possible is the fact that Black is unable to block the position with ...e6-e5.

The natural-looking **11.♞c3** allows Black to complete his development, prepare ...e6-e5 and secure the important outpost on b4. **11...♗d7**

In this critical position White has the following continuations at his disposal:

A) **12.e4 e5 13.dxe5** This is an introduction to a sound plan. White wants to have total control of d5, and after the eventual exchange of the knight transform his advantage into a strong passed pawn.

Black was ready to meet 13.d5?! with 13...a5.

This is the kind of position that Black is aiming for in this system.

His better control of the dark squares, including the key squares c5 and b4, plus his more active light-squared bishop are strategic elements that work in Black's favour, Rümmele-Rechmann, corr. 1991.

13.♕d2 a5 and 13.♕b3 a5 are covered under 13.e4.

13...dxe5 14.♞d5 ♞fxd5 15.exd5 15.cxd5 a5= and Black's active and well-coordinated forces compensate for the opponent's strong passed pawn. **15...♕c7** It is better to play 15...e4!?N 16.♞d4 ♕b6

with an unclear position with chances for both sides. **16.♞g5 ♗f5 17.d6±** Kvisla-Zhao Xue, Gibraltar 2013;

B) **12.♕b3 a5 13.♖fd1** 13.e4 e5 14.♖ad1 ♕c7= Cheparinov-

Moiseenko, Khanty-Mansiysk (blitz) 2013. **13...♕c7 14.♖ac1 ♖ac8 15.♘d2** and now:

B1) **15...♖ed8** 15...b6=. **16.♘ce4 ♘e8** 16...♘xe4!? 17.♘xe4 d5∞. **17.♕a3 b6∞** with a solid position for Black, Stone-Dizdar, Makarska 1993;

B2) Also possible is **15...e5 16.dxe5** 16.♘de4 ♘xe4 17.♗xe4 (17.♘xe4?! d5↑) 17...h6∞. **♖xe5 17.♕a3 h5** Better is 17...♗c6 with equal play. **18.b3 ♖ce8 19.♘f3 ♖c5 20.♘d4 ♕b6 21.h3 ♖ce5 22.♕b2** White has a slight plus, Bilobrk-Hulak, Sibenik 2006.

C) **12.♕d2 a5**

C1) **13.e4 e5** Now White has a pleasant choice:

C11) **14.♖fd1 ♕c8 15.♖ac1 ♗g4 16.b3 ♘c6 17.dxe5 dxe5 18.♕e3 ♗xf3 19.♗xf3 ♘d4 20.♘b5±** Pinter-Hulak, Medulin 2002

C12) **14.♖fe1 ♖c8 15.b3 b5 16.cxb5 ♕b6 17.dxe5** 17.♖ac1 ♗xb5 18.♘xb5 ♖xc1 19.♕xc1 ♕xb5= Gligoric-Cebalo, Yugoslavia 1987. **17...dxe5 18.♗f1 ♗g4 19.♖e3±** and Black fails to secure sufficient compensation for the pawn.

C2) **13.♕f4 ♕e7 14.♕h4 b6 15.b3 ♖ac8 16.♖ac1 ♗c6=** Jumabaev-Maletin, Nizhnij Tagil 2007;

C3) **13.♖fd1 ♗c6 14.♘e1 ♗xg2 15.♘xg2 ♖c8 16.♘e3 d5 17.cxd5 exd5=** Lerner-Kortchnoi, Chalkidiki 2002.

11...♘c6

A better option is to accept the offered central pawn with 11...♘xe4 12.♕e1

and now the following beautiful and unexpected double strike justifies the aggression: 12...♘xg3 13.hxg3 ♘c2 14.♕c3 ♘xa1 15.♘bd2 ♗d7 16.♖xa1 ♗c6 17.d5 exd5 18.♘d4± Miranda-Bujdak, corr. 2008.

12.e5 dxe5 13.dxe5 ♘d7

The exchange of queens brings no relief: 13...♕xd1 14.♖xd1 ♘d7 15.♘c3 ♘dxe5 16.♘xe5 ♘xe5 17.♘b5⧸ with more than adequate compensation for the pawn.

14.♕e2 ♕c7 15.♖e1 a6 16.♘c3 ♖b8 17.♖ad1±

Thanks to his faster development and more space, White has the upper hand, Navara-Amin, Reykjavik 2013.

Conclusion

The idea to support the thematic push ...e6-e5 with 8...♖e8 is bound to be shelved after the game Navara-Amin, Reykjavik 2013. The critical position is reached after 9.a3 ♘c6 10.axb4 ♘xb4, when by utilizing the tactical opportunities in the position White defeats the opponent's strategy that was previously seen in numerous tournaments: 11.e4!.

Black's options are to accept the pawn sacrifice with 11...♘xe4, or to play 11...♘c6 and allow White to build a powerful centre. Either way, White is better.

In case of 9...bxa3 10.♖xa3 ♘c6 11.♘c3 e5, the second critical position is reached, which is also to White's advantage: 12.dxe5 dxe5 13.♘g5!? proves that 8...♖e8 is indeed a waste of time.

Exercises

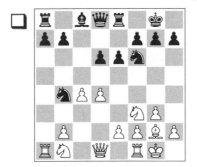

9.1 (1) Find the plan.
(solution on page 445)

9.1 (2) Find the plan.
(solution on page 445)

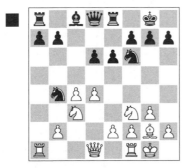

9.1 (3) Find the plan.
(solution on page 445)

Chapter 9.2

The Direct 8...♘c6

1.d4 e6 2.c4 ♗b4+ 3.♗d2 c5 4.♗xb4 cxb4 5.♘f3 ♘f6 6.g3 0-0 7.♗g2 d6 8.0-0 ♘c6

Here White has the choice between the energetic 9.a3 and 9.♘d2, which develops a piece, but is somewhat passive.

9.a3!
We have seen this strategically important move played on move 6, 7, and 8, and now on move 9 as well, after white completes the kingside development. We will first examine the alternatives:

A) **9.♘bd2**

This is a logical developing move, but with a downside: the white queen surrenders the control of the d4-square, which gives Black greater chances to force the opponent to close the centre after the planned ...e6-e5.

A1) **9...e5 10.d5** With the knight on d2 White has no better options as 10.e3 is met with 10...♗f5!?=; and 10.dxe5 dxe5 gives Black a nice position thanks to the passive ♘d2. **10...♘b8** Now we examine three replies:

A11) **11.c5** Stopping Black from using c5 as the building-block for his strategy. However, Black is not without chances thanks to his mobile e5-pawn:

A111) **11...e4!** Black is burning all his bridges behind him! **12.♘g5 e3**

A1111) **13.♘de4 dxc5** Weaker is 13...exf2+? 14.♖xf2± Baryshpolets-Gavrilov, Pardubice 2009. **14.fxe3 ♘bd7 15.♘xf6+ ♘xf6 16.♕d3 h6 17.♘e4 ♘xe4 18.♕xe4 ♗d7 19.♕f4 ♕b6 20.b3 f6=** Both sides have weaknesses in their pawn formations, leading to a complicated and double-edged position, Gertners-Grasis, corr. 2010;

A1112) **13.fxe3 dxc5 14.♕c2** 14.♕b3 ♗g4 15.♖f2 ♘bd7 16.♘ge4 ♘xe4 17.♘xe4 ♕b6 18.♘d2 ♘e5 with equal play. **14...♘bd7 15.d6 h6 16.♘ge4 ♗g4 17.♖f3 b6 18.h3 ♘ge5 19.♖f2 ♗b7** and in this unusual position both sides have their chances, Rybka 2.3.1 mp-Rybka 2.3.1 mp, Internet 2007.

A112) **11...dxc5** is weak because **12.♘xe5** gives White faster development and the better pawn structure. **12...♖e8** Weaker is 12...♘xd5?! due to 13.♘b3 ♘c7 14.♕xd8 ♖xd8 15.♘xc5± with powerful activity orchestrated by White's minor pieces. **13.♘dc4** 13.♘d3±. **13...b5 14.♘c6 ♘xc6 15.dxc6 ♕e7 16.c7 bxc4 17.♗xa8 ♕xc7 18.♗f3±** Fauland-Radnetter, Vienna 2011.

A12) **11.a3** White picks the moment to play this thematic move when Black cannot respond with ...a7-a5. **11...♘a6 12.♘e1 ♗f5**

A simple move with a well-defined aim: Black wants to tempt his opponent into playing e2-e4, further weakening the dark squares. In addition, Black is ready to exchange his bishop for the knight, securing the important outpost on c5, with potential excursions to b4. For example:

A121) **13.♘d3 ♗xd3 14.exd3 ♕b6** and his control of the dark squares gives Black equal play, Rybka 2.0 Beta mp-Rybka 1.2f, Internet (blitz) 2006;

A122) **13.♘c2 bxa3 14.♖xa3 ♗xc2 15.♕xc2 ♘b4 16.♕c3 a5 17.e4 ♘d7 18.♖d1 b6 19.♘f1 ♘c5** and Black has the upper hand because the white bishop is inferior to the ♘c5;

A123) **13.e4 ♗g4 14.f3** After 14.♗f3 Black can exchange the bishops, or check whether White is in the mood for a draw after 14...♗h3 15.♗g2 ♗g4=. **14...♗d7=** and Black has achieved his goal of weakening the dark-square complex.

A13) **11.♘e1**

This is a standard response in this type of position. The knight makes way for the advance f2-f4 and aims for d3, from where it controls the key squares c5 and b4. Now:

A131) 11...a5 is a logical move: before placing the knight on a6, Black wants to prevent the b2-b4 push. **12.♘d3 ♘a6 13.a3 ♗f5** with the already seen scenario leading to the weakening of the dark squares (also possible is 13...bxa3 14.♖xa3 ♗d7= Petkevich-Terrieux, Stockholm 2009): **14.e4 ♗g4 15.f3** (Villavicencio Martinez-Narciso Dublan, Maspalomas 2000) and now Black had the chance to play **15...♗d7!?N** with chances for both sides;

A132) 11...♘a6 12.♘d3 ♖e8 12...♘d7 is met with 13.a3 ♕b6 14.axb4 ♘xb4 15.♕b3 ♘xd3 16.♕xb6 ♘xb6 17.exd3 ♗f5 18.♖a3±

and Black failed to maintain control of the b4- and c5-squares in Mulyar-Shulman, Wheeling 2013. **13.e4 ♕b6 14.a3 ♗g4** – see under 12.♘e1.

A2) 9...♖e8 also deserves attention, for example: **10.e4 e5 11.d5 ♘b8**

A21) 12.c5!? This thematic pawn sacrifice allows White to make progress and fight for the initiative. The idea behind this pawn sacrifice is to prevent the black knight from reaching c5.

12...dxc5 13.♕c2 ♘bd7 14.♘c4♟ and White has the compensation for the pawn, but not more;

A22) 12.♘e1 is harmless: **12...a5** (also possible is 12...♘a6 13.♘d3 ♕b6 14.a3 ♗g4⇄ with chances for both sides, Sachdev-Mastrovasilis, Gibraltar 2013) **13.♘d3 ♘a6** and now:

A221) 14.♕e2 ♕b6= Black has total control of the key squares c5 and b4, with exactly the type of the position he strives for, Kalantarian-Spiridonov, Issy les Moulineaux 1994;

A222) 14.a3 ♗g4!

This thematic move forces White to make concessions. Black's aim is to weaken the dark squares or to disrupt the coordination of his opponent's minor pieces. **15.f3** 15.♕c2 is not as strong: 15...♗e2 16.♖fe1 ♗xd3 17.♕xd3 ♘c5∓ and Black has a mighty knight on c5. **15...♗d7∞** The standard, well-known position has been reached, with chances for both sides, Novikov-J. Horvath, Hungary 1993.

B) 9.d5 This move is not without appeal as it wrecks the opponent's pawn structure, but it also closes the diagonal for the g2-bishop, and commits White to defending the d5-pawn. **9...exd5 10.cxd5 ♘e7!?** Now White has the choice between defending the pawn with 11.♘e1 or 11.♘h4, or give it away with 11.♕d4, taking aim at b4 and leaving Black with the weak pawn on d6:

B1) 11.♘e1 ♕b6 Also good is 11...♗d7 12.♘c2 ♕b6 13.♘e3 ♘f5 14.♘xf5 ♗xf5 15.♘d2 ♖ac8 16.♘b3 ♖fe8= and Black's activity easily compensates for the pawn structure defects, Vladimirov-Anand, Moscow 1989. **12.♘c2 ♖e8**

B11) 13.e4 ♘g6 14.♖e1 14.♕d4 ♘xe4 15.♕xb6 axb6 16.♖e1 b3 17.♖xe4 ♖xe4 18.♗xe4 bxc2 19.♗xc2 ♘e5=. **14...b3?!** Better is 14...♗d7N with equal chances, and Black maintaining active play. **15.axb3 ♕xb3 16.♘d2±** Jasnikowski-Zolnierowicz, Warsaw 1990;

B12) 13.♘e3 ♘f5 14.♘c4 ♕c7 15.♕d3 ♘d7 with good play for Black, Polugaevsky-Arnason, Akureyri 1988.

B2) 11.♘h4 ♗g4 11...♕b6 12.e4 ♗g4 13.♕b3 a5 14.h3 a4 15.♕d3 ♗d7 16.♖e1 ♖fc8∞ with chances for both sides, Leko-Naiditsch, Dortmund 2006. **12.h3 ♗d7 13.e4 ♕c8 14.♔h2 ♕c5∞** with a complicated position, Braun-Ilincic, Budapest 2006;

B3) 11.♕d4 ♘exd5 12.e4 ♘c7 13.♕xb4 ♘c6 14.♕a4 ♕b6! 14...d5 leads to an equal position after 15.exd5 (15.e5 ♘e4 16.♘c3 ♘xc3 17.bxc3 ♗e6= Van der Sterren-Kortchnoi, Wijk aan Zee 1987) 15...♘xd5 16.♘bd2 (16.♖d1 ♕f6=) 16...♕f6= Delchev-Guliev, Balagüer 2007. **15.♘bd2 ♗e6** 15...♕xb2= Kortchnoi. **16.♘c4 ♗xc4 17.♕xc4** and now:

B31) 17...♖ae8 18.♘h4 ♕xb2 19.♖ab1 ♕d4 20.♕xd4 ♘xd4 21.♖xb7 ♘xe4 22.♖xa7 d5= L.B. Hansen-Naiditsch, Novi Sad 2009;

B32) More logical is **17...♖fe8!**

18.♘h4 18.♘d2 ♖ac8∓; White was hoping to organize a siege of the potentially weak d6-pawn, but Black's activity more than compensates for it. **18...g6∓** Black has a clear advantage thanks to his more active pieces.

9...bxa3

White has three ways to get the pawn back. He is more active after 9...♗d7 10.d5 exd5 11.cxd5 ♘e7 12.axb4 ♘exd5 13.♘c3 ♘xc3 (13...♘xb4 14.♕xd6 ♘c6 15.♖fd1±) 14.bxc3 ♕c7 15.♕d4 ♗b5 16.♖fe1 a6 17.♘h4↑ with the idea of playing ♘f5, Otero Acosta-Macieja, Puebla 2013; and 9...♖e8 10.axb4 ♘xb4 11.e4! is covered in Chapter 9.3 under 9...♘c6.

10.♖xa3

The rook capture preserves c3 as the place for the knight.

A) 10.♘xa3 deserves attention, for example: **10...e5 11.♘b5** The aggressive 11.b4 is harmless: 11...e4 12.♘g5 ♗f5 13.b5 ♘e7= Werle-Antic, Rethymnon 2009. **11...♗g4** 11...a6 is a waste of time, as after 12.dxe5 dxe5 13.c5± White obtains a great outpost on d6, Nisipeanu-Iordachescu, Eforie Nord 2009. Now:

A1) 12.d5 ♘b4 13.♖xa7 ♖xa7 14.♘xa7 ♗d7 15.♕b3 ♕a5♔ with sufficient compensation for the pawn, Zhou Weiqi-Wang Yue, Danzhou 2011;

A2) The alternative is **12.h3 ♗h5?!** It is better to play 12...♗xf3N 13.♗xf3 e4 14.♗g2 a6 15.♘c3 ♖e8∞ with approximately equal play. **13.d5 ♘b4 14.♖xa7 ♖xa7 15.♘xa7±** Black no longer has the option of restricting the white knight with ...♗d7 and compensating the lack of a pawn, A, David-Galopoulos, Halkis 2010.

B) 10.bxa3?! White has no reason to close the a-file and split the pawns on the queenside, which indirectly weakens the c4-pawn, for example: **10...♗d7!? 11.♘c3 ♘a5=**

10...e5 11.♘c3

This is the right reaction to Black's activity in the centre: White brings his last undeveloped piece into play, maintaining the tension. This way White keeps the choice of either exchanging on e5 or closing the centre with d4-d5.

A) 11.h3

A1) 11...♖e8 12.e3 ♗f5 13.♘c3 a6 For 13...h6 see line A2, 11...♗f5. **14.♘h4** 14.dxe5!? dxe5 15.♕b3 ♕e7 16.g4 ♗g6 17.♖d1 ♖ad8 18.♘h4±. **14...♗d7 15.♘f3 ♖c8** 15...♗f5. **16.♕b1?!** Better is 16.dxe5 ♘xe5 17.♘xe5 dxe5 18.♕b3 ♕c7 19.♖d1±. **16...exd4 17.exd4 ♘b4 18.b3 b5 19.♘a2 a5**

∓ Cioara-Naiditsch, Plovdiv 2012;

A2) 11...♗f5!? 12.♘c3 h6 13.e3 ♖e8 14.♔h2 14.♕b3±. **14...♗g6?!** Better is 14...e4 15.♘d2 ♘b4∞ with chances for both sides. **15.♕b3±** Markus-Antic, Kavala 2009.

B) 11.d5 does not lead to an advantage for White after **11...♘b4 12.♘c3 ♕c7 13.♘d2 a5 14.♕b1 ♗d7 15.♖c1 b6=** and Black has full control of the c5 and b4 outposts, with good play, Sieciechowicz-Macieja, Warsaw 2012.

11...♗g4

Finishing the development of his minor pieces, and indirectly pressing against the d4-pawn. White can now fight for an advantage with 12.dxe5 or 12.h3; closing the centre with 12.d5 is not as strong.

11...♖e8 is covered under 8...♖e8.

12.dxe5!

The right move at the right time! This exchange simplifies the position and relieves the pressure on the d4-pawn, while White keeps strategic advantages like the strong light-squared bishop on the open h1-a8 diagonal and the potential knight sortie to d5.

A) **12.h3 ♗xf3 13.♗xf3 ♘xd4** 13...exd4 14.♘b5 ♕b6 15.♘xd6 ♘e5 16.♘f5!. **14.♗xb7 ♖b8 15.♗g2 ♖xb2 16.e3 ♘e6 17.♖xa7±** and Black has more weaknesses to defend than his opponent, Antic-Perunovic, Subotica 2008;

B) **12.d5** is the move that both sides need to assess with care. White chases the knight away and gains space, but at the same time closes the diagonal for his own light-squared bishop, and surrenders control of the c5-square. **12...♗xf3 13.♗xf3 ♘b4 14.♕d2 a5 15.♘b5** Or 15.♗g2 ♘d7 16.♘b5 ♘c5= Naumkin-Drasko, Arco 2012. **15...b6 16.♗g2 ♖c8∞** with chances for both sides. Dubov-Sandipan, Moscow 2012.

12...dxe5 13.♕b3

This is a simple and straightforward way for White to improve his position. The d1-square is freed for the as yet inactive rook on f1, while here the queen attacks the unprotected black pawn on b7.

13...♕e7

14.e3

White's domination on the central squares gives him an obvious advantage. Apart from d5, White now controls another important central square: d4.

In case of 14.♘d5 Black can equalize with 14...♘xd5 15.cxd5 ♗xf3 16.♕xf3 ♘d4 17.♕d3 a6 with the idea of playing ...♘b5 18.d6 ♕d7 (weaker is 18...♕xd6?! because of 19.e3 ♘b5 20.♗xb7 ♖ab8 21.♗xa6 ♕xd3 22.♖xd3 ♘c7 23.♗c4 ♖xb2 24.♖d7! ♘e6 25.♖a1±) 19.♖c3 ♖fd8 20.e3 ♘b5 21.♖c5 ♕xd6 22.♕xd6 ♘xd6 23.♖xe5 ♔f8 24.♖d1 ♖ac8 25.♖ed5 ♔e7 and the draw is not far away.

14...♖fd8 15.♖fa1

White threatens the unpleasant ♘d5. It is also good to immediately occupy the central square: 15.♘d5!? ♘xd5 16.cxd5 ♗xf3 17.♗xf3 ♘b4 18.♖fa1± and Black has problems because of the unstable knight on b4.

15...♗xf3 16.♗xf3 e4

Black is practically forced to limit the scope of the strong light-squared bishop, thus endangering his own e-pawn.

17.♗g2±

White keeps the threat of ♘d5 in the air, and maintains the pressure against his opponent's queenside pawns, Banikas-Amin, Khanty-Mansiysk 2010.

> ### Conclusion
>
> As you can see, the natural-looking 8...♞c6 does not prevent White from obtaining an advantage because of the simple but effective plan with which White activates his pieces on the queenside: 9.a3! bxa3 10.♖xa3 e5 and now 11.♞c3. Black completes the development of his forces with 11...♝g4, but when the d-file is opened with 12.dxe5 dxe5, followed by the active 13.♕b3, the initiative is firmly in White's hands.

Exercises

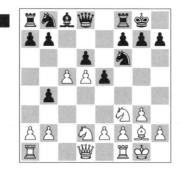

9.2 (1) Find the plan.
(solution on page 445)

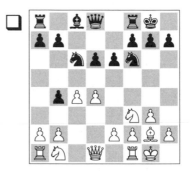

9.2 (2) Find the plan.
(solution on page 445)

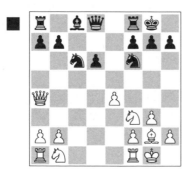

9.2 (3) Find the plan.
(solution on page 446)

Chapter 9.3

Strengthening b4: 8...a5

1.d4 e6 2.c4 ♗b4+ 3.♗d2 c5 4.♗xb4 cxb4 5.♘f3 ♘f6 6.g3 0-0 7.♗g2 d6 8.0-0 a5

This continuation is stronger than the frequently-played and natural-looking moves 8...♘c6 and 8...♖e8, and it represents the lifeline for the entire 3...c5 system. Black aims to first strengthen his important b4 outpost, and then decides on whether to attack the centre with ...e6-e5 or develop the queenside.

First we go back to the position after 6...0-0 and see what happens if White plays a2-a3 earlier.

7.♗g2

7.a3 is met with 7...♕c7! 8.♘bd2 and in this move order the a2-a3 advance loses its primary purpose because it fails to secure the c3-square for the knight: 8...bxa3 9.♖xa3 b6 10.♗g2 ♗b7 11.0-0 d6 12.b4 ♘c6 13.b5 (or 13.♕b1 a5 14.bxa5 ♘xa5 15.♖c1 h6 16.♖ac3 ♖fc8 with an equal position, Almeida Quintana-Uribe, Bogota 2012) 13...♘a5 14.♕a1 ♖fc8 15.♖c1 and in this even position the opponents agreed to a draw, Sosonko-Timman, Rotterdam 1997.

7...d6

This move is an integral part of all of Black's plans in the 3...c7-c5 system. Similar to 6.e3 variations, here Black also prepares the advance ...e6-e5.

193

8.0-0

It is possible to play **8.a3** instead, but after **8...bxa3 9.♖xa3 ♕c7 10.b3** Black has two rock-solid plans at his disposal:

A) **10...b6 11.0-0 ♗b7 12.♘c3 a6!?** This is a relatively new plan in this well-known and theoretically important position. Black builds a flexible pawn formation with the aim of advancing ...b6-b5 at the right opportunity, and eventually simplifying with ...♘e4. **13.♕d2 ♖c8 14.♖c1 ♘bd7 15.♖aa1 ♘e4 16.♘xe4 ♗xe4 17.♕f4 ♘f6 18.♘d2 ♗xg2 19.♔xg2 a5=** With the queens on the board and the flexible pawn structure, Black can successfully fight against his opponent's extra space, Gordon-Yakovenko, Legnica 2013;

B) Or the already covered plan with **10...♘c6 11.0-0 ♘b4 12.♕d2 a5 13.♘c3 ♖d8** 13...♗d7!? deserves attention, not disclosing the destination of the ♖f8 yet. In case of 14.e4 e5 15.♖aa1 ♖fe8 transposes into the position in the main line that has been covered under 9.a3. **14.♖aa1 ♗d7 15.♖fd1 ♖ac8 16.♖ac1 ♕b8 17.♖a1?!** It is better to play 17.e4!?±. **17...b5 18.cxb5 ♕b6 19.♖dc1 ♗xb5=** Zaltsman-Arnason, New York 1989.

8...a5!

White usually continues with queenside development with 9.a3, 9.♘bd2 or 9.♕d3.

9.a3

This unassuming but strategically important advance is there as a possibility since White's 6th move. It serves the double function of opening the a-file for the rook, and freeing the c3-square for the knight.

9.♘bd2 After 9.♕d3 the queen is on the right diagonal, but probably not on the right square. The c2-square looks like a safer and more natural choice. 9...b6!? is the simplest way to even the chances. Because of the awkward position of the white queen, there is no need for Black to prepare the blockading ...e6-e5 advance as in the 9. ♘bd2 variation. 10.a3 (10.e4 is an option, but Black easily equalizes with 10...♗b7 11.♘bd2 e5=; if 10.♘g5 d5=) 10...bxa3 11.♖xa3 ♗b7 12.♘e1 (12.♘c3 ♘c6=) 12...♗xg2 13.♔xg2 ♘c6= Thejkumar-Satyapragyan, Gurgaon 2010.

White places the knight on the modest d2-square, supporting the centre without exchanging the opponent's doubled b-pawn. White has the upper hand in the centre, so it is logical to seek an advantage by advancing one or more central pawns. For his part, Black needs to finish the development of his forces and neutralize White's central activity.

With this in mind, we look at two rather different plans:

1. Black continues with the development of his forces, preparing to meet the potential e2-e4-e5 thrust with 9...♕c7, 9...♖e8 or 9...♘c6, followed by ...e6-e5. As part of this strategy, Black keeps his bishop on the c8-square, looking for the opportunity to activate it on the h3-c8 diagonal.

2. Black immediately develops the light-squared bishop with 9...b6, al-

lowing his opponent to play e4-e5 and getting ready to undermine the white centre in hypermodern style.

A) **9...♛c7** It may seem unusual, but this early queen move is Black's best chance to equalize. It gives him extra control of the critical e5-square. White has a choice between three appealing continuations: 10.e4, 10.♖c1 and 10.♛c2. **10.e4** 10.♖c1 b6 11.e4 ♝b7 12.♖e1 e5 13.♘h4 (13.♘f1 is covered under 10.e4) 13...♘c6= Rychagov-Predojevic, Kavala 2009; 10.♛c2 ♘bd7 11.a3 (11.e4 e5=) 11...bxa3 12.♖xa3 b6 13.♖c3 ♝b7= Fier-Mekhitarian, Sao Paulo 2009. **10...e5!**

Black is blocking the most dangerous of White's central pawns, the one on e4, greatly reducing the mobility of the centre. The standard advance ...e6-e5 is more efficient in the systems in which White places his ♘b1 on d2, because for the time being Black is safe from the ♘d5 incursion.

Organizing this important strategic manoeuvre, which is possible via f1, is going to be time-consuming for White. Having the knight on d2 does not help when it comes to controlling the important squares d4 and c5 either.

On the other hand, you need to keep in mind that White dictates the play in this position. He has developed his forces,

and has a tad more control of the centre as he has an extra pawn there. Besides, the ♘d2 is patiently waiting for its chance to spring to life with c4-c5 and ♘c4, or with e2-e4-e5 and ♘e4. Black has yet to equalize.

11.♖c1 is a natural developing move. White aims to undermine the position of the black queen and gets ready to play c4-c5. Also possible is 11.c5 dxc5 12.dxe5 ♘g4∞ with an unclear position and chances for both sides, Lintchevski-Ovod, Plovdiv 2012. **11...b6**

Black strengthens his control of the key c5-square, while clearing b7 for the bishop.

A1) **12.♖e1!?** Rarely seen in practice, this natural move has the potential to make life difficult for Black. It is a useful developing move, which also clears f1 for the knight manoeuvre ♘f1-e3-d5. We examine three possibilities for Black: 12...♝b7, 12...♝g4 and 12...♘c6.

A11) **12...♝g4** Even though after **13.h3 ♝xf3 14.♘xf3 ♘c6 15.dxe5 dxe5 16.c5!** White does have some initiative thanks to the active ♖c1, still Black has the chance to completely neutralize White's initiative because of the rather inactive ♝g2;

A12) **12...♘c6** Black is actively developing his forces, but this move allows

White to activate the ♖c1 to a powerful effect: **13.c5! bxc5 14.dxc5 dxc5 15.♖xc5±** The rook is well-placed on c5 and White keeps a small edge;

A13) **12...♗b7 13.♘f1!?N** (13.♘h4 transposes to the game Rychagov-Predojevic, Kavala 2009, covered under 9...♕c7 10.♖c1) Transferring the knight to d5 is probably White's best bid for an advantage. It is surprising that we do not see this important position more often in practice. We will look into several possible continuations for Black. **13...♘bd7** Black completes the development of his forces by placing the knight on the somewhat passive d7-square, but intending to use the light-squared bishop to keep an eye on the critical d5- and e4-squares. If 13...♗xe4 14.♖xe4 ♘xe4 15.♘h4±; 13...♘c6 14.♘e3±; 13...♘xe4 14.♘e3±. **14.♘e3 ♗xe4 15.♘d5♗**

White's initiative is in full swing, but after the following more-or-less forced sequence we end up in an equal endgame: **15...♘xd5 16.cxd5 ♗xf3 17.♖xc7 ♗xd1 18.♖xd7 ♗g4 19.♖xd6 exd4 20.♖e4 ♗f5 21.♖xd4 ♖ab8!** The black rook defends the pawn and steers clear of the critical h1-a8 diagonal. **22.♖c6** 22.♗e4 ♗xe4 23.♖xe4 ♖fd8=. **22...♖fc8 23.d6** 23.♖dc4 ♔f8=. **23...♗e6=**

White is practically a pawn up because of his superior pawn structure, but is unable to stop Black from reducing the material and blocking the passed pawn.

A2) **12.h3** is a prophylactic move which unfortunately gives Black the time to complete his development and solve all his opening problems: **12...♗b7 13.♕e2 ♘bd7** Also good is the active 13...♘c6 14.d5 ♘b8⇄ and with the knight on c5 Black can look forward to a good middlegame. **14.♖fe1 ♖fe8 15.♕e3 ♖ac8=** Black has reached an equilibrium in the centre with well-positioned pieces. The position is equal, Raykin-Pavoni, ICCF email 2002.

B) **9...b6** and now:

B1) **10.e4 ♗b7 11.♖e1** For 11.♕c2 see 10.♕c2. **11...♕c7**:

B11) **12.h3** 12.♖c1 is covered under 10.♖c1. **12...e5 13.♖c1 ♘c6 14.♘f1** (Worek-Westerberg, Pardubice 2013), and now Black had the opportunity to play **14...♘e7!?N** with a satisfactory position since the white centre has been dealt with, and the potentially damaging ♘f1-e3-d5 manoeuvre is not easily applicable;

B12) Harmless is **12.e5 dxe5 13.dxe5 ♘fd7** and now: **14.♕c2** 14.♘e4 ♗xe4 (14...♘xe5? 15.♘xe5 ♕xe5 16.♘d6+−) 15.♖xe4 ♘c6=. **14...h6 15.♘e4 ♗xe4** It is possible to munch the offered pawn with 15...♘xe5!? 16.♘xe5 ♕xe5 17.♖ad1 ♕c7∞ and White has difficulty proving that he has enough for the pawn. **16.♕xe4 ♘c6 17.♘g5 hxg5 18.♕xc6 ♕xc6 19.♗xc6 ♖ad8 20.♖ad1 ♘c5** with a good endgame for Black.

B2) **10.♕c2** White places the queen on the b1-h7 diagonal, in support of the advance e2-e4-e5 and possibly ♘g5. We examine 10...♗b7, which allows White to advance the e-pawn, and 10...♕c7, which immediately takes aim at the e5-square.

B21) **10...♗b7** Now the e-pawn is heading for Black's half of the board in anticipation of a kingside attack: **11.e4**

Seeing no obstacles in front of the e-pawn, White springs into action. There are only a few games with this variation, but because of the strategic significance of the position, we look into 11...♘c6, 11...♘fd7 and 11...♕c7,

and we also examine the theoretical novelty 11...♘bd7!?N.

B211) **11...♘c6**

12.e5 A better move is 12.d5!?. Here's an example of how White effectively uses his d-pawn to obtain an advantage: 12...♘e5 13.♘xe5 dxe5 14.♖fd1 with a small edge for White. **12...dxe5 13.dxe5 ♘d7 14.♖fe1 ♘c5** with equality, Koch-Saiboulatov, Belgium 2003;

B212) **11...♘fd7?!** This flexible move neutralizes White's main threat, the e4-e5 advance, but leads to a somewhat passive position. It is hard to develop counterplay in this position where White has a space advantage, a powerful centre and better piece development. **12.e5** White has no reason to be hasty. It is better to first place the rooks optimally on the d-file and the e-file, or to activate the rook with a2-a3. (12.♖ad1±). **12...dxe5 13.♘xe5** 13.dxe5 ♘c6⇄ is covered under 11...♘c6. **13...♗xg2 14.♔xg2 ♘xe5 15.dxe5 ♘c6 16.♘f3 ♘d4 17.♕e4** and in this equal position the players agreed to a draw in Haba-Stocek, Lazne Bohdanec 1999;

B213) **11...♕c7?** This move is now a mistake due to **12.e5 dxe5 13.dxe5 ♘fd7 14.♘g5!±** and Black loses control over the dark squares, for example **14...g6 15.♗xb7 ♕xb7 16.f4**;

197

B214) 11...♘bd7!?N Although it is a quite natural way to finish the development, this move has so far not been tested in practice. **12.e5** With no obstacles in the way, White's centre springs to life. **12...dxe5 13.dxe5 ♘g4** Everything now hangs on how successful the attack is. White will either succeed in pressing against the kingside, or be forced to defend his compromised centre. **14.♖ad1** No advantage is offered by 14.h3 ♘gxe5 15.♘xe5 ♗xg2 16.♘xf7 ♖xf7 17.♔xg2 ♘c5= with the idea of playing ...♕d3. Black has a weaker pawn structure, but more active pieces, which in this simple endgame is enough for equality.

How can Black respond now? White has an active rook on the d-file, the e5-pawn is indirectly protected, and h2-h3 threatens to condemn the black knight into passivity. To shed light on this important position, we analyse several continuations, depicting the strengths and weaknesses of the central pawn formation.

B2141) 14...♖b8! Finding this strong defensive move over the board is not an easy task, having in mind that the queen remains in the vis-à-vis with the ♖d1. **15.♘e4 ♕e7 16.♘eg5** 16.♘fg5?! ♘dxe5 17.♘xh7 ♖fd8∓. **16...g6 17.♖fe1 ♘c5 18.h3 ♘h6** Weaker is

18...♘xe5 19.♖xe5 f6 20.♖xc5 bxc5 21.♘e4±. **19.g4 f6 20.exf6 ♕xf6** with equal chances in a position in which both sides have weaknesses to defend;

B2142) 14...♕e7 The queen and the rook are no longer on the same file, and Black maintains the control of the important g5-square, but it appears that White still has some initiative. For instance: **15.♖fe1 ♖ad8 16.h3 ♘h6** The black knight is temporarily out of action, allowing White to fight for an advantage with **17.♘b3** or **17.♘e4**;

B2143) 14...♕c7 Abandoning the g5-square in order to win the e5-pawn is a risky proposition: **15.♘g5 g6 16.♗xb7 ♕xb7 17.♘de4 ♘dxe5** 17...♘gxe5? is a mistake. White's attack gains in strength thanks to some lovely tactical opportunities:

18.♕e2! (with the idea f2-f4) 18...♖ad8 19.f4 ♘c6 20.f5! exf5 21.♖xf5! ♕c7 22.♖xf7!.

And White wins.

18.h3 18.♕e2♔. **18...f6 19.♘xe6** 19.hxg4 fxg5 20.♘xg5 ♕e7=. **19...♖fe8 20.♘d4 ♖ad8 21.hxg4 ♖xd4 22.♘xf6+ ♔f8=**;

B2144) 14...♘gxe5? 15.♘xe5 ♗xg2 16.♘xd7 ♗xf1 17.♘xf1+−

B22) 10...♕c7!?N Black is in no hurry to play ...♗b7, and prepares to block the e-pawn should White advance with e2-e4. In addition, the black queen is safer on the c-file compared to the variations after 10.♖c1. We will examine 11.e4 and 11.♘g5.

B221) 11.e4 e5 Black has no problems whatsoever in this type of position, because the two most dangerous plans for White, transferring the knight to d5 and c4-c5, are both incompatible with having the queen on c2. For instance: **12.♖fe1 ♘c6 13.♖ac1** 13.dxe5 dxe5 14.c5 ♗g4=. **13...♗g4=**;

B222) 11.♘g5!? ♗b7 11...♖a7!?. **12.♗xb7 ♕xb7 13.♘de4 ♘xe4 14.♕xe4** 14.♘xe4 ♕e7=. **14...♕xe4 15.♘xe4 ♖d8 16.♖ac1 ♔f8** with a somewhat passive, but defensible endgame.

C) 9...♖e8

Similar to the 9...♕c7 variation, Black is getting ready to halt the advancing e-pawn, but here he keeps the option of placing the queen on b6. This strategy works well if White continues with the central push 10.e4, but it is ineffective against the clever 10.♖c1!. In this case, White gets the advantage by exploiting his opponent's slow development:

C1) 10.e4 As stated, with the rook on e8 this plan is not the best that White can come up with. **10...e5**

An important middlegame position with the typical central pawn structure has been reached.

C11) 11.h3 ♘c6 12.d5 ♘b8 13.a3 ♘a6 14.♘e1 ♕b6 15.♘d3 ♘d7= We have seen this before: as soon as White closes the centre with d4-d5, Black obtains the important outpost on c5 and gets counterplay by utilizing the dark squares, Flumbort-Ilincic, Budapest 2012;

C12) 11.a3 bxa3!N 11...♘a6 12.c5!± Iskusnikh-Khachatryan, Yerevan 2004. **12.bxa3** It is risky to play 12.♖xa3?! because of 12...♘c6 13.d5 ♘b4↑ and Black has the nice b4-square for his knight, and a comfortable position to play thanks to his domination on the dark squares. **12...♗g4 13.♕b3 ♘bd7=** (13...b6=);

C13) 11.c5 exd4N 11...dxc5 12.dxe5 ♘fd7 13.♘c4 with a clear advantage for White, Purtseladze-l'Ami, Istanbul 2005. **12.cxd6 ♗g4 13.e5** 13.♖e1?! ♘c6∓. **13...♖xe5 14.♘c4 ♖e8 15.♕xd4 ♘c6 16.♕d2 ♗e6=**;

C14) 11.d5 This move leads to Black's favourite set-up. White secures extra space for himself, but surrenders the important c5-square and the mobility of his d-pawn. **11...♘a6 12.♘e1 ♘c5 13.♕e2 ♕b6** The position is approximately equal. Thanks to his superior control of the dark squares, Black enjoys easier play, Mladenovic-Bogdanovski, Paracin 2013;

C15) 11.♖e1 ♗g4 12.h3 ♗xf3 13.♘xf3 ♘c6= with the idea ...♕b6.

C2) 10.♖c1!

C21) 10...b6 11.c5!? This is not the only option, but it is sufficient for an advantage. **11...bxc5 12.dxc5 ♖a6** With 12...d5 Black closes the diagonal, restricting the activity of the opponent's light-squared bishop, and takes away the potentially powerful c4 outpost from the white knight. On the downside, White now has the passed pawn on c5: 13.♘d4!↑; 12...dxc5 13.♘b3±. **13.♕b3±** (Shulman-Ivanov, St. Louis 2011) More challenging is 13.♘c4!?N dxc5 14.♕xd8 ♖xd8 15.♖fd1♔ and Black is under intense pressure;

C22) 10...e5 With the underdeveloped queenside and without the white pawn on e4, this thematic move is insufficient for equality. **11.dxe5 dxe5 12.c5 ♕e7** 12...e4?! 13.♘g5 e3 14.♘de4± with a clear advantage for White due to the obvious difference in development and activity. **13.♘c4±** Shulman-Mertens, Reykjavik 2012.

D) 9...♘c6 This is a natural developing move, but in this case it is insufficient for equality. In this particular position it is hard for Black to neutralize White's faster development and strong centre, while having to recalculate after every move what happens if White plays d4-d5 or c4-c5.

Black's best bet is to postpone the development of his knight and wait for the opponent to commit before reacting. The black knight is of great importance for maintaining activity on the queenside and for keeping White at bay. The knight can be placed on c6 to press against the centre, or utilize the dark squares b4 and c5 via ...♘a6 or ...♘d7.

10.♖c1 ♕e7 Black is getting ready to play ...e6-e5 by placing the queen on e7 instead of c7, thus avoiding the vis-à-vis with the ♖c1. However, after **11.♕c2!±** (11.e4 e5⇄; 11.c5 dxc5 12.dxc5 ♖d8!⇄; 11.h3 ♖d8 12.e4 e5⇄ Garmendez Gonzalez-Cordova, Mexico City 2012) it is hard to suggest an acceptable plan for Black. For example: **11...e5** 11...b6 12.♖fd1!± with the idea to play d4-d5. **12.d5 ♘b8 13.c5±** and Black fails to sufficiently control the c5-square.

9...♘a6

This is the main point behind Black's plan which started with 8...a5. Black does not have to resolve the tension as in the chapters 9.1 and 9.2, because his knight is ready to occupy the b4-square.

10.axb4

White compromises, so that he can finish his piece development on the queenside, allowing the black knight to land on b4.

With White's last move in mind, it is not consistent to give up the fight for the c3-square and play **10.♘bd2 ♕c7**. The c7-square is probably the optimal place for the queen. It keeps e5 under tabs, and also allows the ♗c8 to come to life with ...b7-b6 and ...♗b7.

A) 11.axb4 makes Black's job easier. Since White has already committed the knight to d2, there is no need to let the black knight occupy b4 in a hurry: 11...♘xb4 12.♖c1 b6 13.♘e1 ♗b7 14.♗xb7 and the opponents agreed to a draw in Shankland-Shulman, Arlington 2013. After 14...♕xb7 the position is completely equal;

B) 11.♕c2 ♗d7 12.♖ac1 ♖ac8 with mutual chances, Cifuentes Parada-Granda Zuniga, Rio Hondo 1987.

C) **11.♖c1** and now:

C1) **11...b6 12.♘e1 ♗b7 13.♗xb7 ♕xb7 14.axb4 ♘xb4 15.♘c2** and in this equal position, the players agreed to a draw, Nanu-Berescu, Baille Olanesti 2010;

C2) Also possible is **11...♖d8!? 12.♘e1** (12.♘g5!?) **12...e5 13.♘d3** (13.e3!? ♗g4=) **13...♗f5 14.e4 ♗g4**. As seen before, this dance of the black bishop aims to weaken the dark squares in White's camp even more, or to disrupt the harmonious development of White's minor pieces.

15.f3 ♗d7 Mission accomplished – the bishop retreats to its natural destination, d7. **16.axb4 ♘xb4 17.♘xb4 axb4 18.♕b3 ♕b6 19.c5 dxc5 20.♘c4 ♕a7 21.dxe5 ♘e8** and Black enjoys a slight edge thanks to his mobile and potentially dangerous queenside majority.

10...♘xb4 11.♘c3

In this theoretically important position, we examine the following moves for Black: 11...b6!?, 11...d5?!, 11...♗d7?! and 11...♕c7!?.

11...b6

Played in the spirit of the Queen's Indian! In the variations with 6.e3, where White puts the bishop on the f1-a6 diagonal, we've praised the activity of Black's 'Queen's Indian' bishop on b7. What happens when both White and Black go for the fianchetto? Can the ♗b7 successfully oppose White's ♗g2? Black has something entirely different on his mind. He does not care about

201

neutralising the activity of the ♗g2, but develops his bishop to a6, putting pressure on the sensitive c4-pawn.

A) **11...d5** is inconsistent: **12.♘e5 b6 13.cxd5** 13.♖c1±. **13...♘fxd5 14.e4 ♘e7 15.d5±** Melkumyan-Berescu, Albena 2013;

B) **11...♗d7** is too slow: **12.e4±** Black has no time to block the e4-pawn with ...e6-e5. Besides, the ♗d7 is rather passive, diminishing the pressure that Black exerts on the central squares;

C) **11...♕c7** Despite the fact that the MegaBase 2013 only lists two games with this move, we are of the opinion that this queen move is solid, and that it gives Black realistic chances to equalize. The queen attacks the pawn on c4, and also supports the ...e6-e5 push.

C1) **12.b3** Now Black gets good practical chances with 12...♗d7 or 12...♖d8:

C11) **12...♗d7**

13.e4 e5 In this position we take a close look at three possible continuations for white: 14.dxe5, 14.h3 and 14.♕d2.

C111) **14.dxe5 dxe5 15.♘d5 ♘fxd5 16.exd5 ♖ad8** With a double-edged position. White's passed pawn is strong, but several important dark squares are under Black's control;

C112) **14.h3 ♖fe8 15.♕d2** 15.♕e2 leads to an interesting possibility for Black: 15...exd4 16.♘xd4 d5⇄

with chances for both sides.
15...♖ad8 16.♖fd1 ♕b6 17.♖ac1 ♗c6 18.♖e1 h6∞ Even though White still enjoys a spatial advantage, Black compensates for this with his active pieces;

C113) **14.♕d2 ♖fe8** To 14...♗g4 with the idea of playing ...♘c6 and pressing against the d4-pawn, White can respond with 15.♘e1 ♘c6 16.♘c2± and keep the better control of the centre and, with it, a small edge.

C1131) **15.♖fc1!?N** deserves attention, with the idea of obtaining control along the c-file after the possible exchange of the knight on d5. For example: **15...h6** Weaker is 15...♗c6 16.dxe5 dxe5 17.♘d5 ♗xd5 18.cxd5 ♕b6 19.♖c4±. **16.dxe5 dxe5 17.♘d5 ♘bxd5 18.cxd5 ♕b6** with approximately equal chances;

C1132) **15.♖fe1 ♖ad8** Black is anticipating the birth of a passed d-pawn after the knight exchange on d5. **16.♘d5** 16.h3!?. **16...♘fxd5 17.cxd5** 17.exd5 f6∞. **17...♗g4!?** Black wants to exchange his bishop so that he could have better control of the central squares e5 and d4. 17...f6∞ is worth considering. It leads to a complex position with chances for both sides. **18.♖ec1** Or 18.dxe5 ♗xf3 19.♗xf3 ♖xe5∞ with plenty of activity for Black. **18...♕b6 19.dxe5 ♗xf3 20.♗xf3 ♖xe5** with chances for both sides.

Black has well-positioned, active pieces and good play on the dark squares.

C12) **12...♖d8**

With this move Black wants to save a tempo for his light-squared bishop and place it on g4 after the thematic ...e6-e5. However, the more natural place for the rook is on the e-file, especially after the planned ...e6-e5.

13.e4 A weaker option is 13.♕c1 ♗d7 14.♖d1 h6 15.♕b2 ♗c6 16.♖ac1 ♕e7= Fernandez Rivero-Ortega, Havana 2013. **13...e5 14.h3!** White prevents the liberating move 14...♗g4, and maintains the tension in the centre. After 14.♕d2 ♗g4 15.♖fe1 (15.♘e1 ♕b6=) 15...♘c6= Black has brought to fruition one of the main ideas of the opening, and has a good position. **14...♗d7 15.♕e2 ♖e8 16.♖fd1 ♖ac8 17.♖ac1±** and with his well-supported centre and extra space for his forces, White has a slightly

better position, Ju Wenjun-Emelin, St Petersburg 2009;

C13) It is too early for **12...e5** because of the weak d6-square: **13.dxe5 dxe5 14.♘b5±** followed by ♕d6 and Black is in difficulties.

C2) In the recent game Meier-Anand, Baden-Baden 2013, White offered a pawn on c4 with **12.♖c1**.

It is perfectly OK to accept the pawn sacrifice with 12...♕xc4!? 13.♘e4 ♕a6 14.♘xf6+ gxf6 15.♕d2∞ even though the attack on the weakened kingside gives White some compensation. But the former World Champion responded with the simple developing move **12...♗d7**, which led to an equal game after **13.♘d2 ♖fd8**. Here Black has the opportunity to test the new strategic idea. Since White has not locked in his light-squared bishop with e2-e4, Black postpones the topical ...e6-e5, maintaining the flexible pawn structure in the centre, and keeping the option of closing the diagonal with ...d6-d5. **14.♘de4 ♘e8** 14...♘xe4!? also deserves attention: 15.♘xe4 ♖ac8 16.♕d2 h6 17.b3 ♕b8 18.♕f4 ♗e8= with the idea of playing ...d6-d5. **15.b3 ♕b6 16.e3 d5!** Thanks to his flexible pawn formation, Black has the option of continuing in the spirit of the Closed Catalan by shutting down the diagonal for the ♗g2.

17.♘c5 ♗c6 18.♘5a4 ♕c7 19.c5 ♘f6
The knight moves to d7, which will lead to full equality as soon as ...b7-b6 is played. **20.♖e1 ♘d7 21.♗f1 b6 22.cxb6 ♘xb6 23.♘xb6 ♕xb6**

with an even position.

The idea 11...b6 has been seen in only a few practical games. Nevertheless, we will examine four possible continuations for White: 12.♘e5, 12.♘e1, 12.♘a2 and 12.e4.

12.♘e5

A) **12.♘e1 d5 13.♘c2** 13.cxd5 ♘fxd5 14.♘d3 ♘xd3 15.♕xd3 ♗a6 16.♕d2 ♘xc3 17.bxc3 ♖c8 18.♖fb1 ♕c7 19.e3 and the players agreed to a draw in this equal position, Dzindzichashvili-Christiansen, Long Beach 1993. **13...♗a6 14.♘e3 ♗b7=** and the position is completely even, Jumabaev-Akopian, Moscow 2012;

B) **12.♘a2** This simplification only brings the game closer to a draw.

12...♘xa2 13.♖xa2 ♗a6 14.b3 ♖c8 15.♖c2 d5!? 16.♘e5 ♕d6= The black bishop is not inferior to its ♗g2 counterpart. The position is equal, with chances for both sides, Medvegy-Chatalbashev, Zalakaros 2008;

C) **12.e4?!** weakens the white centre because of **12...♗a6 13.b3** (or 13.e5 ♘e8∓) **13...d5∓** and Black's light-squared bishop is more dangerous than its colleague on g2.

The text is a direct attempt to refute Black's strategy by utilizing the diagonal that is currently under White's control. However, Black has a way to neutralize his opponent's initiative.

12...♖b8
Weaker is **12...dxe5 13.dxe5** (13.♗xa8 does not work because of 13...exd4 14.♘b5 e5 15.♗g2 ♕e7 16.♕d2 ♗e6 17.b3 ♘d7 18.e3 ♘c5 19.♕b2 dxe3 20.fxe3 ♕g5∓ with strong compensation for the minor material loss, Kunte-Kasimdzhanov, Pune 2004) **13...♖b8** (similarly, 13...♖a7 14.exf6 ♕xf6 15.♕d6± leads to a powerful initiative for White on the queenside, Zlotnik-Gomez Jurado, Naron 1993) **14.exf6 ♕xf6** (Schüler-Smith, Pardubice 2010) and now White had the opportunity to take control of the d-file with **15.♕d6!N** and put his opponent's queenside under heavy pres-

sure. For instance: **15...♗a6** Or 15...♗b7 16.♗xb7 ♖xb7 17.♖fd1±. **16.c5 ♖fd8 17.♕c7 bxc5** 17...♖dc8?! 18.♕a7±. **18.♖xa5±**

13.♘d3

13.♘c6 leads to complete equality after 13...♘xc6 14.♗xc6 ♗a6 15.♕a4 d5=.

13...♘xd3

13...d5!?N deserves attention: 14.cxd5 (14.♘xb4 axb4 15.♘a2 dxc4 16.♘xb4 ♗b7=) 14...♘fxd5 15.♘xd5 ♘xd5= and Black brings the bishop to a6 or b7 with an about equal position.

14.♕xd3

With 14.exd3 White wants to strengthen the potentially weak c4-pawn, but it spoils the pawn formation in the centre: 14...♗d7 15.♖e1 ♖e8 16.♕d2 ♕c7 17.♖ac1 ♗c6 18.♘e4 ♗xe4 and even though Black repairs the opponent's pawn structure, his extra control of the dark squares and the possibility of closing the central h1-a8 diagonal for the white bishop are guarantees for good play: 19.dxe4 e5=.

14...♗a6 15.b4 ♕c7 16.♘b5 ♗xb5

16...♕d7= with the idea of playing ...d6-d5.

17.cxb5 axb4 18.♗c6 d5 19.♖fb1 ♕e7 20.♖a4 ♘e4 21.♖axb4 ♕f6

A better option is 21...f5!?. Black wants to play ...f5-f4 and launch an attack on the white king. This move also prevents f2-f3 followed by e2-e4, which occurred in the game and brought the awkwardly placed light-squared bishop back into play. White can win the control of the a-file, but in that case Black obtains strong counterplay on the kingside, thanks to his highly mobile knight and the fact that the white bishop is cut off from protecting its king.

For example: 22.f3 ♘d6 23.e3 h5 24.♖a4 h4↑ with a strong kingside initiative.

22.f3 ♘d6 23.♖a4 h5 24.e4 ♕g6∞

Black has some counterplay to compensate for the lost a-file, but after managing to carry through e2-e4 White has every reason to feel optimistic, Kunte-Moiseenko, Montreal 2006.

Conclusion

In this chapter we have examined a promising strategy for Black, which commences with supporting the important b4 outpost with 8...a5. The first critical position is reached after 9.a3 ♘a6 10.axb4 ♘xb4 11.♘c3. As the best and simplest solution for Black, we advocate developing the light-squared bishop with 11...b6. The bishop is well placed on a6, and in combination with ...d7-d5 gives the position the nature of a Closed Catalan, with equal chances for both sides.

The second critical position arises after 9.♘bd2, after which we suggest 9...♕c7 for Black. This continuation supports ...e6-e5, which is the key advance after White pushes his e-pawn. Black then goes for the fianchetto, and places his knight on c6 or d7, depending on what his opponent does.

The verdict for the entire 3...c5 system: playing 3...c5 and ending up with the pawn on b4, away from the centre, is an unusual strategy, but as practice shows, it is fully justified.

In Chapter 9.3 we have examined the strategy that is most frequently used by the leaders of the white pieces:

1. Going for the fianchetto in combination with placing the knight on c3. As the best option for Black, we recommend strengthening the b4 outpost with 8...a5, and developing the bishop on b7 or a6. The knight on c3 forces Black to keep his e-pawn on e6 for better control of the d5-square.

2. If the knight goes to d2 in combination with the e2-e4 advance, Black obtains a nice position by placing the queen on c7 and playing for ...e6-e5, taking into account that the white knight cannot easily reach the weakened d5-square. In Chapters 6, 7, and 8 the white bishop is placed on d3 or on e2, and its black counterpart reigns supreme on the central diagonal. For this reason, it is a good idea to go for the fianchetto. Similarly to other positions in which White advances his e-pawn, the best response for Black is to block the centre with ...e6-e5. Apart from stopping the advance of White's potentially dangerous e-pawn, the black e5-pawn attacks the d4-pawn. This often forces White to relieve the tension, either by dxe5 or by playing d4-d5, which takes the mobility out of his central formation and clears an excellent outpost, c5, for the black knight.

The 3...c7-c5 system is a paradox. Its unusual nature causes many strong players, as well as chess-playing programs, to err when analysing it and when encountering it over-the-board. The system is rich in strategic plans, hypermodern in nature, and has no shortage of tactical possibilities and beautiful combinations.

Compared to the 'tabiyas' of modern chess, 3...c7-c5 is a rarely seen guest. This gives it a special appeal in this era of computers and rapid theoretical advances, which threaten original thinking. For young players, this system paves the way towards great tournament results, and helps them develop their own original approach to modern opening theory.

Exercises

9.3 (1) Find the plan.
(solution on page 446)

9.3 (2) Find the plan.
(solution on page 446)

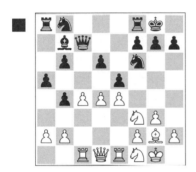

9.3 (3) Find the plan.
(solution on page 446)

Section III

The Eingorn System: 3...a5

1.d4 e6 2.c4 ♗b4+ 3.♗d2 a5

This is the Accelerated Bogo-Indian, or, as some authors rightly call it, the Eingorn System, since grandmaster Viacheslav Eingorn made the greatest contribution to the development of this not so rare variation. What is in fact the idea of this system, in which Black defends the bishop on b4 with the a-pawn and postpones the natural development of his king's knight?

Black defends the bishop with the a-pawn, hoping for an exchange on b4, when he could activate his rook along the a-file and disable the development of the white queen's knight on the c3-square. This system seems to work better in comparison with the 3...c5 system, since here the rook's pawn is used, which has lower strategic value in the opening due to its distance from the centre.

This way Black can save the c-pawn for the battle in the centre. By postponing the development of the king's knight, Black saves a tempo and uses it for his d-pawn, in order to be able to act more quickly in the centre. It has to be emphasized that Black often opts for the regular Bogo-Indian, choosing the right moment for ...♘g8-f6, which is also one of the ideas of the system we are analysing. Contrary to the opponent's idea, White usually tends to force the opponent to exchange or retreat the bishop on b4.

Chapter 10

The Accelerated Bogo: Deviations

In Chapter 10 we will analyse a few not very frequent continuations: 4.♘c3 and 4.e4.

4.♘c3

White aims for a Nimzo-Indian type position with ♗d2 and ...a7-a5 inserted, where the main idea is to gain the bishop pair with a2-a3. Although we often end up in the positions that we have analysed under 4.♘f3 ♘f6 5.♘c3, both sides can opt for other, more original paths.

Black has a wide choice of options, but we will focus on the natural 4...♘f6

and the not so usual 4...d6 or 4...d5, which Black uses to bring about original positions.

4.e4 It is not unusual that White places all three central pawns on the fourth rank so early. In the system with 1...e6 Black often allows the opponent to create a full centre in order to block or attack it with the typical pawn attacks ...e6-e5, ...d7-d5 or ...c7-c5.

We will look at two appropriate ways of neutralizing the white centre: A) 4...d5 and B) 4...d6!.

A) **4...d5!?** A typical move to break up the white centre or exchange the central pawns.

A1) **5.cxd5 exd5 6.e5** With the exchange on d5, White eliminates the possibility of creating a weakness on the d-file, but pays for it by opening a diagonal for the black light-squared bishop. **6...♘e7**:

A11) **7.♘c3 c5** A good option is 7...0-0 8.♗d3 (8.a3 ♗xc3 9.bxc3 c5 10.h3 ♘bc6 11.♘f3 ♗f5 12.♗e2 ♗e4) 8...♗f5 Nikolic-Larsen, Niksic 1983. **8.a3 ♗xc3 9.bxc3** White manages to maintain the stability of his centre, but now has an important strategic task to prevent the exchange of light-squared bishops, which would considerably weaken his light squares. **9...♘bc6 10.♗b5** 10.♗e3 0-0 11.♗d3 ♗f5=. **10...♕b6 11.♕a4 ♗d7** A good option is 11...0-0 12.♘e2 ♘f5=. **12.♖b1 0-0=** And Black manages to complete the opening stage successfully, Alexandrov-Roiz, Warsaw 2005;

A12) It is risky to play **7.♘f3 c5 8.a3 ♗xd2+ 9.♘bxd2 cxd4 10.♗d3 ♘bc6 11.0-0 h6** 11...a4!?. **12.♖e1 ♕b6 13.♖b1 0-0∞**. White will have problems to prove compensation for the pawn, Graf-Hillarp Persson, Benidorm 2003.

A2) In case of **5.e5 ♘e7 6.♘f3 ♘bc6!?∞** Black increases the pressure on the d4-pawn. Also a good option is 6...c5!?⇄, after which the white centre does not pose any threats. **7.♗c3** 7.♘c3 dxc4 8.♘b5 ♗xd2+ 9.♕xd2 ♗d7 10.♗xc4 ♘b4 11.0-0 ♗c6= with a comfortable position for Black. **7...b6 8.cxd5 ♘xd5 9.♗d3 ♗a6 10.♗xa6 ♖xa6 11.0-0 ♗e7 12.♘bd2 ♖a8 13.♖e1 ♕d7=** Sapunov-Ibragimov, Moscow 1999;

A3) **5.a3!** The only continuation that enables White to continue fighting for an advantage. **5...♗xd2+ 6.♘xd2** and now:

A31) **6...♘c6 7.♘gf3 ♘ge7 8.♗e2 0-0 9.0-0 dxe4 10.♘xe4 ♘f5 11.d5 exd5 12.cxd5 ♘ce7 13.♘c3 c6 14.dxc6 ♘xc6 15.♕xd8** This exchange leads to a draw. A better option is 15.♗c4! ♘d6 16.♗a2± and White is slightly better thanks to the good coordination of his pieces. **15...♖xd8 16.♖ad1 ♗e6 17.♖xd8+ ♖xd8 18.♖d1 ♖xd1+ 19.♗xd1** The players agreed to a draw in this equal position, Bagirov-Eingorn, Minsk 1983;

A32) **6...dxe4 7.♘xe4 ♘f6 8.♘c3 0-0 9.♘f3 ♕e7** Neither is the position completely equal after 9...b6 10.♗e2 ♗b7 11.0-0 ♘bd7 12.♖e1 ♘e4 13.♘xe4 ♗xe4 14.♗d3 ♗xd3 15.♕xd3 a4 16.♖ad1± Summerscale-Ward, Swansea 1995. **10.♗e2 ♖d8 11.♕c2 c5 12.dxc5 ♕xc5** 12...♘a6 13.0-0 ♘xc5 14.♖ad1 ♗d7 15.♖fe1 h6 16.h3 ♗e8 17.♘d4± with a more active position for White. **13.0-0 ♘c6 14.♖ad1 ♗d7 15.♘a4 ♕e7 16.♗d3 ♗e8 17.♖fe1±** White has the initiative, Danielian-Pähtz, Wijk aan Zee 2012;

A33) For **6...♘e7 7.♘gf3 ♘bc6** see under 6...♘c6.

B) **4...d6!**

Black wants to block the opponent's e-pawn with ...e6-e5 and attack the most vulnerable central pawn on d4, which, because of the bishop on d2, is difficult to defend. So, in the end, White will be forced to close the centre with d4-d5 or to exchange with dxe5.

B1) **5.♘f3 ♘f6 6.♕c2** 6.♗d3 e5= 7.dxe5?! dxe5 8.♘xe5 ♕d4∓; 6.e5 dxe5 7.dxe5 ♘e4=. **6...e5!=**

And now we have a typical scenario which is often seen in the King's Indian. The white pawn on e4 is blocked, and the central pawn on d4 will be exchanged or will lose mobility if White opts for d4-d5.

Of course, we should keep in mind that the events in the centre are not isolated from the other events on the board. If the dark-squared bishops hadn't been exchanged, the situation in the centre would have been completely different.

It is known that in the King's Indian, White successfully supports the trio in the centre with the dark-squared bishop, regardless whether the trio is mobile with the white pawn on d4 or blocked with the white pawn on d5.

7.dxe5 This exchange is usually a strategic mistake in this type of pawn structure, as White loses control of the d4-square, and it is rarely seen except in such positions in which the d5-square

or the d-file can be used. With 7.d5 White uses the full centre to expand his space, but the weakness on c5 will be a more important factor, since the black bishop will be activated next, completing Black's development. 7...♗g4 8.♗e2 ♘a6∓ After the closure of the centre with d4-d5, the stronghold on c5 is of special importance since Black can place the knight there. **7...dxe5 8.♘xe5?! ♕d4∓** Black will return the pawn and have a better position.

B2) **5.a3 ♗xd2+ 6.♕xd2 e5 7.♘e2** White leaves the f3-square for the pawn. However, such extravagant plans early in the game can only cause White problems. 7.dxe5 dxe5 8.♕xd8+ ♔xd8 9.♘f3 ♘c6=; without the dark-squared bishops Black cannot have problems in this type of ending; a better option is 7.♘f3=. **7...♘f6 8.♘bc3 0-0 9.f3 ♘c6 10.d5 ♘b8** The standard idea. Black spends time to get control of the c5-square. **11.b3 ♘a6 12.♘g3 ♘c5 13.♖b1 c6 14.♗e2 cxd5 15.cxd5 a4!**

Now, thanks to the conquest of the c5-square, Black gets the b3- and d4-squares or exerts pressure on the a3-pawn. **16.b4** A better option is 16.♘xa4 ♘xa4 17.bxa4 ♖xa4 18.0-0 ♖xa3 19.♕b4 ♖a2 20.♖fc1=. White has a pawn less, but has sufficient compensation for a draw thanks to his active and well-coordinated pieces. **16...♘b3 17.♕d3 ♗d7 18.♗d1 ♘d4∓** In a very interesting and instructive way, Black centralizes the knight and gets a better position, Sahovic-Eingorn, Lvov 1984;

B3) **5.♕g4?!** For 5.♘c3 e5 see under 4.♘c3. The aggressive text move, known from the French Defence, only causes White problems because of the peculiar position of the dark-squared bishops and White's unprotected centre. **5...♘f6** Better would be 5...♕f6N 6.♘c3 ♘c6∓ and White will lose the d4-pawn without sufficient compensation. **6.♕xg7 ♖g8 7.♕h6 ♘c6⊒** Dorsch-Georg, Dos Hermanas 2004.

4...♘f6

With this natural continuation, Black accepts the possibility of switching to a Nimzo-Indian type position, with ♗d2 and ...a7-a5 inserted. Both players will be trying to prove the value of their extra move, on which the assessment of the future positions will depend to a great extent. White can continue in the manner of the Nimzo-Indian with 5.a3, 5.e3, 5.♕c2, 5.♗g5, 5.g3, or 5.♘f3, or opt for a more original position with 5.e4.

For 4...d5!? 5.e3 ♘f6 6.♗d3 (6.♘f3 is covered in Chapter 11) 6...0-0 see under 5...0-0.

4...d6?! A flexible continuation in the style of our system. Black builds an elastic pawn structure while preparing for ...e6-e5 or ...c7-c5. However, White has an effective plan which easily renders Black passive.

A) **5.e3** This modest move is an introduction to a simple but solid plan. White plans ♗d3 with ♘ge2 and then to gain the bishop pair with a2-a3, with a slight but stable advantage. Black has a choice between several logical continuations, but White can confidently and successfully follow the same scheme in all cases.

A1) **5...f5**

Black calls the 'Dutch pawn' to help control the e4-square, but it seems that this is not enough for equality. **6.♗d3 ♘f6 7.♕c2 0-0 8.♘ge2** It's obvious that besides his excellent control in the centre, White will also gain the bishop pair with a2-a3. **8...♘c6 9.a3 ♗xc3 10.♘xc3** A good option is 10.♗xc3±. **10...e5 11.d5 ♘e7 12.f4** 12.f3!?. **12...exf4 13.exf4 c6 14.dxc6 ♘xc6 15.0-0±**

White has better chances with the bishop pair, Levitt-Adams, London 1992;

A2) **5...♘f6 6.♗d3** For 6.♘f3 see Chapter 13. **6...b6** In this passive position, Black relies on the strength of the light-squared bishop on the central diagonal h1-a8, but White is not obliged to put his king's knight on f3. 6...e5 is covered under 5...e5. **7.♘ge2!**

A flexible developing move that highlights the effectiveness of White's strategy. White preserves the flexible pawn structure in the centre, while planning to gain the bishop pair with a2-a3. **7...♗b7 8.0-0 d5** With a tempo less, Black goes for the variation analysed under 5.e3 0-0. Other continuations also favour White thanks to his space advantage and strong centre, for example 8...0-0 9.a3 ♗xc3 10.♘xc3±. **9.cxd5 exd5 10.♘g3 g6 11.a3 ♗e7 12.e4 dxe4 13.♘gxe4 0-0 14.♗h6 ♖e8 15.♘g5 ♘d5 16.♕g4 ♘d7 17.♗c4 ♘7f6 18.♕h3±** Tomashevsky-Papin, Loo 2013;

A3) **5...e5 6.♗d3! ♘f6 7.♘ge2!** This proves to be the most effective plan against Black's set-up, regardless whether the knight is on d7 or c6 or whether the light-squared bishop is activated with ...b7-b6 or with ...e6-e5.

The point is that, if the white knight is on f3, Black has good counterplay thanks to the threat of winning a piece with ...e5-e4. **7...0-0 8.0-0** A critical position for the assessment of Black's set-up with the modest ...d7-d6, either before or after ...♘g8-f6. Interestingly, none of the authors who have dealt with these systems has taken this promising position for White into consideration. We will look at several logical continuations which occur in practice:

A31) **8...♖e8 9.a3 ♗xc3 10.♘xc3** 10.♗xc3!? ♘bd7 11.♘g3±; the bishop pair and his good central control favour White. **10...♘c6 11.d5 e4 12.♗c2 ♘e5 13.♘xe4 ♘xe4 14.♗xe4 ♕h4 15.♕c2 ♘g4 16.h3 ♘xf2 17.♗xh7+ ♕xh7 18.♕xh7+ ♔xh7 19.♖xf2±** and White has a pawn more, though Black has some drawing chances;

A32) **8...exd4 9.exd4 h6 10.a3 ♗xc3 11.♘xc3 ♘c6 12.d5** Another option is 12.♗e3!?, not fearing the loss of the bishop pair after 12...♘g4 since after 13.♕f3 White has other strategic advantages; above all his strong centre and better piece coordination. **12...♘e5 13.♗e2 ♖e8 14.♖e1 ♗f5 15.♗f1 ♕d7 16.♗e3 ♘eg4 17.♗d4 ♖xe1 18.♕xe1 ♖e8 19.♕d2 ♕e7 20.f3 ♘e5 21.b4±** White has better chances thanks to his bishop pair and space advantage, Feller-Edouard, Nimes 2009;

A33) **8...♘c6 9.a3 ♗xc3 10.♗xc3** A weaker option is 10.bxc3 ♕e7 11.♘g3 ♗d7 12.♕b1 ♖fe8 13.d5 ♘d8 14.e4 b6 15.h3 ♘b7∞ with chances for both sides, Krush-Gulko, ICC INT 2013. **10...♖e8 11.d5 ♘b8 12.♘g3±**

White is better thanks to his bishop pair good central control, Arencibia Rodriguez-Gulko, Merida 2002.

B) **5.e4** Not many players would resist this principled move. However, practice and analyses have shown that Black has greater chances to reach an equal position than after the modest but more solid 5.e3. **5...e5!** A thematic move, immediately attacking the weak pawn on d4. **6.a3 ♗xc3 7.♗xc3 ♘f6** Now the pawn on e4 should be defended:

B1) **8.f3 exd4 9.♕xd4 0-0** 9...♘c6 10.♕e3 0-0 11.♘e2 ♘d7 12.♘d4 ♘c5 13.♘xc6 bxc6 14.b4 ♘a4 15.♗d4 ♗e6 16.♖d1 ♕e7 17.♗d3

... and now, in the game Karagianis-Sher, Schaumburg 2006, Black could have opened the a-file with 17...axb4!N and after 18.axb4 ♖fb8↑, which would have given him more options despite the opponent's bishop pair. **10.♘e2 ♘c6 11.♕d2 ♘d7 12.♘g3 ♘c5 13.♕c2** A better option is 13.♖d1∞ with chances for both sides. **13...♕h4** 13...♘g5∓. **14.0-0-0 ♘e5∞** Tisdall-Kortchnoi, Haifa 1989;

B2) **8.♗d3 exd4 9.♗xd4 ♘c6 10.♗c3 0-0** 10...♘e5!?=. **11.♘e2 ♖e8 12.f3 ♘e5 13.0-0 b6 14.♖c1 ♘fd7 15.♘g3 ♘xd3 16.♕xd3 ♘e5 17.♕d1 f6=** and Black has good chances to draw, Sorin-Giaccio, Pinamar 2002;

C) **5.♘f3** is covered in Chapter 13.

5.a3

This continuation does not secure the bishop pair for White, which minimizes White's chances to get the upper hand.

A) **5.e3**

This continuation, together with 4.♕c2, is very popular in the regular Nimzo-Indian and gives White better chances of an advantage. However, what this means with our extra moves will be seen after Black's best and most popular reply:

A1) **5...0-0** The best choice in the Nimzo-Indian with e2-e3. Black makes a useful move while waiting to see the opponent's plan, not giving any hints regarding his choice of pawn structure and queenside development. **6.♗d3** White has two ways to develop his king's knight. **6...d5!** This is the main pillar of Black's strategy, regardless of where White puts his king's knight. This classical thrust, on which numerous opening systems are based, neutralizes White's advantage in the centre and, also importantly, combines very well with the pawn on a5. **7.♘ge2** This flexible continuation is good in those positions where Black has played ...d7-d6 and ...e6-e5. Here, White loses control over the important central square e5 for no reason. After 7.cxd5 exd5 8.♘ge2 Black wants to justify the pawn on a5 and chooses the plan in which the light-squared bishop on a6 is exchanged: 8...b6 9.0-0 ♗a6 10.♗xa6 ♘xa6 11.f3 ♖e8 12.♕c2 c5 and Black equalizes relatively easily, Gustafsson-Fressinet, Oberhof 2011; 7.♘f3 is covered in Chapter 11.

Black has a pleasant choice between two different plans: A11) 7...dxc4 and A12) 7...b6.

A11) **7...b6 8.0-0**

A111) **8...♗b7 9.cxd5 exd5 10.♖c1 ♖e8 11.f3 ♗f8 12.♕b3** 12.♕e1 deserves attention, with the idea ♕e1-h4,

which we can find in the corresponding system in the Nimzo-Indian, for example 12...♗a6!? 13.♗xa6 ♘xa6 14.a3 c5⇄. **12...♘a6 13.a3** 13.♘f4!? c5 14.♗b5 ♖e7 15.♖fe1∞. **13...c5 14.♗b1** 14.♗b5!?. **14...♖b8 15.♖fe1 g6 16.♕c2 ♘c7∓** Black's pieces are more effective, Sundararajan-Fominikh, Mumbai 2004;

A112) Attention should also be paid to **8...♗a6N 9.b3 ♘c6!?** with the idea ...e6-e5. Black wants to exploit the fact that with the knight on e2 White has less control of e5. **10.f4** 10.♕c2 e5⇄. **10...♘e7!** White seems to have a strong centre, backed up by his pieces. However, the following sequence shows that it is vulnerable. **11.a3 ♗xc3 12.♘xc3 dxc4 13.♗xc4** 13.bxc4?! c5∓. **13...♗xc4 14.bxc4 ♘f5∞** with chances for both sides.

A12) **7...dxc4 8.♗xc4 ♘bd7 9.♕c2 c5 10.a3 cxd4 11.♘xd4 ♗c5 12.♘cb5 ♘e5 13.♗e2 b6!?N** This is better than 13...♗xd4 14.♘xd4 ♗d7 15.e4 ♕b6 16.♗c3 ♖fc8 17.♖d1 ♘g6 18.0-0 and White kept better chances thanks to the bishop pair in I. Sokolov-Bauer, Nancy 2012. **14.♘b3** 14.0-0 ♗b7 15.♖ad1 ♗xd4 16.♘xd4 (16.♗c3 ♕d5↑) 16...♖c8↑ and Black takes the initiative, for example 17.♕b1 (17.♗c3 ♘d5) 17...♗e4. **14...♗b7 15.♘xc5 bxc5 16.f3** 16.0-0 ♗e4 17.♕d1 ♕b8 18.♗c3 ♖d8 19.♕a4 ♗c6 20.♖ad1 ♘d5⇄. **16...c4 17.0-0 ♕b6 18.a4 ♖fd8⇄** Black is doing well with his active and well-coordinated pieces.

A2) **5...b6** usually leads to the positions analysed under 5...0-0. However, some of them have independent significance. **6.♗d3 ♗b7** 6...0-0 7.♘ge2 (7.♘f3 is covered in Chapter 14.1) 7...d5 is covered under 5...0-0. **7.♘ge2**

One of the ideas of this move is to re-capture with the knight after the exchange on c3. For 7.♘f3 see Chapter 14. **7...0-0** 7...♗xg2 8.♖g1 ♗f3 9.♖g3 ♗h5 10.♕c2 with strong compensation. **8.a3** 8.0-0 d5 is covered under 5...0-0. **8...♗xc3** 8...♗e7 9.e4!?±. **9.♘xc3 d5** After 9...♗xg2 White's attack develops incredibly quickly: 10.♖g1 ♗b7 11.e4 ♘e8 12.♕h5 g6 13.0-0-0♔ with a strong attack on the black king. **10.0-0 c5 11.dxc5 bxc5 12.♘e2 ♘bd7 13.♗c3 a4 14.♕c2** and now with **14...♕c7!?N** in the game Peralta-Marin, Sabadell 2011, Black could have obtained a satisfactory position. For example: **15.♖ac1** 15.♘g3 ♘e5=. **15...dxc4 16.♗xc4 ♘e5⇄**;

A3) 5...d6?! 6.♗d3! is covered under 4...d6.

B) **5.♕c2**

In the manner of the Classical Nimzo-Indian, preparing to build a full

centre with e2-e4 and obtaining the bishop pair with a2-a3. However, Black now has more time to play in the centre. A good choice is the classical 5...d5. We will also look at the flexible 5...d6:

B1) **5...d6** is a flexible continuation often seen in this system. In this particular position, White can now gain the bishop pair while preserving his space advantage:

B11) **6.♘f3**

B111) **6...♘c6 7.a3 ♗xc3 8.♗xc3 ♕e7** Black chooses a not so popular variation from the Nimzo-Indian. **9.e4 e5 10.d5 ♘b8 11.♗d3 a4** Or 11...♘bd7 12.b4 axb4 13.axb4 ♖xa1+ 14.♗xa1 0-0 15.0-0 c5 16.♗c3 ♕d8 17.♖a1 ♕c7 18.♘d2 and White has better chances with his space advantage and bishop pair, Georgiev-Bogdanovski, Skopje 2012. **12.c5 0-0 13.♖c1 ♗g4 14.cxd6 cxd6 15.♘d2 ♘h5 16.♘c4 ♘f4 17.♗f1 b5 18.♘e3** Now the black army retreats. **18...♗d7 19.g3 ♘h5 20.♗e2 ♘f6 21.0-0 ♖e8 22.♗d3 ♘a6 23.f4±** Arngrimsson-Stupak, Pardubice 2013;

B112) **6...♘bd7 7.♗g5!?** For 7.a3 ♗xc3 8.♗xc3 ♕e7 see under 6.a3. **7...h6 8.♗h4 b6 9.e3 ♗b7 10.♗d3** With this move order Black does not manage to realize the standard plan of ...♗xc3, ...g7-g5 and occupying the important central square with ...♘e4, which we will tackle in Chapter 14: **10...♗xc3+** 10...e5?! 11.dxe5 ♘xe5 12.♘xe5 dxe5 13.0-0-0 ♗xc3 14.♗e4 ♕c8 15.♗xb7 ♕xb7 16.♕xc3 ♘d7 17.♖d5± Epishin-Smyslov, Biel 1993. **11.bxc3** 11.♕xc3 g5 12.♗g3 ♘e4 13.♕c2 f5 14.0-0-0 ♕f6∞ M. Marin. **11...0-0 12.0-0 e5 13.♗f5 ♕e8⇄** M. Marin.

B12) **6.a3! ♗xc3 7.♗xc3 ♕e7** Without this move, Black cannot organize his play on the dark squares **8.♘f3**

Everything is ready for e2-e4-e5. Black has to block the opponent's e-pawn immediately, which can be done with the flexible but passive move 8...♘bd7 or the active but risky move 8...♘c6. **8...♘bd7** Passive, but it saves time and does not expose the knight to an attack with d4-d5.

White can continue with either 9.e4 or the modest 9.e3 (8...♘c6 is covered under 6.♘f3).

B121) 9.e4 e5 10.♗d3 a4 Black uses the a-pawn to reduce the mobility of the white queenside pawns, but it's not enough for equality. **11.0-0 0-0**. Now:

B1211) 12.♖fe1 White first wants to place the rooks on the central files before taking serious measures. **12...b6** The move 12...c5 is strategically justified with the bishop pair in mind, but we should not forget Black's lack of space and the possibility for White to open up the position with f2-f4: 13.d5 ♘e8 14.g3 ♘c7 15.♘h4± Delchev-Zelcic, Nova Gorica 2004. **13.♖ad1 ♗b7 14.♘d2** 14.c5!? bxc5 15.dxe5 ♘xe5 16.♘xe5 dxe5 17.♗b5±. **14...♘h5 15.♘f1 ♘f4 16.♘e3 ♕g5⇄** Saucey-Kalinin, Mulhouse 2002;

B1212) 12.♘h4!? It is not strange that with his good control of the centre and his bishop pair, White can choose from among several plans. He wants to move the knight to f5 or, after g2-g3,

relocate it via g2 to the ideal square e3. Here the knight controls the critical squares d5 and f5, and the road will be free for the f2-f4 push. **12...exd4 13.♘f5 ♕d8 14.♘xd4±** Landa-Zaragatski, Germany 2013.

B122) 9.e3

With this weak move, White cannot have great expectations. **9...0-0** Inaccurate is 9...b6 10.b4 axb4 11.axb4 ♖xa1+ 12.♗xa1 ♗b7 13.♗e2 0-0 14.0-0 ♖a8 15.♗b2 ♕d8 16.♖a1 ♖xa1+ 17.♗xa1 ♕a8 18.♗b2 ♕a2 19.♘d2± Nikolaidis-Antic, Paleros 2012. **10.♗e2 b6** A good option is 10...a4. Black uses the e-pawn to reduce the mobility of the white queenside pawns and thus prevents White from gaining space there: 11.0-0 ♖e8 12.♖fe1 b6 13.e4 e5 14.♗f1 ♗b7 15.d5 ♘c5 16.♘d2 ♘h5 17.g3 g6 18.♗b4 ♗c8 19.♗g2 ♗d7 with chances for both sides, Bogner-Nikolic, Germany 2010.

B1221) 11.0-0 ♗b7 12.♘d2 12.♖fd1 ♘e4 13.♗e1 f5⇄ with good play in the centre and on the kingside, Girya-Dzagnidze, Geneva 2013; on 12.b4 Black can aim for the standard aggressive set-up in the centre with 12...♘e4 13.♗b2 f5⇄ with counterplay on the kingside. **12...a4 13.e4** A weaker option is 13.b4?! since after 13...axb3 14.♕xb3 e5 15.♗d3 ♘h5

16.♕d1 g6 17.d5 ♘c5∓ Black has a better pawn structure and better chances, Biriukov-Eingorn, St Petersburg 1996. **13...c5!?** Former World Champion Tal opts for a complicated battle, allowing the opponent to push the e-pawn. A simpler way to get equal chances is 13...e5. **14.e5 ♘e8 15.f4 cxd4 16.♗xd4 dxe5 17.fxe5 ♘xe5 18.♗xb6 ♘d6⇄** with the idea ...♘f5, Gligoric-Tal, Belgrade 1968;

B1222) In the event of the logical **11.b4**, a good option is **11...♗b7**. Black allows the opening of the b-file as he would be less active on the a-file. For example: 11...axb4 12.axb4 ♖xa1+ 13.♗xa1 ♗b7 14.0-0 with a more promising ending for White – see under 9...b6. **12.bxa5** 12.0-0 ♘e4 13.♗b2 f5⇄. **12...♗e4 13.♕d1 bxa5 14.0-0 ♖fb8⇄**;

B2) **5...d5!?** 5...b6?! 6.e4±.

This classical attack on the centre is not common in our system, but the tempi spent on placing the white queen on c2 and the black pawn on a5 increase its energy and secure a satisfactory position for Black.

B21) **6.♘f3**

B211) **6...0-0 7.♗g5** With the queen on c2 and the black pawn on a5, this pin can only cause White problems. For 7.e3 see Chapter 11.

B2111) **7...c5 8.dxc5 ♘a6** 8...h6!?. **9.a3 ♗xc5** 9...♗xc3+ leads to a weaker ending, as Black has not inserted ...h7-h6 and so does not have the active ...g7-g5 and ...♘e4: 10.♕xc3 ♘xc5 11.♗xf6 ♕xf6 12.♕xf6 gxf6 13.cxd5 ♖d8 14.♖d1 ♘a4 15.dxe6 ♗xe6 16.e3±. **10.0-0-0?!** A better option is 10.♖d1!±. **10...h6 11.♗h4 ♗e7=** Le Roux-A. Sokolov, Haguenau 2013;

B2112) **7...h6!**

More comments on this move under line B23) 6.♗g5 h6.

B21121) **8.♗h4 c5 9.dxc5 ♘a6N** 9...dxc4?! 10.e3± Lagunow-Ronin, Novosibirsk 1989; it is also possible to play 9...♘bd7!?. Now, on **10.a3** (10.cxd5 ♘xc5 11.e3 g5 12.♗g3 exd5 13.♗e2 ♘fe4 14.0-0 (14.♗e5 ♗f5↑) 14...♗xc3 15.bxc3 ♗f5⇄) Black plays **10...♗xc3+ 11.♕xc3 g5! 12.♗g3** (12.♘xg5?! hxg5 13.♗xg5 ♘e4∓) **12...♘e4 13.♕c2 ♘axc5↑**. Before White brings the king into safety, Black will take the initiative with ...♗d7 or ...♕b6. This variation clearly shows the value of the extra pawn move ...a7-a5;

B21122) **8.♗xf6 ♕xf6 9.a3** 9.e3 c5!, see Chapter 11. **9...♗xc3+ 10.♕xc3 dxc4 11.♕xc4 ♘c6 12.♖d1 e5** 12...♖d8!? leads to equality without any risk: 13.e3 e5 14.d5 ♘e7= with the idea ...c7-c6. **13.d5 ♘e7 14.♕xc7** e4 15.♕e5! The only option for White not to get into a critical position because of the king in the centre **15...exf3 16.♕xf6 gxf6 17.d6 ♘c6 18.d7 ♗xd7 19.♖xd7 ♘e5⇄** Black has a worse pawn structure but a more active position. Lagarde-Fressinet, Pau 2012;

B212) It is risky to follow grandmaster Vadim Malakhatko's idea to exchange the dark-squared bishop via a6: **6...b6 7.♗g5 0-0 8.e3 h6 9.♗h4 ♗e7** Black switches to the Tartakower Variation of the Queen's Gambit Declined with the rare ...a7-a5 instead of ...♗b7. **10.♖d1** 10.cxd5 ♘xd5 11.♗xe7 ♕xe7 12.♖c1 ♘a6 13.♗c4 ♗b7 14.0-0 c5 15.♘xd5 exd5 16.♗xa6 ♗xa6 17.♖fe1 ♖fc8 18.♕b3 ♗c4 19.♕a3 a4= Gligoric-Kurajica, Pula 1980. **10...♗a6!? 11.♘e5 c6 12.cxd5 ♗xf1?!** A better option is 12...cxd5, though after 13.♗xa6 ♘xa6 14.♕e2 ♘b8 15.0-0± White is active and pressures the weakened light squares in Black's camp. **13.dxe6 ♗a6 14.exf7+ ♖xf7 15.♘xf7 ♔xf7 16.d5 cxd5 17.♗xf6 ♗xf6 18.♘xd5±**; Black has serious problems, I. Sokolov-Malakhatko, Jakarta 2013.

B22) 6.cxd5 exd5 7.♗g5 After the exchange on d5, the a5-pawn becomes more important since it controls space on the queenside where Black has a pawn majority. **7...♕d6!?** With the idea ...♘e4. **8.♗xf6 ♕xf6 9.a3 ♗xc3+ 10.♕xc3 c6 11.e3 0-0 12.♘e2 ♘d7 13.♘g3 ♕e7 14.♗d3 ♘f6 15.0-0 h5⇄** and Black gets a good position, Roiz-Istratescu, Belgium 2008;

B23) 6.♗g5 We have already said that this pin does not work well with the queen on c2 and the black pawn on a5, since these factors give Black more time to play in the centre and also make it easier for him to play on the queenside.

6...h6! The typical reaction. **7.♗xf6** On 7.♗h4 Black hits the centre with 7...c5⇄, which has greater effect thanks to the inclusion of ♕c2 and ...a7-a5. **7...♕xf6 8.e3 c5 9.a3 cxd4 10.axb4 dxc3 11.cxd5 0-0 12.bxc3 b6** 12...exd5 13.♘f3 ♘c6 14.bxa5 ♗f5 15.♕b2 ♘xa5↑ and Black has an advantage in development. **13.dxe6 ♗xe6 14.♘f3 ♘c6⧳** Bukal-Sedlak, Zadar 2011.

C) 5.♗g5

Switching to the Leningrad Variation of the Nimzo-Indian Defence in which Black has the extra move ...a7-a5.

C1) 5...a4 With the idea ...a4-a3. Black wants to show immediately that there is good use for the pawn on a5. **6.a3 ♗xc3+ 7.bxc3 c5?!** The standard move from the regular Leningrad Variation. However, with the pawn on a4 this version is weaker because of the weakened queenside. **8.d5! d6 9.e3** Black now has a choice between two types of position with 9...exd5 and 9...e5, but both of them lead to inferior positions: **9...exd5** In an attempt to play the well-known theoretical position from the Leningrad, Black captures a pawn but enables the opponent to become active. Here we have pawns on a3 and a4 in comparison with the regular Leningrad, which seems to suit White better, due to the weakness of the dark squares in Black's camp. However, 9...e5 would not be a better choice because of the pawn on a4. **10.cxd5 ♘bd7 11.♗d3 ♕a5 12.♘e2 ♘xd5 13.0-0 c4 14.♗c2** 14.♗xc4? ♘5b6−+. **14...♘xc3** Attention should be paid to 14...0-0!?, which is the main move in the Leningrad by the way. **15.♘xc3 ♕xc3 16.♗f4** 16.♕xd6!?♾. **16...0-0 17.♗xd6 ♖e8 18.♗b4 ♕e5 19.♗xa4±** and the push of the pawn to a4 has not been justified;

C2) **5...h6** Usually good, except in those cases where White can exploit the weakening of the pawn structure around Black's king. **6.♗h4 b6 7.f3** 7.e3 ♗b7 8.♘e2 0-0 9.a3 ♗e7=; for 7.♘f3 ♗b7 see Chapter 14.1. **7...d5!** This neutralization of the white centre is possible since Black has the pawn on a5. If not, White would capture a piece with ♕a4+. **8.cxd5** After 8.e3 ♗a6↑ Black is the one who controls the game. **8...exd5 9.e3 0-0 10.♗d3 ♖e8⇄**;

D) **5.g3 d5!**

Logical, and the best reaction. Black immediately attacks the weak pawn on c4, which is especially effective when the white queen's knight is on c3. **6.cxd5** 6.♘f3 is covered in Chapter 14.4. **6...exd5 7.♘f3 0-0 8.♗g2 ♘bd7 9.0-0 ♖e8 10.♖c1 c6=** Black has an excellent position. The pawn on a5, which controls space on the queenside, is of better use to Black than the bishop on d2 is to White, since its natural place is on f4, Brethes-Fressinet, Calvi 2013;

E) **5.e4**

An exciting idea, well known from the French Defence. White offers his important central pawn in exchange for the pawn on g7, normally the main protector of the castled black king. Black can accept with 5...♗xc3 or ignore it with either a counterstrike in the centre by 5...d5 or the suspicious 5...d6?!.

E1) **5...♗xc3 6.♗xc3 ♘xe4 7.♕g4 d5** A weaker option is 7...♘xc3 8.♕xg7 ♔e7 9.bxc3 ♕g8 10.♕e5 d6 11.♕e3 ♘d7 12.♘f3±. White has successfully realized his idea. Black's king will be unsafe for a long time, I. Sokolov-Gofshtein, Villarrobledo 2007. **8.♕xg7 ♕f6!** It is a good thing for Black that White has to exchange the queens because of the threat on f2. However, not all of Black's problems have been solved. **9.♕xf6 ♘xf6**

Black's position is obviously inferior because of his weaker pawn structure and White's bishop pair; however, in this particular position he has the practical possibility of exchanging the light-squared bishops via a6 and get a stronghold on d5, after the potential exchange of the c- and d-pawns. In that case, Black will have a satisfactory position. **10.f3 ⧍g8 11.⧍f2 ⧍c6 12.⧍e1 b6 13.cxd5 ⧍xd5 14.⧍c4 ⧍ce7 15.⧍e2 ⧍a6 16.⧍xa6 ⧍xa6 17.a3 ⧍d7=**

Black has realized all his strategic aims by exchanging the light-squared bishops and placing the knight on the central square d5, Weischede-Eingorn, Hamburg 1999;

E2) 5...d5 6.e5 ⧍e4

E21) In case of **7.⧍f3 0-0 8.a3** (8.⧍d3 ⧍xd2 9.⧍xd2 c5⇄) **8...⧍xc3 9.bxc3 b6 10.⧍d3 ⧍a6=** Black has real possibilities to trade off both White's bishops and obtain equal chances;

E22) **7.⧍xe4 7.a3 ⧍h4!?⇄. dxe4 8.a3** A weaker option is 8.⧍xb4?! axb4∓.

An unusual position in which Black has two pairs of doubled pawns, but also better chances and the initiative! Also, the brave black pawns have vacated the a-file and thus increased the power of the black queen and rook. The black pawn on e4 causes additional problems, since it prevents White from developing naturally with ⧍f3 and ⧍d3, Housieaux-Kosten, Nimes 2009. **8...⧍xd2+ 9.⧍xd2 0-0** 9...c5! 10.dxc5 ⧍d7⇄ M. Marin.

E221) **10.⧍e3 f5 11.exf6 ⧍xf6 12.⧍e2 ⧍c6 13.⧍d1**

E2211) **13...e5?!** Black should wait for the white knight to move, losing control of d4, before he carries out this central strike. **14.d5 ⧍e7 15.⧍g3 ⧍f5 16.⧍xf5 ⧍xf5 17.⧍e2 ⧍h4 18.c5±** Akobian-Kraai, San Diego 2006;

E2212) A better option is **13...⧍d7!N**

and if **14.♘c3 e5!**. White is late with his development, so his better structure does not mean anything here. **15.dxe5** On 15.d5 Black can centralise the knight: 15...♘d4! would lead to problems for White. **15...♘xe5 16.♗e2 ♖ae8 17.♘xe4** 17.0-0 ♘f3+ 18.♗xf3 exf3 19.♕xf3 ♕xf3 20.gxf3 ♗h3 21.♖fe1 ♖xe1+ 22.♖xe1 ♖f6↑. **17...♕g6⯾** Black has maximal activity and excellently coordinated pieces for the pawn.

E222) **10.0-0-0**

E2221) **10...b5!N**

A typical move in positions with opposite castling. Black wants to open files as soon as possible for an attack. **11.cxb5 c6 12.♔b1 cxb5 13.♗xb5 ♕b6 14.♗c4** 14.a4 ♘a6 15.♘e2 ♘c7⯾. **14...♘c6 15.♘e2 ♗b7⯾**;

E2222) **10...f6 11.f4 b5!? 12.♘e2** A better option is 12.cxb5 c6 13.♔b1 cxb5 14.♗xb5 and with the weakness caused by ...f7-f6, Black will have difficulty to prove compensation for the pawn. **12...b4 13.a4 ♗b7 14.♕e3 ♘d7** with equal chances, Cmilyte-Eingorn, Hamburg 2005.

E3) **5...d6?! 6.e5!** Now the bishop on d2 demonstrates its great qualities. **6...dxe5 7.dxe5 ♗xc3** A weaker option is 7...♘fd7 8.♕g4 g6 9.♘f3 ♘c6 10.0-0-0± Ippolito-Ibragimov, Ledyard

2008. **8.♗xc3 ♕xd1+ 9.♖xd1 ♘e4 10.♗d4 ♘c6 11.♗d3 ♘xd4 12.♗xe4 ♘f5 13.♘f3 ♘e7** and now the simple **14.♖d2!±**, preventing the opponent from developing with ...♗d7.

F) For **5.♘f3 b6!** see Chapter 14.1.

5...♗xc3 6.♗xc3 ♘e4

With this simple move, Black shows the opponent that the move a2-a3 was premature.

7.♕c2 ♘xc3

Also possible is 7...f5 8.g3 b6 9.♗g2 ♗b7 10.♘f3 0-0 11.0-0 d6 12.b4 ♘d7 13.♘d2 ♘df6 14.♘xe4 ♗xe4 15.♕b3 a4 16.♕a2 ♗xg2 17.♔xg2 ♕d7= Severina-Volkov, Kazan 2012.

8.♕xc3

8...0-0

With White's king still in the centre, Black hopes to organize satisfactory counterplay. However, with correct play White will be able to enter a favourable ending.

8...b6!?N A good idea. Black postpones castling, not allowing the opponent to fianchetto his bishop first.

A) **9.e4 ♗b7 10.♕g3** 10.♕e3 0-0 11.♘f3 d6 12.♗e2 ♘d7 13.0-0 e5⇄; 10.♗d3 f5!?⇄. **10...0-0 11.♗d3 d6 12.♘f3 ♘d7 13.♖d1 ♕e7 14.0-0 e5⇄** In these lines, Black easily gets equal chances;

B) **9.♘f3 ♗b7** With this order Black does not have to lose time on ...♖a8-a7.

10.g3 d6 11.♗g2 ♘d7 12.0-0 0-0= In this position with reduced material, in which Black controls the important e4-square, a draw is the most probable outcome.

9.g3!

Of course, White wants to fianchetto first and take some advantage from that. 9.♘f3 b6 10.g3 ♗b7 11.♗g2 d6 12.0-0 ♘d7 13.♖ad1 ♘f6=

9...b6!?

Other plans are possible too, but Black wants to neutralize the strong white bishop on g2 at any cost.

10.♗g2 ♖a7 11.♘f3 ♗b7 12.0-0 a4!

With this move, Black not only reduces the mobility of the white pawns on the queenside, but also activates the rook via the excellent square a5.

13.♖fe1 d6 14.c5?!

This seems risky without the support of the white rooks.

A better option is 14.♖ad1, although after 14...♘d7 15.e4 ♕a8 16.♘h4 ♖a5⇄, with his flexible pawn structure and active pieces, Black can probably deal successfully with White's strong centre.

14...bxc5 15.dxc5 ♗xf3 16.♗xf3 d5 17.♖ad1 c6∓

White will have problems with maintaining the pawn on c5 because of the threat of ...♘d7 and ...♖a5, Maiorov-Istratescu, Bastia 2013.

Conclusion

In the critical position occurring after 4.♘c3 ♘f6, which is similar to the Nimzo-Indian, White has many continuations and switches that lead to positions which we have covered in other chapters. However, it is important that the extra move ...a7-a5 fits well into this Nimzo-Indian type position, especially in those lines where White plays ♗g5 at some point, or transfers to positions (by cxd5 exd5) in which Black has a pawn majority on the queenside.

By the way, the use of the rook's pawn is reflected in the space control on the queenside, the support for the dark-squared bishop on b4, or the creation of a stronghold on c5 by preventing b2-b4.

In the critical position, in which White tries to gain an advantage by creating a strong centre with 4.e4, we recommend the flexible 4...d6 and next ...e6-e5 and an attack on the white pawn trio in the centre, especially the d4-pawn. This is the best way to neutralize the strength of the opponent's centre, usually relying on the useful exchange of the dark-squared bishop, without which this story would certainly have a different end.

Exercises

10 (1) Find the plan.
(solution on page 447)

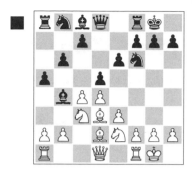

10 (2) Find the plan.
(solution on page 447)

10 (3) Find the plan.
(solution on page 447)

Chapter 11

The Direct Central Thrust 4...d5

1.d4 e6 2.c4 ♝b4+ 3.♝d2 a5 4.♘f3 d5

Of course, Black can play 4...♘f6 first and then attack the centre with 5...d5, as we have explained in the last chapters, but this order is directed against players who like fianchetto systems, for it shuts the door to some important lines.

By the way, this is another possibility, in addition to 4...d6, with which Black attempts to use an extra tempo, by not moving the king's knight, to achieve his goals. In this line, Black must be prepared to face positions which may appear by transposition in different openings, such as the Bogo-Indian, the Queen's Gambit, the Nimzo-Indian, the Queen's Indian, or the Catalan, considering the extra moves: the white bishop to d2 and the black pawn to a5.

White has a wide choice of continuations: 5.g3, 5.e3, 5. ♘c3, 5. ♝b4, and the best continuations: 5.a3! and 5.♛c2.

5.g3
With a Catalan-type position. This is a safe and stable opening system where White relies mostly on his strong fianchettoed light-squared bishop and play along the c-file.
Black can now play the natural move 5...♘f6 and move on to the main line which is covered in Chapter 14.3; however, he has an opportunity to immediately capture the pawn on c4 and use

the extra tempo, acquired by not moving the knight to f6, to prevent the opponent's standard continuations.

A) **5.e3**
5...♘f6

A1) **6.♝d3 0-0 7.0-0 b6**

A11) **8.a3 ♝d6** With a pawn on b6, Black logically opts for a more active position of his dark-squared bishop. **9.♘c3 ♝b7 10.♖c1** and now a good move is **10...dxc4!?N** 10...♘bd7

11.cxd5 exd5 12.♘b5± and White will keep the bishop pair; 10...♘e4 11.cxd5 exd5 12.♘b5± Lerner-Pavasovic, Vienna 1994. **11.♗xc4 ♘bd7=** with the idea ...c7-c5, for example: **12.♕e2** 12.♘b5 ♗e7!?=; 12.♖e1 is covered under 8...dxc4. **12...c5 13.♘b5 ♗b8 14.♖fd1 ♕e7⇄** White has already placed his rooks on central files but his opponent also has strategic assets. This primarily refers to his control of the important e4-square and his bishops that are dangerously directed at the white king;

A12) **8.cxd5 exd5 9.♕c2 ♗b7 10.♘e5 ♗d6 11.♘c3 c5 12.♘b5 c4 13.♗e2 ♘c6 14.f4 ♘b4 15.♕d1 ♘e4 16.a3 ♘c6=** Postny-Istratescu, Nancy (rapid) 2013.

A2) **6.a3 ♗e7** A weaker move is 6...♗xd2+ 7.♘bxd2 0-0 8.♕c2±, see under 5.a3. **7.♘c3 0-0 8.♗d3** On 8.♖c1 Black should employ an active plan, just like after the text, targeting positions with an isolated d5-pawn, when developing the white bishop on d2 makes the least sense: 8...c5!?N 9.cxd5 exd5 10.dxc5 ♗xc5 11.♗e2 ♘c6 12.0-0 ♖e8∞. In relation to standard positions with the isolated pawn, both sides have strategic flaws here: Black has a weakness on b5 with the pawn on a5, and White has an inactive bishop on d2. **8...c5!?** Black does not fear the isolated pawn on d5, because the placement of both White's bishops is inadequate here. **9.cxd5 exd5 10.dxc5 ♗xc5 11.♕c2 ♘c6 12.♘b5 ♕e7 13.♖c1 ♗b6 14.♗c3 ♗g4 15.0-0** 15.♘fd4 ♘e4⇄. **15...♗xf3 16.gxf3 ♖ad8 17.♖cd1 d4! 18.exd4 ♖d5♔** with the idea ...♖h5, Knaak-Psakhis, Yerevan 1988.

A3) **6.♘c3**

Now we have a sort of Nimzo-Indian with the insertion of ♗d2 and ...a7-a5. But is the pawn on a5 useful? We will see in the following analyses. **6...0-0** This is a crossroads for White, who usually opts for one of the following continuations: 7.♗e2, 7.♕c2, 7.cxd5 7.a3 or 7.♗d3.

A31) **7.♗e2 b6** For 7...dxc4 8.♗xc4 b6 9.0-0 see 8...dxc4. **8.0-0 ♗b7** 8...♗a6!?. **9.♖c1 ♘bd7** 9...dxc4 10.♗xc4 is covered under 8...dxc4. **10.♕c2 ♖c8** Better is 10...dxc4N 11.♗xc4 c5! with a good position. **11.cxd5 exd5 12.♖fd1 ♖e8 13.♘b5 ♗xd2 14.♖xd2** With 14.♘xd2!? White would still have slightly better chances. **14...♘e4 15.♖dd1 c5 16.dxc5 bxc5 17.♘c3 ♘df6** and Black has evened the odds, Halkias-Sokolov, Helsingor 2012;

A32) **7.♕c2**

A321) **7...c5 8.dxc5** Better is 8.a3!? ♗xc3 9.♗xc3±. **8...♗xc5 9.♗e2 ♘c6**

10.a3 d4 11.exd4 ♘xd4 12.♘xd4 ♗xd4 13.0-0 ♗d7 14.♖ad1 e5 15.♗g5 h6 16.♗h4 ♗c6∞ Ehlvest-Kortchnoi, Puhajarve 2011;

A322) **7...b6 8.cxd5** 8.♗d3 ♗a6 9.b3 c5 10.a3 ♗xc3 11.♗xc3 ♘bd7 12.cxd5 ♗xd3 13.♕xd3 ♘xd5 14.♗b2 a4 with a pleasant game for Black, Macieja-Rashkovsky, Moscow 2002. **8...exd5 9.♗d3 ♗b7** This leads to a more complex battle. Black can also play 9...♗a6!=. Without the light-squared bishops, White cannot count on any sort of advantage, Almond-Winants, Kusadasi 2006. **10.0-0 ♗e7** and now:

A3221) **11.♖ac1 c5 12.dxc5 bxc5 13.♘a4 c4!?** Black wants to move the active knight to c6 (of course, it is possible to develop the queen's knight with 13...♘bd7!?∞, typical for positions with hanging pawns. **14.♗e2 ♘c6 15.♖fd1 ♕c7 16.b3 ♗a3 17.♘b2 ♘b4 18.♕b1 ♕e7 19.♗c3 cxb3 20.axb3 ♘e4 21.♗d4 ♘c6 22.♖c2 ♗d6⇄** Bensdorp-Atalik, Wijk aan Zee 2006;

A3222) Here is a newer game with mistakes to learn from. **11.♘e5 c5 12.dxc5?!** Moving the white knight to e5 does not combine well with this deterioration in the centre and the transition into a position with hanging pawns. Better is 12.♕a4!? in order to stop the development of the black knight with ...♘c6. **12...bxc5 13.♘a4?! ♕d6∓ 14.♗c3? d4−+** Gunina-Nakhbayeva, Astana 2013.

A33) **7.cxd5 exd5 8.♗d3 ♗g4** Another good move is 8...b6 9.0-0 ♗a6 10.♗xa6 ♘xa6=. Without the light-squared bishops, White cannot achieve anything. **9.♕c2 ♗xf3 10.gxf3** Here it is safest to not waste time with 10...♖e8 11.0-0-0∞ (Tomazini-Zelcic, Sentjur 2010), but immediately attack the cen-

tre with **10...c5!?N 11.dxc5 ♗xc5 12.0-0** (12.♘b5 ♗b4=) **12...♘c6 13.♘b5 ♗b4=**;

A34) **7.a3** White is wasting time, so Black chooses a plan involving an exchange of the light-squared bishops. **7...♗xc3 8.♗xc3 b6 9.b3 ♗a6 10.a4** 10.♗d3 a4=. **10...c5 11.♗e2 cxd4 12.♘xd4 dxc4 13.bxc4 ♘bd7 14.♗b2 ♘c5 15.0-0 ♘fe4 16.♖a3 ♖c8 17.f3 ♘d6⇄** Tosic-Sedlak, Vrnjacka Banja 2013;

A35) **7.♗d3**

7...b6 8.0-0 Black has three real options here, leading him into three different types of position: 8...♗b7, 8...dxc4 and 8...♗a6.

A351) **8...♗b7 9.cxd5 exd5** and now White has a choice between three options:

A3511) **10.♘e5** This is a standard plan in this type of position. For a while, Black will have to endure the opponent's unpleasant knight on e5. By the way, a similar position often occurs in the Nimzo-Indian with the following order: 1.d4 ♘f6 2.c4 e6 3.♘c3 ♗b4 4.e3 0-0 5.♗d3 d5 6.♘f3 b6 7.cxd5 exd5 8.0-0 ♗b7 9.♘e5 etc. **10...♘bd7 11.f4** And now Black has a choice: **11...c5** This leads to more complications. The alternative is the simple 11...♗xc3 12.♗xc3 (12.bxc3 ♗a6=) 12...♗a6 13.♗xa6 ♖xa6 14.♕d3 ♖a8 15.♘c6 ♕e8 16.b4 ♘e4= Piket-Anand, Monte Carlo 1999. **12.a3 ♗xc3 13.♗xc3 c4** Black compensates for the lack of the bishop pair with a majority of pawns on the queenside and control of the critical e4-square. **14.♗c2 b5 15.♖f3 ♖a6 16.♖g3 ♕e7 17.♕e1 ♖fa8 18.♖d1 ♘b6 19.♘g4 ♘xg4 20.♖xg4 ♘d7=** with chances for both sides. l'Ami-Anand, Wijk aan Zee 2011;

A3512) **10.a3** and now:

A35121) **10...♗xc3 11.♗xc3 ♘e4** 11...♗a6!?. **12.♕c2** and a draw was agreed in this somewhat better position for White, Cvitan-Kurajica, Zadar 2008;

A35122) **10...♗d6 11.♘e5 c5 12.f4 ♘c6 13.♘b5 cxd4** A better option is 13...♗e7∞. **14.exd4 ♘e7?!** 14...♘e4±. **15.f5±** Kasparov-Kortchnoi, Zürich 2006.

A3513) **10.♕c2** is covered under 7.♕c2.

A352) **8...dxc4!?** In the spirit of the Queen's Gambit Accepted, so as to open up the central diagonal h1-a8 for his light-squared bishop. White will have the advantage in the centre because of his mobile pawns, but Black intends to neutralize them at the right moment with ...c7-c5. **9.♗xc4 ♗b7 10.♖c1 ♘bd7 11.a3 ♗d6 12.♖e1** 12.♕e2 is covered under 8.a2-a3. Now:

A3521) **12...♘e4 13.♘xe4 ♗xe4 14.♗c3 ♕e7 15.♘d2 ♗b7 16.e4 ♗f4 17.g3 ♗h6 18.f4 ♖ad8 19.♕e2±** Vachier-Lagrave-Le Roux, Le Port Marly 2013;

A3522) **12...c5!?N**

This appears to be the right time for this liberating attack on the centre. Black has levelled the game, for example: **13.♕e2** 13.e4?! cxd4 14.♘xd4 ♘e5∓. **13...♕e7 14.♖ed1 ♖fd8**

A353) **8...♗a6** is the third option:

A3531) **9.♕e2 ♘bd7 10.cxd5 10.♖fd1 ♖c8 11.a3 ♗xc3 12.♗xc3 c5 13.♖ac1 cxd4 14.♗xd4 ♕c7=** Andreikin-Stocek, Warsaw 2005. **10...♗xd3 11.♕xd3 exd5 12.♖ac1 c6 13.♘e2 ♕c7 14.♖fd1 ♖fe8 15.♕c2 ♖ec8 16.a3 ♗f8 17.a4 ♗d6 18.♘c3 ♗b4 19.♘e2 ♗f8 20.♘c3 ♕d6=** Peralta-Ivanchuk, Barcelona 2006;

A3532) **9.b3 ♘bd7 10.♕e2** With the idea e2-e4.

A35321) **10...c5 11.a3** Or 11.cxd5 cxd4 12.♘xd4 ♗xd3 13.♕xd3 ♘c5 14.♕e2 ♗xc3 15.♗xc3 ♘xd5= Babula-Zelcic, Austria 2005. **11...♗xc3 12.♗xc3 cxd4 13.exd4** 13.♗xd4 ♘c5=. **13...a4=** and Black will exchange the light-squared bishops;

A35322) A move which deserves attention is **10...♗b7 11.a3 ♗xc3** (it is better to keep the dark-squared bishop with 11...♗d6= or 11...♗e7=) **12.♗xc3 ♘e4 13.♗b2 f5 14.♘d2** and White has higher odds with the bishop pair, Szekeres-Toth, Budapest 2009.

B) **5.♘c3** White aims for a Nimzo-Indian type of position which, with the exception of the white knight on f3, we covered in Chapter 10. **5...♘f6 6.♗g5** 6.e3 is covered under 5.e3.

We now have a Ragozin system with the black a-pawn on a5 instead of a7. As already stated, in positions where White moves his dark-squared bishop to the kingside, the significance of the pawn on a5 increases, not only because of the option of advancing with ...a5-a4, but also because of the control of space on the queenside and the support for his dark-squared bishop on b4. **6...h6!** Again this important relieving move. **7.♗xf6** 7.♗h4 g5 8.♗g3 ♘e4 9.♕c2 h5 10.h3 a4∞ with the idea ...a4-a3. **7...♕xf6 8.e3 0-0**

With the bishop pair and an extra move in comparison with the regular Ragozin, Black has good prospects. In fact, White must be careful not to end up in an inferior position. For example:

B1) **9.♖c1** 9.♗e2!?= is probably the safest way for White to stay out of trouble. **9...c6 10.♗d3 ♘d7 11.0-0 ♕e7 12.a3 ♗d6 13.e4 dxc4 14.♗xc4 e5⇄** Khalifman-Lobron, Brussels 1992. This was a blitz game, but one that is important for our book;

B2) On **9.♕c2 c5!** in the game Lobron-Short, Dortmund 1995, White did not find the right plan so he got an inferior position: **10.cxd5** Better is 10.a3 cxd4 11.♘xd4 ♗xc3+ 12.♕xc3 ♘c6 13.♘b5=. **10...exd5 11.a3 ♗xc3+ 12.bxc3 c4! 13.♕b2 ♖a6∓**

C) **5.♗xb4**

This exchange usually reduces White's chances for an advantage, as it activates the opponent's rook along the a-file and puts a black pawn on b4, which disrupts the natural development of the white queen's knight. **5...axb4** The pawn on b4 changes the image of this strategically more desirable position for White: **6.e3 ♘f6 7.♘bd2 0-0 8.♗d3 b6 9.0-0 c5** with clearly equal chances, since Black can, without any problems, harmoniously arrange his remaining minor pieces on the queenside.

D) **5.♕c2!?**

White defends the pawn on c4, reserving various possibilities for his minor pieces. What is interesting is that this early queen move gives White more chances of an advantage than the previous seemingly logical continuations.

The point is that the defence of the c4-pawn with the queen is better than the defense with e2-e3, since that way White does not close the diagonal c1-h6 for his dark-squared bishop, so he will have the opportunity to play, after a2-a3 and the retreat of the black bishop to e7, a kind of Queen's Gambit with ♗d2-f4 or ♗d2-g5, where he will be the one to benefit more from the inserted a2-a3 and ...a7-a5.

5...♘f6 6.a3!? Just like in the variation with 5.a3!, which will be analysed below, here White also prefers Queen's Gambit positions where he can benefit from the inserted moves a2-a3 and ...a7-a5. For 6.e3 0-0 7.♘c3 see under 5.e3; for 6.g3 see Chapter 14.4. **6...♗e7** 6...♗xd2+ 7.♘bxd2 0-0 8.e3± is covered under 5.a3. **7.♘c3 0-0** As stated before, White has not closed the diagonal with e2-e3 so he can try ♗d2-g5 or ♗d2-f4 now.

8.♗g5 Though it has not yet been used in practice, the move 8.♗f4!? also deserves attention. **8...♘bd7**

Now the question is where the inserted moves a2-a3 and ...a7-a5 are more useful for White. Is it in the system with D1) 9.e3 or in the exchange line D2) 9.cxd5 ?

D1) **9.e3** Entering a position from the Queen's Gambit, where ...a7-a5 is an inadequate response to a2-a3. **9...c6 10.♖d1!?±** (Riazantsev-Bocharov, Ulan Ude 2009) With a different move order we have arrived in a Queen's Gambit position which commonly arises after the following moves: 1.d4 d5 2.c4 e6 3. ♘c3 ♘f6 4. ♘f3 ♗e7 5. ♗g5 0-0 6.e3 ♘bd7 7.♕c2 (more frequent is 7.♖c1) 7...c6 8.a3 and now 8...a5 is not good;

D2) **9.cxd5 exd5 10.c3 c6 11.♗d3 ♖e8 12.0-0 ♘f8 13.♖ab1 ♘g6** The other popular line is 13...♘e4!?. **14.b4 axb4** 14...♗d6 Kramnik-Kasparov, Frankfurt 1999. **15.axb4 ♗d6⇄**

This was seen in the game Miladinovic-Boudriga, Monastir 2013.

By transposition we have reached a famous theoretical position, the so-called Exchange Variation of the Queen's Gambit with the rarely played moves a2-a3 and ...a7-a5 inserted. Usually this position occurs after 1.d4 d5 2.c4 e6 3.♘c3 ♘f6 4.cxd5 exd5 5. ♗g5 ♗e7 6.e3 c6 7. ♕c2 ♘bd7 8.♗d3 0-0 9. ♘f3 ♖e8 10. 0-0 ♘f8 11.a3 a5. Usually here the main line is entered with 12.♖ab1 ♘g6 (or 12...♘e4) 13.b4 with play for both sides.

E) **5.a3!**

Who would have thought this? Out of so many already mentioned natural continuations, a move with the rook's pawn turns out to be the best. Still, we remain convinced that this is the proper reaction to the early 4...d5, because White moves into positions similar to the Queen's Gambit in which the inserted a2-a3 and ...a7-a5 suit him.

Black can move the bishop back with E1) 5...♗e7 or E2) 5. ..♗d6, or exchange it with E3) 5...♗d2:

E1) **5...♗e7 6.♘c3 ♘f6 7.♗f4 0-0 8.e3 c5** Black has other continuations which would also not solve his opening problems, and the pawn on a5 will only increase these problems, since it is not useful for Black in this type of position. **9.dxc5 ♗xc5 10.♕c2±** Malakhatko-Mietus, Krakow 1999 (or 10.♖c1±,

Astasio Lopez-Nicolas Zapata, Linares 2013). In order to further explain why the insertion of the moves with the a-pawns suits White better, we will give here the regular line in the Queen's Gambit: 1.d4 d5 2.c4 e6 3.♘c3 ♘f6 4.♘f3 ♗e7 5.♗f4 0-0 6.e3 c5 7.dxc5 ♗xc5 and now on 8.a3 it is not a good idea to respond with 8...a5?! (8...♘c6!).

E2) **5...♗d6 6.c5!?±** Of course, another good move is 6.♘c3±;

E3) **5...♗xd2+** After White has wasted time with a2-a3, this exchange usually makes the game easier for Black and takes him close to full equality. However, in this case the move ...d7-d5 is already played, which deprives Black of the opportunity to use more convenient plans which include ...d7-d6 or ...b7-b6. **6.♘bxd2 ♘f6 7.e3 0-0 8.♕c2 ♘bd7 9.♖c1 c6 10.♗d3 ♕e7 11.0-0** with an advantage for White thanks to his better control of the centre and better development, Eingorn-Pira, St Quentin 2001.

5...dxc4!?

Now White usually chooses either 6.♕c2 or 6.♗g2. We will also investigate 6.a3, although this continuation is more common in positions with the white knight on c3, when White acquires the bishop pair after ...♗xc3.

The main line 5...♞f6 is covered in Chapters 14.3 and 14.4.

6.♗g2

A) **6.♕c2 ♗xd2+ 7.♞bxd2** Black has an extra tempo because he has not played ...♞f6, so 7.♕xd2 is no longer effective for White because of 7...b5. 8.♗g2 (in the aforementioned line where Black has a knight on f6, White has ♕d2-g5 here, with an attack on g7 and b5, see Chapter 14.3) 8...♗b7 9.0-0 ♞d7 (Black develops easily, without any difficulties, thanks to the extra pawn) 10.a4 b4 11.♕c2 ♞gf6. Now is the time to return the extra pawn in order to preserve a healthy position. For example: 12.♞bd2 0-0 13.♞xc4 ♗e4 14.♕d2 c5=. **7...b5 8.a4 c6** and now:

A1) **9.♗g2 ♞f6 10.♞e4** 10.0-0 0-0 is covered in Chapter 14.3. **10...♞d5 11.0-0 ♞a6 12.♞c3 ♞ab4 13.♕d2 ♗a6 14.♞e5♔** White has compensation for the pawn, but only for a draw, Nguyen-Malakhatko, Jakarta 2013;

A2) **9.b3 cxb3 10.♞xb3 ♞f6 11.♗g2**

11...b4! This is a move which has several strategic benefits for Black: 1. it creates a strong supported passed pawn for the ending, 2. it opens the diagonal f1-a6 for the activation of his light-squared bishop, and 3. it secures a potential stronghold for the black knight. If 11...♞d5!? 12.0-0 b4 13.♞e5 f6

14.♞xc6 ♞xc6 15.♕xc6+ ♗d7 16.♕c4 ♖c8 17.♞c5 ♞c3=; 11...0-0 12.0-0 is covered under 11.b3. **12.♞e5♔**

White has compensation, but it is not enough for more than a draw, Nikolaidis-Eingorn, Koszalin 1999.

B) **6.a3**

White forces the bishop to declare its intentions, while risking, at some point, the demobilization of his now weakened pawn structure with ...a5-a4. Black has two options, which usually lead him into two very different types of position: B1) in the spirit of our system, 6...♗xd2+ and B2) the Catalan type position with 6...♗e7.

B1) **6...♗xd2+ 7.♞bxd2 b5 8.a4** 8.♗g2?! a4! and White has lost his most important attacking possibility, a2-a4, which would compensate for the lost pawn. **8...c6 9.♗g2 ♞f6** 9...♞e7!?.

10.0-0 0-0∞ White has compensation for the pawn, but he has no advantage. By the way, we have entered a position which is covered in Chapter 14.3, except that there White already has a queen on c2 – here he has lost a tempo by moving the a-pawn twice;

B2) **6...♗e7**

This is a new version of the Open Catalan with a2-a3 and...a7-a5 inserted. Once again, we face the key question: which side benefits from this? In general we can state that both sides have shown their cards too soon and, in a way, both sides are weakened; however, the following analysis of a game in MegaBase 2013 should shed some more light on this important matter.

7.♕a4+ ♗d7 8.♕xc4 ♘f6 Black can prevent the invasion of the opponent's knight with 8...♗c6!?N, which also leads to a more common type of Catalan; for example: 9.♗g2 ♘f6 10.♘c3 ♘e4! (exchanging the important white knight in order to take control of the squares e4 and e5) 11.♗f4 ♘xc3 12.♕xc3 0-0 13.0-0 ♗d6 14.♗d2 ♘d7 15.♖fd1 ♘f6 with equal play. **9.♘e5 ♘c6** 9...♗c6!? is also possible, although after 10.♘xc6 ♘xc6 11.e3 ♕d5 12.♕xd5 exd5 13.♘c3 ♘d8 14.♗d3 White has a small but long-term advantage thanks to his bishop pair. **10.♘xd7** Better is 10.♗g2!?

0-0 11.♘c3 ♗e8 12.♘xc6 ♗xc6 13.♗xc6 bxc6 14.♖c1 with an easier and more pleasant game for White. **10...♕xd7 11.♗c3**

B21) **11...♕d5 12.♕xd5 exd5 13.♘d2 0-0** Black has equal chances in spite of the opponent's bishop pair, which is hard to activate in this type of position. Besides, the move a2-a3 has made the game on the queenside easier for Black, Van Wely-Andersson, Monaco (blind) 1997;

B22) It may be safer to aim for a draw with **11...♖d8!? 12.e3** A weaker move is 12.♗g2?!, for example 12...♘xd4 13.♕xd4 ♕xd4 14.♗xd4 ♖xd4 15.♗xb7 0-0 16.♗f3 ♖b8∓ Black has been the first to activate his pieces and he obtains heavy pressure on the queenside. **12...e5! 13.♗g2 exd4 14.exd4 ♘xd4 15.0-0 0-0!? 16.♗xb7 ♕g4!=** with the idea ...♘e2.

6...♘c6!

Black has not developed the king's knight yet, so he is playing with an extra tempo, which forces his opponent to change his course and decide on how to defend his d4-pawn. By the way, the variation with a knight on f6 is explained in Chapter 14.3.

White can defend the pawn in one of two ways: 7.♗c3 or 7.e3.

7.e3

In case of the natural continuation 7.♗c3 ♘ge7 8.a4 0-0 9.0-0 b6 10.e4 (10.♕c2 ♗a6 11.♖d1 ♕e8 12.♘g5 g6 13.e4 ♖d8 14.♘a3♔

... with certain compensation, but only for a draw, Kamsky Istratescu, Achaea 2012) 10...♗a6∞

... the question is whether White's full centre is enough compensation for a pawn, Jankovic-Edouard, Aix-les-Bains 2012.

7...♘f6

More flexible is **7...♘ge7**. Black intends to defend his weak c4-pawn with ...b7-b5, so he develops the knight to a more passive square to protect its fellow soldier on c6. **8.0-0 0-0** and now:

A) **9.♕c2**

A1) **9...b5 10.a4** 10.♘e5!?. **10...♗a6 11.axb5 ♗xb5**

A11) **12.♖c1 ♖b8 13.♗c3 ♗d6** Better is 13...♘d5! with a complex game: 14.e4?! ♘xc3 15.bxc3 ♗e7 16.♘bd2 a4↑ and White encounters problems in the ending. **14.♘bd2** After 14.♘g5! ♘f5 15.♘e4± Black will have a hard time defending the pawn on c4 and harmonizing his pieces. **14...♘d5∞** Postny-Istratescu, Bastia 2013;

A12) Better is **12.♘e5!** ♗xd2 12...♖b8 13.♘xc4±; 12...♘xe5? 13.♗xb4±. **13.♘xc6 ♗xc6** 13...♘xc6 14.♕xd2 c3 15.♕xc3 ♗xf1 16.♔xf1±. **14.♗xc6 ♘xc6 15.♘xd2±** and Black remains with a weak pawn on the c-file: **15...♕d5 16.♖a4 ♖fb8 17.♖xc4**

A2) **9...e5** does not work because of **10.♘xe5** (a weaker move is 10.dxe5?! ♗f5 11.e4 ♗g4∓) **10...♘xe5 11.dxe5 ♗f5** (if 11...♕d3 12.♕xd3 cxd3 13.♖c1 c6 14.a3 ♗xd2 15.♘xd2± Black will be in serious trouble because of his pawn on d3; 11...♘c6 12.f4 ♕d3 13.♕xd3 cxd3 14.a3 ♗c5 15.♖c1 ♗a7 16.♘c3±) **12.e4 ♗g6 13.♕xc4±** and White keeps the extra pawn.

B) 9.♕e2 e5!? 10.♘xe5 ♘xe5 11.dxe5 ♕d3 A better option is 11...♘c6!N 12.f4 ♗f5!⇄. With the queen on c2, this variation is not available to Black. 13.e4 ♗g4! 14.♕xg4 ♕d4+ 15.♔h1 ♕xb2 with chances for both sides. **12.♕xd3 cxd3 13.a3** 13.♖c1!. **13...♗c5 14.♖c1 ♗b6∞** Georgescu-Doncea, Bucharest 2012.

8.0-0 0-0

Now it is not easy for White to decide from which square to attack the opponent's pawn on c4 with his queen, since both squares have their strong and weak points.

9.♕c2

Among other things, White considers taking control of the diagonal b1-h7.

9.♕e2 b5 9...♗d6! with the idea ...e6-e5, see Chapter 14.3; 9...e5?!, see Chapter 14.3. **10.♘e5** Better is 10.a4! bxa4 11.♕xc4±. **10...♘xe5 11.♗xa8 ♘d3 12.♗g2 c5⊒** Mikhalchishin-Kupreichik, Tbilisi 1976.

9...e5!

The safest choice in the position where the white queen is on c2.

A) 9...♗d6!? with the idea ...e6-e5. **10.♘a3!?N** This seems to be the only option for White to continue the fight for the advantage. 10.♕xc4 e5 is covered in Chapter 14.3. **10...♗xa3** 10...e5? 11.dxe5 ♘xe5 12.♘xe5 ♗xe5 13.♘xc4±. **11.bxa3**

11...♕e7 The important move 11...b5, on which Black relies in this type of position, is not good with the queen on c2 because of 12.♘e5! and after 12...♘xe5 13.♗xa8 ♘d3 14.♗xa5 ♘d5 Black cannot achieve compensation like in positions with the queen on e2 due to a small but significant detail: 15.a4!± and the queen on c2 prevents the important move 15...b4. See the analysis in Chapter 14.3. **12.♕xc4∞** with a complicated and unclear position;

B) 9...♗xd2 10.♘bxd2 b5 Neither can Black achieve a draw with 10...♘b4 11.♕xc4 b6 12.♖fc1 with an advantage for White, characteristic of Catalan-type positions. **11.♘e5 ♘b4** 11...♘xe5?! 12.♗xa8 ♘d3 13.♗g2±; Black does not have enough compensation for the sacrificed material. **12.♕b1** Better is 12.♕c1!? with the intention to break up the black pawns with a2-a4 and b2-b3, so it is good to maintain control of the c3 and c4-squares. For instance: 12...♖a6 13.a4 c6 14.b3±. **12...♖a6∞** White has compensation for the pawn but only enough for a draw.

10.dxe5

10.♘xe5 ♘xe5 11.dxe5 ♘g4 With the queen on e2 White would have a better game here with f2-f4!. See Chapter 14.3. **12.♗xb4?!** A better option is 12.a3 ♗xd2 13.♘xd2 ♘xe5 14.♘xc4 ♘xc4 15.♕xc4 c6=. **12...axb4 13.♕xc4 ♕e7**

14.♘d2 ♘xe5 15.♕c2 ♖d8 16.♘b3 c6 17.h3 ♗e6 18.♘d4 ♗d5∓ Sharevich-Sudakova, Sochi 2006.

10...♘g4 11.a3

There is no other path for White.

**11...♗xd2   12.♘bxd2   ♘gxe5
13.♘xe5**

13.♘xc4 ♘xf3+ (it is better to take another knight: 13...♘xc4!N 14.♕xc4 ♕f6 15.♘d4 ♘xd4 16.♕xd4 ♕xd4 17.exd4 ♖a6!=) 14.♗xf3 ♕f6 15.♗e4 h6 16.♖ac1 ♗h3 17.♖fd1± White's chances are slightly better due to his more active pieces, but Black has real chances to achieve a draw in the end, Zaltsman-Bass, New York 1983.

13...♘xe5	**14.♘xc4**	**♘xc4**
15.♕xc4	**c6**	**16.♖ad1**	**♕e7**
17.♖d2 ♗e6 18.♕c3 ♖fd8		

With equality, Miton-Stocek, Philadelphia 2006.

Conclusion

In this chapter, we have explained that after 4.♘f3 Black has an interesting alternative: the early ...d7-d5. By not making the main move 4...♘f6, Black gets an extra tempo to play in the centre, thus preventing White from applying the standard variations in the fianchetto system with 5.g3. We also saw how Black managed to level the chances with this early thrust also against several other common continuations, such as 5.e3, 5.♘c3 and 5.♗xb4.

White, on the other hand, has opportunities to demonstrate the drawbacks of this early attack in the centre. It is true that the ways to achieve this are somewhat unexpected: by moving the rook pawn 5.a3!, and probably also with the continuation 5.♕c2!?, with which White turns the tide by entering positions similar to the Queen's Gambit, where the extra moves a2-a3 and ...a7-a5, work better for White's position.

Let us remind ourselves that after 4.♘c3, which we covered in a previous chapter, no. 10, the classical move ...d7-d5 worked well, since in that Nimzo-Indian type position, the pawn on a5 was more than useful.

Exercises

11 (1) Find the plan.
(solution on page 447)

11 (2) Find the plan.
(solution on page 447)

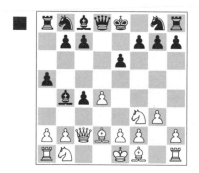

11 (3) Find the plan.
(solution on page 447)

Chapter 12

Nimzo-Type 4.♘f3 d6: The Fianchetto 5.g3

1.d4 e6 2.c4 ♗b4+ 3.♗d2 a5 4.♘f3 d6 5.g3

The bishop on b4 will disappear at some point, so Black begins to build an adequate pawn structure which will obviously serve the purpose of controlling the dark squares in the centre. However, generally speaking, Black declares himself prematurely in the centre with this move, just as he does with 4...d5 which we considered in the previous chapter.

5.g3 is the most frequent continuation which, apart from 5.♘c3 (covered in Chapter 13), gives White the best chances in the fight for the advantage in response to Black's early declaration in the centre with 4...d6.

Black usually chooses 5...♘f6 with the idea of ...♘d7 and ...e6-e5, or 5...♘c6 with the same idea ...e6-e5 but one move earlier.

5...♘c6!?
Black develops his queenside knight first to attack the centre with ...e6-e5 as soon as possible.
With 5...♘f6, Black returns to the usual Bogo-Indian positions: **6.♗g2 ♘bd7** A flexible but passive development of the black knight. 6...♘c6 7.0-0 e5 8.♗g5 is coverd under 5...♘c6 6.♗g2 e5 7.0-0 ♘f6. **7.0-0** Here we will analyse three moves:

A) **7...♗xd2?!** This trade doesn't comply with the idea of the system, since now there is no point in 3...a5. **8.♕xd2 0-0?! 9.♘c3** and now:

A1) **9...♖e8 10.♖ad1!?** White plays a useful developing move, planning the trade on the e5-square and play on the d-file in the case of the standard reaction ...e6-e5. **10...♕e7** If now 10...e5 11.dxe5 ♘xe5 12.c5!±. **11.e4 e5 12.♖fe1±**

With a typical advantage for this type of position, Naumkin-Djurovic, Belgrade 1988;

A2) **9...e5 10.dxe5!?** The simplest way to get a better position, using his superior development, and trying to show that the move ...a7-a5 is simply a waste of time and a weakening of Black's position. **10...♘xe5** On 10...dxe5 11.♘b5!± Black would face even greater problems. This short variation may show us how Black ruins the a5-pawn with the unnecessary exchange of the bishop on d2, Shestakov-Guburov, Kolontaevo 1997. **11.♘xe5 dxe5 12.♕xd8 ♖xd8 13.♖fd1** with easy play, and obviously a better and more active position for White.

B) A weak move would be **7...0-0?** because of **8.♗g5** and Black will have to give up a pawn to save his dark-squared bishop: **8...a4** No better is 8...d5 9.c5 h6 10.♗xf6 ♕xf6 11.♕b3 b6 12.a3 ♗xc5 13.dxc5 bxc5 14.♕c2± Vassiliev-Goumas, Golden Sands 2013. **9.a3 ♗a5 10.♕xa4±** Gunina-Zhai Mo, Beijing 2012;

C) **7...e5** Practically the only move. **8.♘c3** With the knight on d7 Black doesn't pressure the d4-pawn, so White can calmly develop his queenside knight. **8...0-0**

A critical position and an important crossroads for White in the system with

the black knight on d7. White usually chooses between 9.♕c2, 9.a3, 9.e3 and 9.dxe5:

C1) **9.♕c2** The most commonly played continuation. White takes the e4-square under control, at the same time clearing the first rank for the activation of his rooks. **9...♖e8** A logical developing move which Black uses to activate his rook, supporting, among other things, the advance of his e-pawn.

C11) **10.a3** Now this plan of capturing the bishop pair is not as efficient as is the case where White first exchanges the pawns on e5, which we cover under 9.dxe5 below. **10...♗xc3 11.♗xc3 e4!** **12.♘g5** In response to the other retreats, Black has a ready plan: 12.♘d2 e3∞ with mutual chances; or 12.♘e1 d5∞ with mutual chances. **12...♕e7 13.d5 h6 14.♘h3 ♘e5** 14...a4!?∞ with the idea of ...♘c5. **15.f3 ♗f5 16.fxe4 ♗h7 17.♘f2 ♘ed7 18.♕d2 ♗xe4**

With better perspectives for Black, courtesy of his slightly better pawn structure, Zhou Weiqi-Xiu Deshun, Xinghua 2013;

C12) 10.♖ad1

A logical developing move, but as after 10.a3 in line C11, it enables Black to get a more active game by pushing the e-pawn: **10...e4! 11.♘g5 ♗xc3 12.♗xc3** A weaker move would be 12.bxc3 ♕e7 13.f3 e3 14.♗c1 ♘b6⇄ 15.d5? h6 16.♘h3 ♘xc4 17.♖d4 ♘e5 18.f4 ♘eg4∓ Nikolic-Benjamin, Groningen 1993. **12...♕e7 13.d5** If 13.♕c1 h6 14.♘h3 ♘b6 15.b3 a4 16.d5 axb3 17.axb3 ♗g4 18.♕b2 ♘bd7 19.f3 ♗f5= Shneider-Thinius, Bad Zwesten 2006. **13...h6 14.♘h3 ♘e5 15.f3 ♗f5∞**

With mutual chances, Damljanovic-Markus, Skopje 2011;

C13) 10.e4

With this move, White takes over the dominance of the centre and with it gains some space advantage. What's left is to place his rooks on d1 and e1, so that in the upcoming middlegame this strategic plus may gain him some material or an otherwise substantial advantage. Both players have an identical pawn structure in the centre, as is the case in certain theoretical positions of the King's Indian, but the differences in the positions of the dark-squared bishops will here and there still significantly influence the further planning on both sides.

Black can 1. prolong the pressure in the centre with 10...c6, but this plan might hamper his game due to the weakening of the d6-pawn; or 2. open the centre, in the search for a more active game with 10...exd4, which gives him satisfactory play.

C131) 10...c6 Also a frequently-seen move in this structure, which controls the important d5-square and vacates the squares on the a4-d8 diagonal for the black queen, but it has the flaw of weakening the d6-pawn. **11.♖ad1**

C1311) Now the exchange **11...exd4** makes less sense because of the weakened d6-pawn. **12.♘xd4 ♘e5** A weaker move would be 12...♘c5?! because after 13.♖fe1 White has the strategic threat of a2-a3, by which he wins the bishop pair and further weakens the d6-pawn: 13...♗g4 (or 13...♕b6 14.a3 ♗xc3 15.♗xc3±) 14.f3 ♗d7 15.a3 ♗xc3 16.♗xc3± and without his dark-squared bishop, Black's d6-pawn is a strategically weak spot, Van Wely-Nikolic, Monaco (blindfold) 1998.

C13111) **13.♘ce2** White wants to exchange the dark-squared bishops and press on d6. **13...h6 14.h3 ♗xd2 15.♖xd2 ♕b6 16.♖fd1** with pressure;

C13112) **13.♘a4 ♗g4 14.f3 ♗d7** With the idea ...b7-b5. A weaker move would be 14...♗xd2 15.♖xd2 ♗d7 16.f4 ♘eg4 17.♕d3± A. David-Winants, France 2009. **15.c5** 15.♗c1?! b5 16.a3 bxa4 17.axb4 axb4 18.f4 ♘g6 19.e5 dxe5 20.♘xc6 ♕c8 21.♘xe5 ♗f5 22.♕d2 ♗e4↑. **15...dxc5 16.♗xb4 axb4** A weaker move would be 16...cxb4?! because of 17.f4±. **17.♘xc5 ♕b6 18.f4 ♗g4!**

19.fxe5 ♗xd1 20.♖xd1 ♖xe5 21.♘db3 ♖xa2=;

C13113) **13.b3** A simple, yet strong move. White defends the c4-pawn and also vacates the b2-square after which his bishop can move to the a1-h8 diagonal. **13...♗d7** If 13...♗g4!? 14.f3 ♗d7 15.♗c1± and it is not easy for Black to find an active plan. **14.h3 ♗c5 15.♗e3±** White has a real chance to turn his space advantage into something more substantial later in the game, Demuth-Winants, France 2009.

C1312) **11...♕c7** and now:

C13121) Nothing is achieved by **12.d5 ♗xc3 13.♗xc3 cxd5 14.cxd5 b5 15.♕b1 ♘c5 16.♖fe1 b4 17.♗d2 h6 18.♖c1 ♕b8 19.♗f1 ♗a6** with easy play and an equal position, Christensen-Hansen, corr. 1993;

C13122) However, a noteworthy tactical assault, which exploits the black queen's position, is **12.c5!?N exd4** (or 12...dxc5 13.dxe5 ♘xe5 14.♘xe5 ♕xe5 15.♗f4 ♕e6 16.a3 ♗xc3 17.♕xc3 and White has more than sufficient compensation thanks to his bishop pair and good control on the dark squares) **13.cxd6 ♕b6 14.♘a4 ♕a7 15.a3 ♗xd2 16.♖xd2 ♘xe4 17.♖xd4 ♘df6 18.♖fd1±** and White has an unpleasant supported passed pawn on the d-file;

C13123) **12.♖fe1 exd4!?N** Better than 12...b6 13.a3 ♗xc3 14.♗xc3± Moranda-Babula, Lublin 2009.

13.♘xd4 ♘e5⇄ Black has active play for his lack of pieces in the centre. For example: **14.♗g5** 14.b3 ♗g4↑ 15.f3? ♗c5∓. **14...♘xc4 15.♗xf6 gxf6 16.♗f1 ♘e5 17.f4 ♗c5 18.♔g2 ♘g6∞**

C132) 10...exd4 Giving way in the centre, yielding more space to his opponent, but also activating his passive pieces, especially the knight on d7 and the bishop on c8. **11.♘xd4 ♘e5** 11...♗c5 is a solid alternative as long as there is no rook on d1, because in that case White could simply put the bishop back on c1. 12.♘f5 After other knight moves Black has a satisfactory game. 12...♘e5 13.b3 ♗d7 14.♖ad1 h6 with a position we have covered under line C1321) 12...♗c5. **12.b3** 12.♗g5 c6 (12...h6! 13.♗xf6 ♕xf6 14.♘d5 ♕d8 15.♘xb4 axb4 with an excellent position for Black) 13.♘a4 h6 14.♗f4 ♘g6 15.♗e3 ♘g4 16.♗c1± Van Wely-Fressinet, Aix-les-Bains 2012;

C1321) 12...♗c5!? 13.♘f5 h6 14.♖ad1 ♗d7 Black is a little lacking in space, but all his pieces are functional and with them a considerable chance fpr full equality in the upcoming battle. **15.♗c1** (15.h3 a4⇄ Swapnil-Esen, Golden Sands 2012) **15...♕c8 16.♗b2 a4 17.♔h1 axb3 18.axb3 ♗a3!?** In case of 18...♗xf5 19.exf5± White is better off thanks to his bishop pair, Moranda-Bartel, Warsaw 2012.

With the text Black wants to exchange or displace the opponent's bishop. **19.♗a1** 19.♗xa3 ♖xa3=. **19...♗c5** with equal chances, since a1 is not a logical square for the white bishop;

C1322) 12...a4!? Black makes use of the opportune moment to increase his activity on the a-file. **13.h3** 13.♘cb5 ♗xd2 14.♕xd2 c6 15.♘c3 axb3 16.axb3 ♖xa1 17.♖xa1 h6 18.♖a8 ♕b6 19.♘a4 ♕c7= and Black gradually neutralizes his opponent's initiative, Andriuschenko-Kashlyak, corr. 2008; 13.♘xa4 ♗xd2 14.♕xd2 ♘xc4= Cernousek-Polak, Slovakia 2012; 13.♖ad1 axb3 14.axb3 ♗d7= Van Wely-Babula, Warsaw 2005. **13...axb3 14.axb3 ♖xa1 15.♖xa1 ♗c5 16.♘ce2 ♕e7 17.♗c3 ♗d7 18.♖e1 ♕d8∞** White has a space advantage in the centre, but Black's active pieces are ready for counterplay on the weakened squares in case White charges with f2-f4 or b3-b4, Erdös-Babula, Graz 2013.

C2) 9.a3

This is also one of the standard plans with the knight on c3. White gains the bishop pair, freeing the d2-square for his knight in case Black advances his e-pawn. **9...♗xc3 10.♗xc3** and now:

C21) 10...♘e4 11.♗e1± With the idea of ♘xe5. With the bishop pair,

White has better chances. **11...exd4** On 11...♕e7, in the game Khalifman-Lobron, Brussels (rapid) 1992 White could have gained an advantage immediately with 12.♘xe5!±; for 11...♘ef6 12.dxe5 dxe5 13.♗c3± see under 10. a3. **12.♘xd4 ♖e8 13.♕c2±**

White will be able to strengthen his position unhindered with ♖ad1, f2-f3, e2-e4, ♗c3, and with his space surplus and bishop pair he will gain an undisputed advantage;

C22) 10...e4 11.♘d2! In the line with the inserted moves ♕c2 and ...♖e8, Black has the simple ...e4-e3 with good play. Here White manages to block the aggressive black pawn with e2-e3 and then attack and trade it with f2-f3. For 11.♘g5 ♖e8 12.♕c2 ♕e7 see under 10.a3. **11...♖e8** 11...e3?! 12.fxe3 ♘g4 13.♖f3±. **12.e3** If 12.f3 e3∞ with mutual chances, Krivousas-Kveinys, Kaunas 2001. Now:

C221) With **12...b6!?** Black wants to destroy his opponent's main threat of f2-f3 by playing ...♗b7: **13.b4** 13.f3 ♗b7=. **13...axb4 14.axb4 ♗b7 15.♖xa8 ♕xa8 16.♕c2 b5!?∞** A thematic pawn sacrifice with which Black conquers the blockade square d5 and thus is able to disconnect White's dark-squared bishop from the game for some time.

Although the engines give a considerable advantage for White here, Black has a real chance to hold the position thanks to White's inactive dark-squared bishop;

C222) 12...d5?! Unfortunately, this logical blocking move, aimed against the activities of White's bishop pair, does not work, since White gains a considerable initiative by opening up the f-file: **13.f3! exf3 14.♕xf3 c6 15.g4!?** White has superior development, so he immediately moves in for the attack, aiming at the weakened f7-square. Also possible is the simple 15.♖ae1 with the idea of e3-e4. when White has better development and a clear advantage. **15...h6 16.h4±** Goldin-Rohde, Philadelphia 1992;

C223) 12...♘b6!?N

13.♕c2 13.f3 exf3 14.♕xf3 ♘a4 with equal chances. **13...♗f5 14.b4 a4=** Of course, Black does not want to open the position and activate White's bishop pair. **15.♗b2** With 15.d5 White opens up his dark-squared bishop but also gives new life to his knight via the e5-square: 15...♘bd7, with an unclear position. **15...d5**

The white bishops are neutralized for a long time. The chances are equal.

C3) **9.e3** In case of a trade on d4, White wants to recapture with his pawn and keep the full centre. However this unnecessary double defence neglects the e4-square, which allows Black to obtain equal chances. **9...e4** The calmer 9...♖e8 also works: 10.a3 ♗xc3 11.♗xc3 ♘e4!?.

Now this aggressive move is good, since White has lost a tempo with e2-e3 and therefore Black has more active play against White's bishop pair. It is useful to compare this position with the variation covered under 9.a3 where

White hasn't played e2-e3. 12.♗e1 ♕e7∞ with mutual chances.

10.♘g5 A more passive move is 10.♘e1 ♕e7 11.♘e2 ♘b6 12.b3 ♗g4↑ and Black takes matters into his own hands, Hertneck-Zelcic, Salzburg 2003. **10...♗xc3 11.♗xc3 ♖e8 12.b3** 12.f3 exf3 13.♕xf3 h6 14.♘h3 ♘b6⇄ with good play for Black. **12...♘f8 13.f3 exf3 14.♕xf3 h6 15.♘xf7** A practically forced trade, because after 15.♘h3 the simple response is 15...♗xh3 16.♗xh3 ♕e7 and in spite of his bishop pair, White is the one with the problems due to his serious weaknesses on the e-file. **15...♔xf7 16.e4 ♕e7 17.e5 dxe5 18.dxe5 ♕c5+ 19.♔f2 ♖xe5 20.♗xe5 ♕xe5 21.♖ae1 ♕d6=**

White has certain compensation, but only for a draw, Deep Junior 13-Vitruvius 1.11C, Internet 2012;

C4) **9.dxe5**

The introduction to a simple yet dangerous plan. Many black players underestimate the value of this exchange, because they tend to think it facilitates their position.

However, this opening up of the position, especially of the d-file, suits White's active pieces. Black can use either his knight or his pawn to capture on e5, but either way there is no equality for him:

C41) 9...dxe5 With the white knight on f3 Black's pawn has better prospects on e5. However Black's bishop remains detained on c8 so White easily overtakes his opponent in development and activity, which gives him the better chances:

C411) White has less chance of an advantage after **10.♘d5 ♗d6** (10...♘xd5 11.cxd5±; 10...♗xd2 11.♕xd2 c6 12.♘xf6+ ♕xf6 13.♖ad1 ♖e8 14.♘g5 ♘c5 15.♘e4 ♘xe4 16.♗xe4 ♗g4= Koch-Ellers, Germany 2000) **11.♕c2** (11.♗c3 ♘e4= Hartl-Sedlak, Lienz 2013) **11...c6** (11...h6 12.♘xf6+ ♕xf6 13.♗e3 ♗c5 14.♕e4 ♖e8= Hernando Rodrigo-Garcia Ilundain, Torrevieja 1997) **12.♘xf6+ ♘xf6=**;

C412) 10.a3! ♗c5 Even after 10...♗xc3 11.♗xc3 ♕e7 12.♕c2 White has an easy game and better chances with his bishop pair, for

example 12...♕c5? 13.♗b4!+−; 10...♗d6 11.♕c2 c6 12.♖ad1±; 10...♗e7 11.♕c2 c6 12.♖fd1 ♕c7 13.♘a4 b6 14.h3 ♖b8 15.♗e3 ♗a6 16.♖ac1± Arencibia Rodriguez-Bruzon Batista, Montreal 2012. **11.♕c2 h6 12.♖fd1 ♕e7 13.♘a4 e4 14.♘xc5 ♘xc5 15.♘d4** White's bishop pair gives him the better chances, Tancik-Stankovic, Subotica 2012.

C42) 9...♘xe5 Black uses this moment to simplify the position and open up his light-squared bishop. **10.♘xe5 dxe5** and now:

C421) On **11.♕c2** Black has a nice tactic that leads to a position with the different-coloured bishops and equal chances: **11...♗f5!N** On 11...c6 White puts his plan into action with 12.♖fd1 ♕c7 13.♘a4 ♗e6 14.♗e3 with a more active position and better chances, Gagarin-Nikolenko, Moscow 1989.

12.♕xf5 ♕xd2 13.♗xb7 ♖ad8! On b8 the rook seems to be less effective: 13...♖ab8 14.♘e4 ♘xe4 15.♕xe4 ♕xb2 16.♗d5± and Black has yet to improve the positions of his queen and bishop, though he still maintains chances to equalize. **14.♘e4** 14.♘d5 ♘xd5 15.♗xd5 ♕xe2= Zappa Mexico II-Toga II, Internet 2009. **14...♘xe4 15.♕xe4** 15.♗xe4 g6 16.♕f3 ♕xb2=. **15...♕xb2 16.♗d5 ♔h8=**;

C422) 11.a3! is the best continuation if we follow the idea of the trade on e5, since without the d-pawn and the white knight on f3 the advance of Black's e-pawn loses all meaning. Black has many options for his dark-squared bishop, but not one of them guarantees him a carefree position:

C4221) 11...♗e7 Passively, not wanting to move the bishop to c5 because of the attack by the white knight with ♘a4. **12.♕c2 c6 13.♘a4** It seems that Black's three last moves have become standard in the line with 9.dxe5. **13...♗e6** And now for White all roads lead to Rome, it would seem: **14.♗e3** 14.♖ad1 ♕c7 15.c5 ♘d7 16.f4 f6 17.f5 ♗f7 18.♗e3 ♖ad8 19.♗e4± also works; or 14.♖fd1 ♕c7 15.c5 ♖fd8 16.♘b6 ♖a6 17.♗g5±. **14...♘d7 15.♖fd1** 15.♖ad1± also works. **15...♕c7 16.♖d2 ♖fd8 17.♖ad1±**

Black has developed his pieces and defended all the critical points, but his active play vanishes without a trace. White has ideal activity and piece coordination but nothing substantial so far. Still, the odds favour him, Spark 1.0-Nemo 1.0.1b, Internet 2012;

C4222) 11...♗d6 essentially changes nothing. After **12.♕c2 c6 13.♖ad1** White has a better position;

C4223) Giving up the bishop pair in this open position with **11...♗xc3?!** is practically the worst possibility. After **12.♗xc3** White has a clear advantage;

C4224) 11...♗c5 Black's bishop is the most active on this square, but the problem is that it will be exposed to attack with ♘a4. **12.♕c2 c6** Strategically speaking an unavoidable move. Black must limit the influence of the strong light-squared bishop on g2 and take control of the important d5-square:

C42241) 13.♖fd1 ♕e7 14.♘a4! Now Black faces the unpleasant choice of either giving up his dark-squared bishop or making peace by passively retreating. **14...♗e6** 14...♗a7 15.c5±; 14...♗d6? 15.♘b6±. **15.♘xc5 ♕xc5 16.♖ac1±** White has better chances with his bishop pair, Sargissian-Moiseenko, Ningbo 2011;

C42242) 13.♘a4! The white knight aims at the strong black bishop and the weakened b6-square. **13...♗a7** 13...♕e7 is not good because of 14.♘xc5 ♕xc5 15.b4 with a clear advantage (a weaker move would be 15.♗b4 because after 15...axb4 16.axb4 Black has the intermediate move 16...♗f5!=); 13...♗e7 14.♗e3±. **14.♖ad1 ♕e7** 14...♕c7 15.c5±. **15.c5**

± Zhidkov-Kveinys, Kurgan 2001.
6.♗g2 e5

The starting position of the so-called Accelerated Bogo-Indian, where Black combines the ...a7-a5 push with a delay of the development of his kingside knight. White usually chooses between 7.0-0, 7.d5, 7.dxe5, 7.♗xb4 and 7.a3.

7.0-0

A) **7.d5** Gaining space with tempo, but as we know this typical shutting down of the centre also has its flaws: 1. it releases the pressure in the centre, 2. it shuts down his own light-squared bishop's diagonal and 3. it loses control of the central squares c5 and e5. Black can respond with the trade on d2 or by retreating with 7...♘ce7 or 7...♘b8:

A1) **7...♘ce7!?** With the bishop on the b4-square, retreating the knight to e7 is reasonable, because it can be activated with ...c7-c6 with pressure on White's centre. **8.♗xb4** 8.0-0 ♘f6 9.♘c3 0-0 10.a3 ♗c5 11.♘e1 ♗f5 12.♗g5 ♘d7 13.♘d3 ♗a7 14.e4 ♗g6 15.♘b5 ♗b6 16.b4 h6 17.♗d2 f5∞ with mutual chances, Tregubov-Fressinet, Bastia 2011. **8...axb4 9.0-0 ♘f6 10.♘bd2** 10.♕d2 c5 11.dxc6 ♘xc6 12.♖d1 ♗e6⇄ Black has good play with his active pieces, Kasimdzhanov-Turov, Nancy (rapid) 2011. **10...0-0** and now:

A11) **11.♕b3 c5 12.a3** and now with the simple **12...bxa3N** (instead of 12...b5?! when after the simple

13.cxb5 Black is worse, as in the game Epishin-Mundorf, Paderborn 2012) **13.♖xa3 ♖xa3 14.♕xa3 b5** Black could have gained equal chances;

A12) A weaker move would be **11.♘e1 c6 12.dxc6 bxc6 13.♘d3 ♗f5!N 14.c5** If 14.♘xb4 ♖b8 15.♘xc6 ♘xc6 16.♗xc6 ♖xb2∓ with more than sufficient compensation, due to the excellent coordination of Black's pieces. **14...♗xd3 15.exd3** 15.cxd6 ♗b5 16.dxe7 ♕xe7∓. **15...d5∓**

A2) **7...♘b8** has no independent significance because after **8.0-0 ♗xd2** we switch to the positions covered under A3) 7...♗xd2+;

A3) The exchange **7...♗xd2+**, after which Black transposes into the positions covered under 3...♗xd2+, is part of the logical plan in the positions where Black has weakened the dark squares. We shall examine all three recaptures:

A31) **8.♘fxd2** A solid choice. White plans c4-c5 and the knight jump to c4, and will develop the queenside knight to the natural c3-square. **8...♘b8** and now:

A311) **9.♘c3 ♘d7 10.a3 f5 11.b4 ♘h6**

We have already seen that in this type of position the black knight has good manoeuvring capabilities even from the edge of the board. It is also good to develop the knight to its natural square with 11...♘gf6!? 12.0-0 0-0 13.♘b3 axb4 14.axb4 ♖xa1 15.♕xa1 f4 16.♕a5 ♘g4⇄ 17.♘b5?! fxg3 18.hxg3 ♕g5→ M. Marin. **12.0-0 0-0 13.♖c1 b6**

With good chances for both sides, Sadler-Conquest, Hastings 1996;

A312) Freeing the c4-square for the knight also works: **9.c5!? ♘f6** It might not be the best course of action to break up one's own pawn structure in the centre with 9...dxc5?! because of 10.♘c4♾ with obvious compensation for White due to the increased activity of his pieces. **10.cxd6 cxd6 11.♘c3 0-0 12.♘c4 ♘a6 13.♘b5 ♘e8 14.0-0 ♘c5 15.♕d2 b6** With the idea ...♗a6. Black has a real chance to gradually stop the white initiative and reach full equality.

A32) **8.♘bxd2** Also a logical move, aiming to develop his minor pieces quickly. **8...♘b8**

A321) Nothing comes from the thematic **9.c5 ♘f6 10.0-0** After 10.cxd6 cxd6 11.0-0 0-0 12.♘c4 b5 13.♘e3 ♘a6 14.♖c1 ♗d7∓ Black achieves all his goals, Cmilyte-Muzychuk, Beijing (blind) 2012. **10...0-0 11.♘c4 b5 12.cxb6 cxb6 13.♘fd2** With 13.a4 White puts another pawn on a light square. After 13...♘a6 14.♘fd2 ♘c5 Black also has an unchallenged knight

on c5, with excellent play. **13...b5 14.♘e3 ♘a6** with equal chances. Fedder-Ward, Copenhagen 1992;

A322) **9.0-0 ♘f6** 9...♘h6 is another popular idea: 10.e4 0-0 11.b3 ♘a6 12.a3 ♗d7 13.♘e1 c6 14.♘c2 cxd5 15.cxd5 ♘c5 (15...♗b5!?) 16.♘e3 f5 17.b4 axb4 18.axb4 ♖xa1 19.♕xa1 ♘a6 (19...♘xe4↑) 20.exf5 (20.♕a5!±) 20...♘xf5 21.♘xf5 ♗xf5= Meduna-Eingorn, Haifa 1989. **10.♘e1** If 10.e4 0-0 11.♘e1. **10...0-0 11.e4** and now:

A3221) **11...♘a6 12.♘d3 c6⇄** The thematic 12...♗g4 is covered under 3...♗d2.

Black compensates for his lack of space with counterplay on the dark squares, Del Prado Montoro-Hoffman, Ponferrada 1991;

A3222) **11...c6 12.♘d3 ♘bd7!?** The introduction to an interesting plan. Black doesn't place the knight on the natural a6-square, but saves this square for his light-squared bishop (we saw 12...♘a6 in the previously mentioned game under 11...♘a6). **13.♖c1 ♖e8 14.♖c3 b6 15.♕c2 ♗a6 16.♖e1 ♖c8∞** with play for both sides, Kachiani Gersinska-Epishin, Willingen 1999.

A33) **8.♕xd2**

A331) **8...♘b8** The knight is directed to c5 as quickly as possible. **9.♘c3 ♘a6 10.0-0**

Black is awarded for his courage in delaying the development of his kingside knight and now has a choice between two solid positions for it: h6 and f6. **10...♘h6** Black wants a mobile f-pawn and he is not afraid to move the knight to the edge of the board, especially since White has no dark-squared bishop. 10...♘f6!? – it is fascinating to see the development of the kingside knight only on the tenth move. Is there really no limit to the theory of chess? Also interestingly, we now enter a position covered under 3...♗xd2+. **11.♘e1 0-0** and now:

A3311) The aggressive **12.f4** can only bring trouble for White after **12...exf4 13.gxf4**. If he captures with the rook or the queen, White will also have a strategically inferior position because he loses control of the important e5-square. **13...f5** 13...♖e8!?. **14.♘d3 ♗d7 15.♖ae1 ♕f6 16.e3 b6 17.b3 ♔h8 18.♘e2 ♘c5 19.♘xc5 bxc5∓**

Black has several plans to choose from in a strategically pleasant position, Pinter-Eingorn, Dortmund 1988;
   A3312) **12.♘d3 ♗d7 13.b3 f5**

With equality, Petran-King, Budapest 1989.

A332) A more passive move is **8...♘ce7?!** because without the bishop on b4, Black cannot activate his knight with ...c7-c6 because of the weak d6-pawn: **9.♘c3** 9.♕g5!? is unusual but noteworthy, since it is not an easy decision for Black how to defend his g7-pawn. **9...♘f6 10.0-0 0-0 11.e4 ♘d7** On 11...♗d7 play could continue as follows: 12.♘e1 ♘g6 13.♘d3 and White has the brighter position since the knight on d3 supports the important squares f4, e5, c5 and b4, unlike the lost black knight which has distanced itself from the control of the critical squares. **12.♘e1 f5 13.♘d3±** With the idea of f2-f4. Shulman-Akobian, Upper Lake (blitz) 2009.

B) **7.dxe5** White simplifies the position by taking the pressure off of the centre but keeps in mind the conquering of the bishop pair. **7...dxe5 8.♘c3**

B1) **8...♘ge7!** On this square the knight is less active, but but Black thus keeps the f-pawn mobile and keeps the option of limiting White's mobility.

9.a3 ♗xc3 10.♗xc3 ♛xd1+ 11.♖xd1 f6 12.b3 White must not allow the thematic ...a5-a4!, restricting the mobility of his queenside pawns. **12...♗e6 13.♘d2 ♔f7 14.0-0 ♖hd8=**

Black has a healthy position, with active and harmonious pieces, which is quite enough for the fight against the strong bishop pair, Jelen-Sher, Ptuj 1993;

B2) Also functional and natural is **8...♘f6** to save the e7-square for the black queen, though in that case after a2-a3 and the practically forced trade on c3, White's dark-squared bishop will have a strong influence on the a1-h8 diagonal. For example: **9.0-0 0-0 10.a3 ♗xc3 11.♗xc3 ♛e7 12.b4!** White wishes to immediately use the power of his dark-squared bishop, not allowing the thematic ...a5-a4. If 12.♛c2 a4! – the typical move, restricting White's queenside. In this structure the c4-pawn and the b3-square are es-

pecially vulnerable and Black often invades there. That is why White later resorts to the trade of the a-pawn with b2-b3, but this only turns one problem into another, because White's pawns get separated: 13.e3 ♖e8 14.h3 e4 15.♘d2 ♗f5 16.b3 axb3 17.♛xb3 b6 with equal chances since White compensates for the weak pawn structure with his strong dark-squared bishop, Potkin-Vitiugov, Tiumen 2012.

12...♗g4 On 12...♖d8 in the game Abdalla-Borovikov, Cappelle la Grande 2012, White could have kept his edge with 13.♛c2!?N e4 14.♘g5 e3 15.f4± due to his strong dark squared bishop and mobile queenside pawns. **13.♛b1 axb4 14.axb4 ♖xa1 15.♛xa1 ♘e4 16.b5 ♘xc3 17.♛xc3 ♗xf3 18.♛xf3 ♘d4** Even worse is 18...♘a5 19.♛c3 b6 20.♗d5± with a great difference in value between the bishop and the knight. **19.♛xb7 ♘xe2+ 20.♔h1 ♛c5 21.♛d5±** and White has excellent winning chances, Rybka 4.1-Gull II b2, Internet 2012.

C) **7.♗xb4** We have already said that this exchange favours the opponent, since it activates his rook on the a-file and denies White's queenside knight its natural developing square. **7...axb4 8.d5 ♘b8 9.0-0 ♘f6 10.♘bd2 0-0 11.♘e1 ♘a6** Also possible is the simple

11...c5 with mutual chances, Piket-Psakhis, Leeuwarden 1993. **12.♘d3 ♗f5!?N**

Black has strategic threats in ...e5-e4 or ...♗xd3 and so provokes an additional weakening of the white position. **13.e4** Of course, had the dark-squared bishops still been on the board, then this move would strengthen White's position. But in this instance White further limits his light-squared bishop on g2 and additionally weakens the dark squares. **13...♗g4** We are already familiar with this idea, which he uses to force a weakening of the g1-a7 diagonal. **14.f3 ♗d7⇄**

... with the idea of ...c7-c6, with good play on the dark squares;

D) **7.a3** This currently unnecessary move grants Black some extra time to get a comfortable position. **7...♗xd2+ 8.♕xd2 ♘f6 9.dxe5** If 9.♘c3 0-0

10.0-0 ♗g4 and Black easily equalizes. **9...♘xe5 10.♘xe5 dxe5 11.♕xd8+ ♔xd8 12.♘c3 c6** with an excellent endgame for Black, Lieb-Eingorn, Bad Wörishofen 1997.

After 7.0-0, Black can continue pursuing the plan of the Accelerated Bogo-Indian with 7...exd4 or move into the regular Bogo-Indian with 7...♘f6:
7...exd4
Black has an extra tempo because he hasn't played ...♘f6, so his opponent doesn't have the unpleasant pin with ♗g5. With **7...♘f6** we enter one of the variations of the Bogo-Indian which commonly develops in the following move order: 1. d4 ♘f6 2. c4 e6 3. ♘f3 ♗b4 4. ♗d2 a5 5. g3 d6 6. ♗g2 ♘c6 7. 0-0 e5. **8.♗g5**

White intends to play a2-a3, trapping the bishop. **8...exd4** Black is practically forced to give way in the centre and centralize the White's pieces to clear c5 for the bishop's retreat. **9.♘xd4 ♘xd4** A weak move would be 9...♗d7? 10.a3 ♗c5 11.♘b5 ♖c8 12.♘1c3 h6 13.♗xf6 ♕xf6 14.♘d5 ♕d8 15.♖b1 0-0 16.b4 axb4 17.axb4 ♗a7 18.♘xa7 ♘xa7 19.b5! and Black is in danger of losing, Dreev-Apicella, Kemer 2007. **10.♕xd4 h6 11.♗xf6 ♕xf6 12.♕xf6 gxf6 13.a3 ♗c5 14.♘c3 c6 15.e3.**

Black's bishop pair can't compensate for his bad pawn structure. White is better and has an easy game, Giri-Ivanchuk, Reggio Emilia 2012.

Now comes a series of forced moves.
8.♘xd4 ♘xd4 9.♗xb4 axb4 10.♕xd4 ♘f6

In this critical position White has a plan he can use to continue the fight for a strategic edge. It involves putting the rook on d1 and the knight on e3.

Weaker would be **10...♕f6** (also, 10...♕g5?! 11.♘d2 ♘f6 12.♘b3± with the idea of c4-c5) because after **11.♕d2** White has pressure on the weaknesses on the d-file, with better chances: **11...c5 12.♖d1 ♖a6 13.a3!** 13.♕c2 ♕e7 14.♘d2 ♘f6 15.♘f1 0-0 16.a3 bxa3 17.♖xa3 ♖xa3 18.bxa3 ♖e8∞ Pedersen-Epishin, Koge 2013.

13...♘e7 14.♖a2 0-0 15.b3± By trading the a- and b-pawns, White gets rid of his only weakness, but Black has a permanent defect in his queenside structure. **15...♖b6 16.axb4 ♖xb4 17.♖a3 b5?!** This sacrifice ruins Black's position even further. **18.cxb5 d5 19.♖c1 ♖xb5 20.♘c3 ♖b4 21.♘a4 ♗f5 22.♘xc5 ♖fb8 23.♕xb4 ♖xb4 24.♘d7!** and White wins, Nikolic-Psakhis, Moscow 1990.
    11.♖d1!
With the idea of ♕d2.
    A) **11.♘d2 0-0**

White has slightly better development and pressure on the central diagonal. However, Black has sufficient counterplay due to his pressure on the a-file. The push 3...a5 with the delayed development of the kingside knight to f6 have clearly proved their worth in this position. We'll take a look at three logical continuations for White:

A1) 12.♘b3 c5 13.♕d3 ♕e7 14.♖fd1 ♖a6 15.a3 ♖b6⇄ Petrukhina-Pähtz, Moscow 2009;

A2) 12.♘e4 ♘xe4 13.♗xe4 ♖e8 Let's see how the machine plays the endgame: 13...♕g5!? 14.♔h1 ♖b8 15.f3 ♗e6 16.♖g1 ♕e5 17.♕xe5 dxe5 18.♗d5 ♖bd8 19.♖gd1 c6 20.♗xe6 fxe6 21.b3 c5 22.♔g2 ♔h8 23.♖xd8 ♖xd8 24.a3 ♖a8 25.a4 ♖d8 26.♔f2 g6 27.♔e3 ♔g7 28.h4 ♔f6 29.g4 h5 30.♖g1 ♖d4↑. An instructive endgame, played phenomenally by the machine, which eventually won, Witz Alpha21-Critter 0.34, Internet (blitz) 2013. **14.♗f3 ♕g5=** Jelling-L.B. Hansen, Denmark 1997;

A3) 12.♖fe1

A31) 12...♕e7!? 13.♘f1 c5 13...♕e5= Marin. **14.♕d2 ♗e6** Worthy of attention is 14...♘g4!?N 15.h3 ♘e5 16.♘e3 ♗e6 17.♘d5 ♕d8 18.b3 ♖a6⇄. **15.♘e3 ♖a6 16.a4 bxa3 17.♖xa3 ♖b6 18.♕c3** In this slightly better position for White, the players agreed a draw, Holst-Topalov, Aalborg 1991;

A32) 12...♖e8 13.♘f1 ♘g4! 14.c5 dxc5 15.♕xc5 ♕e7 16.♕xe7 ♖xe7 17.♖ed1 ♖e8 18.h3 ♘f6 19.♘e3 ♖a7=

B) 11.c5 dxc5 12.♕xc5 ♕e7 13.♖c1 ♕xc5 14.♖xc5 c6 and now:

B1) 15.♖c4 b3 16.♘c3 Weaker would be 16.a3 ♗e6 17.♖d4 ♖d8 18.♖xd8+ ♔xd8 19.♘c3 ♔c7 20.♖d1

♘d7 21.f4 ♘b6 22.♖d3 ♖e8 23.♔f2 f6 24.♗f3 ♗f7 25.♖d4 ♘c4 26.♘d1 b5↑ Magerramov-Fingorn, Uzhgorod 1988; or 16.a4 ♗e6 17.♖b4 0-0-0∓ Antonsen-L.B. Hansen, Naestved 1991. **16...♔e7** 16...♗e6!? 17.♖b4 bxa2 18.♖xb7 0-0=. **17.a3 ♗e6∞**;

B2) 15.♖xc6?! bxc6 16.♗xc6+ ♔e7 17.♗xa8 ♖d8 18.f3 ♗a6 19.♗c6 ♖d1+ 20.♔f2 ♖h1∓ Boos-Trella, Paderborn 2012.

11...♖a6

11...0-0 12.c5±.

White has multiple options here, but only one of them fits the plan that gives him hopes for a better middlegame:

12.♘d2!

A natural developing move with which the knight aims towards the ideal e3-square. Surprisingly, no one has played this move yet.

12.c5 ♕e7 13.♕xb4 dxc5 14.♕f4 0-0 15.♘c3 ♖b6= was seen in Garza Marco-Sedlak, La Roda 2013; 12.♕d2 c5 13.♕e3+ ♕e7 14.♕xe7+ ♔xe7= was Pliasunov-Totsky, St Petersburg 2000; **12.b3 0-0 13.a3 ♕e7=** was Gleizerov-S. Schneider, Stockholm 2012.

12...♕e7!

Black should exchange queens as soon as possible, before White organizes his pieces by placing the knight on e3.

White maintains the situation after the natural **12...0-0 13.♘f1 ♖e8** 13...♕e7 14.♘e3 ♖e8 15.♘d5 ♘xd5 16.cxd5 (leaving b4 and c7 weak) 16...♕xe2? 17.♗f1±. **14.♘e3**

The knight is on the ideal square, with the option of strengthening the position with ♘d5 or attack the b4-pawn. It is hard to find an active plan for Black, but the game could continue as follows: **14...h5!?** Black wants to play ...♘g4 in order to chase away or exchange the well-placed white knight and so achieve active play on the e-file.

It is too late to aim for the queen trade on e5: 14...♕c7 15.♘d5 ♘xd5 16.cxd5± and Black has weaknesses on b4 and c7; if 14...♘d7? 15.♕d2±.

A) **15.h3** White takes the important b4-square under control, but in this case, his pawn structure on the kingside becomes more sensitive. **15...♖a5!** Black changes his plans for the queen-side rook, and places it on e5, in order to achieve active play on the kingside. **16.♕d2 ♖ae5 17.♕xb4 ♘e4!** By capturing the pawn with the queen, White has left his kingside more vulnerable.

Also worthy of consideration is 17...♖xe3!? 18.fxe3 ♘e4⦶ and Black has sufficient compensation for a draw, since the prophylactic h2-h3 has evidently weakened White's kingside. **18.♘d5 h4 19.g4 ♘xf2 20.♔xf2 ♗xg4 21.hxg4? ♖xe2+ 22.♔g1 h3∓**;

B) **15.♕d2 ♘g4 16.♘d5 c5 17.h4** with a minimal advantage for White, since his pieces are placed more naturally. Weaker would be 17.♗f3 h4⇄.

13.♘f1 ♕e5 14.♘e3

White does not achieve enough with 14.♕d2 0-0 15.♘e3 h5 16.♘d5 ♘xd5 17.cxd5 ♗g4 with equal chances; or 14.♕xe5+ dxe5 15.♘e3 ♔e7 16.c5 (16.♘d5+ ♘xd5 17.♖xd5 ♗e6= with the idea of ...♖ha8) 16...c6 17.♘c4 ♗e6 18.♘xe5 ♖ha8 and Black regains the pawn with equal play.

14...♕xd4 15.♖xd4 c5 16.♖d3 ♔d8

With the queens off, the black king should be placed on c7.

17.a4 bxa3 18.♖axa3 ♖xa3 19.♖xa3 ♔c7 20.♖b3 ♖e8 21.♗f3 h5 22.h4 g6=

And Black is close to full equality.

Conclusion

As a response to the most frequently played move 5.g3, Black has two plans at his disposal:

A. A swift attack on the centre with 5...♞c6 and ...e6-e5; or

B. switching to a regular Bogo-Indian with 5...♞f6, where after the popular 6...♞d7,(6...♞c6 7.0-0 e5 allows 8.♗g5, which usually leads Black into an inferior endgame) Black also pushes through ...e6-e5, but one move later.

We feel that plan A with the swift attack on the centre (1.d4 e6 2.c4 ♗b4+ 3.♗d2 a5 4.♞f3 d6 5.g3 ♞c6 6.♗g2 e5) gives Black a practically equal endgame, whereas plan B is employed more frequently. Among top players the game becomes quite curious and problematic for Black after the opening of the centre with (1.d4 e6 2.c4 ♗b4+ 3.♗d2 a5 4.♞f3 d6 5.g3 ♞f6 6.♗g2 ♞d7 7.0-0 e5 8.♞c3 0-0) 9.dxe5!?.

Exercises

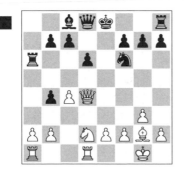

12 (1) Find the plan.
(solution on page 448)

12 (2) Find the plan.
(solution on page 448)

12 (3) Find the plan. *(solution on page 448)*

Chapter 13

Nimzo-Type 4.♘f3 d6: The Solid 5.♘c3

1.d4 e6 2.c4 ♗b4+ 3.♗d2 a5 4.♘f3 d6 5.♘c3

In this chapter, besides the solid 5.♘c3 we will examine the rarely played continuations 5.e4, 5.e3 and 5.a3.

5.♘c3

The natural continuation we analysed on move 4 in Chapter 10. White makes a move that is characteristic of the Nimzo-Indian, planning to gain the bishop pair after a2-a3.

A) In reply to **5.e4** Black usually blocks with ...e6-e5, so as to neutralize White's early formed pawn trio in the centre. **5...♘f6 6.♗d3** It is insane to advance in the centre without support: 6.e5 dxe5 7.dxe5 ♘e4=. **6...e5 7.♘c3** 7.dxe5? dxe5 8.♘xe5 ♕d4∓. Now:

A1) **7...♗g4 8.d5?! ♘bd7** Black is playing one of his favourite types of position with control of square c5. **9.h3 ♘c5 10.♗c2 ♗h5 11.♕e2 ♗g6∓** Berezovsky-Eingorn, Bern 1993;

A2) Another good move is **7...exd4 8.♘xd4 ♘c6 9.♘xc6** 9.♗e3 ♘g4↑. **9...bxc6 10.0-0 0-0⇄**

B) **5.e3** is a continuation that does not cause much trouble for Black: **5...♘f6** Also possible is 5...♗xd2+ 6.♘bxd2 ♘d7 7.♕c2 b6 (or 7...♘gf6 8.♗d3 0-0 9.0-0 b6 10.♘g5 h6 11.♘ge4 ♗b7=) 8.♗d3 h6 9.♗e4 ♖a7 10.0-0 ♘e7 11.♖fd1 0-0= Burmakin-Epishin, Schwäbisch Gmünd 2013. Now:

257

B1) White gains nothing by **6.♘c3 ♘bd7 7.♗d3 e5**. As we can see, Black conducts his favourite plan with ease and is already threatening to win the opponent's piece. **8.♕c2 0-0 9.0-0 ♖e8** Black activates a rook while at the same time renewing the threat of winning a piece. **10.♘e4** 10.e4 This two-step with the e-pawn cannot bring White anything good: 10...exd4 11.♘xd4 c6 12.♖ae1 ♘e5 13.h3 ♗c5= 14.♗e3? ♗xh3∓ and White surrendered to the former World Champion, having lost a clean pawn, in Spraggett-Smyslov, Montpellier 1985. **10...♘xe4 11.♗xe4 ♘f6** And Black is at least equal, Bacrot-Fressinet, Calvi (rapid) 2013;

B2) **6.♗d3 ♕e7 7.0-0** 7.e4 e5= Borsuk-Drasko, Cappelle la Grande 2013; 7.♕c2 e5= Löffler-Zelcic, Austria 2004. **7...e5 8.a3 ♗xd2 9.♘fxd2!**

The only way for White to make progress. **9...0-0 10.♘c3 ♖e8 11.h3 ♘bd7 12.♖c1** with a more active position for White, Christiansen-Speelman, London 1982.

C) **5.a3 ♗xd2+ 6.♕xd2 ♘f6** 6...♘c6 7.♘c3 ♘f6 8.g3 0-0 9.♗g2 a4 10.♕c2 ♗d7 11.0-0 ♘a5 12.♘d2± Kanakaris-Antic, Paleochora 2009. **7.♘c3 ♘bd7** Now White usually plays one of the next moves:

C1) **8.g4!? 0-0** 8...♘xg4?! 9.♖g1 ♘gf6 10.♖xg7± with the idea of ♘f3-g5; a better move is 8...h6 9.0-0-0 d5∞. **9.g5 ♘e8 10.0-0-0 b6 11.h4±** Pap-Babula, Hungary 2011;

C2) **8.e3 0-0 9.♗d3 e5 10.0-0 ♖e8 11.♕c2 ♕e7** 11...h6 12.♗f5 c6 13.♖ad1 ♕c7 14.h3 ♘f8 15.♗xc8 ♖axc8 16.dxe5 dxe5 17.♘d2 ♖cd8 18.c5 ♘e6 19.♘b3 g6 20.♘a4 ♘d5 21.♘d2 ♕e7∞ Jobava-Suba, Brasov 2011. **12.♘d2 ♘f8 13.♘de4 ♘xe4 14.♗xe4 c6 15.d5 c5 16.♗d3 ♗d7 17.♖ae1 ♘g6 18.f3 ♖f8 19.f4 f5 20.g3 ♖ae8 21.♕d2 ♕f6∞** Bricard-Jussupow, Kaufbeuren 1993;

C3) **8.e4 e5 9.♗d3 0-0 10.0-0 ♖e8 11.♖fe1 exd4 12.♘xd4 ♘c5 13.♗c2 a4 14.h3 ♘fd7** 14...♗e6!? 15.♘xe6 ♖xe6=. **15.♘f3 ♘b6 16.e5↑** Houska-Mohannad, Dubai 2013;

C4) **8.g3** and now:

C41) **8...0-0 9.♗g2 e5 10.0-0 exd4 11.♘xd4** 11.♕xd4 ♘c5 12.♖ad1 ♖e8 13.b4 axb4 14.axb4 ♘a4= Pcola-Benjamin, Yerevan 1996. **11...♘b6** 11...a4!?=. **12.♕c2** 12.b3 a4 13.♘d5 ♘fxd5 14.cxd5 axb3 15.♘xb3 ♗d7= Borovikov-Kosten, Sautron 2005; for 5.g3 see Chapter 11. **12...c6** A weaker move is 12...♘xc4 13.♘cb5±. Black must return a pawn and hence disrupt his pawn structure. For example: 13...c6 (13...d5 14.b3±) 14.♕xc4±.

13.♘d1 ♖e8 14.b3 ♕e7⇄
Tworuszka-Jakubowski, Krynica 1998;

C42) A risky move is **8...e5 9.dxe5 ♘xe5** (9...dxe5 10.♗h3±) **10.♘xe5 dxe5 11.♕g5** (11.♕xd8+ ♔xd8 12.0-0-0+ ♔e7 13.♘d5+ ♘xd5 14.♖xd5 f6 with a draw in this equal position, Antal-Groszpeter, Kecskemet 2013) **11...0-0 12.♕xe5±** Zaja-Sedlak, Bosnjaci 2013.

5...f5!?

Black wants better control of the centre because all his problems are caused by the opponent's future bishop pair and his ability to create a strong centre with e2-e4.

A) **5...♘c6 6.a3 ♗xc3 7.♗xc3 ♘f6 8.♕c2 ♕e7** is covered under 6...♕e7.

B) **5...♘f6** is a return to the standard Bogo-Indian defence. **6.♕c2** and now:

B1) **6...♘bd7 7.a3 ♗xc3 8.♗xc3** After winning the bishop pair, next on the agenda is the advance of the e-pawn, so Black must prepare to block it. **8...♕e7** On 8...0-0 after 9.e4± Black has no time to block the opponent's e-pawn. Now:

B11) **9.e4 e5 10.♗d3** White is already better. He was the first to finish his development, he has the bishop pair, and a better control of the centre. Besides, White has kept the mobility of his central pawns d4 and c4, which gives him more possibilities in the upcoming battle. 10.dxe5 dxe5 11.b3 0-0 12.♗d3 ♘h5 13.0-0 ♘f4= was seen in Granda Zuniga-Garcia Gonzales, Havana 1986; 10.d5 ♘c5 11.♘d2 a4 12.♗e2 ♗d7= was Iotov-Cvek, Novi Sad 2009. **10...0-0 11.0-0**

B111) In case of **11...a4?!** as in the game Delchev-Zelcic, Nova Gorica 2004, White could have obtained a clear advantage with **12.c5!N**

12...dxc5 Or 12...exd4 13.cxd6 ♕xd6 (13...cxd6 14.♘xd4±) 14.♗xd4 ♘g4 15.♕c3± **13.dxe5 ♘g4 14.e6! fxe6** A bad move is 14...♕xe6? 15.e5!± and Black is near defeat. **15.♖fe1±** White has more than enough compensation for the pawn due to Black's disarrayed pieces and weak pawn structure;

B112) **11...b6 12.b4 axb4 13.axb4 ♗b7** Now is a good moment to decide on the pawn structure in the centre: **14.d5!?** With more space and the bishop pair, White has better chances. **14...♖fc8 15.♖fd1 c6 16.♘d2 c5 17.b5**;

B113) **11...exd4 12.♘xd4 ♘c5 13.♖fe1 ♖e8 14.f3 ♗d7 15.♗f1 a4 16.♖ad1**. White has more space, a strong dark-squared bishop, and better chances.

B12) More passive is **9.e3 0-0 10.♗e2** 10.♗d3 e5! 11.♗f5 (11.♘g5 h6 12.♘e4 ♘xe4 13.♗xe4 exd4 14.♗xd4 ♖e8 15.♗d3 ♘e5= 16.♗e2?! ♕g5↑) **11...♖e8 12.dxe5 ♘xe5=** Sturua-Eingorn, Swidnica 1997.

Black can continue with 10...a4, which strategically devalues the movements of the opponent's b-pawn, or with the natural development of his light-squared bishop with 10...b6. This continuation usually evolves also into positions covered under 10...a4;

B121) **10...a4** In this type of position, White's plan includes playing with the b-pawn, so Black deprives him of that possibility with this simple move. Now White may play with the b-pawn but after the exchange on b3 he will have a weaker pawn structure. **11.0-0 b6 12.♘d2 ♗b7 13.e4** 13.♘f3 ♗xf3 14.♘xf3 c5= Campbell-Johansen, Khanty-Mansiysk 2010; 13.♗d3 c5= with the idea ...♖fc8 and play along the c-file; 13.f4 c5 14.♖ae1 ♖fc8 15.♗d3 d5 16.cxd5 exd5∞ with play on both sides, Kanko-Karner, Finland 1993. **13...c5!?** 13...e5=.

14.e5 14.♖fe1 cxd4 15.♗xd4 ♖fc8 with equal chances, Sakaev-Eingorn, Moscow 1991; 14.d5?! cannot be played because of 14...exd5 15.cxd5 ♘xd5∓. The text is appealing, but after **14...♘e8 15.f4 cxd4 16.♗xd4 dxe5 17.fxe5 ♘xe5 18.♗xb6 ♘d6!⇄** Black has at least equal chances. In the game, Grand Master Gligoric played imprecisely: **19.♗d4?!** and after **19...♘f5 20.♗xe5 ♕c5+ 21.♖f2 ♕xe5**

... the ex-World Champion had more active pieces and a better position in Gligoric-Tal, Belgrade 1968;

B122) **10...b6 11.0-0 ♗b7**

12.♘d2 White should take control of the important square e4, because Black intends to play the standard ...♘e4 with ...f7-f5 next. If 12.♖fd1 ♘e4 13.♗e1 f5 with chances for both sides, Girya-Dzagnidze, Geneva 2013 (13...a4!?=); if 12.b4 ♘e4 13.♗b2 f5∞ with chances on both sides in a type of position that can arise by various move orders and various openings, Zulfic-Ad. Horvath, Canberra 2013. **12...a4!** And Black should not miss this useful prophylactic move, with which we enter the position covered under 10...a4.

B2) The variation **6...♘c6 7.a3 ♗xc3 8.♗xc3 ♕e7** is covered under 6...♕e7;

B3) **6...♕e7**

7.a3 Another possible move is 7.e4 e5 8.dxe5 dxe5 9.♘d5 with a minimal advantage; if 9...♗e2 ♗xc3 10.♗xc3 ♘c6=. As we have said, White's main idea behind the continuation 6.♘c3 is to win the bishop pair. **7...♗xc3 8.♗xc3** With a strong dark-squared bishop on the board, White is already threatening with a dangerous charge with his e-pawn to square e5, therefore the other side has no time for castling but must immediately prepare to block with ...e6-e5. As usual, this can be done with either the active 8...♘c6 or the passive 8...♘bd7.

8...♘c6 For 8...♘bd7 see under 6. ..♘bd7. By conducting ...e6-e5, Black will now exert stronger pressure on the critical square d4, which will force the opponent to an immediate declaration regarding his pawn structure in the centre. By the way, this position occurs more frequently in the order of the Nimzo-Indian: 1.d4 ♘f6 2.c4 e6 3. ♘c3 ♗b4 4. ♕c2 ♘c6 5. ♘f3 d6 6. ♗d2 ♕e7 7.a3 ♗xc3 8. ♗xc3 a5.

9.e4 e5 10.d5 A practically forced closure of the centre, which is not the case with the black knight on d7, where White can maintain the mobility of his d4- and c4-pawns for longer and preserve control of square c5. However, here White has time to attack the stronghold on c5. **10...♘b8**

This is a critical position and an important crossroads for White. He can develop with either 11.♗d3 or 11.♗e2 or play the active 11.c5:

B31) **11.b4!? axb4 12.axb4 ♖xa1+ 13.♗xa1 0-0 14.♗e2 ♘a6 15.♗c3 ♗g4 16.0-0±** Golod;

B32) **11.♗d3**

White wants to finish his development and then use the extra space and the bishop pair for something more substantial.

B321) **11...♘bd7 12.b4!** At the right moment, otherwise Black would arrest White's play on the queenside with 12...a4. **12...axb4 13.axb4 ♖xa1+ 14.♗xa1 0-0 15.0-0** White has more space and the bishop pair. The odds are in his favour, Georgiev-Bogdanovski, Skopje 2012;

B322) **11...a4** This prophylactic move, keeping the pawn on b2, is not effective unless Black has significant control over square c5: **12.c5 0-0 13.♖c1±** and Black has only weakened his position by moving the pawn forward, Arngrimsson-Stupak, Pardubice 2013;

B323) With **11...0-0 12.0-0 ♘h5** Black improves the position of his knight, but he has no time to eliminate the opponent's light-squared bishop: 13.♖fe1 ♗g4 14.♘d2 ♘f4 15.♗f1± and White's chances are better since he can start action on the queenside;

B324) 11...♘h5!N With the idea ...♘f4, attacking the d3-bishop and the g2-pawn. **12.0-0** 12.c5 0-0 13.0-0 ♘f4 14.cxd6 cxd6 15.♗d2 ♘xd3 16.♕xd3 f5=; 12.g3 ♗h3=. **12...♘f4 13.♗d2 ♘xd3 14.♕xd3 0-0=**

B33) 11.♗e2 Now Black cannot play ...♘h5 because of 12.♘xe5±, but with the bishop on e2 he has other options:

B331) 11...♗g4 12.0-0

B3311) 12...♗xf3 13.♗xf3 a4 14.♖ae1 ♘bd7 15.♖e3 ♘c5 16.♗d1± Black has a stronghold for his knight, but White still has better chances because he can, at a favourable moment, open up the position for his bishop pair;

B3312) 12...a4 13.♘h4!

White takes his knight to the edge of the board bearing three strategic ideas in mind:

1. to exchange his weaker light-squared bishop,

2. to perform f2-f4, thus activating his dark-squared bishop and his rook on f1, and

3. to potentially go to f5.

13...♘xd5 13...♗d7 14.f4± Krush-Koneru, Hyderabad 2002; 13...♘fd7 14.♗xg4 ♕xh4 15.♗h3 0-0 16.♖ae1 ♕e7 17.♖e3 ♘c5 18.♖g3 ♘bd7 19.f4±; 13...♗xe2 14.♕xe2 g6 15.f4±. **14.exd5 ♕xh4 15.f4±** Tkachiev-Delchev, France 2001;

B3313) 12...0-0 13.b4 ♘h5 14.h3 (14.bxa5 ♘f4♔) **14...♗xf3 15.♗xf3±**

B332) 11...0-0 12.0-0 a4 Obstructing White's basic queenside plan of b2-b4.

B3321) 13.♘d2 ♘bd7 Black has completely neutralized the opponent's game on the queenside. However, this is not the end of the story, as the battle now moves on to square e5 and to outwitting each other about the typical attack with f2-f4.

14.♖ae1 ♖e8 Since the only active plan White is now left with is an attack by f2-f4, a black rook on the e-file and the possibility of moving a black knight to g6 via square f8 are good ideas. **15.♗f3** 15.♗d1 b6 16.♖e3 ♘f8 17.f4 exf4 18.♖xf4 ♘6d7 19.♖g3 ♘g6 20.♖f1 ♘c5 21.♕b1 ♗d7∞.

Black has succeeded in neutralizing the opponent's initiative and securing enough play for himself. **15...♘c5** with a complex position and chances for both sides, Jiretorn-Richards, Varna 2002. (A move which deserves attention is 15...b6!?, keeping the possibility of ...♘f8.)

B3322) **13.c5 ♗g4!**

We have seen that this continuation is not effective with the bishop on d3 because White can then simply move the knight back to d2.

14.♗b4 Or 14.cxd6 cxd6 15.♘e1 ♗xe2 16.♕xe2 ♘a6 17.♘d3 ♖ac8 18.f3 ♘d7= Portisch-Tal, Skelleftea 1989. **14...♘a6 15.♗xa6 ♖xa6 16.♘d2 ♘h5 17.f3** 17.g3 f5⇄ with counterplay on the kingside. **17...♗d7 18.cxd6 cxd6 19.♕c7 b5** with equal chances, Odirovski-Heffalump, Internet 2008.

B34) **11.c5!**

White does not want to allow a blockading black knight on c5, so he pushes his c-pawn, which changes the position completely.

With this thrust White has several strategic goals in mind:

1. creating a weak pawn on d6 and a weak square on b6;

2. opening the diagonal f1-a6 for his light-squared bishop;

3. opening the c-file;

4. freeing square c4 for his knight, from where it can pressure the d6- and a5-pawns as well as the b6-square.

11...0-0 12.cxd6 cxd6 13.♘d2 ♘bd7 14.♗e2 ♘c5 Neither did the exchange of the bishop on a6 achieve equality after 14...b6 15.0-0 ♗a6 16.♗xa6 ♖xa6 17.b4 ♖c8 18.♕d3 ♖a7 19.♖fc1, when Black remained in a more passive position with weak light squares, Babujian-Harutjunyan, Poti 2013. **15.b4 axb4 16.axb4 ♖xa1+ 17.♗xa1 ♘a6** and now:

B341) **18.♕b1 ♗g4!** This is a good idea. Black wishes to exchange off the active white bishop or otherwise force f2-f3, enabling more active play for himself with ...♘h5. **19.f3** On 19.♗xg4 ♘xg4 20.0-0 ♖c8 (or 20...♕g5 21.♘f3 ♕g6=) 21.h3 ♘f6 chances are equal, Matheis-Borwell, corr. 2008. **19...♗d7**

B3411) After **20.♘c4** serious complications could arise: **20...♘h5!? 21.g3 f5 22.f4** 22.0-0=. **22...exf4 23.♗xh5 fxe4 24.0-0 ♗b5** with an equal position. Let us also mention that in the event of 18.♕b3 this variation does not work for Black. **25.♕c2** 25.♕b3 f3 26.♗g4 ♘c7≅. **25...f3 26.♗g4 ♕c7=;**

B3412) **20.0-0 ♘h5!N** A weaker move is 20...♖c8 21.♘c4± with the idea ♘b6, Bareev-Gulko, New Delhi 2000. **21.♖f2** 21.g3 ♕g5 hands Black the initiative. **21...♘f4=**

B342) **18.♕b3**

18...♗g4 We have seen this tap-dancing of the black bishop several times, with the intention to weaken the opponent's dark squares. **19.f3 ♗d7 20.♘c4 ♘c7** A weak idea is 20...♘h5 21.g3 f5 because of 22.f4!±. **21.♕e3** A better move is 21.0-0, for example 21...♘h5 22.g3 b5 23.♘e3±. **21...♘h5 22.g3 ♗b5 23.0-0 f5 24.exf5 ♘xd5**

With equal chances, Carlsen-Ivanchuk, Nice (rapid) 2009. A rapid game, but one between two Grand Masters, so we award it a central place in our attempts to better explain this important theoretic variation.

Now we go back to the main line.

After 5...f5!? White can play 6.a3, 6.e3, 6.♕c2 and 6.g3.

6.a3

White is consistent in his intention to win the bishop pair, however the big question is whether this is the right moment for it, as he will lose control of the critical square e4.

A) **6.e3** This calm move in the spirit of the central systems may give White the best chances in the battle for the lead because he does not relinquish the control of the important e4-square. **6...♘f6 7.♗d3 0-0 8.♕c2** A simple but efficient plan. White has taken control of the critical point, e4, and now plans to win the bishop pair as well with a2-a3:

A1) Black cannot obtain square e4 with **8...b6** because of **9.0-0 ♗b7 10.d5!±** and due to the pressure on the diagonal b1-f5, White destroys the flexibility of the opponent's centre. For example: **10...♕e7** 10...exd5 11.♘g5 dxc4 12.♗xf5 g6 13.♗e6+ ♔h8 14.a3 ♗c5 15.♘a4±. In addition to the weakened position of his king, Black will also leave the opponent in possession of the bishop pair. White has more than enough compensation for the lost pawn. **11.♘d4!**

A typical and instructive strategic picture. This method of play is characteristic for this type of pawn structure and can also be observed in other move orders and openings. **11...exd5 12.♘xf5 ♕f7 13.♘xd5 ♘xd5 14.cxd5 ♗xd2 15.♕xd2 ♗xd5 16.e4 ♗e6 17.♖ac1!** White prevents the opponent's development and controls important squares on the c-file. **17...♗xf5 18.exf5 d5 19.♖fe1 c5 20.♗b5±** And Black is still not developed and at the verge of losing a pawn on d5 or b6;

A2) **8...♘c6**

A21) **9.0-0 ♗xc3! 10.bxc3** 10.♗xc3 ♘b4=. **10...♕e8 11.♘e1 ♕h5 12.f3 e5 13.♗c1 ♖e8 14.d5 ♘d8 15.e4 f4∞**

with play for both sides, Yaroshenko-Lev, Odessa 2000;

A22) With **9.d5** White wants to reduce the mobility of the opponent's central pawns by exerting pressure on the diagonal b1-h7, however after **9...♘e5** Black keeps his central pawns connected and mobile: **10.♘xe5** 10.♗e2 ♘xf3+ 11.♗xf3 e5⇄. **10...dxe5 11.0-0-0 e4 12.♗e2 ♕e7 13.h3 exd5 14.♘xd5 ♘xd5 15.cxd5 ♗d6 16.♗c3 ♗d7** with play for both sides, Matnadze-Marin, Barcelona 2011;

A23) **9.a3!** White avoids the opponent's opportunity to exchange one of his bishops with 9...♗xc3 10.♗xc3 ♘b4 or to disturb his pawn structure with 10.bxc3. **9...♗xc3 10.♗xc3 ♘e7**

A231) **11.0-0-0** Queenside castling is tempting because White can gain better control of the centre and he also has the bishop pair. Nevertheless, Black has the option to use ...b7-b5! to attack the white king. **11...♗d7 12.♖hg1 b5! 13.cxb5 ♕e8 14.h3?! ♗xb5 15.♗xb5 ♕xb5∓** Bareev-Eingorn, Minsk 1987;

A232) A safer move is **11.0-0N ♗d7** (11...b6 12.♘d2 ♗b7 13.b4±; with the bishop pair and somewhat more space, White has slightly better chances) **12.♘d2** and with good control of the centre and the bishop pair, White's chances improve;

B) **6.g3** Fianchettoing the light-squared bishop is usually a good idea in our Accelerated Bogo-Indian, however, in combination with a knight on c3 it seems to reduce White's chances of an advantage. **6...♘f6 7.♗g2 0-0 8.0-0 ♘c6 9.a3 ♗xc3 10.♗xc3 ♘e4**

In practice White has played three different moves here, but nowhere did he achieve anything substantial:

B1) **11.♕c2 a4 12.♘d2 ♘xc3 13.bxc3** 13.♕xc3 ♕f6 14.e3 e5=. **13...e5 14.e3 ♗d7 15.♖ab1 b6=** Babula-Maze, Dresden 2007;

B2) **11.♗e1 ♕f6 12.e3 e5=** Postny-Bauer, France 2010;

B3) **11.♖c1 e5** 11...a4!?. **12.d5** 12.dxe5 ♘xc3 13.♖xc3 dxe5 14.♕d5+ ♔h8 15.♕xd8 ♖xd8 16.♘g5 ♖e8=. **12...♘e7 13.♗e1** and now in the game Hübner-Gulko, Istanbul 2000, Black could have obtained nice play with **13...♗d7!⇄**, for example **14.♕c2** 14.b4?! axb4 15.axb4 ♖a2 16.b5 ♕a8↑. **14...c6 15.dxc6 ♗xc6⇄**

C) **6.♕c2 ♘f6 7.e3 0-0 8.♗d3** is covered under 6.e3.

6...♗xc3 7.♗xc3 ♘f6 8.b3

White ensures a retreat for his dark-squared bishop in case of ...♘e4.

A move which deserves attention is **8.b4**, so as to maintain control over square c5, because White plans to acti-

vate his dark-squared bishop with d4-d5. **8...0-0** 8...axb4 9.axb4 ♖xa1 10.♕xa1 b5!? M. Marin. **9.e3 ♕e7 10.♗d3 ♘e4 11.♗b2±** Tikkanen-Noritsyn, Istanbul 2012.

8...0-0

White can develop his light-squared bishop along the f1-a6 diagonal with 9.e3 or fianchetto it with 9.g3.

9.e3

This continuation provides better chances for White than 9.g3, since it reduces the possibility of the exchange of light-squared bishops. We shall analyse the usual 9...♘e4 and the new plan 9...b6.

White has less chances of an advantage with the fianchetto: **9.g3 b6 10.♗g2 ♗b7 11.0-0**

A) **11...♘bd7!?N 12.d5** 12.♘g5 ♗xg2 13.♘xe6 ♕e7 14.♘xf8 ♗xf1 15.♘xd7 ♘e4 16.♔xf1 ♘xc3∞ and White has a little more trouble. **12...♘c5 13.♘g5 exd5 14.cxd5 h6 15.♘h3 g5∞**;

B) **11...♕e8 12.♘d2** White allows the exchange of light-squared bishops and therefore loses his greatest strategic asset. Better would be 12.d5 ♘e4 13.♗b2 ♘d7 14.dxe6 ♕xe6 15.♕c2 ♖ae8⇄. **12...♗xg2 13.♔xg2 ♘bd7 14.♕c2 ♕h5⇄** with an excellent game for White, for the opponent's dark-squared bishop is not so impressive in this type of position, Muir-Luther, Lyngby 1990.

9...♘e4

Would anyone dare to say this thematic move is not the best? However, White's plan given below left a strong impression on us and forced us to search for an alternative: **9...b6!?N**

Black continues his development, wishing to establish maximum control of the squares e4 and d5. Essentially this plan differs from the one after 9...♘e4, since its intention is to use the control of square d5 to decrease the value of the standard attack with d4-d5. **10.♗e2** 10.d5 runs into 10...e5 and if then 11.♗e2 Black has an active and interesting plan with 11...♘bd7 12.0-0 ♘c5 13.b4 ♘ce4 14.♗b2 ♘g4⇄ with complicated play; 10.♗d3 ♘e4 11.♗b2 is covered under 11.♗d3. **10...♗b7 11.0-0 ♘bd7 12.♘d2** What else? d4-d5 does not work. **12...♕e8⇄** White has the bishop pair and a flexible pawn structure in the centre. But Black has his strategic assets as well, for example: **13.f3 ♕h5 14.♗d3** 14.♕e1 ♖ae8 15.b4 e5⇄ 16.bxa5?! exd4↑. **14...e5 15.♕c2** 15.d5 ♘c5 16.♗c2 b5!?⇄ with the idea of ...a5-a4. **15...e4 16.fxe4?? ♘g4-+**

10.♗b2 b6

Black continues building his best offensive line-up with a fantastic Queen's Indian bishop on b7.

11.♗e2!

This calm developing move gives the best chances in the fight for the lead. **11.♗d3** is more active, but at the critical moment it prevents White from playing the important strategic attack 13.d5!, as it stands in the way of the queen. **11...♗b7 12.0-0 ♘d7**

A) **13.♕e2**

13...♖f6 13...♕e7!? – now that White's main strategic threat is gone, Black can without any pressure improve his position and prepare an attack on the white king, or perhaps an attack on the centre with ...c7-c5: 14.♘d2 ♖f6 15.f3 ♘xd2 16.♕xd2 ♖h6. **14.d5 ♖h6**

A1) **15.dxe6** This backing down and opening of the diagonal for the black light-squared bishop often creates a scene for nice tactical attacks by Black.

15...♘dc5 16.♗c2 ♘xe6⇄ Here is an obvious result of the bad exchange on e6. Almost all of Black's pieces are now involved in the action against the opponent's king. **17.g3?!** It is now quite difficult to find a good defensive plan – there probably isn't one. **17...♕e8** White cannot successfully ward off the strong attack, for example:

A11) **18.♗xe4 fxe4 19.♘d4 ♘g5** With the idea ...♕e8-d7. **20.♕g4** 20.h4 ♖xh4! 21.gxh4 ♘f3+–+. **20...♖g6–+**;

A12) White is losing even faster after **18.♘d4 ♘xd4**

A121) **19.♗xd4**

Now Black has two possible instructive wins: 19...♘g5 20.f3 ♕h5–+ or 19...♘d2 20.♕xd2 ♖xh2 21.e4 ♕h5 22.♕d1 ♕h3 23.♕f3 g5–+.

A122) **19.exd4 ♘xg3!**

20.♕xe8+ ♖xe8 21.fxg3 ♖e2–+ Rahmanov-Javakhadze, Nakhchivan 2013.

A2) Better is **15.♘d4 ♕h4 16.h3 ♘dc5** (16...♘g5?! 17.♗xf5±) **17.♗xe4 fxe4 18.b4 ♘d3 19.♘xe6 ♗c8 20.♗c3 ♗xe6 21.dxe6 ♖xe6 22.bxa5 bxa5 23.♖ab1±**.

B) **13.♕c2**

B1) **13...♕e7 14.♘c1±** with the idea of f2-f3, Polugaevsky-Speelman, London 1984;

B2) **13...♕e8 14.♘d2 ♘xd2 15.♕xd2 e5 16.f4 e4 17.♗e2 d5 18.a4** with a minimal advantage for White, Hiarcs 13.2 MP-Komodo 1.3, Johan 2011;

B3) **13...♘g5?!** Wrong idea. Black offers his strong centralized knight for an exchange after which he can say goodbye to his attack on the white king. **14.♘xg5 ♕xg5 15.f4 ♕g6 16.d5 ♘c5 17.♖f3±** Now White leads the dance. With his dark-squared bishop activated, he clearly has the better chances, Bouwmeester-Hyldkrog, corr. 1985;

B4) **13...♖f6!**

It is now time for Black to start the dance. By the way, activating a rook along the sixth rank is a basic motif and the most important link in Black's plan to attack the white king in order to confront the opponent's active and harmonious line-up with the bishop pair.

A common move is **14.d5** (14.c5 bxc5 (another possibility is 14...dxc5 15.dxc5 ♘dxc5 16.♗xf6 ♕xd3

17.♕xd3 ♘xd3 and Black has enough play for a draw) 15.dxc5 ♘exc5 16.♗xf6 ♕xf6⩲ Polugaevsky-Psakhis, Moscow 1983) **14...♖h6 15.♘d4** In the line 15.♗xe4 fxe4 16.♕xe4 ♘c5∓ we see the difference with the lines in which White is allowed to play b2-b4, said a great theoretician, grandmaster M. Marin, to one of this book's authors. **15...♘dc5 16.f3 ♕h4** 16...♕g5!? M. Marin **17.h3 ♘xd3 18.♕xd3 ♘g5** Black threatens 19...♘h3, immediately winning. **19.♖f2** Another defence is not visible. **19...♖g6 20.♔f1 ♖f8** and now:

B41) **21.♘xe6 ♘xe6 22.dxe6 ♖xe6∓**;

B412) **21.♕c2 ♗c8** With the idea of ...e6-e5. **22.dxe6 ♗xe6∓** and Black still maintains the initiative;

B413) **21.dxe6? ♘e4! 22.♖c2** 22.fxe4 ♕xf2+−+. **22...c5! 23.♘b5 ♘g3+ 24.♔g1**

24...♗xf3−+
11...♗b7 12.0-0 ♘d7

This is a critical position. On the point of entering the centre and entering a direct battle, Black has come out of the opening with a defined pawn structure and developed minor pieces. A basic characteristic of Black's further plan is an attack on the opponent's king, so he wants to move his major pieces to the kingside.

White has also completed his development with a flexible pawn structure and the bishop pair, which will decide his future plans, the essence of which will lie in the activation of the bishop pair with d4-d5.

White can play the principled 13.d5! or the schematic 13.♕c2, with complicated positions, where Black is actually leading in the attack.

13.d5!

White uses the position of his queen on d1 to play this thematic move which:

1. opens up the diagonal for his dark-squared bishop;

2. limits the effect of Black's aggressive light-squared bishop; and

3. frees square d4 for his knight.

13.♕c2

This brings about an unclear and complicated theoretical position which usually occurs in the Nimzo-Indian order: 1.d4 ♘f6 2.c4 e6 3.♘c3 ♗b4 4.♕c2 0-0 5.a3 ♗xc3 6.♕xc3 b6 7.♘f3 ♗b7

8.e3 d6 9.♗e2 ♘e4 10.♕c2 a5!? 11.b3 f5 12.♗b2 ♘bd7 13.0-0.

A) Since there is no tempo gain for White with f2-f4 Black can try **13...♘g5!?**

White can choose between:

A1) **14.♘e1 ♘h3+** A better move would be 14...♖f6N 15.f3 ♖h6 16.♘d3 ♕e8⇄ with the idea of ...♕h5. **15.♔h1 ♕h4 16.f3±** Kruppa-Pavlov, Rivne 2005;

A2) **14.d5 ♘xf3+ 15.♗xf3 ♕g5 16.e4** 16.♖ad1!?. **16...f4 17.♕d1 ♘e5 18.♗xe5 ♕xe5 19.♗g4 ♗c8** and in this equal position the opponents agreed to a draw, Bykhovsky-G. Kuzmin, Irkutsk 1983;

A3) **14.♕d1 ♘xf3+ 15.♗xf3 ♗xf3 16.♕xf3 a4!?=** Radovanovic-Lajthajm, Srebrno Jezero 2013;

A4) **14.♘xg5 ♕xg5 15.d5** 15.g3 ♘f6∞. **15...exd5 16.♗f3 c6 17.cxd5 c5⇄;**

A5) **14.♘d2 ♘h3+** Weaker is 14...♖f6?! 15.d5 ♖h6 16.f4±. **15.♔h1 ♕h4 16.f3 ♘g5** and now:

A51) **17.d5 ♘f6 18.♗d3** 18.♖ae1 ♘h5⇄. **18...♖ae8 19.♖ae1 ♖e7** With the idea ...exd5. **20.dxe6 ♘h5 21.♔g1 f4 22.♘e4 ♘xe4 23.♗xe4 ♗xe4 24.♕xe4 ♖fe8 25.♕d4 ♖xe6=;**

A52) **17.♔g1 ♖f6 18.g3 ♕h3 19.d5 ♖g6** A better move would be

19...♖h6N 20.♖f2 ♕h5∞. **20.f4 ♘e4 21.♘xe4 fxe4 22.♕xe4±** Pepito 1.59.2-Arasan 13.2, Internet 2011.

B) **13...♖f6!**

Black has completed his development and now he cannot stop with his attack because his opponent has the bishop pair and the possibility to kick away the knight on e4. A small delay or a passive plan would soon land Black into an inferior position. **14.d5!** And White mustn't waste any time either. He uses his d-pawn as an outpost behind which he can activate his forces, in particular his dark-squared bishop.

Obviously, Black only has three options:

B1) **14...♖h6** Black activates his rook in order to attack the white king along the h-file as this will disable White's main idea with ♘f3-d4. **15.♖ad1** A weaker move is 15.♘d4 ♕h4→. **15...♘f8?!** This move makes sense if White has already captured on e6. Now it is just passive. 15...e5∞ would give chances for both sides. For the opponent's bishop pair, Black has active counterplay on the kingside. **16.g3±** Bocharov-Romanov, St Petersburg 2005;

B2) **14...e5 15.♘h4!±** with the idea ♘f5. Now Black must close the 6th rank with ... g7-g6 and so render worthless his plan to attack the white king;

B3) **14...♖g6** and now:

B31) **15.♖ad1 e5**

B311) **16.b4** Depriving the black
knights from the important square c5,
but giving White more time to regroup
and prepare for the attack. **16...♕e7** Or
the typical 16...c6⇄ in order to en-
hance the effect of his light-squared
bishop. **17.♖fe1** White frees square f1
for his light-squared bishop, so that he
can move it to g2 and improve his defensive options. **17...♖f8 18.♗f1 ♗c8**
With each move, Black improves the
position of his pieces. ...c7-c6 or ...♖h6
are alternatives to be explored.
19.♘d2?! It is too late for this defensive
manoeuvre, because it allows Black's
queen sortie. A better move would be
19.g3∞ when the fight continues re-
lentlessly and the outcome is unclear.
**19...♕h4 20.♘f3?! ♕h5 21.♕e2
♘df6−+**

All of Black's pieces are attacking, leading inevitably to White's defeat,
Shipov-Balashov, Krasnoyarsk 2003;

B312) A better move is **16.♘d2 ♕h4
17.♘xe4 ♕xe4 18.♕xe4 fxe4 19.f4
exf3 20.♗xf3** with equal chances, for
example: **20...♖f6** Or 20...♘f6 with
real chances for a draw but with a risky
position for the black rook, for example
21.♗e2 ♗c8∞. **21.♗g4 ♗c8=**

B32) **15.♘d4!?**

B321) **15...♕g5 16.g3 ♘f8 17.♖ad1
♖e8 18.♗f3±** Zhao Xue-Karjakin, Cap
d'Agde 2006;

B322) **15...♘f8?!** Black activates his
knight by returning a pawn. **16.g3 exd5
17.cxd5 ♗xd5 18.♘xf5** With the
knight on f8 Black cannot attack, so his
position is already critical as White has
many threats. **18...♕g5** 18...♘g5
19.f3+−. **19.♖ad1 ♕xf5 20.♖xd5 ♕e6
21.♗c4 c6 22.♖e5+−** Czakon-Bartel,
Lublin 2008;

B323) **15...exd5 16.♘xf5 ♘dc5**
16...d4!?N deserves attention, for
instance 17.♘g3 ♘xg3 18.fxg3 ♕e8
19.exd4 ♕e3+ 20.♔h1 ♗e4 21.♕d1
♖f6 22.♗f3 ♖af8 23.♗c1 ♗xf3
24.♗xe3 ♗xd1 25.♖fxd1 ♖e6 26.♖e1
♖fe8 27.♗d2 ♖e4⩲. For the minus
pawn Black has enough play to draw.
17.cxd5 17.♘g3 ♖h6 18.♘f5 ♖g6=.

17...♕g5 17...♗xd5!? 18.f3 ♕g5
19.♗c4 ♗xc4 20.♕xc4+ ♘e6 21.♘e7+

271

♕xe7 22.♕xe4 ♖e8=. **18.♘g3 ♘xg3 19.hxg3 ♗xd5 20.b4 ♗e4 21.♕c3 ♘e6 22.g4 h5 23.f3±** Deep Rybka 4-Deep Rybka 4, Internet 2010.

13...e5

A weak move is 13...exd5? because of 14.♘d4 ♕e7 15.cxd5 ♗xd5 16.♘b5± and Black will lose material.

14.♘d2!N

14.♘e1 ♕g5 A typical move which activates the queen and prevents the relieving f2-f3. **15.f4 exf4?!** Black does not need to hand the d4-square to his opponent. A better option is 15...♕e7 16.♘f3 c6 17.dxc6 ♗xc6=. With his good control of the centre, Black compensates for the opponent's bishop pair. 16.exf4 ♕e7 17.♘c2± Kelecevic-Hirzel, Grächen 1999.

14...♕h4

Here Black can also play:

A) **14...♘xd2 15.♕xd2 ♘c5** 15...e4 16.b4 ♕g5 17.♗c3±. **16.♕c2±** with the idea b3-b4;

B) **14...♘ef6 15.f4±** As we have seen several times before, the d-pawn and f-pawn are the main actors in the realization of White's most important strategic plan: activating his bishop pair while limiting the activity of the opponent's pieces;

C) **14...♕g5 15.f4±** and White will conveniently exchange the knight on e4;

D) **14...♖f6 15.f4!±** A tempting option, but weaker, is 15.♘xe4. After 15...fxe4 Black, with a doubled pawn on e4, slows down the activation of White's dark-squared bishop. For example: 16.♕c2 ♖h6 17.f4 (17.♕xe4?! ♘c5∓ 18.♕c2? ♕h4 19.h3 ♗c8−+) 17...exf3 18.♖xf3 ♕h4 19.h3 ♖f6 20.♖af1 ♖af8=.

15.f4 ♘xd2 16.♕xd2±

White has the better chances in this typical position with the bishop pair.

Conclusion

In this chapter we have examined:

1. the flexible 4...d6, which allows Black to create some original positions with ...f7-f5, but we have also included:

2. positions where Black plays ...e6-e5 and creates a more common formation: knights to f6 and c6 (or d7) and queen to e7.

We can conclude that in both cases Black did not achieve a satisfactory game – he obtained no positions that could be recommended for practical play.

In the first critical variation with 5.♘c3 f5 6.a3 ♗xc3 7.♗xc3 ♘f6 8.b3 0-0 9.e3 we suggested, instead of the standard jump 9...♘e4, a new plan with 9...b6!? which we believe is good enough to ensure an equal game. But we were not able to find the antidote to White's simple plan involving 6.e3, ♗d3, and ♕c2, where he first takes control over the important central square e4, and then wins the bishop pair with a2-a3.

In the second part, where after 5.♘c3 Black plans an attack on the centre with ...e6-e5, White also gained an advantage, regardless of whether the black knight was on c6 or d7. With the knight on d7 White had better chances thanks to the mobility of his centre with his pawn on d4 and the bishop pair, whereas with the knight on c6, White had to close the centre with d4-d5, but as we saw in the critical game Carlsen-Ivanchuk, the black player fails to create the standard stronghold on c5.

Based on the work from the previous chapter, no. 12, as well as this one, where after 4.♘f3 we considered Black's early declaration of his intentions in the centre – in the previous chapter with 4...d5 and in this one with 4...d6 – to use the extra tempo by omitting the main move 4...♘f6 to enter certain original positions, we can state that the outcome is not desirable for Black, although some positions and variations could be used as surprise weapons in tournaments.

Therefore, after 4.♘f3, play the natural 4...♘f6! and then make an assessment based on your opponent's set-up as to what pawn structure you should form in the centre. Our analyses of the main lines after 4.♘f3 ♘f6 start in Chapter 14.

Exercises

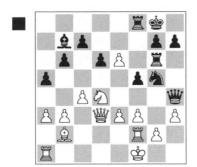

13 (1) Black to play and win.
(solution on page 448)

13 (2) Black to play and win.
(solution on page 448)

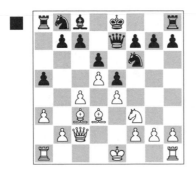

13 (3) Find the plan.
(solution on page 449)

Chapter 14

The Regular Bogo: 4.♘f3 ♘f6

1.d4 e6 2.c4 ♗b4+ 3.♗d2 a5 4.♘f3 ♘f6

This development of the king's knight brings us back to the much better known tracks of the regular Bogo-Indian, which is not the case in the system of the so-called accelerated Bogo-Indian, where Black delays the development of the king's knight, to try and create original and unusual positions which are, however, risky.

White may choose between the solid lines 5.♘c3 or 5.g3, and the rarely used 5.a3, 5.e3 and 5.♕c2.

Chapter 14.1

The Nimzo Move 5.♘c3

1.d4 e6 2.c4 ♗b4+ 3.♗d2 a5 4.♘f3 ♘f6 5.♘c3

With this sequence White mainly opts for the conquest of the bishop pair and for positions in the spirit of the Nimzo-Indian. The key question will once again be: which side benefits more from the inserted moves ♗d2 and ...a7-a5 ? Let us remember, based on the work from the previous chapters, that in positions similar to the Nimzo-Indian the a5-pawn was mostly useful to Black because it defended his bishop and controlled space on the queenside, as opposed to positions such as in the Queen's Gambit, where White would usually manage to expose the pawn as a weakness and use this to his advantage.

We will analyse 5...b6 and the solid 5...0-0. Black often chooses 5...d6 or 5...d5 as well, but we have covered those moves in Chapters 13 and 12.

A) **5.g3** see Chapter 14.2;

B) After **5.e3** Black has a wide selection of solid systems: 5...d5 (Chapter 11); 5...d6 (Chapter 13); or 5...0-0, which usually transposes into those systems; for 5...b6 6.♘c3 see under 6.e3;

C) **5.♕c2** and now: 5...d6 6.♘c3 ♘bd7 7.a3 ♗xc3 8.♗xc3 ♕e7 (Chapter 13) or 5...d5 6.g3 (Chapter 14.4).

D) **5.a3**

An unpleasant continuation for Black. White intends to move into positions which we have covered in the first part of the book in the Andersson system, but with extra moves on the a-file which he wants to turn in his favour. Let us recall that with this continuation White obtained an advantage in the variation with 4.♘f3 d5, which we have covered in Chapter 11.

5...♗xd2+ 5...♗e7 is weaker since after 6.♘c3 d5 7.♗f4± we arrive at the familiar variation of the Queen's Gambit, where the extra moves on the a-file are more useful to White – Chapter 11.

6.♕xd2

More passive is 6.♘bxd2 d6 (for 6...d5 see Chapter 11) 7.e3 (7.e4 e5 8.dxe5 (weaker is 8.d5?! a4 (also good is 8...0-0!?∓) 9.g3 ♘bd7 10.♗g2 ♘c5 11.♕c2 0-0 12.0-0 ♗g4∓ Ivlev-Iljin, Astrakhan 2013) 8...dxe5 9.♘xe5 ♕d4 10.♘d3 ♘c6 11.♕e2 0-0♗) 7...♕e7 8.♗d3 e5 9.♕c2 0-0 (9...exd4 10.♘xd4 0-0 11.0-0 ♘a6= Pallardo Lozoya-Belezky, Cullera 2007) 10.0-0 ♖e8 11.dxe5 dxe5 12.♘g5 h6 13.♘ge4 ♘xe4 14.♘xe4 ♗e6 15.♘c3 ♘d7= Dao Thien Hai-Ghaem Maghami, Al Ain 2008.

After the queen capture, both sides will seek positions in which they will be able to justify their pawns being on the a-file. Black actually has two modes of play where the a5-pawn can have a function: ...b7-b6 with control of the central diagonal, or ...d7-d6, preparing an attack on the centre with ...e6-e5. Let us examine the fianchetto with 6...b6, and the elastic 7...d6, which usually moves into positions under 6...0-0, and the flexible 6...0-0 itself.

D1) With **6...b6** Black arrives in time to establish control over the central diagonal and the e4-square. **7.♘c3 ♗b7 8.e3** 8.♕f4!?, with the idea of e2-e4, resembles the lines covered in Andersson's system (under 3...♗xd2). **8...♘e4 9.♕c2 ♘xc3 10.♕xc3 0-0 11.♗e2 d6 12.0-0 ♘d7 13.b4 ♕e7 14.♘d2 f5=** Lucas-Meijers, Werther 2013;

D2) **6...d6 7.♘c3 0-0** is covered under 6...0-0;

D3) **6...0-0 7.♘c3 d6**

On 7...d5 White moves from 8.e3 into the position where the a5-pawn is clearly not useful in the black position, as it makes the queenside more vulnerable. This type of position is covered in Chapter 11.

With the text, Black prepares a thematic attack on the centre with ...e6-e5, seeking positions in which the a5-pawn will be useful. White has the following options: the less efficient fianchetto 8.g3 (due to the c4-pawn's vulnerability), the humble 8.e3, and the active 8.e4.

D31) White has less chances to get an advantage with **8.g3** because after the natural moves **8...♘bd7 9.♗g2 e5 10.0-0** Black can play **10...exd4!** with the idea to try and turn the moves on the a-file to his advantage. In this particular position the landmark is the weakness on c4 and b3. **11.♘xd4** 11.♕xd4 ♘c5⇄ with the idea ...♘c5-b3 and ...a5-a4. **11...♘b6** There

277

are two ways for White to defend the c4-pawn: **12.♕c2** 12.b3 a4⇄ and the a5-pawn has demonstrated its qualities, Borovikov-Kosten, Sautron 2005. **12...c6** 12...♞xc4?! is weaker due to 13.♞b5± and White will return the pawn, thereby disrupting the opponent's pawn structure. **13.♞d1** 13.♞e4 ♞xe4 14.♗xe4 g6=; **13...♖e8 14.b3 ♕e7 15.♞e3** and now we have the game Tworuszka-Jakubowski, Krynica 1998, where with **15...♕e5!?N 16.♖ad1 ♞g4 17.♞xg4 ♗xg4 18.♖fe1 ♕c5** Black could have obtained equality;

D32) **8.e3 ♞bd7 9.♗d3 e5 10.0-0 ♖e8 11.♕c2 h6** Also possible is 11...♕e7 12.♞d2 ♞f8 (12...c6!?) 13.♞de4 ♞xe4 14.♗xe4 (14.♞xe4 ♗f5=) 14...c6 15.d5 c5 16.♗d3 ♗d7 17.♖ae1 ♞g6 18.f3 ♖f8 19.f4 (a better option is 19.♗f5 when White is slightly better thanks to his more mobile pawns and control over b5) 19...f5 20.g3 ♖ae8 with play for both sides, Bricard-Jussupow, Kaufbeuren 1993. **12.♗f5** 12.♞d2 c6 13.♞de4 exd4 14.exd4 ♞xe4 15.♞xe4 (15.♗xe4 ♞f6=) 15...♞f6=. **12...c6** Black wants to move the queen to c7, but he seems to be prematurely weakening the dark squares in the centre.

12...♕e7!?N deserves attention.

The idea is ...♞b6. For example: 13.♖fd1 (13.♞b5 ♞f8 14.♗xc8 ♖axc8=) 13...♞h6 14.♗xc8 ♖axc8 15.dxe5 dxe5 16.♞e4 ♞xe4 17.♕xe4 c6=.

13.♖ad1 ♕c7 14.h3 ♞f8 15.♗xc8 ♖axc8 16.dxe5 dxe5 17.♞d2 ♖cd8 18.c5 ♞e6∞ and Black is close to equality, Jobava-Suba, Brasov 2011;

D33) **8.e4 ♞c6** It is risky to immediately play 8...e5 because of 9.dxe5 dxe5 10.♕xd8 ♖xd8 11.♞xe5 ♖e8 12.f4± and clear compensation for the minus pawn is not to be seen, Sebenik-Babula, Legnica 2013. **9.♗e2 e5** Black provokes a reaction from the opponent's d-pawn, thus giving greater importance to his own a5-pawn. **10.d5 ♞e7 11.c5 ♞g6 12.cxd6 cxd6 13.g3 ♗h3 14.♞g5 ♗d7⇄** Raimbault-Eingorn, Metz 2002.

Back to the main line after **5.♞c3**.

5...b6!

Black develops a bishop on the central diagonal, directly opposing White's plans in the centre or a fianchetto of the white bishop. Now, for instance, White is not in time with 6.♕c2 to carry through e2-e4 due to 6...♗b7, unlike in the system with 4...d6 5.♞c3 ♞f6 6.♕c2, which was covered in Chapter 13.

Black can also play **5...0-0**, an elastic sequence with which Black makes no declarations in the centre and on the queenside, while on the other hand it increases the force of the opponent's plan with ♗g5 since, among other things, ... h7-h6 and ... g7-g5 will become more risky due to a decrease in the safety of the black king.

We shall analyse the moves 6.e3 and 6.♗g5. For 6.♕c2 d5 see Chapter 11; 6.a3 ♗xc3 7.♗xc3 b6 8.e3 ♘e4= (8...♗b7 9.♗e2 d6 10.0-0 is covered under 7.♗e2).

A) **6.e3**

We now have a Nimzo-Indian with the extra moves ♗d2 and ...a7-a5. Black can respond in the spirit of our systems with 6...d6 or 6...b6, or with the classic 6...d5, which often leads to positions where Black has hanging pawns.

6...d6 6...b6 7.♗d3 ♗b7 is covered under 5...b6; for 6...d5 see Chapter 11. Now:

A1) **7.♗d3 e5!** Black threatens to win a piece for the pawn with ...♗xc3 and ...e5-e4. **8.dxe5 dxe5 9.♕c2** Weaker is 9.♘xe5?! ♘c6 10.♘xc6 ♕xd3∓. **9...♘bd7 10.0-0-0** Safer for White is 10.0-0=. **10...♗xc3 11.♗xc3 ♕e7 12.♘g5 h6 13.h4 ♖e8** with chances for both sides, Davies-Kindermann, Wijk aan Zee 1982;

A2) **7.♗e2 b6** 7...♗xc3 8.♗xc3 ♘e4= Tunik-G. Kuzmin, Yalta 1996.

8.0-0 ♗b7 9.a3 ♗xc3 10.♗xc3 ♘e4 11.♗e1 11.♘d2 ♘xc3 12.bxc3 f5 13.♗f3 ♗xf3 14.♘xf3 ♘d7 15.♕d3 ♕e7= Ivanov-Polugaevsky, Toluca 1982. **11...♘d7 12.♘d2 ♘xd2 13.♗xd2 f5 14.f3 e5=;**

A3) **7.♕c2 ♘bd7** A good move, which leaves open the possibilities of ...♕e7 or ...b7-b6. **8.a3** For 8.♗d3 e5 9.0-0 ♖e8 see Chapter 13. **8...♗xc3 9.♗xc3 ♕e7** An economic and flexible set-up. Black is now waiting for ♗d3, on which he will play ...e6-e5, or for ♗e2 so as to play ...b7-b6. **10.♗d3** On 10.♗e2 we can fianchetto the light-squared bishop with 10...b6!?. **10...e5 11.♘d2** Also nothing is achieved by 11.♗f5 ♖e8 12.dxe5 ♘xe5= Sturua-Eingorn, Swidnica 1997. **11...♖e8** 11...exd4!N

Black uses the pin along the e-file to reduce the power of the opponent's centre with this exchange. 12.♗xd4 ♖e8 13.0-0 b6 14.b4 ♗b7 with equal chances. White has the bishop pair but Black has the opportunity of counterplay by ...♘d7-e5. **12.0-0 e4 13.♗e2±** White's position is more promising thanks to the bishop pair, Da Silva-Delgado Ramirez, Maringa 2013.

B) **6.♗g5** and now:

B1) **6...d6 7.e3 ♘bd7 8.♕c2 e5 9.♗e2** 9.dxe5 dxe5 10.0-0-0 ♗xc3

11.♕xc3 ♕e7 with chances for both sides, Pein-Kosten, Sunningdale 2008. **9...h6 10.♗h4 exd4 11.exd4** 11.♘xd4 ♖e8 12.0-0 ♗xc3 13.bxc3 (13.♕xc3 g5 14.♗g3 ♘e4 15.♕c2 ♕e7 16.♖ae1 ♘dc5⇄) 13...♘c5⇄. **11...♖e8 12.0-0 ♗xc3 13.bxc3 b6 14.♖ac1** 14.♖fe1!? ♗a6 15.♘d2 ♕e7 16.♖ad1 ♕f8 17.♘f1±. **14...♗a6 15.♘d2 ♕e7 16.♕c1 ♕f8 17.♗d3** 17.♗f3 d5=. **17...d5 18.♕c2** The players agreed to a draw in this equal position, Pert-Lalic, Swansea 2006;

B2) 6...d5 7.e3 ♘bd7 8.cxd5 exd5 9.♗d3 ♖e8 10.0-0 c6 11.♕c2 The Exchange Variation of the Queen's Gambit. **11...g6 12.h3 ♗e7** We have entered a familiar position from the Exchange Variation, where Black has made a premature declaration with ...a7-a5. Therefore his opponent will, instead of the most often applied plan with ♖b1 and b2-b4, move on to another, also good, standard plan with ♖ae1, and take the battle to the centre. **13.♗f4 ♘f8 14.♘e5 ♘h5 15.♗h2 ♗d6 16.♖ae1 f6 17.♘g4 ♗xh2+ 18.♔xh2 ♕d6+ 19.♔g1 ♔g7 20.♘h2 f5 21.♘a4 ♗e6 22.♘f3 ♘d7 23.♘c5±** I. Sokolov-Skembris, Portoroz 1993;

B3) 6...h6 7.♗h4 d6 8.e3 ♘bd7 9.♗e2 ♗xc3+ 10.bxc3 b6 11.♘d2 ♗b7 12.f3 e5 13.e4

A well-known theoretical position from the Nimzo-Indian with the extra move ...a7-a5.

13...♕e8 14.♗f2 14.0-0 ♘h5⇄. **14...♘h5 15.g3 g6** 15...♕e7!?N 16.0-0 ♘hf6 17.♖b1 ♘h7∞ with play for both sides. **16.0-0 ♘g7∞** White has the bishop pair, but Black has enough play thanks to the doubled white pawns on the c-file, Savon-Taimanov, St Petersburg 1995.

6.♗g5

The main line and a critical test of the move 6...b6. White assumes a nearly identical hybrid position of the Queen's and Nimzo-Indian that usually occurs after 1.d4 ♘f6 2.c4 e6 3.♘f3 (or first 3.♘c3 ♗b4 4.♘f3 b6 5.♗g5) 3...b6 4.♘c3 ♗b4 5.♗g5, but where Black has a pawn on a7 instead of a5.

White can also try 6.e3, 6.g3 or 6.a3. We will examine them here:

A) 6.e3

White develops calmly in the spirit of the central systems of the Nimzo-Indian, whose main idea is to create a stable centre in harmony with active pieces. With e2-e3, White limits his dark-squared bishop, so Black has more possibilities to continue. With 6...♗b7 he may activate the light-squared bishop on the central diagonal h1-a8, and be the first to establish control of the critical e4-square, or he may play solidly with 6...0-0 followed by ...d7-d5 (as covered in Chapter 11). The straightforward 6...♗xc3 7.♗xc3 ♘e4 is, according to grandmaster Viacheslav Eingorn in his book *A Rock-Solid Chess Opening Repertoire for Black*, enough for a draw.

6...♗b7 The safest plan for Black is probably the one starting with 6...0-0 because after 7.♗d3 d5 8.0-0 he has a choice between three solid continuations: 8...♗a6, 8...♗b7 and 8...dxc4, as covered in Chapter 11. **7.♗d3 0-0 8.0-0** A strategic crossroads for Black. He may choose between two altogether different position types: the flexible but rather passive 8...d6 and the active 8...d5 (covered in Chapter 11).

For 8.♕c2 d6 (for 8...d5 9.cxd5 exd5 10.0-0 see Chapter 11) 9.0-0 ♘bd7 10.e4 e5 see under 8.0-0.

8...d6

Black has established control over the central diagonal and the e4-square, so he now builds a flexible structure, with the intention of finishing his development with ...♘b8-d7. Here White usually chooses one of the ways to resume the battle for the critical e4-square, such as: 9.♖e1, 9.♕e2, 9.a3 or 9.♕c2.

With 8...d5, Black may move on to the solid positions covered in Chapter 11, however, the above-mentioned move order with 6...0-0 is better because Black then preserves the possibility of the excellent ...♗c8-a6.

A1) **9.♖e1** White supports e2-e4 with the rook, but Black can now calmly develop his last piece. **9...♘bd7** 9...♗xc3 10.♗xc3 ♘e4 (11.♖c1 f5=) 11...♗xe4 12.♘d2 ♗b7 (12...♗g6!?) 13.e4 ♘d7 14.♘f1 (14.♖e3!?) 14...e5 15.d5 ♘c5 16.♘g3

♗c8 17.♖f1 ♕h4 18.♕e2 f5 19.exf5 ♗xf5 20.♘xf5 ♖xf5∓ Sadler-Roktim, Hove 1997. **10.e4 e5 11.a3** 11.d5 ♘c5 12.♗c2 ♗c8 (12...♗a6!?) 13.h3 h6 14.a3 (14.b3 ♘h7 15.a3 ♗xc3 16.♗xc3 f5 17.exf5 ♗xf5 18.♗xf5 ♖xf5 19.b4 axb4 20.axb4 ♖xa1 21.♗xa1 ♘d7⇄ Rodriguez Lopez-Caruana, Calvia 2006) 14...♗xc3 15.♗xc3 a4 16.♘d2 ♘h7 17.f4 exf4 (17...f6!?) 18.e5 ♗d7 19.♕f3± Wells-Emms, England 2013.

Now Black plays an important intermediate move: **11...exd4! 12.♘xd4** A weaker option is 12.axb4 dxc3 13.♗xc3 axb4 14.♗xb4 ♖e8 15.♘d2 ♘c5∓. **12...♘e5!** Again an intermediate move. Black has an excellent game thanks to his strong pressure on the opponent's centre, Bobotsov-Najdorf, Lugano 1968;

A2) **9.♕e2** does not enable White to get control of the e4-square because of the simple **9...♗xc3 10.♗xc3** and now Black is the first to take control of e4: **10...♘e4** 10...♗e4 11.♘d2 ♗xd3 12.♕xd3 ♘bd7 13.e4 e5 14.♖fe1 ♘h5 15.♘f1 ♕g5 16.♖ad1 ♖ae8 17.b3 ♖e6!?.

With equal play, Elianov-Moiseenko, Kiev 2011.

11.♗xe4 ♗xe4 12.♘d2 ♗b7 13.e4 White occupies the centre and has a space advantage, but also a more passive bishop, which evens out the chances. **13...♘d7 14.d5 ♕e7** Another good option is 14...♕h4 15.f4 exd5 16.exd5 ♖ae8 17.♕f3 f5 18.g3 ♕e7= Macchiagodena-Chripko, ICCF email 2009. **15.♕g4 e5 16.f4 f6=** Chiburdanidze-Speelman, Lippstadt 2000;

A3) **9.a3** also gives Black some time to consolidate the e4-square and organize play on the kingside: **9...♗xc3 10.♗xc3 ♘e4 11.♗xe4** 11.♗e1 f5 12.♘d2 ♕g5! 13.f4 ♕g6 14.♘xe4 ♗xe4 15.♗xe4 fxe4 16.b4 axb4 (another good option is 16...♘c6!? with the idea of moving the knight via e7 to the strategic f5-square) 17.axb4 ♘d7∞ with play on both sides, Stamenkov-Kosic, Struga 2011. **11...♗xe4 12.b4** 12.♘d2 ♗d3= Paidousis-Andersen, Tel Aviv 1964. **12...axb4 13.axb4 ♖xa1 14.♗xa1 ♘d7** 14...♘c6!?=. **15.♘d2 ♗b7 16.♕c2=** Böhmer-Meijers, Wiesbaden 2013;

A4) **9.♕c2 ♘bd7** A riskier move is 9...♗xf3 10.gxf3 ♘c6 11.a3 ♗xc3 12.♗xc3 ♘e7 13.♔h1 ♘g6 14.♖g1± and with his maximally active pieces, White has all the preconditions to increase his advantage and force his opponent into a critical position, Elianov-Alexandrov, Moscow 2003.

After the text, White usually chooses between 10.e4 and 10.a3.

10.e4 After 10.a3 ♗xc3 11.♗xc3, in addition to the pair of bishops, White has more space and should be better. However, grandmaster Bronstein unexpectedly reached a more promising ending from this position: 11...♖e8 12.♘g5 (12.b4!?) 12...h6 13.♘e4 ♘xe4 14.♗xe4 ♗xe4 15.♕xe4 a4= 16.♖ad1 f5 17.♕c6 ♖a7 18.♗b4 ♕c8

19.♖c1 ♘f6 20.c5?! (this seems logical, as White wishes to increase the effectivity of his pieces) 20...bxc5 21.dxc5 d5 22.♗c3 ♕a6 23.♕xa6 ♖xa6 24.♗xf6 gxf6 25.♖fd1 ♖b8∓.

Although Black's structure is not appealing, thanks to his more functional rooks due to the pressure on the b2-pawn, he is doing better, Porat-Bronstein, Amsterdam 1964.

10...e5

A critical position. Black has blocked the e-pawn with standard moves and partially neutralized the opponent's centre, but White still has not lost the chance to achieve an advantage, as he can maintain the mobility of his d4-pawn.

A41) **11.d5** As we know, this closing of the centre with the intention to occupy more space and relieve the tension, tends to lead to strategically desirable positions for Black. In this situation, White gives up his light-squared bishop at an early stage, which provides his opponent with the opportunity to play on the light squares and to open the position with ...f7-f5: **11...♘c5 12.♖fe1 ♘xd3 13.♕xd3 h6 14.b3 ♗c8 15.h3 ♘h7 16.a3 ♗xc3 17.♕xc3 f5 18.exf5 ♗xf5↑**

Black has an excellent game, thanks to the bishops and the opened f-file, Hübner-Short, Brussels 1987.

A42) **11.♘d5!?** A provocative move. White wants his opponent to weaken his position with ...c7-c6. **11...♗xd2 12.♕xd2 ♖e8**

A421) **12...c6!?** Black does not want to face an unpleasant white knight in the centre, so he grants his opponent's wish by closing in his bishop and weakening the d6-pawn. Still, White does not benefit much from this: **13.♘c3 ♖e8 14.♖fe1 ♘f8 15.♖ad1 ♘g6 16.♗f1** A move that deserves attention is 16.dxe5!? dxe5 (16...♘xe5?! 17.♗e2±) 17.♘a4!? with the idea of c4-c5, with a minimal advantage for White. **16...♕c7 17.d5** 17.dxe5 dxe5 18.♕d6 ♕xd6 19.♖xd6 ♖ad8=. **17...c5 18.g3 ♗c8 19.h3∞** Black has a healthy position, but with a little extra space, his opponent has a minimal advantage, Van der Sterren-Rashkovsky, Baku 1983;

A422) **12...c5?!** This move directly benefits White. Black cannot stand the strong central knight for long, so after the exchange on the d5-square, White will have a strong protected passed pawn: **13.dxe5 ♘xe5 14.♘xe5 dxe5 15.♖fe1 ♕d6 16.♗c2 ♗xd5 17.exd5±** Kasparov-Urday Caceres, Lima 1993. **13.♖fe1** and now:

A4221) **13...exd4!?** Black gives way in the centre so as to get more active play. Besides giving extra space to the opponent, this also increases the strength of White's pieces. **14.♘xd4 ♘c5 15.f3** Many pawns as well as the bishop on light squares are strategically undesirable, but his space advantage and fantastic knights in the centre give White a more promising game. **15...c6 16.♘c3 ♕c7** Even 16...♕e7 does not promise Black a draw: 17.♗c2 ♕f8 18.♘f5 ♖ad8 19.♖ad1 and White is doing better, with more space and more active pieces, Vera Gonzalez Quevedo-Rodriguez Cespedes, Cuba 1984. **17.♗f1 ♖ad8 18.♖ad1** Better is 18.♘f5 ♘e6 19.♖ad1 d5 20.cxd5 cxd5 21.e5± Kasparov. **18...d5!∞** After this liberating thrust, Black has more realistic chances of a draw, Kasparov-Tal, Niksic 1983;

A4222) **13...♘f8!?** An attractive move by Taimanov. Before the relieving ...c7-c6, he relocates the knight to e6 to attack d4. **14.g3?!** White puts the cart before the horse and loses his main strategic assets. A better move was 14.♖ad1 ♘6d7 15.♗c2!? (with the idea ♗a4) 15...♘e6 (15...a4!?) 16.♗a4 and White is doing better thanks to his strong centre and maximally active pieces. **14...♘6d7 15.♗f1 ♘e6** Black has already levelled the chances thanks to the ill-timed 14.g3.

16.b3?! And after this unnecessary move, Black takes the game into his own hands. **16...c6 17.♘e3 ♘xd4 18.♘xd4 exd4 19.♕xd4 c5! 20.♕xd6 ♘e5 21.♕xd8 ♘f3+ 22.♔h1 ♖axd8** Black will return the pawn, thus maintaining a better position, Cvitan-Taimanov, Baku 1983.

B) **6.g3**

Another position where the fianchetto of the light-squared bishop and the knight on c3 are not the best combination, since it leaves the c4-pawn exposed.

B1) **6...♗b7 7.♗g2 0-0 8.0-0 d6**

Black has established control over the central diagonal and the e4-square, so he now builds a flexible structure, with the intention of finishing his development with ...♘d7.

8...♘e4!? is a simple option to draw and also avoid a lot of theory: 9.♘xe4 ♗xe4 10.♗f4 (10.♗xb4 axb4=) 10...a4 11.♖c1 h6 12.♘e5 ♗xg2 13.♔xg2 ♗d6 14.e4 ♗xe5 15.♗xe5 d6 16.♗f4 ♘d7 17.♕d3 ♕e7 18.♖fe1 e5 19.♗e3 ♕e6 20.h3 ♖ae8 21.♕c2 exd4 22.♗xd4 c5 23.♗e3 ♕xe4+∓ Johannessen-Kortchnoi, Drammen 2004.

8...d5 is possible, but it leads to more passive positions: 9.cxd5 ♗xc3 (9...exd5 10.♖c1 ♖e8 11.♗f4± Llanes Hurtado-Ubilava, Zafra 2004) 10.bxc3 ♗xd5 11.♗g5 ♘bd7 12.♕a4; White has a more promising position with the bishop pair.

Now:

B11) **9.cxd5 exd5 10.♘xd5 ♘xd5** Weaker is 10...♗xd2 11.♕xd2 ♘bd7 12.♘d4 ♘c5 13.♖fe1 ♗xd5 14.cxd5± Eljanov-Zubov, Poltava 2006. **11.cxd5 ♘d7 12.♘d4 ♕f6 13.♗xb4 axb4 14.♕d2 ♖a5= 15.♖fc1 ♘c5 16.♖e1 ♖fa8** with a good game for Black, Spark 1.0-Stockfish 1.9.1, Internet 2011;

B12) **9.♖c1 ♘bd7 10.♗g5 ♗xc3 11.♖xc3 h6 12.♗xf6 ♘xf6 13.♘e1** 13.♘d2 ♗xg2 14.♔xg2 c5 15.♖d3 ♕c7= Richert-Klimm, Germany 2000. **13...♗xg2 14.♘xg2 ♕e7 15.♕d3 e5 16.♘e3 e4 17.♕c2 c6 18.♕a4 ♖fc8 19.a3 g6 20.♕c2 a4=** Mensch-Kuzubov, Zürich 2009;

B13) **9.♗g5** is a risky move which allows the disruption of White's own pawn structure on the queen's wing: **9...♗xc3 10.bxc3 ♘bd7 11.♖e1 h6 12.♗f4** 12.♗xf6 ♘xf6 with at least an equal game for Black. **12...♖e8 13.♖b1 ♗e4 14.♖b2 e5 15.♗c1 ♕e7∓** Sekano-Lalic, Haarlem 1994;

B14) **9.♕c2 ♘bd7 10.♖e1** 10.♖ad1 ♗xc3 11.♗xc3 ♗e4 12.♕c1 ♕b8 13.a4 ♕b7 14.b3 d5 15.♗h3 c6 16.♘d2 ♗g6 17.♗g2 b5.

With equality, Romanov-Andreikin, Moscow 2011.

10...♗xc3 11.♗xc3 ♗e4 12.♕d2 12.♕a4 c5 13.♘h4 ♕c7 with good play for Black, Bacrot-Kortchnoi, Cannes 1998; 12.♕c1 c6 13.♕f4 ♕e7 (13...♕b8 14.b3 b5= Kumic-Nestorovic, Novi Sad 2013) 14.♗h3 b5= Banikas-Kryvoruchko, Paleochora 2011. **12...♕b8 13.♖ad1 b5 14.cxb5 ♕xb5 15.♗f1 ♗b7 16.♘h4 ♘e4 17.♕c2 f5** with good play for Black, Naumkin-Fedorchuk, Cesenatico 2011.

B2) **6...♗a6**

Black quickly develops a piece while attacking the most vulnerable pawn in the opponent's position.

After **7.b3** Black has a pleasant choice between two continuations: 6...0-0 followed by ...c7-c6 and ...d7-d5, then, in the event of an exchange, capture with the c-pawn and activate the rook on the c-file; or attack the vulnerable c-pawn

immediately with 6....d5, and then in the event of an exchange on d5, take back with the e-pawn and activate his rook on the e-file:

B21) **7...0-0 8.♗g2 c6 9.a3 ♗e7 10.♗g5 d5 11.♗xf6** 11.♘e5 ♘fd7 12.♗xe7 ♕xe7=; 11.0-0 ♘bd7 12.♕d3 c5 13.♘b5 ♗xb5 14.cxb5 ♘e4 15.♗xe7 ♕xe7 16.♘e5 ♘xe5 17.dxe5 f5 with an excellent position for Black. **11...♗xf6 12.cxd5 cxd5 13.0-0 ♘d7 14.♕d2 ♗e7**

And with his active bishop pair Black has better chances, Karpov-Jussupow, Linares 1992;

B22) **7...d5 8.cxd5** This release of the tension in the centre is a consequence of the weakness of the c4-pawn, all due to the hapless combination of the light-squared bishop and the knight on c3. Now the diagonal f1-a6 and the e-file are opened, but in favour of Black, because it improves the effectivity of his bishop on a6 and a future rook on e8. **8...exd5 9.♗g2** 9.a3 ♗e7 (9...♗xc3 10.♗xc3 0-0 11.♗g2 ♖e8=) 10.♕c2 c5 11.♗h3 ♘c6 12.♗e3 0-0 13.0-0 ♖e8 14.♖fd1 h6= Girya-Zhao Xue, Kazan 2013. **9...0-0 10.0-0 ♖e8 11.♖e1 ♘bd7 12.a3** A weaker move is 12.♖c1 c6 13.♘b1 ♗b7 14.a3 ♗d6 15.♗c3 ♘e4 16.♗b2 f5∓ and Black has taken control of the centre, Birbrager-

Bronstein, Soviet Union 1967. **12...♗f8=** Black has a good position, Siebrecht-Fridman, Schwetzingen 2013.

C) **6.a3** In this particular position this move is a waste of time, since Black easily compensates for the conquest of the bishop pair with excellent play along the central diagonal h1-a8. **6...♗xc3 7.♗xc3 ♗b7 8.♗d2?!** White wants to activate his bishop, but this will cost him time, which his opponent will use to quickly prepare an amassment of troops for an attack on the white king. 8.e3=. **8...d6 9.♗g5 a4 10.e3 ♖a5** With the idea 11...♗xf3, winning a piece. **11.♗h4 ♘bd7 12.♗d3 ♕a8 13.0-0 g5** Black is not afraid to make this charge as he has excellent support from his pieces. **14.♗g3 h5 15.h4 gxh4 16.♘xh4 ♖g8 17.♖e1 ♖ag5∓**

A beautiful and strategically instructive picture. Rarely do we see positions where one side manages to maximally activate and harmonize all their pieces in relatively few moves, offering a graphic display of the two most important strategic elements:

1. Activity
2. Piece coordination.

White is in a critical position, facing an onslaught of black pieces, Chernuschevich-Eingorn, France 2004.

We go back to the main line **6.♗g5**.

Black may continue 6...♗b7 or try to prove the value of his a-pawn with 6...a4, making immediate use of the extra move.

6...♗b7

6...a4!? With the idea ...a4-a3. **7.a3 ♗xc3+ 8.bxc3 ♗b7 9.e3** Here Black usually opts for: a) an aggressive plan with 9...♖a5 combined with the advance of his g- and h-pawns; or b) the standard plan with 9...d6 followed by ...♘bd7, ...♕e7 and ...e6-e5:

A) **9...♖a5** With the idea 10...♗xf3. **10.♗h4 d6 11.♘d2!** We have already commented on this standard continuation under 9...d6. We will add that usually in this position Black plays actively with ...g7-g5 and ...h7-h5, which is not to say that his opponent has a subordinate position, and does not have his own chances. By keeping both bishops and a flexible pawn structure, White can start a long and complex battle. **11...g5** 11...♘bd7 12.f3 h5 13.♗d3 g5 14.♗f2 h4 15.h3 ♘h5 16.♖b1 ♕a8 17.♕c2 ♔e7 18.♔d1 ♗c6 19.♖e1 ♗b7 20.♖b4 ♗c6 21.♔c1 ♗b7 22.♔b1 ♗c6 23.♔a1 with slightly better chances for White thanks to his bishop pair and space advantage in the centre, Pinter-Turov, Austria 2011. **12.♗g3 ♘bd7** 12...h5 13.h3 (better is

13.h4 g4 14.f3 with slightly better chances, as White maintains the mobility of his pawn centre and the activity of his bishop pair) 13...♘bd7 14.f3 ♕e7 15.♗d3 e5 16.e4 h4 17.♗f2 ♘h5. Black has effectively neutralized White's bishop pair and mobile pawn centre, so he can count on equal chances, Pert-Rochev, Bunratty 2007.

13.f3 ♕e7!?N 13...♖g8 14.♗e2 h5 15.e4 h4 16.♗f2 ♕e7 17.♖b1 c5?! 18.♗d3 ♔d8?! 19.0-0± Khalifman-Alexandrov, St Petersburg 1996.

The text is played with the idea of ...e5-e4. **14.♗e2** 14.h4 g4! 15.fxg4 h6⊜. Weaknesses in the position are the pawns on g4 and g2 and the diagonal h1-a8 and the central square e4. 14.♗d3 e5 15.♕e2 e4 16.♗c2 exf3 17.gxf3 ♔d8∞. **14...h5 15.h4 g4 16.e4** 16.fxg4? hxg4∓. **16...♖g8 17.♗f4 gxf3 18.gxf3 ♘h7∞;**

B) **9...d6**

Black makes a move that is necessary in this type of position, while maintaining the possibility of a transition into plan A with ...e6-e5, usually supported by 10...♕e7 or 10...♘bd7, or plan B: the activation of his rook along the fifth rank with 10...♖a5, which is particularly effective if White plays 10.♗d3:

B1) **10.♗d3 ♖a5!**

10...♕e7, planning to advance the e-pawn, does not work in this case because of the simple 11.0-0 e5 (or 11...♘bd7 12.♘d2±) 12.♘d2±.

11.♗h4 ♘bd7 12.♖b1 12.e4 ♕a8⇄ and White must compromise his pawn structure by playing d4-d5; 12.0-0 ♕a8 13.♘e1 g5 14.♗g3 h5↑

A nice and instructive picture of the activity and harmony of Black's entire battle force.

12...♕a8 13.♖b5 ♗c6 14.♖xa5 ♕xa5 15.♕c2 ♕h5 16.♗xf6 ♘xf6 17.e4

♕**g4** 17...0-0!? 18.0-0 e5 with a more promising game for Black. **18.0-0 ♗xe4 19.h3 ♕f4** Epishin-Turov, Helmond 2012;

B2) **10.♘d2!?**

A typical move and a better reaction than 10.♗d3 to Black's unusual but effective plan of activating his rook via a5. White's plan is to ensure with f2-f3 the retreat of his dark-squared bishop and neutralize the opponent's pressure along the a8-h1 diagonal, especially on e4. However, this standard move also costs time, so Black can successfully apply his standard back-up plan: the advance of his e-pawn, by either 10...♘bd7 or 10...♕e7!.

B21) **10...♖a5 11.♗h4** is covered under 11.♘d2;

B22) **10...♘bd7** After this developing but routine move, which is given here in order to better understand the essence of the position, White is able to realize his plan of keeping the dark-squared bishop and creating a flexible pawn structure: **11.f3 ♕e7 12.♗d3 e5 13.♕e2!?** Thus White manages to neutralize Black's combined strategic threats of ...h7-h6 and ...exd4, and can fight for the upper hand. A weaker move is 13.0-0 h6 14.♗xf6 (14.♗h4?! does not work because of 14...exd4∓ with the idea of 15...♕e3) 14...♘xf6 with a good posi-

tion for Black. **13...h6 14.♗h4 0-0 15.0-0 ♖fe8 16.♖ae1 g5 17.♗g3 e4 18.♗c2 exf3 19.gxf3↑** White has a space advantage in the centre and a potentially dangerous bishop pair.

B23) **10...♕e7!?N**

Now White has no time for ♗d3 and ♕e2, as in the previous line.

11.f3 e5 Now White will have to either exchange his dark-squared bishop or make it passive due to the strategic threat of ...exd4 combined with ...h7-h6. **12.♗d3** 12.♗e2 h6 13.♗h4 ♘bd7 14.♗f2 0-0=. **12...h6 13.♗xf6 ♕xf6**

With a balanced game.

Now we go back to the position after **6...♗b7**.

7.e3 h6

For 7...a4 8.a3 ♗xc3+ 9.bxc3 see under 6...a4.

8.♗h4 g5

A logical plan, well-known from the Nimzo-Indian. Black will compensate for the opponent's bishop pair with a strong central knight on e4 and by disrupting the opponent's pawn structure with ...♗xc3.

9.♗g3 ♘e4 10.♕c2 d6 11.♗d3 ♗xc3+ 12.bxc3

Now Black has two known standard continuations, leading to completely different types of positions: the active 12...f5 and the solid, simplifying 12...♘xg3.

12...f5

12...♘xg3 13.fxg3 Or 13.hxg3 g4 14.♘h4 ♘d7 15.0-0 ♕g5 16.♖ab1 0-0-0 with an unusual position with play for both sides, Pelletier-Abergel, Warsaw 2005. **13...♘d7 14.0-0 ♕e7 15.♗e4 ♗xe4 16.♕xe4 0-0** White has more space and more activity, but also many doubled pawns, which gives Black a realistic chance to achieve full equality. **17.♕d3 f6** Better is 17...f5N 18.e4 fxe4 19.♕xe4 ♘f6 20.♕e2 ♖ae8 21.♖ae1 ♕g7 with equal chances. **18.e4 ♕h7 19.♖ae1** with slightly better chances for White thanks to his advantage in the centre, Khalifman-Elianov, Moscow 2012.

13.d5

Without this thematic move, with his weaker pawn structure and inactive bishop pair White would soon end up in an inferior position.

13...♘a6

With the idea of ...♘a6-c5. 13...♘d7 is also possible, with the idea of ...♘d7-c5, which comes down to the same thing except that Black does not have at his disposal the additional reply to 14.♗xe4 which we will see below.

14.♘d4

We have seen White's last two moves together several times in this type of position. In case of 14.♗xe4 there follows 14...fxe4 15.♕xe4 ♕f6 16.0-0 0-0-0 17.♕xe6+ ♕xe6 18.dxe6 ♗xf3!? (this solid move would not be possible with a black knight on d7 because White could then play the intermediate move 19.exd7 with check) 19.gxf3 ♘c5 20.♔g2 ♘xe6= Black has a good game because of his superior pawn structure.

14...♘ac5 15.0-0

Compared to the original theoretical position in the Nimzo-Indian, which usually occurs after 1.d4 ♘f6 2.c4 e6 3. ♘c3 ♗b4 4. ♘f3 b6 5. ♗g5 ♗b7 6.e3 h6 7. ♗h4 g5 8. ♗g3 ♘e4 9. ♕c2 d6 10. ♗d3 ♗xc3+ 11.bxc3 f5 12.d5 ♘a6 13. ♘d4 ♘ac5 14.0-0, our position, with the pawn on a5 instead of a7, seems weak if we look at the white knight on d4, but this will not affect the assessment of the position if we choose the following continuation:

15...♕e7

With the idea ...0-0-0.

In case of 15...♕f6, after 16.♗xe4 fxe4 17.f4↑ White has a certain initiative.

16.f3   ♘xg3   17.hxg3   exd5 18.♘xf5   ♕d7   19.cxd5   ♗xd5 20.e4   ♗b7 21.♗c4 0-0-0

with play for both sides.

> ### Conclusion
> In this chapter we began the analysis of the regular Bogo-Indian, with the focus on the variation 4.♘f3 ♘f6 5.♘c3 b6!. With this move order Black can successfully meet the opponent's fianchetto system 6.g3 with the active 6...♗a6, and he can meet the central system 6.e3 with 6...♗b7 or 6...0-0!?, followed by 7.♗d3 d5 and ...♗a6. After 6.♗g5 we have seen how Black can either successfully make use of his extra move with 6...a4!? or implement his plans modelled to the regular Nimzo-Indian.

Exercises

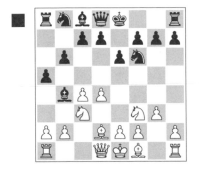

14.1 (1) Find the plan.
(solution on page 449)

14.1 (2) Find the plan.
(solution on page 449)

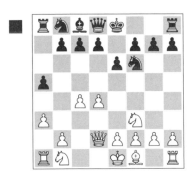

14.1 (3) Find the plan.
(solution on page 449)

Chapter 14.2

Queen's Indian Type 5.g3 b6

1.d4 e6 2.c4 ♗b4+ 3.♗d2 a5 4.♘f3 ♘f6 5.g3 b6

5.g3 represents the best continuation and the most complex task for the Bogo-Indian player. Black has several options, although in fact only three solid ones, which lead him to three utterly different types of positions.

In this chapter we shall analyse the Queen's Indian position type with 5...b6, or first 5...0-0 and then ...b7-b6, as well as the more rarely played 5...♘e4.

The Catalan-type positions with ...d7-d5 are explained in Chapters 14.3 and 14.4.

5...b6

Black combines the Bogo-Indian with the solid Queen's Indian. However, it is not too late for the position to also acquire characteristics of the Catalan Opening, as White has played g2-g3. Incidentally, this commonly seen scenario of positions mixing or one opening becoming another only tells us that systems, especially complete openings, can hardly be studied in isolation, that is, independently of other systems or openings.

A) 5...0-0 6.♗g2 b6

For 6...d5 see Chapter 14.3; see Chapter 12 for 6...d6.

7.♘e5 Now White is master of the central diagonal. However, this knight jump is most likely harmless, especially since Black has still not made a declaration regarding the position of his d-pawn.

7.0-0 &a6 (7...&b7 is covered under 5...b6) 8.♕c2 (see under 7.♕c2) or 8.b3 (see under 7.b3) or 8.♘e5 ♖a7 (see under 7.♘e5).

7...♖a7 8.0-0 Now Black can play, with relief, 8...d6, or first exchange the bishops with 8...&xd2 and then chase the opponent's knight away from the centre. That is why these two continuations using different move orders usually lead to the same positions:

A1) 8...&xd2 9.♕xd2 A weaker move is 9.♘xd2 d6 10.♘d3 c5! (with knights on the d-file, this attack is more efficient than the usual plan with ...e6-e5 for Black does not need to worry about the pawn's weakness on d6) 11.dxc5 bxc5= , resulting in a good position for Black due to his excellent control of the centre and his possibility to develop his pieces freely, Geler-Kosic, Cetinje 2013. **9...d6 10.♘d3** 10.♘f3 is covered under 8.. .d6. **10...&b7 11.♘c3 &xg2 12.♔xg2 c5** The standard plan is also possible here: 12...♘bd7 13.f3 e5, although after 14.e4 exd4 15.♘b5 ♖a8 16.♘xd4 ♘e5 17.♖ac1 ♘xd3 18.♕xd3 ♖e8 19.♖fd1 ♘d7 we arrive at a typical middlegame where White has slightly better chances thanks to his small spatial advantage in the centre; 20.♕c3± J. Horvath-Aleksic, Montecatini Terme 1999. **13.d5** Black has no problems after 13.♘e1 cxd4 14.♕xd4 ♘c6 15.♕d2 ♖d7 16.♘f3 d5 17.cxd5 ♘xd5= Agzamov-Jussupow, Frunze 1981. **13...exd5 14.cxd5 a4 15.b4 ♘a6 16.b5 ♘c7 17.♘b2 ♕e8 18.♕d3 ♘g4 19.♘c4 ♘e5 20.♘xe5 ♕xe5=** Mikhalevski-Fedorchuk, Trieste 2009;

A2) **8...d6**

This is a natural reaction whereby Black returns the opponent's aggressive knight to its territory and continues the development of his queenside. 9.♘f3 Returning to the same place. The question imposes itself as to whether the invasion of the white knight on e5 has served any purpose. Still, there are some benefits for White as well. The bishop on b4 has become vulnerable due to the threat of &d2-f4(g5), so Black is forced to make a usually undesirable exchange. 9.♘d3 &xd2 is covered under 8...&xd2. **9...&xd2 10.♕xd2** A weaker move is 10.♘bxd2?! because of 10...c5!⇄ and Black has a good game in the centre, thanks to the passive knight on d2. **10...&a6 11.b3**

11...c6!? A seemingly passive but strategically useful move. Black has cleared the 7th rank for his queen's rook, and his fourth pawn on the 6th rank is also ready for action. Now the plan with

11...c5 is not the best solution because after 12.♘c3± White continues with his natural development, thus exerting pressure on the d-file. Therefore, in this type of position Black most often leans towards plans with ...e6-e5 or ...d7-d5, although they all, of course, have their own strategic pros and cons. **12.♕f4!** In case of the natural 12.♘c3 Black quickly levels the chances by activating his light-squared bishop with 12...b5! 13.cxb5 cxb5 14.♖fc1 ♘bd7= Meins-Lobron, Germany 2000. **12...♖e7** Black is obviously preparing to attack the centre using the e-pawn. If 12...b5 13.♘bd2 bxc4 14.bxc4 ♕c7 15.e4 (15.♖ab1 ♘bd7=) 15...♘bd7 16.e5±. **13.♖d1 ♕c7 14.♘c3** For now White has a more viable position due to his more active pieces, however Black has the option to level the chances with an opportune attack on the centre with ...e6-e5. **14...♗c8 15.♕d2** 15.e4 e5=. **15...♘a6 16.♖ac1 ♖fe8 17.h3 h6 18.♘e1 ♗d7 19.♕b2 ♕b8 20.a3 e5 21.dxe5 dxe5 22.b4** 22.♘c2!?. **22...e4!** Black uses his assets in order to occupy more space and limit the action of the opponent's minor pieces. **23.e3** 23.♘c2?! e3→. **23...axb4 24.axb4 ♕c8 25.♔h2 ♖e5 26.♘e2 c5!=** He also establishes control over other important parts of the board. Both sides have their chances, Pelletier-Fedorchuk, Fort-de-France 2013.

B) **5...♘e4** is a rarely played move although Black has a strong strategic idea: to put a knight on d3 or to force the opponent to an exchange of dark-squared bishops on b4. **6.♗g2** Weaker is 6.♗xb4 axb4= and Black gets an open a-file. **6...0-0 7.0-0 ♘xd2 8.♘bxd2±** Black takes the dark-squared bishop and gains the bishop pair, but he loses more

since he is weaker in the centre and behind with his development.

6.♗g2

And now, as usual, Black can play to neutralize the effect of the opponent's bishop with 6...♗b7, to play the pseudo-active 6...♗a6 or to first castle 6...0-0, and then decide where to move the light-squared bishop, which usually transposes into positions of the first two continuations.

6...♗b7

This position is also commonly arrived at in the Queen's Indian move order: 1.d4 ♘f6 2.c4 e6 3.♘f3 b6 4.g3 ♗b7 5.♗g2 ♗b4 6.♗d2 a5.

6...0-0 is covered under 5...0-0.

A major alternative is **6...♗a6**, an active approach to the position. White has three options of defending the pawn on c4:, A) 7.b3, B) 7.♘e5, and C) 7.♕c2.

A) **7.b3** makes the game easier for Black on the queenside because of the option ...a5-a4: **7...0-0 8.0-0** Black can now continue in the spirit of the Queen's Indian with 8...♗b7 or the Catalan with 8...d5.

A1) **8...♗b7** Black returns to the central diagonal after the opponent has weakened his queenside with b2-b3, bearing in mind the potential ...a5-a4, with play along the a-file. **9.♘c3 ♘e4** A simple and useful exchange. Not only does it secure a significant position for his light-squared bishop on e4, but it also facilitates a potential ...a5-a4. **10.♘xe4 ♗xe4 11.♘e5 ♗xg2 12.♔xg2 ♘c6 13.♘f3 d5 14.♖c1 ♗a3 15.♖c2 ♕d7 16.♗c3 a4=** Vyzhmanavin-Christiansen, Manila 1992.

A2) **8...d5!?**

White wants to continue the play against the pawn on c4, thus giving the position Catalan characteristics. We will examine three natural reactions for White: 9.♕c2, 9.♘e5 and 9.cxd5.

A21) **9.♕c2 c6 10.♗f4 ♘bd7 11.♘bd2 ♘h5!** Black is the first to make his thematic move, not giving the opponent the time to take the initiative with e2-e4. **12.♘g5** 12.♗g5 ♘hf6 13.e4 h6 14.♗f4 g5 15.♗e3 ♘g4⇄. **12...♘df6 13.♖fd1?!** 13.♗e5=. **13...♘xf4 14.gxf4 ♕e7∓** Pinter-Makarichev, Rotterdam 1988;

A22) **9.♘e5 c6 10.a3** A weaker option is 10.cxd5?! cxd5 11.a3 ♗d6 12.♗f4 ♕e7∓ and White has no good solution for the weakness on a3, S. Larsen-Jussupow, Copenhagen 2003. **10...♗e7 11.♘c3 ♘fd7 12.♘xd7 ♘xd7 13.♘d2 ♖c8=** Razuvaev-Jussupow, Soviet Union 1984.

A23) With the exchange **9.cxd5** White has got rid of the vulnerable c4-pawn but he also activates the opponent's pieces.

In this particular position, it seems that Black can, aside from the standard reaction 9...exd5, also resort to 9...♘xd5!?, thus creating a dynamic position thanks to his active bishops:

A231) **9...exd5** A position type where the pawn structure in the centre is usually more agreeable to White. However, the bishop on d2 and White's weakened queenside provide Black with enough counterplay: **10.♘c3 ♖e8 11.♖e1 ♕e7** 11...♘c6!? with the idea of ...♘f6-e4. **12.♘g5 ♗b7 13.e4 ♗xc3 14.♗xc3 ♘xe4 15.♕h5 h6 16.♘xe4 dxe4 17.♗xe4 ♗xe4 18.f3 ♘d7 19.♖xe4 ♕d6 20.♖ae1 ♘f6=** Rhode-Backe, ICCF email 2001;

A232) **9...♘xd5!?** Black relinquishes control of the centre, hence giving a chance to the opponent's e-pawn and dangerous Catalan bishop to demonstrate their strength. Now:

A1) **10.a3 ♗e7 11.♘c3** 11.♖e1 c5 12.♘c3 (12.e4 ♘f6⇄) 12...♗b7 13.♘xd5 ♗xd5 14.e4 ♗b7 15.♗c3 cxd4 16.♘xd4 ♘d7 with an equal position. **11...♘d7 12.♖e1 c5 13.e4 ♘xc3 14.♗xc3** and now in the game Ree-Kuligowski, Wijk aan Zee 1983, Black could have achieved a satisfactory game with **14...cxd4!N**

15.♗xd4 A weaker move is 15.♘xd4?! ♖c8 16.♗b2 ♘c5∓ and Black's light-squared bishop is more valuable than the respected Catalan bishop; 15.♕xd4 ♘f6=. **15...♕c7⇄**;

A2) 10.♖e1 c5 11.e4 ♘f6 A better option is 11...♘e7!N 12.a3 ♗xd2 13.♕xd2 cxd4 14.♘xd4 ♘ec6! 15.♘f3 (15.♘xc6 ♘xc6∓) 15...♘d7↑ with the idea of ... ♘d7-c5. **12.a3 ♗xd2 13.♘bxd2±** Magerramov-Makarichev, Moscow 1991.

B) 7.♘e5

Practice shows that this attractive move does not accomplish much by forcing the opponent's rook to a7, since we often encounter positions where the expelled black rook performs many useful strategic tasks from a7:

- it supports the light-squared bishop on b7;

- it clears the a8-square for its queen, with possible pressure along the a-file;

- or it is presented with a possibility to be activated through the 7th rank by moving to the c- or e-file.

7...♖a7 8.0-0 0-0 Now we will examine the following logical continuations: 9.♗b4, 9.♗g5 and 9.♕c2.

B1) 9.♗g5 ♗e7 10.♕c2 h6 11.♗f4 and now simply **11...d6!?N 12.♘d3** (12.♘c6?! ♘xc6 13.♗xc6 d5∓; 12.♘f3 c5 13.dxc5 bxc5⇄ and with excellent control of the centre and good options to activate his pieces, Black has no reason to fear) **12...c5 13.dxc5** (13.d5 exd5 14.cxd5 b5↑) **13...bxc5⇄** again with a familiar pawn structure in the centre which gives Black a good game. Moreover, White must be careful, as the central black pawns are mobile and this structure is known to have made life difficult for a number of players;

B23) 9.♗xb4 axb4 10.a3 d6 11.axb4 dxe5 12.dxe5 ♘g4 13.b5 ♘xe5 14.♕xd8 14.b3 ♕e7 15.♕d4 f6

16.bxa6 ♖d8 17.♕e3 ♖xa6=. **14...♖xd8 15.b3 ♔f8 16.♖a2 c6 17.♘c3 cxb5 18.cxb5 ♖d4 19.♖fa1 ♖b4 20.♖a3 ♘ed7 21.bxa6 ♘c5 22.♗b7 ♘xb7 23.axb7 ♖xb7=** Lerner-Makarichev, Moscow 1981.

B3) 9.♕c2 c5!

Black is taking advantage of the absence of the opponent's knight to control d4, so he rushes to conveniently exchange the pawns and open the c-file.

It is also possible to make a transition into a Catalan position type with 9...d5!? 10.♖d1 c6 11.♗xb4 (11.♗f4!? ♗d6 12.♘d2 with a complex and unclear position because of the black rook's position on a7) 11...axb4 12.a3 (White wants to free himself from the pressure along the a-file, however, also possible is 12.♘d2!? ♗b7 13.♘d3 ♕e7 14.c5 bxc5 15.♘xc5∞ with a minimal advantage for White) 12...♗xc4 13.♘xc4 dxc4 14.♕xc4 c5 15.♘d2 bxa3 16.♖xa3 ♖xa3 17.bxa3 cxd4 18.♘f3 ♕d6 19.♕xd4 ♕xa3 20.♕xb6= Dreev-Grischuk, Moscow 2006.

10.dxc5 Nothing is achieved by 10.♗xb4 cxb4 (another good move is 10...axb4=). 11.♘d2 ♖c7⇄ Gozzoli-Jussupow, France 2009. **10...♗xc5 11.♘d3** 11.♘c3?! d5 12.cxd5 ♘xd5↑ Mochalov-I. Botvinnik, corr 1988. **11...♗e7 12.♗f4** and now, in the game

Lputian-Makarichev, Moscow 1989, with **12...d5!N**

Black could have simply levelled the chances.

C) **7.♕c2!** is the usual defence of the c4-pawn. White does not want to weaken the queenside with b2-b3 or jump to the centre too soon with ♘e5. **7...0-0 8.0-0** Here Black has a lot of possibilities, but none of them seems to provide him with a satisfactory game:

C1) **8...c5** For this continuation, the position of the black knight on e7 would clearly be more suitable. **9.♖d1!** In practice, Black has tried **9...♗xd2** (9...d5 10.♗g5 with the idea of a2-a3; 10...cxd4 11.cxd5±, P.H. Nielsen-Postny, Khanty-Mansiysk 2011; after 9...♖a7 10.e4!± Black has no satisfactory solution to the threat e4-e5, Lobron-Jussupow, Germany 1991) **10.♘bxd2 ♘c6 11.dxc5 bxc5 12.♘e4 ♘xe4 13.♕xe4 ♖b8 14.b3 ♕f6** (14...a4!?) **15.♖ac1 ♖fd8 16.♖d6 ♗b7 17.♕e3 ♕b2 18.♖cd1** Karpov-Piket, Monaco 1996;

C2) **8...♗b7** This tap-dancing of the black bishop amounts to the loss of a tempo in this position. It makes sense when Black can conduct a plan with ...c7-c5 or if he has at least provoked the weakening of the opponent's queenside with b2-b3. **9.♗g5** 9.♗e3. **9...h6** 9...♗e7 10.♘c3± and White

builds a position which we explain elsewhere in this chapter with an extra tempo under 6...♗b7. **10.♗xf6 ♕xf6 11.a3 ♗e7 12.♘c3** Weaker is the immediate 12.e4 because of 12...♕g6 13.♘e5 ♕h7 14.♘c3 d6 15.♘d3 ♘c6 16.♘b5 ♗f6 17.d5 ♘d4 18.♘xd4 ♗xd4⇄ and the black bishop pair is more dangerous than the opponent's centre, Nikolic-Perunovic, Vrnjacka Banja 2007. **12...g6** 12...d5 13.♘e5±. **13.e4±** The white centre is more dangerous than Black's bishop pair, which is difficult to activate, Beliavsky-Lafuente, Leon 2008;

C3) **8...c6** Black intends to play the Closed Catalan, where ...a7-a5 is not very popular. **9.♗f4** Or 9.♗g5 ♗e7 10.♘bd2 d5, which leads to one of many original versions of the Catalan, where Black has made the rare move ...a7-a5 but White has played the rare ♗g5: 11.♘e5 ♘fd7 12.♗xe7 ♕xe7 13.♘d3 ♘f6 14.♖fe1 ♖d8 15.♖ad1 ♘bd7 16.e4± Ilincic-Raicevic, Nis 1996. **9...♗e7 10.♘bd2 d5±** See Chapter 14.3.

C4) With **8...d5** Black enters an unfavourable version of the Queen's Indian: **9.cxd5 exd5 10.♗g5 ♗e7 11.♘c3±** Ivanchuk-Turov, Kusadasi 2006.

Back to the position after **6...♗b7**.
7.0-0 0-0

A critical position. White has a wide selection of continuations, but his best chances for an advantage are with 8.♗f4 and 8.♗g5. 8.♘c3 was explained in Chapter 14.1.

8.♗f4

White is already threatening with c4-c5 to block the black bishop's retreat.

Let us take a look at **8.♗g5**. White is ready to give up his bishop pair in order to take control of e4 and create a full centre. **8...♗e7** and now:

A) **9.♘c3** is a natural developing move which, however, allows a significant simplification: **9...♘e4 10.♗xe7 ♕xe7 11.♕d3 ♘xc3 12.♕xc3** It is easier for Black after the unnecessary doubling of pawns with 12.bxc3 f5 13.♘e1 ♗xg2 14.♘xg2 ♘c6 15.f4 ♕a3 16.♘e3 ♘e7 17.♕c2 ♕d6 with chances for both sides. Avrukh-Rodshtein, Acre 2013. **12...d6** Black has one extra piece in relation to the system of Ulf Andersson which we explained in Chapter 3.1: 1.d4 e6 2.c4 ♗b4+ 3.♗d2 ♗xd2+ 4.♕xd2 ♘f6 5.♘f3 0-0 6.g3 b6 7.♗g2 ♗b7 8.♘c3 ♘e4 9.♕c2 ♘xc3 10.♕xc3 ♕e7 11.0-0 d6. As we can see, here Black has made the useful move ...a7-a5. Now:

A1) **13.♘e1 ♗xg2 14.♘xg2 ♘c6!?** A nice strategic idea. Black devalues the opponent's main plan with e2-e4 and

♘g2-e3 by provoking his d-pawn to move. Of course, the flexible but more passive 14...♘d7!? is also possible, although after 15.e4 e5 16.♘e3 White's position is a bit more promising thanks to his small space advantage and more active knight. **15.d5** 15.e4?! e5 16.d5 ♘d4!?. **15...♘e5 16.e4 ♖ae8 17.♖ae1 ♘d7** Black has performed a circle dance with his knight and spent time, but he has provoked the opponent's move d4-d5, thereby depriving him of a potential stronghold on said square, as we can see in the game Cvek-Polak below. **18.f4 ♘c5** and the pawn on a5 has demonstrated its qualities in this position: **19.b3 exd5 20.exd5 ♕d7** with equal chances;

A2) **13.♖ae1** A wise move order. White does not exchange the bishops until the black knight has declared its intentions. **13...♘d7 14.♘h4 ♗xg2 15.♘xg2 ♘f6 16.e4 e5 17.f3 exd4 18.♕xd4 ♖fe8 19.♘e3** with a small space advantage for White but also with real chances for Black to achieve a draw, Cvek-Polak, Czechia 2013.

B) **9.♕c2** is the only continuation that gives White any chance for an advantage (M. Marin). For example:

B1) **9...♘a6 10.♘c3 ♘b4 11.♕b3 ♘e4 12.♗xe7 ♕xe7 13.a3 ♘a6 14.♖ad1 ♘xc3 15.♕xc3 ♗e4 16.♖fe1 c5 17.dxc5 ♘xc5 18.b4 axb4 19.axb4 ♘a6 20.♘e5 ♗xg2 21.♔xg2**

21...f6? Better is 21...♖fd8 22.♘d3 ♖ac8 23.b5 ♘c5 with chances of complete equality. **22.♘xd7±** Mamedyarov-J. Polgar, Geneva (rapid) 2013;

B2) **9...♗e4 10.♕d2 ♗b7 11.♘c3 ♘e4** 11...h6 12.♗xf6 ♗xf6 13.e4± (13.♕c2 is cover under 9...h7-h6). **12.♘xe4 ♗xe4 13.♗xe7 ♕xe7 14.♕f4 ♗xf3 15.♗xf3 ♖a7±** Dzhumagaliev-Barlakov, Barnaul 2011;

B3) **9...h6 10.♗xf6 ♗xf6 11.♘c3** 11.♘g5?! hxg5 12.♗xb7 ♖a7 13.♗f3 ♗xd4∓.

11...g6
Black prevents a tactical attack from the opponent with ♘f3-g5 and secures an escape square for his dark-squared bishop but allows the opponent to create a full centre.

An idea deserving attention is to prevent e2-e4 with 11...d5!? 12.♖fd1 ♘a6 13.a3 ♕e7 14.cxd5 exd5 15.♖ac1 ♖fd8 16.♕b3 ♖d6 17.♘e1 ♖ad8 18.e3 c5⇄. Black has a vulnerable pawn on d5 but also counterplay because of his bishop pair and a potential pawn majority on the queenside, Bruzon Batista-Nisipeanu, Linares 2013.

In the event of 11...d6 12.♘g5 hxg5 13.♗xb7 ♖a7 14.♗g2 c6 15.♖ad1 ♖c7 16.e3 ♘d7 White is doing a little better thanks to the greater activity of his

pieces, but Black has chances to achieve equality, Rodshtein-Bacrot, Porto Carras 2011.

12.♖ad1 d6 13.h4 h5 14.e4 ♘d7 A typical position with an eternal question: are the bishop pair and a flexible pawn structure enough to oppose the opponent's powerful centre? **15.e5** 15.♖fe1 ♗g7 16.♘b5 ♕b8 17.d5 e5 18.b3 ♕d8 19.a3 ♗h6 20.b4 ♘f6 with play for both sides and equal chances, Karpov-Kortchnoi, Tilburg 1986. **15...♗g7 16.d5 ♘xe5 17.♘xe5 ♗xe5 18.dxe6 ♗xg2 19.exf7+ ♔xf7 20.♔xg2 ♗xc3 21.♕xc3 ♕f6 22.♕xf6+ ♔xf6** with an equal ending, Kasparov-Karpov, London/Leningrad 1986.

We return to the line with **8.♗f4.**
 8...♗e7
We have made a transition into Classical Queen Indian (1.d4 ♘f6 2.c4 e6 3.♘f3 b6 4.g3 ♗b7 5.♗g2 ♗e7 6.0-0 0-0 7.♘c3), where it is common to play 7...♘e4 and not ...a7-a5.

On the other hand, White also plays a rare line with ♗f4, so what we actually have on the board is a new original position where two rare moves have been used.
 9.♘c3 ♘e4

A significant move in the battle for control over the critical e4-square and the attempt, after the exchange of the knights, to stabilize his light-squared bishop on it.

Let us examine a more recent continuation – the most promising 10. ♘b5!, as well as the usual continuations which, however, give White only slim chances to accomplish anything: A) 10.♖c1, B) 10.♕c2 and C) 10.♘xe4.

10.♘b5!

With this continuation White justifies the position of his bishop on f4, as opposed to natural and usual continuations, where Black achieves satisfactory play with his standard set-up ...d7-d6, ...♘bd7 etc., emphasizing the shortcomings of White's bishop on f4:

A) **10.♖c1 d6 11.♕d3 ♘xc3 12.♖xc3 ♘c6** On 12...♘d7?! White used a mating motif with 13.♘g5! ♗xg5 14.♗xb7 ♖b8 15.♗xg5 ♕xg5 16.♗c6± to enter a better endgame with a strong bishop and better control of the centre in Farago-Polak, Austria 2012. **13.e4**

13...♗f6 A move which deserves our attention is 13...♘xd4!?N 14.♕xd4 (or 14.♘xd4 e5 15.♗e3 exd4 16.♗xd4 ♖b8= with the idea ...♗e7-f6) 14...e5 15.♘xe5 ♗f6 16.c5 dxe5 17.♕xd8 ♖fxd8 18.♗e3 b5 19.c6 ♗c8=. **14.e5 dxe5 15.dxe5 ♕xd3 16.♖xd3±** Sargissian-Timman, Antwerp 2009;

B) **10.♕c2** Just as in the previous line, White continues to strengthen his position, but the inadequate position of the bishop on f4 minimizes his chances in the battle for the lead. **10...♘xc3 11.♕xc3** There is also no advantage with 11.bxc3 ♕c8 (11...♖a7 12.e4 d6 13.♖fe1 ♘d7= Dautov) 12.e4 d6 13.♖fe1 ♘d7 14.♖ad1 a4 15.h4 ♖e8 16.♗h3 ♗f8 17.d5 e5 18.♗e3 ♕d8 19.♔g2 ♗c8 20.♖h1 ♗e7 21.♕e2 ♘f6= Epishin-Ikonnikov, Nuremberg 2012. **11...d6** and now White can play three logical moves:

B1) **12.♖fd1 ♘d7 13.♖ac1 h6 14.♕d3 f5** with equal chances, Van Wely-Salov, Amsterdam 1996 (another good move is 14...♘f6!?=);

B2) **12.♕c2 f5 13.♘e1 ♗xg2 14.♘xg2 ♘c6 15.♖ad1 ♗f6=** Andreikin-Lenic, Moscow 2011.

B3) **12.♖ad1 ♘d7** 12...f5 13.h4 (13.c5!?) 13...h6 14.♗c1 ♗f6 15.♕d2 ♕e8 16.d5 e5 17.e4 ♗c8 18.exf5 ♗xf5 19.♕e3 ♘a6∓ Abramovic-Gulko, Biel 1993. **13.♖fe1?! ♘f6 14.♕c2 ♗e4** A standard set-up of the black pieces in this type of position, which provides Black with an equal game. **15.♕c1 ♕b8 16.♗f1?!** Better is 16.♘d2 ♗xg2 17.♔xg2=. **16...c5∓** and Black takes the initiative, Ratkovic-Nestorovic, Paracin 2013.

C) The exchange **10.♘xe4** is in Black's favour, providing him with an easy and balanced game. **10...♗xe4**

We will take a look at several options for White, but Black has a response to everything, with an easy and balanced game:

C1) **11.♘e1 ♗xg2 12.♘xg2 d6 13.e4 ♗f6** Or 13...♘d7!?= with the idea ...e6-e5, making use of the unfavourable position of the white dark-squared bishop. **14.♗e3 e5 15.d5 ♗g5 16.♕c2 ♘d7** Ligterink-Short, Marbella 1982;

C2) **11.♖c1 d6 12.♕d2 ♘d7 13.♖fd1 ♕c8 14.♘e1 ♗xg2 15.♘xg2 ♗f6 16.♗g5 ♕b7=** Bukic-Ostojic, Ljubljana 1981;

C3) **11.d5 ♗f6 12.♕d2 ♘a6 13.♖ad1 ♘c5 14.b3 d6=** Sargissian-Lysyj, Mainz 2007.

10...♘a6

The black knight must be moved to the edge of the board. White has three attractive moves: 11.♖c1, 11.♘d2 and 11.d5.

No good is 10...d6? due to the thematic pin with 11.♘d2 f5 (11...♘xd2 12.♗xb7 ♘xf1 13.♗xa8+−) 12.♘xe4 ♗xe4 13.♗xe4 fxe4 14.♕c2± and White wins a clean pawn, Kracht-Borwell, ICCF email 2008.

11.♖c1

A) **11.♘d2** is an excellent alternative. White immediately uses the pin along the central diagonal in order to achieve a small but stable advantage. The most tenacious move for Black is **11...♘xd2** (11...f5 12.♘xe4 ♗xe4 (it is harder after 12...fxe4 13.d5! and Black will lose a pawn on e4: 13...c6 14.♘d6 ♗xd6 15.♗xd6 cxd5 16.♗xf8 ♕xf8 17.cxd5 ♗xd5 18.♕d4 and with his extra material White has a clear advantage, Goganov-Bocharov, Moscow 2012) 13.♗xe4 fxe4 14.♘c3 d5 15.cxd5 exd5 16.♕a4± with the idea ♕c6. Black has great difficulties with his weakened light squares. **12.♗xb7 ♘xf1 13.♕xf1 c6 14.♗xa8 ♕xa8 15.♘c3 ♕b7** Another possibility is 15...exd5!?, although after 16.cxd5 Black faces an unpleasant choice between two inferior endgames: 1. 16...cxd5, when his weak b5-square could cause him problems, or 2. 16...exd5, when he is left with an unpromising pawn structure. Nevertheless, in both cases, Black has chances to achieve a draw because of the reduced material: 16...cxd5 17.♖c1 ♖c8 18.h4 h6 19.a3 ♕b7 20.♘b5↑ with a certain initiative thanks to White's strong knight on b5 and good piece coordination; or 16...exd5!? (instead of taking with the c-pawn, Black opts for an unpopular pawn structure so as to maintain control of the important b5-square) 17.♖c1 ♕b7 18.♕d1↑ and White has an easier game and a permanent initiative thanks to Black's pawn structure.

16.e4 d6 16...d5? 17.exd5 cxd5 18.cxd5 exd5 19.♖e1± and Black is in a critical position due to his disconnected pieces and weakness on the d5-square. **17.d5** It is probably better to first improve the position and not rush with the advance in the centre with 17.♖d1!?±, when it is very difficult to find an acceptable plan for Black. **17...♖d8 18.♖d1±** Narciso Dublan-Gonzalez Gambau, Manresa 2007;

B) To **11.d5** Black must react with **11...d6!?N**. Weaker is 11...c6 12.dxc6 dxc6 13.♘bd4 c5 14.♘b5 ♕c8 (14...f6 15.♘d2± Narayanan-Ashwin, New Delhi 2013) 15.♕c2 and White is better thanks to his more active pieces, So-Megaranto, Guangzhou 2010.

And now in the event of **12.♘d2** (12.♘fd4 exd5 13.cxd5 ♗xd5∓ and there is no visible compensation for the lost pawn) **12...exd5 13.cxd5 ♘xd2 14.♕xd2 ♕d7 15.♘d4 ♘c5 16.♖ac1 ♗f6⇄** Black has a good position because the invasion of the opponent's knight on c6 does not disturb his game.

11...d6 12.a3
White continues with useful prophylactic moves while waiting for the right time for ♘f3-d2.
On 12.♘d2 Black has chances to achieve equality after 12...♘xd2 13.♗xb7 ♘xf1 14.♕xf1 ♘b4 15.♗xa8 ♕xa8 16.a3 ♘a6 17.♕g2 f5.

12...f5

A calm move which deserves attention is 12...c6!?N 13.♘d2 ♘xd2 14.♕xd2 ♕d7 15.♘c3 c5 16.♗xb7 (16.d5 e5 17.♗e3 ♘c7∞) 16...♕xb7 17.d5 e5 18.♗e3 ♕d7 19.♕d3 ♘c7 20.♗d2 f5 21.f3 ♖ab8∞ with the idea ...b6-b5 and chances for equality.
13.♘d2 ♘xd2 14.♗xb7 ♘xf1 15.♕xf1 g5
Black weakens the position of his king, probably because he does not like the position after 15...c6 16.♗xa8 ♕xa8 17.♗xd6±.
16.♗d2 c6
16...♖b8? 17.♗xa6 c6 18.♘c3 ♕c7 19.b4+−; 16...♕d7? 17.♕g2±.
17.♗xc6 ♖b8 18.d5 e5 19.b4⩲

For his slight material minus, White dominates a great part of the board and has more than enough compensation, Iturrizaga Bonelli-Marin, Leon 2012.

Conclusion

In this chapter we considered positions where after 5.g3 Black attempts to achieve equality by following the model of the Queen's Indian with 5...b6. After 6.♗g2 we analysed the main line 5... ♗b7 and 5...♗a6. In case of the pseudo-active 5...♗a6 White relatively easily achieves a better game with 6.♕c2!, since with his pawn on a5 and bishop on a6 Black could not find a satisfactory plan, whether he entered positions with Queen's Indian or Catalan characteristics, or tried to neutralize the white centre with ...c7-c5.

In the main line, where the critical position occurs after 5.g3 b6 6.♗g2 ♗b7 7.0-0 0-0, White has two real chances to fight for the advantage: 8.♗f4 and 8.♗g5. After 8.♗f4 ♗e7 9.♘c3 ♘e4 White has many continuations, but 10.♘b5! has been the only one to provide an advantage for White. In the second case, after 8.♗g5 ♗e7 9.♕c2 h6 10.♗xf6 ♗xf6 11.♘c3, we propose two continuations for Black which lead him into totally different types of positions:

1. 11...g6!? from the World Championship match between Garry Kasparov and Anatoly Karpov, where Black wages a strategically uncertain battle with the bishop pair against the opponent's full centre,

2. the classical 2. 11...d5 with which Black, in the spirit of the Queen's Gambit, confronts the opponent's centre and builds up counterplay on the dark squares.

Exercises

14.2 (1) Find the plan.
(solution on page 449)

14.2 (2) Find the plan.
(solution on page 450)

14.2 (3) Find the plan.
(solution on page 450)

Chapter 14.3

The Bogo-Catalan Gambit: 5.g3 d5 6.♗g2

1.d4 e6 2.c4 ♗b4+ 3.♗d2 a5 4.♘f3 ♘f6 5.g3 d5

This is one of the most important positions in our book. Not only because of the logical reaction to the white bishop's fianchetto, but also because it provides the best opportunities for Black to level the game. Otherwise, theoretically speaking, Black makes a transition into a type of position where ideas of the Bogo-Indian (a black bishop on b4) and the Catalan (characterized by the pawn structure in the centre and a bishop on g2) are combined. Although the continuation essentially leads to complex Catalan positions, which are not the topic of this book, it would be ungrateful to not consider this principled response for the simple reason that we would not be able to show the real value of the Bogo-Indian opening. It would also be useful to remind ourselves of the continuation ...d7-d5 one move earlier, when Black delays the development of his king's knight (Chapter 11).

In this Chapter we will examine 6.♗g2 and the drawish 6.cxd5, whereas we will leave the third natural move 6.♕c2 for the next Chapter, 14.4.

6.♗g2

White continues with his development, leaving the pawn on c4 undefended, but this is a common scene in the Catalan Opening. Black can react in practically the same way as after the move 6.♕c2, which we will investigate in Chapter 14.4; therefore, the continuations regularly intertwine and often lead to the same positions. We will analyse: the open positions with 6...dxc4; closed positions with 6...c6; 6...0-0, which often transposes into one of the first two continuations, the extravagant option 6...♘e4, and 6...♘c6, which usually transposes into the system of Smyslov/Taimanov already covered under 6...dxc4.

6.cxd5 is a continuation which causes White to lose his chances in the battle for advantage, because with it he loses more than he accomplishes. White opens the e-file and the diagonal h3-c8 to the opponent, so as to stop having to worry about the pawn on c4. Besides, we know that this exchange of pawns on d5-square is usually justified, when in this type of position Black plays ...b7-b6. **6...exd5 7.♗g2 0-0 8.0-0 ♖e8 9.♘c3 c6=** Black has nothing to be concerned about in this type of position with a Carlsbad structure in the centre, where the white bishop is normally on d3 instead of on g2. Here it is limited by Black's pawn chain, Weiss-Bauer, Austria 2013.

6...dxc4

A principled and most common response, and probably the most important test for the Bogo-Catalan continuation 5...d5. Black accepts the pawn sacrifice on c4, thus fulfilling the opponent's wish and opening a diagonal for the bishop on g2. However, Black also wins something with this continuation because, first of all, he has an extra pawn, and also the black queen can be more active along the freed d-file.

A) **6...0-0** A logical developing move. Black does not yet declare his intentions with the pawn structure in the centre.

However, with this move order, Black virtually decides on systems with ...c7-c6 or ...c7-c5 since the popular systems we covered under 6...dxc4 and 6...♘c6 do not work well when Black spends time on castling.

A1) With **7.a3** White unnecessarily wastes time, since Black has an excellent back-up square in store for his bishop. **7...♗e7 8.♕c2** and now:

A11) **8...b6 9.cxd5 exd5 10.♗f4 c5 11.♘c3** with a characteristic advantage for a Queen's Indian type position, Lajthajm-Certic, Belgrade 2012;

A12) And why not **8...c6!?**

with a transition into a Catalan-type position where White has played the rather unnecessary move a2-a3?. For example: **9.0-0 ♘bd7 10.♗f4 b6!** No, this important move is not risky because instead of ♖d1, White has his pawn on a3, so ♘e5 is not effective. Black is ready with his development and has a solid position known from the Closed Catalan, with motifs like ...♘h5 or ...♗a6 with pressure on the pawn on c4. **11.♖d1 ♗a6 12.♘bd2 ♘h5 13.♘e5?!** Better is 13.♗e3=. **13...♘xf4 14.gxf4 ♖c8∓** Leiva Rodriguez-Mareco, Lima 2013.

A2) For **7.♕c2** see Chapter 14.4;

A3) With **7.0-0**, White again gives Black an option to, in addition to playing the Closed Catalan with 7...c6, play a solid variation with an extra pawn after 7...dxc4:

A31) **7...dxc4 8.♕c2** Here Black only has one good move, but a solid one, with 8...♗xd2. Also possible are 8...b5 or 8...♘c6 but now these lead to inferior positions:

A311) **8...b5** 8...♘c6 9.♕xc4 ♕d5 10.♕d3 is covered under 6...dxc4; for 10.♖c1 see Chapter 14.4.

9.a4! bxa4 9...c6? is not possible because of 10.axb5 ♗xd2 and now White can use the strength of the Catalan bishop with 11.♘fxd2! ♕xd4 (Black is also doing badly after 11...♘d5 12.♕xc4 cxb5 13.♕xb5± and White has a clean extra pawn, Bacrot-Gharamian, Bastia (rapid) 2012) 12.♘xc4 (another good move is 12.bxc6±, Le Quang Liem-Bukavshin, Moscow (rapid) 2013) 12...♕c5 13.♘ba3 with a clear advantage for White, Oll-Nei, Espoo 1989; also it is now too late for 9...♗xd2 because White can open the diagonal for the Catalan bishop with 10.♘fxd2! ♖a7 11.axb5 ♕xd4 12.♘xc4 with a clear advantage, Hoffman-Dorin, Buenos Aires 2001. **10.♖xa4** Another good move is 10.♘a3 ♗b7 11.♘xc4 ♘bd7 12.♖fd1 ♘b6 13.♘xb6 cxb6 14.♗xb4 axb4 15.♖xa4 ♗e4 16.♕b3 ♖xa4 17.♕xa4

♕d6 18.♘e5± Antic-Rajkovic, Kragujevac 2009. **10...♗b7 11.♗xb4** 11.♕xc4 ♗d5 12.♕d3 ♗e4 13.♕e3 ♘c6 14.♘c3 ♗c2 15.♖a2 ♖b8=. **11...axb4 12.♖xa8 ♗xa8 13.♘bd2!** White will return the pawn, preserving the better pawn structure and a characteristic advantage for this type of position. **13...c5** An understandable idea. Black would like to free himself from the most troublesome pawn in the Open Catalan. **14.dxc5** and now:

A3111) **14...♕a5 15.♕xc4±** Karpov-Piket, Monaco 1999;

A3112) Black has better chances to level the game with **14...♗xf3 15.♗xf3** (15.♘xf3 ♕d5 16.♖c1 c3 17.bxc3 ♕xc5 18.cxb4 ♕xb4=) **15...♕d4 16.♖d1 ♕xc5 17.♕xc4↑**. White preserves the initiative because of the weak pawn on b4 and his more active pieces.

A312) **8...♗xd2!**

This is a necessary exchange in order to play ...b7-b5. **9.♘bxd2 b5** White now has to strike with 9.a4 or 9.b3, otherwise he will have no compensation for the minus pawn:

10.a4 is White's main attack on the queenside. After 10.b3 cxb3 11.♘xb3 ♗b7 12.♖fc1 ♗d5 13.♘bd2 (White is not doing well even after 13.♕xc7 ♕xc7 14.♖xc7 ♘a6 15.♖cc1 a4 16.♘c5 ♘xc5 17.dxc5 b4=) 13...♘a6

14.e4 ♗b7 and White will have a hard time showing compensation for the pawn, Georgiev-Bukavshin, Legnica 2013. With 10.a4 White opens the a-file and emphasizes the weakness of Black's important b-pawn. Now: **10...c6** 10...b4?! 11.♘xc4 ♗b7 12.♖ac1 ♗e4 (12...♘bd7 13.♖fd1± with the idea ♘fe5 and Black will hardly be able to solve his problems on the c-file) 13.♕d1 ♘bd7 14.♘fe5 ♗xg2 15.♔xg2± with strong pressure on the queenside.

After 10...c6 we get a critical position in which both sides have a rather difficult task showing that their ideas are justified: White needs to show that he has enough compensation for being one pawn short and Black that his troubles are temporary and that in the end the extra pawn will help him to at least achieve a draw.

In general, Black has an undeveloped queenside and more weaknesses, but also an extra pawn. White can maximally activate and harmonize his pieces, but it will not be easy to turn this into something substantial, if such a thing is even possible.

We shall analyse 11.♖fd1, 11.♘e5, 11.e4 and 11.b3.

A3121) **11.♖fd1** White makes a useful move by placing the king's rook on

the best square and waiting for the development of events. Of course, he still has in mind the ideal arrangement with b2-b3, e2-e4 and ♖ac1, which creates the most difficulties for the opponent.

A31211) **11...♕b6** and now:

A312111) **12.e4 h6** Directed against White's strategic threat of e4-e5 and ♘g5. **13.e5** 13.b3 cxb3 14.♘xb3 ♘bd7 15.e5 ♘d5 16.♘fd2 ♗a6 17.♘e4∞. **13...♘d5 14.♘e4 ♘a6∞**;

A312112) **12.b3 cxb3 13.♘xb3 ♘bd7 14.♘e5** 14.e4 h6 is covered under 12.e4; 14.♖dc1 ♗b7 15.♘c5 b4!∞. **14...♘xe5 15.dxe5 ♘d5 16.e4 ♘b4 17.♕c3 bxa4 18.♖xa4 ♗a6 19.♖xa5=**;

A312113) **12.♘e4** 12.♘e5 ♘d5!=. **♘bd7 13.♘e5 ♘xe4 14.♗xe4 ♘xe5 15.dxe5 h6 16.axb5 ♕xb5 17.♕c3 a4=**.

A31212) **11...♘d5 12.e4** 12.♘e4 f6∞. **12...♘b4 13.♕c3 ♗a6 14.b3 ♘d7 15.bxc4 bxc4 16.♘xc4±**

Both sides have a typical structure in the centre which occurs in some other openings as well, such as the Queen's Indian. White has better control of the centre and a slightly better pawn structure. Black has an opportunity to eliminate his weaknesses with ...c6-c5, but after d4-d5 White will have a strong passed pawn.

A31213) **11...♘a6**

The black knight moves to the desirable b4-square. There are very few practical games, but analyses show that this position is playable for both sides.

12.b3 A thematic move, and the most frequent. White wishes to accentuate the weakness of the opponent's queen's pawns as much as possible. **12...♘b4 13.♕b2** After 13.♕c1 cxb3 14.♘xb3 bxa4 15.♘c5 White gets compensation, but only to level the game, Dydyshko-Alexandrov, Minsk 1996. **13...cxb3** 13...♗a6 14.♘e5 ♖c8 (after 14...♘fd5 15.bxc4 bxc4 16.♘exc4 White has better chances due to his highly mobile centre. Besides, it will be difficult for Black to eliminate the weakness on c6) 15.bxc4 bxc4 16.♘dxc4⩲. **14.♘xb3** White undoubtedly has enough compensation for the pawn, in the sense that he has a strong and mobile centre, great piece activity, and the option to exert pressure on Black's many weaknesses, such as the c6- and a5-pawns and the e5- and c5-squares. However, Black has an extra pawn and the option to return it at the right time and so neutralize his strategic weaknesses, the most important one being his passive light-squared bishop. For example: **14...♘bd5!** Black wants to strengthen his position on the queenside with ...b5-b4 and ...♘c3. If 14...♗a6 15.♘e5⩲.

15.♘e5 b4 This is a good decision. Black continues pursuing his idea, not considering the defence of his weak pawn on c6. With 15...♕b6 Black can keep the pawn, but after 16.♖dc1⩲ White puts a lot of pressure on Black's queenside and has more than enough compensation for the pawn. **16.♘xc6** White wins back the pawn but frees two diagonals for the opponent's light-squared bishop. **16...♕b6 17.♖dc1 ♗d7!N**

From this diagonal the black bishop will put the a4-pawn under pressure, and so White's stronger defensive piece will be restrained. 17...♗b7 makes perfect sense; however, in a game between two strong machines, Houdini 3 Pro-Deep Rybka 4.1, Internet (blitz) 2013, after 18.♘e5 ♘c3 19.♘c5 ♗xg2 20.♖xc3 ♕a7 21.♖cc1 ♗b7, White limited the black bishop's activity with 22.f3 ♘d5 23.e4 ♘e7 and after

24.♘c4± had better chances due to his more active knights. **18.♘e5 ♖fc8 19.♘c5 ♕d8** and Black has equal chances in the endgame. In fact, if White does not exchange the pieces on d7 and d5, which leads to a draw, Black will play ...♗d7 and all his pieces will be functioning.

A3122) With the aggressive **11.♘e5** White accomplishes nothing because of **11...♘d5**

And now White should probably look for a draw with **12.axb5 cxb5 13.b3 c3 14.♗xd5 ♕xd5 15.♕xc3 f6 16.e4** (16.♘d3 ♘c6 17.e3 ♗b7↑) **16...♕d6 17.♘ef3 ♘c6 18.♖fc1 ♘b4 19.♕e3 ♗b7 20.e5=** as 12.e4?! ♘b4 13.♕c3 ♘d7∓ leaves Black with an extra pawn and better chances (Bunzmann-Pelletier, Lausanne 1999);

A3123) **11.e4** White wants to show that he has compensation for the pawn with his control of the dark squares and potential attack against the black king. However, this, somewhat hasty, advance of the e-pawn provides Black with counterplay because it creates certain weak points: **11...♘a6 12.e5 ♘b4 13.♕b1 ♘fd5 14.♘e4 ♗a6** Or 14...h6∓, Agaragimov-Brkic, Plovdiv 2012. **15.♖d1 ♘d3∓** And Black takes advantage of the unprepared advance of the

opponent's e-pawn, Grigoryan-Laznicka, Yerevan 2007;

A3124) **11.b3** We have already mentioned, in addition to the attack with a2-a4, the significance of this offensive move with which White tries to expose the opponent's pawn weaknesses on the queenside as soon as possible. **11...cxb3 12.♘xb3**

A31241) **12...b4** leads to an unclear, static position with a passive light-squared bishop, where White has compensation for the pawn: **13.e4!** If 13.♘e5 ♘d5 14.e3 (14.♘xc6 ♘xc6 15.♕xc6 ♖a6 16.♕c4 ♘c3∓ Jianu-Favarel, Condom 2013) 14...♘c3∞ White will have a hard time finding compensation for the minus pawn since 15.♘xc6? ♘xc6 16.♗xc6 ♖a7∓ does not work and White is in serious trouble as he is facing threats along the c-file and the f1-a6 diagonal.

13...♘bd7

A312411) After **14.♖fd1** Black can choose:

A3124111) **14...♗b7 15.♖ac1 ♕e7 16.♘fd2** 16.h4 c5 17.e5 ♗xf3 18.♗xf3 ♘d5=. **16...♘b6 17.♘c5 ♖fd8 18.e5 ♘fd5 19.♘de4 ♗a6∞**, White has compensation for the pawn but the chances are even, Reich-Jäderholm, corr. 2007;

A3124112) **14...♕b6 15.e5 ♘d5 16.♘g5 g6 17.♖dc1** Weaker is 17.♕e4?! h6! 18.♘xe6 ♘7f6! 19.exf6 ♗xe6∓; Black skilfully defends himself and obtains a better game. **17...♘c3 18.♘e4 ♘xe4 19.♕xe4 ♗b7 20.h4⨀**

A312412) Weaker is to return the material with **14.♕xc6 ♖a6 15.♕c2 ♗b7** This activates the light-squared bishop, which gives Black a good game, for instance: **16.♘e5** Weaker is 16.♘fd2 ♕a8 17.♖fc1 ♖c8∓ Song-Favarel, Pau 2012. **16...♘xe5** Or 16...♕a8 17.♘xd7 ♘xd7 with an excellent position for Black, Inarkiev-Zhou Weiqi, Jiangsu Wuxi 2008. **17.dxe5 ♘g4 18.♕e2** 18.♕c5 ♕b8 19.♘xa5 ♗a8 20.♖ab1 ♕xe5 21.♘b3=. **18...♘xe5 19.♕b5** Black is walking on thin ice, and now is the time to seriously consider the variations! **19...f6!∓** 19...♘c6? 20.♖fd1 ♕c7 21.e5± with the idea ♖c1; 19...♕c7 20.♖fc1 ♕b8 21.♘xa5±. **20.♕xb7?? ♖b6 21.♕a7 ♘c6−+**

A31242) **12...♗a6!** This is a flexible continuation which does not require Black to decide about his b-pawn; therefore, at least for a while, he prevents the opponent from realizing his most dangerous plan with e2-e4. Analyses of the following games demonstrate that it is difficult for White to get good play with one pawn less:

A312421) **13.♘c5 b4** and now:

A3124211) **14.♖fd1 ♘d5 15.♘e5 ♕e7 16.♖d2 f6 17.♘c4 ♗xc4 18.♕xc4 ♘d7 19.e4 ♘xc5 20.exd5 ♘e4 21.♗xe4 cxd5 22.♗xd5 exd5 23.♕xd5+ ♕f7** with a better endgame for Black thanks to his superior pawn structure, Heinsohn-Talos, corr. 2012;

A3124212) **14.♖fe1 ♘d5 15.e4** A more cautious move is 15.♘e5 although Black has 15...♘c3 16.e3 ♕d6∞ with the idea ...f7-f6. Here it will also be difficult for White to find compensation for the pawn. **15...♘c3 16.e5 ♘d7∓** Black has an extra pawn and a clear advantage, Saric-Pavasovic, Rijeka 2005;

A312422) **13.♖fc1 bxa4 14.♘c5 ♗b5 15.♘xa4 ♘bd7** with little compensation for White, Mihajlovic-Blagojevic, Cetinje 2009;

A312423) **13.♘e5 bxa4 14.♖xa4 ♗b5 15.♖a2 a4 16.♕d2 ♘fd7∓**;

A312424) **13.axb5 ♗xb5 14.♘c5 ♘bd7∓** with little compensation;

A312425) **13.♖fd1 bxa4 14.♘c5 ♗b5 15.♘e5 ♕d6** After 15...♘d5 16.♗e4 g6 17.♕d2 ♕e7 18.♗c2 ♘a6 19.♗xa4 ♘xc5 20.dxc5 ♕c7 21.f4 ♖fd8∓ Black has a clean extra pawn. **16.♘c4** 16.♘xa4 ♘bd7=. **16...♕c7 17.♘a3** Better is 17.♘xa4 ♘a6 18.♘e5. White is a pawn short, but he is on the right track to balance the position. **17...♘d5** A better move is 17...♘a6!N

18.♘xa4 ♖ab8 and it is not easy for White to play with one pawn less since the black pieces are active as well. **18.♖dc1 ♕e7 19.♘xa4 ♘a6** 19...♖a7!=. **20.♘c3** 20.♘xb5! cxb5 21.♗xd5 ♘b4 22.♕c5 ♕xc5 23.♖xc5 ♘xd5 24.♖xb5±. **20...♘ab4 21.♕d2 ♗a6∓** Black's pawns are scattered but he has an extra one, Romanishin-Landa, Reggio Emilia 2007.

A32) 7...c6 Also possible is first 7...♘bd7 and then 8.♕c2 c6. This is a favourite structure with many players, directed against the activity of the famous Catalan bishop. **8.♕c2 ♘bd7 9.♗f4** Or 9.c5. **9...♗e7**

Since the dark-squared bishops have left their Bogo-Indian positions, we now have the original position of the Closed Catalan with the rarely played move

...a7-a5 (the main line is with 9...b6 and the development of the bishop on b7 or a6). This position can arise in different move orders, the most common one being 1.d4 ♘f6 2.c4 e6 3.♘f3 d5 4.g3 ♗b4 5.♗d2 ♗e7 6.♗g2 0-0 7.0-0 c6 8.♕c2 ♘bd7 9.♗f4 a5, which was also employed by Veselin Topalov in his world championship match against Vladimir Kramnik. We shall pay a little more attention to this critical position, because Black has a solid position and he only needs to develop his light-squared bishop to completely level the game. Of course, one of the important questions is: can the pawn on a5 fit into any useful plan for Black?

A321) 10.♘bd2 White plans the thematic e2-e4. **10...♘h5!**

This is one of the most important standard ideas in this opening type, particularly effective when the retreat squares c1 and d2 are occupied. **11.♗e3 b6 12.♖ac1 ♗a6=**;

A322) A risky move is **10.♘c3 dxc4 11.e4** Weaker is 11.♖ad1 ♘d5∓ Gorse-Hera, Triesen 2009. **11...b5 12.♖ad1 ♗b7** and it is difficult for White to prove that his full centre is enough to make up for the lost pawn, Donchenko-Gajewski, Deizisau 2013;

A323) 10.b3 With the idea ♘c3. This, however, gives Black time to set up an anti-Catalan position with 10...b6 11.♖d1 (11.♘c3 ♗a6=). **11...♗a6** Black has realized his set-up, where the pawn on a5 seems useful:

A3231) Now the typical sortie **12.♘e5** is not dangerous because White has spent time on b2-b3. Moreover, White must be extra careful not to land into an inferior position. **12...♘xe5** Another good move is 12...♖c8 13.♘c3 ♘xe5 14.dxe5 ♘d7 15.♕b2 ♗g5!?= Shengelia-Sargissian, Porto Carras 2011. **13.♗xe5** 13.dxe5?! ♘d7∓ with the idea ...g7-g5. **13...♖c8=** Verat-Chuchelov, Cappelle la Grande 1999;

A3232) **12.♘bd2 ♘h5 13.♗e3** Weaker is 13.e4 ♘xf4 14.gxf4 ♖c8 and Black has better chances with his bishop pair and better pawn structure, Jirka-Polak, Strmilov 2005. **13...♗d6** 13...♘hf6 14.♗f4 ♘h5=. **14.♘g5** 14.♗g5 f6 15.♗e3 f5 with an excellent position for Black. **14...♘hf6** Black's pieces are more naturally placed; he has an excellent position, Kiss-Chernin, Hungary 1999;

A3233) **12.♘c3 dxc4!?** 12...♖c8 13.e4 dxc4 14.♕e2 ♗b4 15.♖ac1 ♗a3 16.♖b1 ♗b4 17.♖bc1 ♗a3 18.♖b1 ♗b4 19.♖bc1 with a draw by move repetition, Buscara-Lazarev, Pau 2012.

The pawn on a5 plays a useful role in this line. **13.e4** 13.bxc4 ♗xc4 14.♘d2

♗a6 15.♗xc6 ♖c8∓. **13...cxb3 14.axb3 ♖c8∞** White faces the difficult task of proving that his strong centre is sufficient compensation for the pawn, since the black a-pawn is in the right place.

A324) **10.♖d1!**

An important developing move and White's best chance for an advantage. The strength of this continuation primarily lies in White's ability to respond to the usual ...b7-b6 with the thematic ♘e5!. Black, however, also has other interesting ideas, which may render this variation of the Closed Catalan with a pawn on a5 useful for practical play. This especially refers to plans where the aforementioned pawn is useful for play on the queenside.

We shall begin with the most logical continuations, where Black plans to transpose into a Dutch Stonewall with 10...♘h5 or 10...♘e4, then to the rarely played 10...b5 and the patient continuation 10...h6 (Black awaits the development of the white queen's knight) and 10...a4. Finally, we shall analyse the standard 10....b6, which in this variation with a pawn on a5 leads Black into a difficult position.

A3241) **10...♘h5** The best and generally accepted method of fighting the opponent's strong bishop on f4. **11.♗c1** We will analyse three continuations for Black leading to three different types of position: the logical but unambitious 11...♘hf6, which is at the same time a manner of offering a draw if the opponent returns the bishop to f4, the risky 11...b5 and the energetic 11...f5.

A32411) 11...♘hf6 12.♘bd2!? b6
After 12...b5 13.c5 ♕e8 14.e4 White has better chances because of the weak black light-squared bishop, Marin-Pogorelov, Barcelona 1993. **13.e4±**

This is a well-known theoretical position, but a weaker version of it for Black, since he has a pawn on a5 instead of a developed bishop on b7 or a6, Govciyan-Lazarev, Guingamp 2010;

A32412) **11...b5** Black wants to close the queenside before moving on to the Stonewall, where he usually leads the action in the centre and on the kingside. However, White has an instructive possibility to open the centre and create an advantage thanks to the disconnected black pieces:

A324121) **12.c5** Black usually benefits more from closing the queenside, if White does not have better control of the e4-square. **12...f5** Strengthening his control of e4. Black now only has to activate his passive light-squared bishop in order to level the game. However, in this type of Stonewall, Black also has at

his disposal an active plan on the king's wing with ...♗f6, ...g7-g5-g4 etc.
We will look at three continuations for White:

A3241211) **13.♘e5 ♘xe5 14.dxe5 ♗d7** 14...g5 15.♘d2 ♕e8 16.♘f3 ♕g6 17.♘d4 ♗d7∞ Ponfilenok-Shaposhnikov, Kazan 2010. **15.♗e3 g5 16.♗d4 ♘g7 17.♘d2 g4 18.a4 b4 19.f3 h5 20.h3 ♕e8 21.♗f2 ♗d8 22.hxg4 hxg4 23.f4 ♘h5 24.♕b3 ♗c8 25.♗d4 ♖a7 26.♔f2 ♖h7 27.♖h1 ♗a6=** Black has arranged his forces appropriately and has nothing to fear in this blocked position, Wojtaszek- Macieja, Chotowa 2009;

A3241212) **13.♘c3**

13...g5 13...b4!? If the activation of the black light-squared bishop is with tempo, then why not? 14.♘a4 ♗a6∞. While White is organizing the manoeuvre of his queen's knight to the ideal d3-square, or organizing his play in relation to the black pawn on b4, Black is moving his king's knight to e4, ensuring functionality for all his pieces, with equal chances. For example: 15.a3 ♖e8 (prior to moving the knight to e4, Black must insure himself against White's threat of ♘g5) 16.b3 ♕c7 17.♘b2 ♘hf6 18.♘d3 ♕b7 19.♗f4 ♘e4∞. **14.a3 ♗f6 15.♕d2 h6** 15...g4!? 16.♘e1 ♗g7 17.e3 ♘hf6∞. **16.h4 g4**

17.♕xh6 gxf3 18.♕xh5 fxg2 19.♕g6+ ♔h8 20.♕h6+ ♔g8 21.♕g6+ and the game Rahman-Ghaem Maghami, Doha 2003, ended in perpetual check;

A3241213) **13.b3 ♗f6** With a knight on h5, the opening of the diagonal for his light-squared bishop with 13...b4?! does not work because after **14.a3!** Black faces an unpleasant choice of which weakness to keep, the one on b4 or a5. **14...♗a6** 14...bxa3 15.♖xa3 ♗a6 16.♕a2±. **15.axb4 axb4 16.♖a4±**

Since activating the light-squared bishop on the diagonal f1-a6 is risky, Black concentrates on strengthening his position in the centre and on the kingside, planning ...e6-e5 and activation of his light-squared bishop on the diagonal h3-c8. **14.♗b2 ♕c7** Taking control over some critical squares in the centre, which is another basic idea of the Dutch Stonewall. 14...b4?! is still weak because after 15.a3 ♗a6 16.axb4 axb4 17.♖a4± the pawn on b4 is lost. **15.♘bd2 g5** Black is expanding on the kingside as well, and planning to drive the opponent's knight away from taking control of the e5-square. **16.a3** Of course, White does not wish to wonder whether or not ...b5-b4 is possible, so he is preparing to block with b3-b4. **16...g4 17.♘e1 ♗g7** A smart move.

Black frees the f6-square for his knight and the f-file for his rook on f8. **18.♘d3 e5 19.dxe5 ♘xe5 20.♘xe5 ♗xe5 21.e3 ♕g7 22.♖ab1 b4** with an equal position, Kizov-Kasimdzhanov, Plovdiv 2010;

A324122) **12.cxd5** Sometimes this exchange is the best solution. **12...cxd5 13.e4!**

This poses a problem for Black. White takes advantage of the knight's absence from f6 to open up the centre. Now everything seems to be forced: **13...dxe4 14.♕xe4 ♖b8 15.♕e2** Another good move is 15.♘e5 ♘hf6 16.♕c2 ♘xe5 17.dxe5 ♘d7 18.♘c3 ♗b7 19.♘e4 ♗d5 20.♕e2± Markus-Dorfanis, Skopje 2012. **15...♘hf6 16.♗f4 ♖b6 17.♘e5 ♘d5 18.♗xd5 exd5 19.♘c3 ♘xe5** Probably weaker is 19...♘f6 20.♘xb5 ♗a6 21.a4 ♘e4 22.♖dc1 ♕e8 23.♖c7

... with an edge for White, Kramnik-Topalov, Elista 2006. **20.dxe5 d4 21.♗e3 dxe3 22.♖xd8** This is White's only chance if he wants to continue the battle since 22.♕xe3 after 22...♗g5 23.♕c5 ♗e7 24.♕e3 ♗g5 25.♕c5 ♗e7 leads to move repetition, as was the case in two elite games: Radjabov-Topalov, Wijk aan Zee 2007 and Cheparinov-Ponomariov, Porto Carras 2011. **22...exf2+ 23.♔xf2** 23.♕xf2 ♗xd8 24.♘d5 ♖c6 25.♕d4 ♖e8 26.h4 ♖c4 27.♕a7± Borroni-Dullemond, corr. 2009. **23...♖xd8 24.♖d1 ♗c5+** Weaker is 24...♖e8 25.♘d5 ♗c5+ 26.♔g2 ♗b7 27.g4 ♖d8 28.♕f3 ♗f8 29.♔g3± Aberbach-Salzmann, Lechenicher SchachServer 2009. **25.♔g2 ♗b7+ 26.♔f1 ♖e8 27.♘xb5±** Even the strongest machines have difficulties assessing this insane position.

A32413) **11...f5!?**

We choose the Dutch Stonewall because then we have the best chance that the pawn on a5 will be of value. **12.b3** 12.♘c3 ♗d6 13.♘g5 ♘df6 14.c5 ♗c7 15.f4 ♘e4= Wang Hao-Anand, Stavanger (blitz) 2013. **12...♕e8 13.♗a3** The exchange of the dark-squared bishops is an important strategic goal in this type of position, although this often gives the opponent the time to organize counterplay in the

centre with ...e6-e5, while the white knight on a3 is being brought back into the game. 13.♘c3 ♗d6 14.♘a4 with the idea ♘b2-d3 and control of the critical point e5: 14...♘hf6 15.♘b2 ♘e4 16.♘d3 b6 17.♘fe5 ♗b7 18.♗f4 ♗a3 with chances for both sides. **13...♗xa3 14.♘xa3 ♘hf6 15.♕b2** This is another commonly seen move in this type of position, for it controls the critical e5-square and frees the c2-square for the travel of his passive knight to the ideal square d3. **15...♘e4 16.♘c2 b5!?N** This is better than 16...b6 17.♘ce1 ♕e7 18.♖ac1 ♗b7 19.♘d3± when White has arranged his pieces ideally for this type of position by controlling the critical points e5 and f4. The odds are in his favour, Admiraal-Peralta, Wijk aan Zee 2013.

The attack against the pawn on c4 must be under constant control by both sides as it can change the assessment of the position in a heartbeat. In this particular position, due to the white knight's position on c2, the advance c4-c5 or the exchange would be in favour of Black. **17.c5** 17.cxb5 cxb5= and White is the one who needs to be careful. **17...f4!** Naturally, Black does not miss the opportunity to open up the f-file for his rook and thereby indirectly facilitate the liberating attack on the centre with ...e6-e5 thanks to the weakness of the white pawn on f2. **18.♘ce1 fxg3 19.hxg3 e5=**

A3242) **10...♘e4**

A black knight is definitely more effective on e4 than on the edge of the board like in the previous line, but we should not forget that the white dark-squared bishop has remained on an excellent square, f4. We shall observe three natural reactions for White:

A32421) **11.♘bd2** A more passive development of the queen's knight but it is closer to a critical e5-square in relation to its position on c3 **11...f5 12.♘e5 ♘xe5 13.♗xe5 ♘d6!?** In case of 13...♗d7 14.♘f3 (14.f3 ♘d6 15.e4 a4∞ with play on both sides) 14...♗e8 15.♘e1, by maintaining control of the critical e5-square, White preserves slightly better chances.

The black knight moves to f7 to strengthen the control of the critical e5-square. **14.♖ac1 ♘f7 15.♗f4 ♗f6 16.♘f3 g5 17.♗e3 ♕e7∞** In the spirit of the Dutch Stonewall, Black keeps under control the important squares e4 and e5 and has actual chances to fully even the game since he can easily solve the problem of the development of his light-squared bishop on d7 or, after ...b7-b6, on a6 or b7;

A32422) **11.♘fd2 f5 12.♘xe4 fxe4 13.♘c3** Weaker is 13.f3 exf3 14.♗xf3 ♗g5 15.♗xg5 ♕xg5= Sundararajan-Peralta, Barbera del Valles 2009. **13...♘f6 14.♕b3** 14.f3 exf3 15.exf3 dxc4 with a complex position and chances for both sides. **14...♔g4!N** 14...♔h8 15.f3?! (better is 15.c5!?∞) 15...exf3 16.♗xf3 dxc4 (better is 16...a4! 17.♕c2 dxc4∓. 17.♕xc4 ♘d5= Raznikov-Peralta, Arinsal 2009.

15.♖f1 a4 16.♕c2 16.♘xa4?! dxc4 17.♕c2 ♕xd4∓. **16...♖xf4 17.gxf4 e3♔♔**;

A32423) **11.♘c3 f5** Black has established control over the e4-square, and now the assessment of the position primarily depends on the battle for the other critical point, e5. After 11...g5 in the game Bareev-Renet, France 1995, White accomplished more with 12.♗e3 f5 13.♘xe4 fxe4 14.♘d2 ♗f6

15.f3 exf3 16.exf3 ♖f7 17.♖e1 ♘f8 18.♖ad1 ♗d7 19.♘b3 b6 20.♘c1 ♘g6 21.♘d3± . **12.♘e5** White achieves nothing by 12.♘xe4 fxe4 13.♘e5 ♘xe5 14.♗xe5 ♗f6=. **12...♘xe5 13.♗xe5 ♘d6 14.c5** 14.♗xd6 ♗xd6 15.e3 ♖b8 16.c5 ♗c7 17.f4 ♗d7 with play for both sides, Bacrot-Kamsky, Elista 2007.

14...♘c4! 14...♘f7 15.♗f4 ♗f6 16.♘a4± . **15.♗f4 b6 16.cxb6** With 16.b3 ♘a3 17.♕b2 bxc5 18.dxc5 ♗xc5 19.♖ac1 White has compensation for the pawn but only in the sense of equal chances. **16...♘xb6∞** Black is very near full equality since he will be able to rid himself of his weaknesses with ...c6-c5. Here we see the significance of the black knight's position on b6 instead of on f7, for it prevents the paralysis of the black queenside with ♘a4.

A3243) **10...b5!?**

This is a logical continuation if we want to incorporate the move ...a7-a5 into some useful plan. Apart from that, in this order – first 10...♘h5 and then ...b7-b5 – Black excludes White's dangerous push 13.e4!, which we explained under 10...♘h5. The downside is that after the best reaction 11.c5 ♘h5, White has the additional move 12.e3!.

By the way, apart from ...b7-b6, which leads to calm development and usually more tension in the centre, the continuation ...b7-b5 is the most important strategic idea in Closed Catalan positions. Black immediately wants his opponent to declare his intentions on the queenside – either he will by exchange open the c-file, with play on the queenside, or he will close the queenside with c4-c5 and move the game to the centre and the kingside.

Of course, there is also a third strategic solution for White: to maintain the tension with b2-b3, but after the exchange of the b-pawns on c4 and ....♗a6, this makes the black light-squared bishop more valuable.

A32431) After **11.cxb5 cxb5** we have:

A324311) **12.♘e5 ♗b7 13.♘c6** and now:

A3243111) 13...♕e8 14.♘xe7+ ♕xe7 15.♕c7! 15.♘d2 ♖fc8=. Black has established control over the c-file and has levelled the chances in spite of the opponent's bishop pair, Hoffmann-Khairullin, Vlissingen 2009. **15...♖fb8 16.♗d6** 16.♗g5= Bitan-Kunte, Kolkata 2012. **16...♕e8 17.♘d2** 17.♘c3?! ♗a6 18.♕xa5 b4 19.♗xb8 ♕xb8∓. **17...♖a7 18.♕c2 ♖c8 19.♕d3 b4 20.♖dc1 ♖aa8 21.♕b5 ♗a6 22.♕xa5±** although Black is close to equality;

A3243112) 13...♗xc6!N 14.♕xc6 ♕b6 15.♕xb6 ♘xb6 16.♘c3 b4 17.♘b5 ♘a4! A simple move with an understandable idea. Black ties the opponent's rook to the defence of the pawn on b2, in order to establish control over the c-file. **18.♖ab1** Weaker is 18.b3?! ♘c3 19.♘xc3 bxc3 20.♖ac1 ♖fc8↑ and Black takes over the game thanks to his strong passed pawn. **18...♖fc8 19.♘c7 g5! 20.♗e5** (20.♘xa8?! gxf4∓) **20...♖a7 21.♖dc1 ♘g4 22.♘b5 ♖xc1+ 23.♖xc1 ♖a8=;**

A324312) 12.♗c7 ♕e8 Now let us examine the following continuations:

A3243121) 13.a4 b4 14.♖c1 ♗a6 15.♕d1 ♗d8 16.♗f4 ♕e7 17.♖c6 ♘e4 18.♘bd2 ♗b7 19.♖c2 ♗b6 20.♘b3 ♖fc8= Dziuba-Macieja, Wroclaw 2011;

A3243122) 13.♕c6 ♗a6 13...♖a7=. **14.♘a3?** A better move is 14.♘bd2 b4∞. **14...b4∓** Ott-Fridman, Bad Wiessee 2012;

A3243123) 13.♖c1 ♗a6 14.♘bd2 ♗d8 14...b4 15.♗f1 a4 16.♘e5 ♗b5∞ Nguyen Duc Hoa-Adhiban, Ho Chi Minh City 2012; 14...a4!?. **15.♘b3 a4 16.♘c5 ♗xc7 17.♘xd7 ♕xd7 18.♕xc7 b4 19.e3 ♕xc7 20.♖xc7 ♖fc8 21.♖ac1 ♖xc7 22.♖xc7 ♗c4 23.a3 bxa3 24.bxa3 ♖b8**

= Markowski-Macieja, Wroclaw 2010.

A32432) 11.b3

This defensive move usually leads to levelled positions because Black's light-squared bishop gains significance along the diagonal f1-a6. For example, in the game Gonzalez de la Torre-Ladron de Guevara, Zornotza 2012, instead of the more passive 11...♗b7, Black could have showed the strength of his light-squared bishop with:

A324321) 11...♗a6!N 12.c5 12.♘bd2 bxc4 13.bxc4 ♖c8= – we will cover this under 11...bxc4. **12...b4** The fact that Black did not exchange the b-pawns is obviously strategically justified because White would probably be using the b-file, whereas now Black is using the b-pawn to take control of the important c3-square. **13.♖e1 ♘e4 14.♘bd2** 14.♘e5 ♘xe5 15.♗xe5 f6 16.♗f4 e5↑. **14...♘c3 15.♘b1 ♘e4=;**

A324322) Another possibility is to

play first **11...bxc4 12.bxc4 ♗a6 13.c5**
A good reaction. White occupies space
on the queenside which, supported by
the strong bishop on f4 and future activity along the b-file, may cause trouble for Black. 13.♘bd2 makes sense because it develops a piece and defends
c4. However, this way the black bishop
is given greater value for it exerts pressure on c4: 13...♖c8= with the idea
...c6-c5. Black has clearly emerged from
the opening without any problems and
can also make active plans. **13...♘e4
14.♘e5 ♘xe5 15.♗xe5 f6 16.♗f4 f5
17.♘c3** White's chances are slightly
better thanks to his more promising
pawn structure in the centre.

A32433) 11.c5! ♘h5 In case of
11...b4 with the idea to activate the
bishop on the diagonal f1-a6, White
has the simple move 12.♘bd2, when
he has time to conduct the thematic
e2-e4 with better chances, because now
12...♘h5 does not work due to
13.♗d6±; in case of 11...♘e4 White
has 12.a3!± and Black has trouble activating his passive light-squared bishop.
As we can see from the last two obser-
vations, Black fights to achieve two strategic goals:1. to activate his light-
squared bishop with ...b5-b4 and
...♗a6 and 2. to take control of the
critical e4-square.

A324331) 12.e3!?

White offers the opponent an exchange after which he has the bishop
pair but in a rather closed position.
12...f5 12...♘xf4 13.exf4 b4 14.a3
♗a6 15.axb4 axb4 16.♘bd2 ♕c7
17.♗f1± and the advanced black
pawn is in great danger on the opponent's territory. **13.♘bd2 ♘hf6
14.♘g5 ♘b8 15.♘h3 ♗d7 16.f3 ♗e8
17.♘f2±** Bauer-Fernandes, San
Sebastian 2009;

**A324332) 12.♗d6 ♗xd6 13.cxd6
♗b7!** 13...♘b8 14.♘bd2± Meier-
Postny, Copenhagen 2010.

14.♘bd2 14.♘e5 ♘hf6 15.♘d2
♕b8∞ and White will be a pawn short.
**14...♕b8 15.e4 ♕xd6 16.e5 ♕e7
17.a4 b4 18.♖ac1 g6∞** and White faces
a long and difficult struggle with a minus pawn, Komodo 4-Critter 1.2 6CPU,
Internet 2011;

A324333) 12.♘e5?! ♘xe5 13.dxe5?
Better is 13.♗xe5 f6 14.♗d6 ♗xd6
15.cxd6 ♕xd6 16.♘d2 ♗d7
17.♘b3≅, but only for a draw.
13...♕c7 14.♕c3 f6 with a winning
advantage for Black, Kizov-Hera, Skopje
2011;

A324334) 12.♗c1 f5 is covered under 10...♘h5 11.♗c1 b5 12.c5.

A3244) 10...h6!? is a strange and
rarely played move that hides an interesting idea.

Many would wonder whether it is even possible to play this opening, where Black spends time on moving pawns on the h- and a-file, leaving his light-squared bishop undeveloped on c8.

The meaning of the text move is not easy to perceive, for it has a primarily waiting character. Only after the white queen's knight is developed, Black decides on his own plan. We have seen in the previous lines that, in case the white knight is developed on d2, the white dark-squared bishop loses two important retreat squares after the thematic ...♘h5, and in case of the knight's development on c3, Black can simply take the pawn on c4.

A32441) **11.♘bd2 ♘h5 12.♗e3 ♘hf6** With the idea ...♘g4. **13.♗f4 ♘h5=**;

A32442) **11.♘c3 dxc4 12.♘e5 ♘xe5 13.dxe5 ♘d5 14.♖ac1 ♗d7 15.♘e4 b5 16.a3 ♕c7** It will be difficult for White to prove compensation for the pawn, Bianchi-Arizmendi Martinez, Lille 2013;

A32443) **11.b3 b6 12.♘c3 ♗a6⇄** Lubczynski-Lafuente, Barcelona 2008;

A32444) **11.♘e1 b6 12.♘d2 ♘h5 13.♗e5 ♗a6 14.♘d3 ♖c8 15.♖ac1 ♘hf6=** Kozul-Topalov, Heraklio 2007;

A32445) **11.♘e5** This well-known aggressive invasion of the white knight is more dangerous when Black has played ...b7-b6. This way it seems to

come down to the exchange of the knight and a simplification of the position without any visible benefits for White. **11...♘h5!** A weaker move is 11...♘xe5 12.dxe5 ♘d7 13.cxd5 cxd5 14.e4± and Black has serious problems, Phoobalan-Laxman, New Delhi 2013. **12.♗c1** 12.♗d2 ♘hf6 13.♘d3 b6= with the idea ...♗c8-a6; 12.♗e3 ♘hf6 13.♘d3 b6 14.♘d2 ♗a6⇄. **12...♘hf6** Having deactivated the white dark-squared bishop and weakened the white knight's stronghold on e5, Black returns the knight to its natural square, while planning the exchange on e5:

A324451) **13.♘xd7 ♗xd7 14.♘d2 c5!** A correct reaction. Black immediately activates his bishop pair. **15.cxd5 exd5 16.dxc5 ♖c8 17.♕d3 ♖e8 18.♘f1 ♗xc5 19.♗e3 ♕b6=** Black compensates for the weak pawn on d5 with the greater activity of his pieces, Sakaev-Dizdar, Plovdiv 2008;

A324452) Nor is anything achieved by **13.♘d3** (13.♗f4 ♘h5=) **dxc4 14.♕xc4** (14.♘e5 ♘xe5 15.dxe5 ♘d5∞ 16.♕xc4?! ♗e3∓) **14...e5!**

... with equality.

A3245) **10...a4** The simplest way to prove that the pawn on a5 is useful. However, Black does not achieve a satisfactory game by advancing his rook pawn: **11.♘e5** and now:

A32451) **11...♕a5 12.♘c3 ♕a6 13.♖ac1** Better is 13.♘xd7 ♗xd7 14.c5±. **13...dxc4 14.♘e4 a3 15.♘xc4 axb2 16.♖b1 ♕a4 17.♖xb2 ♕xc2 18.♖xc2 ♘xe4 19.♗xe4 ♘f6 20.♗f3 ♘d5∞** with real chances to level the game, Beliavsky-Eingorn, Leningrad 1990;

A32452) **11...♘h5 12.♗c1 ♘hf6 13.♘d3 ♕a5 14.♘d2 ♕a7 15.♘f3±** The black light-squared bishop is still out of the game, Kachiani Gersinska-Jussupow, Germany 2012.

A3246) **10...b6**

This standard plan with the development of the bishop on b7 or a6 would clearly benefit more from a rook on c8 than a pawn on a5. **11.♘e5! ♘xe5** 11...♗b7 12.♘c3 ♖c8 13.e4± and White has realized all his ideas in this opening while leaving his opponent in a tight spot, Kallai-Kiss, Hungary 2003. **12.dxe5 ♘d7 13.cxd5 cxd5 14.e4±**

White's chances are better due to his greater activity and the fact that the black queenside is not yet developed. If we compare this position with the one with the insertion of b2-b3 and ...♗a6 (under 10.b3) we see that the assessment turns in favour of Black, which clearly shows the importance of each tempo in this type of position, Drozdovskij-Makarov, Rijeka 2010.

Now we turn to Black's alternatives on move 6.

B) **6...♘e4**

Black breaks the rules of the opening by moving the same piece twice, but his idea is understandable and appealing:

1. to trade the white dark-squared bishop and gain the bishop pair, or
2. to coerce White into a usually unfavourable exchange on b4:

B1) **7.♗xb4 axb4 8.♘bd2** 8.♕b3 ♘c6=. **8...♘c6 9.0-0 0-0 10.e3 ♘xd2** 10...f5 11.♕b3 ♕d6 12.♖fd1 ♗d7 13.cxd5 exd5 14.♘e5±. **11.♘xd2±** White has a healthier pawn structure but Black has not lost his chances for a draw, Lou Yiping-Eshbaev, Jakarta 2012;

B2) **7.0-0 ♘xd2** Black achieves his aim and gets the bishop pair, but the question is if it is effective. **8.♘bxd2 0-0 9.♕c2** A Catalan type position, where it seems that Black has lost too much time in order to get a non-functional bishop pair. 9.c5 a4 10.a3 ♗xd2 11.♕xd2 ♘c6 12.♕f4 ♗d7 13.e4 dxe4 14.♕xe4 ♘a5= Rotstein-Wegerer, Latschach 2011. **9...♘c6** 9...c6 10.e4± Traito Taimanov, Leningrad 1987. **10.♖ad1 ♗xd2** Then why waste time with 6...♘e4 ? **11.♖xd2±** White has a healthier and more active position, Bany-Becker, Porz 1989;

C) **6...c6 7.♕c2 0-0 8.0-0** is covered under 6...0-0;

D) **6...♘c6 7.♕c2** (for 7.0-0 dxc4 see under 6...dxc4) **7...dxc4** is covered under 6...dxc4.

Back to the main line. White usually chooses between two natural continuations: 7.♕c2 or 7.0-0.

7.♕c2

7.0-0 is a typical reaction. White first finishes the development of his kingside and only then decides whether he will play on the queenside or in the centre. We will analyse: A) 7...♘c6 and B) 7...0-0. In case of 7...♗xd2 or 7...b5 it is relatively easy for White to achieve a better game.

A) **7...♘c6**

A1) **8.♗g5 h6 9.♗xf6 ♕xf6 10.a3** 10.♘c3 0-0 11.♘b5 ♖d8 (another good move is 11...♘a7 12.a3 ♗d6=

Giri-Nakamura, Hoogeveen 2012) 12.♕c2 e5 with a solid game for Black. **10...♗d6** and now:

A11) **11.♕a4 0-0 12.♕xc4 e5 13.d5 ♘d4 14.♘xd4 exd4 15.♘d2 b5 16.♕d3 ♗f5 17.♕xb5?!** A better move is 17.♗c4=. **17...♖ab8 18.♕c4 ♖xb2∓** Wang Yue-Bitoon, Jakarta 2011;

A12) **11.♘c3 0-0 12.e3 e5 13.d5 ♘a7!** 13...♘e7 14.♘d2 b6 15.♘xc4 ♗a6 16.♖c1± Wells-Kortchnoi, London 2009. **14.♘d2 b5 15.a4 ♗d7** Weak is 15...♗f5 16.axb5± ♗d3?! 17.♖xa5+− Gonzalez de la Torre-Korneev, Elgoibar 2011. **16.♕c2** 16.axb5 ♘xb5 17.♘ce4 ♕e7 18.♘xc4 ♗b4= Hera-Hort, Triesen 2011. **16...♗b4** 16...♖fb8!? 17.axb5 ♘xb5 18.♘ce4 ♕e7 19.♘xc4 ♗b4 with chances for both sides. Now: **17.♖fc1** 17.axb5 ♘xb5 18.♘xb5 ♗xb5 19.♘xc4 a4 20.♖fc1 ♗d6 21.♘d2 ♖fb8= Markus-Beliavsky, Turin 2006; 17.♖fd1 bxa4 (if 17...♖ab8 18.axb5 ♘xb5 19.♘xc4± the a5-pawn is a weakness) 18.♘xa4 ♘b5 19.♘xc4 ♖fb8= Vinchev-Klauner, ICCF email 2011.

17...c6 17...♖fb8!?. **18.♘de4 ♕g6 19.dxc6 ♗xc6 20.axb5 ♘xb5 21.♘xb5 ♗xb5 22.♘c3 ♕xc2 23.♖xc2 ♖ab8=** Ragger-Blagojevic, Novi Sad 2009.

A2) After **8.e3** Black has two plans: the solid 8...0-0 with the idea to return the pawn and attack the centre with

...e6-e5, and the risky 8...♖b8 with the idea to continue the game with an extra pawn:

A21) **8...0-0 9.♕e2** Regaining the pawn and taking the initiative as in the regular Catalan. 9.♕c2 ♗d6 10.♕xc4 (for 10.♘a3 see Chapter 11) 10...e5 leads to the same position.

A211) **9...♗d6!**

Another standard idea in these positions. Black uses the time it takes his opponent to retake the pawn on c4 to perform the liberating ...e6-e5 and obtain a satisfactory position.

A2111) **10.♕xc4 e5 11.dxe5 ♘xe5 12.♘xe5 ♗xe5 13.♗c3 ♕e7 14.♗xe5 ♕xe5 15.♕c3 ♕e7 16.♘d2 c6** and Black levels the chances, Fernandez-Mekhitarian, Maringa 2013;

A2112) Also possible is **10.♘a3 ♗xa3 11.bxa3 b5** and now:

A21121) **12.a4 ♗a6 13.axb5 ♗xb5 14.♘e5 ♘xe5 15.dxe5** 15.♗xa8?! ♕xa8 16.dxe5 ♘e4∓ with strong compensation for Black due to his dangerous c-pawn and the opponent's weak light squares. **15...♘d5 16.♖fb1 c6 17.a4 ♗a6 18.♕e1 ♕c7 19.♗xa5 ♕xe5 20.e4 ♘f6 21.♗c3 ♕c7 22.♖d1⩲** White has compensation for the pawn but, objectively speaking, the position is likely to end in a draw, Micic-Karacsony, ICCF email 2010;

A21122) **12.♘e5 ♘xe5 13.♗xa8 ♘d3 14.♗xa5 ♘d5 15.♖ab1** 15.a4 b4⩱. 15...♗d7 16.♗b7 ♕b8 17.♗xd5 exd5 18.a4 c6 19.♖fd1 ♕c8 20.axb5 cxb5⩲ Petrov-Daubenfeld, ICCF email 2011.

A212) A sharp and risky move is **9...e5 10.♘xe5 ♘xe5 11.dxe5 ♘g4 12.f4 ♗f5 13.e4!? ♕d4+ 14.♔h1 ♗c8 15.♘c3 ♖d8** 15...♗c5 16.h3 ♘f2+ 17.♔h2 ♖a6∞. **16.♖ad1 ♗xc3 17.bxc3 ♕d3 18.♗f3 ♕xe2 19.♗xe2 b5 20.♔g2** and White had better chances with a strong centre and the bishop pair in Shirov-Kortchnoi, Carlsbad 2007;

A213) **9...b5?!** is covered in Chapter 11.

A22) **8...♖b8** Black moves away from the dangerous diagonal, planning to keep the extra pawn with ...b7-b5. **9.♕e2 b5 10.a4 ♗a6 11.axb5** 11.♖d1! 0-0 12.♘e5 ♘e7 13.axb5 ♗xb5 14.♘c3⩲, Victor Bologan in *The Powerful Catalan*. **11...♗xb5 12.♗c3** 12.♘c3 ♗xc3 13.bxc3 ♘e4 14.♖a3 with compensation, but not for more than a draw. **12...0-0**

... and it is not easy for White to show what he has gained for the pawn, Ernst-I. Sokolov, Maastricht 2013.

B) **7...0-0 8.♗g5** 8.♕c2 ♗xd2 9.♘bxd2 b5 is covered under 6...0-0.

B1) **8...b5!?** leads to very complicated positions:

B11) 9.a4 bxa4 10.♘e5 ♖a7 and now:

B111) 11.♘a3 ♗a6 11...c3! 12.bxc3 ♗xc3 13.♖b1 ♗a6 14.♘b5 ♗xb5 15.♖xb5 with compensation, but only enough for equality. **12.♘axc4 h6 13.♗d2 ♗b5∞** I. Schneider-Fridman, Germany 2013;

B112) 11.♘xc4 ♗a6 12.♘ba3 h6 13.♗e3 ♘d5 14.♕xa4 ♘xe3 15.fxe3 c5∓ Kekelidze-Moradiabadi, Abu Dhabi 2007;

B113) 11.♖xa4 ♗b7 12.♗xb7 ♖xb7= Grischuk-Mamedyarov, Khanty-Mansiysk 2013.

B12) 9.♘e5 ♖a7! On a7, the rook may support the development of its bishop. Weaker is 9...♖a6 10.a4 bxa4 11.♘xc4 ♘bd7 12.♘c3 c5 13.♘xa4± Kramnik-Navara, Prague 2008. **10.a4** 10.♘c3 ♗b7!. **10...♗b7=** Black neutralizes White's Catalan Bishop and stops the opponent's initiative, Khotenashvili-Nakhbayeva, Tashkent 2013;

B13) 9.♘c3 ♗a6 9...c6 10.♘e5⩲. **10.a4 bxa4 11.♕xa4** Weaker is 11.♘xa4 h6 12.♗xf6 ♕xf6 13.♕c2 ♖a7 14.♖fd1 ♘d7.

It is not going to be easy for White to prove compensation for the pawn, Ernst-Landa, Vlissingen 2013.

11...♗b7!N After 11...h6?! 12.♗xf6 ♕xf6 13.♘e5± White has more than sufficient compensation for the pawn, Fridman-Khenkin, Germany 2013.

12.♗xf6 12.♕a2 ♘bd7 13.♕xc4 c5=. **12...♕xf6 13.♕b5 ♖a7 14.♖fd1 ♗a6 15.♕h5 ♘d7=**

B2) 8...♘c6 and now:

B21) 9.♘c3 h6 10.♗xf6 (10.♗f4?! ♘d5∓) **10...♕xf6** is covered under 7...♘c6;

B22) 9.e3 h6 10.♗xf6 ♕xf6 11.a3 ♗d6 12.♘fd2 For 12.♘c3 e5 see under 11.♘c3. **12...e5 13.d5 ♘b8 14.♘c3 b6 15.♘xc4 ♗a6 16.♘e4 ♕e7 17.♕c2 ♘d7** with mutual chances, Iskusnikh-Riazantsev, Ekaterinburg 2013.

Back to the main line.

With 7.♕c2, White clearly wants to take back the pawn, keeping the strategic advantages that are characteristic for this type of position (the Catalan bishop and a strong mobile centre). By the way, this position can appear from various move orders, but a very popular order with elite players is the one from

the Catalan Opening: 1.d4 ♘f6 2.c4 e6 3.♘f3 d5 4.g3 dxc4 5.♗g2 ♗b4 6.♗d2 a5 7.♕c2. For example, this was the order used in the first game of the World Championship match between Kramnik and Topalov in 2006.

We will analyse several different continuations for Black, the most important one being 7...♗xd2+, which prevents White from simply regaining the pawn on c4 and preserving his strategic assets; a more passive but solid system devised by Taimanov and Smyslov with 7...♘c6, the risky 7...b5 and 7...b6, and 7...♖a6, an interesting but also risky move by Kortchnoi.

7...♗xd2+

This is a necessary exchange if Black wants to play ...b7-b5.

A) **7...♘c6**

A move played by the old masters, Mark Taimanov and Vassily Smyslov. Black postpones the exchange of the bishop because he wants to make the best of his defence with ...a7-a5. **8.♕xc4 ♕d5** The main idea of the system. Black wants a queenless middlegame, which his opponent ultimately cannot avoid due to the weakness of his pawn on d4:

A1) **9.♕xd5** We already emphasized that this exchange changes the essence of the position in Black's favour, since it strengthens his centre and opens the di-

agonal for the troublesome light-squared bishop on c8. **9...exd5**

A11) **10.a3 ♗xd2+ 11.♘bxd2 a4⇄** and Black easily keeps the balance on both wings;

A12) **10.♘c3** This is a natural developing move but it provides Black with a greater choice of solid options: 10...♗g4, Taimanov's move 10...♗f5, and Smyslov's move 10...♗e6:

A121) **10...♗g4 11.e3** 11.♘b5 0-0 (also a good move is 11...♗xf3 12.♗xf3 ♔d7 13.♖c1 ♗xd2+ 14.♔xd2 a4= with the idea ...♘a5) 12.♖d1 ♘e4⇄. **11...0-0 12.h3 ♗f5 13.g4 ♗xc3 14.bxc3 ♗d3** 14...♗e4!?. **15.♘g1 b5** A better move is 15...♘e4∓.

Peter Wells states in his commentary that the position is balanced. **16.♘e2 ♖fb8 17.f3 b4 18.♔f2 b3 19.♘c1 b2 20.♘xd3 bxa1♕ 21.♖xa1≅** Van Wely-Piket, Wijk aan Zee 2001;

A122) **10...♗f5!?** It is interesting that Taimanov moved his light-squared bishop exclusively to f5. **11.♘b5 0-0-0 12.♖c1 ♗xd2+ 13.♘xd2 ♖he8 14.e3 ♖e7 15.♘f3** and the players agreed to a draw in this good position for Black, Sosonko-Taimanov, Wijk aan Zee 1981;

A123) **10...♗e6 11.♖c1** In the event of 11.0-0 Black has 11...♘e4!⇄; and after 11.e3, as in the game, 11...a4. **11...a4!** Black makes maximal use of the a-pawn and the postponed exchange of the dark-squared bishops to destabilize the opponent's queenside. **12.♘b5 ♗xd2+ 13.♔xd2 ♘d8 14.♘e5 ♖a5!** A simple but effective move. Black drives the aggressive white knight back and obtains better play on the queenside. **15.♘xc6+** 15.♖xc6 ♖xb5 16.♖xe6 fxe6 17.♘f7+ ♔e7 18.♘xh8 ♖xb2+ 19.♔d3 ♖xa2♙ Black has enough compensation for a draw since the opponent's knight has no way out. **15...bxc6 16.♘c3 ♔e7 17.♘d1 ♔d6 18.f3 c5! 19.dxc5+ ♖xc5 20.♖xc5 ♔xc5 21.♘c3 ♔b4∓**

and Black has a more promising ending as he is in charge on the queenside, Browne-Smyslov, Las Palmas 1982.

A13) **10.0-0 ♗g4!**

Black completes his development with tempo and indirectly attacks the central pawn on d4. It is possible to simply play

10...♗xd2 11.♘bxd2 ♘e7 12.♖fe1 0-0 13.♘g5 h6 14.♘h3 ♘f5 15.e3 ♘d6 16.f3 c6 17.♘f2 ♖e8 18.♖ad1 a4⇄ with chances for both sides, Vakhidov-Iordachescu, Tashkent 2012.

A131) **11.♗e3 ♘e4!** A multipurpose move. It prevents the development of the white queen's knight, frees the f-pawn, and controls the important squares d6 and g5.

A1311) **12.h3 ♗e6** The more passive 12...♗xf3 is also possible, for example 13.exf3 ♘f6 14.a3 ♗e7 15.♘c3 ♘d8 16.f4 c6∞ Burger-Taimanov, Budapest 1982. **13.♗f4 0-0-0 14.♘a3 ♗xa3 15.bxa3 ♘c3 16.♖fe1 ♘b5 17.♖ac1 f6 18.a4 ♘d6 19.h4 ♘c4↑** Delorme-Marin, Bratto 2010;

A1312) **12.♖c1 f6 13.h3** 13.♘c3 0-0-0 14.♘b5 ♖he8 15.♗f4 ♗d6=. **13...h5 14.g4?!** This unnecessary advance of the g-pawn hands the initiative over to Black. **14...♗f7 15.♗f4 ♔d7 16.e3 g5 17.♗h2 h5 18.a3 ♗d6 19.♗xd6 ♘xd6 20.♘c3 hxg4** 20...♘e7∓. **21.hxg4 ♘e7 22.b3 ♗e6 23.♘e1 c6∓** Kuligowski-Pokojowczyk, Gdynia 1982.

A132) **11.e3 ♘e4!** This is an important move, just like in the previous line. **12.♗c3** 12.♗xb4 axb4 13.♘bd2 ♗xf3 14.♘xf3 ♖a5 15.a4 ♔d7 16.♗h3+ ♔d6 17.♗f5 ♖ha8↑ with an excellent position for Black, Vladimirov-Taimanov, St Petersburg 1995. Now:

A13211) **12...♔e7?! 13.♖c1 ♖hc8 14.♘fd2 ♘f6 15.a3 ♗d6** and now in the game Arkell-Speelman, Birmingham 2001 White could have obtained a clear advantage with **16.f3!N** 16.♘f3 ♗e6 17.b3 ♘e4 18.♗e1 ♘b8 19.♘c3 ♘xc3 20.♗xc3 h6 21.♘e1 ♘d7 22.♘f3 ♔d8 23.b4 axb4. **16...♗d7 17.e4±;**

A13212) 12...♗xf3?! In this particular position Black has no reason to give up his bishop pair. **13.♗xf3 f5 14.♖c1 ♔d7 15.a3 ♗d6 16.♗e1 a4 17.♗d1 b5 18.f3 ♘f6 19.♘c3 ♘a7 20.♗c2 g6 21.e4** White's chances are better thanks to the bishop pair. Diachkov-Yanvarev, Korolev 1999;

A13213) 12...0-0 Black is the first to finish his development. **13.♖c1 ♗e7 14.♗e1 ♖fd8 15.♘fd2 ♘f6 16.♘b3 ♗f5 17.♘c5 ♖db8 18.♘xb7 ♘xd4 19.exd4 ♖xb7 20.♘c3 ♖d8 21.♘a4 ♘e4 22.b3 ♗a3 23.♖d1 ♖a7 24.f3 ♘d6=** Rybka 3-Rybka 3, Internet (blitz) 2009.

Now we go back to the position after 8...♕d5.

A2) 9.♕d3!

A sensible decision. White does not wish to exchange the queens on square d5 and so after ...exd5 strengthen the opponent's centre and open the diagonal h3-c8 for the black light-squared bishop, thus limiting the actions of his own bishop on g2. Black can continue with the basic idea of the system, which involves the exchange of queens with 9... ♕e4 or 9...♕f5, or he can play the more serious 9... 0-0 with the idea ...♖fd8.

A21) 9...♕e4

Black's game is usually easier without the queens in Catalan positions because it does not have a comfortable place and not as much activity in the middlegame as the white queen. **10.♕xe4 ♘xe4** The position is simplified but White has preserved the strong activity of his light-squared bishop along the central diagonal h1-a8. Usually, White fights for an advantage with one of the following continuations: 11.a3, 11.♘c3 or 11.♗xb4.

A211) A weak move is **11.a3** because after **11...♘xd2** (also possible is 11...♗d6, where Black focuses on playing... e6-e5: 12.♗e3 ♘f6 13.♘c3 ♗d7 14.♗d2 a4 15.e4 e5= Payen-Istratescu, Dieppe 2012) **12.♘bxd2** Black can move the bishop back and play a passive but solid position with the bishop pair:

A2111) 12...♗d6 Black saves the e7-square for his king. **13.♘c4 a4 14.♖c1 ♘a5 15.♘fd2 ♘xc4 16.♖xc4 16.♘xc4 ♗e7⇄. 16...♗d7 17.♘e4 ♔e7 18.♘xd6 cxd6 19.♔d2 d5 20.♖c7 ♖hb8 21.♖hc1 ♖a6 22.e4 dxe4 23.♗xe4 ♔d6 24.♖7c4 ♖b6** with equal chances towards the endgame, Saric-Zelcic, Plitvicka Jezera 2013;

A2112) 12...♗e7 13.♖c1 0-0 14.0-0 a4 As we can see, advancing to a4 has become the typical idea in this type of position, because it brings a great strategic advantage for Black. Black takes space on the queenside and vacates the a5-square for his knight or rook. **15.e3** 15.♘c4 ♗d8 16.♖fd1 ♘a5 17.♘fd2 c6. The key move would be ...a5-a4, with the general idea to stop the combined influence of the bishop on g2 and rook on c1: 18.♗e4 ♗c7 19.♘xa5 ♖xa5 20.♘b1 ♗d7 21.♘c3 ♗b6⇄ and Black prepares to open up the centre with ...c7-c5, to activate his bishops. Kouatly-Polugaevsky, Toluca 1982. **15...♗d7 16.♖c3 ♖fb8 17.♖fc1 ♗d8 18.♘e4 ♗e8 19.♘c5 ♖a7 20.h4 h6 21.♘d2 ♘a5 22.♘d3 ♖a6 23.♔h2 ♖a7 24.♘b4 ♔f8 25.♖c5 c6∞** Black is temporarily passive, but the bishops and his solid position allow him sufficient counterplay, especially in the long run, Sasikiran-Zhang Zhong, Zaozhuang 2012.

A212) The humble **11.e3** grants Black relatively easy recuperation: **11...♘xd2 12.♘fxd2 a4 13.a3 ♗e7 14.♘c3 ♗d7 15.♖c1 ♘a5 16.♘ce4 ♗c6 17.0-0 0-0 18.f4 ♖fd8 19.♘c5 ♗xc5 20.♖xc5 ♗xg2 21.♔xg2 c6=** Garcia Palermo-Marin, Benasque 2010;

A213) **11.♗xb4**

This is probably the best choice. White exchanges the dark-squared bishop as he does not want to give the opponent the bishop pair. From here on, he will rely on typical strategic assets in the

Catalan, such as the active light-squared bishop on g2, the strong pawn centre and pressure on the c-file.

A2131) **11...axb4** Black gains an open file and pressure on the a2-pawn, which is undoubtedly useful, but practice shows that the b4-pawn is also weak, which means that White has the upper hand. **12.♘bd2 ♘xd2** 12...♘d6 13.0-0 ♔e7 14.♖fc1 f6 15.e3 ♗d7 16.♘e1 ♖hc8 17.♘d3± and the b4-pawn constitutes a serious weakness, Giemsa-Lagunow, Berlin 2007. **13.♔xd2**

A21311) **13...0-0** Black develops his other rook, but pointlessly moves the king away from the centre. **14.♖hc1 ♖a5 15.e3 ♗d7 16.♘e1 ♖fa8 17.♘d3 ♖xa2 18.♖xa2 ♖xa2 19.d5** Another possibility is 19.e4!?. With the king on g8, Black can't protect his c7-pawn: 19...♔f8 20.d5 exd5 21.exd5 ♘d8 22.♖xc7 ♗f5 23.♗f1 ♗xd3 24.♗xd3 ♖xb2+ 25.♔e3±. **19...exd5 20.♗xd5± ♖a5 21.♗xc6 ♗xc6 22.♘xb4 ♖b5 23.♖c4 ♗e8 24.♘d3 ♗c6 25.♔c3±** Bochev-Chiru, corr. 2010;

A21312) **13...♔e7**

A logical decision in the endgame. Instead of castling, Black moves his king closer to the centre. **14.♖hc1**

A213121) **14...♖a5 15.♘e1!** 15.e3 ♗d7= with the idea of ...♖ha8. With the king on e7, this represents a more favourable version when compared to the variations with 13...0-0. **15.♘xd4 16.♖xc7+ ♗d7 17.♘c2 ♘xc2 18.♔xc2 ♖c8 19.♖xc8 ♗xc8 20.♔b3 b6 21.♔xb4±** White has an extra pawn and Black a more active rook, but that is not enough compensation;

A213122) **14...♖d8 15.e3 e5 16.♖xc6!?** Necessary if White wants to fight on. **16...bxc6 17.♘xe5 ♗b7!?N** 17...♖d6 18.♘xc6+ ♔f8 19.♘xb4±, Sosonko-Herzog, Lucerne 1982. Now the best way for White to continue the fight is to guard his knight and not to force a trade. For example: **18.♘d3!?** 18.♘xc6+?! ♔f8∓; on 18.♗xc6, 18...♖a5 is the only move, but it's enough to allow Black to fight on equal footing: 19.♘c4 ♖c5! (19...♖a7?! 20.♗xb7 ♖xb7 21.♘a5 ♖b6 22.♖c1 ♔d7 23.♘c4 ♖f6 24.♘e5+ ♔c8 25.♘d3±) 20.♗xb7 ♖xc4 with play for both sides, but objectively this is a draw. **18...♖a5** 18...♖db8 19.♘c5⩲ with pressure, which offers White sufficient compensation. **19.♔c2 ♖b8 20.♘c5 ♔d6 21.e4 ♗c8 22.e5+ ♔e7 23.♗xc6↑**

A2132) **11...♘xb4**

All would be perfect if the threat to c2 were real. However:

A21321) **12.♘a3 f6** 12...♘d6 13.0-0 ♔e7 (13...♗d7 14.♖fc1±) 14.♖fc1 c6

15.♘b1 f6 16.♘bd2 ♖d8 17.a3 ♘a6 18.e3 ♗d7 19.♗f1 ♗e8= Cifuentes Parada-Vehi Bach, Pamplona 2003 **13.♘d2** A better option would be 13.♘b5 ♔d8 14.0-0 ♗d7 15.♘c3 ♗c6 16.♖fc1±. **13...♘d6 14.0-0 ♗d7 15.♖fc1 ♗c6 16.e4** Better is 16.♘ac4 ♘xc4 17.♘xc4 ♗xg2 18.♔xg2 ♘c6 19.e3 0-0-0=. **16...0-0-0↑** Sosonko-Hartmann, Germany 1983;

A21322) **12.♘bd2 ♘c2+ 13.♔d1 ♘xd2 14.♔xc2 ♘xf3 15.♗xf3 c6 16.♖ac1 a4 17.♖hd1 ♔e7 18.♖d3 ♖a5 19.♖a3 ♖d8 20.e3 e5=** Pharaon 3.5.1-Deep Shredder 11, Internet 2007;

A21323) **12.0-0!** White calmly finishes his development, shoving that his opponent's knights, while seemingly active, do not bother him in the least. **12...♘d6**

An important defensive move, because the knight on d6 guards many critical squares. After 12...♔e7 13.♖c1 ♘a6 14.♘e5 ♘d6 15.♘d2 ♖d8 16.e3 ♖a7 17.♗f1 ♘e8 18.a3± White's pieces are more naturally placed, and he has better chances, Vaulin-Faibisovich, Swidnica 2000; 12...f6 13.♖c1 c6 14.♘c3 ♘d6 15.e4 ♔e7 16.a3 ♘a6 17.e5 ♘f7 18.exf6+ gxf6 19.♖e1± Beliavsky-Ljubojevic, Linares 1991; a weaker move would be 12...♘c2? because of 13.♘e1±. **13.♘c3 ♘d5** A logical idea.

Black wants to further simplify the position, using the knight which no longer contributes anything on b4. **14.♖ac1 ♘xc3 15.♖xc3 c6** Also an important move, defending against White's increasing initiative on the c-file and the Catalan diagonal. **16.e3 ♔e7** The possibility of keeping the king in the centre is an important resource in Black's defensive strategy, because it eases his play in this passive endgame. **17.♘e5** White has no trouble activating and coordinating his pieces. **17...♗d7** As we see, Black's play is also easy in this position, because his moves are more or less forced. Black opens up the 8th rank to activate the kingside rook, and the bishop may be put on e8, because after ...f7-f6 it can be activated on the h5-e8 diagonal. **18.♖d1 ♖hc8±**

The players agreed to a draw in this slightly passive, but otherwise solid position for Black. This endgame is typical for the variation we are investigating. White almost always ends up with more active and better-coordinated pieces, but it is difficult to force a breakthrough or anything substantial in this simplified position where Black has a well-placed king and a solid position, Biriukov-Krogius, St Petersburg 1996.

A22) 9...♕f5 10.♕xf5 exf5 With this exchange of the queens, Black increases

his control over square e4 and ensures activity for his light-squared bishop via square e6; however, the question is whether this comes at a greater price: the doubling of pawns on the f-file. **11.0-0**

A221) **11...0-0 12.a3** After 12.♘c3 ♗xc3!? 13.bxc3 ♖e8 14.♖fe1 ♘e4 15.♖ac1 ♗e6 16.♖c2 f6 17.h4 ♗c4 18.♗f4 ♘e7 19.♘d2 ♘xd2 20.♗xd2 c6= Black had the opponent's bishop pair under control and had equal chances in Hagström-Hagen, ICCF email 2011. **12...♗d6** 12...♗xd2 13.♘bxd2 a4 14.♖ac1±. **13.♘c3 ♗e6 14.♖ac1 a4 15.♘b5 ♘e4 16.♗e3 ♖a5 17.♘xd6 cxd6 18.♘d2** with slightly better chances for White thanks to his better pawn structure, Bocheva-Daubenfeld, ICCF email 2011;

A222) **11...♗e6 12.♖c1 ♗d5 13.e3 ♘e4 14.♗e1 0-0 15.♘fd2 ♖fe8 16.♘c3 ♘xc3 17.bxc3 ♗xg2 18.cxb4! ♗d5 19.b5 ♘b4 20.a3 ♘d3 21.♖c3 ♘xe1 22.♖xe1 c6 23.♖b1** with better odds in the endgame due to White's better pawn structure, Giri-Landa, Mulhouse 2011.

A23) **9...0-0**
A231) **10.♘c3 ♕h5**

By putting the queen on h5 and the rook on d8, Black improves his tactical possibilities and increases the dynamics in the position, especially if it is possible to attack the centre with ...e6-e5. Still, with the undeveloped bishop on c8, this plan is riskier than the previous ones involving the exchange of queens and the transition to the endgame. White has several pleasant options: to exploit the pseudo-active position of the black queen with the prophylactic 11.a3 or 11.h3, or to directly threaten the black queen with 11. ♘h4:

A2311) **11.a3** The right time to gain the bishop pair, because a retreat by the black bishop would result in White's superiority in the centre. **11...♗xc3 12.♗xc3 ♖d8 13.♕c2 ♕f5!** Black can do nothing better than exchange the queens, because his plan with ...e6-e5 is devalued with the arrival of the white bishop at c3. **14.♖c1** After 14.♕xf5 exf5 15.0-0 ♗e6= Black has no problems. **14...♕xc2 15.♖xc2 ♗d7 16.♗d2 ♗e8 17.0-0 ♘e4 18.♗f4** White has better chances with his bishop pair, C. Hansen-Andersson, Hinnerup 1995;

A2312) **11.h3 ♖d8 12.a3** 12.g4 ♕g6 13.♕xg6 hxg6 14.e3 a4 15.a3 ♗f8 16.♖d1 ♘a5 17.g5 ♘d7 18.h4 ♘b3 19.♘e4 b6 20.♗c3 ♗b7∞ Atalik-Speelman, Germany 2000. **12...♗xc3** 12...♗e7 13.♖c1±. **13.bxc3 ♕g6 14.♕xg6 hxg6 15.♗g5** and Black must continue to fight to level the game, Fridman-Bartel, Dresden 2008;

A2313) **11.♘h4** With the idea ♗f3. By directly threatening to win the opponent's queen, White forfeits his control of the critical square e5, which facilitates Black's plan: **11...e5 12.d5 e4! 13.♗xe4** A weaker move is 13.♘xe4 ♘xd5∓. **13...♗xc3!? 14.♗xc3** A bad move is 14.bxc3? ♘e5 15.♕d4 ♘xe4 16.♕xe4 ♖e8∓. **14...♘b4 15.♗xb4 axb4 16.♗g2 ♖e8 17.e3 b6⇄** Black has enough compensation for the pawn.

A232) Another possibility is **10.0-0**, although after **10...♖d8!?** Black has better chances to show the worth of his dynamic plan. **11.♘c3** 11.e3?! e5∓. **11...♕h5** 11...♗xc3?! 12.bxc3 would strengthen the opponent's centre and render Black's plan pointless.

Now White has several options but he must be careful when choosing his move, for there is still the threat of ...e6-e5.

A2321) **12.a3?! ♗c5!N** 12...♗xc3?! 13.bxc3± Naumkin-Zelcic, Saint Vincent 2001.

13.e3 13.♘b5 e5∓. **13...e5↑**;

A2322) **12.♕c4?! e5 13.dxe5 ♘g4 14.h3?** Better is 14.h4 ♘gxe5 15.♕f4 ♗g4↑. **14...♘gxe5∓** and Black will take on h3 and keep an extra pawn, Manea-Iordachescu, Galati 2007;

A2323) **12.h3 e5 13.g4 ♕g6** 13...♗xg4?! 14.hxg4 ♘xg4 15.d5 ♘d4

16.♖fd1 ♖a6 17.♘e4±; analyses show that White can defend himself in this crazy position and keep the upper hand. **14.♕xg6 hxg6 15.dxe5 ♘xe5 16.♘xe5 ♖xd2 17.♖fd1 ♖xd1+** 17...♗xc3 18.bxc3 ♖xd1+ 19.♖xd1 ♗e6 20.♗xb7±. **18.♖xd1** White's pieces are all active and harmoniously placed, and he holds a certain initiative, but Black can hold thanks to the bishop pair. For instance: **18...♗d6 19.♘c4 ♗e7 20.♗f3** 20.g5 ♘e8 21.h4 ♔f8=. **20...c6 21.♘b6 ♖b8 22.♘xc8 ♖xc8 23.♘a4 g5=**

A2324) **12.♗g5 ♗e7 13.♕b5** 13.e3 e5⇄ Lipinsky-Thinius, Germany 1999. **13...a4!↑** With the idea ...♖a5. If 13...♖a6 14.♗xf6 ♕xb5 15.♘xb5 ♗xf6= Wells-Kosten, Torquay 2013. **14.♗f4?!** 14.♗xf6 ♕xb5 15.♘xb5 ♗xf6 16.e3 ♖a5 17.♘a3! e5!=. **14...e5!N** Black opens up his light-squared bishop with the intention to capture the opponent's queen. A weaker move is 14...♕xb5 15.♘xb5↑, Baginskaite-Stein, San Francisco 2005. **15.dxe5 ♖a5** And White must give up the queen for rook, knight and pawn: 16.♕xa5 16.♕c4? ♗e6−+. **16...♘xa5 17.exf6 ♗xf6 18.♗xc7 ♖e8∓;**

A2325) **12.♗f4!?**

This move gives White the best chances. He prevents ...e6-e5 and at the same time attacks the pawn on c7. **12...♘xd4**

12...♗d6 with chances for a level game, Jakobsen-Kristiansen, Denmark 1988. **13.♗xc7 ♘xf3+** Better is 13...♖d7 14.♘xd4 ♖xc7 15.♗f3 ♕h3 16.♘db5 ♖d7 17.♕c4 ♖d8∞ with chances for a draw. **14.♕xf3 ♕xf3 15.♗xf3±** Rogers-Wells, London 1983.

B) **7...b5**

This doesn't work well because of **8.a4** and now Black has to break up his queenside with **8...bxa4** (8...c6 is not advisable due to 9.axb5, and after 9...♗xd2+ White opens up his notorious Catalan bishop with 10.♘fxd2!±. **9.♘e5 ♖a6 10.♕xa4+ ♗d7 11.♘xd7** 11.♕c2!? ♗b5 12.e3 0-0 13.♘a3±. **11...♕xd7 12.0-0 0-0 13.♕xd7 ♘fxd7 14.♗xb4** 14.♖c1!? c5 15.♖xc4±. **14...axb4 15.♖xa6 ♘xa6 16.♗b7 ♘db8 17.♖c1 c5 18.♖xc4↑** Tkachiev-Moiseenko, Santo Domingo 2002;

C) **7...b6** With the bishop on g2 this continuation is very risky. **8.0-0** Also good is 8.a3 ♗xd2+ 9.♘fxd2± Sharevich-Sudakova, Vladimir 2007; 8...♗e7!?. **8...0-0** For 8...♗b7 9.♗xb4 axb4 10.♕xc4 see 8. ♗g2. **9.♗g5 ♗a6 10.♖d1 ♖a7 11.♘e5±** White has more than enough compensation for the pawn, Kunte-Juswanto, Kuala Lumpur 2005;

D) **7...♖a6** is a very interesting idea from Kortchnoi. The black rook moves away from the dangerous diagonal, indirectly defending the c4-pawn.

D1) **8.0-0!**

Correctly delaying the capture on c4, due to 8...♖c6. The question remains: can Black justify the presence of the rook on a6? **8...b5 9.a4 c6 10.e4 ♘bd7 11.♘c3♕** with strong compensation for White, among other things because of the unusual position of the black rook, Akshayraj-Predke, Moscow 2012;

D2) **8.♘a3 ♗xa3** 8...♕d5!? 9.0-0 b5 10.♖ad1 ♘c6 11.♗e3 ♕h5∞. **9.bxa3 b5 10.♖b1 ♗d7 11.♘e5 0-0 12.a4 b4 13.♕xc4 ♗xa4=** Marin-Kortchnoi, Reggio Emilia 2008;

D3) Nothing is achieved by **8.♕xc4** (or 8.♗xb4 axb4 9.♕xc4 ♖c6 10.♕xb4 ♖c1+ 11.♔d2 ♘c6 12.♕a4 ♖c5!= with the idea ...♖a5) **8...♖c6 9.♕b5 ♗d7 10.0-0 ♖b6 11.♕d3 ♗b5 12.♕e3 ♘d5 13.♕e4 ♘f6 14.♕e3 ♘d5=** and the black pieces are dancing nicely, Tratar-Kortchnoi, San Sebastian 2011;

8.♕xd2

Oddly enough, White once again uses the queen instead of the more logical recapture with the knight. However, this paradoxical continuation was also played in the first game of the World Championship match between Kramnik and Topalov in 2006, and it has a better

reputation than the developing move 8.♘bxd2, because now Black's key strategy, with 8...b5, can be countered with 9.♕g5

For 8.♘bxd2 b5 9.a4 c6 10.0-0 0-0 see under 6...0-0.

8...c6

With the idea ... b7-b5. Weaker is 8...b5 due to 9.♕g5! 0-0 10.♕xb5±.

White retrieves the pawn and completely destroys the black pawn structure on the queenside, Laznicka-Kosten, Austria 2008.

9.a4

9.♘e5 b5 and now:

A) **10.a4 ♖a6?!** A better move would be the thematic 10...♘d5!N

with the idea of ...f7-f6 and Black has the position under control. **11.♘c3±** and Black's position is already critical because he is about to lose either his b-pawn or his c-pawn, while also falling behind in development, Delchev-Guerra Mendez, Benasque 2013;

B) Reclaiming the pawn with **10.♘xc6** serves no purpose due to **10...♕c7!=**, Gavrilidis-Skaperdas, Achaea 2012. Weaker would be 10...♕b6?! because of the not so apparent knight jump 11.♘e7! and in case of 11...♗b7 12.♘c8!± when Black loses material due to the fork on d6;

C) **10.b3** White doesn't give his opponent any time for the defensive ...♘d5! as in the variation with 10.a4. **10...cxb3**

C1) **11.♘xc6?! ♕b6?!** 11...♕c7!∓. **12.♘xb8?!** 12.♘e7! (the motif known from line B) 12...♗b7 13.♘c8! ♗xc8 14.♗xa8±. **12...♗b7∓** Kornev-Landa, Krasnoyarsk 2007;

C2) Better would be **11.axb3 0-0 12.0-0** (nothing comes from 12.♘xc6 ♘xc6 13.♗xc6 ♖a7∞ 14.♗xb5? ♕d5−+) **12...♗b7 13.♖c1 ♕b6 14.e3⩲**. White has the usual compensation for this type of position, but only enough for a draw.

9...♘e4!

A relatively new move, with the general idea of defending the c4-pawn from d6, which seems to disturb White's plans more than the usual 9...b5.

9...b5, (weaker is 9...0-0 because of 10.♘a3±) which is the move known

from the World Championship match Kramnik-Topalov, Elista 2006, also works: **10.axb5 cxb5 11.♕g5** The idea of the move 8.♕d2. **11...0-0 12.♕xb5 ♗a6 13.♕a4 ♕b6 14.0-0** 14.♘bd2 ♗b5 15.♕a3 ♘c6 16.0-0 ♖ab8 17.♖fc1 ♘xd4 18.♘xd4 ♕xd4 19.♘f3 ♕b6 20.♕xa5 ♕xa5 21.♖xa5 ♗c6 22.♖xc4 ♗xf3 23.♗xf3 ♖xb2 with obvious equality, Leko-Kramnik, Dortmund 2009. **14...♕xb2 15.♘bd2 ♗b5 16.♘xc4 ♗xa4 17.♘xb2 ♗b5** and now:

A) **18.♘e5 ♖a7** Black is very close to a draw, but he still has to take care of his a-pawn:

A1) **19.♘bc4!**

White has a better endgame thanks to the weak a5-pawn. **19...♘bd7** If 19...a4, possible is the simple 20.♖fb1 ♗xc4 21.♘xc4 ♘d5 22.♖a3 when White is slightly better, as Black will hardly be able to save the a5-pawn. **20.♘xa5** 20.♖fc1± Bologan, *The Powerful Catalan*. **20...♘xe5 21.dxe5 ♘d7 22.f4 ♗xe2 23.♖fe1 ♗h5 24.♘c6 ♖c7 25.♖ec1±** White is slightly better, thanks to his better coordinated pieces and space advantage, Guskov-Klimakovs, Lechenicher schachserver 2009;

A2) **19.♘bd3 ♘bd7** 19...♘fd7 20.♖fb1 ♘xe5 21.♖xb5 ♖xd3 22.exd3 a4 23.♖a3 ♘d7 24.♗c6 ♘f6 25.♖b4

♖d8 26.♖axa4 ♖xa4 27.♖xa4 and White still has chances, Gleizerov-Luther, Predeal 2007. **20.♖fb1** 20.♘c6!? ♗xc6 21.♗xc6 ♖c8 22.♖fc1 g6 and Black is very close to a draw. **20...♘xe5 21.♖xb5 ♘xd3 22.exd3=** and the opponents agreed to a draw in Ushenina-T. Kosintseva, Rijeka 2010;

A3) **19.♗f3 ♘bd7** Black is close to full equality, Kramnik-Topalov, Elista 2006.

B) A more passive approach is **18.♘d2** although White has the healthy idea of attacking his opponent's c-pawn from b3: **18...♖a7** Weaker would be 18...♗c6 19.♘b3 ♗xg2 20.♔xg2± and Black loses his a-pawn, Gupta-Greenfeld, Chennai 2011. **19.♖fe1 ♖c8=** Gupta-Maheswaran, Kochi 2011.

To the text, White has four reasonable replies:
10.♕c2
A) **10.♕e3**

Perhaps the best position for the queen, because she defends the vulnerable pawns on d4 and e2 here. In this manner, White drastically hampers Black's ideal plan with ....♘b4 and ...b6 with the idea of ...♗b7. **10...♘d6 11.♘bd2**

A1) **11...0-0 12.0-0 b5 13.♕f4 ♗b7** 13...f6!? 14.♘e4 ♘xe4 15.♕xe4 ♖a7∞; Black has more passive pieces, but also an extra pawn, meaning that both sides are decently equipped for the

remainder of the game. **14.e4** 14.♘g5!? with the intention of ♘ge4. **14...♘a6∞**

With chances for both sides, Ju Wenjun-Kosteniuk, Istanbul 2012;

A2) **11...♘a6!?N**

Intending to move the knight to solid ground on b4. **12.0-0 ♘b4 13.♖fc1 b5** Black manages to defend his extra pawn, but White has sufficient compensation for a draw thanks to the excellent potential of his pieces. **14.♘e4** 14.♘e5 ♖a6=. **14...♘d5 15.♘xd6+ ♕xd6 16.♕d2 0-0=;**

B) **10.♕c1 ♘d6 11.♘fd2** 11.♘a3 b5∞. **11...0-0 12.♘a3 ♖a7** 12...♖a6!? is a bold idea, and a good one. Black uses the opportunity to activate his rook on the b-file, thanks to his control of b4. **13.♘axc4 ♘xc4 14.♕xc4 ♖b6 15.♕c3 ♖b4 16.e3 e5 17.dxe5 ♗e6 18.f4 ♕b6⯑** Sage-Schunck, ICCF email 2012. **13.♘dxc4 ♘xc4 14.♕xc4 b6 15.♕c3 ♗a6 16.♘c4 ♖d7 17.e3 ♕c7**

18.♘e5 ♖dd8 19.♘xc6 ♖c8 20.♘xb8 ♕xb8 21.♕d2 e5! and Black has the initiative, Stockfish 2.2.2-Rybka 4.1, Internet 2012;

C) **10.♕f4** and now:

C1) **10...♘d6 11.♘a3 ♘a6 12.♘e5 0-0 13.0-0 ♘b4 14.♘axc4 ♘xc4 15.♘xc4 b6 16.♖fd1** 16.♘e5 ♗a6 17.♖fc1 ♖c8 18.♘xc6 ♘xc6 19.♖xc6 ♖xc6 20.♗xc6 ♗xe2=. **16...♗a6=** With this same plan Black gets satisfactory positions after all White's queen retreats. The black knight heads for the strong outpost on b4 and the light-squared bishop becomes active on the f1-a6 diagonal, Cioara-Landa, Germany 2012;

C2) Also possible is **10...♕b6!?**

C21) **11.0-0** 11.♕xe4? ♕xb2∓. ♕xb2 12.♘bd2 ♘c3 13.♕e3 ♘d5∞ White has compensation for the pawn, but cannot hope for more than a draw;

C22) **11.♘bd2 ♘xd2 12.♕xd2 ♘d7 13.0-0 0-0 14.♕c3 e5 15.♕xc4** 15.dxe5 ♖e8 16.♖fd1 ♕b4∞ with mutual chances. **15...exd4 16.♕xd4 ♕xd4 17.♘xd4 ♘c5 18.♖fc1 ♘e6=** Cumming-Leimgruber, ICCF email 2010.

10...♘d6 11.♘bd2 ♘a6 12.♘xc4 ♘b4 13.♘xd6+ ♕xd6 14.♕d2 14.♕c3 0-0 15.0-0 b6 16.♘e5 ♗a6 17.♘c4 ♗xc4 18.♕xc4 ♖ac8 19.♖fd1 ♖fd8= Wagner-Saric, Sibenik 2012.

14...0-0 15.0-0 ♖d8 Or 15...b6 16.♖ac1 ♗a6 17.♖fd1 ♖ac8 18.♗f1 ♖fd8= Ragger-Wojtaszek, Porto Carras 2011.

16.♖fd1 b6 17.♕c3 ♗a6 18.♖d2 ♖ac8 19.♖ad1 ♕e7=

Black isn't behind in terms of piece activity and coordination, Hammer-Carlsen, Sandnes 2013.

Conclusion

In this chapter we focussed on one of the main lines, 5.g3 d5! 6.♗g2. We covered some open positions with ...dxc4 and some closed positions with ...c7-c6.

In the critical position emerging after 6.♗g2 dxc4 7.♕c2, the best continuation for Black is 7...♗xd2!. The optimal response for White is 8. ♕xd2 (since 8. ♘bxd2 leads to unclear positions, where it is difficult for White to prove his compensation for the minus pawn). After the logical 8...c6 9.a4, the best move for Black is 9...♘e4! and moving the knight to d6, as was recently played in the game Hammer-Carlsen, Sandnes 2013.

In the system of Vassily Smyslov and Mark Taimanov, emerging after 6...dxc4 7.♕c2 ♘c6 8.♕xc4 ♕d5, White should play 9.♕d3!, although after 9...♕e4 there is nothing better than to trade queens with 10.♕xe4 ♘xe4. Now the right plan for White is 11.♗xb4 ♘xb4 12. 0-0!. What we suggest in this critical position is 12...♘d6!? and then the logical 13.♘c3, further simplifying. In the ensuing endgames Black's position is passive, but solid and relatively easy to play.

In the Closed Catalan, the critical position arises after 6.♗g2 0-0 (or 6...c6 before 7...0-0) 7.0-0 c6 8.♕c2 ♘bd7 9.♗f4 ♗e7. Here White has several options, but the best chances are provided by 10.♖d1!. As we have seen, both players are on a slippery slope, but we believe Black can dabble with, or even apply in practical play continuations such as 10...♘h5, 10...♘e4, 10...b5 and 10... h6.

Exercises

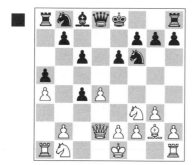

14.3 (1) Find the best plan.
(solution on page 450)

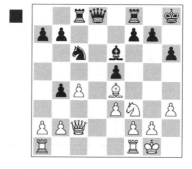

14.3 (2) Find the plan.
(solution on page 450)

14.3 (3) Find the plan.
(solution on page 451)

Chapter 14.4

The Solid 5.g3 d5 6.♕c2

1.d4 e6 2.c4 ♗b4+ 3.♗d2 a5 4.♘f3 ♘f6 5.g3 d5 6.♕c2

Defending the pawn on c4 is a good choice if White wants a safe and solid game. Compared to the variation 6.♗g2 dxc4, White here rejects the positions where he sacrifices the pawn on c4, but by moving the queen early he creates the preconditions for the opponent's attack on the centre with ...c7-c5.

Black has a wide choice of options, but we will examine 6...dxc4, 6...0-0, 6...c5, 6...♘c6 and 6...c6.

6...dxc4

The most frequent move in this position: White fianchettos his light-squared bishop. Strategically speaking, the capture on c4 weakens Black's control of his centre and opening the central diagonal h1-a8 increases the effectiveness of the famous Catalan bishop. On the other hand, it takes White some time to regain the pawn, which Black uses to activate the queenside or organize play in the centre.

A) The continuation **6...0-0** is used by players who wish to attack the opponent's centre on the next move with ...c7-c5, or else to play the Bogo-Catalan with ...c7-c6. **7.♗g2** In this position, which can also arise by switching White's 6th and 7th moves, Black has two systems he can play: A1) 7...c5 and the universal 7...c6, which we explained in Chapter 14.3. Other continuations such as A2) 7...♘c6, A3) 7...dxc4 and A4) 7...♘e4 lead Black into more problematic positions:

A1) **7...c5** is a natural reaction in the centre to the white queen's sortie, which we will also see on move 6.

A11) On **8.dxc5** Black acquires a mobile pawn pair in the centre with **8...d4 9.♗xb4** 9.0-0 ♗xc5 10.♗g5 ♘c6 11.♘bd2 ♗e7= with a good game for Black, Behrhorst-Marie, Naujac sur Mer 2013. **9...axb4 10.♘bd2 ♘c6 11.0-0 ♕e7 12.♘b3** 12.♘g5 e5 13.♘de4 ♗f5 14.♘xf6+ ♕xf6 15.♘e4 ♕g6⩲. **12...e5 13.♘g5 h6 14.♘e4 ♗f5 15.♘xf6+ ♕xf6 16.♗e4 ♗xe4 17.♕xe4 ♕e6⩲** Black has enough compensation thanks to his active pieces and better control of the centre, Bocharov-Kosten, Izmir 2004;

A12) **8.cxd5! 8...cxd4** 8...♕xd5 9.♘c3±. **9.♘xd4 ♕b6 10.e3** 10.♘f3 ♗xd2+ 11.♘bxd2 exd5 12.0-0 ♘c6=; Black can easily activate his other pieces, which is enough to level the game, Postny-Filippov, Sibenik 2012.

A121) **10...exd5 11.0-0 ♘c6 12.♘xc6** White must change the structure as he cannot favourably maintain the d4-square.

A1211) **12...bxc6**

In the new structure, Black's pawn on d5 has become stronger, but the c6-pawn is a new target.

A12111) **13.♘c3** This natural developing move is flawed, as it grants more freedom to the opponent's light-squared bishop:

A121111) **13...♗g4!?** prevents the opponent from activating his rook on the d-file, and in case of an expulsion by h2-h3, Black will withdraw the bishop to the b1-h7 diagonal. **14.♖ac1 ♖fc8 15.a3 ♗d6 16.h3 ♗h5 17.♘a4 ♕b5?!** This is a logical move, but this position of the black queen provides White with the opportunity to limit the action of Black's light-squared bishop. Better is 17...♕d8!? 18.♗c3 (18.♘c5 ♗g6⩲; 18.f4) 18...♗g6 19.♕e2 ♘e4 20.♗d4 ♖ab8⇄.

After the text, **18.f4!** is best, with the idea to use g3-g4 and f4-f5 to lock the opponent's light-squared bishop out of the game. Less good is 18.♘c5? ♗g6 19.♕c3 ♖e8= Lekic-Markus, Petrovac 2004 – better is 19...♕b8! with the idea...♗d6-e5, for example 20.b4 axb4 21.axb4 ♖a2∓ 22.♖a1? ♖c2−+. **18...h6** After 18...♗e2 White can take advantage of the black queen's position with 19.♘c3! ♕c4 20.♘xe2 ♕xe2 21.♖fe1 ♕b5 22.♗c3± and White is in the lead with the bishop pair. **19.g4 ♗g6 20.f5 ♗h7 21.♗c3 ♘d7 22.♗d4 f6 23.e4±;**

A121112) A more passive move is also possible: **13...♗e6 14.♖fc1**

A1211121) **14...♕a7 15.♘a4** This logical continuation allows Black to move the c6-pawn. A better move is 15.a3!? ♗e7 16.♘e2↑ and it is not easy for Black to anticipate where the white knight will move. **15...c5!** Black takes the opportunity to prevent the oppo-

nent's knight to be moved to c5.
**16.♗c3 ♗xc3 17.♘xc3 ♖ab8 18.♖d1
d4 19.exd4 cxd4 20.♘e4 ♘xe4
21.♗xe4 h6=** Gagarin-Zelcic, Zadar
2003;

A1211122) **14...♖fc8 15.♘a4** 15.a3
♗e7 16.♘e2 (16.♘a4!? also deserves
attention, for example 16...♛c7
17.♗c3 ♖ab8 18.♕d2↑ ♘e4 19.♗xe4
dxe4) 16...g6⇄. **15...♛b5 16.♗f1
♛b8 17.♗xb4 axb4 18.♘c5 ♛e5
19.♕d2 ♘e4 20.♘xe4 dxe4** A better
move would be 20...♛xe4!N 21.♗g2
♛e5 22.♕xb4 ♖cb8 23.♕d4 ♛xd4
24.exd4 ♖xb2=. **21.♕xb4 ♗xa2
22.♕b7±** Burmakin-Luther, Graz 2004.

A12112) **13.♖c1!**

White immediately demonstrates his
good appetite to the newcomer on c6,
and forces the opponent to focus on its
defence, preventing the active move
...♗g4. By the way, positions with
hanging pawns in the centre are highly
complex and many books have been
written on the subject. This book's limited space does not allow for a full explanation; nevertheless, it needs to be
emphasized that the pawn structure in
the centre is one of the main markers in
the assessment of the position. Still, as
we shall see in the further analyses, the
tiniest details may often affect this assessment.

We shall analyse the defensive move
13...♗d7, the tactically interesting
13...♘e4, and the new ideas 13...♖b8
and 13...♛b8, which is an attempt to
treat this position more actively and use
the potential dynamic power of the
hanging pawns. In the end, we will examine an analysis by grandmaster
Dragan Kosic which starts with the strategically paradoxical exchange of the
dark-squared bishops with 13...♗d2!?.

A121121) **13...♗d7** A natural reaction. Black defends his pawn, but this
defensive, passive strategy makes it easier for White to achieve his plan, whose
goal is to block the movements of the
opponent's hanging c6-pawn:

A1211211) **14.♗c3!?**

By attacking the opponent's knight on
f6 White provokes the exchange of the
dark-squared bishops, which, considering the pawn structure, clearly works in
his favour.

14...♗xc3 Also interesting is 14...♛d8!?.
Black makes this modest defensive move
with the intention to accomplish more
than with the exchange of the bishops.
15.♗d4! (Black's hanging pawns will
have difficulties when the white knight
is on a4, so White clears the path for it
via c3, centralizing his bishop at the
same time) 15...♖e8 (of course, Black
strengthens his position as well by acti-

vating his pieces and planning to centralize his knight on e4) 16.♘c3 ♖b8 17.♘a4 ♘e4 with a complex and unclear position.

Black has a strategic drawback in the sense of the hanging pawns, but White still has a rook on a1, which he would certainly like to see on the d-file.

15.♘xc3 ♖fb8 Black seeks play on the b-file. A move which also deserves attention is 15...♖fc8!? with the idea to activate the black bishop. **16.♘a4 ♕a7 17.♘c5 ♗e8 18.b3 ♘d7 19.♘d3** White does not need to simplify the position and make life easier for his opponent, since he has a greater choice of squares for his knight. **19...♘f6 20.♖d1 h6 21.♖ac1±** White has more active pieces and control over the dark squares in the centre, which is, by the way, characteristic of positions with hanging pawns, Kozul-Zelcic, Zagreb 2013;

A1211212) With **14.♘c3** White finishes his development, bearing in mind the thematic plan with ♘c3-a4-c5. **14...♖fe8** 14...♕a7 15.♘a4 ♖fb8 16.♗c3 ♗xc3 17.♕xc3 ♖b4 (17...h5!? 18.♘c5 h4) 18.b3±, Blagojevic-Winants, Istanbul 2012. **15.♘a4 ♕d8 16.♗xb4** This is a good and strategically interesting exchange. Black has even less chance to move his weak pawn from c6 due to the weakened

dark squares, whereas a new threat for him appears on the a-file in the form of the passed a-pawn. If 16.♘c5 ♗xc5 17.♕xc5 ♘e4=. **16...axb4 17.♘c5 ♗g4 18.h3 ♗e6 19.a3 bxa3 20.bxa3** The difference in the mobility of the a- and c-pawns is obvious. Also good is 20.♖xa3±. **20...♘d7 21.a4 ♘xc5 22.♕xc5**

White is better since the pawn on c6 remains blocked and weak, as opposed to the pawn on a4 which has good opportunities to advance, Koziak-Ovseevich, Mukachevo 2012.

A121122) **13...♘e4**

This is a risky move. Black sacrifices a pawn on e4 in order to achieve active play on the light squares. **14.♗xb4 axb4** Black is also worse after 14...♕xb4 15.a3 ♕b8 16.♗xe4 dxe4 17.♘c3± with a clearly disarrayed position. Now: **15.♕xc6** Better is 15.♗xe4

dxe4 16.♘d2!± and Black has permanent problems on the c-file. A weaker move is 16.♕xe4 ♗b7!♔

... with the idea ...c6-c5, with a good game for Black on the light squares; or 16.♕xc6?! ♕xc6 17.♖xc6 ♖d8∓ and the white queenside is stalemated. **15...♕xc6 16.♖xc6 ♗d7 17.♖c7** 17.♖c2 ♖xa2! (17...b3 18.♖c7 ♖xa2 19.♖a7∞) 18.♖xa2 b3=. **17...♖fd8 18.♗xe4** 18.a3!? deserves attention, for instance: 18...♗e6 19.♔f1 ♖a5 20.♔e2 with the idea ♘b1-d2. It is difficult for Black to show compensation for the pawn. **18...dxe4 19.♘d2 ♗h3 20.♖c2** 20.♘xe4?! ♖xa2∓. **20...♖d3** A better move is 20...♖a5♔. **21.♖e1?** 21.♘xe4±. **21...♖xa2 22.♘xe4 b3 23.♘c5 bxc2 24.♘xd3 ♖a8∓** and Black has more than enough compensation thanks to the dangerous c-pawn, Farago-Voiska, Porto San Giorgio 2008; A121123) **13...♖b8**

Black does not want to waste any time defending the hanging c6-pawn, but rather seeks counterplay along the b-file. White can react in several ways, although only one of them gives him a chance to fight for an advantage:

14.♘c3! White completes his development, intending to follow the recipe of the great strategist Aron Nimzowitsch, and permanently block the opponent's weak spot on the c-file with the standard manoeuvre ♘a4-c5. After 14.♗xb4 ♕xb4 15.b3 ♗e6 16.♘c3 ♖fc8= Black does not need to be concerned; and it is a waste of time to play 14.♗c3?! ♗xc3 15.♕xc3 ♕xb2 16.♕xb2 ♖xb2 17.♖xc6 ♘g4↑ and White is in trouble on the kingside. Finally, 14.♕xc6 ♕xc6 15.♖xc6 ♗xd2 16.♘xd2 ♖xb2 17.♘b3 ♘g4 gives mutual chances.

14...♕d8 15.♘a4 It is better to drive away the black bishop first with 15.a3! ♗d6 16.♘a4 ♗d7 17.♘c5 (with the idea ♘d7) 17...♗g4 18.b4 axb4 19.axb4±. White has a permanent initiative on the queenside, especially against the c6-pawn. **15...♘g4!** Black takes advantage of the fact that his opponent cannot capture on c6 to move the knight to e5. As we can see, one small detail can significantly influence the assessment of the variation which started with 15.♘a4. We will take a look at several logical options for White:

16.b3 16.♗xb4 ♖xb4 17.b3 ♘e5⇄; 16.♗c3 ♗xc3 17.♕xc3 ♖e8 18.♕xc6 d4!♔ 19.exd4 (19.♕c7=) 19...♘xf2 (also good is 19...♗b7 20.♕c2 ♗xg2 21.♔xg2 ♕d5+ 22.♔g1 ♕xd4♔ with the idea of ...♘e5) 20.♖e1= (20.♔xf2 ♕xd4+ 21.♔f1 ♗d7∓). **16...♘e5⇄** By moving the knight to e5, the dynamic power of Black's position has obviously increased. For example, **17.♗c3** 17.f4 does not lead anywhere either; after 17...♘g4 18.h3 ♘f6⇄ Black will have enough counterplay; a bad move is 17.h3? due to 17...♗xd2 18.♕xd2 ♗xh3!∓. **17...♗xc3 18.♕xc3 ♖e8 19.♘c5 ♖b4 20.♘d3 ♘xd3 21.♕xd3 ♗d7=**; his active pieces and the possibility to play ...a5-a4 provide Black with equal chances;

A121124) **13...♕b8**

Black uses tactical motifs to give his light-squared bishop a more active role, instead of the defensive one with ...♗d7.

A1211241) **14.♗xb4** Generally speaking, with this pawn structure in the centre, this exchange of light-squared bishops should benefit White because it weakens the opponent's dark squares, thus reducing his chances to eliminate his weaknesses with ...c6-c5. **14...axb4** By capturing with the a-pawn, Black intends to centralize his queen with ...♕b8-e5, although on the other hand he gives the opponent a potential passed a-pawn after a2-a4. 14...♕xb4 15.♘d2 ♗e6 16.♘b3 ♖fc8 17.♘c5↑. **15.♘d2** After 15.♕xc6 Black solves his problems with 15...♗f5! 16.♕c7 ♕xc7 17.♖xc7 ♖fc8 18.♖xc8+ ♖xc8 19.♘d2 ♖c2=. **15...♗e6!** The point of 13...♕b8. The light-squared bishop does not have to move to the passive d7-square, which is usually required for the knight in order to break the blockade of the critical c5-square and push the backward c-pawn. White can now only try and create a passed a-pawn with 16.a4 or first block the opponent's c-pawn: **16.♘b3** 16.a4 bxa3 17.bxa3 (in case of 17.♖xa3 ♖xa3 18.bxa3 c5⇄ Black solves his main strategic problem and has equal chances in the endgame) 17...♖c8⇄ and the c-pawn is mobile: 18.♘b3?! c5∓. **16...♖c8 17.♘c5 ♕e5** White has managed to achieve his strategic aim with the blockade of the pawn on c6, but in the meantime his opponent has also been working hard and has managed to maximally activate his troops, achieving an equal game. For instance: **18.a4 bxa3 19.bxa3** 19.♖xa3=. **19...♖a5!? 20.a4 ♗f5 21.♕c3 ♕xc3 22.♖xc3 ♖ca8=**

A1211242) **14.♕xc6 ♗f5!**

With the idea ...♖f8-c8. **15.♕c7** 15.♗xb4 axb4 16.♕c7 ♕xc7 17.♖xc7 ♖fc8 18.♖xc8+ ♖xc8 19.♘d2 ♖c2 20.♘b3 ♖xb2 21.♘d4 g6=; 15.♘c3? ♗d7−+ and the white queen has nowhere to go. **15...♗xd2 16.♘xd2 ♕xb2 17.♕c3** 17.♕f4?! ♖ac8↑. **17...♕xc3 18.♖xc3 ♖fc8 19.♖ac1** 19.♖xc8+ ♖xc8 20.♘b3 a4 21.♘d4 ♗d3=. **19...♖xc3 20.♖xc3 a4⇄** Would anyone make this seemingly meaningless move? However, the pawn on a4 provides Black with active play along the b-file. Another option is 20...g6 with an equal ending.

A1211243) **14.♘c3!** Just like in the line with 13...♖b8 this developing move gives White the best chances, for example: 14...♗e6 14...♗a6 15.a3 ♗e7 16.b3!± with the idea ♘c3-a4 (16.♘a4 ♗c4⇄) ; 14...♗g4 15.a3 ♗e7 16.e4± (16.♘a4 ♖c8⇄) **15.a3 ♗e7 16.♘e2** 16.♘a4 ♖c8⇄. **16...♖c8 17.♘f4↑** with a slightly better game for White;

A121125) **13...♗xd2** is a strategically undesirable exchange, but with the idea to move the opponent's knight away from the critical a4-square. **14.♘xd2** In the event of 14.♕xd2 ♗f5 15.♘c3 a4⇄ Black has a satisfactory game.

A1211251) **14...♗a6 15.♘b3±** and Black does not have enough play for the weaknesses along the c-file (15.♕xc6 ♕xb2=) ;

A1211252) **14...♗e6** Black moves the bishop to a more active square, reserving d7-square for his knight. Still, after **15.♘b3 ♖fc8** (15...♖ab8 16.♕xc6 ♕xc6 17.♖xc6 a4 18.♘c5±) **16.♕c5!** White has a better game than his opponent. (with 16.♘c5 ♘d7 17.♘xd7 ♗xd7= White keeps his minimal advantage thanks to his more compact pawn structure);

A1211253) **14...♖b8!?**

This is a proposition by grandmaster Dragan Kosic. Black does not want to assign his light-squared bishop with a passive role by moving it to d7. Now:

A12112531) After **15.♕xc6** awith **15...♕xc6 16.♖xc6 ♖xb2↑** Black is the first to strike due to his pressure on the second rank;

A12112532) **15.♘b3 a4!** Black insists on simplification and moves into the ending. If 15...♗d7 16.♘c5±. **16.♘c5 ♕xb2 17.♕xb2 ♖xb2 18.♘xa4 ♖b4 19.♘c5 ♗f5** With the idea ...♘d7 (19...♘d7?! 20.♘d3±). **20.a4 ♖a8 21.a5 ♘d7** Black continues the simplifications by exchanging the opponent's most dangerous blockade piece. **22.♗f1** 22.f3 ♖b5 23.♘xd7 ♗xd7 24.a6 ♖b6 25.♗f1 ♔f8 also with an equal ending. **22...♘xc5 23.♖xc5 ♗d7=** Black has virtually sailed into the harbour of the draw;

A12112533) **15.b3!** White defends the pawn on b2, with the intention to activate his knight on f3. After the forced **15...♗d7 16.♘f3** White has the better game because his knight actively comes into play via e5 or d4. For example: 16.♕c5 a4 17.bxa4 ♕xc5 18.♖xc5 ♖b2♙. **16...♖fc8** Or 16...♖fe8 17.♘d4 with a more promising game for White since he can easily strengthen the blockade of c5 with ♕c2-c5. **17.♘e5 ♕c7 18.♘xd7 ♕xd7 19.♖d1** Black is in an inferior position as it will be difficult for him to activate his position with ...c6-c5 or ...a5-a4.

A1212) **12...♕xc6!?N**

Black chooses to keep a weak pawn on d5 instead of c6. However, this position is less dynamic, especially if there are slim chances that Black can play ...d5-d4.

A12121) **13.♘c3! ♗e6 14.a3 ♗e7 15.♕d3** White has a more favourable game. His plan is simple: to move the rooks to the c- and d-file and attack Black's weak squares on d4 and b5 with his queen or knight;

A12122) In the event of the queen exchange **13.♕xc6 bxc6 14.♖c1 ♗d7** Black has an equal game, since he can prevent White's standard and most dangerous plan of moving the knight to a4. For instance: **15.a3** 15.♘c3 a4⇄. **15...♗e7 16.♘c3 a4** Another option is 16...♖fb8!?⇄. **17.e4 d4 18.♘e2 c5 19.e5 ♘g4 20.♗xa8 ♖xa8 21.♗f4** 21.f4 ♗b5∓. **21...g5♔** Black has less chances of achieving a draw after:

A122) **10...♘xd5 11.♘c3 ♘xc3** 11...♘c6 12.♘xc6 bxc6 13.0-0 ♗a6 14.♖fd1±. **12.bxc3 ♗e7 13.♖b1 ♕c7 14.0-0 ♘d7 15.♖fd1** White is doing better since the pawn on a5 significantly weakens Black's position on the queenside, Pelletier-Ovseevich, Basel 2011;

A123) Or **10...e5?!**

A risky pawn sacrifice, usually preferred by players who are more tactically inclined. However, White has a pleasant choice from among several continuations: **11.♘e2** It is also possible to return the pawn with 11.♘f3!? ♘xd5 12.a3! (12.♘xe5? ♘xe3−+) 12...♗d6 13.0-0±; or play 11.♘f5!?±. **11...♗g4 12.♘bc3 ♖c8 13.♕d1 ♘bd7** Black activates his troops and harmonizes his pieces, which provides him with certain compensation for the pawn. **14.h3** Better is 14.0-0 ♘c5 15.h3 ♗f5 16.a3 ♗xc3 17.♗xc3± when it will not be easy for Black to show enough compensation for the minus pawn in the centre. Now:

A1231) **14...♗h5 15.0-0 ♘c5 16.g4 ♗g6 17.♘g3±** and it is difficult for Black to prove compensation for the pawn, Tukmakov-Kachiani Gersinska, Lenk 2000;

A1232) The move **14...♗f5!?N** deserves attention, with the idea ...♗d3, for example **15.a3** 15.0-0 ♗d3 16.♖e1 ♗c4♔ (with the idea ...♘d7-c5) 17.e4?! ♗c5!∓; 15.e4?! ♘c5!∓. **15...♗xc3 16.♗xc3** 16.♘xc3?! ♗d3∓. **16...♘e4 17.g4 ♗g6 18.0-0 ♘xc3 19.♘xc3 ♕xb2=**

345

A2) 7...♘c6 Black wants to play the Smyslov/Taimanov variation. **8.0-0 dxc4 9.♕xc4 ♕d5** Because both sides have castled, White now has an additional possibility: **10.♖c1!?** For 10.♕d3 see Chapter 14.3. **10...♖d8 11.♕xd5 exd5 12.♗f4 ♗g4 13.e3 ♖d7 14.♘c3** Better is 14.a3 ♗e7 15.h3 ♗e6 16.♘c3 ♘h5 17.♗e5±. **14...♘h5 15.♘b5 ♘xf4 16.gxf4 f6 17.a3 ♗f8** And Black has equal chances with his bishop pair, Babula-Jirovsky, Zlin 1997;

A3) 7...dxc4

In this move order, where Black has spent time on castling, opening the centre with ...dxc4 loses its effectiveness, since after **8.♕xc4** Black has no promising plans left to emerge safely from the opening. For example: **8...♘c6** Or 8...b6. Here, also due to the time Black has spent on castling, he is late to act on the queenside, unlike in the line we saw under 7...b6: 9.♗xb4 ♗a6 10.♕b3 axb4 11.♕xb4± as Black does not have enough compensation for the pawn, Helmers-Rantanen, Lucerne 1982. It's also no good to sacrifice a pawn with 8...♕d5 9.♕xc7 ♘c6 10.♘c3 ♕c4 11.♕b6 ♖d8 12.e3 ♘d5 13.♕b5 ♕xb5 14.♘xb5± and Black has absolutely nothing to show for the pawn, Short-Slavin, Gibraltar 2011. **9.♘c3!** Why allow the system of Vassily Smyslov

when White has this simple developing move with which he establishes control of the critical e4- and d5-squares? True, Black could capture this knight with ...♗xc3, but this would lead to other problems and another type of advantage for White. For instance:

A31) 9...♘d5 10.a3 10.0-0±. **10...♘xc3** and now in the game Vidit-Ageichenko, Moscow 2012, with **11.axb4 ♘e4 12.bxa5 ♘xd2 13.♘xd2** White could have obtained an easy game and better chances in the ending;

A32) 9...♖e8 With the idea ...e6-e5. **10.0-0 e5 11.dxe5 ♘xe5 12.♘xe5 ♖xe5 13.♗e3±** and White's pieces are better coordinated (13.♗f4 ♖c5⇄);

A33) 9...e5?!

10.d5?! A better move is 10.dxe5!N ♘g4 11.♗f4±. **10...♗xc3 11.♗xc3 ♕xd5 12.♕xd5** and the opponents reached a draw in the game Blagojevic-Pikula, Cetinje 2013, because after **12...♘xd5 13.♘xe5 ♘xc3 14.♘xc6 bxc6 15.bxc3 ♖b8=** Black is active enough for a draw;

A34) 9...♘e7 10.♘e5 ♘fd5 11.a3 ♗d6 12.♘e4 White moves into the centre although this way he is blocking the path for his e-pawn. The move 12.♘b5!?N deserves attention, for example 12...♗xe5 (12...b6? 13.e4±) 13.dxe5 ♗d7 14.♘d4!? and White has better chances thanks to his bishop pair. **12...b6 13.♕c2 h6 14.0-0 ♗a6 15.♖fe1 ♖c8 16.♘c6 ♘xc6 17.♕xc6 ♕e8 18.♕xe8 ♖fxe8** and the opponents agreed a draw in this approximately equal position, Piket-Yermolinsky, Groningen 1998.

A4) **7...♘e4** This idea, where Black invests too much time in order to capture the bishop pair or force White to exchange the dark-squared bishops on b4, we have also seen in Chapter 14.3 under 6.♗g2 ♘e4. **8.♗xb4** White refuses to grant Black the bishop pair, so he opts for this exchange which is, however, rarely useful to him. White has better chances for an advantage after the natural 8.0-0± ♘xd2 9.♘bxd2, see Chapter 14.3. **8...axb4 9.♘e5** A safer option is 9.♘bd2. **9...f6** A better option is 9...c5!N. **10.♘d3 ♘c6 11.e3 f5 12.0-0 b3** 12...♕e7 13.cxd5 exd5 14.♘d2± with a more agreeable position for White. **13.♕xb3 ♘a5 14.♕c2 dxc4 15.♘c1±** With the following moves ♘d2 and ♘e2 White will have a more natural and more active position, Stohl-Murdzia, Czechia 2010;

A5) **7...c6** Usually, after **8.0-0 ♘bd7 9.♗f4 ♗e7** this transmutes into positions which we have explained in Chapter 14.3.

B) **6...c5**

7.a3 7.cxd5! cxd4 8.♘xd4 0-0 9.♗g2 is covered under 6...0-0. The text favours the opponent, since after **7...♗xd2+ 8.♘bxd2 cxd4 9.cxd5 exd5 10.♘xd4 0-0 11.♗g2 ♕b6 12.♘2f3 ♘c6⇄** White's capture on c6 is not a good idea because of the fact that the b-file has been weakened with a2-a3. In the following game, White played **13.♕b3** and after **13...♖a6** (13...♕xb3=) **14.♕xb6?!** (better is 14.♕d3, leaving the rook on a6, for example 14...♕xb2 (14...♖e8=) 15.♖b1 ♕a2 16.0-0⩲ and White has enough compensation for the pawn, but he only plays for a draw) **14...♖xb6 15.b3 ♗g4 16.♖b1 ♘e4↑** Black took the initiative in Georgiev-Khenkin, Serbia 2008;

C) **6...♘c6** Black wants to play the Smyslov/Taimanov system with ...dxc4 and ...♕d5, which we covered in Chapter 14.3. In this particular position we have an independent line if White plays **7.a3!?**, a move we have seen with various move orders. White wants his opponent's bishop on b4 to declare itself. For 7.♗g2 dxc4 8.♕xc4 ♕d5 see Chapter 14.3.

Obviously, there are three possibilities now: moving the bishop to e7, or to d6, or exchanging it with 7...♗xd2:

C1) **7...♗e7!**

8.♗g2

C11) **8...dxc4** Black opens the diagonal to the dangerous Catalan bishop but he also activates his queen on d5, which otherwise has no prospects with the knight on c6. **9.♕xc4 ♕d5 10.♕d3** Now Black can again opt for the exchange of queens with ...♕e4 or play more seriously with the pseudo-active ...♕f5 or ...♕h5:

C111) **10...♕e4** The principled move. **11.♕xe4 ♘xe4 12.♗f4 ♗d6 13.♘e5** After 13.♗e3 ♘f6 14.♘c3 ♗d7 15.♗d2 a4 16.e4 e5⇄ by transposition we have entered the game Payen-Istratescu, Dieppe 2012, Chapter 14.3. Now the best reply is **13...♘xd4!?N** 13...♗xe5 14.dxe5 ♘c5 15.♘d2± and Black will have serious problems on the queenside, Kallai-Iskov, West Berlin 1987. **14.♗xe4 f5 15.♗d3 g5 16.♘d2** 16.♗xg5 ♗xe5 17.♘d2 ♗d7⇄. **16...gxf4 17.gxf4 ♗xe5 18.fxe5 ♗d7 19.♖g1 ♗c6⇄** and Black levels the odds;

C112) **10...♕f5 11.♕xf5 exf5 12.♘c3 ♗e6 13.♗f4** 13.♘b5 0-0-0 14.♖c1 ♖d5⇄. **13...0-0-0** with chances for both sides, Cserna-Sydor, Ruse 1984;

C113) **10...0-0 11.♘c3 ♕h5 12.0-0 ♖d8 13.♕c4 ♗d7 14.♖fe1 ♘d5 15.e4 ♘b6 16.♕d3 a4 17.h3±** Ribli-Smyslov, London 1983.

C12) After **8...0-0 9.0-0** it is not easy for Black to find a satisfactory plan: **9...a4 10.♖d1** Or 10.cxd5 exd5 11.♘c3 ♗d7 12.♗f4±, Deglmann-Taimanov, Fürth 2000. **10...♗d7 11.♗e1 dxc4 12.♘e5** 12.♕xc4 ♘a5 13.♗xa5 ♖xa5 14.♘c3 ♗c6∞. **12...♘xe5 13.dxe5 ♘d5 14.♕xc4 ♕b8** 14...c5!?N deserves attention, for instance: 15.♗xd5 b5 16.♕f4 exd5 17.♖xd5 ♕c8⧯) **15.♘c3±** Vernay-Sulava, France 2008;

C13) **8...♘e4 9.♗f4 a4 10.♘c3 ♘xc3 11.♕xc3 ♖a6 12.0-0 ♖b6 13.♖fd1 0-0 14.♖ab1 ♗d7 15.♕c2±** with a more active position for White.

C2) **7...♗d6!?**

A rarely used but active move, with the standard idea ...dxc4 and ...e6-e5. Black also provokes the opponent to play c4-c5, with which White could gain space with tempo, but this would also keep the central diagonal closed for his bishop on g2.

C21) **8.♗g2 0-0 9.0-0 dxc4 10.♕xc4 e5 11.d5 ♘e7 12.♘c3** 12.e4 c6 13.dxc6 ♗e6 14.♕e2 ♘xc6⇄. **12...c6** Another less than satisfactory idea is 12...b6 13.♖fe1 ♗a6 14.♕b3 ♘d7 15.♕c2±. **13.dxc6 bxc6 14.♗g5** White has fewer weaknesses and a better game, Pinter-Raaste, Helsinki 1983;

C22) After **8.c5 ♗e7** Black gets the option of counterplay on the queenside with ...b7-b6 or he could capture the e4-square in the spirit of the Dutch Defence. For example: **9.♗g2 0-0**

C221) **10.0-0 ♘e4!** Since the plan with ...b7-b6 is not effective here, Black captures the e4-square with a view to creating an arrangement in the spirit of the Dutch Defence and activating the light-squared bishop with ...♗c8-d7-h5. **11.♖d1** After 11.♘c3 f5

12.♗f4 ♗d7∞ Black has an opportunity to strengthen his position with ...♗f6 and ...♗d7-e8-h5. **11...♗d7 12.♘c3 f5⇄** Ftacnik-Cvetkovic, Strbske Pleso 1978;

C222) After **10.♘c3** in the game Gheorghiu-Muse, Hamburg 1984, Black could have taken the initiative with **10...b6!N 11.cxb6 cxb6** when it would be difficult for White to find a good plan against ...♗a6 and ...♖c8. For instance: **12.♕a4** 12.♘a4 ♗d7 13.0-0 ♖c8↑ and Black is the first to take action; 12.0-0 ♗a6↑ with the idea ...♖c8. **12...♕d7!?∞** with the idea ...♗a6.

C3) **7...♗xd2+** With a knight on c6 and without a dark-squared bishop, Black will lose his chances of getting active play. **8.♘bxd2 0-0 9.♗g2 ♘e7 10.0-0 c6 11.b4±** With an active position and a space advantage. **11...axb4?! 12.axb4 ♖xa1 13.♖xa1 dxc4 14.♕xc4 ♘ed5 15.♘e5 ♗d7 16.♘b3 ♕b8 17.♘c5±** with a clear strategic advantage for White, Moranda-Jedynak, Krakow 2013.

D) **6...c6 7.♗g2 b6!?** Black is rushing into the well-known arrangement in the Closed Catalan with ...♗a6 and ...♘bd7. By the way, this variation, which was often used by grandmaster Alexander Alexandrov, has almost disappeared from use nowadays, among other things because with an early ...b7-b6 Black loses the additional option of a transition into the Dutch Stonewall, which will be discussed a bit further on. 7...0-0 is covered under 7...c7-c6. **8.0-0**

D1) **8...♗a6**

D11) **9.♗xb4!** This exchange usually works in Black's favour, but here we have a position where this is not the case.

White exchanges the bishops because he wants to defend the pawn on c4 with a knight on d2, finishing the development of his queenside, and he will solve the problem on the a-file with the simple a2-a3.

Now everything seems to be forced: **9...axb4 10.♘bd2 ♘bd7 11.a3** White seizes the opportunity to take control of the a-file. **11...bxa3 12.♖xa3 ♗b7 13.♖fa1 ♖xa3 14.♖xa3 0-0 15.b4!** With simple moves, White activates the rook on the a-file and gives himself some breathing room by creating better prospects on the queenside. **15...♕c7 16.c5** The thematic 16.e4!? is also good, for example: 16...♘xe4 17.♘xe4 dxe4 18.♘g5 c5 19.dxc5 bxc5 20.b5 h6 21.♘xe4±. **16...♖a8 17.♖xa8+ ♗xa8 18.♕a4** White has better chances after 18.e4! ♘xe4 19.♘xe4 dxe4 20.♕xe4±. **18...♗b7 19.e3 ♕b8 20.♘b3 ♕a8 21.♕xa8+ ♗xa8=** White has a small space advantage and more active pieces, however, since the position is quite simplified, Black has chances to achieve a draw, Psakhis-Alexandrov, Polanica Zdroj 1997;

D12) In case of **9.b3** Black has the time to realize his plan and create his favourite set-up: **9...0-0 10.♖d1 ♘bd7 11.♗f4 ♖c8** By provoking the opponent's move b2-b3, Black has managed to complete his development first, and with his favourite set-up as well. **12.♘bd2**

12...♘h5 Another good option is 12...c5!?⇄. **13.♗g5 f6 14.♗e3 f5 15.a3 ♗d6∞** with a good and active position for Black, Döttling-Alexandrov, Mainz 2006.

D2) It is also possible to play **8...0-0**

... although White now has a greater choice of solid continuations: 8.♗f4 and 8.♗g5, threatening to shut off the black bishop with c4-c5, or exchanging the dark-squared bishop with 8.♗xb4:

D21) 9.♗f4

D211) 9...♗d6 10.♗xd6 ♕xd6 11.♘bd2 ♗a6 12.♖ac1 ♘bd7 13.e4 ♘xe4 14.♘xe4 dxe4 15.♕xe4 c5 16.♖fd1 ♖ad8 17.dxc5 ♕xc5 18.b3± White has a small but stable advantage, characteristic for this type of ending with the pawn majority on the

queenside, Matlakov-Ionov, St Petersburg 2010;

D212) 9...♗a6 10.c5! With the idea a2-a3 **10...a4 11.♗d6** Also good is 11.a3 ♗a5 12.cxb6 ♕xb6 (12...♗xb6 13.♘c3±) 13.♘c3 ♗xc3 14.bxc3±. White's dark-squared bishop ensures a long-term initiative. **11...♖e8 12.♕xa4 bxc5 13.dxc5!** 13.♗xc5 ♗xc5 14.dxc5 ♘bd7 15.♕c2 ♘e4∓ Vaulin-Alexandrov, Sochi 1997. **13...♕a5 14.♕xa5** Better is 14.♕c2!N ♘e4 15.a3 ♗xc5 16.b4 ♗xf2+ 17.♖xf2 ♕d8 18.♗c5± when Black does not have enough compensation for the lost material. **14...♗xa5⧲** Krasenkow-Moldobaev, Blagoveschensk 1988.

D213) 9...♗e7 Contrary to similar positions covered in Chapter 14.3, Black here plays ...b7-b6 instead of ...♘d7. His idea is obviously to activate his light-squared bishop as soon as possible on a6 or b7, although this would rule out the options ...♘h5!? and ...♘e4!?, with which he could make a transition into a Dutch Stonewall type position. **10.♖d1 ♗a6 11.♘e5 ♘fd7 12.cxd5 cxd5** 12...♘xe5? 13.d6!±. **13.e4 ♘xe5 14.♗xe5** 14.exd5 ♘g6 15.d6±. **14...♗b7 15.♘c3** A better move would be 15.exd5!? ♗xd5 16.♗xd5 ♕xd5 17.♘c3 ♕b7 18.d5 ♘d7 19.♗d4± and it is not easy for Black to stabilize his position. **15...♘c6 16.exd5 ♘b4 17.♕b3 ♘xd5 18.♘xd5 ♗xd5 19.♗xd5 a4 20.♕f3 ♕xd5 21.♕xd5 exd5=** Cernousek-Cvek, Slovakia 2011.

D22) 9.♗g5 With the idea c4-c5. **9...♗e7 10.♘bd2 ♗a6 11.♖fe1** Another good move is 11.♘e5 ♘fd7 12.♗xe7 ♕xe7 13.♘d3±. **11...♘bd7 12.e4 ♖c8 13.♖ad1±** Shipov-Mochalov, Minsk 1993;

D23) Exchanging with **9.♗xb4** is also possible, although after **9...axb4 10.♘bd2 ♗b7**, by Black's cunning move order, White's move a2-a3 is stripped of its value and the thematic threat e2-e4 is neutralized. **11.e4**

11...♘bd7 A better option is 11...dxe4!N 12.♘xe4 c5⇄. **12.cxd5 exd5** 12...cxd5 13.e5 ♘e4 14.♖fc1±. **13.exd5 ♘xd5 14.♖fe1 ♘7f6 15.♘e5 ♖c8 16.♕b3 ♖c7 17.♘d3 c5 18.dxc5 bxc5 19.♘c4** and White exerts a lot of pressure, Georgiev-Ermenkov, Budapest 1993.

7.♕xc4

Of course, White does not wish to keep the opponent's pawn on c4 even for another move. In fact, this is why he opted for the early 7.♕c2.

For 7.♗g2 see Chapter 14.3.

7...b6!

Considering that there are still no threats on the long h1-a8 diagonal,

Black immediately moves into action along the diagonal f1-a6. By the way, this active plan is probably Black's best chance to level the chances and emerge successfully from the opening.

For 7...♘c6 8.♘c3!± (for 8.♗g2 ♕d5 see Chapter 14.3) 8...0-0 9.♗g2 see 6...0-0.

8.♗g2

A weaker move is 8.♗xb4 ♗a6 9.♕b3 (9.♕c2 axb4 10.♗g2 0-0 is covered under 10.♗b4) 9...axb4 10.♕xb4 ♘c6 11.♕c3 ♗b7 12.e3 ♘e4 13.♕b3 (or 13.♕c2 ♕d5∓) 13...♘a5 14.♕a4+ ♔f8 15.♕d1 ♕d5∓. Black has more than enough compensation for the pawn because of the threat 16...♘b3 and White's weakness on the diagonal h1-a8.

8...♗a6!

This is a normal scenario in this type of position. Black wants to obtain counterplay on the diagonal f1-a6.

Black cannot be satisfied with just opposing the Catalan bishop with **8...♗b7** due to **9.♗xb4 axb4 10.0-0** (nothing is achieved by 10.♕xb4 ♘c6 11.♕c4 ♘xd4=) **10...♘a6 11.♘bd2** (a weaker move is 11.a3 ♗d5 12.♕d3 0-0 13.♘bd2 bxa3 14.bxa3∞. In order to have an advantage in the centre, White disrupts his pawn structure on the queenside, Landa-Schneider, Germany

2008) **11...0-0 12.♖fd1 ♕e7 13.♘e5 ♗xg2 14.♔xg2 c5 15.♕b5** and White has the upper hand in the ending, Ribli-Lekic, Neum 2004.

9.♕c2 0-0

Black has calmly castled, leaving it to the opponent to find a solution, in addition to dealing with the pressure from the black light-squared bishop on the e2-pawn. In practice, there are three ideas to solve this problem: 10.a3, 10.♗xb4 and 10.♘c3.

Not 9...♘bd7?! 10.♘e5±.

10.a3

A) **10.♗xb4** After this rare exchange, Black easily fulfills his objectives in the opening and obtains active play: **10...axb4 11.0-0 ♗b7 12.♘bd2 ♕e7 13.e4 ♖a7 14.♖fe1 ♖c8=** All black pieces are functioning, Parker-Speelman, Birmingham 2001;

B) **10.♘c3** This natural move also accomplishes nothing. **10...♗b7** A safer move is 10...♘bd7!?N 11.0-0 ♖c8= with the idea ...c7-c5. **11.0-0 ♗xc3 12.♗xc3** A move that deserves attention is 12.♕xc3!? ♘e4 13.♕c2 ♘xd2 14.♕xd2 ♘d7 15.♖fd1 ♖c8 16.♖ac1 ♕e7 17.♕f4 c5 18.dxc5 ♘xc5 19.♘e5↑. **12...♗e4 13.♕d2 ♘c6 14.♖fd1 ♕d5 15.♕f4 ♖ac8 16.♘e1?!** Better is 16.♗f1 ♗xf3 17.♕xf3 ♕xf3 18.exf3 ♘d5=. **16...♗xg2 17.♘xg2**

♖fd8 **18.♖d2 ♕e4** A better move is 18...b5!∓ with the idea 19.b3? b4 20.♗b2 e5∓. **19.f3 ♕xf4 20.♘xf4=** Dizdarevic-Vukovic, Kladovo 1991.

10...♗xd2+

An option that deserves attention is **10...♗e7!?N 11.♘c3 ♘bd7 12.0-0 ♖c8** with the idea ... c7-c5, with a rich and highly complex position. Here is a possible variation: **13.♖ad1 c5 14.♗f4 cxd4 15.♖xd4** 15.♘xd4?! e5 16.♘c6 ♖xc6 17.♗xc6 exf4∓. **15...♗c5 16.♖d2 ♕e7 17.♖fd1 ♖fd8 18.♕a4 h6∞**

11.♘bxd2!?N

The knight's recapture makes castling difficult as e2 is hanging, but the opponent's ...c7-c5 is also prevented.

After **11.♕xd2 ♘bd7 12.♘c3** it is easy for Black to realize **12...c5** and after **13.0-0 ♖c8** the opponents quickly agreed a draw in a clearly equal position in Wojtkiewicz-Gulko, San Diego 2004. After the text Black has two ways to continue: with the prophylactic and complex 11...♖a7 with the idea ...c7-c5, or the straightforward 11...♘d7.

11...♖a7!?

Black moves the rook away from the endangered diagonal and plans the relieving ...c7-c5 and ...♖c7.

With **11...♘bd7** Black is the first to finish his development, with the intention to continue with ...c7-c5 and finish the opening successfully. **12.♘e5!** There is no better option. **12...♘xe5 13.dxe5 ♘d5 14.♘e4** It seems as if White has some initiative, since Black's pawn majority on the queenside is hampered due to the potential weakness of the d6-square. Still, it is unclear what White can do to improve his position, while Black can realize his plan with play along the d-file. Here is another variation suggested by a Bogo-Indian aficionado, grandmaster Dragan Kosic: **14...♕e7 15.0-0 ♖fd8 16.♖fd1 h6** Black has the intention to play ...♕e8 and ...♘e7 so he protects the critical g5-square from the invasion of the opponent's knight. **17.♖d2** 17.♖d4 ♖d7 18.♖ad1 ♖ad8∞. **17...♖ac8 18.♖ad1 ♕e8 19.e3 ♗b5∞** With the idea ...♘e7 and simplification on the d-file.

After the text White has three real continuations: 12.♘c4, 12.♖c1 and 12.♖d1. Analyses show that in all these cases Black achieves a satisfactory, approximately equal game since he has time to develop and realize the thematic ...c7-c5 push.

12.♘c4

White makes his castling possible and prevents the opponent's ...c7-c5, but he loses control of the e4-square.

A) **12.♖c1 c5 13.dxc5 ♖c7 14.♘e4** If 14.b4 bxc5 15.bxc5 ♕e7 Black will return the pawn, with equal chances. **14...♘xe4 15.♕xe4 ♖xc5 16.♖xc5 bxc5 17.0-0 h6!? 18.♖c1** 18.♘e5 ♕d2=. **18...♘d7** with an equal ending. In compensation for his separated queenside pawns, Black has counterplay against the b2- and e2-pawns;

B) **12.♖d1 c5 13.dxc5 ♖c7 14.♘e4 ♕e7 15.♘fg5 ♘xe4 16.♘xe4 f5!?**

17.♘c3 ♕xc5 18.0-0 ♘d7∞ Black has finished his development and has a satisfactory game.

12...♗b7

Black retreats his bishop to the h1-a8 diagonal, because apart from exerting control on the e4-square, Black indirectly threatens the pawn on d4.

13.♘ce5

A gambit is also possible: 13.0-0 ♗xf3 14.♗xf3 b5!? 15.♘e5 ♕xd4 16.♘d3≌, but this suffices only for a draw.

13...♗e4 14.♕c3 c5 15.0-0

15.dxc5 ♖c7 16.b4 axb4 17.axb4 bxc5 18.bxc5 ♕d5 and Black returns the pawn, with equal chances.

15...♖c7 16.♖ac1 ♘bd7=

And Black's opening has been successful; chances are level.

Conclusion

As we have seen in this chapter, with an early 6.♕c2 White wishes to retake the pawn on c4, but this gives Black an opportunity to attack the centre with 6...c5 or first 6...0-0 and then ...c7-c5. Still, we recommend as the most promising plan for Black 6...dxc4 and then 7.♕xc4 b6!, with fast development of the queenside. Black can activate the bishop with tempo on the diagonal f1-a6. There are few practical games, but nevertheless we can see, based on the work in previous chapters, that Black is able to finish his development without any problems and realize the typical break ...c7-c5, which provides him with equal chances in the end.

Exercises

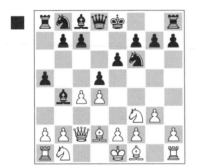

14.4 (1) Find the best plan.
(solution on page 451)

14.4 (2) Find the plan.
(solution on page 451)

14.4 (3) Find the plan.
(solution on page 451)

Part II: 3.♘d2

Chapter 15

3...♘f6 4.♘f3 0-0

If he wants to strive for a more complex game, White plays 3.♘d2. The knight is not on the natural c3-square, but White maintains the option of gaining the bishop pair with the move a2-a3, and, in the long term, maintaining a slight advantage.

In this move order we recommend 3...♘f6 and transferring to the regular Bogo-Indian. Instead of the standard surrender of the bishop, after 5.a3, we will cover the variation which, quite understandably, has increased in popularity for the last couple of years. Namely, after 5.a3, Black withdraws his bishop to e7, allowing White to grasp a full pawn centre. Things aren't that simple, however. Black can undermine White's centre, and the position of the knight on d2 is certainly not the most fortunate.

This position has similarities with the Morozevich Variation in the Tarrasch Variation of the French Defence.

Chapter 15.1

Deviations

1.d4 e6 2.c4 ♝b4+ 3.♘d2

Certainly, with such a specific move order, other possibilities, such as 3...b6, 3...c5, 3...f5 or 3...d5 also deserve our attention, though they are not the subject of this book. Let's take a look at some examples from recent times.

A) **3...b6 4.a3 ♝xd2+ 5.♕xd2 ♝b7 6.♘f3 f5** Thanks to this move order, Black has the opportunity to further strengthen his control of the e4-square. **7.g3 ♘f6 8.♝g2 0-0 9.0-0 ♕e8 10.b4 d6 11.♝b2 ♘bd7 12.♖ac1 ♝e4 13.a4 a5 14.b5 ♕h5 15.♝a3 ♝b7 16.♕c2 ♝e4 17.♕d2 ♝b7**

18.♕c2 18.♕e3!? certainly deserves attention, with some advantage for White. The idea is 18...♘e4 19.♘d2 ♘df6 20.f3 ♘xd2 21.♕xd2±. **18...f4 19.gxf4 ♝xf3 20.♝xf3 ♘g4 21.♝xg4 ♕xg4+ 22.♔h1 ♕xf4** with complex play and excellent chances for Black, Gelfand-Grischuk, Paris 2013;

B) **3...c5 4.a3 ♝xd2+ 5.♕xd2 cxd4 6.♘f3 ♘f6 7.♘xd4** Moving into the standard Bogo-Indian, this is one of the standard continuations for Black. **7...0-0 8.e3 d5 9.cxd5 ♕xd5 10.♘b5 ♕c6 11.f3 e5 12.e4 a6 13.♘c3 ♝e6 14.♕f2 ♝b3 15.♝e2 ♕e6 16.0-0 ♘c6 17.♝e3 ♖fd8 18.♝d1 h6 19.♖c1 ♖d3 20.♝e2 ♖d7 21.♝d1 ♖d3 22.♝e2 ♖d7 23.♝d1 ½-½** Gelfand-Andreikin, Moscow 2013;

C) With **3...f5** Black gains additional control over the e4-square: **4.g3 ♘f6 5.♗g2 0-0 6.♘f3 a5 7.0-0 b6 8.♘e5 ♖a7 9.♘d3 ♗xd2 10.♕xd2 ♗b7 11.♗xb7 ♖xb7 12.b3 ♕e7 13.♗b2 d6 14.d5 e5 15.f4 e4 16.♘e1 ♖f7 17.♘c2** White's advantage is obvious. The position is open, White's dark-squared bishop dominates the board, with ideal coordination of the other pieces. **17...c5 18.dxc6 ♘xc6 19.♘e3 ♘e8 20.a4 ♘b4 21.♖ad1±** P.H. Nielsen-Nikolic, Barcelona 2012;

D) **3...d5**

D1) **4.♘f3 ♘f6**, transferring into standard positions, is a continuation which doesn't belong to the topic of this book;

D2) **4.a3 ♗e7** Giving up the bishop pair at this early stage with 4...♗xd2+, with a defined pawn structure in the centre, doesn't promise Black equality. Normally, when one gives up one's dark-squared bishop, as in this case, it is better to place the pawns on the dark squares, compensating for the weaknesses of these squares. After 5.♗xd2 ♘f6 6.♘f3 0-0 7.♕c2 ♘e4 8.♗f4! c6 9.e3 ♘d7 10.♗d3 f5 11.h3 ♕f6 12.g4! g6 13.g5 ♕e7 14.h4, with complete domination on the dark squares and positional control all over the board, White's initiative is unstoppable:

14...♘d6 15.cxd5 exd5 16.h5 ♖f7 17.hxg6 hxg6 18.♖h6 1-0 (38) Cebalo-Etmans, San Bernardino 1989. **5.e4 dxe4 6.♘xe4 ♘f6 7.♘c3 c5** and now:

D21) **8.♗f4**

8...0-0 At this point Black could have played a more active move: 8...cxd4! with the idea 9.♘b5 0-0 10.♘c7 e5! 11.♗xe5 ♘c6 12.♗g3 ♖b8 13.♘b5 ♕a5+ 14.b4 ♘xb4→. **9.dxc5 ♗xc5 10.♘f3 ♘c6 11.♗e2 ♕e7 12.0-0 ♖d8 13.♕c2 b6 14.♖ad1 ♗b7 15.b4 e5 16.♗g5 ♘d4 17.♘xd4 ♗xd4 18.♘b5 h6 19.♗h4 g5 20.♗g3 ♘e4** with an unclear position, Rodshtein-Kogan, Ashdod 2006;

D22) **8.♘f3 cxd4 9.♘xd4** 9.♕xd4 0-0 10.♕xd8 ♖xd8 11.♗f4 ♘c6 12.♗e2 b6 13.0-0 ♗b7 14.♖fd1 h6 15.h3 g5 16.♗e3 with equal chances in the semi-endgame, Karpov-Galego, Seixal 2001. **9...♘c6 10.♗e3 ♘xd4 11.♕xd4 ♕xd4 12.♗xd4 ♗d7 13.♗e2 0-0 14.0-0 ♖fd8 15.♖fd1 ♗c6 16.♗e3 ♘e4 17.♘xe4 ♗xe4 18.f3 ♗c2 19.♖xd8+ ♖xd8** After these massive exchanges the game is close to a draw, Jussupow-Istratescu, Switzerland 2013.

3...♘f6 4.♘f3 0-0

Of course, Black has other continuations, such as 4...b6, 4...d5, and 4...c5. However, the variation covered in this book is the one we honestly recommend, with plenty of dynamic and active play for Black. Among other things, the move order 1.d4 e6 is primarily suitable for players of the French Defence, and the position in the main line of the Bogo-Indian has a lot of similarities with the Tarrasch Variation.

5.e3

A) **5.♕c2 c5 6.dxc5 ♗xc5 7.a3 b6 8.b4 ♗e7 9.♗b2 d6 10.g4!?**

An aggressive move, typical for grandmaster Shakhriyar Mamedyarov, before Black sets up a typical Hedgehog position. **10...♗b7 11.g5 ♘h5 12.e3 a5 13.♖d1 axb4 14.axb4 ♘d7** The computer, of course, recommends capturing the pawn: 14...♘xg5 15.♘e4 ♗f6 16.♘xf6+ ♘xf6 17.♘g5 ♘bd7 18.♖g1 e5 19.♗d3 g6 20.h4 with compensation for the pawn and an unpleasant initiative for White. **15.♖g1 ♕c7 16.♗d3 g6 17.♔e2 ♖fc8 18.♖a1 ♗f8 19.♖xa8 ♗xa8 20.♖a1** with a complex middlegame, Mamedyarov-Dominguez Perez, London 2012;

B) **5.g3 b6** 5...d5 6.♗g2 b6 transposes into the line with 5...b6 and ...d7-d5 (B2 below). **6.♗g2**

B1) **6...♗b7 7.0-0 c5** and now:

B11) **8.a3 ♗xd2 9.♕xd2 d5 10.cxd5 ♗xd5 11.dxc5 bxc5 12.b4 ♘bd7 13.♕e3 cxb4 14.axb4 a5 15.b5**

15...♘b6 15...♕b8!? 16.♗a3 ♖c8 with unclear play. **16.♕d4 ♘c4 17.♗f4 ♕e7 18.b6** with White's advantage, Ponomariov-Fedorchuk, Kiev 2012;

B12) The gambit move **8.d5!?** deserves attention:

8...exd5 9.♘h4 ♗xd2?! Or 9...♖e8!? 10.♘f5 (10.cxd5 ♗xd5 11.♗xd5 ♘xd5 12.♘c4) 10...♗a6 with complicated play. **10.♗xd2 ♘e4 11.cxd5 ♖e8?! 12.♗f4 d6 13.♕d3 ♗a6 14.♕c2 ♘f6 15.♘f5 ♖xe2 16.♕c3 ♘bd7 17.♖fe1!** with a decisive initiative for White, Ivanisevic-Antic, Kragujevac 2009;

B2) **6...d5 7.0-0 ♗b7 8.cxd5 exd5 9.♘e5 ♖e8 10.♘df3 ♘e4 11.♗f4 ♗d6** 11...♗f8 12.♕a4 f6 13.♘d3 c5 14.dxc5 bxc5 15.♘d2 ♕d7 (15...♘xd2 16.♗xd2 ♖xe2 17.♕d1 ♖e6 18.♘f4 ♖d6 19.♖e1⩲) 16.♕c2 ♘xd2 17.♗xd2 ♘a6 18.e3 ♔h8 19.♖fe1 ♖ac8 20.♖ad1 with complications, Yakovenko-Alexeev, Moscow 2012. **12.♖c1 c5 13.dxc5 bxc5 14.♘d3 ♘a6 15.♘d2 ♗f8 16.♘xe4 dxe4 17.♗e3 ♕b6 18.♘f4 ♖ad8 19.♕b3 g6** with an unclear position, Ivanisevic-Nikolic, Banja Koviljaca 2013.

5...b6

5...d5 6.a3 ♗e7 is partially covered under 5.a3.

6.♗d3 ♗b7 7.0-0

7.a3 ♗xd2+ 8.♕xd2 d6 9.♕c2 c5 10.dxc5 dxc5 11.b3 ♕e7 12.♗b2 a5 13.0-0 ♘bd7 14.♕c3 ♖fd8 15.♖fd1 ♘e8 16.♕c2 ♘f8 17.a4 f6 with near equality, Grischenko-Romanov, Sochi 2012.

7...d5

7...c5 8.a3 ♗xd2 9.♗xd2 d6 10.b4 ♘bd7 11.♗c3 ♕e7 12.dxc5 dxc5 13.♗e2?!

Unnecessarily passive play – 13.♕c2!? deserves attention, for example 13...♖fd8 with complications typical for this type of position. White has the bishop pair; in return, Black is trying to block the position and especially gain control of the dark squares and limit the white dark-squared bishop with the e5/f6 pawn structure. 13...♘e4 14.♗b2 ♖fd8 15.♕b3 ♘df6 16.♖ad1 ♖xd1 17.♖xd1 ♖d8 18.h3 h6 19.♗c2 with ideal control of the centre by Black, Likavsky-Jobava, Austria 2012.

8.cxd5 exd5 9.b3 ♗d6 10.♗b2 ♕e7 11.♘e5 c5 12.f4 ♘c6 13.♖c1 ♖ac8 14.♕f3 cxd4 15.exd4 ♗a3 16.♖ce1 ♘xe5 17.♖xe5 ♕b4 18.♗xa3 ♕xa3

And Black takes the initiative, Shengelia-Georgiev, Vienna 2012.

Conclusion

As we have seen in this chapter, secondary continuations by White give Black a great deal of freedom in choosing his course of action. Black has no difficulties in levelling the game – quite the contrary, he can play in a more ambitious manner.

The continuation 5.e3 is harmless in this move order. First 5.a3 and then e2-e3 seems more precise for White.

Exercises

15.1 (1) White threatens ♘b5. Does Black have an active way to prevent it?
(solution on page 451)

15.1 (2) With his last move ...c7-c5 Black is trying to equalize in the centre. Does White have a dynamic option to prevent this?
(solution on page 452)

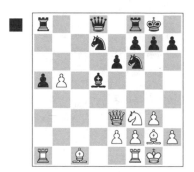

15.1 (3) Find Black's most economical set-up.
(solution on page 452)

Chapter 15.2

5.a3 ♗e7: The Slow 6.e3

1.d4 e6 2.c4 ♗b4+ 3.♘d2 ♘f6 4.♘f3 0-0 5.a3 ♗e7 6.e3

5.a3 is the most principled move, and is in the spirit of the position. For the last couple of years, **5...♗e7** has been the most popular reply, and also one that has been applied by many grandmasters. The idea is simple: Black allows White to create a full pawn centre with 6.e4, trusting that it can be undermined with 6...d5.

This has created a new crossroads for white players. Apart from the standard 6.e4 (the main line, covered in Chapters 15.4-15.6), other possibilities may be considered, like 6.e3, 6.g3, the less popular 6.b4, and of course 6.♕c2 (followed by e2-e4, transferring to some of the main lines. In this chapter we take a look at the option 6.e3. This is certainly not a harmless continuation, however White's idea is to slowly continue development and gradually build up his position. Black has to be careful with choosing his plan.

Let's first of all consider **6.g3**. Now:

A) **6...d5 7.♗g2 b6 8.0-0 ♗b7 9.♘e5** 9.b3 ♘a6!? 10.♗b2 c5 11.♖c1 ♖c8 12.dxc5 bxc5 13.♘e5 ♕b6 14.♕c2 d4 15.e4 dxe3 16.fxe3 ♗xg2 17.♔xg2 ♕b7+ 18.♔g1 ♘b8 with excellent chances for Black, Kanakaris-Markidis, Achaea 2012. **9...♕c8 10.cxd5 exd5 11.♘df3 ♘e4 12.♗f4 ♕e6 13.♕b3 f6 14.♘d3 ♘c6! 15.♗e3 ♘a5 16.♕a2 ♘c4 17.♗c1 g5 18.♖e1 ♖ac8 19.b3 ♘cd6** and Black takes over the initiative,

363

Iturrizaga Bonelli-Delgado Ramirez, San Jose 2009;

B) **6...b6 7.♗g2 ♗b7 8.b4** 8.0-0 c5 9.b3 cxd4 10.♗b2 ♕c7 11.♗xd4 d6 12.♕b1 ♘bd7 13.♕b2 ♖ac8 14.♖ac1 ♕b8 15.♖fd1 ♖fd8 16.♘f1 d5 17.cxd5 ♗xd5 18.♘e3 ♗e4 19.b4 ♕b7 20.♖xc8 ♖xc8 21.♖c1 with an equal position, Shulman-Akopian, Ningbo 2011. **8...c5 9.bxc5 bxc5 10.e3 cxd4 11.exd4 ♘c6 12.0-0 ♘a5 13.♖e1 ♖c8 14.♗f1 ♗a6 15.♕a4 ♕c7 16.♖a2 ♗xc4 17.♘xc4 ♘xc4 18.♖c2 ♕b7 19.♖xc4 ♕xf3 20.♖xc8 ♖xc8 21.♕xa7 ♘g4** with a slight advantage for Black, Nyzhnyk-Miroshnichenko, Denizli 2013.

6...d5

6...b6 7.♗d3 ♗b7 8.0-0 c5 9.b3 d6 10.♗b2 ♘bd7 and now:

A) 11.a4 a5 12.♕e2 ♖e8 13.♖fd1 ♕c7 14.♘b1 cxd4 15.♘xd4 ♘c5 16.♗c2 ♖ad8 17.♘a3 ♕b8 18.♖ac1

with an unclear position, Mirzoev-Miroshnichenko, Denizli 2013;

B) **11.♕e2 ♖e8 12.b4 ♗f8** Practically the most efficient plan for Black, with the direct threat e4-e5. **13.♖fd1?!** Logical, but not optimal (13.♗c2∞). **13...e5 14.dxe5 dxe5 15.♗f5 ♕c7?!** Black could have captured the pawn as there is no compensation: 15...cxb4 16.axb4 ♗xb4. **16.b5 e4** With 16...g6!? again, Black could have maintained his advantage: 17.♗xd7 (17.♗h3 e4∓; 17.♗c2 e4∓) 17...♘xd7 with the advantage of the bishop pair and a slightly better position for Black. **17.♘g5 ♖ad8 18.♗xd7!** The point: Black must ruin his pawn structure, since the knight on f6 must keep the queen from intruding on h5, which is why the intermediate move 16...g6 was needed. **18...♖xd7** 18...♘xd7 19.♕h5!. **19.♗xf6 gxf6 20.♘h3 ♖ed8** with equal chances, Grigorov-Antic, Sunny Beach 2009.

7.♗d3

7.b4 seems overly ambitious and allows Black a typical attack on the queenside: **7...a5 8.b5 c5 9.♗b2 ♘bd7 10.♗e2 b6 11.♘e5 ♗b7 12.cxd5 ♘xd5** 12...exd5!?. **13.♘c6 ♗xc6 14.bxc6 ♘b8 15.dxc5 bxc5 16.♕a4 ♕c7 17.♗b5 ♖c8 18.♕g4 ♗f6 19.♗xf6 ♘xf6 20.♕c4 ♘xc6 21.♕xc5 ♕b7!–+** Williams-Fressinet, Haguenau 2013.

7...b6 8.0-0 c5

The most precise move order – it is important to stop White's space occupation by b2-b4.

If **8...♗b7 9.b4 c5** After 9...dxc4 10.♘xc4 ♘bd7 11.♖b1 ♖b8 12.b5 a6 13.a4 axb5 14.axb5 c6 15.bxc6 ♗xc6 16.♘ce5 ♘xe5 17.♘xe5 ♗a8 18.♗d2 White is a little better, Karpov-Grischuk, Moscow 2008. **10.bxc5 bxc5 11.♖b1 ♕c7 12.cxd5 exd5 13.dxc5 ♘bd7 14.♘b3 ♘e4 15.♕c2 ♖fc8 16.♗b2** with a pleasant position for White, Kalesis-Antic, Eretria 2011.

9.b3 ♗b7

9...cxd4 10.exd4 ♘c6 10...♗b7 11.♕e2 a5 12.♗b2 a4 13.b4 dxc4 14.♘xc4 ♘bd7 15.♘fe5 ♘d5 16.♘xd7 (16.g3±) 16...♕xd7 17.♘e5 ♕d8 18.♕e4 g6 19.b5 with unclear play, Kempinski-Istratescu, Warsaw 2012. **11.♗b2 ♗b7 12.♕e2** An older continuation. A lot more threatening seems 12.♖c1!? ♖e8 13.♖e1 ♗f8 and now:

14.c5!. That's the idea: when the knight is on c6, White has this unpleasant move at his disposal. Of course, with the flexible position of the knight on d7, this move isn't possible. 14...bxc5 15.dxc5 a5 16.♗b5 ♘d7 17.b4 axb4 18.axb4 ♖b8 with an advantage for White, Ponomariov-Vitiugov, Saratov 2011. **12...♖e8 13.♖ac1 ♗f8 14.♖fd1**

♖c8 15.♗c2 ♕c7 16.♘f1 ♗a6 16...g6!∞. **17.♘e3 ♕b7 18.♘e5 dxc4 19.bxc4**
Black has lost the coordination between his pieces. Besides, relinquishing the centre with ...dxc4 is not a good idea unless there is some strategic benefit to it. That isn't the case here and it is only a matter of time before White will break through, with the typical structure of hanging pawns and White's ideal control of the d5-square by the knight on e3, maintaining the positional pressure.

10.♗b2

There is always a dilemma in this type of position: whether to place the knight on the flexible d7-square or the more active c6-square. Practice shows that it is better to make the flexible knight move here:

10...♘bd7 11.♕e2 cxd4 12.exd4 ♖e8 13.♖ad1 ♕c7 14.♘e5 dxc4 15.♘dxc4 b5 16.♘xd7 ♕xd7 17.♘a5 a6 18.♘xb7 ♕xb7 19.♖c1 ♖ec8 20.g3 ♕d5 21.♕e3 ♕d7 22.♖xc8+ ♖xc8 23.♖c1 ♘d5

With good chances for Black. The bishop pair doesn't provide White with an advantage, considering that the bishop on b2 is passive, Neverov-Sjugirov, Taganrog 2013.

> **Conclusion**
>
> What is important to remember at the end of this chapter is that White's secondary lines are not harmless, and they still require precise play by Black. After 6.e3 we recommend a flexible set-up for Black, with an attack on the centre via ...b7-b6/c7-c5 and a flexible position for the knight on d7!

Exercises

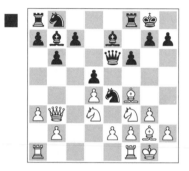

15.2 (1) Find the way to take over the initiative!
(solution on page 452)

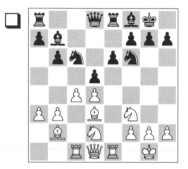

15.2 (2) In such positions we recommend a flexible position for the knight on d7, not on c6. White to play, prove our recommendation and gain an advantage!
(solution on page 452)

15.2 (3) Make use of Black's better development in a powerful way!
(solution on page 453)

Chapter 15.3

5.a3 ♗e7: The Subtle 6.♕c2

1.d4 e6 2.c4 ♗b4+ 3.♘d2 ♘f6 4.♘f3 0-0 5.a3 ♗e7 6.♕c2

This is an interesting move order, favoured especially by grandmaster Zdenko Kozul. In addition to transposing to the main line with 7.e4, White has additional options of 7.g3 and 7.e3. We will devote most of our attention to the theoretical duel with 7.e4, considering that the other possibilities aren't a real challenge for Black.

6.b4

The attempt to capture space on the queenside, at such an early stage, gives Black additional possibilities, for example: **6...a5 7.b5 c5 8.dxc5** In case of

8.bxc6 bxc6 9.c5 d6 10.cxd6 ♕xd6 11.e4 ♕c7 12.♗b2 c5 13.dxc5 ♗xc5 14.♗xf6 gxf6 15.♗c4 ♗b7 16.0-0 ♖d8 17.♕e2 ♘c6 18.♖fc1 ♕e7 and here the bishop pair guarantees Black a pleasant game in the long run, Moiseenko-Vitiugov, Ningbo 2011. **8...♗xc5 9.♗b2 b6 10.g3 ♗b7 11.♗g2 ♗e7 12.0-0 d6 13.e4 ♘bd7 14.♘d4 ♕c7 15.♕e2 ♖fe8 16.f4 e5 17.♘f5 ♘c5 18.♘xe7+ ♕xe7 19.f5 ♖ac8 20.♖ae1 h6** with excellent chances for Black, Shirov-Tomashevsky, Sochi 2012.

   6...d5 7.e4

A) **7.g3**

7...b6 8.♗g2 ♗b7 8...c5!? 9.dxc5 bxc5 10.0-0 ♗b7 11.cxd5 exd5 12.♖d1 ♘bd7 13.♘h4 ♖e8 (13...♕b6 14.♘f5 ♖fe8 15.e4 ♗f8 16.exd5 ♗xd5 17.♘c4 ♕e6 18.♗xd5 ♘xd5 19.b3 ♘7b6 20.♘fe3 ♘xe3 21.♘xe3 ♖ac8 22.♗b2 c4 23.♘xc4 ♘xc4 24.bxc4 ♕xc4 ½-½ Kizov-Antic, Skopje 2011) 14.♘f5 ♗f8 15.♘c4 ½-½ Kozul-Dizdar, Medulin 1997. **9.0-0 ♘bd7 10.b4 dxc4 11.♘xc4 c5 12.♕b2 cxd4 13.♕xd4 ♘e4 14.♗b2 ♗f6 15.♕e3 ♗xb2 16.♘xb2 ♘df6 17.♘e5 ♖c8** with equal chances, Kozul-Predojevic, Rijeka 2010;

B) **7.e3 b6 8.♗d3 c5 9.0-0 cxd4 10.exd4 dxc4 11.♘xc4 ♗b7 12.♘ce5 ♕d5 13.♗g5 ♖c8 14.♕e2 ♘c6** with an unclear position, Laylo-Ni Hua, Ho Chi Minh City 2012;

C) **7.b4 b6 8.♗b2 ♗b7 9.c5 a5 10.e3 axb4 11.axb4 ♘c6 12.♖xa8 ♕xa8 13.♗c3 bxc5 14.dxc5 d4! 15.exd4 ♘d5 16.b5 ♘cb4 17.♗xb4 ♘xb4 18.♕b1 ♗xf3 19.♘xf3 ♕a3 20.♔d2** with an attack for Black, which unfortunately doesn't win (1-0, 27) Kozul-Palac, Sibenik 2012.

7...c5

With this move we transpose to one of the main branches. We will give the most important games and some rich analysis with plenty of possibilities for both sides.

8.dxc5 dxe4 9.♘xe4 ♘xe4 10.♕xe4 ♘c6 11.b4

11.♗f4 f5 and now:

A) **12.♕e3 ♕a5+ 13.♕d2 ♕xd2+ 14.♗xd2** 14.♔xd2 ♗xc5 15.♗e3 ♗e7 16.b4 (16.♔c3 ♗f6+) 16...f4 with an initiative for Black. **14...e5 15.♗c3** 15.b4 e4↑. **15...e4 16.♘d4**

A1) **16...♗xc5 17.♘xc6 bxc6 18.b4** 18.♗e2 ♖d8 19.b4 ♗e7 20.0-0 ♗e6 21.♖fd1 ♔f7 22.f3 ♗g5 23.fxe4 ♗e3+ 24.♔f1 fxe4 25.♔e1 c5 26.♖ab1 ♗d4 27.♔d2 g5 28.♔c2 ♔g6 29.bxc5 ♗xc5 30.♖f1 ½-½ Kosulin-Petrov, LSS email 2007. **18...♗e7 19.0-0-0** 19.♗e2 ♗e6 20.0-0 a5 (20...♖ad8 21.♖ad1 ♔f7 22.♗d4 ♖d7∞) 21.b5 cxb5 22.cxb5 ♖fc8 23.♗d4 ♗c4 24.♗xc4+ ♖xc4 25.♗e3 ♔f7 with chances for both sides in the endgame, Javorsky-Bucek, ICCF email 2010. **19...a5 20.bxa5 c5** with a complex endgame, Manso Gil-Galanov, ICCF email 2008;

A2) 16...a5!?N A new and interesting attempt to create more tension. **17.♘xc6 bxc6 18.b4 ♗e6** Black has compensation for the sacrificed pawn, due to his better piece development. In addition, there are many tactical possibilities, so let's see what may follow:

A21) 19.♔d2 f4! 19...♗h4 20.f3 axb4 21.axb4 ♖xa1 22.♗xa1 ♖a8 23.♗b2 ♖a2 24.♔c1 ♗e7 25.fxe4 fxe4 26.♔b1 ♖a4 27.♗c3±. **20.♗e2 e3+ 21.fxe3 fxe3+ 22.♔e1** 22.♔d3 ♗f5+ 23.♔xe3 ♖ae8→. **22...axb4 23.axb4 ♖xa1+ 24.♗xa1 ♖b8 25.♗c3 ♗xc5!;**

A22) 19.♗e2 axb4 20.axb4 ♖xa1+ 21.♗xa1 ♖a8 22.♗c3 ♖a3 23.♔d2 ♖a2+ 24.♔d1 f4 25.♖e1

25...♗g5!♟ 25...♗f6 26.♗xf6 gxf6 27.♗h5 f5 28.b5 ♖xf2 29.♖e2 ♖f1+ 30.♔c2±. **26.♗h5 e3 27.fxe3 fxe3 28.h4 ♗h6 29.♗e2 g6** 29...♗f5 30.b5 g6 31.b6 ♗g7 32.b7 ♗xc3 33.b8♕+ ♔g7 34.♕c7+ ♔g8 35.♕d8+

With a draw.

30.♗d3 30.b5 cxb5 31.c6 ♗g7 32.♗f3 ♗xc3 33.♖xe3 b4 34.♖xe6 b3 35.c7 ♖d2+=. **30...♗g7 31.♗xg7 ♖d2+ 32.♔c1 ♖xd3 33.♗h6 ♖c3+ 34.♔b2 ♖xc4 35.♖xe3 ♔f7=** We see that after this interesting novelty, Black has a very rich game in all lines.

B) 12.♕c2 and now:

12...♗xc5!? An active approach! If instead 12...♕a5+ 13.♗d2 (13.♕d2 ♕xd2+ leads to the endgame which we mentioned in the previous text, with excellent chances for Black) 13...♕c7 14.b4 (14.0-0-0 e5↑) 14...a5!↑ △ 15.♖d1 axb4 16.axb4 e5. **13.♖d1 ♕f6 14.♗g5** 14.b4 e5 (14...♘d4!?) 15.♗g5 ♕g6∞ with the idea 16.bxc5 e4 17.♖d6 ♕h5. **14...♕g6 15.b4**

15...e5! Black makes good use of his development advantage, denying White a harmonious positioning of his pieces.

16.♕c1 16.bxc5 e4 17.♖d6 ♕h5 18.♕d2 exf3 19.gxf3 ♕xf3 (19...♖e8+!? 20.♗e2 ♗e6→) 20.♕d5+ ♕xd5 21.cxd5 ♘e5 22.♗f4 ♘f7 23.♔d2 ♖e8 24.♗d3 ♘xd6 25.♗xd6 b6 26.♗b5 ♖d8 27.♗c6 bxc5 28.♗e7 ♗d7

An interesting position, but it ends in a draw after 29.♗xa8 ♖xa8=. **16...f4 17.bxc5 e4 18.♖d6 ♕h5∞**

The position is getting more tense and Black has outstanding chances. Let's look at some of the options:

B1) **19.♕d2 exf3 20.♕d5+ ♔h8 21.♗xf4 ♕e8+ 22.♗e3 ♘e5 23.h3 ♗d7 24.g4 ♖d8 25.♗d3** 25.♕xb7 ♗c6 26.♕b1 ♖b8→. **25...♗c6 26.♕d4 ♕e7 27.♗f5 ♘f7 28.♖d5 ♖fe8 29.♗c2 ♘e5 30.♖d6 b6!∞**;

B2) **19.♗xf4 exf3 20.♕d2 ♕xc5 21.gxf3 ♕xa3 22.♗e2 ♕a1+ 23.♕c1 ♕a5+ 24.♗d2 ♕c5 25.♖d5 ♕e7 26.♕c3 ♗f5 27.♗e3**

27...♕b4?! Bad judgment, with which Black relinquishes his advantage after an otherwise excellently played game. 27...♘b4! 28.♖d2 ♖ad8 29.0-0 ♖xd2 30.♕xd2 ♖d8 31.♕c3 ♗d3 32.♖e1 ♗xe2 33.♖xe2 ♘c6∓. **28.♕xb4 ♘xb4 29.♖b5 ♘c2+ 30.♔d2 ♘xe3 31.fxe3 b6** ½-½ Koneru-Antic, Kavala 2009.

11...f5 12.♕b1

A) **12.♕d3?!N** This attempt to go into the endgame with a material advantage doesn't give White a satisfactory game. **12...♕xd3 13.♗xd3 e5 14.b5** 14.♗e2 e4 15.♘g5 h6 16.♘h3 ♘d4 17.♗d1 ♗f6 18.♖b1 ♗e6↑. **14...e4 15.bxc6 exf3 16.gxf3 bxc6 17.♔d1** 17.♗e3 f4 18.♗d2 ♗xc5; 17.♗d2 ♖d8 18.♔e2 ♖e8 19.♔f1 ♗e6 20.♗e3 ♖ad8 21.♗e2 f4. **17...♗xc5 18.♗e3 ♗d6 19.♔c2 c5 20.♖ad1 ♖d8 21.♖he1** 21.g5 ♖e8 22.♗e4 fxe4 23.♖xd6 exf3∓. **21...h6 22.h4 ♖b8 23.♖b1 ♗d7∓** due to his superior pawn structure;

B) **12.♕e3 ♗f6!N**

Just in time! **12...e5 13.♗b2 e4 14.♖d1 ♕e8 15.♘d4 ♗f6 16.g3 a5 17.b5 ♘e5 18.♗e2 ♕f7 19.0-0 ♗d7** (19...♘xc4 20.♗xc4 ♕xc4 21.♖c1 ♗xd4 22.♕xd4 ♕xd4 23.♗xd4 with White's advantage in the endgame, where the presence of the opposite-coloured bishops isn't helping Black) **20.♕c1 ♖ac8 21.a4** with a solid advantage for White, Le Quang Liem-Bocharov, Moscow 2008. **13.♖b1 e5∓ 14.♗b2 e4 15.♖d1 ♕e8 16.♘d4** 16.♗xf6 f4!. **16...f4 17.♕e2 e3→** with a decisive attack for Black;

C) **12.♕c2 a5 13.b5 ♘d4 14.♘xd4 ♕xd4** ½-½ Kozul-Cvitan, Rijeka 2009.

12...e5 13.♗b2 ♗f6 14.♕d1 ♕e7
Being one pawn down isn't a big price to pay for Black's developmental advantage and initiative!

15.♕b3 a5 16.0-0-0 axb4 17.axb4 e4↑ 18.♘e1 f4 19.♘c2 ♗g4

19...♗f5!↑.

20.f3 exf3 21.gxf3 ♗xb2+ 22.♔xb2 ♕f6+ 23.♔b1 ♗f5 24.♗d3

24...♖a7
24...♘d4!?N 25.♕b2 ♘xf3 26.♕xf6 ♖xf6 27.♗xf5 ♖xf5 with excellent chances for Black in the endgame.

25.♕b2 ♕f7?! 26.♗xf5 ♕xf5 27.♖hg1
With an advantage for White, Navara-Hracek, Prague 2012.

Conclusion

We have seen an abundance of possibilities for both sides in this chapter. The most important thing is that White's conquest of the centre in the main line with e2-e4 gives Black an array of dynamic options with a more than satisfactory game. After the standard ideas, plenty of new ones have been presented, along with theoretical novelties! We are trying to be objective, yet one gains the impression that Black is able to play for more than just a draw!

Exercises

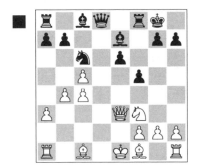

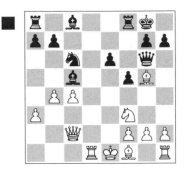

15.3 (1) Black is a pawn down but has better development. How to continue?
(solution on page 453)

15.3 (2) It looks as if White has seized a space advantage and is close to completing his development. How should we prevent this?
(solution on page 453)

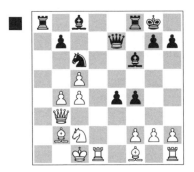

15.3 (3) There is only a single move to develop the bishop and continue the initiative. The question is: where to go?
(solution on page 453)

Chapter 15.4

5.a3 ♗e7: Main Line 6.e4 d5 7.♗d3

1.d4 e6 2.c4 ♗b4+ 3.♘d2 ♘f6 4.♘f3 0-0 5.a3 ♗e7 6.e4 d5 7.♗d3

Unquestionably this position bears a great resemblance with the Morozevich Variation of the Tarrasch Defence with an extra tempo for White. However, one of the moves is not really useful. This primarily concerns the c4-pawn, which, combined with the knight on d2, doesn't exert sufficient pressure on Black's centre. On the contrary, it gives Black an opportunity to undermine White's centre.

7...c5 8.dxc5

Though it is not the most popular, we find this continuation to be the most unpleasant for Black. White proposes to enter the endgame, where he has a small space advantage and where Black must play precisely. In case Black refuses to play the endgame with 8...dxe4, White simply maintains the pressure in the centre without advancing the e-pawn to e5. 8.e5 ♘fd7 will be covered in Chapters 15.5 and 15.6.

8...dxe4

If Black aims for a more complex game, with queens on the board, then **8...a5!?** presents a serious, though more risky, alternative:

A) **9.0-0 dxe4 10.♘xe4 ♘bd7 11.♘xf6+ ♗xf6**

12.♘d2?! 12.♕c2! h6?! 13.♗f4 ♘xc5 14.♗h7+ ♔h8 15.♖ad1. **12...♕c7 13.♘e4 ♗e7 14.♗e3 f5 15.♘d6 ♘xc5 16.♘xc8 ♖axc8 17.♗c2 ♗f6∞** Abasov-Hracek, Sibenik 2009;

B) **9.♕e2** and now:

B1) **9...dxe4 10.♘xe4 ♘a6 11.♗f4**
11.0-0 ♘xe4 12.♗xe4 ♘c5 13.♗c2±;
11.b4? axb4 12.axb4 ♘xb4 13.♖xa8
♘xd3+−+. **11...♘xe4 12.♕xe4 g6
13.0-0-0** 13.♕e2. **13...♘xc5 14.♕e3
♗d7?!** 14...♕b6 15.♔b1 f6∞. **15.♗h6
♕c7** 15...♖e8 16.♘e5±. **16.♗xf8 ♗xf8
17.♘e5 ♗g7 18.♘xd7 ♘xd7 19.♔b1
♘c5 20.♗e2 a4**

With certain compensation due to the
strong dark-squared bishop, but also
the opened d-file, which unlike in certain Sicilian Dragon position presents
the possibility of an exchange of major
pieces, Navara-Stocek, Czechia 2006;

B2) **9...h6 10.cxd5?!**

It is not necessary to activate the passive
c8-bishop! 10.0-0± ♘c6 11.♗c2 dxe4
12.♘xe4 ♘xe4 13.♗xe4 ♗xc5
14.♗e3. **10...exd5 11.♖b1 a4 12.0-0
♘bd7 13.h3 dxe4 14.♘xe4 ♘xc5**

15.♘xf6+ ♗xf6∞ Miljkovic-Arsovic,
Vrnjacka Banja 2010.
    **9.♘xe4 ♘xe4 10.♗xe4 ♕xd1+
11.♔xd1 ♗xc5**

Certainly the most frequently played
move, but the other possibilities for
Black need to be considered. White
wants to take control of the queenside
with b2-b4. Black should prevent this
in either by playing 11...a5 or with the
active 11...f5 – in both instances, there
is dynamic play in the endgame.

A) **11...a5** and now:

A1) **12.♗e3 f5 13.♗c2**

13...♘d7 13...♘c6!? is a serious alternative, with dynamic play in the semi-
endgame despite the minus pawn:
14.♔e2 e5. **14.♔e2 a4 15.♖ad1 ♘xc5
16.♗xc5 ♗xc5 17.♘e5 b6 18.♖he1 g6
19.f4 ♖e8** with a slightly more pleasant
endgame for White, Khurtsidze-N.
Kosintseva, Tbilisi 2011;

374

A2) 12.♔e2 f5 13.♗c2

13...a4?! 13...♘c6! is a developing move which grants Black a satisfactory game, for example 14.♗a4 ♗f6∞. **14.♗f4 ♘d7 15.♗d6 ♔f7 16.♖ad1±** ♘xc5 17.♘e5+ ♔f6 18.♗xc5?! 18.f4 ♖a6 19.♗c7±. **18...♗xc5 19.♘d7+ ♗xd7 20.♖xd7 ♖fd8** Miljkovic-Antic, Vrnjacka Banja 2010;

A3) **12.♗f4 ♗xc5 13.♔e2 f5 14.♗c2 ♘c6 15.♖hd1 a4 16.♔f1 b6** 16...♗e7 17.♗d6 ♗xd6 18.♖xd6 e5. **17.♔g1 h6 18.♗d6 ♖f7 19.♖d2** 19.♗xc5 bxc5 20.♖d6 ♖c7∞ 21.♖ad1 g5 22.h3 ♔g7 23.g4 ♘a5 24.♘e5 ♖b8 25.♗xa4 ♖xb2 26.gxf5 ♗e2 27.♘g4 exf5 28.♘f6 ♗ce7 29.♘h5+ ♔h7 30.♘f6+ ♔g7. **19...♗xd6 20.♖xd6 ♖c7 21.♖ad1 ♔f8 22.♘d4 ♘xd4 23.♖1xd4 b5**

With counterplay in the endgame, Gelfand-Ivanchuk, Biel 2009.

B) **11...f5 12.♗c2 ♗f6 13.♖b1 e5** 13...♖d8+ 14.♔e1 e5 15.♗g5 ♗xg5

16.♘xg5 h6?! (no need to improve the knight's position – 16...♘c6!?) 17.♘f3 e4 18.♘e5± Kovalenko-Maletin, Magnitogorsk 2011. **14.♗g5 ♗xg5 15.♘xg5 ♘c6 16.♗a4 ♖d8+ 17.♔c2 ♘d4+ 18.♔c3 h6?!** 18...♘e2+N 19.♔b3 ♘d4+ 20.♔c3=. **19.♘f3 ♘e2+ 20.♔b3 e4 21.♘e5 ♗e6 22.♖bd1 ♘d4+ 23.♔c3 ♘e2+ 24.♔b3 ♘d4+ 25.♔c3 ♘e2+** ½-½ Pacheco-Mareco, Lima 2013.

12.b4

12.♔e2 a5 12...f5!? 13.♗c2 ♘c6 14.b4 ♘d4+ 15.♘xd4 ♗xd4 16.♖b1 e5∞. **13.♗e3 ♘a6 14.♖hd1 ♗xe3 15.♔xe3 ♘c5 16.♗c2 a4 17.♖d6 ♗d7 18.♘e5 ♗e8 19.♖ad1 f6 20.♘d3 ♖c8 21.♘xc5 ♖xc5 22.♖xe6 ♖xc4 23.♗e4 ♗c6 24.♗xc6 bxc6** with nearly equal chances in the endgame, Jia Haoxiang-Kunte, Subic 2009.

12...♗e7

Capturing the pawn with **12...♗xf2** is a risky move, which allows White to take the initiative in the endgame: **13.c5 f5 14.♗b1 ♘c6 15.♗a2 ♖d8+ 16.♖d2** 16.♔e2 ♗d4 17.♖d2 ♗f6 18.♖xd8+ ♘xd8. **16...♖xd2+ 17.♗xd2**

17...b5?! 17...♘d4 18.♖f1 ♘xf3 19.♖xf2 ♘xh2 20.♗f4 ♘g4 21.♖d2 ♔f7 22.♖d8 e5 23.♗d2♙ **18.♗a2 ♔f8 19.g4 ♗d7 20.♖f1±** Khenkin-Ulibin, Borzhomi 1988.

13.♔c2
13.♗b2 a5 14.c5 ♘a6 15.♔e2 f5 16.♗d3 ♘c7 17.♗c4 ♘d5 18.♗e5 b6? 18...♖d8!? 19.♖hd1 ♔f7∞ with the idea 20.h3 g5. **19.♗xd5** 19.c6!?± axb4 20.axb4 ♖xa1 21.♖xa1 ♗xb4 22.♖a7. **19...exd5 20.cxb6±** Gupta-Khukhashvili, Kavala 2009.

13...a5 14.♗d2 ♘d7 15.♔b3 ♘f6
There is no reason to refrain from the thematic 15...f5!, opting for more active play. Pushing the centre pawns with ...f7-f5 and ...e6-e5 is Black's main plan.
16.♗c2 b6 17.♗e3 ♖b8 18.♗f4 ♖a8 19.♗e3 b5±
½-½ Malakhatko-Maletin, Dubai 2009.

Conclusion

Though it is not very popular with white players, moving to the endgame might present a great challenge for Black. We feel that this continuation is unjustly neglected. Our recommendations grant Black a satisfactory game, but don't forget to strive for active play!

Exercises

15.4 (1) Find a satisfactory and active way to compensate for the pawn!
(solution on page 451)

15.4 (2) Find the plan.
(solution on page 453)

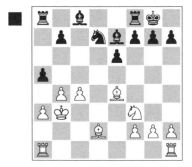

15.4 (3) Find an active move!
(solution on page 454)

Chapter 15.5

5.a3 ♝e7: Main Line 6.e4 d5 7.e5 ♞fd7 8.♝d3

1.d4 e6 2.c4 ♝b4+ 3.♞d2 ♞f6 4.♞f3 0-0 5.a3 ♝e7 6.e4 d5 7.e5 ♞fd7 8.♝d3

We are reaching the boiling point. In this chapter, we start the analysis of White's most direct and most principled line. It would seem that everything is ready for taking the initiative: the full pawn centre, better piece development, a space advantage and Black's pieces badly clustered... but things aren't that simple! By means of attacking the centre with ...c7-c5, Black will start freeing squares for his pieces. We will present an array of possibilities that are interesting for club players and professionals alike, so buckle up, we're taking off!

First we consider the alternative to 7.e5:

7.cxd5 exd5 8.e5 ♞fd7 9.♝d3 c5 and now:

A) **10.0-0 ♞c6 11.♖e1 a5 12.♝c2 ♖e8** 12...♕c7 13.♞b3 c4 14.♞bd2 b5

15.♞b1 ♞b6 16.♞c3 b4 17.axb4 ♞xb4 18.h3 ♝e6 19.♞g5 ♝xg5 20.♝xg5 ♞xc2 21.♕xc2 ♕d7 22.♕d2± Iotov-N. Kosintseva, Dallas 2013. **13.♞f1?!** Better would be 13.h3 a4!♾.

We shall leave it up to our readers to analyse this position! **13...cxd4 14.♗f4 ♕b6 15.♖b1 ♘f8 16.h3**

16...♗e6 16...♘e6!? 17.♗g3 ♗d7∓. **17.♘1d2 ♘g6 18.♗g3 f6 19.exf6 ♗xf6 20.♗d3 ♗f7 21.♕c2** White faces a tough battle for equality, Nyzhnyk-Bluvshtein, Groningen 2010;

B) **10.h4 h6 11.♗g5?!** 11.♗b1!? – a similar position has been covered in the section containing 9.h4!? but without the inclusion of cxd5 exd5, which suits Black well. See the next page. **11...cxd4 12.e6** 12.♗b1 ♘xe5 13.♘df3 ♘bc6–+. **12...♘e5 13.exf7+ ♘xf7 14.♘xf7 ♖xf7 15.♕h5 ♕d6 16.♘f3 ♘c6 17.♗d2**

17...♕e6+ 17...♗d7! is a developing move maintaining a clear advantage for Black: 18.0-0! ♖af8 19.♖ae1 ♗f5∓. **18.♔f1 ♕g4 19.♕xd5 ♗e6 20.♕e4 ♕xe4 21.♗xe4 ♖d8∓** Ding Liren-Zhou Jianchao, Beijing 2009.

7...♘fd7 8.♗d3 c5 9.h4!?

The latest and most modern attempt by White in this line. White wants to swiftly make use of Black's cramped position, so before Black manages to free some squares for his pieces (with ...c7-c5, for example), White prepares a direct attack on the king. This is no small matter and Black should be cautious!

9...g6
I believe this is the best reaction.

A) The immediate counter-strike **9...f5** causes big damage in Black's position: **10.cxd5 exd5 11.♘g5 ♕b6 12.♕f3 ♕c6 13.♕h5!?** A typical aggressive approach by grandmaster Cheparinov! 13.♗xf5↑. **13...h6 14.♘df3 b6 15.e6 ♘f6 16.♕f7+! ♖xf7 17.exf7+ ♔h8 18.♘e5 g6 19.♘xg6+?!** 19.♘xc6 ♘xc6 20.♘f3 ♔g7 21.♗b5 and White is better. **19...♔g7 20.♘xe7 ♕b7 21.♘g6 ♘bd7?** A logical developing move, but a mistake under the continuous pressure. 21...♘fd7 22.♗xf5 ♘f8 23.♗xf8 hxg5∞. **22.♘e6++–– ♔xg6 23.h5+ ♔xf7 24.♘d8+ ♔g7 25.♘xb7 ♗xb7 26.f3 cxd4 27.♗f4 ♖e8+ 28.♔f2 ♘c5 29.♗xf5 ♗c8 30.♗g6 ♖f8 31.♗e5 ♘e6 32.♖hd1 ♗d7 33.♗xd4 ♘f4 34.♖ac1** 1-0 Cheparinov-Georgiev, Sunny Beach 2012;

B) **9...h6?!** A question mark alone would possibly be better, since after the following analysis the reader will see that this move isn't enough to equalize, in fact White is ahead! **10.♗b1!**

This is the main idea. Against 11.♕c2, Black prepares the defence ...♘f8.

B1) White is better after **10...♘c6 11.♕c2 f5 12.exf6 ♘xf6 13.dxc5 ♗xc5 14.0-0** 14.cxd5 gives Black unnecessary activity: 14...♕xd5 15.0-0 ♗d7. **14...♗d6 15.b4 ♘e7?!** 15...♘e5 gives better chances, although White keeps the initiative. **16.♗b2 ♘f5 17.♕b3 ♔h8 18.♗xf5 exf5 19.♖fe1± ♘e4 20.♖ad1 ♗e6 21.♕e3 ♕e7 22.♕xh6+ ♔g8 23.♗xg7 ♖fe8 24.♘xe4 fxe4 25.♗b2** 1-0 Ding Liren-Thavandiran, Athens 2012;

B2) **10...cxd4 11.cxd5 exd5 12.♕c2** White can also try different moves, but it seems that the queen is better on c2, controlling square c5. If 12.♘b3 ♘c6 13.♕d3 f5 14.♗f4

14...♕c7?! (better is 14...♘c5! 15.♘xc5 ♗xc5 with an unclear position) 15.♕e2 (simpler is 15.0-0± ♘dxe5 16.♘xe5 ♘xe5 17.♕g3 ♗d6 18.♖c1 ♕e7 19.♘xd4 ♘c4 20.♗xd6 ♘xd6 21.♗a2 with an initiative) 15...♕b6 16.♗a2 ♖e8 17.0-0-0 ♗f6 18.♘bxd4 ♘xd4 19.♖xd4 ♘xe5 20.♔b1 ♗d7?? (20...♖e7) 21.♗xe5 1-0 Shulman-Ludwig, Philadelphia 2012. **12...f5 13.♘b3 ♘c6 14.♗f4 ♕b6** The intermediate 14...d3 doesn't change the character of the position: 15.♕xd3 ♘c5 16.♘xc5 ♗xc5 17.♗a2 ♗e6 18.b4 ♗b6 19.♖d1 ♕e7 20.0-0 ♖ad8 21.♖fe1± Lupulescu-Smith, Albena 2013. **15.♗a2 ♖e8 16.0-0** 16.0-0-0 is also promising: 16...♕a6 17.♔b1 ♘b6 18.♘bxd4 ♘xd4 19.♘xd4± ♘c4 20.♖h3 ♔h8 21.♖g3 (better is 21.♖c3!) 21...♗xh4 22.♖h3 ♗e7 23.e6 ♗f8 24.g4 (24.♗xc4 dxc4 25.♗e5 and White keeps an advantage) 24...♗xe6 25.g5 ♖ac8∞ 26.gxh6 g6 (26...g5!) 27.♗xc4 (27.♘f3!) 27...♖xc4∞ Wojtaszek-Korobov, New Delhi 2012. **16...♘f8 17.♖ad1±**

White keeps a stable advantage due to his better pawn structure, for example: **17...♘e6 18.♕d2 ♗d7 19.♘bxd4 ♘cxd4 20.♘xd4 ♘xd4 21.♕xd4 ♕xd4 22.♖xd4 ♗e6**, Rodshtein-Andreev, Cappelle la Grande 2013;

B3) 10...♖e8 11.♕c2 ♘f8 12.dxc5 a5

B31) Again, **12...♗xc5** is not enough to equalize: **13.cxd5 ♕xd5 14.♘e4 ♗e7**

15.♗xh6! A smashing blow. Black simply doesn't have a satisfactory defence. 15.0-0± ♖d8 16.♘c3 ♕c4 17.♖e1 ♘c6 18.♖e4 ♘d4 19.♖xd4 ♖xd4 20.b3 ♕c7 21.♘xd4 ♕xe5 22.♘f3 ♕h5 23.♘e2 ♗d7 24.♘f4 ♕b5 25.♗b2 ♖c8 26.♕d3 ♕a5 27.♗a2 ♗b5 28.b4 1-0 Bartel-Womacka, Gibraltar 2013. **15...gxh6 16.♖h3 ♕a5+** 16...♘c6 17.♖g3+ ♔h8 18.♕c1+−; 16...♘g6 17.♘c3 ♕a5 18.♖g3+−. **17.b4 ♗xb4+ 18.axb4 ♕xb4+ 19.♔f1 ♘bd7 20.♖g3+ ♔h8 21.♕c1 ♘h7 22.♕xh6 ♖g8 23.♕xh7+ ♔xh7 24.♘f6+ ♔h6 25.♘xg8+ ♔h5 26.♖g5+**

1-0 Kacheishvili-Shahade, Saint Louis 2011;

B32) 12...a5! The point. Black wants to stabilize the centre, preventing b2-b4, by following up with either ...♘a6 or ...♘bd7.

B321) White achieves nothing after **13.♘b3 ♘bd7 14.♗f4 a4 15.♘bd4 ♘xc5 16.♗a2 dxc4** (16...♘g6!∓) **17.♗xc4 ♗d7 18.h5 b5 19.♗e2 b4 20.0-0 ♕b6 21.♘d2 ♖ec8 22.♘c4** ½-½ Avrukh-Fedorchuk, Sibenik 2012;

B322) **13.♘f1!**

This is the right direction for the knight.

B3221) **13...♘c6** doesn't help Black too much:

14.♗xh6!? Again this blow! However, 14.♘g3! is even stronger. White's idea is so simple: ♘h5 followed by ♖h3! and his attack is unstoppable! For instance, 14...b6 15.♘h5 bxc5 16.♖h3+− Knaak. **14...gxh6** 14...♗xc5 15.♗e3±. **15.♖h3** The position is quite difficult for Black and he has to work very hard in order to neutralize White's initiative. Let's have a look: **15...f5 16.♕d2 ♔h7 17.cxd5 exd5 18.♘e3 ♘xe5** What else? **19.♘xe5 ♗xc5 20.f4 ♗xe3** 20...♘g6 21.♘xg6 (21.♕xd5 ♘xf4 22.♕xc5 ♘xh3 23.gxh3 b6 24.♕c3 ♕xh4+ 25.♔d1 ♗e6 looks promising for Black: 26.♘xf5 ♖ad8+ 27.♔c1 ♕g5+ 28.♕e3 ♗xf5 29.♕xg5 hxg5 30.♗xf5+ ♔g7∓) 21...d4 22.♘e5 dxe3 23.♕xd8 ♖xd8 24.♗a2 b6 25.♖g3 ♗a6 26.♗e6 ♗c8 27.♗f7 and White is slightly better. **21.♖xe3 d4 22.♖e2 ♕xh4+ 23.♔f1** 23.♔d1?! ♗e6∓. **23...♖a6 24.♔g1 ♘g6 25.♘xg6 ♖xe2 26.♘f8+ ♔g7 27.♕xe2 ♔xf8 28.♕e5 ♕e7 29.♕h8+ ♔f7 30.♕xc8 ♕e1+ 31.♔h2 ♕h4+=** Of course, there is still the impression that White could have played better somewhere;

B3222) **13...f6 14.exf6 ♗xf6 15.♘g3±**;

B3223) **13...♘a6 14.♗xh6!** That's it! amazing preparation! This new idea by grandmaster Kapnisis puts 9...h6 under a question mark! **14...♘xc5** If Black accepts the challenge with 14...gxh6 15.♖h3 f5 16.♕d2 ♔h7 17.cxd5 ♗xc5 – we leave this position to our dear readers to do some homework. Certainly they will find that White has more than just compensation here! **15.♘g3!** 15.♗e3±. **15...gxh6 16.♕c1 dxc4 17.♕xh6 ♘d3+ 18.♔f1 ♘h7 19.♘g5 ♗xg5 20.hxg5 ♕xg5 21.♕xh7+ ♔f8 22.♗xd3 cxd3 23.♕xd3 ♕xe5 24.♖e1 ♕xb2 25.♕d6+ ♔g8 26.♖h4 ♕b5+ 27.♔g1 ♕g5 28.♖h5 ♕g6 29.♘e4 f6 30.♖e3 ♖a6 31.♖g3** 1-0 Kapnisis-Markidis, Patras 2013;

B323) **13.0-0 ♘a6 14.♖d1 ♘xc5 15.♘b3 b6 16.♗e3 ♗b7!** Active play!

17.♘xc5 ♗xc5 18.♗xc5 bxc5 19.cxd5 ♗xd5 20.♗a2∞ 20.♕xc5 ♕b8∞, Ragger-Babula, Graz 2013. **20...♖c8 21.♗c4** If 21.♗xd5 exd5 Black takes over the initiative. **21...♘g6 22.♖d2 ♘e7 23.♕c3 ♕c7!**

24.♖e1?! 24.♖ad1. **24...♗xf3!** The right decision, just in time. **25.♕xf3 ♖ed8∓** In such a position, the knight simply dominates the bishop, having the flexibility to move to the g6-, c6- and f5-squares and attacking the advanced white pawns: **26.♖c2?! ♘f5∓** Milanovic-Antic, Pozarevac 2013.

C) It speaks for itself that **9...cxd4?** backfires in view of **10.♗xh7+** (Navara-Dzagnidze, Erevan 2014) when Black cannot take the bishop: 10...♔xh7? 11.♘g5+ and wins.

10.h5

A) **10.cxd5** changes the direction of the game by playing in the centre: **10...exd5 11.h5 cxd4 12.♘b3 ♘c6 13.♗f4 ♖e8 14.hxg6 fxg6** There was no reason to be afraid to open the h-file. More accurate was 14...hxg6 15.0-0 ♗f8 16.♖e1 ♕b6 17.♕c2 ♗g7 18.e6 ♖xe6 19.♖xe6 fxe6 with complicated play. **15.0-0 ♘f8** Too passive. **16.♘bxd4 ♘xd4 17.♘xd4±** Gordievsky-Oparin, Loo 2013;

B) **10.b4** Playing on both wings gives Black enough time to consolidate in the centre: **10...cxd4 11.♕e2 ♘c6 12.cxd5 exd5 13.e6 ♘f6 14.♘g5 ♗xe6 15.♘xe6 fxe6 16.♕xe6+ ♔g7∓ 17.0-0**

17...♘h5 17...♕d7! and Black is slightly better. **18.♘f3 a6 19.♘g5 ♖f6 20.♕e2± ♕d6 21.♖e1 h6 22.♘e6+ ♔f7**

23.♗xg6+!+− ♔xg6 24.♕g4+ ♔h7 25.♕xh5 ♖g8 26.♘g5+ ♔g7 27.♖e6 ♕xe6 28.♘xe6+ ♖xe6 29.♗f4 ♖d8 30.♖d1 ♖f6 31.♖d3 ♔h7 32.♖g3 ♖df8 33.♕g4 ♖6f7 34.♗xh6 1-0 Khotenashvili-Dzagnidze, Geneva 2013.

10...cxd4 11.♕c2

A) **11.hxg6** is the most principled re-action, opening up the h-file. The point is that Black also has an open f-file, as an additional defensive resource! **11...fxg6 12.♕c2 ♕e8** and now:

A1) **13.0-0**

A11) **13...♘c5 14.♘xd4 ♘xd3 15.♕xd3** White is slightly better. **15...♘c6 16.cxd5 exd5 17.♘2f3 ♗g4**

18.♗h6 ♖f7 19.e6 ♖f6 20.♖ae1 ♗xf3 21.♘xf3 ♖d8 22.♘d4± Jankovic-Roiz, Plovdiv 2012;

A12) **13...♘c6** looks more logical, simply developing another piece: **14.♖e1 a5 15.cxd5 exd5 16.♗b5 ♘c5 17.♘b3**

A121) **17...♗f5?!** is not enough for equality: **18.♕d1 ♗g4 19.♘bxd4±**, Kozul-Arsovic, Sarajevo 2012;

A122) **17...♖xf3!N**

Just in time! **18.♘xc5** 18.gxf3 ♘e6 and Black has more than compensation due to White's weak king. **18...♖f5 19.♗d2 ♕f7** with an unclear position;

A123) **17...d3!?N**;

A2) **13.♘b3 ♘c6 14.♗h6 ♖xf3** Again, just in time. **15.gxf3 ♘dxe5 16.f4 ♘xd3+ 17.♕xd3 ♗f6** White has played too ambitiously, now it is Black's turn. His bishop pair and central pawns give him a promising advantage. **18.0-0-0 ♕f7 19.♘d2**

19...♗d7 19...e5! was just simpler, the bishop should go to f5, for example 20.cxd5 ♕xd5 21.♖dg1 ♘e7 22.♘e4 ♗h8↑. **20.♖dg1 ♖c8 21.♔b1 ♗h8 22.♔a1 ♘e7 23.cxd5 exd5 24.♘f3 ♗f5 25.♕b3 ♘c6 26.♘h4 ♗e6 27.♖g5?!** 27.f5 ♗xf5 28.♘xf5 ♕xf5 29.♕xb7±. **27...♘e7 28.♕xb7 ♘f5 29.♕xf7+ ♔xf7 30.♘f3 d3 31.♖gg1 ♘d4** 31...♖c2! — a rook on the second rank has priority. **32.♘g5+ ♔e7** with unclear play, Kogan-Spraggett, Catalunya 2013.

B) **11.cxd5 ♘c5** Better is 11...exd5.

12.♗b1 12.d6!N deserves attention: 12...♘xd3+ 13.♔f1 and White has an initiative. **12...exd5 13.♘xd4 ♘c6 14.♘2f3 ♘e4 15.♗h6 ♖e8 16.hxg6 hxg6 17.♘xc6 bxc6 18.♕c1 ♗a6 19.♗xe4 dxe4 20.♗g7 g5∞ 21.♕xc6 ♕b6?!** 21...f6! with mutual chances. **22.♕xe4 ♕g6 23.♕xg6 fxg6**

24.♗h8! An unusual move, but the best one! **24...♖ac8 25.e6 g4 26.♘d4 ♖c5 27.f4 gxf3 28.gxf3±** Nyzhnyk-Miroshnichenko, Mamaia 2013.

11...♘c5

There's no reason to waste time with **11...♕e8**. This move only works after the immediate 11.hxg6 fxg6 as then after 12.♕c2 White is threatening 13.♗xg6. **12.♘b3 ♘c6 13.♗f4** White is slightly better thanks to his perfect control in the centre and he can slowly build up positional pressure. **13...dxc4 14.♗xc4 ♘b6 15.♗d3 ♘d5 16.♗h6 ♗d7 17.♕e2 ♕d8 18.♘bd2?!** 18.hxg6N hxg6 19.♕e4±. **18...♖c8?!** 18...♖e8. **19.g3 ♕c7 20.♔f1∞** Ding Liren-Tomashevsky, St Petersburg 2012.

12.♗f1

Keeping the bishop seems to be more logical than:

A) **12.hxg6 ♘xd3+ 13.♕xd3 fxg6 14.♘xd4** Centralising the queen gives Black a tempo for development, with excellent play: 14.♕xd4 ♘c6 15.♕e3 ♖f7 (better was the immediate 15...♕b6 16.♕xb6 axb6 17.b3 g5 18.♗b2 ♗d7∓ with the option of ...♗d7-e8-g6) 16.b3 ♕b6 17.♕xb6 axb6 18.♗b2 ♗d7 19.0-0 g5 20.cxd5 exd5 21.♖fe1 with an unclear position, Ionov-Mishuchkov, St Petersburg 2012. **14...♘c6 15.♘xc6 bxc6 16.♕h3 ♖f7∓**

This quiet defensive move defends against all White's activity over h-file. Black is better thanks to his bishop pair and the possibility to open up the position and playing along the open files and diagonals, Shulman-Kaidanov, Saint Louis 2012;

B) **12.cxd5** and now:

B1) **12...♘xd3+!?** deserves attention, viz. **13.♕xd3 ♕xd5∞** 13...exd5 14.♘xd4 ♘c6 15.♘2f3 ♗g4 16.♗h6 ♖e8∞. **14.♘e4** and now:

B11) **14...♗d7 15.♗h6 ♖e8** 15...♘xe5 16.♘xe5 ♕xe5 17.f4! – an important intermediate move: 17...♕a5+ (17...♕d5 18.♗xf8 ♔xf8 19.hxg6 hxg6 20.0-0-0±) 18.b4 ♕d8 19.hxg6 fxg6 (19...hxg6 20.♗g5!+−) 20.♗xf8 ♕xf8 21.♕xd4±. **16.♗g5!?** ♘xe5 16...b6!? 17.♗xe7 ♖xe7 18.0-0!? (18.♘f6+ ♘xf6 19.exf6 ♖c7 20.hxg6 fxg6 21.♔d2 ♕d6!= Leitao in *Chess Informant*) 18...♗b7 19.♖fe1 ♖f8 20.h6∞. **17.♘xe5 ♕xe5 18.f4** 18.hxg6 fxg6 19.f4≋. **18...♕a5+ 19.♔f2 ♕a6 20.♕xa6** 20.♕h3 e5 21.♕h4 ♗f5−+. **20...bxa6 21.♘f6+ ♗xf6 22.♗xf6 ♗b7=;**

B12) **14...♘c6 15.♗h6** and now:

B121) **15...♘xe5 16.♘xe5 ♕xe5 17.f4!;**
B122) **15...♖e8 16.♗g5 ♘xe5 17.♘xe5 ♕xe5 18.hxg6** with equality (Antic): **18...fxg6 19.f4 ♕g7 20.♖c1≋;**

B123) **15...♗d7 16.♗g5** 16.♗xf8 ♖xf8 17.♖d1 ♘xe5 18.♘xe5 ♕xe5 19.♕xd4 ♕xd4 20.♖xd4 ♗c6, Leitao. **16...♘xe5** 16...♕a5+ 17.♕d2 ♕xd2+ 18.♔xd2→; 16...♗xg5!? 17.♘fxg5 ♘xe5 18.♕h3 ♔g7 19.hxg6 h5!∞ Antic. **17.♘xe5 ♕xe5 18.♗xe7 ♗b5 19.♕f3 f5 20.hxg6 hxg6 21.a4 ♗c6 22.♕g3 ♕xg3 23.♘xg3±** Leitao;

B14) **15...♕a5+? 16.♕d2 ♕xd2+ 17.♔xd2± ♖d8 18.hxg6 fxg6 19.♗g5 h5** 19...♗xg5+ 20.♘exg5 h5 21.g4!↑ hxg4 22.♖h6+−. **20.g4** 20.♗xe7 ♘xe7 21.g4+−. **20...♗xg5+ 21.♘fxg5** 21.♘exg5 ♘a5 (21...♖d5 22.gxh5 ♘xe5 23.♘xe5 ♖xe5 24.♖ag1→) 22.♖ag1 ♘c4+ 23.♔c2→. **21...♘xe5 22.gxh5 ♘c4+ 23.♔e1 ♗d7 24.b3** 24.hxg6!? ♔g7 25.♔e2 ♔xg6 26.♖ag1 ♔f5 27.♖h6!↑. **24...♘a5 25.♖c1± ♗c6?! 26.hxg6+−** Giri-Naiditsch, Wijk aan Zee 2014;

B2) **12...exd5 13.♘xd4** 13.hxg6 ♘xd3+ 14.♕xd3 fxg6 15.♘xd4 (15.♘b3 ♗f5) 15...♘c6 16.♘2f3 ♗c5∞. **13...♘c6 14.♘2f3 ♘xd4 15.♘xd4 ♕c7∞ 16.♗f4 ♘xd3+** The beginning of a wrong plan. **17.♕xd3 ♕c4?! 18.♕xc4** 18.♕d2! could secure an advantage. **18...dxc4 19.♖c1± b5 20.♘xb5 ♖b8 21.♘d6 ♖xb2 22.♘xc4 ♖a2≋** Smirnov-Landa, Loo 2013.

C) **12.♗e2 ♘c6! 13.b4 d3 14.♗xd3 ♘xd3+ 15.♕xd3**

15...dxc4 15...g5!? looks risky but deserves attention, just in order to keep tension in the centre. **16.♕xc4 ♕d5 17.hxg6 fxg6 18.♕e2?!** 18.♗b2∞ was more precise. **18...♘d4** That is the difference. **19.♘xd4 ♕xd4 20.♖b1 ♗d7** Black has an advantage. **21.♖b3**

21...♗c6 21...♕d5!−+; decisive centralization! **22.♖d3 ♕f4∓** Ding Liren-So, Khanty-Mansiysk 2011.

12...d3   13.♗xd3   ♘xd3+ 14.♕xd3 dxc4

14...b6!N

We recommend that Black keep the pressure on the centre and keep the critical squares e4 and c4 under control, thereby limiting the mobility of White's pieces, primarily the knight on d2! **15.♕e3 g5** with the idea **16.♘e4 h6∞**.

15.♕e3

An interesting try is to trade the queens: 15.♕xd8 ♖xd8 16.hxg6 fxg6 17.♘e4 ♘c6 18.♗g5!⩱

18...h5 19.♗xe7 ♘xe7 20.g4 b5 With a very dynamic position and compensation for the sacrificed material, for example:

21.♘f6+ 21.♘fg5!?. **21...♔g7 22.gxh5 gxh5 23.♖xh5 ♖h8 24.♖xh8 ♔xh8 25.0-0-0** White is better. **25...♔g7 26.♖g1+ ♔f8 27.♖h1 ♘f5 28.♖h7 ♘g7 29.♘g5 ♗b7 30.♘d7+ ♔g8 31.♘f6++−** Fabian-Mareco, Villa Martelli 2013.

15...g5 16.♘e4 h6

17.♘fxg5!? hxg5
17...♗xg5 18.♕g3↑.

18.♕g3 ♔h8 19.♗xg5 ♗xg5 20.♘xg5

A very difficult position to evaluate. Perhaps an engine can find a defence, but in a practical human game it is quite unpleasant for Black.

20...♘c6 21.♖d1 ♕c7 22.f4 ♖g8 23.♕e3 b5 24.♖d6 ♗b7 25.f5

25...♛e7?

The decisive mistake. Now White's attack is unstoppable. 25...♘d4!.

26.♘e4 ♛f8 27.fxe6 ♘xe5 28.e7 ♘d3+ 29.♚f1

1-0, Cheparinov-Mchedlishvili, Leon 2012.

Conclusion

In this line, which is very popular at the moment, we have proved that White's initiative can be neutralized, but only with 9...g6, a move that justifies the whole white idea of 9.h4. But don't forget, Black also strives for active play and for the opening of the f-file, so: active play and initiative whenever and wherever the circumstances on the board allow it!

Exercises

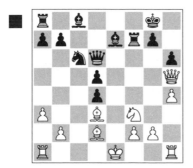

15.5 (1) Find the move.
(solution on page 454)

15.5 (2) How to continue the attack?
(solution on page 454)

15.5 (3) Find the move. *(solution page 454)*

Chapter 15.6

5.a3 ♗e7: Main Line 6.e4 d5 7.e5 ♗fd7 8.b4

1.d4 e6 2.c4 ♗b4+ 3.♘d2 ♘f6 4.♘f3 0-0 5.a3 ♗e7 6.e4 d5 7.e5 ♘fd7 8.b4

In this final chapter with the line 3.♘d2, we consider a way for White to take control of the queenside before developing his pieces to the optimal squares, White wants to slow down the central counterattack ...c7-c5. And again, seemingly Black has passive play, but he can still achieve counterplay without difficulty!

8...a5 9.b5 c5 10.cxd5

A) **10.♗b2 cxd4**

A1) **11.♗xd4 ♘c5**

A11) **12.♕c2 ♘bd7 13.♗e2 b6 14.cxd5** 14.0-0 ♗b7 15.♖fd1 ♖c8 16.♕b2 ♕c7 17.♖ac1 ♕b8 18.cxd5 exd5!

An important move in this type of position. Black vacates the important

e6-square for a regrouping of his knights. Recapturing with the bishop guarantees equality, but capturing with the pawn is more ambitious! 19.♘b1?! ♘e6 20.♗e3 ♗c5 21.♗xc5 ♘dxc5∓ Livner-Antic, Paleochora 2009. **14...exd5 15.0-0 ♗b7** and now:

A111) **16.a4 f6**

Important! This move isn't necessary as it creates unnecessary weaknesses in Black's camp. Better is 16...♖c8!? or 16...♘e6!?, in both cases with an excellent position for Black. **17.exf6?!** 17.e6! ♘xe6 18.♗d3♕ with the idea 18...g6 19.♗xg6 hxg6 20.♕xg6+ ♘g7 21.♘g5. **17...♗xf6 18.♘b3 ♖c8 19.♕b2 ♘xb3 20.♕xb3 ♘c5 21.♕a2 ♗xd4 22.♘xd4** and Black is a little better, Gupta-Xiu Deshun, Subic 2009;

A112) 16.♖fe1 ♘e6 17.♗b2 ♖c8 18.♕b1 ♘dc5 19.♘d4 ♘xd4 20.♗xd4 ♘e6 21.♘f3 ♗c5 22.♕b2 ♕e7 23.♗d3 g6∓ Korobov-Zhou Jianchao, Khanty-Mansiysk 2011;

A113) 16.♖ac1 ♘e6 17.♗b2 ♖c8 18.♕f5 ♘dc5 19.♘d4 ♘xd4 20.♗xd4 ♘e6 21.♗b2 g6 22.♕g4 h5 23.♕g3 ♗h4 24.♖xc8 ♗xc8 25.♕e3 d4 26.♕e4 d3 with an initiative for Black, Macieja-Bartel, Warsaw 2010.

A12) 12.♗e2 ♘bd7 13.0-0 b6 14.cxd5 exd5

A121) 15.♖e1 ♗b7 16.♕b1 ♖e8 17.♗d1 ♗f8 18.♗c2 g6 19.a4 ♖c8 20.♕b2 ♘e6 21.♗b3 ♗g7 22.♖e3 ♗h6 23.♖d3 ♘dc5 This ideal set-up for Black and the lack of coordination between White's pieces grant Black a significant advantage, Zhou Jianchao-Bocharov, Moscow 2007;

A122) 15.♗b2 ♗b7 16.♖e1 ♖e8 17.♘f1 ♘e6

It is very important to remember this regrouping of Black's knights via the e6-square, which grants him complete freedom in making a dynamic plan. In such positions, if you have the choice between capturing with the bishop or with the pawn on d5, the authors suggest you take with the pawn! And let us not forget that the d5-pawn is a passed pawn, not an isolated one! **18.♘e3 ♘dc5 19.♘f5 ♗f8 20.♗f1 ♖c8 21.♘3d4 g6** with a perfect set-up for Black, Cramling-Hou Yifan, Kemer 2007.

A2) 11.cxd5 exd5

A21) 12.♗e2 ♘c5 13.♘xd4 ♘bd7 14.f4 ♘b6 15.a4

Although it seems that White has stabilised his position, Black has several great options and even a few tactical assaults! If 15.0-0 ♘ba4 16.♖b1 ♘xb2 17.♖xb2 ♕b6 18.♔h1 ♘e4 19.♘xe4 dxe4 20.♕a4 ♖d8 with better odds for Black, Van Wely-Van den Doel, playchess.com 2011.

A211) 15...♗h4+ 16.g3 ♗h3 17.♗f1 ♗xf1 18.♔xf1 ♗e7 18...♕d7!? 19.♔g2 ♗e7. **19.♘f5 g6 20.♘xe7+ ♕xe7 21.♗d4 ♘c4 22.♘f3 ♖ac8 23.♔g2 ♘e4** with a great game for Black, Van Wely-Guliev, Baku 2007;

A212) 15...f6!?N 16.0-0 16.exf6 ♗xf6 17.0-0 ♕e7∓. **16...fxe5 17.fxe5 ♗d7**∞;

A213) 15...♗g4!N

A tactical strike with which Black takes over the initiative. We shall take a look at one of the possibilities and leave our readers to check out the rest! **16.0-0 ♗xe2 17.♕xe2 ♘bxa4** Plain and simple: Black has a material and positional advantage.

A22) **12.♗xd4 ♘c5 13.♗xc5 ♗xc5 14.♗d3 ♕e7 15.0-0 ♗xa3 16.♕b3 ♗b4 17.♕xd5 ♘d7 18.♕e4 g6 19.♕f4 ♘c5** Black takes over the control in the centre, and the passed pawn and the mighty bishop pair give him the advantage, Anastasian-Yakovenko, Moscow 2007;

A23) **12.♘b3 a4 13.♘bxd4 ♘c5** 13...♕a5+! a great moment for a new move, taking over the initiative! **14.♕d2 ♕xd2+ 15.♔xd2 ♘c5** with a better endgame for Black due to the excellent coordination of his pieces and the exposed white king. **14.♗e2 ♕b6** ½-½ Rindlisbacher-Gonda, Budapest 2013.

B) **10.♗d3 cxd4 11.♕c2 h6 12.♗b2** 12.cxd5 transposes to another type of position, covered further on. **12...♘c5 13.♗h7+ ♔h8 14.♗xd4 b6 15.cxd5 exd5 16.0-0 ♘bd7 17.♗f5 ♘e6** 17...♗b7! is a more precise move that prevents White's continuation in the game. **18.♗b2** (18.♕c6! capturing the

material, is the most principled continuation, and Black will have to work hard to compensate for the sacrificed material: 18...♖b8 19.♕xd5 ♗b7 20.♕c4 ♖c8 21.♕e2. **18...♘dc5 19.♖fd1 ♗b7** 19...♘d7!, developing the piece with tempo should be the first option to consider! The idea is 20.a4 ♖c8 21.♕b1 ♘f4 22.♘d4 ♗xf5 23.♘xf5 ♘cd3 with great play for Black. **20.♘b3 ♘a4** 20...♖c8!? 21.♘bd4 ♕c7 22.♖ac1. **21.♘bd4 ♘xb2 22.♕xb2** with an unclear position, Potkin-Iordachescu, Serpukhov 2008.

10...exd5 11.♗d3 cxd4

Black is temporarily in a tight spot and it is very important to free the c5-square for a further regrouping of his pieces, especially the knights.

12.♘b3
12.♕c2

A) **12...♔h8 13.♘b3 f6** The authors have already mentioned earlier in this chapter that they are not fond of this move, unless it is absolutely necessary! **13...a4!**

As we have mentioned earlier, it is important to develop the pieces and free the c5-square for Black's regrouping. Time is a very important factor in this type of position. 14.♘bxd4 ♘c5⇄ with the idea 15.♗xh7 ♘b3!. **14.exf6 ♘xf6 15.♘bxd4 ♗g4 16.0-0 ♘bd7 17.h3 ♖c8 18.♕a2 ♗xf3 19.♘xf3 ♕b6 20.♗b2±** Berczes-Saric, Rogaska Slatina 2009.

B) **12...♘c5** is an interesting pawn sacrifice of the pawn which gains Black time to develop his pieces dynamically. **13.♗xh7+ ♔h8** with a complex position, with possibilities for both sides. Let us look at some of the options:

B1) **14.0-0N** A piece sacrifice which certainly deserves attention:

B11) **14...♕b6 15.♗d3 ♘bd7 16.♘b3 ♘xb3 17.♕xb3 ♘c5 18.♕c2 ♘e6** 18...♗d7 19.♘xd4 ♖ac8 20.♗f5 ♘e6 21.♕d1 ♔g8 22.♗e3±. **19.♗d2 a4 20.♕b2 ♗d7 21.♖ac1 ♖fc8 22.h4 ♔g8 23.h5 ♗d8 24.h6** 24.♗e2!±. **24...gxh6 25.♗xh6 ♘c5** with an unclear position;

B12) **14...g6 15.♗xg6 fxg6 16.♕xg6** and now:

16...d3 16...♗f5! 17.♕h5+ ♗h7 18.♘xd4♛. **17.♕h6++** 17.♗b2 ♘e6 18.g3 ♕e8 19.♕xd3 ♘d7 20.♕xd5 ♘dc5 21.♘c4 ♕g6∓. **17...♔g8 18.♕g6+ ♔h8 19.♗b2→**

B2) **14.♘xd4** is perhaps the simplest continuation, allowing White to maintain his material advantage and leaving Black the possibility of capturing with the bishop on h7 in return for a strong initiative: **14...♘bd7** 14...g6?! 15.♗xg6 fxg6 16.♕xg6 ♕e8 17.♕h6+ ♔g8 18.0-0 ♕f7 19.♘2f3 ♕g7 20.♕xg7+ ♔xg7 21.♗g5 ♖e8 22.♗xe7 ♖xe7 23.♖fe1

With an edge for White.

B21) **15.♘2f3!** The most principled move, developing a piece and defending the pawn. **15...♕e8 16.♗f5** and now:

B211) **16...♘xe5! 17.♘xe5 ♗d6 18.f4 ♗xf5 19.♕xf5 f6 20.0-0 fxe5 21.♕h3+ ♔g8 22.♘f5 ♕e6** with excellent play for Black;

B212) 16...♗d6 17.♘xd7 17.0-0 ♘xe5 18.♗b2 f6 19.♘h4 ♕h5 20.g3±. **17...♘xd7 18.0-0 ♘xe5 19.♘g5!±;**

B213) 16...♗f6 17.0-0 ♘xe5 18.♘g5 ♗xf5 19.♕xf5 ♗xg5 20.♗xg5 f6 21.♗e3 g6 22.♕h3+ ♔g8 23.♖ad1±

B22) 15.f4?! ♕b6 Of course, Black is not satisfied with a draw: 15...g6 16.♗xg6 fxg6 17.♕xg6 ♖xf4 18.♕h6+ ♔g8 19.♕g6+ ♔h8=. Now:

B221) 16.♗f5 ♘e6 17.♘e2 ♘dc5 18.a4 g6 19.♗d3 19.♗xg6 fxg6 20.♕xg6 ♗h4+! – it is important to deny White the g3-square as he will need the entire 3rd rank for the rook manoeuvre a3-h3. 21.g3 ♗d8 22.♗b2 ♗d7∞. **19...♘xd3+ 20.♕xd3 ♘c5 21.♕d4 ♗f5 22.♗a3 ♘d3+ 23.♔f1 ♕xd4 24.♘xd4 ♗xa3 25.♖xa3 ♖ac8 26.g3** with more active play and compensation for the material in the endgame;

B222) 16.♗d3 f6 17.♘2f3 17.♘f5 ♖e8. **17...fxe5 18.fxe5 a4 19.♗e2 ♘b3! 20.♘xb3 axb3 21.♕xb3** 21.♕c3 ♘c5 22.♗e3 ♘e4 23.♕xb3 ♕a5+ 24.♔f1

24...d4!. **21.♘xe5 22.♗e3** 22.♘xe5 ♕f2+ 23.♔d1 ♕d4+. **22...♘xf3+ 23.♗xf3 d4 24.♗f2 ♗e6 25.♕b2 ♕a5+∓;**

B3) 14.♗d3 ♘bd7 15.0-0 ♘xd3 16.♕xd3 ♘c5 17.♕xd4 ♗f5 18.♕e3

♗d3 19.♖e1 ♗xb5 20.a4 ♗xa4 21.e6 ♗c2 22.exf7 ♖xf7 23.♖a3 b6 24.♘e5 ♖f6 25.♘g4 ♖g6 26.♘e5 ♖f6 27.♘g4 ½-½ Berczes-Meier, Germany 2008;

C) 12...h6!?

C1) 13.0-0 b6 13...♘c5 14.♗b2 ♘xd3 15.♕xd3 ♘d7 16.♗xd4 b6 17.♕e3 ♘c5 18.a4 ♗e6. **14.♖e1 ♘c5 15.♘xd4 ♘e6 16.♗b2 ♗c5 17.♘2f3 ♘f4 18.♖ad1 ♘xd3 19.♕xd3 ♕e7 20.h3 a4 21.♖e2 ♖a5 22.♖de1 ♗e6 23.♖c1 ♖e8 24.♖d1 ♖a8 25.♘f5 ♗xf5 26.♕xf5 ♗xa3 27.♗xa3 ♕xa3 28.♖xd5 ♕e7 29.♖d6 ♖a7 30.♖a2 ♘d7 31.♕e4 ♕xd6 32.exd6 ♖xe4 0-1** Andriasian-Hess, ICC 2008;

C2) 13.♘b3 a4 14.♘bxd4 ♘c5

White is at an important crossroads and must decide how to continue.

C21) 15.0-0 ♘xd3 16.♕xd3 ♘d7

C211) 17.e6 ♘c5 18.exf7+ ♖xf7 19.♕g6 ♕d6 20.♕xd6 ♗xd6 21.♗e3 ♗d7∓ 22.♖fc1?! 22.♖fd1 ♘e4∓ **22...♘b3! 23.♘xb3 axb3 24.♖cb1** (24.♖ab1? ♗xa3 25.♖d1 b2 26.♘d4 ♖c8 27.f3 ♖c3 28.♔f2 ♖e7−+) **24...♖xf3 25.gxf3 ♗e5−+;**

C212) 17.♗b2 ♘c5 and now: **18.♕c2** 18.♕e2 ♕b6 19.h3 ♗d7∓; the queen being on e2 instead of c2 doesn't generally change the evaluation of the position, Black has the upper hand. **18...♕b6 19.♖ad1 ♗d7**

His excellent control in the centre gives Black an undisputed advantage. Let us look at the options for White:

C2121) **20.e6 fxe6 21.♘e5 ♗xb5 22.♘g6** 22.♖fe1 ♗f6 23.♘g6 ♗d3!−+. **22...♗xf1 23.♘xe7+ ♔f7 24.♘xd5 exd5 25.♖xf1 ♔g8! 26.♘f5 ♖f7 27.♗d4**

27...♕c6!−+;

C2122) **20.♘f5 ♗xf5 21.♕xf5 ♕xb5** with a material advantage for Black.

C213) **17.♗e3 ♘c5 18.♕c2 ♗g4 19.h3** 19.♘f5 ♘b3 20.♖ad1 ♗xa3. Now:

C2131) **19...♗xf3 20.gxf3** 20.♘xf3 ♘b3 21.♖a2 (21.♖ad1 ♗xa3) 21...d4 22.♖d1 ♕d5. The squares in front of the passed pawn in the centre are unblocked, Black has the advantage. **20...♖c8 21.♕d1** 21.♕f5 ♘b3∓. **21...♕d7 22.♔h2 ♘e6** 22...f6 23.f4 fxe5 24.fxe5 ♘e4∓. **23.♕xa4?** 23.♘f5

♗c5∓; 23.♖g1 ♗c5 24.♘xe6 ♕xe6∓. **23...♘xd4 24.♗xd4 ♖c4 25.♕d1 ♗c5 26.♗xc5 ♖h4−+**

C2132) **19...♗h5 20.♘f5 ♘b3 21.♖ad1 ♗xa3 22.♕a2 ♗b4** 22...♗xf3!∓ 23.gxf3 ♕c8 24.♕b1 ♕e6 25.f4 ♖fc8 26.♔h2 ♗f8 27.♕d3 ♖c4 28.♖g1 ♖ac8−+. **23.g4 ♗g6 24.♘3d4 ♗xf5 25.gxf5 ♗c3!∓**

Pavlidis-Antic, Thessaloniki 2011.

C22) **15.♗h7+ ♔h8 16.0-0 ♘b3 17.♘xb3** 17.♖b1 ♘xc1 18.♖bxc1 ♗xa3 19.♖a1 ♗e7 20.♗f5 a3 △ 21.♗xc8 ♖xc8 22.♕xc8 ♖xc8 23.♘f5 ♗f8 24.♖fd1 ♖c5∓; 17.♖a2 ♘d7 18.e6 ♘f6 19.♗f5 ♗c5∓. **17...axb3 18.♕d3 ♘d7 19.♗e3 b2 20.♖ab1 ♘b6!∓ 21.♖xb2 ♖xa3 22.♕b1 ♘c4 23.♖e2 ♘xe3 24.fxe3 ♕b6 25.♗d3 ♗c5 26.♖fe1 ♗e6** with a great advantage for Black;

C23) **15.♗f5 ♘b3!∓**

This thematic move keeps troubling White, whose pieces are overloaded. **16.♘xb3 axb3 17.♕xc8 ♕xc8 18.♗xc8 ♖xc8∓ 19.♘d2** 19.♘d4? ♗b4+ 20.♗d2 b2. **19...♘d7 20.♘xb3 ♘xe5 21.0-0 ♘d3∓**;

C24) **15.♗e3 ♘xd3+ 16.♕xd3 ♘d7 17.♘f5 ♘c5 18.♘xe7+ ♕xe7 19.♗xc5** If White captures the pawn with 19.♕xd5 Black gets plenty of compensation: 19...♘b3 20.♖a2 ♗f5 21.♕d6 ♕xd6 22.exd6 ♗d3 23.b6 ♖fe8∓ and White has a material advantage, but his pieces are paralysed. **19...♕xc5 20.0-0 ♗d7 21.♖ab1 ♖fc8 22.h3 ♕c4 23.♕d2 ♗f5 24.♖bc1 ♕d3 25.♕xd3 ♗xd3 26.♖fd1∓** Smirin-Demchenko, St Petersburg 2012;

12...a4 13.♘bxd4 ♘c5 14.♗c2
If **14.0-0**:

A) **14...♘bd7 15.♘f5 ♘xd3 16.♕xd3 ♘c5 17.♘xe7+ ♕xe7 18.♕xd5 ♘b3** 18...♗e6!?♾ 19.♕d6

♕xd6 20.exd6 ♖fd8 21.♗f4 ♘e4 22.♖fd1 ♘c3 with a complex endgame. **19.♗g5 ♕e6 20.♖ad1** ½-½ Lputian-Gulko, Erevan 1996;

B) **14...♗g4?!**

15.♗c2 15.♗f5! and Black is late blocking e6: 15...♘h5 16.♖e1 ♘bd7 17.e6!↑. **15...♘bd7 16.♖e1 ♘b6 17.h3 ♗d7 18.♗d2 ♘e6** Better is 18...♘c4 19.♗b4 ♖e8 20.♘e2 ♗xb5 with excellent play for Black as well as a material advantage, Elianov-Khismatullin, Dresden 2007. **19.♕b1** 19.♘f5!±. **19...g6 20.♗b4 ♘c4 21.♗d3 ♖c8 22.♗c2 ♗xb4 23.♕xb4 ♘xd4 24.♘xd4** and now:

B1) **24...♕b6 25.♘f3?** 25.♖ad1 ♖fe8 26.♗xa4 ♖xe5 27.♖xe5 ♘xe5 28.♗b3 ♘c4 29.a4 ♕c5=. **25...♕xb5∓**;

B2) **24...♖e8 25.♘f3 ♘xe5 26.♘xe5 ♖xc2 27.♕xa4** with unclear play, Potkin-Navara, Dagomys 2008.

14...♘bd7
After 14...g6 15.0-0 ♘bd7 16.♗h6 ♖e8 17.♕d2 ♘f8 White is slightly better, Vovk-Van den Doel, Vlissingen 2009.

15.0-0
15.♘f5 ♘b3 16.♗xb3 axb3 17.0-0 ♘xe5 18.♘xe7+ ♕xe7 19.♕xb3 ♘xf3+ ½-½ Berczes-Predojevic, Sarajevo 2011. Perhaps Black could have been ambitious and continued with 19...♘c4!?.

15...♘b6 16.♖e1 ♖e8 17.h3 ♗d7

18.♘f5

18.♗d2!? is an interesting try by grandmaster Sergey Volkov. There can follow **18...♘c4 19.♗b4 ♕b6** and now:

A) **20.♖a2?!** An unnatural position for the rook. **20...g6 21.♕c1**

A1) **21...♗xb5 22.♕h6 ♗f8 23.♕f4♙** It would appear that White has certain compensation for the pawn, though, in the long run, Black's defensive possibilities are excellent;

A2) **21...♖ac8 22.♕f4 ♗f8 23.♘g5** 23.♖aa1!? ♗g7 24.♖e2 ♖e7∞. **23...♖e7∓ 24.♗xc5 ♕xc5 25.e6 fxe6 26.♘dxe6 ♕d6−+;**

A3) **21...f6** and now:

A31) **22.♕f4 fxe5 23.♘xe5 ♕f6 24.♕xf6 ♗xf6 25.♗xc5 ♗xe5 26.♖d1** 26.♖aa1?

26...♗f6!−+. **26...♗f6 27.♗b4∞** still with slightly better odds for Black;

A32) **22.♗xc5 ♗xc5 23.♗e4 ♘xe5 24.♗xd5+ ♔g7 25.♘xe5 ♖xe5 26.♖xe5 fxe5 27.♘f3 ♖c8** with a complex position in which we still think Black has the upper hand with his bishop pair.

A321) **28.♕a1 ♗xb5 29.♖c2** 29.♕xe5+ ♕f6 30.♕xf6+ ♔xf6 31.♗xb7 ♖b8 32.♗d5 ♖d8 33.♗e4 ♖d1+ 34.♔h2 ♖c1↑

And Black has the initiative.

29...♕f6 30.♕b1∞ 30.♗xb7 ♖c7 31.♗e4 ♗d6 32.♖xc7+ ♗xc7 33.♕b2 ♗d7 34.♕b7 ♕d6∞;

A322) **28.♕g5?!⇄ ♕f6?!⇄** 28...♖e8∓ 29.♘xe5 ♗d6 30.♘f3 ♕xb5 Without a doubt, the bishop pair and the weak a3-pawn give Black the advantage. **29.♗xb7 ♖c7∞** Volkov-Markidis, Kavala 2012;

B) **20.♖b1**

Certainly a more natural spot for the rook . Let us look at the analyses:

B1) 20...♘e4!?

B11) 21.♗xe4   21.♗xe7   ♖xe7
22.♗xe4 dxe4 23.♖xe4 ♕g6∞; 21.e6
fxe6 **21...dxe4 22.e6** 22.♖xe4?! ♕g6∓.
**22...♗xe6 23.♖xe4 ♘xa3 24.♘xe6
fxe6** 24...♘xb1 25.♘xg7. **25.♗xa3
♗xa3 26.♖xa4 ♗c5∞**

B2) 20...♘e6 and now:

B21) 21.♗xe7 ♘xd4 **22.♕xd4**
22.♗b4 ♘xc2 23.♕xc2 ♕xb5∓.
22...♕xd4 23.♘xd4 ♖xe7 24.♖b4

♖xe5 25.♖xe5 ♘xe5∞ 26.♖xa4 ♖xa4
27.♗xa4 ♘c4 28.♗b3 ♔f8 29.a4 ♔e7
30.♗xc4 dxc4 31.a5 ♔d6 32.a6 bxa6
33.bxa6 ♔c7∓;

**B22) 21.♕d3 g6 22.♘xe6 ♗xe6
23.♗xe7 ♖xe7 24.♘d4** 24.♖b4 ♕c5∞.
24...♗d7 **25.♘f3** 25.f4 ♗f5−+.
25...♗f5∓

**18...♗xf5 19.♗xf5 ♘c4 20.♘d4
g6 21.♗g4 ♘e4**

And Black takes the initiative,
Cheparinov-Vitiugov, Moscow 2011.

Conclusion

Regardless of the fact that the authors have a subjective view
concerning the continuation recommended here, and considering they also have it in their arsenal, we have tried to give objective opinions and analysis in all variations. We feel that Black has
a satisfactory game in all the lines. And not just a satisfactory
game, but we recommended an abundance of dynamic and active possibilities in the fight for an initiative.

We feel that this continuation will not lose popularity in the future – quite the contrary! But as they say, the gauntlet has been
thrown down before the white player, and it will be very interesting to see how things develop in the future, especially in the
matches between top players.

In the meantime we recommend to all Bogo-Indian fans, if they
haven't done so already, to try out and adopt this rather unusual
variation as it gives Black an excellent game!

Exercises

15.6 (1) Find the best move.
(solution on page 455)

15.6 (2) How to continue development with black?
(solution on page 455)

15.6 (3) How to complete development and how to get compensation for the minus pawn?
(solution on page 455)

Part III: 3.♘c3

For players preferring the Nimzo-Indian as White, 3.♘c3 is certainly the logical choice. Compared to the standard positions, Black has additional possibilities, considering that the g8-knight is still on its starting square. As we shall see, many of the positions in this line are unorthodox, but we feel that Black can achieves satisfactory play.

Chapter 16

3...c5

3...c5 is the continuation we recommend. Other possibilities should definitely be considered, but they are not the subject of this book.

Chapter 16.1

Central Play: 4.♘f3 d5

1.d4 e6 2.c4 ♗b4+ 3.♘c3 c5 4.♘f3 d5

With 4.♘f3 White opts for natural piece development and now it is up to Black to choose the correct game plan. White's other options are not satisfactory in the fight for the initiative. They are listed further below. First we will examine a few alternatives for Black to the move 3...c5.

A) **3...b6** 4.e4 ♗b7 5.♕c2 ♗xc3+ 6.bxc3 ♘e7 7.♘f3 d6 8.♗d3 ♕d7 9.0-0 ♘bc6 10.♗e3 ♘a5 11.♘d2 ♗a6 12.f4 f5 13.d5 0-0 14.♖ae1 exd5 15.cxd5 ♗xd3 16.♕xd3 ♖ae8 17.c4 c6 18.♗d4 fxe4 19.♘xe4± Volkov-Khismatullin, Moscow 2013;

B) **3...f5 4.g3!**

The most precise move order. It is very important to stop the fianchetto of the black light-squared bishop, completing an ideal set-up of the black pieces. If 4.♕c2 b6! 5.a3 ♗xc3+ 6.♕xc3 ♘f6 7.♘f3 ♗b7 8.g3 0-0 9.♗g2 d6 10.0-0 ♕e8 11.b4 ♘bd7 12.♗b2 ♕h5 13.d5 e5 14.♘h4 f4 15.♕f3 ♕g5 16.♗h3 b5! Gonda-Pap, Gyula 2013. **4...♘f6 5.♗g2 0-0 6.♘f3 d6 7.0-0 ♗xc3 8.bxc3 ♘c6 9.♘d2?!** 9.♖b1±. **9...e5 10.c5 e4 11.cxd6 cxd6 12.e3 ♗e6 13.♕e2 ♖c8 14.c4 d5 15.♖d1 ♗f7 16.♗a3 ♗h5∓** Salem-Amin, Istanbul 2012;

C) **3...d5** This is the move we will meet in the next phase as well, after 4.♘f3. It is always a serious alternative for Black.

C1) **4.a3** 4.♘f3 ♘e7 5.♗d2 c5 6.a3 ♗xc3 7.♗xc3 cxd4 8.♗xd4 0-0 9.e3 ♘bc6 10.♗c3 b6 11.♕c2 h6 12.cxd5 exd5 13.♗e2 ♗f5 14.♕a4 ♗e4 15.0-0 a6 16.b4 b5 17.♕b3± Van Wely-I. Sokolov, Malmö 2013. **4...♗xc3+ 5.bxc3 c5 6.e3 ♘e7**

In this specific move order in the opening, game plans with the knight on e7 will be frequent in the upcoming chapters! **7.♗d3** 7.♘f3 ♘bc6 8.♗d3 dxc4 (8...b6 9.0-0 ♗a6 10.cxd5 ♗xd3 11.♕xd3 ♕xd5 12.♖d1 ♘a5 13.♕b5+ ♘ec6 14.a4 0-0 15.♗a3 ♖fd8 16.h3 cxd4 17.cxd4 ♖ac8 18.♖ac1 ♘b8 19.♘d2 h6 20.♗e7 ♖e8 21.♗b4 ♘ac6 22.♗c3 ♘e7± Onischuk-Nogueiras Santiago, Buenos Aires 2005) 9.♗xc4 ♕c7 10.0-0 0-0 11.♗a2 h6 12.e4 ♖d8 13.♗e3 b6 14.♕e2 ♗b7 15.♖ad1 ♘g6 16.♗c1 ♘ce7 17.♖fe1 ♖ac8 18.♗b1 ♗c6 19.♗b2± Grigoriants-Nisipeanu,

Mamaia 2013. **7...dxc4 8.♗xc4 ♕c7 9.♕e2 0-0 10.♗b2 ♘bc6 11.♘f3 e5 12.♖d1 ♗g4 13.d5?! e4 14.dxc6 exf3 15.gxf3 ♕xc6 16.e4 ♗e6 17.♗b5 ♕c7 18.c4? a6 19.♗a4 ♕a5+−+** Beliavsky-Yu Yangyi, Tromsø 2013.

4.♘f3

A) If **4.dxc5 ♗xc3+ 5.bxc3 ♕a5** and now:

A1) **6.♕d4 ♘f6 7.f3 ♘c6 8.♕e3 0-0 8...b6!**

9.cxb6 axb6 10.♕d2 ♗a6 11.e4 ♘e5∓. 9.h4? e5 10.g4 ♘d4 11.♕d2 ♘e6 12.♖b1 ♕xc5 13.e4 d6 14.♖b5 ♕c7 15.♗a3 ♖d8 16.♘h3 b6∓ Popovic-Nikcevic, Herceg Novi 2006;

A2) **6.♗d2 ♘f6 7.f3 ♘c6 8.♘h3 0-0 9.♘f2 ♕xc5 10.♕a4 d5 11.♘d3 ♕xc4 12.♕xc4 dxc4 13.♘b2 e5 14.e4 ♗e6 15.♗xc4 ♗xc4 16.♘xc4 ♖ac8 17.♔e2 ♘d7 18.♘d6 ♖c7 19.♘b5 ♖cc8 20.♘d6 ♖c7 21.♘b5 ♖cc8 22.♘d6** draw agreed, Hebden-Arkell, Buxton 2012;

A3) **6.♘f3 ♘f6**

A31) **7.e3**

7...0-0 7...♘a6!. **8.♘d4 ♘e4 9.♗b2 ♘xc5 10.♘b3 ♕c7 11.♘xc5 ♕xc5 12.♕b3 d6 13.♖d1 ♖d8 14.♗a3 ♕e5 15.c5 d5 16.c4 ♘c6 17.♗e2 dxc4** 17...d4!∞. **18.♖xd8+ ♘xd8 19.♕xc4 ♕d5 20.♕xd5 exd5 21.♔d2±** Alekhine-Keres, Bad Nauheim 1936;

A32) **7.♕c2 ♘a6 8.♘d2 ♘xc5 9.g3 d6 10.♗g2 ♗d7 11.0-0 ♖c8 12.♘b3 ♕a4 13.♗f4 ♘c6 14.♗xc6+ ♖xc6 15.♖fd1 e5 16.♗e3∓** Kahn-Tolnai, Budapest 1993;

A33) **7.♘d2 ♘a6 8.♘b3 ♕xc3+ 9.♗d2 ♕e5 10.♖c1 ♘e4 11.♗e3 ♘axc5 12.♗d4 ♕c7 13.♗xg7 ♖g8 14.♗d4 ♘xb3 15.axb3 ♕a5+ 16.♗c3 ♘xc3 17.♕d2 b5 18.cxb5 ♗b7 19.♖xc3 ♕xb5↑↑** Hebden-Arkell, Amsterdam 2012;

A4) **6.♕b3 ♘a6** 6...♘f6 7.f3 ♘a6 8.♗e3 0-0 9.♘h3 b6 10.cxb6 ♖b8 11.♗d4?! axb6 12.♕b5 d6 13.♕xa5 bxa5 14.0-0-0 e5 15.♗f2 ♗xh3 16.gxh3 ♖fd8± Schuurman-Komarov, Bratto 2006. **7.♗e3** 7.♗d2 ♘xc5 8.♕b4 ♕c7∓; 7.♕a3 ♕xc5 8.♕xc5 ♘xc5 9.♘f3 ♘f6 10.♘d4 ♔e7 11.f3 d6 12.♗a3 ♗d7 13.e4 ♖hc8 14.♗e2

♘e8 15.♔d2 f6 16.♖he1 ♘a4 17.♘c2 ♔f7 18.♘e3 ♖c7∓ P. Schmidt-Keres, Parnu 1936. **7...♘e7!**

Black uses all of the specific features of his position as well as the atypical move order, which grants him flexible play. **8.♘f3 ♘c6 9.g3 ♘xc5 10.♕c2 b6 11.♗g2** 11.♘d2 ♕a4!. **11...♕a4!↑**

B) **4.a3 ♗xc3+ 5.bxc3 ♘c6** 5...b6!?; 5...f5 6.e4 fxe4 7.♕h5+ g6 8.♕xc5 ♘c6 9.h4 ♕a5 10.♕xa5 ♘xa5 11.h5 gxh5 12.♖b1 b6 13.c5 ♘f6 14.♗g5 0-0 15.♗xf6 ♖xf6 16.♖xh5± Astaneh Lopez-Arkell, Bunratty 2013. **6.e3** 6.e4 b6 7.♘f3 ♘ge7 8.♗d3 ♗a6 9.♗g5 h6 10.♗h4 ♘a5 11.♕e2 d6 12.0-0 ♖c8 13.♖ac1 ♕d7∞ 14.e5 d5 15.cxd5 ♗xd3 16.♕xd3 (Khismatullin-Rakhmanov, Khanty-Mansiysk 2013) 16...♘xd5!N

17.c4 ♘f4 18.♕e4 g5 19.♗g3 ♕b7∞. **6...d6** 6...b6!?N

Very unusual in modern chess: a theoretical novelty on move 6! Black has an excellent game and can take a creative approach to the upcoming middlegame, for example: **7.♘f3 ♗a6 8.♗d3 ♘a5 9.dxc5** (9.♕e2 ♖c8!) **9...♕c7! 10.e4 ♘e7∞. 7.♗d3 e5** and now:

B1) **8.♘f3 f5!**

Complete control of the e4-square is the key to Black's game. 8...♘f6 would transpose to the Hübner Variation of the Nimzo-Indian. **9.♗c2 ♘f6** with good play for Black;

B2) **8.♘e2 f5! 9.e4 f4 10.g3 f3 11.♘g1 cxd4 12.cxd4 ♘xd4 13.h3 ♘f6 14.♗e3 0-0 15.♗xd4 exd4 16.♘xf3 ♖e8 17.♕e2 ♗d7∓** Alexandrov-Komarov, Kherson 1991;

B3) **8.d5 ♘ce7 9.e4 ♘g6 10.♘e2 ♘h4** 10...♘f6 11.0-0 0-0 12.f3 ♗d7 13.♗e3 ♖b8 14.a4 ♕a5 15.♕d2 ♘h5∞. **11.0-0 g5 12.♘g3 h6 13.♘f5 ♘xf5 14.exf5 ♗d7 15.♖e1 ♕f6 16.g4**

♕g7 **17.f3 h5 18.♖a2∓** Spirin-Eingorn, Metz 2009.

4...d5 5.e3

We feel this is the most solid move to maintain the advantage of the first move. Other possibilities lead to complicated play:

5.cxd5 exd5 6.dxc5 6.♗g5 f6 7.♗d2 ♘c6 8.dxc5 ♗g4 9.♕a4 ♗xf3 10.gxf3 ♘e7 11.0-0-0 ♗xc5 12.♗h3 0-0 13.♗e6+ ♔h8 14.♗f4 d4 15.♘e4 ♗b6 16.♔b1 ♘g6 17.♗g3 f5 18.♘d6 f4 19.♘f7+ ♖xf7 20.♗xf7 ♘ge5∓ Dubov-I. Sokolov, Aix-les-Bains 2011. **6...♘c6 7.e3** 7.♗g5 ♘ge7 8.e3 0-0 9.♗e2 ♕a5 10.0-0 ♗xc3 11.bxc3 ♕xc5 12.♖c1 ♗e6 13.♘d4 ♘g6 14.♕b3 h6 15.♕xb7 ♘xd4 16.cxd4 ♕b6 17.♕xb6 axb6 18.♗f4 ♘xf4 19.exf4 ♖xa2 20.♗f3 Mamedyarov-Movsesian, Moscow 2008. **7...♘f6 8.♕c2** 8.♗e2 0-0 9.0-0 ♗xc5 10.b3 a6 11.♗b2 ♗a7 12.♕d3 ♗e6 13.♖fd1 ♕e7 14.♖d2 ♖ad8 15.♖ad1 ♗g4 16.♕b1 ♗xf3 17.♗xf3 d4 18.exd4 ♘xd4 19.♘e4 ♘xf3+ 20.gxf3 ♘xe4 21.♕xe4 ♕g5+ 22.♕g4 ♗xf2+∓ l'Ami-Sokolov, Hilversum 2006. **8...0-0 9.♗e2 ♗xc5 10.0-0 ♕e7 11.b3 ♗g4 12.♗b2 ♖fd8 13.♖ad1 ♖ac8 14.♘a4 ♗d6 15.♕b1 ♘e4 16.♕a1 ♘e5! 17.♘d4 ♕h4 18.f4 ♗xe2 19.♘xe2 ♘g4−+** Wiedenkeller-Stefansson, Istanbul 2012

5...♘e7

An attempt to play creatively in the opening phase. Considering the positioning of the central pawns and the natural development of the white pieces, it probably does not grant Black full equality. Certainly, the logical alternative is the putting the knight on the natural square f6: 5...♘f6 6.♗d3, with transposition to the Nimzo-Indian.

6.♗d3

6.♗d2 cxd4 7.♘xd4 ♘bc6 8.a3 ♗d6 9.♘f3 a6 10.♕c2 0-0 11.♗d3 h6 12.0-0 ♗d7 13.cxd5 exd5 14.♘e2 ♖c8 15.♗c3 ♗g4 16.♘ed4 ♗b8 17.h3 ♘xd4 18.♘xd4 ♕d6 19.f4 ♗d7 20.♕f2 ♗a7∞ Wang Yue-Barsov, Doha 2006

6...♘bc6 7.0-0 dxc4 8.♗xc4 0-0 9.a3 ♗a5

9...cxd4 10.axb4 dxc3 11.bxc3 ♕c7 12.♕b3 ♖b8 13.♗e2 b5 14.e4 a6 15.♗e3 ♗b7 16.c4 bxc4 17.♕xc4± ♖fc8 18.♖fb1 ♘g6 19.♕c5 ♕d8 20.♕h5 h6 21.♘e1 ♕f6 22.♗f1 ♘xb4 23.♖a4 ♘c6 24.♘d3 ♗a8 H. Hernandez Carmenatcs-Nogueiras Santiago, Havana 2010.

10.♕d3 a6 11.dxc5 ♕xd3 12.♗xd3 ♗xc3 13.bxc3 ♖d8 14.♖d1 e5

15.♗b2?

15.e4N is a natural move that allows White to keep his advantage.

15...♖xd3 16.♖xd3 e4 17.♖d2 exf3 18.gxf3∓

Arab-Nogueiras Santiago, Turin 2006.

Conclusion

We have considered an array of game plans after 3.♘c3 that are possible due to the specific move order in the opening. It is important to remember and understand that, in certain positions, having the knight still on g8 may provide Black with additional control of the e4-square with ...f7-f5 followed by ...♘f6, or with the more flexible ...♘e7. The best game plan for White, we find, is to develop naturally. More on this in the following chapters!

Exercises

16.1 (1) Find the best plan to play against White's pawn structure!
(solution on page 455)

16.1 (2) Find the plan. Should Black take a pawn on c5, and if so, with which piece?
(solution on page 455)

16.1 (3) Find the plan.
(solution on page 456)

Chapter 16.2

Transpositions: 4.♘f3 ♘f6

1.d4 e6 2.c4 ♗b4+ 3.♘c3 c5 4.♘f3 ♘f6

After the standard move 4.♘f3, we think that Black ought to respond in the same manner, i.e. move his knight to the standard f6-square! In this move order, we will consider the transposition to the Kasparov Variation of the Nimzo-Indian. Regardless of the specific order of moves by Black, the transposition is possible, and besides the Kasparov Variation, the Hübner Variation is also recommended.

5.g3

5.e3 ♘c6 transposes to the Hübner Variation of the Nimzo-Indian.
   5...cxd4 6.♘xd4 ♘e4 7.♕d3 7.♕c2

This move has gained popularity lately, however it does not pose a problem to Black. The easiest way is to take the c3-pawn with the knight and thus to damage White's pawn structure. Other options are very hazardous for Black.

A) **7...♘xc3**

The recommended plan. White has an edge in development and has the diagonals and files open. However, Black can complete his development slowly and with caution, and later in the game the weak pawns on the unprotected c-file may become objects of attack for him. If Black plays well, the position is unclear:
8.bxc3 ♗e7 9.♗g2 d6 9...0-0 10.0-0 a6 11.♖b1 ♕c7 12.♕b3 d6 13.♗xb7 ♗xb7 14.♕xb7 ♖a7 15.♕xc7 ♖xc7 16.♖b6 ♖xc4 17.♗d2 ♘d7 18.♖xa6 ♘c5 19.♖a7 ♗f6 20.♖b1 ♘e4 21.♗e1 ♖xc3 22.♘b5 ♖c2 23.♔f1 h5∞ Pogromsky-Predke, Loo 2013. **10.0-0 a6 11.♖b1 ♕c7 12.♖d1 ♘d7 13.♕a4**

13...0-0 13...♖b8!? 14.♘b3 0-0. Now:
A1) **14.♘b3 ♖b8 15.♗f4 g5** 15...e5 16.♗e3 ♘f6 17.♕b4∞; 15...♘e5 16.c5 dxc5 17.♘a5⩲. **16.♗e3 ♘e5**

17.♘a5?! 17.♘d2 ♗d7 18.♕a3∞. **17...♗d7 18.♕b4 b5∓ 19.♗d4 ♘xc4?!** 19...♖fe8 20.♗xe5 dxe5 21.c5 ♗xc5 22.♖xd7 ♗xb4 23.♖xc7 ♗xa5 24.♖c6 ♖ec8 25.♖xa6 ♗xc3∓; 19...♗g6! 20.♘b3 bxc4 21.♕a5 ♕c8!∓. **20.♘xc4 ♕xc4 21.♕b2** 21.♗e5! ♕xb4 22.cxb4 ♖b6 23.♗d4=. **21...♕c7** 21...♗c6 22.♗a7 ♗xg2 23.♗xb8 ♗d5 24.♗a7↑. **22.♕d2 ♗c6 23.♗xc6 ♕xc6 24.♗e3 f6**

... with a clear advantage for Black, Mastrovasilis-Antic, Valjevo 2011.
A2) **14.♘b5 ♕b8 15.♘d4 ♕c7** 15...♕c5!? 16.♕a3 ♕c7 △ 17.♘b5 axb5 18.♕xa8 ♘a4 19.♗d2 ♕xc4⩱. **16.♘b5=;**

B) **7...♕a5**
B1) **8.♗g2!**

The point. White wants to gain an advantage in development by temporarily sacrificing a piece. **8...♘xc3 9.0-0** and now:

B11) 9...♘c6 10.bxc3 ♗xc3 11.♘b3
B111) 11...♘d4 12.♘xd4 ♗xd4 13.♖b1

13...0-0 13...d6!? 14.♖d1 ♗c5 15.♗xb7 ♗xb7 16.♖xb7 ♕a6 17.♕b3 0-0 18.♗b2 ♖ac8 19.♕b5 ♕xa2 20.♖a1 a6 21.♕xa6 ♕xa6 22.♖xa6 ♖a8 23.♘c6 ♖fb8 24.♖xb8+ ♖xb8 25.e3 h5 Stocek-Ad. Horvath, Sydney 2013. **14.♖d1 ♗c5 15.♖b5 ♕c7 16.♗f4 e5 17.♖xc5 ♕xc5 18.♖d5 ♕b4 19.♗xe5 ♖e8 20.♗e4↑** Wojtaszek-Hracek, Aix-les-Bains 2011;

B112) 11...♕e5 12.♖b1 12.♗f4 ♕f6 13.♖ab1 ♗e5 14.e3 ♗xf4 15.exf4 0-0 16.♘c5 d5 17.♘xb7 ♗xb7 18.♖xb7 ♘a5 19.♖c7 ♘xc4 20.♖xc4 dxc4 21.♗xa8 ♖xa8 22.♕xc4 g6 23.♕c7 ♕d4 24.♖b1 Radjabov-Gashimov, Elista 2008. **12...♕f6 13.♘c5 ♗e5 14.♗a3 ♕e7 15.♕d3 a5 16.♘xb7**

With a winning advantage, Feller-Iordachescu, Khanty-Mansiysk 2011.

B12) 9...♘a4

The attempt to save the piece brings Black even bigger problems: **10.a3 ♗e7 11.♘b5 ♘xb2 12.♗d2 ♕d8 13.♗f4 d6 14.c5 0-0 15.cxd6 ♗f6 16.♘c7 ♘c6 17.♗xc6 bxc6 18.♘xa8 e5 19.♗e3 ♗h3 20.♕xb2 ♗xf1 21.♖xf1 ♕xa8 22.♖d1±** Matlakov-Diu, Taganrog 2011;

B13) 9...♘xe2+ 10.♕xe2 ♘c6 11.♘b3 11.♗e3 ♗e7 12.♖fd1 ♕e5 13.♕d2 0-0 14.♘b5 a6 15.♘d6 ♗xd6 16.♗f4 ♗b4 17.♕xb4 ♘xb4 18.♗xe5 ♘c6 19.♗d6 ♖e8 20.b4± P.H. Nielsen-B. Savchenko, Konya 2012. **11...♕d8 12.♗xc6 bxc6 13.c5 ♗a5 14.♕g4 0-0 15.♗h6 g6 16.♘xa5 ♕xa5 17.♕d4+−** Stocek-Tan, Philadelphia 2010;

B2) 8.♘b5 a6 9.♕xe4 axb5 10.♗d2 bxc4 11.♕xc4 ♘c6 12.♗g2 d5 13.♕h4 0-0 14.0-0 ♕b6∓ 15.b3 ♕a5 16.a3 ♗xc3 17.b4 ♗xb4 18.axb4 ♕xa1 19.♖xa1 ♖xa1+ 20.♗f1 ♖d1 21.♗c3 d4 22.♗b2 e5 23.f4 ♘e7 24.♔f2 ♘f5 25.♕h3 ♘e3 Shishkin-Hracek, Koszalin 1999;

B3) 8.♗d2 ♘xd2 9.♕xd2 ♘c6 10.♘xc6 bxc6 11.♖c1 0-0 12.a3 ♗e7∓ 13.♗g2 d5 14.0-0 ♖b8 15.♖fd1 ♖d8 16.cxd5 cxd5 17.♘xd5 ♖xd5 18.♗xd5 ♕xd2 19.♖xd2 exd5 20.♖c7∞ Hawelko-Wojtkiewicz, Slupsk 1989;

B4) 8.♘b3? ♕f5 9.♗d2 9.♘d2 ♕xf2+ 10.♔d1 ♗xc3 11.♕xe4 f5

12.♕d3 ♗f6∓ Kremenietsky-Popov, Moscow 1999. **9...♕xf2+ 10.♔d1 ♘xd2 11.♕xd2 ♘c6 12.a3 ♗xc3 13.♕xc3 0-0−+ 0-1** Menendez Solar-Petkov, Gijon 2007.

The transposition to the Kasparov Variation of the Nimzo-Indian does not improve White's position. Black has many possibilities to equalize. From among them we recommend the following two, which provide active possibilities in the fight for the initiative:

7...♗xc3+

7...♘xc3 is the second option, which until recently was very popular with grandmasters. Let us look into the options, supported by the excellent comments of grandmaster Postny in *ChessBase Magazine* and further analyses by the authors of this book:

8.bxc3 ♗e7 and now:

A) **9.♘b5**

A1) **9...0-0?!**

10.♗f4 ♘a6 11.♗g2 would be in White's favour: **11...♘c5** The alternatives aren't better: 11...f6 12.♕d2 ♘c5 13.♗c7 ♕e8 14.♗d6 ♗xd6 15.♕xd6 ♘a6 16.♕d4 ♕e7 17.0-0 ♕c5 18.♘d6 ♖b8 19.♖fd1 ♕xd4 20.cxd4 ♘c7 21.♖ab1± Czebe-Gyimesi, Hungary 1997; or 11...d5 12.cxd5 exd5 13.♕xd5 ♕a5 14.0-0 ♖d8 15.♕e4± Ribli-Majeric, Pula 2001; or 11...♕a5 12.0-0 d5 13.cxd5 ♗d7 14.a4 exd5 15.♗xd5± Granara Barreto-Fernandez, Villa Martelli 2007. **12.♕e3 ♕a5 13.0-0**

A11) **13...f6**

14.♘c7?! This is tempting, but it gives Black a chance to fight back. 14.♗c7! ♕a4 15.♖fd1 is positionally sound and much more annoying. White clearly has the initiative. Now:

A111) **14...♖b8? 15.♘d5+−**;

A112) **14...e5 15.♗xe5! fxe5** 15...d6 16.♗xd6 ♗xd6 17.♘xa8 ♗d7 18.♖ad1 ♖e8 19.♕d2 ♗e5 20.♗xb7±. **16.♕xe5 ♗f6** 16...♖f6 17.♘xa8 ♗d6 18.♕e8+ ♖f8 19.♕h5+−. **17.♗d5+ ♔h8 18.♕d6 ♖d8 19.♘xa8+−**;

A113) **14...d6! 15.♘xa8 g5 16.♖ab1 gxf4 17.♕xf4 f5∞**

A12) **13...a6? 14.♘c7 ♖a7 15.♘d5!** Now Black is in big trouble, as White gets full control of the dark squares. **15...exd5 16.♕xe7 dxc4 17.♕e3 ♖d8** bitious than 16... dxc5. Black has already grounds to play for more than equality. If 16...dxc5 17.♗xc5 ♗g4 18.♗g2 ♖d8 19.♕e3 b6 20.♕e4 ♗d7 21.♗a3 ♘d4 22.♖c1 ♘b5 23.♕b4, Agrest-Ftacnik, Khanty-Mansiysk 2010. **17.♗g2** 17.♕xd5 ♗e6. **17...♗e6 18.f4** 18.♗xd5 ♖d8. **18...0-0 19.0-0 e4 20.♕b5**

20...♘a5!N 20...f5 21.♖ab1 ♖f7 22.♖fd1 ♖d7 23.♖b2 ♖c8∞ Babujian-Van Wely, Tromsø 2010. **21.f5** 21.♖ab1 ♘c4 22.♗d4 ♖fb8. **21...♗d7 22.♕b4 ♘c4 23.♗d4 b6 24.f6 g6∓**

Back to the position after 8...♗e7.

B) 9.♗g2:

B1) 9...a6 10.0-0 0-0:

B11) 11.♖b1!? ♕c7?! In case of 11...♘c6 12.♗f4 (White gets very little after 12.♘xc6?! dxc6 13.♗e3 e5) 12...♕a5 13.♖fd1↑ it won't be easy for Black to complete his development.

12.♗f4 d6 12...e5? 13.♘f5±. **13.c5! e5** 13...♕xc5 14.♗xb7 ♗xb7 15.♖xb7 ♖e8 16.♖fb1±. **14.♘f5 ♗xf5** 14...exf4 15.cxd6 ♗xf5 16.dxc7 ♗xd3 17.cxd3 ♘c6 18.♖xb7 ♘a5 19.c8♕ ♖axc8 20.♖xe7 ♖xc3 21.♗d5 ♖xd3 22.♖d7±. The difference between the minor pieces is huge. **15.♕xf5 exf4 16.♖xb7 ♕d8 17.♖d1! fxg3 18.hxg3** with a very strong initiative for the piece;

B12) 11.♖d1

11...♕c7?! 11...d6 is the right move here, transposing to the recent encounter Mamedyarov-Karjakin, Moscow 2010. **12.♗f4 d6 13.c5!**

B121) 13...e5 14.cxd6 ♕xd6 15.♘f5 ♕f6 15...♗xf5? 16.♕xf5 ♕f6 17.♕xe5+−. **16.♘xe7+ ♕xe7 17.♗e3** (Jumabaev-Babujian, Martuni 2009) and the strong bishop pair promises White a stable advantage;

B122) 13...♕xc5 14.♘b3 ♕b6 15.♗xd6 ♖d8

16.♗xe7! The queen sacrifice is perfectly correct. 16.♗c5 ♖xd3 17.♗xb6 ♖xc3 is playable for Black. **16...♖xd3 17.♖xd3 ♘d7 18.♖ad1** 18.♘c5 ♘xc5 19.♖d8+ ♕xd8 20.♗xd8 ♗d7 21.♗e7 ♖c8 22.♖d1 ♗e8 23.♗xc5 ♖xc5 24.♗xb7±. **18...h6 19.c4!** 19.♖xd7? spoils the advantage, for example: 19...♗xd7 20.♖xd7 ♕b5. In normal conditions three pieces can overcome a queen, but here White's forces are not well coordinated: 21.♖xb7 ♕xe2 22.c4 a5 23.♗f1 ♕xa2 24.♘d4 a4 25.♘b5 a3 26.♘xa3 ♖xa3 27.♗xa3 ♕xa3 28.♖c7 ½-½ Le Quang Liem-Ghaem Maghami, Ha Long City 2009. **19...♕c7 20.c5 a5** 20...♘f6 21.♖d8+ ♔h7 22.♗xf6 gxf6 23.♖f8 ♔g7 24.♖dd8 with complete domination; 20...♖a7 21.♗d6 ♕d8 22.♗b8! ♖a8 23.♗f4 and after the forthcoming c5-c6 Black will suffer heavy material losses. **21.♗d6 ♕d8 22.c6 bxc6 23.♗f4 ♕b6** 23...g5 24.♗xc6 a4 25.♘c1 gxf4 26.♗xa8±. **24.♖d6 ♖a6 25.♖xc6 ♕xc6 26.♗xc6 ♖xc6 27.♘xa5±**

B2) 9...0-0

B21) 10.♘b5 Now 10...♘c6 would transpose to the line with 9.♘b5, but Black has another option: **10...a6! 11.♘d6 ♘c6 12.c5 ♕a5 13.♗xc6** 13.♗e3 ♘e5 14.♕c2 ♗xd6 15.cxd6 ♘c4⇄. **13...bxc6 14.♗e3 ♗xd6**

15.cxd6 ♕d5= Bezold-Volke, Austria 2001;

B22) **10.0-0**

B221) **10...♘a6 11.♖d1** 11.♘b5?! ♘c5 12.♕d4 d6 13.♖d1 e5 14.♕d2 ♕a5 15.♗a3 ♗e6 16.♗b4 ♕b6 17.♕e3 ♖ac8 18.♘d5 ♖fd8 19.♖ab1 ♕a6∓ Parker-Topalov, Singapore 1990. **11...♘c5 12.♕e3** 12.♕c2?! – the queen is too passive here, for example: 12...d6 13.♗e3 ♗d7 14.♘b5 ♗xb5 15.cxb5 ♕c7=. Now:

B2211) **12...♕a5**

13.♗d2?! 13.a4! d6 14.♗a3 ♗d7 15.♘f5 exf5 16.♕xe7±. **13...♘a4 14.♖ab1 ♕c7 15.♕d3 a6 16.♗f4 d6 17.♘b3 ♖d8 18.c5 ♘xc5 19.♘xc5 ♕xc5 20.♗xb7 ♗xb7 21.♖xb7 ♗f8 22.♕f3 ♕f5 23.e4 ♕f6 24.♕e3 h6 25.♕d3 ♖ac8=** Kuthan-Schlosser, Austria 2009;

B2212) **12...d6 13.♗a3 ♗d7 14.♖ab1 ♖b8 15.♗xc5 dxc5**

16.♘b5 16.♘c6! bxc6 17.♖xb8 ♛xb8 18.♖xd7 ♛b1+ 19.♗f1 ♖e8 20.♛f4. Despite the symmetrical pawn structure and opposite-coloured bishops, it won't be easy for Black to equalize. White's rook is very active compared to its counterpart. **16...a6 17.♘d6 ♛c7 18.♛f4??** A tactical oversight. 18.♘xb7 ♗a4 19.♖d2 ♖fd8 20.♖db2=. **18...♗a4! 19.♖d2 ♗xd6??** Returning the favour. 19...e5! 20.♛xe5 ♖fd8 would win a piece. **20.♖xd6** Now the position is back to 'normal'. White has a slight edge. **20...♖fd8 21.♖xd8+ ♛xd8 22.h4 b6 23.♖b2 h6 24.♖d2±** P.H. Nielsen-Hracek, Germany 2007.

B222) **10...d6**

11.♖d1 11.♖b1 is met by 11...♘d7=. **11...a6** This is the right move order here! Now:

B2221) **12.♘b3 ♛c7 13.♗a3** 13.♗f4 e5 14.♗e3 ♘d7 15.♘d2 f5 16.♖ab1 ♖b8 17.♗a7 ♖a8 18.♗e3 ♖b8 19.♗a7 ♖a8 20.♗d5+ Nakamura avoids the repetition of moves, but his desire to play for a win in this position was based on self-confidence rather than on objective evaluation. 20...♔h8 21.♛e3 ♘f6 22.♗b6 ♛d7 23.f4 ♛e8 24.♘f3 ♛h5 25.♔h1 ♖e8 26.♛g1 ♘xd5 27.cxd5 ♗f6

With an edge for Black, Nakamura-Karjakin, Wijk aan Zee 2010. **13...♖d8 14.♖ab1 ♘c6 15.f4?**

15...b6? Missing a neat tactical trick: 15...♘e5! 16.fxe5 dxe5 and Black gains back the bishop on a3 and is clearly better. **16.♖d2 ♗b7 17.♛e3 d5 18.♗xe7 ♘xe7 19.c5 b5∓** Ibraev-Iordachescu, Dubai 2010;

B2222) **12.♘f3 ♘d7 13.♗a3 ♘c5 14.♗xc5 dxc5 15.♛xd8 ♖xd8 16.♘e5 ♖b8 17.♖ab1 ♖xd1+ 18.♖xd1 ♔f8 19.♘d7+ ♗xd7 20.♖xd7 b6=** Agrest-Iordachescu, Dresden 2008;

B2223) **12.♗a3 ♛c7 13.♖ab1 ♖d8 14.♛e3 ♗f8 15.♘f3 ♗e7 16.♛b6 ♛xb6 17.♖xb6 ♘d7 18.♖b2 ♘c5 19.♖bd2 ♖e8 20.♗xc5 dxc5 21.♘e5 ♔f8 22.♖b1±** Grischuk-Karjakin, Monaco 2011;

B2224) **12.♗e4 h6 13.♛f3 ♘d7!**

The b7-pawn is of little significance. For Black it is far more important to complete his development. **14.♖b1** 14.♗xb7?! ♘e5 15.♕g2 ♗xb7 16.♕xb7 ♗f6∓. The sacrifice of the b7-pawn is temporary. Black has solved the problem of his queenside development and will soon gain the pawn back, keeping a superior pawn structure. **14...♕c7 15.♗c2** 15.♗xb7? ♘e5 16.♕g2 ♖b8 17.♗e4 ♗d7∓. **15...♘e5** 15...♕xc4...

Somewhat risky, but principled. **12.♗e3** 12.♗c1 ♘e5 13.♕c2 ♘xc4 14.e4 ♕a5 15.♖b1 ♘a3 16.♗xa3 ♕xa3 17.e5 d5 18.f4 gxf4 19.♖xf4 f5 20.exf6 ♗xf6 21.♖bf1 ♕e7∞ Nakamura-Karjakin, Monaco 2011. **12...♘e5 13.♕e4 d6 14.♘f3 f5 15.♕d4 ♘f7 16.♖fd1 ♗f6 17.♕d3 ♗d7 18.c5 d5∞** Schekachev-Fedorchuk, Coubertin 2009;

B2232) **11.♖d1**

... would allow White to create a messy position with 16.♗xh6! gxh6 17.♕g4+ ♗g5 18.f4. **16.♕h5 ♗f6 17.♖b4** 17.♗xh6 gxh6 18.♕xh6 ♘g6 19.♗xg6 fxg6 20.♕xg6+ ♕g7∓. **17...♖d8∓ 18.♘f3 ♗d7 19.♗e3 ♘xf3+ 20.♕xf3 ♗c6 21.♗e4 ♗xe4 22.♕xe4 ♖d7 23.♖db1 d5 24.♕f3 b5∞** Mamedyarov-Karjakin, Moscow 2010.

B223) **10...♘c6**

B2231) **11.♗f4 g5!**

B22321) **11...♘e5 12.♕e4 ♕a5** 12...♘xc4 13.♘xe6 fxe6 14.♕xc4 d5 15.♕d3±. **13.♗f4** 13.♘b3 ♕c7 14.♗f4 f6 15.c5 ♖b8=; 13.♘b5 a6 14.♕xe5 ♗f6 15.♕c5 axb5 16.cxb5 ♕xc3 17.♕xc3 ♗xc3 18.♖b1 ♖xa2∓. **13...♘g6 14.♘b3 ♕xc3 15.♖ac1 ♕b4 16.♗c7** White has excellent compensation for the sacrificed pawn;

B22322) **11...♕a5 12.♘b3 ♕c7 13.c5** A typical squeezing move in this opening line. **13...b6** Otherwise it's hard for Black to complete his development. **14.&f4** Forcing a certain concession. **14...e5 15.&e3 &b8** 15...f5?! 16.a4 f4 17.&c1 &h8 18.&a3. **16.&e4± h6 17.&d5** 17.cxb6 axb6 18.&d2 b5 19.&ab1±. **17...&h8 18.&f5 bxc5 19.&h5 d6 20.&xf7 &g4 21.&xg4 &xf7 22.&d2 &f8 23.&e4±** Jianu-Fedorchuk, Plovdiv 2008.

C) **9.&f4 d6 10.&b5 e5 11.c5!**

The only way to fight for an opening initiative. If 11.&e3 a6 12.&a7 &d7 13.&g2 &c6 14.&xc6 &xc6 15.&xc6+ bxc6 16.0-0 0-0= Mastrovasilis-Fedorchuk, Cappelle la Grande 2010. **11...exf4 12.cxd6 0-0 13.dxe7 &xe7 14.&g2 &d8 15.&d4 &c7!** Black shouldn't take on g3 before White castles, so as not to open the h-file. **16.0-0 fxg3** Now is the right moment for this. **17.hxg3**

17...&a6! The natural 17...&c6?! is an inaccuracy. I like the plan of bringing the

knight to c5. 18.&ab1 &d7 19.&fd1 &a5 20.&e4 g6 21.&f3 &c6 22.&xc6 &xd1+ 23.&xd1 &xc6 24.&d5 &e8 25.c4±. Now White enjoys long-lasting pressure, as his bishop is superior to the knight. 25...&e7 26.&g2 h5 27.&d3 &g7 28.&f4± Ponomariov-Gashimov, Astrakhan 2010. **18.&fd1 &d7 19.&ab1** 19.&b5 &xb5 20.&xb5 &c5=. **19...&c5 20.&c4 &ac8 21.&d5 &a4** 21...&f8=. **22.&xb7 &xd1 23.&xc8 &xe2 24.&xe2 &xc8=**

Back to the main line.
8.bxc3 &c5

Black has given up the bishop pair but instead he plays on White's pawn structure. In the further course of the game, White attempts to open up the position and highlight the domination of the bishop pair. Black gradually finishes his development obtains a great game.
9.&f3
White blocks the development of the black light-squared bishop on the optimal diagonal. Other options are:

A) **9.&e3 b6 10.&g2 &b7 11.&xb7 &xb7** and now:

A1) 12.&a3 &c6 (12...&a6 13.&f5 &f6 14.&d6+ &xd6 15.&xd6 &c8 16.&d1 &xc4 17.0-0 &xc3 18.&d2 &c4 19.&e5↑ Vazquez Igarza-Granda Zuniga, Benasque 2013.

13.♘xc6 13.♘b5 ♘ca5 14.♗b4 a6 15.♕d4 f6 16.♗xa5 bxa5 17.♘d6+ ♘xd6 18.♕xd6 ♖c8 19.♕xa6 ♕c7 20.0-0 ♕xc4 21.♕xa5 ♕xc3 22.♕h5+ ♔e7 23.♕g4 ♔f7 24.♕h5+ ♔e7 25.♕g4 ♔f7 26.♕h5+ Fridman-Meier, Baden-Baden 2013. **13...dxc6 14.♕e5 ♕f6 15.♕c7 ♕xc3+ 16.♔f1 ♕xa3 17.♕xc6+ ♔e7 18.♕c7+ ♔f6 19.♕f4+ ♔e7 20.♕c7+ ♔f6 21.♕f4+ ♔e7 22.♕c7+ ♔f6** with a draw by repetition in Socko-Wojtaszek, Lublin 2011;

A2) **12.♕e4 ♘c6 13.♘xc6 dxc6**
A21) **14.0-0!? 0-0 15.♗a3**

15...♘c5 15...♖e8! 16.♕xc6 ♘a5∞. **16.♗xc5 bxc5 17.♕xc6 ♕d2 18.♕f3 ♖fd8±** Li Chao-Zhou Weiqi, Qinhuangdao 2011;

A22) **14.♗a3 ♕c7 15.♕d4 f6 16.♕e4 ♔f7 17.0-0 c5 18.♖ad1 ♘d6 19.♕f4 ♖hd8∓** Sipos-Gonda, Zalakaros 2009;

A23) **14.♕xc6+ ♕d7 15.♕xd7+ ♔xd7 16.♗a3 ♖hc8 17.0-0-0+ ♔e8 18.♖d4 ♖c7 19.♖h4 h6 20.♖d1 ♖ac8∞** Drazic-Perunovic, Vrnjacka Banja 2010.

B) **9.♕d2**

9...b6 10.♘b5 0-0 11.♘d6 ♗b7 12.f3 12.♘xb7 ♘xb7 13.♗g2 ♘c6 14.♗a3 ♖e8 15.♖d1 ♕f6 16.0-0 ♖ed8 17.f4 ♖ac8 18.g4?! d6 19.g5 ♕e7 20.f5 ♘e5∓ Parker-Adams, England 2003. **12...♗c6 13.♗a3 ♘ba6 14.♗g2 f5 15.0-0 e5! 16.♖ad1 ♕e7 17.f4 e4 18.♕d4 ♖f6 19.♖d2 ♖af8 20.e3 ♖h6 21.♖fd1 ♖ff6! 22.♘b5 d6∓** Ivanisevic-Grigorov, Kallithea 2009;

C) **9.♕c2 b6 10.♗g2 ♗b7 11.♗xb7 ♘xb7 12.♕e4** transposes to 9.♕e3.

9...d6 10.♗g2
10.♗a3

10...0-0 11.♗g2 11.♖d1 ♕a5 12.♘b5 ♗d7 13.♗b4 ♕xa2 14.♗xc5 dxc5 15.♘c7 ♗a4∓ P.H. Nielsen-Ivanchuk,

Havana 2007. **11...♘bd7 12.♕e3** 12.0-0 ♘e5 13.♕f4 ♘xc4 14.♘c6 bxc6 15.♕xc4 ♗a6 16.♕d4 ♕a5 17.♗b4 ♕c7 18.♗xc5 dxc5 19.♕e3 ♖ab8∓ Garcia Roman-Malakhatko, Rhone 2008. **12...♘b6 13.♗xc5 ♘xc4 14.♕d3 dxc5 15.♕xc4 cxd4 16.♕xd4** 16.cxd4 ♕a5+ 17.♔f1 ♖d8↑. **16...♕c7 17.0-0** 17.♖d1 e5 18.♕b4 a5 19.♕b3 ♗e6 20.♗d5 ♗xd5 21.♖xd5 a4 22.♕b4 ♕c6∞ Kozlov-Adams, Turin 2006. **17...♗d7 18.♖fb1 ♗c6 19.♕c5**

19...h6? 19...♖fc8 20.♗xc6 b6 21.♕b4 ♕xc6 22.♖d1 h6 23.a4=. **20.♗xc6 bxc6 21.♖b2±** Mastrovasilis-Antic, Thessaloniki 2011.

10...e5

Black consistently takes control of the dark squares, taking into account that he had already given up his dark-squared bishop. Black restricts White's dark-squared bishop and at the same

time forces him to declare his intentions with the knight in the centre.

11.♕e3

A) **11.♘b3**

11...♘ba6 and now:

A1) **12.♗a3 ♕c7 13.♖d1 ♗e6 14.♘xc5 ♘xc5 15.♗xc5 ♕xc5 16.♕xb7 ♖c8 17.♗d5 ♗xd5 18.♕xd5 ♕xd5** 18...♕xc4 19.♕xd6 ♕xc3+ 20.♔f1↑ Moiseenko-Gyimesi, Maalot-Tarshiha 2008. **19.♖xd5 ♖xc4 20.♖xd6 ♖xc3 21.0-0 ♔e7 22.♖a6 ♖c7=** Kuzubov-Gyimesi, Bornholm 2008;

A2) **12.0-0 0-0 13.♗a3 ♕c7**

A21) **14.♖fd1 ♗e6 15.♘xc5 ♘xc5 16.♗xc5 ♕xc5 17.♕xb7 ♗xc4**

A211) **18.♕xa8 ♖xa8 19.♗xa8 ♗xe2 20.♖d2 ♗g4!N** 20...♗b5 21.♖ad1?! (21.♖b1∞) 21...♗a4 22.♖c1?! (22.♖xd6) 22...h5∓ Wang Yue-Gyimesi, Beijing 2008. **21.♖b1 g5∓**;

A212) **18.♕b4 ♖ad8** 18...♖ac8?! 19.♖xd6 ♗xe2 20.♖d5 ♕xc3 21.♕xc3 ♖xc3 22.♖xe5 ♖c2 23.♖e7 a5 24.♗d5± Sedlak-Antic, Kragujevac 2009. **19.♖d2 a5 20.♕xc5 dxc5 21.♖ad1 ♖xd2 22.♖xd2 ♖b8 23.♗d5 ♗a6∞ 24.♗b3 ♔f8 25.♖d5** 25.f3 f6 26.♔f2 ♔e7. **25...c4 26.♗a4 ♖b1+ 27.♖d1 ♖b2**;

A22) **14.♕e3 ♗e6 15.♘xc5 ♘xc5 16.♗xc5 dxc5 17.♗d5** and now:

A221) **17...♖ae8!**

The beginning of an extremely flexible game plan, aiming to prove that the open d-file does not give an advantage to White, and the position of the bishop on d5 only looks good. If 17...♗d7 18.f4 ♖ae8 19.f5→ Cruz Lledo-Colon Garcia, Granada 2009. **18.♖fd1** 18.♗xe6 ♖xe6 19.♖ad1 e4 20.♖d5 b6 21.♖fd1 ♕c6∞. **18...♗c8! 19.♖d2 ♔h8 20.♖ad1 f5** and Black's pieces are perfectly coordinated.

B) **11.♘f5 ♕f6 12.♘e3 ♕xf3 13.♗xf3 ♗e6 14.♗a3** and now:

B1) **14...♘ba6 15.0-0-0 ♔e7 16.♗g2 ♖ad8 17.f4 f6 18.♖hf1 b6±** Kramnik-Anand, Monaco 2007;

B2) **14...♘bd7!** is more natural, bringing the knight closer to the centre: **15.0-0-0** 15.0-0 ♖c8∞. **15...♔e7 16.♖d2 a5N** 16...♖ac8 17.♖hd1 e4 18.♗g2 ♖c6∞ Pascual Perez-Janosi, LSS email 2008. **17.♖hd1 ♖a6** with good counterplay.

11...0-0

The standard option, although the following alternative should also be taken into consideration: **11...♗e6 12.♘xe6 fxe6 13.♗a3** 13.f4 exf4 14.gxf4 ♕h4+ 15.♕g3 ♕xg3+ 16.hxg3 ♘bd7 17.♗e3 ♖c8 18.♖d1 ♔e7 19.g4 ♘a4∞ Mekhitarian-Leitao, Campinas 2010. **13...♘ba6 14.♖d1 0-0 15.0-0 ♕c7 16.♖d2 ♖ad8 17.♖fd1 ♖f6 18.♔h1 h6 19.f4 exf4 20.gxf4 ♕a5 21.♗c1 ♕a4∞** Romanov-Macieja, Plovdiv 2008.

12.♘b3 ♘ba6 13.♘xc5

13.♗a3

This is an attempt to increase the pressure on the square c5 and to retain the tension.

13...♕c7 14.♖d1 ♗e6 15.♘xc5 dxc5 16.♗d5 ♖ae8 17.0-0 ♕a5 18.♗c1 ♗xd5 19.cxd5 ♕xa2 20.♕d3 ♕a4⯹ Vitiugov-Gyimesi, Plovdiv 2010.

13...♘xc5 14.♗a3 ♕c7 15.♖d1

15...♗e6?!

15...♖e8! Simple and effective. Black avoids tactical attacks and further into the game he will be able to neutralize White's initial advantage.

16.0-0 ♗e6 **17.♗xc5 dxc5 18.♗d5 ♗h3 19.♖fe1 ♖e7∞ 20.♕d2 ♖f8 21.♖ed1 ♔h8 22.♕f3 ♗c8** As we mentioned earlier, this plan is optimal for Black and it ought to be kept in mind. White's domination on the open d-file is only an optical illusion, and the bishop on d5 stands as an obstacle for White's major pieces. Black's chances are exceptionally good!

16.♖xd6 ♕xd6 17.♗xc5 ♕a6 18.♗xf8 ♖xf8 19.c5 ♕xa2 20.0-0±

Kazhgaleev-Ghaem Maghami, Dresden 2008.

Conclusion

In this chapter we have analysed the Kasparov Variation of the Nimzo-Indian Defence. We have suggested two ways for Black to obtain an active game. Not only does Black have no problems equalizing in the gambit line, but his chances also increase in the further course of the game.

It is important to pay attention to the positions and plans that we have highlighted. Also, the basic strategic principles of the game must not be overlooked. From the very beginning, White has the two bishops, open files and diagonals and an advantage in development, so he will aim at opening the position. Black ought to respond in the opposite way: to develop his pieces gradually and seek his chances in the complex middlegame.

Exercises

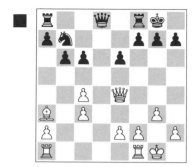

16.2 (1) Find the plan.
(solution on page 456)

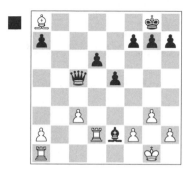

16.2 (2) The bishop is under attack, in which direction should it move?
(solution on page 456)

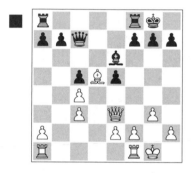

16.2 (3) find the most flexible plan!
(solution on page 456)

Chapter 16.3

The Classical 4.e3

1.d4 e6 2.c4 ♗b4+ 3.♘c3 c5 4.e3

With this continuation White leans towards a classic development of his pieces, and proposes a transition into the Nimzo-Indian. Still, as we will see further in the text, with this order of moves Black does not need to enter the Nimzo-Indian variation that we recommended, the Hübner Variation. But if he wants to play this variation, it would be more precise for White to play 4.♘f3 and on 4...♘f6, 5.e3. In this chapter we will show you why!

4...♘c6 5.♘f3

This is the first crossroads. Apart from this continuation, which we suggest as the main option, White has other possibilities, with dynamic play in the centre:

A) **5.d5**

A1) **5...♗xc3+ 6.bxc3 ♘a5** and now:
A11) **7.♗d3 b6 8.e4 ♗a6 9.♕e2 ♘e7 10.♘f3 0-0** 10...d6 11.dxe6. **11.0-0±**;
A12) **7.e4 b6 8.♗d3 d6 9.♘f3±**;
A2) **5...♘e5!? 6.f4 ♘g6** and now:
A21) **7.e4 e5 8.f5**

8...♕h4+ A more precise move is 8...♗xc3+N 9.bxc3 ♕h4+ 10.♔d2 ♘6e7∞. **9.♔d2 ♕f2+ 10.♕e2 ♕xe2+ 11.♗xe2 ♘6e7 12.a3 ♗xc3+ 13.♔xc3 ♘f6 14.♗f3±** Krysa-Perez Ponsa, Buenos Aires 2013;

A22) **7.♘f3**

A221) **7...♘f6 8.♗d3** 8.dxe6 ♗xc3+ 9.bxc3 dxe6 10.♕xd8+ ♔xd8 11.h4 b6 12.h5 ♘e7 13.h6 gxh6 14.♘e5 ♔e8 15.♖xh6 ♘d7 16.♘xd7 ♗xd7 17.g4 ♗c6 18.a4 ♗e4 19.a5 ♔d7 20.♖h2 ♘c6 21.a6 ♖ag8∓ Richter-Markidis, Rethymnon 2012. **8...0-0 9.0-0 ♗xc3 10.bxc3 exd5 11.cxd5 d6 12.f5 ♘e5 13.♘xe5 dxe5 14.e4 c4 15.♗c2 ♘e8 16.♖f3→**

A222) **7...f5!N**

Increasing his control of the e4-square, which is of vital importance. This move is possible thanks to the move order in the opening, so first ...f7-f5 and then

...♘f6 ! **8.dxe6** 8.♗d2 ♘f6 9.a3 ♗xc3 10.♗xc3 0-0 11.dxe6 ♕e7∞. **8...♗xc3+ 9.bxc3 dxe6∞**;

A223) **7...♗xc3+N 8.bxc3 f5! 9.g4?! fxg4 10.♘g5 ♘f6 11.♗d3 ♘h4**

B) **5.♘e2**

An interesting continuation which also promises a complicated game. The ensuing positions are yet to be tested in practice, but we believe that Black has excellent play:

B1) **5...♘ge7!?** and now:

B11) **6.dxc5!?** 6.a3 ♗xc3+ 7.♘xc3 cxd4 8.exd4 d5∞. **6...♗xc5 7.♘f4 ♘g6 8.g3 ♘xf4 9.gxf4 0-0 10.♗g2**

10...f5 10...e5!?.**11.a3 ♗e7 12.b4 ♗f6 13.♗b2 ♖b8 14.♕b3 b6 15.0-0-0 ♗b7 16.♖hg1 a5 17.♘b5±** Swapnil-Praveen Kumar, Chennai 2013.

B2) **5...cxd4 6.exd4 d5**

B21) **7.a3 ♗xc3+** 7...♗a5 8.b4 ♗c7 9.cxd5 exd5 10.g3 ♘f6 11.♗g2 0-0 12.0-0±. **8.♘xc3** and now:

B211) 8...♘ge7 9.cxd5 9.c5 0-0 10.♗f4 ♘f5∓. **9...♘xd5** 9...exd5 10.♗e3 Martinez Romero-Markidis, Barcelona 2011. **10.♗e2** 10.♗c4 0-0 11.0-0 ♘b6. **10...0-0 11.0-0 ♘de7 12.♗e3 ♘f5 13.d5 ♘xe3 14.fxe3 exd5 15.♘xd5 ♗e6 16.♘f4 ♕f6 17.b4 ♕e5∓** Dijankov-Makarov, Orel 1997;

B212) 8...dxc4 9.♗xc4 ♕xd4N 9...♘f6 transposes to the regular Nimzo-Indian.

10.♕e2 ♕e5 11.♗e3 ♘f6 12.0-0 0-0 13.f4 ♕c7∞

B22) 7.c5 ♘ge7 8.a3 ♗xc3+ 9.bxc3 b6 10.cxb6 axb6 11.♘g3 0-0 12.h4 ♘f5 13.♘xf5 exf5 14.f3 ♘a5 15.♗f4 ♕d7 16.♖b1 ♕c6 17.♔f2 ♗a6 18.♗xa6 ♖xa6 19.♕d3 ♘c4∓ Sadler-Davies, London 1992;

B23) 7.cxd5 exd5 8.a3 ♗a5 9.♘f4 9.g3!?N ♘f6 10.♗g2 0-0 11.0-0 h6 12.b4 ♗b6 13.♗e3 ♗g4±. **9...♘f6 10.♗e2 ♘e4 11.♗d2 0-0 12.0-0**

12...♖e8! 12...♗f5 13.♘xe4 dxe4!? 14.d5 ♗xd2 15.♕xd2 ♕d6 16.♖fd1 ♘e5 17.♖ac1 ♖ac8 18.♕e3 b6 19.b4 h6∞ Piot-Eingorn, St Quentin 2001. **13.♗b5** 13.♘fxd5 ♘xd2 14.♕xd2 ♕xd5. **13...♗f5∓**;

B3) 5...d5

As we stated in the previous chapter, in this type of position it is better to have a knight on f3. Bearing in mind the position of the white knights, Black's strategy in the centre is totally justified! **6.cxd5 exd5 7.dxc5 ♘f6 8.a3 ♗xc5 9.b4 ♗b6 10.♗b2 0-0 11.♘a4 ♗c7∞ 12.♘g3?! d4! 13.exd4** 13.♗xd4 ♘xd4 14.♕xd4 ♕xd4 15.exd4 ♗d7 16.♘c5 ♖fe8+ 17.♗e2 ♗c6 18.f3 ♖ad8∓.

13...♖e8+ 13...♕d5! 14.♕f3 ♖e8+ 15.♗e2 ♕g5∓. **14.♗e2 h5 15.0-0 h4 16.♘h5 ♘d5 17.♗f3 ♘ce7 18.♖e1 ♗f5 19.g3±** Benitah-Eingorn, Metz 2010.

5...♗xc3+

5...♘f6

In this section, we will consider the Hübner variation of the Nimzo-Indian, which represents an additional option for Black: **6.♗d3 ♗xc3+ 7.bxc3 d6**

We have reached a tabiya.

Now it is up to White to choose his game plan:

A) **8.0-0**

8...e5 This is the most precise order of moves. It is important to immediately create a threat with ...e5-e4 and at the same time create an option, in some variations, for Black to play his pawn to g5, while the black king can go to the queenside, by castling queenside or playing ...♔d8. White has several possibilities at his disposal which lead to a complicated game. Let's take a look at them:

A1) **9.d5 ♘e7** 9...e4!? 10.dxc6 exd3 11.cxb7 ♗xb7 12.♕xd3 0-0 13.♘d2

♘g4 14.e4 f5 15.exf5 ♕f6 16.♘f3 ♖ae8 17.♗f4 ♗e4 18.♕xd6 ♕xf5 19.♗g3 ♗xf3 20.gxf3 ♘f6± Melkumyan-Gashimov, Germany 2011.

A11) **10.e4 0-0 11.♘h4**

A111) **11...♔h8 12.g3 ♗h3 13.♖e1 ♘fg8 14.f4**

14...exf4?! 14...♘g6! 15.♘xg6+ fxg6 16.fxe5 dxe5∞. **15.♗xf4 ♕d7 16.♕c2** 16.e5↑. **16...♘g6 17.♘xg6+ fxg6 18.e5 dxe5 19.♖xe5 ♖xf4 20.gxf4 ♕g4+ 21.♔h1 ♕f3+ 22.♔g1 ♕g4+ 23.♔h1 ♕f3+ 24.♔g1 ♕g4+** Gelfand-Grischuk, Astana 2012;

A112) **11...♘g6** Probably the simplest way to establish a balance in the opening. **12.♘f5 ♘f4** 12...♖e8 13.♕f3 ♗xf5 14.♕xf5 ♕d7 15.♕xd7 ♘xd7 16.g3 ♘e7 17.♗d2 ♖f8 18.f4 f6 19.♔g2 ♔f7 20.h4 ♔e8± Wang Hao-Andreikin, Moscow 2013. **13.♗c2 g6 14.♘h6+ ♔h8 15.g3**

15...♘6h5! 16.♘g4 16.gxf4 ♘xf4
17.♘g4 ♕g5 18.f3 h5 19.♗xf4 exf4
20.h4 ♕xh4 21.♘f2 ♖e8→.
**16...♘h3+ 17.♔g2 ♘g5 18.♕e2 ♖b8
19.h3 f6 20.♗d2 b6 21.♖ae1 ♖b7∞**
Akdag-Cesetti, ICCF email 2010.

A12) **10.♕c2**

White's idea is to maintain the control
of the e4-square, preserving the possibility for a wing acttack with the move
f2-f4. **10...0-0 11.♘d2** 11.e4 h6
12.♘h4 ♘g6 13.♘f5 ♘f4 14.♖e1
♘xd3 15.♕xd3 ♗xf5 16.exf5 ♕d7
17.a4 b6∞ Gabrielian-Zhigalko,
Voronezh 2011. **11...h6 12.f4** 12.f3
♘e8 13.e4 ♘g6 14.g3 ♗h3 15.♖f2
♕d7 16.♗a3 a6 17.♔h1 b5 18.♖g1 f5
19.exf5 ♗xf5∓ Farago-Sosonko, Amsterdam 1979. **12...exf4 13.exf4 g6
14.h3**

A121) **14...♘f5 15.♘f3 h5 16.♗d2
♖e8 17.♖fe1 ♗d7 18.♘h2 ♖xe1+
19.♖xe1 ♕f8 20.g4 hxg4 21.hxg4 ♘g7
22.f5±** Naiditsch-Mchedlishvili, Istanbul 2012;

A122) **14...♗f5 15.g4 ♗xd3
16.♕xd3 ♕d7 17.f5↑;**

A123) **14...h5!N** In this type of position, the exchange of light-squared
bishops is one of Black's main strategic
goals. The f5-square is key, but so is the
control of the light squares, therefore
the advance g2-g4 must be prevented.

15.f5 This is the only possible move,
any other option would lead to White's
strategic capitulation, after ...♗f5. The
following sequence is forced, but we
believe that Black gets an excellent
game. If 15.♘f3 ♗f5 16.♘h4 ♕d7!.
**15...♗xf5 16.♗xf5 ♘xf5 17.♖xf5 gxf5
18.♕xf5 ♕e7∞**

A2) **9.♘g5**

As stated above, this move is only one of
several possibilities, besides 9.♘d2 and
9.♕c2, that serve to keep the control
and possible occupation of e4. **9...0-0
10.f4 exd4 11.cxd4 ♖e8 12.d5 ♘b4
13.♗b1 h6 14.♘f3 b5! 15.a3 ♘a6
16.♖e1 bxc4 17.e4 ♖b8 18.h3 c3!
19.♕d3 c4 20.♕xc4 ♘c5∓** Lauber-
Jussupow, Germany 2011;

A3) **9.♕c2 h6 10.♗b2 0-0 11.♘d2
b6 12.♘b3 ♗d7 13.♖ae1 ♖e8
14.♕b1?! e4 15.♗c2 ♗f5 16.f3 ♗h7
17.♘d2 ♕e7 18.f4 ♗f5** Peray-
Steingrimsson, La Massana 2013;

A4) **9.♘d2**

9...0-0 Of course, capturing the pawn, as is well-known, provides White with powerful compensation thanks to his bishop pair, and, above all, thanks to the activation of his dark-squared bishop. Remember that Black's strategy, from the very beginning and with the exchange of the bishop for the knight on c3, is based on neutralizing White's dark-squared bishop and putting his pawns on dark squares, which additionally establishes control over those dark squares.

Therefore, the position should not be opened but blocked, which is after all the main idea of Black's entire system!

If 9...cxd4 10.cxd4 exd4 11.exd4 ♘xd4 12.♖e1+ ♘e6 13.♗a3 0-0! 14.♘b3 ♕d7 15.♖e3 ♕c6 16.♗xd6 ♖d8 17.♗e5 ♘d7 18.♕h5↑ Portisch-Timman, Wijk aan Zee 1978.

A41) **10.♘e4 b6 11.♕f3 ♗b7 12.♕h3** 12.♘g3 ♔h8 13.d5 e4 14.♗xe4 ♘e5 15.♕f4 ♗a6 16.♖d1 g5 17.♕xg5 ♖g8 18.♕h6 ♖xg3 19.hxg3 ♘xe4−+ Kamsky-Anand, Sanghi Nagar 1994. **12...g6** 12...♘xe4!? 13.♗xe4 g6∞. **13.♘g5 ♖e8** 13...♘a5 14.e4→. **14.d5 e4 15.dxc6** 15.♗xe4 ♘e5 16.♗c2 ♕d7 17.♕xd7 ♘fxd7∞. **15...♗c8 16.♕h6 exd3 17.e4 ♗a6** (Zilka-Laznicka, Czechia 2011)

... and now **18.f4!** would have been strong.

A42) **10.♖b1 b6 11.d5 ♘e7 12.♕c2 g6 13.f4 exf4 14.h3?** 14.exf4 ♗f5 15.h3 h5 16.♘f3 ♕d7 17.♖b2 ♖fe8∓ Chuprikov-Shaposhnikov, Voronezh 2008. **14...♘f5 15.♗xf5 ♗xf5 16.e4 ♗d7 17.♖xf4 ♕e7 18.♗b2 ♘h5 19.♖f2 f5 20.♖e1 ♖ae8 21.♗c1 f4↑** Laznicka-Ivanchuk, Havana 2012;

A43) **10.h3 ♖e8 11.d5** 11.dxc5?! e4 12.♗c2 dxc5 13.a4 ♗d7 14.♕e2 b6 15.♖d1 ♕c7 16.♘f1 ♗c6 17.♗b1 ♖ad8∓ Lekic-Antic, Paleochora 2013.

11...♘e7 11...e4! 12.♘xe4 ♘xe4 13.dxc6 bxc6 14.♕c2 f5∞. **12.g4?!** ♘g6 13.f4 exf4 14.exf4 h6 14...h5!?. **15.♘f3 ♘e4 16.f5 ♘h4 17.♗f4 ♘g5 18.♘xg5 hxg5 19.♗d2 ♗d7∞** Navara-Stocek, Karlovy Vary 2005.

B) **8.♘d2** A premature declaration of White's intentions, since Black has not played ...e6-e5. Now Black can play flexi-

bly: **8...0-0 9.0-0 b6 10.♖e1 ♗a6 11.♖b1**
11.♗b2 ♖e8 12.e4 e5 13.d5 ♘e7 14.♘f1
♗c8 15.♗c1 ♘g6 16.g3 ♗h3 17.a4 h6
18.♖a2 ♖b8 19.♘e3 ♗d7 20.♕f3 ♘h7
21.h4 ♘e7∞ I. Sokolov-Michiels, Istanbul
2012. **11...♖c8 12.♕a4 ♗a5 13.e4 ♕d7
14.♕c2 cxd4 15.cxd4 ♖fd8 16.♖e3 ♗xc4
17.♗xc4 d5∓** Kovacs-Palac, Oberwart
2009;

C) **8.e4**

8...e5 and now:

C1) **9.h3 h6 10.♗e3 b6 11.d5 ♘e7
12.a4** 12.♘d2 ♘g6 13.g3 0-0 14.♕c2
♗d7 15.♘f1 ♘h7 16.h4 ♘e7 17.♘d2
f5 18.exf5 ♗xf5 19.g4 ♗xd3 20.♕xd3
♕d7 21.g5 h5 22.♘e4 a6 23.♖g1 ♘f5
Jussupow-Alexeev, Germany 2006.
**12...♗d7 13.♘d2 0-0 14.♘f1 ♘h7
15.♘g3 ♘g6 16.♕d2 ♘h4 17.f4 exf4
18.♗xf4 ♕e7 19.0-0 ♘g6 20.a5 ♘g5
21.♘f5 ♗xf5 22.exf5 ♘xf4 23.♖xf4∞**
Timofeev-Khairullin, Khanty-Mansiysk
2012;

C2) **9.d5**

9...♘e7 10.♘h4 h6

C21) **11.f3 ♗d7 12.a4 ♕c7 13.g3
0-0-0 14.♗d2 ♗h3 15.♕e2 g5 16.♘g2
♖dg8 17.a5 ♘e8 18.♘e3 ♔b8 19.♔d1
♘g7∞** Levin-Khismatullin, St Petersburg 2012;

C22) **11.f4 ♘g6 12.♘xg6 fxg6 13.0-0**
13.fxe5 dxe5 14.♗e3 b6 15.0-0 0-0 16.a4
a5 17.♖b1 ♗d7 18.♖b2 ♖b8 19.♖bf2
♕e7 20.♗c2 g5 21.♗d2 ♕e8 22.♗e1
♕g6 23.♕d3 ♘h5 24.♖xf8+ ♖xf8
25.♖xf8+ ♔xf8 26.♗d1 ♘f4 27.♕c2??

27...♗xa4−+ 0-1 Spassky-Fischer,
Reykjavik 1972. **13...0-0 14.fxe5 dxe5
15.♖b1 b6 16.♖b2 ♕d6 17.♖bf2 ♗d7
18.♕c2 ♘h5 19.♕e2 ♖xf2 20.♖xf2
♖e8 21.♕d1 ♘f4∞** Rubinas-Cesetti,
ICCF email 2010;

C23) **11.h3 ♕c7 12.0-0 g5 13.♕f3
♘fg8 14.♘f5 ♘xf5 15.exf5 f6
16.♕h5+ ♔d8 17.h4 ♕h7 18.g4 ♗d7
19.hxg5 fxg5 20.f3 ♘f6∓** Potkin-
Korobov, Moscow 2010.

6.bxc3 d6!?

As stated at the beginning of this chapter, thanks to the order of moves in the opening, Black has at his disposal, apart from the option to enter the Hübner Variation of the Nimzo-Indian, this flexible manner of developing his pieces, where the g8-knight is moved to e7. We are entering completely unexplored positions now, which we believe will be more often tested in the future. In any case, the authors recommend this system and we claim that Black has excellent chances!

7.♗d3 e5 8.0-0

8.♗e4 ♘ge7 9.dxc5 dxc5 10.♗d5 0-0 11.e4 ♗g4 12.h3 ♗h5 13.g4 ♗g6∞ 14.♕e2 ♕a5 15.♗d2 ♕a4 16.♗e3 ♖fe8 17.0-0 ♘xd5 18.cxd5 ♘a5 19.♘d2 ♗xe4 20.c4 ♗g6∓ Peralta-Oms Pallisse, La Pobla de Lillet 2012.

8...♘ge7 9.♗e4

9.d5 ♘a5 10.♘d2 f5 11.♕h5+ g6 12.♕h6 ♘g8 13.♕g7 ♕f6 and now:

A) 14.♕c7 b6 15.♘b3 ♕e7 16.♕xe7+ ♘xe7 17.♘xa5 bxa5 18.e4

18...f4 18...fxe4!? 19.♗xe4 ♗a6 20.♖e1 ♗xc4∓. **19.♖b1 ♗a6 20.♖b3 ♘c8∞ 21.♖a3 ♘b6 22.♖xa5 ♗xc4 23.♗xc4 ♘xc4 24.♖a4 ♘b6** Sisatto-Nyysti, Jyväskylä 2013;

B) **14.♕xf6 ♘xf6 15.f3 b6 16.e4 f4 17.♘b3 ♗b7 18.♗d2 ♗d7 19.a4 ♔e7 20.a5 ♖hb8 21.axb6 axb6 22.♖fb1 g5∞** Bierbach-Eingorn, Bad Wörishofen 1998.

9...♕c7 10.♗d5 0-0 11.h3 ♘a5 12.dxe5 dxe5 13.e4 ♘xd5 14.cxd5 f6 15.♘d2 b6 16.c4 ♗a6 17.♕c2 ♖ae8 18.♗b2 ♗c8 19.♘b3 ♗b7 20.♖ae1 ♘d6∞

½-½ Mladenov-Eingorn, Cappelle la Grande 2013.

Conclusion

In this chapter, we have examined some complex positions from the Hübner Variation of the Nimzo-Indian, and we have also introduced a flexible and rarely played method for Black, with ...♘ge7. We owe immense gratitude to grandmaster Viacheslav Eingorn, for introducing this system into practice. As already mentioned, certain positions still have to be tested further in practice, but the authors' conclusion for the moment is: Black is OK!

Exercises

16.3 (1) Find the most effective plan!
(solution on page 456)

16.3 (2) Find the most sufficient way to obtain compensation for the sacrificed pawn!
(solution on page 457)

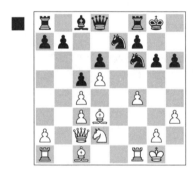

16.3 (3) Find the best plan.
(solution on page 457)

White Takes Space with 4.d5

1.d4 e6 2.c4 ♗b4+ 3.♘c3 c5 4.d5

This is an interesting possibility, which enables White to take more space in the centre in the early stage of the game. In this chapter we will see that this is not a naïve continuation and that it demands careful moves by the black player. Although it is not popular in practice, the move 4.d5 speeds up the pace of the game.

4...♗xc3+ 5.bxc3 d6
A) **5...♕a5!?**

The activation of the queen at this early stage brings with it certain risks. Although we believe that Black can get a good position, this move is not the right choice, though it is an alternative.

A1) **6.♕c2 ♘f6 7.♗g5** 7.♗d2 0-0 8.g3 ♖e8 9.♗g2 ♕a6 10.♗g5 ♕xc4 (10...exd5! 11.cxd5 h6∓) 11.♗xf6 gxf6 12.♘h3≌ d6?! 13.♘f4 ♘d7 14.♗e4 ♘e5 15.♘h5→ Nikolov-Markidis, Rethymnon 2011. **7...♘e4**

A11) **8.♗d2?! f5! 9.♘f3 0-0 10.e3 d6 11.♗d3 ♘d7!**

12.♗xe4 12.dxe6 ♘df6!∓. **12...fxe4** and now:

A111) **13.♘g5 exd5 14.cxd5 ♕a6 15.♘e6 ♘e5 16.♘xf8** 16.♘c7 ♘d3+ 17.♔f1 ♖xf2+ 18.♔g1 ♖xg2+ 19.♔xg2 ♘f4+ 20.exf4 ♕e2+ 21.♔g1 ♗h3

And Black wins.

16...♘d3+ 17.♔d1 ♗g4+−+;

A112) **13.♕xe4 ♘f6 14.♕d3 ♕a6! 15.♕e2** 15.e4 exd5 16.exd5 ♖e8+ 17.♗e3 ♖e4 18.♘d2 ♖e5 19.♕c2 ♗f5 20.♕b2 ♗d3. **15...♗d7 16.a4 ♖ae8**

A12) **8.♗f4 f5 9.♖c1 0-0 10.g4!?**

10...b5?! 10...e5!? 11.♗xe5 d6 12.♗g3 ♕d8♔; 10...♖e8!?∞. **11.gxf5 exf5 12.♗g2 ♗b7 13.♗xe4 fxe4 14.♕xe4 ♘a6 15.♘h3 ♖ae8 16.♕b1 ♕b6 17.♕xb5 ♖e4 18.e3 ♗c8 19.f3 ♖ee8 20.♕xb6 axb6 21.♔f2** 1-0 Grover-Praveen Kumar, Kolkata 2012.

A2) **6.e4**

That's right! Activity is the most important thing, and the weak pawn on c3 is unimportant. In fact, its capture would open additional dark squares for the white bishop. **6...♘f6**

A21) **7.f3!**

White further strengthens his centre and increases his spatial domination. To avoid positional pressure, Black has to be careful and develop his pieces gradually. Capturing the pawn on c3 is too risky and it should only be considered as a possibility after the completion of Black's development − by the way, the threat is stronger than the execution!

A211) **7...d6 8.♘e2 e5** 8...h6 9.♘g3 ♕xc3+ 10.♗d2 ♕a3 11.♗e2 0-0 12.0-0 b6 13.♕c2↑. **9.♗d2 ♘bd7 10.♘g3 ♘b6 11.a4 ♗d7 12.♗d3 h5 13.h4 ♘c8 14.♕b3 ♕b6 15.♕c2 ♘e7 16.0-0 ♕c7 17.♗e2 ♘g6 18.♗f5±** Ilincic-Damljanovic, Belgrade 1995;

432

A212) 7...♕xc3+ 8.♗d2 ♕e5 9.♘e2 exd5 10.cxd5 d6 11.♗c3 ♕e7 12.♘g3 12.g4 ♘a6 13.♘g3 ♘c7 14.♔f2 h6 15.♗c4 b5 16.e5!↑ Khenkin-Pap, Hungary 2008. **12...0-0 13.♕d2 ♘e8 14.♗e2 f5 15.exf5 ♘f6?!** 15...♗xf5 16.0-0±. **16.0-0 ♘bd7 17.♖fe1 ♘b6 18.♖ad1±** Kryakvin-Tomashevsky, Essentuki 2003.

A22) 7.♗d2?!

A221) 7...0-0 8.e5 ♘e4 9.d6?! 9.♗d3 ♘xd2 10.♕xd2±. **9...♘c6 10.♘f3 f5 11.♗d3 ♕d8 12.♕e2 b6 13.♗xe4 fxe4 14.♕xe4 ♗b7 15.♘g5 ♖f5 16.f4 h6 17.♘f3 ♘a5 18.♕d3 ♗a6∓** Saric-Markidis, Skopje 2012;

A222) 7...♘xe4 8.♕g4 ♘xd2 9.♕xg7 ♖f8 10.♔xd2 ♕a3 11.♖c1 d6 12.♘f3±;

A223) 7...d6 8.♗d3 0-0

A2231) 9.♘e2 9.♘f3 exd5 10.cxd5 c4 11.♗c2 ♗g4 12.h3 (12.0-0 ♘bd7) 12...♗h5∞. **9...♖e8 10.♕c2?!** 10.f3 ♘bd7 11.♗f4. **10...exd5 11.exd5 ♘bd7 12.f4 ♘b6 13.♔f2 ♘bxd5 14.cxd5 c4 15.♗xh7+ ♘xh7 16.♗e3 ♘f6−+** Flear-Dorfman, Polanica Zdroj 1992.

B) 5...♘e7!?N

Now we even have a theoretical novelty on the fifth move! We are curious if this interesting position will be tested in the near future.

6.e4 e5 7.♗d3 ♘e7 8.♘e2 ♘g6

We are again entering unexplored positions. If we compare this with Hübner's Variation, we can notice some differences: the white knight is on e2 instead of f3, thus making the pawn advance f2-f4 possible, but Black also has his own advantages: first of all the f6-square is free for other pieces and he has the possible pawn advance ...f7-f5!. Instead, 8...♘d7 9.0-0 ♘f6 10.♘g3 h6 11.♕e2 0-0! 12.♗d2 ♖e8 13.♖ae1 a6 14.h3 ♘g6 15.♘f5 ♗xf5 16.exf5 ♘f4 17.♕f3 ♘xd3 18.♕xd3 ♕d7 19.g4 b5∓ was seen in E. Toth-Kosic, Budapest 2008.

9.♖b1

9.a4 ♘d7 10.♗e3 h6 11.g3 ♘f6 12.h3 0-0 13.♕d2 ♘h7 14.h4 f5 15.exf5 ♗xf5 16.♗xf5 ♖xf5 17.h5 ♘h8 18.g4 ♖f3

19.0-0-0 ♘f7∓ Volkov-Eingorn, Swidnica 1997.

9...♘d7 10.f3 ♕f6!?

Black uses the free f6-square for this interesting manoeuvre performed by the queen.

Thanks to the threat ...♘g6-f4, the next moves are virtually forced, and White loses the coordination of his pieces. Another possibility is 10...♘f6.

11.♕d2

11.0-0 ♘f4!?∞.

11...h6 12.0-0 0-0 13.♕e3 ♕d8

13...♕e7!? may be a logical possibility for Black to enter a similar position with an extra tempo.

14.g3 ♘f6 15.♖f2 ♖b8 16.♕d2 ♖e8 17.♕c2 ♕e7 18.♗e3 ♗d7∞

Berkes-Kosic, Hungary 2011.

Conclusion

In this chapter, we have acquainted ourselves with some unexplored possibilities on both sides. We saw that Black continued to apply the general strategic principles in this type of position, in the battle against White's bishop pair, that is: set up a blockade. The resulting positions are very complex and Black has excellent chances.

As a final conclusion, the continuation 3.♘c3 creates very interesting, dynamic, and unexplored positions. The authors have made an effort to show possibilities for Black to make new and creative moves, but future games will have to show whether we were right or wrong.

Our final conclusion, however, is: Black is OK!

Exercises

16.4 (1) Find the best plan.
(solution on page 457)

16.4 (2) Find the active plan.
(solution on page 457)

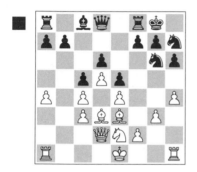

16.4 (3) Find the best plan.
(solution on page 458)

Solutions

Solution 1 (1)

11...h6!? The idea is ...♘h7 and ...f7-f5. **12.♗f1 ♘h7 13.c5 f5 14.♖c1** Here a draw was agreed in Kasimdzhanov-Andersson, Germany 2000. Both sides have good play on the different flanks. However, Black's kingside initiative is clearly more dangerous than the opponent's queenside initiative.

Solution 1 (2)

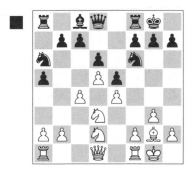

12...♗g4! Black wants to place the bishop on d7, but prior to that forces his opponent to make a strategically inferior move. **13.f3 ♗d7 14.a3 c6↑** Black has good play, especially on the dark squares after the potential ...♕b6, made possible by Black's last move.

Solution 1 (3)

9...c5!? An understandable idea. Black doesn't worry about his lack of space and creates a pawn structure in the centre that is compatible with his light-squared bishop, forcing the opponent to shut down the centre with d4-d5. He will seek counterplay on the queenside with ...a7-a6 and ...b7-b5 or on the kingside with ...f7-f5. **10.d5 ♘a6 11.a3 ♗d7 12.♖b1 ♘c7⇄** Postny-Golod, Biel 2012.

Solution 2.1 (1)

8...exd5 9.exd5 9.cxd5?! ♖e8∓. **9...♘a6!?N** In case of 9...c5 10.♗e2 d6 11.0-0 White has better chances due to his space advantage,

Sherbakov-Kholmov, Smolensk 1986. **10.♗e2 ♘c5 11.0–0 c6! 12.♖fe1 ♖e8 13.♗f1 ♘ce4 14.♘xe4 ♘xe4 15.♕d4 cxd5 16.cxd5 ♘f6** with obviously equal chances.

Solution 2.1 (2)

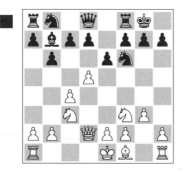

8...c6!? Black is eager to activate his light-squared bishop before his opponent finishes developing and fortifying the centre. **9.d6 c5 10.♗g2 ♘e4 11.♕d3** 11.♘xe4 ♗xe4 12.0–0 ♘c6=. **11...♘xc3 12.♘g5 ♕xg5 13.♗xb7 ♘xe2! 14.♕xe2 ♘c6 15.♗xa8 ♖xa8♕** With a supported knight in the centre, Black has obvious compensation for the slight lack of material, Christiansen-Seirawan, Estes Park 1986.

Solution 2.1 (3)

8...♘c6!? And a hyper-modern chess position emerges. Black is not interested in the centre, but exclusively in the development and activity of his own pieces. **9.♗e2 ♘e7 10.0–0 ♘g6 11.♕e3 d6 12.h3 ♕e7 13.♖ad1 h6 14.♗d3 ♘d7** Black has active pieces and a flexible pawn structure, but less space.

Solution 2.2 (1)

11...c5! 12.0–0 cxd4 13.exd5 d3! 14.♕xd3 exd5= Carlsen-Andreikin, Moscow 2013.

Solution 2.2 (2)

15...♕f6!?N 15...a5 was seen in the game Prusikin-Saric, Rogaska Slatina 2009 **16.♖ed1 ♖ad8** with good counterplay.

Solution 2.2 (3)

13...♕e7! 14.♖fd1 ♖fd8! 15.cxd5 cxd5 16.e4! dxe4 16...d4!?. **17.♕d6 ♕xd6 18.♖xd6 ♘c5=** Sosonko-Ljubojevic, Wijk aan Zee 1988.

Solution 3.1 (1)

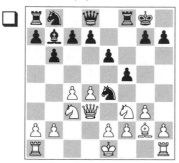

10.♘e5! ♘c5 10...♘d6 11.d5±. **11.dxc5 ♗xg2 12.♖g1 ♗c6 13.0-0-0±** Polugaevsky-Dokhoian, Belgrade 1988.

Solution 3.1 (2)

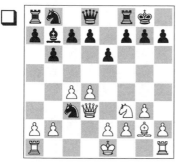

10.♘g5! ♘e4 11.♘xe4 11.♗xe4 ♗xe4 **12.♕xe4 ♕xg5 13.♕xa8 ♘c6 14.♕b7**

♘xd4♔ Euwe-Capablanca, Amsterdam 1931. **11...♘c6 12.0-0±** Sargissian-Yu Yangyi, Ningbo 2011.

Solution 3.1 (3)

10.♕c2 ♕e7 11.e4 e5 12.♘fe1 ♖fe8 13.♖ad1± Kasparov-Akopian, Internet (blitz) 1998.

Solution 3.2 (1)

7...d5!=

Solution 3.2 (2)

8...e5 9.d5 ♘e7 10.0-0 ♘g6 11.g3

11.♘e1 c6⇄. **11...♗h3 12.♖fd1 h6 13.♘e1 ♘h7**⇄

13.♕xe7 ♖xe7 14.e4 ♘5b6 15.♖c2 e5=
Kramnik-Andreikin, Moscow 2013.

Solution 3.2 (3)

15.♘d2N 15.a3 Baumgartner-Schwierzy, ICCF corr 1999. **15...♖fd8 16.♘b3±**

Solution 4.1 (3)

10...dxc4! 11.♖xc4 ♘d5 12.♕d2 ♘5b6 13.♖c2 e5=

Solution 4.1 (1)

9...e5! 10.dxe5 ♘e5 11.♕xd8 ♘xf3+ 12.♗xf3 ♖xd8 13.♘xc4 ♗e6=
Tomashevsky-Nisipeanu, Moscow 2012.

Solution 4.1 (2)

10...dxc4 11.♖xc4 ♘d5 12.♕a3 ♖e8

Solution 4.2 (1)

16...b5! With the idea ...b5–b4. 17.♕xa5 ♕xd6 18.♖c6 ♕b8 19.♖xa6 ♖xa6 20.♕xa6 ♘xe5 21.dxe5 ♕xe5∓
Kramnik-Carlsen, Wijk aan Zee 2011.

Solution 4.2 (2)

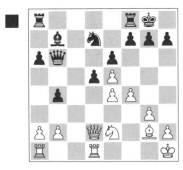

18...f6!N 19.exf6 19.exd5 fxe5
20.dxe6 ♘f6≌. **19...♘xf6 20.♕d4**
♕xd4 21.♘xd4 dxe4 22.♘xe6 ♖fc8
with equality, Ganguly-Markidis, Kavala
2012.

Solution 4.2 (3)

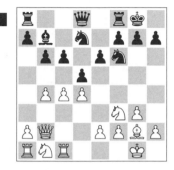

11...dxc4!? Also good is 11...♖b8
12.♘bd2 ♕e7 13.e3 ♖fc8 14.♖c2
c5⇄, Topalov-Carlsen, Nanjing 2010.
12.♖xc4 a5 13.bxa5 ♖xa5 with mutual
chances.

Solution 5.1 (1)

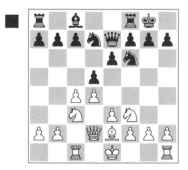

After **9...dxc4 10.♗xc4 c5 11.0–0 ♘b6**
12.♗e2 ♖d8 13.♖fd1 cxd4 14.♘xd4
♗d7 Black achieved equal play in
Kunte-Zvjagintsev, Khanty-Mansiysk
2007.

Solution 5.1 (2)

13...b6! 14.a4 14.b5 c5⇄. **14...a5**
15.bxa5 ♖xa5 16.♖fd1 ♗b7 17.h3
♖ea8⇄ Bacrot-Dominguez Perez,
Makedonia Palace 2013.

Solution 5.1 (3)

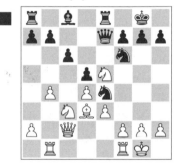

14...♘xc3 15.♕xc3 ♘e4 16.♕c2 g6
17.♖fc1 ♗f5 18.♖b3 a6 19.a4 ♘d6=
Onischuk-Dominguez Perez, Tromsø
2013.

Solution 5.2 (1)

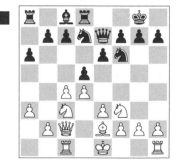

11...dxc4 12.♗xc4 c5 13.♗e2 b5
14.dxc5 ♕xc5 15.b4 ♕e7 16.0–0?
♗b7= Aronian-Carlsen, London 2013.

Solution 5.2 (2)

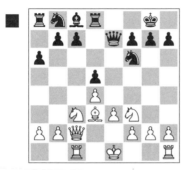

11...♘c6! With the idea 12...♘b4 or
12...♗g4.

Solution 5.2 (3)

8...dxc4 9.♗xc4 c5 10.0–0 ♘c6
11.♖ad1 ♖d8 12.♕c2 12.♕e2 cxd4
13.exd4 a6! was seen in the game
Tomashevsky-Vitiugov, Sochi 2012.
12...cxd4 13.exd4 13.♘xd4 ♗d7=.
13...a6!N 14.a3 b5 15.♗a2 ♗b7 with
mutual chances.

Solution 5.3 (1)

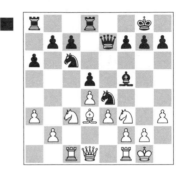

14...♘xc3 15.♖xc3 ♗xd3 16.♕xd3
♘a7! with the idea ...♘c8(b5)-d6.

Solution 5.3 (2)

18...♕d7! With the idea ...♗xh3.

Solution 5.3 (3)

21...♕h4! 22.♖c1 ♘hxf4! 23.exf4
♕xf4 24.♗e2 ♕xd4 25.b5 ♘f4∓
Beliavsky-Makarov, Novosibirsk 1995.

Solution 6 (1)

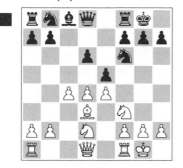

9...exd4!? Black has the option 9...♖e8, but he prefers active play on the dark squares. **10.♘xd4 ♕b6 11.♘2f3 ♘c6 12.♗c2 ♗g4** with mutual chances

Solution 6 (2)

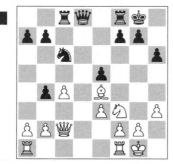

17...♕c7!?N 18.♖fd1 ♘e7⇄ Black controls important central squares, and counts on the centre and the queenside for counterplay.

Solution 6 (3)

11...b3!∓ Black has a clear advantage thanks to the combined threats on the b4- and e4-squares, Eingorn-Kortchnoi, Odessa 2006.

Solution 7 (1)

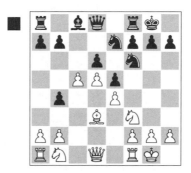

11...♘exd5!N This tactical blow solves all of black's problems in the opening. **12.exd5 e4 13.♗xe4 ♘xe4=**.

Solution 7 (2)

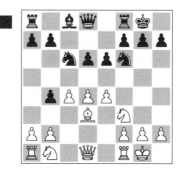

9...♕b6!N As you can see, Black does not have to block the e-pawn immediately. Instead, he is utilizing the dark squares to organize his play. In case of 9...e5 10.d5 ♘e7 (10...♘b8 11.c5!±) 11.♘bd2 (11.c5?! ♘exd5!) 11...♘g6 12.a3 bxa3 13.♖xa3 ♗g4 14.♕c2± White is better. His chances on the queenside are more concrete than is Black's counterplay on the kingside.

10.d5 ♘d4 11.♘bd2 exd5 12.cxd5 ♗g4 with mutual chances.

Solution 7 (3)

13...♘bd7! Since White has opened the b-file, the knight goes to d7 to defend the backward pawn on the b-file. **14.♗f3 ♗xf3** 14...♖ab8 Kramnik-Kosten, Oviedo (rapid) 1992. **15.♕xf3 e5=** (Kramnik)

Solution 8 (1)

12...♘b4!?N By attacking the strong light-squared bishop Black wants to avoid the unpleasant ♕b1, forcing a weakening of his kingside pawns. **13.♗b1 ♘8c6 14.e4 ♘e7∞** Black's flexible pieces keep White's mobile centre under check, and his intention is to activate his queenside majority at the first opportunity.

Solution 8 (2)

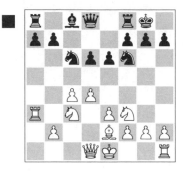

10...♘b4! The knight takes up the outpost on b4, whereas the light-squared bishop aims for b7 or a6. Black's central pawns stay on e6 and d6, allowing the opponent's central pawns to advance and become a target for counterplay. **11.0–0 b6 12.♘e1 a5!?N** With the idea of immediately attacking the weakened c-pawn. Also good is 12...♗b7⇄. **13.♗f3** 13.♘d3 ♗a6⇄ **13...d5 14.cxd5 ♘fxd5 15.♘xd5 ♘xd5 16.♘d3 ♗a6** with the cances for both sides.

Solution 8 (3)

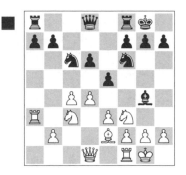

12...a6!?N Safeguarding against the potential problems with the d6-square after the d-file gets opened, or after ♘b5. **13.h3 ♗h5 14.♕d2 ♖c8 15.♖d1 h6 16.dxe5 dxe5 17.♘d5 ♖e8 18.♖b3!? e4 19.♘d4 ♗xe2 20.♘xe2 ♘e5** The position is approximately equal.

Solution 9.1 (1)

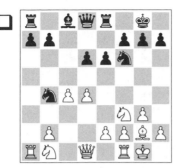

11.e4! This surprising pawn sacrifice, with the clear threat of e4-e5, hits Black's position like a thunderbolt. **11...♘c6** 11...♘xe4 12.♕e1. **12.e5 dxe5 13.dxe5 ♘d7 14.♕e2 ♕c7 15.♖e1 a6 16.♘c3 ♖b8 17.♖ad1** Thanks to his faster development and more space, White had the upper hand in the game Navara-Amin, Reykjavik 2013.

Solution 9.1 (2)

10.♖xa3! Also good is 10.♘xa3 ♘c6 11.♘b5± with the intention to play c4-c5. **10...♘c6 11.♘c3 e5 12.dxe5 dxe5 13.♘g5±** White has more activity and better control over the central squares. As you can see from this example, in this line Black's move ...♖e8 serves no purpose.

Solution 9.1 (3)

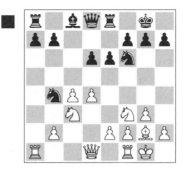

11...♗d7! 11...b6?! 12.♘g5±. **12.e4 e5 13.dxe5** 13.d5?! a5. **13...dxe5 14.♘d5 ♘fxd5 15.exd5** 15.cxd5 a5=. **15...e4!?N 16.♘d4 ♕b6** with mutual chances.

Solution 9.2 (1)

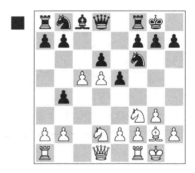

11...e4! **12.♘g5 e3** with mutual chances.

Solution 9.2 (2)

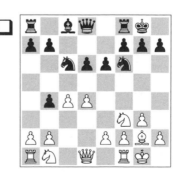

9.a3! bxa3 10.罝xa3 The rook capture preserves c3 for the knight. **10...e5 11.分c3! 奧g4 12.dxe5!** This exchange simplifies the position and relieves the pressure on the d4-pawn, while White is keeping his strategic advantages, like the strong light-squared bishop on the open h1—a8 diagonal and the potential for a knight incursion on d5. **12...dxe5 13.曼b3! 曼e7 14.e3! 罝fd8 15.罝fa1±** White threatens the unpleasant 分d5.

Solution 9.2 (3)

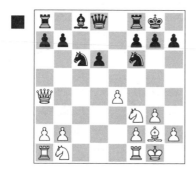

14...曼b6! 15.分bd2 奧e6 15...曼xb2=. **16.分c4 奧xc4 17.曼xc4 罝fe8! 18.分d2** 18.分h4 g6∓. **18...罝ac8∓**

Solution 9.3 (1)

12...奧a6! 13.b3 13.e5 分e8∓. **13...d5!∓** Black's light-squared bishop is more dangerous than its colleague on g2.

Solution 9.3 (2)

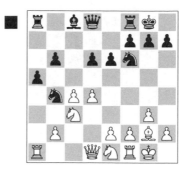

12...d5! 13.cxd5 13.分c2 奧a6 14.分e3 奧b7=. **13...分fxd5 14.分d3 分xd3 15.曼xd3 奧a6 16.曼d2 分xc3 17.bxc3 罝c8 18.罝fb1 曼c7 19.e3** and the players agreed to a draw in this equal position, Dzindzichashvili-Christiansen, Long Beach 1993.

Solution 9.3 (3)

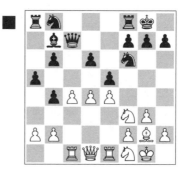

13...分bd7! Black completes the development of his forces by placing the knight on the somewhat passive d7 square, intending to use his light-squared bishop to keep an eye on the critical d5- and e4-squares. If 13...分c6 14.分e3!± **14.分e3 奧xe4! 15.分d5** White's initiative is in full swing, but after a more-or-less forced sequence we arrive at an equal endgame. For example: **15...分xd5 16.cxd5 奧xf3 17.罝xc7 奧xd1 18.罝xd7 奧g4**

Solution 10 (1)

13...b6!?N 13...♗xd4 I. Sokolov-Bauer, Nancy 2012. **14.♘b3 ♗b7 15.♘xc5 bxc5 16.f3** 16.0–0 ♗e4⇄. **16...c4 17.0–0 ♛b6 18.a4 ♖fd8⇄**

Solution 10 (2)

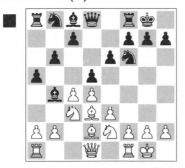

8...♗a6!?N 8...♗b7 Sundararajan-Fominikh, Mumbai 2004. 9.b3 ♘c6 with the idea ...e6-e5. **10.f4** 10.♛c2 e5⇄. **10...♘e7! 11.a3 ♗xc3 12.♘xc3 dxc4 13.♗xc4 ♗xc4 14.bxc4 ♘f5⇄**

Solution 10 (3)

5...d5! 6.cxd5 exd5 7.♗g2 0–0 8.♘f3 ♘bd7 9.0–0 ♖e8 10.♖c1 c6 and Black has a pleasant game.

Solution 11 (1)

9...e5! 10.dxe5 10.♘xe5 ♘xe5 11.dxe5 ♘g4=. **10...♘g4** and Black will recapture the pawn with equal play.

Solution 11 (2)

9...♗d6! with an idea ...e6–e5 with mutual chances.

Solution 11 (3)

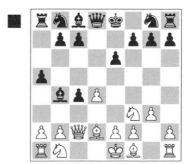

6...♗xd2+!? 7.♘bxd2 After 7.♕xd2 Black develops without problems, for example 7...b5 8.♗g2 ♗b7 9.0–0 ♘d7∞. **7...b5 8.a4 c6 9.b3 cxb3 10.♘xb3 ♘f6 11.♗g2 b4** with mutual chances.

Solution 12 (1)

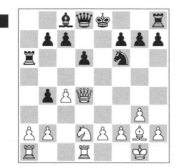

12...♕e7! The best move. Black's goal is to centralize his queen on e5, to offer a simplification into an endgame that is favourable for him. **13.♘f1 ♕e5 14.♘e3 ♕xd4 15.♖xd4 c5 16.♖d3 ♔d8 17.a4 bxa3 18.♖axa3 ♖xa3 19.♖xa3 ♔c7=.**

Solution 12 (2)

8...♘ge7! 9.a3 ♗xc3 10.♗xc3 ♕xd1+ 11.♖xd1 f6 Now Black has the possibility to neutralize his opponent's bishop in the most economical way. **12.b3 ♗e6 13.♘d2 ♔f7 14.0–0 ♖hd8=**

Solution 12 (3)

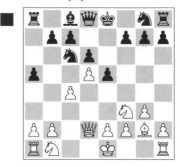

8...♘b8! Taking the shortest route to c5. **9.♘c3 ♘a6 10.0–0 ♘h6!?** Keeping the option to move his f-pawn. **11.♘e1 0–0 12.♘d3 ♗d7 13.b3 f5** with mutual chances.

Solution 13 (1)

21...♘e4! 22.♖c2 22.fxe4 ♕xf2+ 23.♔xf2 fxe4–+. **22...c5 23.♘b5 ♘g3+ 24.♔g1 ♗xf3–+**

Solution 13 (2)

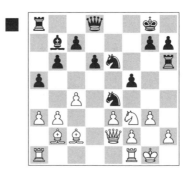

17...♕e8! 18.♗xe4 18.♘d4 ♘xd4
19.exd4 (19.♗xd4 ♘d2
(19...♘g5−+) 20.♕xd2 ♖xh2 21.e4
♕h5−+) 19...♘xg3 20.♕xe8+ ♖xe8
21.fxg3 ♖e2−+. **18...fxe4 19.♘d4
♘g5** With the idea ...♕e8-d7. **20.♕g4
♖g6−+**

Solution 13 (3)

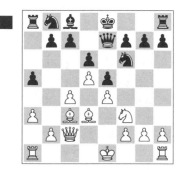

11...♘h5!?N 12.0-0 12.g3 ♗h3⇄.
**12...♘f4 13.♗d2 ♘xd3 14.♕xd3
0-0=**

Solution 14.1 (1)

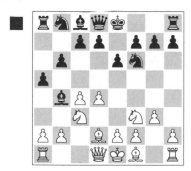

6...♗a6! The combination of the
fianchetto and the knight's development to c3 is not the best for White, as
the c4-pawn becomes vulnerable. **7.b3
d5=** A good plan is also 7...0-0!?
8.♗g2 c6⇄ with the idea ...d7-d5.

Solution 14.1 (2)

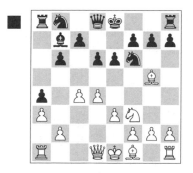

10...♖a5! With the idea 11...♗xf3.
**11.♗h4 ♘bd7 12.♗d3 ♕a8 13.0-0 g5
14.♗g3 h5 15.h4 gxh4 16.♘xh4 ♖g8
17.♖e1 ♖ag5∓**

Solution 14.1 (3)

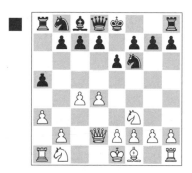

6...b6!? Just in time to take control of
the long diagonal and the e4-square.
7.♘c3 ♗b7 8.e3 ♘e4=

Solution 14.2 (1)

9...c5! **10.dxc5** 10.♗xb4 axb4=.
10...♗xc5 **11.♘d3** **♗e7** **12.♗f4** and
now in the game Lputian-Makarichev,
Moscow 1989, Black could simply level
the chances with **12...d5!**.

Solution 14.2 (2)

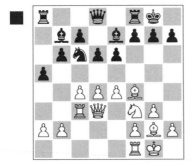

13...♘xd4!?N 13...♗f6 Sargissian-
Timman, Antwerp 2009. **14.♕xd4 e5**
15.♘xe5 ♗f6 16.c5 dxe5 17.♕xd8
♖fxd8 18.♗e3 b5 19.c6 ♗c8=

Solution 14.2 (3)

11...g6!? Another solid plan is
11...d5!?, Bruzon Batista-Nisipeanu,
Linares 2013. **12.♖ad1 d6 13.h4 h5**
14.e4 ♘d7∞ Kasparov-Karpov, Lon-
don/Leningrad 1986.

Solution 14.3 (1)

9...♘e4! A relatively new move, with
the idea to protect the c4-pawn from
d6. **10.♕c2 ♘d6 11.♘bd2 ♘a6** The
knight will have an excellent outpost on
b4. **12.♘xc4 ♘b4 13.♘xd6+ ♕xd6**
14.♕d2 0-0 15.0-0 ♖d8 16.♖fd1 b6
17.♕c3 ♗a6 18.♖d2 ♖ac8 19.♖ad1
♕e7= All Black's pieces are perfectly
coordinated, Hammer-Carlsen, Sandnes
2013.

Solution 14.3 (2)

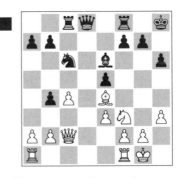

17...♕c7!?N **18.♖fd1** **♘e7⇄** Black
controls important central squares, and
counts on the centre and the queenside
for counterplay.

Solution 14.3 (3)

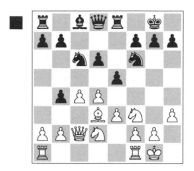

11...b3! and Black has a clear advantage thanks to the combined threats on b4 and e4, Eingorn-Kortchnoi, Odessa 2006.

Solution 14.4 (1)

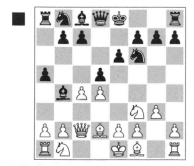

6...dxc4! 7.♕xc4 b6! 8.♗g2 ♗a6 9.♕c2 0-0⇄ with counterplay along the a6-f1 diagonal.

Solution 14.4 (2)

14...♕d8!?N 14...♗xc3 Kozul-Zelcic, Zagreb 2013. **15.♗d4 ♖e8 16.♘c3 ♖b8 17.♘a4 ♘e4⇄**

Solution 14.4 (3)

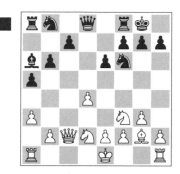

11...♖a7!? With the idea ...c7-c5; 11...♘bd7!?. **12.♘c4** 12.♖c1 c5 13.dxc5 ♖c7♔; 12.♖d1 c5 13.dxc5 ♖c7♔. **12...♗b7 13.♘ce5 ♗e4 14.♕c3 c5 15.0-0 ♖c7 16.♖ac1 ♘bd7⇄**

Solution 15.1 (1)

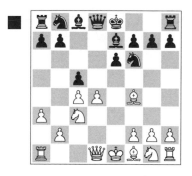

8...cxd4! 8...0–0 9.dxc5 ♗xc5 10.♘f3 ♘c6 11.♗e2 ♕e7 12.0-0 ♖d8 13.♕c2 b6 14.♖ad1 ♗b7 15.b4 e5 16.♗g5 ♘d4 17.♘xd4 ♗xd4 18.♘b5 h6 19.♗h4 g5 20.♗g3 ♘e4∞ Rodshtein-Kogan, Ashdod 2006. **9.♘b5 0–0 10.♘c7**

10...e5! 11.♗xe5 ♘c6 12.♗g3 ♖b8 13.♘b5 ♕a5+ 14.b4 ♘xb4

Solution 15.1 (2)

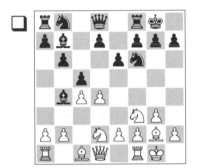

8.d5!? exd5 9.♘h4 ♖e8!? 9...♗xd2 10.♗xd2 ♘e4 11.cxd5 ♖e8 12.♗f4 d6 13.♕d3 ♗a6 14.♕c2 ♘f6 15.♘f5 ♖xe2 16.♕c3 ♘bd7 17.♖fe1!+− Ivanisevic-Antic, Kragujevac 2009. **10.♘f5** 10.cxd5!? ♗xd5 11.♗xd5 ♘xd5 12.♘c4♙. **10...♗a6♙**

Solution 15.1 (3)

15...♕b8!? 15...♘b6 16.♕d4 ♘c4 17.♗f4 ♕e7 18.b6± Ponomariov-Fedorchuk, Kiev 2012. **16.♗a3 ♖c8** with unclear play.

Solution 15.2 (1)

14...♘c6! 15.♗e3 15.♗xc7 g5! **15...♘a5 16.♕a2 ♘c4 17.♗c1 g5 18.♖e1 ♖ac8 19.b3 ♘cd6** with a slight advantage for Black in Iturrizaga Bonelli-Delgado Ramirez, San Jose 2009.

Solution 15.2 (2)

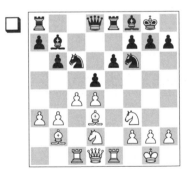

14.c5! bxc5 15.dxc5 a5 16.♗b5 ♘d7 17.b4 axb4 18.axb4 ♖b8 and White was clearly better in Ponomariov-Vitiugov, Saratov 2011.

Solution 15.2 (3)

21...♕b7!–+ Williams-Fressinet, Haguenau 2013.

Solution 15.3 (1)

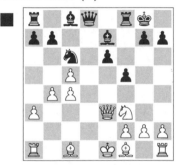

12...♗f6! 12...e5 13.♗b2 e4 14.♖d1 ♕e8 15.♘d4 ♗f6 16.g3 a5 17.b5± Le Quang Liem-Bocharov, Moscow 2008. **13.♖b1 e5♔ △14.♗b2 e4 15.♖d1 ♕e8 16.♘d4** 16.♗xf6 f4!–+. **16...f4 17.♕e2 e3**

Solution 15.3 (2)

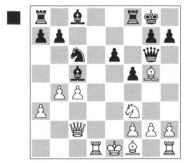

15...e5! 16.♕c1 f4 17.bxc5 e4 18.♖d6 ♕h5∞ Koneru-Antic, Kavala 2009.

Solution 15.3 (3)

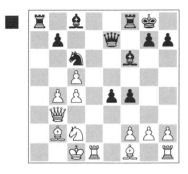

19...♗f5! With full compensation for the pawn! 19...♗g4 20.f3 exf3 21.gxf3 ♗xb2+ 22.♔xb2 ♕f6+ 23.♔b1 ♗f5 24.♗d3∞ Navara-Hracek, Prague 2012.

Solution 15.4 (1)

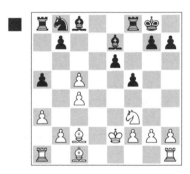

13...♘c6! 13...a4 14.♗f4 ♘d7 15.♗d6 ♔f7 16.♖ad1± Miljkovic-Antic, Vrnjacka Banja 2010. **14.♗a4 ♗f6♔**

Solution 15.4 (2)

16...♘c6!⩱ 16...h6?! (there is no reason to force the knight to move to a better spot and close the centre) 17.♘f3 e4 18.♘e5± Kovalenko-Maletin, Magnitogorsk 2011.

Solution 15.4 (3)

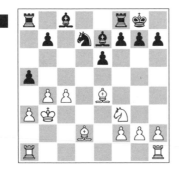

15...f5! Pushing the central pawns with ...f7-f5, ...e6-e5 is one of the most important ideas in such positions: the majority attack! **15...♘f6 16.♗c2 b6 17.♗e3 ♖b8 18.♗f4±** Malakhatko-Maletin, Dubai 2009.

Solution 15.5 (1)

17...♗d7! A simple developing move, which keeps a clear advantage for Black. 17...♕e6+ 18.♔f1 ♕g4 19.♕xd5 ♗e6 20.♕e4 ♕xe4 21.♗xe4 ♖d8± Ding Liren-Zhou Jianchao, Beijing 2009. **18.0–0 ♖af8 19.♖ae1 ♗f5∓**

Solution 15.5 (2)

16.♕f7+! ♖xf7 17.exf7+ ♔h8 18.♘e5 g6 19.♘xc6 Less convincing is 19.♘xg6+?! ♔g7 20.♘xe7 ♕b7 21.♘g6 with unclear play in the game Cheparinov-Georgiev, Sunny Beach 2012. **19...♘xc6 20.♘f3 ♔g7 21.♗b5** with a clear advantage for White.

Solution 15.5 (3)

16...♘g6! There was no reason to give up the centre with 16...dxc4 17.♗xc4 ♗d7 18.h5 b5 19.♗e2 b4 20.0–0 ♕b6 21.♘d2 ♖ec8 22.♘c4 and here a draw was agreed in the game Avrukh-Fedorchuk, Sibenik 2012. **2.♗e3 ♕a5+ 3.♔f1 ♘b3!** with a slight advantage for Black.

Solution 15.6 (1)

13...♕a5+! 13...♘c5 14.♗e2 ♕b6 with a draw in the game Rindlisbacher-Gonda, Budapest 2013. **14.♕d2 ♕xd2+ 15.♚xd2 ♘c5∓** The black pieces have excellent coordination.

Solution 15.6 (2)

13...a4! A very important strategic idea. Black conquers the c5-square! 13...f6 14.exf6 ♘xf6 15.♘bxd4 ♗g4 16.0-0 ♘bd7 17.h3 ♖c8 18.♕a2 ♗xf3 19.♘xf3 ♕b6 20.♗b2 and Black was slightly better in Berczes-Saric, Rogaska Slatina 2009. **14.♘bxd4 ♘c5 15.♗xh7 ♘b3!** and again, Black has a small advantage.

Solution 15.6 (3)

18...♗e6!? 18...♘b3 19.♗g5 ♕e6 20.♖ad1 ½-½ Lputian-Gulko, Erevan 1996. **19.♕d6 ♕xd6 20.exd6 ♖fd8 21.♗f4 ♘e4 22.♖fd1 ♘c3∞**

Solution 16.1 (1)

9...b6!N 10.cxb6 axb6 11.♕d2 ♗a6 12.e4 ♘e5∓

Solution 16.1 (2)

8...♘a6! Developing a piece and taking full control of the e4-square!

Solution 16.1 (3)

8...f5! Full control of the e4-square is essential! **9.♗c2 ♘f6** and Black has more than sufficient play.

Solution 16.2 (1)

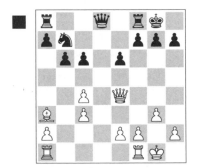

15...♖e8!N 15...♘c5 16.♗xc5 bxc5 17.♕xc6 ♕d2 18.♕f3 ♖fd8± Li Chao-Zhou Weiqi, Qinhuangdao 2011. **16.♕xc6 ♘a5∞**

Solution 16.2 (2)

20...♗g4!N 20...b5 21.♖ad1?! (21.♖b1∞) 21...♗a4 22.♖c1?! (22.♖xd6) 22...h5∓ Wang Yue-Gyimesi, Beijing 2008. **21.♖b1 g5∓**

Solution 16.2 (3)

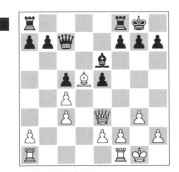

17...♖ae8!N 17...♗d7 18.f4 ♖ae8 19.f5↑ Cruz Lledo-Colon Garcia, Granada 2009. **18.♖fd1** 18.♖xe6 ♖xe6 19.♖ad1 e4 20.♖d5 b6 21.♖fd1 ♕c6∞. **18...♗c8!** A perfect, quite flexible set-up for Black. **19.♖d2 ♔h8 20.♖ad1 f5** with perfect piece coordination.

Solution 16.3 (1)

7...f5!N Improving control of the e4-square is essential! **8.dxe6** 8.♗d2 ♘f6 9.a3 ♗xc3 10.♗xc3 0–0 11.dxe6 ♕e7!∞. **8...♗xc3+ 9.bxc3 dxe6∞**

Solution 16.3 (2)

13...♕d5!N 13...♖e8+ 14.♗e2 h5 15.0-0 h4 16.♘h5 ♘d5 17.♗f3 ♘ce7 18.♖e1 ♗f5 19.g3± Benitah-Fingorn, Metz 2010. **14.♕f3 ♖e8+ 15.♗e2 ♕g5∓**

Solution 16.3 (3)

14...h5!N In such positions, the exchange of the light-squared bishops is the main idea, but Black should first prevent g2-g4 ! If 14...♘f5 15.♘f3 h5 16.♗d2 ♖e8 17.♖fe1 ♗d7 18.♘h2 ♖xe1+ 19.♖xe1 ♕f8 20.g4 hxg4 21.hxg4 ♘g7 22.f5± Naiditsch-Mchedlishvili, Istanbul 2012. **15.f5** Less good is 15.♘f3 ♗f5. **15...♗xf5 16.♗xf5 ♘xf5 17.♖xf5 gxf5 18.♕xf5 ♕e7∞**

Solution 16.4 (1)

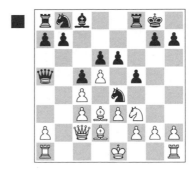

11...♘d7! Developing a piece and taking full control of the e4-square! **12.dxe6** 12.♗xe4 fxe4 13.♕xe4 (13.♘g5 exd5 14.cxd5 ♕a6 15.♘e6 ♘e5!↑) 13...♘f6 14.♕d3 ♕a6! 15.♕e2 ♗d7 16.a4 ♖ae8↑. **12...♘df6!∓**

Solution 16.4 (2)

10...e5!?N 10...b5?! 11.gxf5 exf5 12.♗g2 ♗b7 13.♗xe4 fxe4 14.♕xe4 ♘a6 15.♘h3 ♖ae8 16.♕b1 ♕b6 17.♕xb5 ♖e4 18.e3 ♗c8 19.f3 ♖ee8 20.♕xb6 axb6 21.♔f2 1–0 Grover-Praveen Kumar, Kolkata 2012. **11.♗xe5 d6 12.♗g3 ♕d8∓**

Solution 16.4 (3)

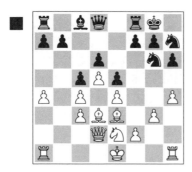

**14...f5 15.exf5 ♗xf5 16.♗xf5 ♖xf5
17.h5 ♘h8 18.g4 ♖f3∓** Volkov-
Eingorn, Swidnica 1997.

Index of Variations

1.d4 e6 2.c4 ♗b4+ (without ...♘f6)

3.♗d2

3...a5

3.♘d2

3.♘c3

1.d4 ♘f6 2.c4 e6 3.♘f3 ♗b4+

4.♗d2

4.♘bd2

4.♘c3

About the Authors

Grandmaster Dejan Antic

Born in Serbia in 1968. Participant, winner and joint winner of many tournaments worldwide, some of which are: Kavala 1996, Zurich 1998, International Open of Belgrade 2001, Charleroi 2005, Las Vegas Masters 2006, Sydney International Open 2007, Tringov Memorial 2009, winner of closed grandmaster tournaments in Jagodina 1998, Sabac 1998, Leposavic 2003 in Serbia. Participant of zonal tournament in Armenia 2002, winner of Australian championship 2008, vice-champion of Yugoslavia 2000 and participants in serval national championships of Yugoslavia and Serbia.

In the period 2004-2008 he was a resident in Australia where he has worked as a chess coach. He was a coach for the chess club Kavala in Kavala, Greece, from 2009-2013. Among his students were two world champions. Co-author of the popular book *The Modern French*, cooperator with Chess Informant for 20 years, author for New In Chess Yearbooks for seven years, and author for ChessBase Magazine.

International Master Branimir Maksimovic

Born in Serbia in 1955, Branimir Maksimovic is a renowned International Master. He often goes for rarely-played variations which are, however, rich in possibilities, in the French and in the Bogo-Indian, which is the subject of this book. His first win of many against top grandmasters was against Efim Geller at the grandmasters' tournament in Nis, Serbia, less than two weeks after Geller won the USSR Championship in 1977.

For the past 30-odd years Branimir Maksimovic has been working as a chess coach in the Serbian city of Nis. His most popular books are *Strategy and Tactics in 1,000 Miniature Games*, and, more recently for New In Chess together with Dejan Antic, *The Modern French* (2012).

Bibliography

1. Mega ChessBase

2. Online ChessBase

3. The Week In Chess

4. ChessBase Magazines, articles by Evgeny Postny and Mihail Marin

5. Online Encyclopedia referential base

6. *The Powerful Catalan* Victor Bologan

7. *A Rock Solid Chess Opening Repertoire for Black* Viacheslav Eingorn

8. *Guide to the Bogo-Indian* Steffen Pedersen

9. New In Chess Yearbook, articles by Dejan Antic

10. *Grandmaster Repertoire 2. - 1.d4 Volume 2* Boris Avrukh

Index of Players

Numbers refer to pages.

The Modern French
Dejan Antic &
Branimir Maksimovic

A Complete Guide for Black

NEW IN CHESS

"Despite my years of experience playing the French with both sides, I found myself learning an incredible amount, particularly regarding the ideas behind many of the common lines that I often employ, but, it turns out, only superficially understand (..) This book compares very favourably to its high quality competitors."
GM David Smerdon, ChessVibes

"I was very impressed by the content, which is detailed, up to date, and has the right blend of variations and verbal explanation."
Steve Giddins, author of '50 Ways to Win at Chess'

"A very interesting book that deservedly has received rave reviews."
GM Jacob Aagaard, author of 'Attacking Manual'

"Certain sections do offer lighter notes with quite extensive verbal explanations. A nice bonus occurs when the authors really want to emphasize a factor, whereupon they label a small section as 'important', just to make sure that the point has been taken (..) I found their suggestions to be coherent and important (..) An excellent piece of work."
GM Glenn Flear

Paperback ✦ 368 pages ✦ € 28.95 ✦ available at your local (chess)bookseller or at newinchess.com ✦ a NEW IN CHESS publication

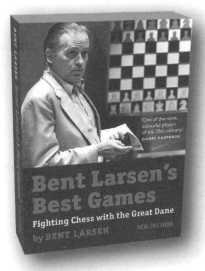